GREEK GRAMMAR

BY WILLIAM WATSON GOODWIN
Ph.D., LL.D., D.C.L.

Revised by
CHARLES BURTON GULICK, Ph.D.
Eliot Professor of Greek Literature
in Harvard University

Aristide D. Caratzas, Publisher
New Rochelle, New York

College Classical Series
Greek Grammar
ISBN (PB): 0-89241-332-8
Exact reprint of the 1930 edition.
Reprinted 1992
by

Aristide D. Caratzas, Publisher
30 Church St., P.O. Box 210
New Rochelle, New York 10802
914/632-8487

PREFACE

"Greek, sir," said Dr. Johnson in one of his *obiter dicta*, "is like lace; every man gets as much of it as he can." This remark, uttered when men still wore lace, threatened to be disastrously true in a contrary sense some two decades ago, when Greek was at its lowest ebb in American education. But the tide has turned, and the very noticeable revival of Greek studies in the colleges and universities of the country makes it appropriate that Goodwin's Grammar should appear in a more modern dress.

In this third edition I have entirely rewritten Parts I and II (Phonology and Inflection), and to a great extent Part III (Formation of Words). Nevertheless, I have kept within the limits imposed by Goodwin in his treatment, which was designed to explain the language on its own soil, without too great inclusion of its pre-history or of Indo-European forms. Thus, for good or for ill, the morphology is expounded without reference to the labio-velar sounds, or to the law of long diphthongs shortened before a consonant; but it is believed that nothing essential to the understanding of forms as they occur in classical literature has been omitted. More details concerning accent have been added. The article, which constitutes a most important development peculiar to the Greek, has been placed where it logically belongs, with the demonstrative pronouns. Adverbs and prepositions have been given a somewhat fuller treatment; and enough has been added from the material afforded by the dialects to answer the need of students of lyric poetry. The classes of verbs have been reduced from eight to five, partly through the simple distinction of thematic and athematic forms, and partly by the assignment of the greater number of verbs to the iota class. In accordance with the desire and the practice of all teachers today, εἰμί, φημί, etc. are treated with other μ verbs and not relegated to a separate category as though they were irregular or anomalous. Quantities are marked in Parts I and II, and occasionally elsewhere. The cross-references have been greatly increased in number, and the Indexes enlarged. Repetition has not been avoided if it could serve the reader better than a cross-reference.

The translation of examples has been revised in the interest of a more contemporary idiom. There is, strictly speaking, no such thing as a "literal translation," and much of the value of Greek as an aid to English depends upon the constant practice of rendering the Greek idiom by the English idiom, with due regard, of course, to the character and style of the author to be translated. Many new examples have been added; my studies in Athenaeus have prompted me to introduce sentences from later authors, including, on occasion, the New Testament.

A lighter hand has been applied in the revision of Part IV. Goodwin was a master in his own field of the moods and tenses, and his exact knowledge combined with common sense produced a lucidity of statement that could hardly be improved. In the treatment of tense as well as of many other topics, Gildersleeve's "Syntax of Classical Greek," produced with the co-operation of Professor C. W. E. Miller, has illuminated much that was little understood before. I have tried to emphasize more distinctly the "character of the action"; this will be especially noted in the exposition of the imperfect and the perfect — "action in a line," and "perfective." I have purposely refrained from reducing Goodwin's account of the cases to fewer categories, believing that the infinite variety and subtlety of the Greek can thereby better be kept in mind.

I have gone farther than Goodwin in the matter of pronunciation, especially in the case of ει; and in the uncertainty as to the exact value of ζ in Attic Greek, I have indicated the English z as an approximate equivalent. No one beyond the borders of the Greek Republic, of course, would follow the Modern Greek as a guide to the value of the ancient vowels and consonants; yet I firmly believe that every teacher today should have at least a slight acquaintance with Modern Greek, if only to realize more vividly the fluency of the language and the continuity of its history. And whatever may be said of the difference between stress and pitch accent, the fact remains that the observance of stress accent is the only device by which we can even remotely approach the ancient enunciation. I regret, therefore, the recent decision of my friends in the Classical Association of England

and Wales to adhere to the quantitative or Latin method of
pronunciation.

In the absence of a brief manual in English on Greek verse,
comparable to that of Masqueray in French, I need not apolo-
gize for retaining Part V, the section on Prosody. Full details
may be studied in the authoritative "Verse of Greek Comedy" by
my late colleague John Williams White, although I cannot follow
him in his abolition of ictus; and in the actual practice of the
classroom, where reading aloud is of the first importance, I have
found that the older system works better. This is a pragmatic
position which by no means denies the force of White's argument
in many cases, and which recognizes fully the fallacy of analogies
drawn from modern music of the West, on which the older system
was largely based.

I am under great obligation to many teachers who have kindly
furnished me with corrections and suggestions inspired by the
last edition. My particular thanks are due to my colleagues
Professors Joshua Whatmough and Carl Newell Jackson. Professor Whatmough read Part I, and Professor Jackson read the
entire book. To their helpful criticism I owe much; neither is
chargeable with responsibility for any doctrine which may be
debatable. To Mr. Byington of the Athenæum Press I am in-
debted for searching criticism, from the point of view of a pro-
found scholar and an accomplished maker of books.

CHARLES BURTON GULICK

CONTENTS

INTRODUCTION

PART I. LETTERS, SYLLABLES, ACCENTS

CONTENTS

FORMATION OF NOUNS

COMPOUND WORDS

PART IV. SYNTAX

SUBJECT AND PREDICATE

APPOSITION

ADJECTIVES

THE ARTICLE

TENSES

I. *Tenses of the Indicative*

II. *Tenses of the Dependent Moods*

A. NOT IN INDIRECT DISCOURSE

B. IN INDIRECT DISCOURSE

III. *Tenses of the Participle*

IV. *Gnomic and Iterative Tenses*

CONTENTS

CONTENTS

CONTENTS XXV

CITATIONS OF GREEK AUTHORS

GREEK GRAMMAR

INTRODUCTION

THE GREEK LANGUAGE AND DIALECTS

The Greek language is the language spoken by the Greek race, which, from a period long before Homer, has occupied the lower part of the Balkan peninsula, the islands of the Aegean Sea, the coasts of Asia Minor, and, later, certain districts in Southern Italy, Sicily, Gaul, and Northern Africa. After the Homeric period the people of this race called themselves by the name **Hellenes,** and their language **Hellenic.** We call them **Greeks,** from the Roman name **Graeci.**

Although conscious of possessing the same speech and the same religion, the Greeks were not politically united. In the Homeric poems (before 900 B.C.) there is no common name to denote the entire race. The Homeric Hellenes were a small tribe in southeastern Thessaly, of which Achilles was king; and the Greeks in general were called by Homer Achaeans, Argives, or Danaans. Later, Greek literature recognized three important divisions which we may conveniently follow here, though they leave out of account many regions and dialects which differed from each other and from the three. These main divisions are **Aeolic, Doric,** and **Ionic.** The **Attic** dialect is closely related to the Ionic.

Aeolic was the language of Lesbos and the Lesbian poets Alcaeus and Sappho. Many traces of it appear in Homer and later poetry. A variety of Aeolic was spoken in Thessaly and Boeotia. **Doric** belongs to Peloponnesus (except Elis and Arcadia), Crete and other islands, Southern Italy, and parts of Sicily. It is the dialect of many lyric poets, and the choral parts of Athenian tragedy have some forms related to it.

In the language of the **Ionians** we must distinguish the **Old** and the **New Ionic.** The **Old Ionic** or **Epic** is the language of the

1

Homeric poems, the oldest literature of the Greeks and therefore of Europe. It exercised a great influence on later poetry, both in diction and in the forms of words. As a spoken language Ionic is found on the coast of Asia Minor, in most of the Aegean Islands, and in Sicily. The New Ionic was the language of Ionia in the fifth century B.C., as it appears in Herodotus (about 484–425 B.C.) and Hippocrates (born 460 B.C.).

The Attic was the language of Athens during her period of literary eminence (from about 500 to 300 B.C.). In it were written the tragedies of Aeschylus, Sophocles, and Euripides, the comedies of Aristophanes, the histories of Thucydides and Xenophon, the orations of Demosthenes and the other orators of Athens, and the works of the philosopher Plato. Old Attic is a name often given to the dialect of the tragedians and Thucydides. New Attic is the language of most of the later Attic writers.

The Attic dialect is the most cultivated and refined form of the Greek language. It is therefore made the basis of Greek Grammar, and the other dialects are usually treated, for convenience, as if their forms were merely variations of the Attic. This is a position, however, to which the Attic has no claim on the ground of age or of more primitive forms, in respect to which it holds a rank below the other dialects.

The literary and political importance of Athens caused her dialect gradually to supplant the others wherever Greek was spoken; but in this very extension to regions widely separated the Attic dialect itself was not a little modified by various local influences, and lost some of its early purity. The language which thus arose, with admixture of many Ionic elements, is called the Common Dialect, or Koiné (ἡ κοινὴ διάλεκτος). This begins with the Alexandrian period, the time of the literary eminence of Alexandria in Egypt, which dates from the accession of Ptolemy II in 285 B.C. The Greek of the philosopher Aristotle (384–322 B.C.) lies on the border line between this and the purer Attic. The name Hellenistic is often given to that form of the Common Dialect which was used by the Jews of Alexandria who made the Septuagint version of the Old Testament (283–135 B.C.) and by the writers of the New Testament, all of whom were Hellenists (that is, foreigners who spoke Greek). The New Testament is in large part written in the popular colloquial language of the time.

Towards the end of the eleventh century after Christ the popular Greek then spoken in the Byzantine Roman Empire began to appear in literature by the side of the scholastic ancient Greek, which had ceased to be intelligible to the common people. This popular language, the earliest form of **Modern Greek**, was called **Romaic** (‘Ρωμαϊκή), since the people called themselves Romans. The name **Romaic** has been little used since Greek independence was established in the last century ; and the present language of the Greeks is called simply Ἑλληνική or Ἑλληνικά, while the country is Ἑλλάς and the people are Ἕλληνες. The literary Greek has been greatly purified during the last half-century by the expulsion of foreign words and the restoration of classic forms ; and the same process has affected the spoken language, especially that of cultivated society in Athens, but to a far less extent. It is not too much to say that the Greek of many of the books and newspapers now published in Athens could have been understood by Demosthenes or Plato. The Greek language has thus an unbroken literary history, from Homer to the present day, of perhaps thirty centuries.

The Greek belongs to a great family of related languages called the Indo-European. These include ancient Indian (or Sanskrit), Persian, Armenian, Albanian, Slavic, Lithuanian, Italic (that is, Latin, Oscan, and Umbrian), Celtic, and Germanic. Greek is closely connected with the Italic languages, as is shown by many striking analogies between Greek and Latin, which appear in both bases and terminations ; but there are also many less obvious analogies between Greek and the Anglo-Saxon element in English, which are seen in words like *me, is, know*, etc.

On the basis of this original kinship an important distinction is drawn between **cognate** and **borrowed** words. Thus, English *is*, Latin es-t, Greek ἐσ-τί are cognate ; but English *mechanic, theatre, telephone*, and thousands of other words, are borrowed (or derived) from Attic Greek.

PART I

LETTERS, SYLLABLES, ACCENTS

THE ALPHABET

1. The Greek alphabet has twenty-four letters:

FORM	EQUIVALENT	NAME		SOUND
A α	a	ἄλφα	*alpha*	ă: papa; ā: father
B β	b	βῆτα	*beta*	be
Γ γ	g	γάμμα	*gamma*	go (also sing, 21)
Δ δ	d	δέλτα	*delta*	do
E ε	ĕ	εῖ, ἔ, ἒ ψῑλόν	*epsilon*	let
Z ζ	z	ζῆτα	*zeta*	gaze
H η	ē	ῆτα	*eta*	French fête
Θ θ	th	θῆτα	*theta*	thin
I ι	i	ἰῶτα	*iota*	ĭ: French petit; ī: pique
K κ	k, c	κάππα	*kappa*	kill
Λ λ	l	λά(μ)βδα	*lambda*	land
M μ	m	μῦ	*mu*	men
N ν	n	νῦ	*nu*	now
Ξ ξ	x	ξεῖ, ξῖ	*xi*	wax
O o	ŏ	οὖ, ὄ, ὂ μῑκρόν	*omicron*	obey
Π π	p	πεῖ, πῖ	*pi*	pet
P ρ	r	ῥῶ	*rho*	run
Σ σ ς	s	σῖγμα	*sigma*	sit
T τ	t	ταῦ	*tau*	tell
Υ υ	(u) y	ῦ, ῦ ψῑλόν	*upsilon*	French u, German ü
Φ φ	ph	φεῖ, φῖ	*phi*	graphic
X χ	ch	χεῖ, χῖ	*chi*	Scotch loch
Ψ ψ	ps	ψεῖ, ψῖ	*psi*	gypsum
Ω ω	ō	ὦ, ὦ μέγα	*omega*	tone

2. At the end of a word the form ς is used, elsewhere the form σ; e.g. σύνθεσις *combination*.

5

3. Three other letters belonged to the primitive Greek alphabet: *vau* or *digamma* (ϝ), equivalent to *w*; *koppa* (Ϙ), equivalent to *q*; and *sampi* (ϡ), which is a graphic combination of *san*, a form of *sigma*, and *pi*. They were used as numerals (**446**), *vau* here having the form ς, which is used also as an abbreviation of στ. *Vau* had not entirely disappeared in pronunciation when the Homeric poems were composed, and the meter of many verses in these is explained only by admitting its presence. Many forms also which seem irregular are explained only on the supposition that ϝ has been omitted (see **102, 266, 267**).

4. The Athenians of the best period used the names εἶ or ἔ for *epsilon*, οὖ or ὄ for *omicron*, ὓ for *upsilon*, and ὤ for *omega*; the present names for these letters are late. Some medieval Greek grammarians used ἒ ψῑλόν (*plain* ε) and ὓ ψῑλόν (*plain* υ) to distinguish ε and υ from αι and οι, which in their time had similar sounds.

VOWELS AND DIPHTHONGS

5. The vowels are α, ε, η, ι, ο, ω, and υ. Of these, ε and ο are always short; η and ω are always long; α, ι, and υ are long in some syllables and short in others, whence they are called *doubtful* vowels.

6. Vowels are *open* or *close* according to the more open or less open position of the mouth in pronunciation. The open vowels, in order of openness, are α, η, ω; the close vowels are ε, ι, ο, υ, the closest being ι and υ.

7. The diphthongs (δί-φθογγοι *double-sounding*) are αι, αυ, ει, ευ, οι, ου, ηυ, υι, ᾳ, ῃ, ῳ. These unite in one syllable two vowels, of which the second is the close ι or υ. All diphthongs are long. The long vowels (ᾱ, η, ω) with ι form the so-called *improper* diphthongs ᾳ, ῃ, ῳ, in which the ι is now usually written below the line and is called *iota subscript*. But with capitals it is written in the line (*iota adscript*): ΤΗΙ ΚΩΜΩΙΔΙΑΙ *to the comedy*. So also Ὤιχετο, but ᾤχετο *he went away*.

8. The diphthongs ει and ου are either *genuine* or *spurious*. Genuine ει, ου either belong to the earliest structure of the language, as in πείθω *persuade* (cf. its perfect πέποιθα), or arise from contraction of ε + ι, as in γένε-ι, γένει *by birth* (**232**). Spurious ει and ου arise from contraction of ε + ε and ε + ο, ο + ε, or ο + ο, as in ἐποίει (for ἐποίεε) *he made*, ἐποίουν (for ἐποίεον) *they made*; or from compensative lengthening (**32**), as in τιθείς (for τιθεντ-s, **70**) *placing*, τούς (for τόν-s, **75**), the accusative plural of the article. In the fourth century B.C. the spurious diphthongs were written like genuine ει and ου (that is, ΕΙ, ΟΥ); but in earlier times they were written Ε and Ο. See **28**.

9. The mark of diaeresis (διαίρεσις *separation*), a double dot over a vowel, shows that this vowel does not form a diphthong with the preceding vowel ; e.g. προϊέναι (προ-ιέναι) *to go forward*, Ἀτρείδης *son of Atreus*.

10. The ι now called subscript was written as an ordinary sound (that is, in the line with the first vowel) as long as it was pronounced. It was no longer sounded after about 200 B.C., though it was sometimes written (always in the line, or *adscript*), sometimes omitted. The *iota subscript* is not older than the eleventh century.

BREATHINGS

11. Every vowel or diphthong at the beginning of a word has either the *rough breathing* (ʻ) or the *smooth breathing* (ʼ). The rough breathing shows that the vowel is *aspirated*, that is, that it is preceded by the sound *h* ; the smooth breathing shows that the vowel is not aspirated. Thus ὁρῶν *seeing* is pronounced *hŏrōn* ; but ὀρῶν *of mountains* is pronounced *ŏrōn*. In Attic words, initial υ is always aspirated, as in ὕδωρ *water*.

12. A diphthong takes the breathing, like the accent (128), upon its *second* vowel. But ᾱ, ῃ, and ῳ (7) have both breathing and accent on the first vowel, even when the ι is written in the line. Thus οἴχεται, εὐφραίνω, Αἵμων ; but ᾤχετο or Ὤιχετο, ᾄδω or Ἄιδω, ᾔδη or Ἤιδη. On the other hand, the writing of ἀίδιος (Ἀίδιος) shows that α and ι do not form a diphthong, and the diaeresis (9) is not needed in writing.

13. The rough breathing was once denoted by H. When this sign was taken to denote ē (which once was not distinguished in writing from ε), half of it (Ⱶ) was used for the rough breathing ; and afterwards the other half (ꓶ) was used for the smooth breathing. From these fragments came the later signs ʻ and ʼ.

14. When a word beginning with the rough breathing is compounded, as in προ-ορῶν *foreseeing*, the aspirate is not written. But it must often have been heard in pronunciation, e.g. in πολυίστωρ, Lat. polyhistor, and it affected consonants preceding it (51, 103).

15. At the beginning of a word ρ is written ῥ, as in ῥήτωρ (Lat. rhetor) *orator*.

a. Older texts often printed ρρ as ῤῥ ; e.g. ἄῤῥητος *unspeakable*, Πύῤῥος *Pyrrhus*.

CONSONANTS

16. The consonants are divided, according to the organs of speech by which they are produced, or according to their sound effect, into stops (also called mutes), double consonants, liquids, nasals, and spirants.

17. Stops or **mutes** are produced by the complete closing of the organ of speech employed in uttering the sound.   There are three *classes* of stops, according to the organ :

Labials (lips)	π β φ	
Palatals (palate)	κ γ χ	
Dentals (teeth)	τ δ θ	

Stops of the same class are called *cognate*.

18. Stops are also of three *orders*, according to the effort of breathing required :

Smooth or Voiceless	π τ κ	
Middle or Voiced (23)	β δ γ	
Rough or Aspirate	φ θ χ	

Stops of the same order are called *coördinate*.

19. The **Double Consonants** are ξ, ψ, ζ. Ξ, pronounced κσ, may represent κσ, γσ, χσ ; κσ, not ξ, is written in compounds of ἐξ (ἐκ) *out of*, as ἐκ-στάς *standing out of*. Ψ, pronounced πσ, may stand for πσ, βσ, φσ. The combinations σδ, γι, or δι give ζ.

a. All these have the effect of two consonants in lengthening a preceding syllable (120).

20. The **Liquids** are λ and ρ.

21. The **Nasals** are μ (a labial), ν (a dental), and *nasal* γ.

a. The nasal γ occurs before κ, γ, χ, or ξ, and has the sound of *n* in *king* or *ink*; compare *Concord* with *concordance*. E.g. ἄγγελος (Lat. angelus) *messenger*; ἄγκυρα (ancora) *anchor*; σφίγξ *Sphinx*.

22. The only **Spirant** in Greek is σ, also called a *sibilant*.

a. Rarely the spirant *y* gave place to ζ; cf. ζυγόν, Eng. *yoke*, Lat. iugum; more commonly to the rough breathing, e.g. ἧπαρ *liver*, Lat. iecur.

23. Voiced sounds are produced when the vocal cords vibrate. All vowels are voiced, as their name denotes (cf. Lat. vocalis).   Of the sounds explained above, β, γ, nasal γ, δ, λ, μ, ν, and ζ are voiced; so also ρ when not initial. Voiced sounds are also called *sonants*.

Voiceless consonants are produced without vibration of the vocal cords; they are π, τ, κ, φ, θ, χ, σ, ψ, ξ. These are sometimes called *surds*.

24. The only consonants which can end a Greek word are ν, ρ, and σ. If others are left at the end in forming words, they are dropped, but μ becomes ν.

E.g. μέλι *honey* for μελιτ (gen. μέλιτ-ος); σῶμα *body* for σωματ (gen. σώματ-ος); ἄλλο *other* for ἀλλοδ (cf. Lat. aliud); ἔλῦε *was loosing* for ἐλῦε-τ; ἔφερον *was carrying* for ἐ-φερο-ντ (cf. Lat. ferunt); ἵππον *horse* for ἱππο-μ (cf. Lat. equum).

25. The only exceptions, and these are apparent, not real, are ἐκ *out of* for ἐξ (**84 a**), and οὐκ or οὐχ *not*, which has another form οὐ. They are pronounced as part of the following word. Final ξ and ψ (κσ and πσ) are not exceptions. For ν movable, see **110**.

26. Lost Sounds. Besides ϝ (**3**), a spirant, other sounds were lost very early (**22**). They include the *semivowels* ι and υ, corresponding to Eng. *y* and *w*; cf. *union, queer*. These left many traces. See **37, 87, 92**.

27. Sonant Liquids and Sonant Nasals. The sounds λ, μ, ν, ρ once performed the function of vowels and had syllabic force; cf. Eng. tab*le*, fath*om*, cott*on*, Fr. timb*re*. In Greek sonant λ is represented by λα or αλ; sonant μ and ν, by α (**218 a**); sonant ρ, by ρα or αρ.

28. The Greek alphabet above described is the *Ionic*, used by the Asiatic Ionians from a very early period, but not sanctioned officially at Athens until 403 B.C. The Athenians had previously used an alphabet which had no separate signs for *ê, ô* (long and open), *ks*, or *ps*. In this earlier alphabet E was used for ἔ *and* ἔ and also for the spurious diphthong ει (**8**), which in some cases is an orthographic device to represent ē (long and close); O for ŏ and ô and for spurious ου (**8**); H was still an aspirate (*h*); Χϟ stood for Ξ, and Φϟ for Ψ. Thus the Athenians of the time of Pericles wrote in official documents ΕΔΟΧϟΕΝ ΤΕΙ ΒΟΙΕΙ ΚΑΙ ΤΟΙ ΔΕΜΟΙ for ἔδοξεν τῇ βουλῇ καὶ τῷ δήμῳ *Resolved, by the Council and People*; ΤΟ ΦϟΕΦΙϟΜΑ ΤΟ ΔΕΜΟ for τὸ ψήφισμα τοῦ δήμου *the decree of the people*; ΗΕϟ for ἧς *of which*; ΗΕΙ for ᾗ *to which*; ΠΕΜΠΕΝ for πέμπειν *to send*; ΧΡΥϟΟϟ for χρυσοῦς *golden*; ΤΟΥΤΟ for both τοῦτο and τούτου *this* and *of this*; ΤΟϟ ΠΡΥΤΑΝΕϟ for τοὺς πρυτάνεις *the prytanes*; ΑΡΧΟϟΙ for ἄρχουσι *they rule*; ΔΕΟϟΟΝ for δεονσῶν *lacking*; ΗΟΠΟϟ for ὅπως *how*; ΧϟΕΝΟϟ for ξένος or ξένους *alien* or *aliens*.

Ancient Pronunciation

[For further remarks on pronunciation, see the Preface.]

29. The pronunciation of ancient Greek varied with the dialect and the period. In general, such differences were represented orthographically, as in Boeotian τιούχα for Attic τύχη *chance*, wherein the pronunciation of υ in Boeotia is shown to be the same as that of Eng. *u* in *futile*. With few exceptions, of which the iota subscript (**7**) is an example, letters actually written were also spoken. The following paragraphs suggest only the approximate equivalents for the Athenian pronunciation of Greek during the century from the death of Pericles (429 B.C.) to the death of Demosthenes (322 B.C.).

a. **Vowels.** The long vowels ᾱ, η, ῑ, were pronounced much like *a* in *father, e* in *fête* (French *ê* or *è*) or in *there* (but without any sound of *r*), *i* in *machine*; ω was probably more open than the *o* in *tone*, more like the *o* in *song*. Originally *v* had the sound of Latin *u* (Eng. *u* in *lunatic, brunette*, or better, Eng. *oo* in *moon*) ; but before the fourth century B.C. it had come to that of French *u* or German *ü* (pronounced by rounding the lips as in whistling, leaving the aperture small, and thus uttering *e* as in *me*). The short vowels *a* and *ι* had the same quality as the long vowels, but shortened or less prolonged ; this is hard to express in English, as our short *a* and *i*, in *pan* and *pit*, have sounds of a different nature from those of *ā* and *ī*, given above. We have an approach to *ă, ĕ, ĭ*, and *ŏ* in the second *a* in *grandfather*, French *é* in *réal*, *i* in *verity*, and *o* in *monastic, renovate*. The sound of *ε* (short, close) was nearer the *e* of *beg* than the *e* of *net*, while that of *o* (close) was certainly not the sound of *o* in *not*; cf. *o* in *consist*.

b. **Diphthongs.** We may assume that the diphthongs originally had the separate sounds of their two vowels, and only later became a single tone. Our *ai* in *aisle*, *oi* in *oil*, *ui* in *quit*, will give some idea of *αι, οι*, and *υι* ; *αυ* was sounded like *au* in Germ. *aus*, Eng. *ou* in *stout*; *ου* like *ou* in *youth*. Likewise the genuine *ει* must have been pronounced originally as *ε* + *ι*, later like *ei* in *rein* (cf. Hom. 'Ατρεΐδης, Attic 'Ατρείδης) ; and genuine *ου* was a compound of *o* and *υ*. But the spurious *ει* and *ου* are written for simple sounds, represented by the Athenians of the best period by Ε and Ο (see **8** and **28**), and sounded as long close *ē* (cf. Fr. *é*) and long close *ō*. We do not know how these sounds were related to ordinary *ε* and *o* on one side and to *ει* and *ου* on the other; but after the beginning of the fourth century B.C. they appear to have agreed substantially with *ει* and *ου*, since ΕΙ and ΟΥ are written for both alike. In *ει* the sound of *ι* appears to have prevailed more and more, so that after 300 B.C. it had the sound of *ī*. On the other hand, *ου* became (and still remains) a simple sound, like *ou* in *youth*. Ευ was pronounced somewhat like *ĕh-oo*, *ηυ* like *ēh-oo*, *ωυ* perhaps like *aw-oo*.

The diphthongs *ᾳ, ῃ*, and *ῳ* were probably always pronounced with the chief force on the first element, so that the *ι* gradually disappeared (see **10**).

c. **Consonants, Nasals, Liquids.** Probably *β, δ, κ, λ, μ, ν, π*, and *ρ* were sounded as *b, d, k, l, m, n, p*, and *r* in English, *ρ* being trilled at the tip of the tongue. Ordinary *γ* was hard, like *g* in *go*; for nasal *γ*, see **21**. Τ was always like *t* in *tin* or *to*; *σ* was generally like *s* in *so*, though before voiced consonants (**23**) it may have been like *z*. Ζ is a compound of *δ* and *σ* (**19**); opinions differ whether it was *δσ* or *σδ*, but the ancient testimony seems to point to *σδ*; cf. 'Αθήναζε *to Athens* from 'Αθήνας-δε *Athens-ward*. In Hellenistic times *ζ* came to the sound of English *z*, which it still keeps. Ξ represents *κσ*, and *ψ* represents *πσ*, although the earlier Athenians felt an aspirate in both, as they wrote *χσ* for *ξ* and *φσ* for *ψ*. The rough consonants *θ, χ*, and *φ* in the best period were *τ, κ*, and *π* followed by *h*, so that ἔνθα was *ἐν-τha*, ἀφίημι was ἀπ-*hιημι*, ἔχω was *ἐ-κhω*, etc. We cannot represent these aspirates in English; our nearest approach is in words like hot*h*ouse, block*h*ead, and up*h*ill, when here the *h* is not in the same syllable with the consonant. In later Greek *θ* and *φ* came to the modern pronunciation of *th* (in *thin*) and *f* (cf. *philosophy*), and *χ* to that resembling *ch* in Scotch *loch* or German *machen*.

Proper division of the syllables is of great importance in the pronunciation. See **118**. In reading prose, the Greek accents (**126**) should be observed.

CHANGES OF VOWELS

30. Vowels undergo many changes in the formation and inflection of words. The process, which is common in other languages, is known as *vowel gradation* (in German grammar *ablaut*). It may involve either the quantity or the quality of the vowel.

31. **Quantitative Gradation.** A short vowel interchanges with a long vowel:

a with η	ι with ῑ
(ᾱ after ε, ι, ρ)	o with ω
ε with η	υ with ῡ

E.g. pres. indic. τῑμά-ω *I honor*, fut. τῑμή-σω; ἐά-ω *I let*, fut. ἐά-σω; τίθη-μι *I place*, τίθε-μεν *we place*; δίδω-μι *I give*, δίδο-μεν *we give*; ἴτυς *willow rim*, ἰτέᾱ *willow tree*; φύ-σις *growth*, φύω *I grow*.

32. **Compensative Lengthening.** When one or more consonants are dropped (especially before σ), a preceding short vowel is often lengthened. Here

a becomes ᾱ	ι becomes ῑ
ε becomes ει	o becomes ου
	υ becomes ῡ

E.g. μέλᾱς *black* for μελαν-s (**75**), στᾱς *standing* for σταντ-s (**70**), τιθείς *placing* for τιθεντ-s (**70**), δούς *having given* for δοντ-s, λύουσι *they loose* for λῡο-νσι, ἔκρῑνα *I chose* for ἐκριν-σα, δεικνύς *showing* for δεικνυντ-s. Here ει and ου are the spurious diphthongs (**8**).

a. In the first aorist of liquid and nasal verbs (**687**), a becomes η when σ is dropped; e.g. ἔφηνα *I showed* for ἐφαν-σα, from φαίνω (φαν-). But after ι or ρ in the stem a becomes ᾱ; e.g. ὑγιαίνω (ὑγιαν-) *be healthy*, aor. ὑγίᾱνα for ὑγιαν-σα, ῥαίνω (ῥαν-) *sprinkle*, aor. ἔρρᾱνα.

33. **Transfer of Quantity.** The combinations ηο (ᾱο) and ηα often exchange quantity. Thus Epic νηός (νᾱός) *temple*, Attic νεώς; Epic βασιλῆος, βασιλῆα *king*, Attic βασιλέως, βασιλέᾱ; Epic μετήορος *in mid-air*, Attic μετέωρος. See **267**.

34. **Qualitative Gradation.** An interchange of vowels and diphthongs of different quality is found in many bases (**169**) and suffixes. Cf. Eng. *seek, sought*; *choose, chose*; *sink, sank, sunk*. A regular series is established, involving *strong grades* and a *weak (vanish) grade*, in which the vowel may be lost entirely.

E.g. λείπ-ω, λέ-λοιπ-α *leave, have left*, weak grade (with loss of ε) ἔ-λιπ-ον *left*; φεύγ-ω, πέ-φευγ-α, weak grade ἔ-φυγ-ον *flee*, φυγ-ή *flight*; πέτ-ομαι *fly*, ποτ-άομαι *flit*, πῐ-πτ-ω *fall*; λέγ-ω *say*, λόγ-ος *word*; φέρ-ω *carry*, φόρ-ος *tribute*, with weak grade in δί-φρ-ος *carrying two, chariot*, cf. Eng. *bear, bore*; τήκ-ω *melt*, ἐ-τάκ-ην *melted*; ῥήγ-νῡμι, ἔρ-ρωγ-α, ἐρ-ράγ-ην *break*; ἐλεύ-σομαι (69), ἐλήλουθ-α, ἤλυθ-ον *go, have gone*; σπεύδ-ω *hasten*, σπουδή *haste*.

a. Such variations arose under very ancient conditions of accent which were not in operation in the historical period. See 585, 806.

b. When, in the weak grade, the syllable which has lost its vowel is followed by one beginning with a vowel, as in πῐ-πτ-ω, δί-φρ-ος, it is easily pronounced. But often combinations of consonants with sonant nasals and liquids occurred which gave rise to the vowel α in the series (27). Thus, τρέπ-ω, τέ-τροφ-α *turn*, τρόπ-ος *way*, but weak grade ἐ-τρά-πην for ἐ-τρ-πην; στέλ-λω *send*, στόλ-ος *expedition*, weak grade ἐ-στάλ-ην for ἐ-στλ-ην *was sent*.

Other Vowel Changes

35. Shortening. A long vowel is often shortened before another vowel (vocalis ante vocalem corripitur); e.g. ἕως *dawn*, Ep. ἠώς; βασιλέων *of kings*, Ep. βασιλήων; τεθνεώς *dead*, for τεθνηώς.

36. Prothetic Vowel. An apparent prefixing of α, ε, ο sometimes occurred before λ and ρ; e.g. ἀλείφω *smear, anoint*, cf. λίπος *fat*; ἐλεύθερος *free*, cf. Lat. līber; so ἀμέλγω *milk*. In Epic it seems to occur also before ϝ occasionally; e.g. ἔεδνα *wedding-gifts* (also ἔδνα), for ἐ-ϝεδνα.

37. Lost Vowels. Diphthongs ending in ι and υ sometimes lose ι and υ, which became semivowels (26), before another vowel; e.g. πο-εῖν to *make*, often on inscriptions and in modern texts for ποιεῖν; βο-ός *of an ox*, for βου̯-ος, nom. βοῦ-ς; νᾱ-ός *of a ship*, for νᾱυ̯-ος, νᾱϝ-ος (266); see βασιλέως (265). See also 258. So ῥέω *flow*, for ῥευ-ομαι, fut. ῥεύσομαι. See also 611.

Collision of Vowels. Hiatus

38. A succession of two vowel sounds in adjoining syllables, though often tolerated in Ionic Greek, was generally displeasing to the Athenians. In the middle of a word this could be avoided by *contraction* (39–48). Between two words, where it is called *hiatus*, it could be avoided by *crasis* (49–53), by *elision* (55–61) or *aphaeresis* (62), or by adding a *movable consonant* (110–116) to the former word.

Contraction of Vowels

39. Two successive vowels, or a vowel and a diphthong, may be united by *contraction* in a single long vowel or a diphthong; φιλέω, φιλῶ; φίλεε, φίλει; τίμαε, τίμᾱ. It seldom takes place unless the former vowel is *open* (6).

40. The regular use of contraction is one of the characteristics of the Attic dialect (48). It follows these four general principles:

41. I. Two vowels which can form a genuine diphthong (7) simply unite in one syllable; e.g. τείχεί, τείχει; γέραϊ, γέραι; ῥάιστος, ῥᾷστος; ὅις (Lat. ovis), οἷς; κλήιθρον, κλῇθρον.

a. The second element in these cases is ι. In Attic, υι is either left uncontracted or becomes ῡ: ὑίδιον, ῡ́διον pig. If υ is the second element, it does not unite with the first: πράυνσις softening.

42. II. When the two vowels cannot form a genuine diphthong, two like vowels (i.e. two a-sounds, two e-sounds, or two o-sounds, without regard to quantity) unite to form the common long (ᾱ, η, or ω). But εε gives the spurious diphthong ει (8), and οο gives the spurious ου (8). E.g.

μνάᾱ, μνᾶ (193); φιλέητε, φιλῆτε; δηλόω, δηλῶ; but ἐφίλεε, ἐφίλει; πλόος, πλοῦς.

43. III. When unlike vowels occur which cannot form a genuine diphthong, one is assimilated to the other.

a. When an o-sound precedes or follows an a- or an e-sound, the two become ω. But οε and εο give the spurious ου (8). E.g.

δηλόητε, δηλῶτε; φιλέωσι, φιλῶσι; τῑμάομεν, τῑμῶμεν; τῑμάωμεν, τῑμῶμεν; but νόε, νοῦ; γένεος, γένους.

b. When an a-sound precedes or follows an e-sound, the first (in order) prevails, and we have ᾱ or η. E.g.

ἐτίμαε, ἐτίμᾱ; τῑμάητε, τῑμᾶτε; τείχεα, τείχη; Ἑρμέας, Ἑρμῆς.

44. IV. A vowel disappears by absorption before a diphthong beginning with the *same* vowel, and ε is always absorbed before οι. In other cases, a simple vowel followed by a diphthong is contracted with the *first vowel* of the diphthong; and a following ι remains as iota subscript. E.g.

μνάαι, μναῖ; μνάᾳ, μνᾷ; φιλέει, φιλεῖ; φιλέῃ, φιλῇ; δηλόοι, δηλοῖ; νόῳ, νῷ; δηλόου, δηλοῦ; φιλέοι, φιλοῖ; χρύσεοι, χρῡσοῖ; τῑμάει, τῑμᾷ; τῑμάῃ, τῑμᾷ; τῑμάοι, τῑμῷ; λύεαι, λύῃ (45 c); λύηαι, λύῃ; μεμνήοιο, μεμνῷο.

45. a. In contracts of the first and second declensions, every short vowel before α, or before a long vowel or a diphthong, is absorbed. But in the *singular* of the first declension εᾱ is contracted regularly to η (after a vowel or ρ, to ᾱ). See 195.

b. In the third declension εα becomes ᾱ after ε, and ᾱ or η after ι or υ. See **269, 309**.

c. In the second person singular of the passive and middle, εαι (for εσαι) gives the common (later) Attic form in ει as well as the regular contract form in ῃ; e.g. λύεαι, λύῃ or λύει. See **582 g**.

d. In verbs in οω, οει gives οι; e.g. δηλόεις, δηλοῖς; οι is found also in the subjunctive for οῃ; e.g. δηλόῃ, δηλοῖ.

e. The spurious diphthongs ει and ου are contracted like simple ε and ο; e.g. πλακόεις, πλακοῦς *cake*; τῑμάου, τῑμῶ; φιλέου, φιλοῦ. Thus infinitives in αειν and οειν have no ι in the contracted forms; e.g. τῑμάειν, τῑμᾶν; δηλόειν, δηλοῦν; whereas τῑμάει (genuine ει) makes τῑμᾷ, and δηλόει, δηλοῖ. See **793**.

f. When three vowels occurred in succession, the last two contracted first, and this diphthong sometimes contracted with the first vowel. E.g. τῑμά-εσαι, 2d pers. sing. ind. pass., lost σ (90), τῑμάεαι became τῑμάῃ, whence τῑμᾷ. Yet Ἡρακλέους *of Heracles* was not contracted further from Ἡρα-κλεϝε(σ)ος. See **48, 241**.

46. The close vowel ι is contracted with a following ι in the Ionic dative singular of nouns in ις (see **257**); and υ may be contracted with ι or ε in a few forms of epic nouns in υς (see **41 a, 260**, and **261**).

a. In some classes of nouns and adjectives of the third declension, contraction is confined to certain cases; see **230–265**. For exceptions in the contraction of verbs, see **486** and **488**. See dialect forms of verbs in αω, εω, and οω, in **659–661**.

47. For TABLE OF CONTRACTIONS, see page 15. In this Table, "sp." after ει or ου means *spurious*, "gen." means *genuine* (8).

48. Whenever contraction does not take place in Attic (40), an original ϝ or ι̯ may be assumed as the hindering cause. E.g.

ἀηδής *unpleasant* for ἀ-ϝηδής, ἐννέα *nine* (cf. Lat. novem), νέος *young* (Lat. novus), Ἡρακλέους for Ἡρακλεϝ-ους (45 *f*), βοός for βοϝος (37), βασιλέως *of a king* for βασιλῆϝος (33), ἐνδεᾱ *deficient*, from an original ἐν-δεϝ-εα.

Crasis

49. A vowel or diphthong at the end of a word may be contracted with one at the beginning of the following word. This occurs in prose as well as in poetry, and is called *crasis* (κρᾶσις *blending*). The *corōnis* (') is placed over the contracted syllable. The first of the two words is generally the article, a relative (ὅ or ἅ), and καί, πρό, ὦ, or δή.

50. Crasis generally follows the laws of contraction (with which it is essentially identical), with these modifications:

a. A diphthong at the end of the first word drops its last vowel before crasis takes place.

TABLE OF CONTRACTIONS

α + α = ᾱ γέραα, γέρᾱ

α + αι = αι μνάαι, μναῖ

α + ᾳ = ᾳ μνάᾳ, μνᾷ

α + ε = ᾱ ἐτίμαε, ἐτίμᾱ

α + ει (gen.)
 = ᾳ τῑμάει, τῑμᾷ

α + ει (sp.)
 = ᾱ τῑμάειν, τῑμᾶν (45 e)

α + η = ᾱ τῑμάητε, τῑμᾶτε

α + ῃ = ᾳ τῑμάῃ, τῑμᾷ

α + ι = αι γέραϊ, γέραι

ᾱ + ι = ᾳ γρᾱ-ίδιον, γρᾴδιον

α + ο = ω τῑμάομεν, τῑμῶμεν

α + οι = ῳ τῑμάοιμι, τῑμῷμι

α + ου (sp.)
 = ω τῑμάου, τῑμῶ (45 e)

α + ω = ω τῑμάω, τῑμῶ

ε + α = η γένεα, γένη
 = ᾱ ὀστέα, ὀστᾶ (45 a)

ε + ᾱ = η χρῡσέᾱ, χρῡσῆ

ε + αι = ῃ λύεαι, λύῃ (45 c)
 = αι χρῡσεαι, χρῡσαῖ
  (45 a)

ε + ε = ει (sp.) ἐφίλεε, ἐφίλει

ε + ει = ει (gen.) φιλέει, φιλεῖ

ε + ει (sp.)
 = ει (sp.) φιλέειν, φιλεῖν

ε + η = η φιλέητε, φιλῆτε

ε + ῃ = ῃ φιλέῃ, φιλῇ

ε + ι = ει τείχεϊ, τείχει

ε + ο = ου (sp.) γένεος, γένους

ε + οι = οι φιλέοι, φιλοῖ

ε + ου = ου (sp.) φιλέου, φιλοῦ

ε + υ = ευ (rare) ἐύ, εὖ (41 a)

ε + ω = ω φιλέω, φιλῶ

ε + ῳ = ῳ ὀστέῳ, ὀστῷ

η + αι = ῃ λύηαι, λύῃ

η + ε = η τῑμήεντι, τῑμῆντι

η + ει (sp.)
 = η τῑμήεις, τῑμῆς (45 e)

η + ει (gen.)
 = ῃ ζήει, ζῇ

η + η = η φανήητε, φανῆτε

η + ῃ = ῃ ζήῃ, ζῇ

η + ι = ῃ κλή-ιθρον, κλῇθρον

η + οι = ῳ μεμνηοίμην, μεμνῴμην

ι + ι = ῑ Χίιος, Χῖος

ο + α = ω αἰδόα, αἰδῶ
 = ᾱ } doubtful; see 304
ο + αι = αι }

ο + ε = ου (sp.) νόε, νοῦ

ο + ει (gen.)
 = οι δηλόει, δηλοῖ (45 e)

ο + ει (sp.)
 = ου (sp.) δηλόειν, δηλοῦν
  (45 e)

ο + η = ω δηλόητε, δηλῶτε

ο + ῃ = ῳ διδόῃς, διδῷς
 = οι δηλόῃ, δηλοῖ
 = ῳ δόῃς, δῷς

ο + ι = οι πειθόι, πειθοῖ

ο + ο = ου (sp.) νόος, νοῦς

ο + οι = οι δηλόοι, δηλοῖ

ο + ου (sp.)
 = ου (sp.) δηλόου, δηλοῦ

ο + ω = ω δηλόω, δηλῶ

ο + ῳ = ῳ ἁπλόῳ, ἁπλῷ

Rarely the following:

υ + ε = ῡ ἰχθύε, ἰχθῦ (41 a)

υ + ι = ῡ ἰχθυίδιον, ἰχθύδιον

ω + α = ω ἥρωα, ἥρω

ω + ε = ω ἥρωες, ἥρως

ω + ι = ῳ ἥρωι, ἥρῳ

ω + ο = ω cf. ῥιγῶντες (497)

b. The article loses its final vowel or diphthong in crasis before α; the particle τοί drops οι before α; and καί drops αι before all vowels and diphthongs except ε and ει. But we have κεἰ and κεἰς for καὶ εἰ and καὶ εἰς.

51. The following are examples of crasis:

τὸ ὄνομα, τοὔνομα; τὰ ἀγαθά, τἀγαθά; τὸ ἐναντίον, τοὐναντίον; ὁ ἐκ, οὐκ; ὁ ἐπί, οὑπί; τὸ ἱμάτιον, θοἰμάτιον (103); ἃ ἄν, ἅν; καὶ ἄν, κἄν; — ὁ ἀνήρ, ἁνήρ; οἱ ἀδελφοί, ἁδελφοί; τῷ ἀνδρί, τἀνδρί; τὸ αὐτό, ταὐτό; τοῦ αὐτοῦ, ταὐτοῦ; — τοι ἄν, τἄν (μέντοι ἄν, μεντἄν); τοι ἄρα, τἄρα; — καὶ αὐτός, καὐτός; καὶ αὕτη, χαὕτη (103); καί ἐστι, κᾆστι; καὶ εἰ, κεἰ; καὶ εἶτα, κᾆτα; καὶ οὐ, κοὐ; καὶ οἱ, χοἱ; καὶ αἱ, χαἱ. So ἐγὼ οἶδα, ἐγᾦδα; ὦ ἄνθρωπε, ὤνθρωπε; τῇ ἐπαρῇ, τῇπαρῇ. Likewise we have προὔργου *helpful* for πρὸ ἔργου *ahead in work*; cf. φροῦδος *vanished* for πρὸ ὁδοῦ, φρουρός *guard* for προ-hορός (14, 103).

52. If the first word is an article or relative with the rough breathing, this breathing is retained on the contracted syllable, taking the place of the coronis; e.g. ἅν, ἁνήρ, for ἃ ἄν, ὁ ἀνήρ.

53. In crasis, ἕτερος *other* takes the earlier form ἅτερος, — whence ἅτερος (for ὁ ἕτερος), θἀτέρου (for τοῦ ἑτέρου), θἀτέρῳ, etc. (50 *b*; 105*f*).

Synizesis

54. In poetry, two successive vowels (or a vowel and a diphthong), not forming a diphthong, are sometimes united in pronunciation for the sake of the meter, although no contraction appears in writing. This is called *synizēsis* (συνίζησις *settling together*). Thus θεοί may make one syllable in poetry; στήθεα or χρῡσέῳ may make two.

a. Synizesis may also take the place of crasis (49) when the first word ends in a long vowel or a diphthong, especially with ἐπεί *since*, μή *not*, ἤ *or*, ἦ (interrog.), and ἐγώ *I*. E.g. ἐπεὶ οὐ may make two syllables, μὴ εἰδέναι may make three; μὴ οὐ always makes one syllable in poetry.

Elision

55. A short final vowel may be dropped when the next word begins with a vowel. This is called *elision*. An apostrophe (') marks the omission. E.g.

δι' ἐμοῦ for διὰ ἐμοῦ; ἀντ' ἐκείνης for ἀντὶ ἐκείνης; λέγοιμ' ἄν for λέγοιμι ἄν; ἀλλ' εὐθύς for ἀλλὰ εὐθύς; ἐπ' ἀνθρώπῳ for ἐπὶ ἀνθρώπῳ. So ἐφ' ἑτέρῳ; νύχθ' ὅλην for νύκτα ὅλην (103).

56. Elision is especially frequent in ordinary prepositions, conjunctions, and adverbs; but it may also be used with short vowels at the end of nouns, adjectives, pronouns, and verbs.

57. Elision never occurs in

a. The prepositions περί and πρό, except περί in Aeolic (rarely before ι in Attic).

b. The relative and conjunction ὅτι *what, that* (ὅτ' is for ὅτε *when*).

c. Monosyllables, except those ending in ε, e.g. δέ, γέ, τέ.

d. The dative singular in ι of the third declension and the dative plural in σι, except in epic poetry.

e. Words ending in υ.

58. The epic, lyric, and comic poets sometimes elide αι in the verbal endings μαι, σαι, ται, and σθαι (θαι). So οι in οἴμοι *woe is me,* and rarely in μοι *to me.*

59. Elision is often neglected in prose, especially by certain writers (as Thucydides). Others (as Isocrates) are more strict in its use. In prose, forms which admit ν movable (**110**) do not suffer elision, except ἐστί *is.*

60. Apocope. The poets and non-literary dialects sometimes cut off a short vowel before a consonant. Thus in Homer we find the monosyllabic forms ἄν, κάτ, and πάρ, for the more usual dissyllabic ἀνά, κατά, and παρά. So Alcaeus: ὸν (= ἀνὰ) τὸ μέσσον *on the main.* Both in composition and alone, κάτ assimilates its τ to a following consonant and drops it before two consonants; e.g. κάββαλε and κάκτανε for κατέβαλε and κατέκτανε — but κατθανεῖν (not καθθανεῖν) for καταθανεῖν (**63** *a*), κὰκ κορυφήν, κὰγ γόνυ, κὰπ πεδίον; and ν in ἄν (for ἀνά) is subject to the changes of **72** and **73**; e.g. ἀμ-βάλλω, ἀλ-λέξαι, ἀμ πεδίον, ἀμ φόνον. So ὑβ-βάλλειν (once) for ὑπο-βάλλειν.

61. A short final vowel is generally elided also when it comes before a vowel in forming a compound word. Here no apostrophe is used. E.g.

ἀπ-αιτῶ (ἀπό and αἰτέω) *demand back,* δι-έβαινον (διά and ἔβαινον) *they crossed over.* So ἀφαιρῶ (ἀπό and αἱρέω) *take away from;* δεχ-ήμερος (δέκα and ἡμέρα) *lasting ten days;* φίλ-ιππος (φιλο- and ἵππος) *fond of horses.* **103.**

Aphaeresis

62. In poetry, a short vowel at the beginning of a word is sometimes dropped after a long vowel or a diphthong, especially after μή *not* and ἤ *or.* This is called *aphaeresis* (ἀφαίρεσις *taking away*), or *inverse elision.* E.g. μὴ 'γώ for μὴ ἐγώ; ποῦ 'στιν for ποῦ ἐστιν; ἐγὼ 'φάνην for ἐγὼ ἐφάνην; ἤ 'μοῦ for ἤ ἐμοῦ.

CHANGES OF CONSONANTS

Doubling of Consonants

63. *a.* A rough stop (18) is never doubled in literary Greek, but πφ, κχ, and τθ are always written for φφ, χχ, and θθ. Thus Σαπφώ, Βάκχος, κατθανεῖν, not Σαφφώ, Βάχχος, καθθανεῖν (60). So in Latin, Sappho, Bacchus.

b. A voiced stop is never doubled in Attic Greek. In γγ the first γ is always nasal (21). The doubling of voiceless stops, liquids, and nasals (73) is due to assimilation; e.g. ἵππος *horse* (ἴκχος, Lat. equus), πολλοί *many* (πολυ-οι), ἐμμένω (ἐν-μένω) *abide by.*

c. Attic has ττ for the σσ of Ionic and most of the other dialects in forms arising from voiceless palatals or dentals with ι (17 ; 94 ; 95); e.g. φυλάττω *guard* for φυλάσσω (base φυλακ-), ἐλάττων *less* for ἐλάσσων (ἐλαχ-), μέλιττα *bee* for μέλισσα (μελιτ-). Also ττ (not for σσ) and τθ occur in a few other words; e.g. 'Αττικός, 'Ατθίς, *Attic* (cf. 66). In tragedy and in Thucydides σσ is an Ionism.

64. Initial ρ is doubled when a vowel precedes it in forming a compound word; e.g. κατα-ρρίπτω *throw down.* So after the syllabic augment (535) ; as in ἔρριπτον (imperfect of ρίπτω). But after a diphthong it remains single ; as in εὔροος, εὔρους *fair-flowing.*

Euphonic Changes of Consonants

65. The following rules (66–109) apply chiefly to changes made in the final consonant of a stem to facilitate pronunciation. They occur when endings are added, especially in forming and inflecting the tenses of verbs and cases of nouns, when compounds are formed, and in other instances to be noted.

66. Consonants before Consonants. Before a dental stop (τ, δ, θ, 17), a labial (π, β, φ) or a palatal (κ, γ, χ) must be co-ordinate (18), and another dental stop becomes σ. E.g.

βτ, φτ : τέτριπται *has been rubbed* (τε-τρίβ-ται); ἔστραπται *is twisted* (ἐ-στραφ-ται).

γτ, χτ : λέλεκται *has been said* (λε-λεγ-ται); δέδεκται *has received* (δε-δεχ-ται).

πδ, φδ : κλέβδην *by stealth* (κλέπ-τω *steal*); γράβδην *scraping* (γράφ-ω *scratch, write*).

πθ, βθ : ἐλείφθην *was left* (ἐ-λειπ-θην) ; ἐτρίφθη *was rubbed* (ἐ-τρίβ-θη).

κθ, γθ : ἐπλέχθην *was plaited* (ἐ-πλεκ-θην) ; ἐλέχθη *was said* (ἐ-λεγ-θη).

ττ: ἀρυστίs *ladle* (for ἀρυτ-τιs, ἀρύτ-ω *draw water*). But cf. **63 c.**

δτ: νενόμισται *is the custom* (νε-νομιδ-ται, from νομίζω *hold as a custom*); ἴστε *you know* (ἰδ-τε, from οἶδα *I know*).

δθ: ἐνομίσθη *was believed* (ἐ-νομιδ-θην, from νομίζω); οἶσθα *thou knowest* (οἰδ-θα).

θτ: πέπεισται *is persuaded* (πε-πειθ-ται, from πείθ-ω *persuade*).

θθ: ἐπείσθην *was persuaded* (ἐ-πειθ-θην).

67. 'Eξ *from* has in composition the form ἐκ before a consonant; e.g. ἐκ-κρίνω, ἐκ-δρομή, ἔκ-θεσιs. **80 a; 84 a.**

68. No combinations of stops except those included in **63** and **66** (those in which the second is τ, δ, or θ) are allowed in Greek. When any such arise, the first stop is dropped; e.g. πέπεικα *have persuaded* for πεπειθ-κα. When γ stands before κ, γ, or χ, as in συγχέω *confound* (σύν and χέω), it is not a stop but a nasal (**21**; **63 b**).

69. Consonants before σ. No stop can stand before σ except π and κ. A labial with σ forms ψ, a palatal ξ, and a dental is first assimilated to form σσ, and one σ is then dropped. E.g.

τρίψω *shall rub* (for τρίβ-σω), γράψω *shall write* (γραφ-σω), λέξω *shall say* (λεγ-σω), πείσω *shall persuade* (πειθ-σω), ᾄσει *will sing* (ἀδ-σει), σώμασι *bodies*, dative (σωμάτ-σι), ἐλπίσι *hopes*, dative (ἐλπιδ-σι), φλέψ *vein* (φλεβ-s), ἐλπίs *hope* (ἐλπιδ-s), νύξ *night* (νυκτ-s), πάσχω *suffer* (πασσχω, παθ-σκω, with transfer of breathing, **105 f**).

70. The combinations ντ, νδ, νθ, when they occur before σ in inflection, are dropped and the preceding vowel is lengthened (**32**). E.g.

πᾶσι *for all* (παντ-σι), γιγᾶs *giant* (γιγαντ-s), δεικνύs *showing* (δεικνυντ-s), λέουσι dat. plur. *lions* (λεοντ-σι), τιθεῖσι dat. plur. *placing* (τιθεντ-σι), τιθείs nom. sing. *placing* (τιθεντ-s), διδούs *giving* (διδοντ-s), σπείσω *shall make libation* (σπενδ-σω), πείσομαι *shall suffer* (πενθ-σο-μαι).

71. a. The combinations λσ, ρσ may become λ, ρ and the preceding vowel be lengthened (**32**); e.g. ἤγγειλα *reported* (for ἤγγελ-σα, from ἀγγέλλω), ἔφθειρα *destroyed* (for ἔφθερ-σα). See **92.**

b. New Attic frequently shows ρρ for ρσ; e.g. Χερρόνησος for Χερσόνησοs *Chersonesus*. But ρσ is retained in βύρσα *ox-hide*, and in the dat. plur.; e.g. χερσί from χείρ *hand* (stem χερ-).

72. ν before Consonants. Before a labial stop ν becomes μ; before a palatal it becomes nasal γ (**21**); before a dental it remains unchanged. E.g.

ἐμπίπτω *fall into* (ἐν-πίπτω), συμβαίνω *come together* (συν-βαίνω), ἐμφανήs *in plain sight* (ἐν-φανήs); συγχέω *confound* (συν-χέω), συγγενήs *akin to* (συν-γενήs); ἐντίθημι *put in*.

73. Before λ, μ, and ρ, ν is assimilated. E.g.

ἐλλείπω *fail* (ἐν-λείπω), σύλλογος *assembly* (συν-λογος), ἐμμένω *abide by* (ἐν-μένω), συρρέω *flow together* (συν-ρέω). So ν is assimilated after λ in ὄλλῡμι *destroy* (for ὀλ-νῡ-μι, 640).

74. But verbs in -νω form the perfect middle (603) in -σμαι, not -μμαι ; e.g. πέφασμαι (from φαίνω *show*) for πε-φαν-μαι, by analogy with forms in -σται arising from a dental before a dental (66, 82). See 499 *d* ; 732.

75. N before σ is generally dropped and the preceding vowel is lengthened (32). Here a becomes ᾱ, ε the spurious diphthong ει (8), ο the spurious ου. E.g.

μέλᾱς *black* (for μελαν-s), εἷς *one* (for ἐν-s, ἑμ-s), λύουσι *they loose* (for λῦο-νσι). See 215 *b* ; 582. So λύουσα *loosing* (for λύοντ-ι̯α, λῦον-σα), λυθεῖσα *loosed* (for λυθεντ-ι̯α, λυθεν-σα), πᾶσα *all* (for παντ-ι̯α, παν-σα). See 95 *b*.

76. N standing before σι of the dative plural appears to be dropped without lengthening the vowel ; e.g. δαίμοσι, apparently for δαιμον-σι. But the dat. plur. of such words originally had the weak grade (34) δαιμν-σι, which would give δαιμα-σι (27), becoming δαίμοσι through force of the other cases. So μέλασι for μελν-σι, φρασί (Pindar) for φρν-σι, Attic φρεσί conforming to the ε in φρένες.

77. The preposition ἐν is not changed before ῥ, σ, or ζ ; e.g. ἐνράπτω *sew into,* ἔνσπονδοι *allies,* ἐνζεύγνῡμι *yoke fast.*

a. Σύν *with* becomes συσ- before σ and a *vowel,* but συ- before σ and a con-sonant or before ζ ; e.g. σύσ-σῑτος *messmate,* σύ-στημα *system,* σύ-ζυγος *paired.*

78. Πᾶν and πάλιν may retain ν in composition before σ or assimilate to σ ; e.g. πάν-σοφος, πάσσοφος *all-wise,* παλίν-σκιος *thickly shaded,* παλίσ-συτος *rushing back.* See 86 *c*.

79. Stops before μ. Before μ a labial stop becomes μ, and a palatal becomes (or remains) γ. E.g.

λέλειμμαι *have been left* (for λελειπ-μαι), τέτρῑμμαι *have been rubbed* (for τετρῑβ-μαι), γέγραμμαι *have been written* (for γεγραφ-μαι), πέπλεγμαι *have been plaited* (πεπλεκ-μαι), τέτευγμαι *have been made* (τετευχ-μαι), τέταγμαι *have been posted* (stem ταγ-).

80. But κ and μ may stand when they come together through vowel gradation (34; 107; 169) ; e.g. κέ-κμη-κα *am tired* (see κάμνω). Both κ and χ may stand before μ in the formation of substantives ; e.g. ἀκμή *edge,* ἀκμών *anvil,* αἰχμή *spear-head,* δραχμή *drachma.*

a. Ἐξ is ἐκ in composition before μ (67) ; e.g. ἐκ-μανθάνω *learn thoroughly.*

81. When γγμ or μμμ would thus arise, they are simplified to γμ or μμ ; e.g. ἐλέγχω *test,* perfect ἐλήλεγμαι (for ἐληλεγχ-μαι, ἐληλεγγ-μαι) ; κάμπτω *bend,* κέκαμμαι *have been bent* (for κεκαμπ-μαι, κεκαμμ-μαι) ; πέμπω *send,* πέπεμ-μαι *have been sent* (for πεπεμπ-μαι, πεπεμμ-μαι). See 499 *b*.

82. Before μ, a dental stop sometimes appears to become σ; e.g. νενόσφισμαι *am separated* (for νενοσφιδ-μαι, from νοσφίζω), πέπεισμαι *am persuaded* (for πεπειθ-μαι, from πείθω). These forms, with their ending -σμαι, are really due to analogy with the 3d sing. νενόσφισται, πέπεισται, where σ arose from a dental before a dental (66, 74). So ἴσμεν *we know* (Hom. ἴδμεν), due to ἴστε (for ἰδ-τε) *you know*; ἆσμα *song* (ἄδω *sing*); νόμισμα *currency* (νομίζω *hold as a custom*); σχίσμα *schism* (σχίζω *split*). But in ἐρετμόν *oar*, ἀριθμός *number*, ῥυθμός *rhythm*, σταθμός *stage*, the dental before μ is unchanged.

83. The Spirant σ. Between consonants or between a liquid and a consonant, σ is dropped; e.g. τέταχθε *you have been posted* (for τεταγ-σθε, 66); ἔσταλθε *you have been sent* (for ἐσταλ-σθε).

84. In compounds σ is retained when it begins the second element of the compound; e.g. ἔν-σπονδοι *allies* (77).

a. Ἐξ *from* drops σ before a consonant in compounds; e.g. ἐκ-ρέω *flow out*, ἐκ-πρεπής *preëminent*; cf. ἐκ τῆς πόλεως *from the city*, but ἐξ Ἀθηνῶν *from Athens*. 25, 67.

85. When σσ arises from inflection, one σ is dropped; e.g. ἔπεσι dat. plur. *words* (Hom. ἔπεσ-σι), ἐτέλεσα *I finished* (Hom. ἐτέλεσ-σα). But σσ, when represented by Attic ττ, never becomes σ; cf. φυλάσσω (63 c).

86. *a.* Compounds of δυσ- *ill* and a word beginning with σ and a vowel retain σσ; e.g. δυσσεβής *impious*; but δύσχιστος *hard to split* (for δυσ-σχιστος, from σχίζω *split*).

b. Σ is usually dropped before μ or ν, with compensative lengthening (32); e.g. εἰμί *I am* (for ἐσ-μι). But σμ may stand when μ belongs to a suffix, e.g. χάσ-μα *chasm* (82), and in compounds of δυσ- *ill*, e.g. δύσμεικτος *hard to mix*.

c. Σ is assimilated (according to the ancient and still current etymology) in Πελοπόννησος for Πέλοπος νῆσος '*Pelops' isle*'; so also in ἔννυμι *clothe* (for ἐσ-νῦμι, Ionic εἴνῦμι), and in the Homeric forms ἀγά-ννιφος *very snowy*, *snow-capped* (ἀγα-σνιφ-), φιλο-μμειδής *laughter-loving* (φιλο-σμειδ-).

d. Adverbs denoting *motion towards* may be formed by -ζε, representing -σδε; e.g. Ἀθήναζε *to Athens* for Ἀθήνας-δε. 19.

87. Loss of σ. Many forms are due to the loss of an original spirant, which may be recognized in earlier Greek or in kindred languages.

88. At the beginning of a word an original σ appears as the rough breathing. E.g.

ἵστημι *set* for σι-στη-μι, Lat. sisto; ἥμισυς *half*, Lat. sēmi-; ἕζομαι *sit*, Lat. sedeo; ἑπτά *seven*, Lat. septem.

a. Initial σ sometimes disappears before μ without trace; e.g. μία *one* for σμια, μειδῆσαι *to smile* for σμειδ- (86 c), μοῖρα *fate*, perhaps for σμορ-ͺα. Compare σμῑκρός and μῑκρός *little*, σμῖλαξ and μῖλαξ *smilax*.

89. In some words both σ and ϝ (or the semivowel υ, 26) have disappeared. E.g.

ἡδύς *sweet* (base σϝαδ-), cf. Lat. suāvis (for suād-uis); Hom. ὅς *his* (for σϝος), Lat. suus.

90. Between vowels σ became *h*, then disappeared. E.g.

γένος *race*, Att. gen. γένους, Hom. gen. γένεος for γενεσ-ος, cf. Lat. gener-is; λύη, λύει *thou ransomest* for λύε-σαι, λύε-αι; ἐ-λύε-σο, ἐλύεο, ἐλύου; ἀληθεσ-ια (cf. ἀληθής *true*), ἀλήθεια *truth*; εἱπόμην *I followed* (for ἐ-σεπ-ομην, cf. Lat. sequor), with transfer of breathing (105 ƒ); εἶχον *I had* (for ἐ-σεχ-ον).

91. There are a few cases of the retention of σ between vowels, as in some -μι forms of the verb, e.g. ἵστα-σαι and ἵστα-σο; also, σ is not dropped when it stands for σσ (85), as in ἐτέλεσα, or when -σι- represents an original -τι-, as in πλούσιος for πλουτ-ιος, λύουσι for λύοντι, or, in general, where its loss would disturb an inflectional system, as in ἔλῡσα, σ being retained because of σ in ἔπρᾱξα.

92. In the first aorist active and middle of liquid and nasal verbs, σ is generally dropped, with compensative lengthening (32); e.g. φαίνω (φαν-) *show*, aor. ἔφην-α for ἐφαν-σα, ἐφην-άμην for ἐφαν-σαμην. So ὀκέλλω (ὀκελ-) *run aground*, aor. ὤκειλ-α for ὠκελ-σα; but poetic κέλλω has ἔκελ-σα. See 71, 687.

93. Consonant Changes before ι. The following changes occur when ι (representing an original *y*, 26) follows a consonant.

94. The palatals κ, χ with such an ι become in Attic ττ, in Ionic and other dialects σσ (63 c); labials give πτ (621). E.g.

κόπτω *cut* for κοπ-ι̯ω; ταράττω *disturb* for ταραχ-ι̯ω, cf. ταραχ-ή *disturbance*; ἥττων *worse* for ἡκ-ι̯ων (357); θᾶττον *sooner* for ταχ-ι̯ον (105 e).

95. The dentals τ, θ with ι may become

a. ττ (σσ, 63 c); e.g. κορύττω, Hom. κορύσσω *equip*, for κορυθ-ι̯ω (cf. κόρυς, stem κορυθ-, *helmet*); μέλιττα *bee* for μελιτ-ι̯α (cf. μέλι, stem μελιτ-, *honey*). The poetical form χαρίεσσα *graceful* does not show a corresponding form in ττ (323).

b. Or, after a long vowel, a diphthong, or a consonant, τ, θ with ι may become σ; after a short vowel σσ, Attic σ; e.g. in the feminine of participles and adjectives (324 b; 332 a), in which ν is dropped with compensative lengthening (32); παντ-, παντ-ι̯α, πάνσα (Thessalian, Cretan, Arcadian, Argive), Hom. and Att. πᾶσα *all*; λῦο-ντ-, λῦοντ-ι̯α, λῦον-σα, λύουσα *loosing*. Hom. μέσσος, Att. μέσος *middle* may come from μετ-σο-s (Boeot. μέττος).

96. After a vowel δ or γ with ι becomes ζ; e.g. φράζω *tell* (for φραδ-ι̯ω, 617, 623); κομίζω *tend* (for κομιδ-ι̯ω); πεζός *on foot* (for πεδ-ιος, cf. Lat. pēs, ped-is); κράζω *screech* (for κραγ-ι̯ω, 589); Ion. μέζων (for μεγ-ι̯ων), Att. μείζων *greater*, comp. of μέγ-ας *great* (357). But after a consonant γ with ι becomes δ; e.g. ἔρδω *do* (for ἐργ-ι̯ω), cf. ῥέζω *do* (for ῥεγ-ι̯ω).

97. Verbs like πράττω *do*, τάττω *arrange*, from stems in γ (πρᾱγ-, ταγ-), seem to violate the principle of 96. They are probably due to analogy, since their futures, πρᾱ́ξω, τάξω, are like the future of φυλάττω (φυλάξω). The analogy was strengthened by verbs like ἁρπάζω, which has two stems, ἁρπαδ- and ἁρπαγ-, giving Hom. future ἁρπάξω, Att. ἁρπάσομαι *snatch away*. Πρᾱ́ττω may have had an earlier stem πρᾱκ- (also πρᾱχ-, cf. πέπρᾱχα). Cf. σφάζω and σφάττω (stem σφαγ-) *slaughter*.

98. Λ with ι becomes λλ; e.g. στέλλω *send* for στελ-ιω; ἅλλομαι *leap* for ἁλ-ιομαι (cf. Lat. salio and 88); ἄλλος *other* for ἀλ-ιος, Lat. alius. 63 *b* ; 628.

99. After αν, αρ, ορ, an ι is transposed and contracted with α or ο. This was called *epenthesis* (ἐπένθεσις *insertion*), though the process is really assimilation ; e.g. φαίνω *show* for φαν-ιω ; χαίρω *rejoice* for χαρ-ιω ; μέλαινα *black* for μελαν-ια, fem. of μέλᾱς (319) ; μοῖρα *fate* for μορ-ια (88 *a*), cf. μέρ-ος *portion*.

100. After εν, ερ, ιν, ιρ, υν, υρ, an ι disappears and ε, ι, or υ is lengthened (ε to ει). E.g.

τείνω *stretch*, for τεν-ιω ; χείρων *worse*, for χερ-ιων ; κείρω *cut the hair*, for κερ-ιω ; κρῑ́νω *separate*, for κριν-ιω ; οἰκτῑ́ρω *pity*, for οἰκτιρ-ιω ; πλῡ́νω *wash*, for πλυν-ιω ; σῡ́ρω *drag*, for συρ-ιω. So σώτειρα, fem. of σωτήρ *savior*, for σωτερ-ια. 630.

101. Before an ι (not the semivowel operating in the preceding cases, 93–100), τ becomes σ in many dialects (not, e.g., in Doric). E.g. Dor. λῦο-ντι *they loose*, λῦο-νσι, Hom. and Att. λύουσι (75), Aeolic λύοισι ; τίθησι *he places*, Dor. τί-θη-τι ; πλούσιος *rich* for πλουτ-ιος (cf. πλοῦτος *wealth*) ; σύ *thou*, Dor. τύ, Lat. tū. 91.

102. Digamma. The Aeolic and Doric retained ϝ, equivalent to English *w* (3), long after it disappeared in Ionic and Attic. The following are a few of the many words in which its former presence is known: ἔαρ *spring* (Lat. vēr), εἴκω *yield* (Eng. *weak*), δῖος *divine* (dīvus), ἔπος *word*, εἶπον *said* (stem ϝεπ-, cf. Lat. voc-is), εἶδον *saw* (for ἐ-ϝιδ-ον, Lat. vid-eo), ἔλπομαι *hope* (Lat. volup-tas), ἔννῡμι *clothe* (for ϝεσ-νῡμι, 86 *c*), ἐσθής *garment* (Lat. vestis), ἐρέω *I shall say* (Lat. ver-bum), ἔσπερος *evening* (vesper), ἴς *strength* (vīs), κληίς, Dor. κλᾱίς, *key* (clāvis), οἶδα *I know* (Eng. *wise*), οἶς *sheep* (ovis, Eng. *ewe*), οἶκος *house* (vīcus), οἶνος *wine* (vīnum), σκαιός *left* (scaevus). See also the cases under the semivowel *u*, 89.

103. Changes in Aspirates. When a voiceless consonant (π, κ, τ) is brought before a rough breathing either by elision, by crasis, or in forming a compound, it is itself made rough. E.g.

ἀφῑ́ημι for ἀπ-ῑ́ημι *let go*, καθαιρέω for κατ-αιρέω *take down*, ἀφ' ὦν for ἀπὸ ὦν *from which*, νύχθ' ὅλην for νύκτα ὅλην *all night* (55, 66). For crasis, see the examples in 51, 53. So οὐχ οὗτος *not he* (115).

<

N B

104. The Ionic generally does not observe this principle in writing, but has (for example) ἀπ᾽ οὗ, ἀπίημι (from ἀπό and ἵημι, 165 *i*).

105. The Greeks generally avoided two rough consonants in successive syllables.

a. In reduplication (544) an initial rough stop (φ, χ, θ) is always made smooth. E.g.

πέφυκα for φεφῦκα, perfect of φύω *grow*; κέχηνα for χεχηνα, perf. of χάσκω *gape*; τέθηλα for θεθηλα, perf. of θάλλω *flourish*. So in τί-θημι *place*, for θι-θημι (612 *b*).

b. The ending θι of the first aorist imperative passive becomes τι after θη- of the tense stem (789 *a*). E.g.

λύθητι *be released* (for λυθη-θι), φάνθητι *be shown* (for φανθη-θι); but 2 aor. φάνηθι *appear* (789 *b*).

c. In the aorist passive ἐτέθην *was placed* from τίθημι (θε-), and in ἐτύθην *was sacrificed* from θύω (θυ-), θε and θυ become τε and τυ before θην.

d. A similar change occurs in ἀμπ-έχω (for ἀμφ-εχω) and ἀμπ-ίσχω (for ἀμφ-ισχω) *clothe*, and in ἐκε-χειρία (ἔχω and χείρ) *truce*. So an initial aspirate is lost in ἔχω (stem ἔχ- for σεχ-, 88, 537), but reappears in fut. ἕξω.

e. There is a transfer of the aspirate in a few verbs which had originally two rough consonants in the stem; e.g. τρέφω (stem τρεφ- for θρεφ-) *nourish*, fut. θρέψω (675); τρέχω (τρεχ- for θρεχ-) *run*, fut. θρέξομαι; ἐτάφην from θάπτω (ταφ- for θαφ-) *bury*; see also θρύπτω, τύφω, and stem θαπ-, in the Catalogue of Verbs. So in θρίξ (227) *hair*, gen. τριχός (stem τριχ- for θριχ-); and in ταχύς *swift*, comparative θάσσων for θαχ-ιων (94). Here the first aspirate reappears whenever the second is lost by any phonetic change. Yet in some forms both rough consonants appear. E.g.

ἐ-θρέφ-θην *was nourished*, inf. θρεφ-θῆναι, τε-θράφ-θαι; τε-θάφ-θαι inf. *lie buried*; ἔ-σχε-θον *I held*; and the imperatives φάθι *say*, γράφηθι *be written*, στρά-φηθι *turn*; epic present φθινύθω *waste*.

f. An aspirate may pass from one syllable to another in early phonetic changes. E.g.

Attic ἕως *dawn*, Hom. ἠώς, Aeolic αὖος for αὐσ-ος, αὐ-ός (90, cf. Lat. a u r-ō r a, from aus-ōsa); ἔννυμι *clothe* (86 *c*) for ϝεσ-νῡμι, ϝεh-νῡμι; πάσχω *suffer* for παθ-σκω (69). So also the rough breathing; e.g. φροῦδος *vanished* from πρὸ ὁδοῦ; φρουρός *watchman* (for προ-ορος). 51.

106. Metathesis. A consonant sometimes shifts its position within a word; e.g. Πνύξ *Pnyx Hill*, gen. Πυκνός; τίκτω *give birth* for τι-τκ-ω, aor. ἔ-τεκ-ον; σκέπτομαι *consider*, Lat. s p e c i o.

107. The term *metathesis* should not be applied to cases like κράτος and κάρτος, θράσος and θάρσος, which arose from a sonant ρ (27); cf. *centre* and *center, apron (αρχη)* ; nor to forms such as βέ-βλη-κα *I have thrown,* τέ-τμη-κα *I have cut,* which are a grade of the dissyllabic bases *belē, temē* (169) ; cf. βάλλω, ἔ-βαλ-ον, βέ-λος, βέλε-μνον ; τέμ-νω, ἔ-ταμ-ον, τέμε-νος, all representing different vowel grades (34).

108. Between μ and ρ or μ and λ the sound of β is developed. E.g.

μεσημβρία *midday* for μεσ-ημρ-ια, from μέσος *middle* and the weak grade (ἠμρ, 34) of ἡμέρα *day,* Hom. ἦμαρ ; μέμβλωκα, epic perfect of βλώσκω *go,* from μολ-, μλω-, με-μλω-κα. Thus the vulgar *chimley* for *chimney* generally becomes *chimbley,* and Lat. camera became Fr. *chambre,* Eng. *chamber.*

a. In such cases the μ before β is lost when it begins a word. E.g.

βροτός *mortal* from μορ-, μρ- (cf. Lat. mor-ior *die*), but ἄ-μβρο-τος *immortal* ; βλίττω *take honey,* from μελιτ-, μλιτ-, cf. μέλι *honey.* See 625.

109. Between ν and ρ a δ is developed ; e.g. in the oblique cases of ἀνήρ *man* (277), gen. ἀνδρός for ἀνρ-ος, dat. ἀνδρί, etc. ; σίνδρων *mischief-maker,* cf. σινα-ρός *mischievous.* Cf. Lat. cinerem and Eng. *cinder.*

Movable Consonants

110. Most words ending in -σι (including -ξι and -ψι), and all verbs of the third personal singular ending in ε, may add ν when the next word begins with a vowel. This is called ν *movable,* ν ἐφελκυστικόν (*dragging after*). It is not found in Herodotus. E.g.

πᾶσι δίδωσι ταῦτα *he gives these things to everybody* ; but πᾶσιν ἔδωκεν ἐκεῖνα *he gave those things to everybody.* So δίδωσί μοι *he gives me* ; but δίδωσιν ἐμοί.

111. ᾿Εστί *is* may also take ν movable, like forms of the third person in σι, or it may admit elision (55 ; 59).

112. The third person singular of the pluperfect active in -ει, and ἤει *went,* may take ν movable ; e.g. ᾔδει(ν) *he knew.* But contracted imperfects in -ει (for -εε), e.g. ἐφίλει, never take ν in Attic.

113. The epic κέ (for ἄν) is generally κέν before a vowel, and the poetic νύν (enclitic) has an epic form νύ. Many adverbs in -θεν (as πρόσθεν) have poetic forms in -θε, which are regular in Herodotus.

114. N movable may be written at the end of a sentence or of a line of poetry. It may be added even before a consonant in poetry (and sometimes in prose) to make a syllable long by position (120). It may be added, by analogy with other neuters, to the pronominal forms τοσοῦτο(ν), τοιοῦτο(ν), ταὐτό(ν).

115. Οὐ *not* is the form used before a consonant or at the end of a sentence, οὐκ before a smooth vowel, and οὐχ before a rough vowel ; e.g. οὐ λύσω *I shall not loose,* οἱ μέν, οἱ δ' οὔ *some, but others not,* οὐκ αὐτός *not he himself,* οὐχ οὗτος *not he* (103). The emphatic form οὐχί is used before both vowels and consonants. Μή *not* inserts κ in μηκ-έτι *no longer,* by the analogy of οὐκ-έτι.

116. Οὕτως *thus,* ἐξ (ἐκς) *from,* are used before a vowel, οὕτω and ἐκ (cf. 84 *a*) before a consonant; e.g. οὕτως ἔχει *so it is,* οὕτω δοκεῖ *so it seems,* ἐξ ἄστεως *out of the city,* ἐκ τῆς πόλεως *out of the city.* Οὕτως is used at the end of a sentence or in answers, *just so!*

SYLLABLES

117. A Greek word has as many syllables as it has separate vowels or diphthongs. The syllable next to the last (ultima) is called the *penult* (p a e n - u l t i m a *almost last*) ; the one before the penult is called the *antepenult.*

118. The following rules, based on ancient tradition, are now generally observed in pronunciation and in dividing syllables at the end of a line:

a. Single consonants, combinations of consonants which can begin a word (which may be seen from the Lexicon), and consonants followed by μ or ν are placed at the beginning of a syllable; e.g. ἔ-χω, ἐ-γώ, ἐ-σπέ-ρα, νέ-κταρ, ἀ-κμή, δε-σμός, ἔ-λε-ξα, δα-ψι-λής, μῖ-κρόν, πρᾶ-γμα-τος, μι-μνή-σκω, πί-πτω.

b. Other combinations of consonants, which cannot begin a word, are divided ; e.g. ἐλ-πίς, ἔν-δον, ἄρ-ματα. So doubled consonants, e.g. πρᾶσ-σω.

c. Compound words are usually divided into their original parts ; but when the final vowel of a preposition has been elided in composition, the compound is perhaps more properly divided as a simple word would be, without regard to the derivation ; e.g. κα-θυ-φαι-ρῶ (from κατά, ὑπό, and αἱρέω), πα-ρά-γω (from παρά and ἄγω) ; so εἰ-σαγ-γε-λί-ᾱ (from εἰς and ἀγγελίᾱ).

Quantity of Syllables

119. A syllable is long by *nature* (φύσει) when it has a long vowel or a diphthong : τῑ-μή *honor,* κτεί-νω *kill.*

120. *a.* A syllable is long by *position* (θέσει) when its vowel is followed by two consonants or a double consonant ; e.g. τρά-πε-ζα *table,* ὄρ-τυξ *quail,* ἱ-στάν-τες *setting.* In ἱ-στάν-τες the first two syllables are long by position.

b. The length of the *vowel* itself is not affected by position. E.g. α was sounded as long in πρᾱσσω *do,* πρᾶγμα *deed,* and πρᾶξις *action,* but as short in τάσσω *arrange,* τάγμα *order,* and τάξις *ordering.*

c. One or both of the consonants which make position may be in the next word ; e.g. the second syllable in οὗτός φησιν *he says* and in κατὰ στόμα *vis-à-vis* is long by position.

121. When a vowel *short by nature* is followed by a stop with a liquid or a nasal, the syllable is *common* (that is, it may be either long or short) ; e.g. τέ-κνον *child*, ὔ-βρις *insolence*, ὔ-πνος *sleep*. But in Attic poetry such a syllable is generally short (*correptio Attica*) ; in Homer it is generally long : πῖκρός *bitter*, Att. πικρός.

122. A voiced stop (β, γ, δ) before μ or ν, and generally before λ, lengthens the preceding syllable by position ; e.g. ἀ-γνώς *unknown*, βι-βλί-ον *book*, δό-γμα *decree*. Exceptions, however, occur *metri gratia*.

123. To allow a preceding syllable to be common (e.g. short instead of long), the stop and the liquid or nasal must be in the same word, or in the same part of a compound. E.g. ἐκ is common (i.e. it may be short) in ἔ-κρῦψα *I hid* (∪ ‿ ∪ or ‿ ‿ ∪) ; but it is always long when a liquid or nasal follows either in composition or in the next word : ἐκ-λέγω *pick out*, ἐκ νεῶν *from the ships* (both ‿ ∪ ‿).

124. The quantity of most syllables can be seen at once. Thus η and ω and all diphthongs are long by nature ; ε and ο are short by nature. See 5.

125. When α, ι, and υ are not measured long by position, their quantity must generally be learned by observing the usage of poets or from the Lexicon. But it is to be remembered that

a. Every vowel arising from contraction or crasis is long ; e.g. α in γέρᾱ (for γέραα) *prizes*, ἄκων (for ἀέκων) *unwillingly*, and κἄν (for καὶ ἄν) *even if*.

b. The combinations ασ and υσ are long when ν or ντ has been dropped before σ (70).

c. The accent often shows the quantity of its own vowel, or of vowels in following syllables.

Thus the circumflex on κνῖσα *savor* shows that ι is long and α is short ; the acute on χώρᾱ *land* shows that α is long ; on τίνες *who?* that ι is short. On βασιλείᾱ *kingdom* the acute shows that the final α is long ; on βασίλεια *queen*, that final α is short. See 126 ; 130 ; 132.

d. Within a word, α, ι, υ are generally short before ζ ; e.g. θαυμάζω *wonder*, νομίζω *think*, ποππύζω *smack*. So before ξ within a word, ι and υ are generally short ; e.g. ὄρτυξ *quail*, στίξω *shall tattoo*.

ACCENT

General Principles

126. a. There are three accents :
The acute (´) ; e.g. ἀθάνατος, ἄνθρωπος, λόγος, αὐτός, δέ.
The grave (`) ; e.g. αὐτὸς ἔφη.
The circumflex (^) ; e.g. πᾶς, τοῦτο, τιμῶν.

b. No accent can stand in any syllable before the antepenult (117). The acute can stand only on one of the last three syllables of a word, the circumflex only on one of the last two, and the grave only on the last.

c. The circumflex can stand only on a syllable long by *nature*.

127. *a.* The Greek accent was not a *stress* accent, like ours, but it raised the musical *pitch* or *tone* (τόνος) of the syllable. This appears in the terms τόνος and προσῳδία, Lat. accentus, and also in ὀξύς *sharp*, and βαρύς *grave*, *flat* (see 129 *a* and *c*), all taken from ancient Greek music. As the language declined, the musical accent gradually changed to a stress accent, which is now its only representative in Greek as in most other languages.

b. The marks and terms of accent were introduced by Aristophanes of Byzantium, an Alexandrian scholar, about 200 B.C., in order to teach foreigners the correct pronunciation of Greek. By the ancient theory every syllable not having either the acute or the circumflex was said to have the grave accent (κἀτἀλὐὠ, now written καταλύω simply); and the circumflex, originally formed thus ⁀, and still ^ in French, was the union of an acute and a following grave. See 137.

128. The accent, like the breathing (12), stands on the second vowel of a diphthong; e.g. αἴρω, μοῦσα, τοὺς αὑτούς. But in the improper diphthongs (ᾳ, ῃ, ῳ) it stands on the first vowel even when the ι is written in the line; e.g. τιμῇ, ἁπλῷ, Ὦι (ᾧ), Ὦιξα (ᾦξα).

129. *a.* A word is called *oxytone* (ὀξύ-τονος *sharp-toned*) when it has the acute on the last syllable, e.g. τίς *who* (interrog.), ἀνήρ *man*, βασιλεύς *king*; *paroxytone* when it has the acute on the penult, e.g. λύω, πάθος, βασιλέως; *proparoxytone* when it has the acute on the antepenult, e.g. ἔλυον, βασιλεύοντος.

b. A word is called *perispomenon* (περι-σπώμενον *drawn round*, circumflexus) when it has the circumflex on the last syllable, e.g. παῖς, ἐλθεῖν; *properispomenon* when it has the circumflex on the penult, e.g. μοῦσα.

c. A word is called *barytone* (βαρύ-τονος, *grave* or *flat-toned*) when its last syllable has no accent (127 *b*). Of course, all paroxytones, proparoxytones, and properispomena are at the same time barytones.

d. When a word throws its accent as far back as possible (130) it is said to have *recessive* accent. This is especially the case with verbs (150). See 142.

e. The term *orthotone* is applied to a word, usually enclitic or proclitic (154), which acquires or retains an accent in certain positions; e.g. ὤν πέρι instead of the usual περὶ ὤν *concerning which* (135). So in English, "Government óf the people, bý the people, fór the people."

130. **Rules for the Accent.** The antepenult, if accented, takes the acute, but it can have no accent if the last syllable is long by nature or ends in ξ or ψ; e.g. πέλεκυς *axe*, ἄνθρωπος *man*; but ἀνθρώπους *men*, προφύλαξ *outpost*.

131. Genitives in -εως and -εων of substantives in -ις and -υς (252), all cases of substantives and adjectives in -ως and -ων of the *Attic* declension (205), and the Ionic genitive in -εω of the first declension (196 *c*), allow the acute on the antepenult; e.g. πόλεως, πόλεων, Μενέλεως, εὔγεως, ἵλεως, Ἀτρείδεω (gen. of Ἀτρείδης). So some compound adjectives in -ως, e.g. ὑψί-κερως *with high antlers.* For the accent of ὥσπερ, οἵδε, ὧντινων, see 163.

132. The penult, if accented, is circumflexed when it is long by nature while the last syllable is short by nature; e.g. μῆλον, νῆσος, ἦλιξ (125 *d*). Otherwise, if accented, it takes the acute; e.g. λόγος, τούτων, ἀνθρώπου, θώραξ.

133. Final αι and οι are counted as short in determining the accent; e.g. ἄνθρωποι, νῆσοι; except in the optative (e.g. τιμήσαι, ποιήσοι, not τίμησαι or ποίησοι) and in οἴκοι *at home.* 153.

134. An oxytone changes its acute to the grave before other words in the same sentence, and no stress whatever should be placed upon a syllable so marked; e.g. τοὺς πονηροὺς ἀνθρώπους (for τοὺς πονηροὺς ἀνθρώπους), ἀπὸ ἵππου.

a. This change, which means that all the syllables of the former oxytone are now of the same tone, is not made before *enclitics* (160), nor before an elided syllable (νύχθ᾽ ὅλην, 55, 140), nor in the interrogative τίς, τί; τί ὁρᾷς *what do you see?* (394) It is not made before a colon or a period. Before a comma modern usage differs, and the tradition is uncertain.

b. The grave accent is occasionally written on the indefinite pronoun τὶς, τὶ (394) to distinguish it from the interrogative τίς, τί.

135. Anastrophe. Dissyllabic prepositions, regularly oxytone, throw the accent back on the penult in two cases. This is called *anastrophe* (ἀναστροφή *turning back, reversion*). It occurs

a. When such a preposition follows its case; e.g. in τούτων πέρι (for περὶ τούτων) *about these matters.*

This occurs in prose only with περί, but in the poets with other dissyllabic prepositions except ἀνά, διά, ἀμφί, and ἀντί. In Homer it occurs also when a preposition follows its verb; e.g. ὀλέσας ἄπο *having destroyed.*

b. When a preposition stands for itself compounded with ἐστίν; e.g. πάρα for πάρεστιν (in poetry also for πάρεισι or even πάρειμι), ἔνι for ἔνεστιν (ἐνί being poetic for ἐν). Homer has ἄνα (for ἀνά-στηθι) *up!* and ἔνι for ἔνεισι.

136. Anastrophe is really the reversion of a preposition to its original use as an adverb, when it was orthotone (129 *e*) and generally more emphatic than its verb. Cf. the sentence-accent in Eng. *go awáy!* Greek ἄπιθι, and the poetic use of ἄνα *up!* (adverb) with the unstressed ἀμ βωμοῖσι *upòn thè áltars.*

Accent of Contracted Syllables and Elided Words

137. A contracted syllable is accented if either of the original syllables had an accent. A contracted penult or antepenult is accented regularly (130; 132). A contracted final syllable, if the original word was oxytone, has the acute; if not, the circumflex. E.g. τῑμώμενος from τῑμαόμενος, φιλεῖτε from φιλέετε, φιλοῖμεν from φιλέοιμεν, φιλούντων from φιλεόντων, βεβώς from βεβαώς, but τῑμῶ from τῑμάω.

This proceeds from the ancient principle that the circumflex comes from ΄ + ΄ (127 b), never from ΄ + ΄; so that τῑμάω gives τῑμῶ, but βεβαὼς gives βεβώς. So Hom. πάϊς boy becomes Attic παῖς, but κληΐς key, κλῄς.

a. Some exceptions to the rule of 137 will be noticed under the declensions. See 209; 304. The analogy of other forms is the cause.

138. If neither of the original syllables had an accent, the contracted form is accented without regard to the contraction; e.g. τῑμᾱ for τῑμαε, εὔνοι for εὔνοοι.

139. In crasis (49) the accent of the first word is lost and that of the second remains; e.g. τᾱγαθά for τὰ ἀγαθά, ἐγᾦδα for ἐγὼ οἶδα, κᾆτα for καὶ εἶτα; τᾶλλα for τὰ ἄλλα; τᾶρα or τᾶρα for τοι ἄρα.

140. In elision, oxytone prepositions and conjunctions, since they are of the nature of proclitics (154), lose their accent with the elided vowel; so also the enclitics (158) τινά and ποτέ. Other oxytones throw the accent back to the penult, but without changing the acute to the grave (134). E.g.

ἐπ' αὐτῷ for ἐπὶ αὐτῷ, ἀλλ' εἶπεν for ἀλλὰ εἶπεν, τίς ποτ' ἀνθρώπων for τίς ποτὲ ἀνθρώπων, φήμ' ἐγώ for φημὶ ἐγώ, κάκ' ἔπη for κακὰ ἔπη.

Accent of Substantives and Adjectives

141. The place of the accent in the nominative singular of a substantive (and the nominative singular *masculine* of an adjective) must generally be learned by observation. The other forms accent *the same syllable* as this nominative, if the last syllable permits (130); otherwise the following syllable. E.g.

θάλαττα, θαλάττης, θάλατταν, θάλατται, θαλάτταις; κόραξ, κόρακος, κόρακες, κοράκων; πρᾶγμα, πράγματος, πρᾱγμάτων; διδούς, διδόντος, διδοῦσιν. So χαρίεις, χαρίεσσα, χαρίεν, gen. χαρίεντος; ἄξιος, ἀξίᾱ, ἄξιον, ἄξιοι, ἄξιαι, ἄξια.

a. The *kind* of accent is determined as usual (130; 132); e.g. νῆσος, νήσου, νῆσον, νῆσοι, νήσοις. See also 143; 145.

142. The following substantives and adjectives have *recessive* accent (129 *d*) :

a. Contracted compound adjectives in -οος (209 *b*).

b. The neuter singular and vocative singular of adjectives in -ων, -ον (except those in -φρων, compounds of φρήν), and the neuter of comparatives in -ων ; e.g. εὐδαίμων, εὔδαιμον (307) ; βελτίων, βέλτῖον (cf. 355) ; but δαΐφρων, δαΐφρον.

c. Many barytone compounds in -ης in all forms; e.g. αὐτάρκης, αὔταρκες, gen. pl. αὐτάρκων ; φιλαλήθης, φιλάληθες (but ἀληθής, ἀληθές) ; this includes vocatives like Σώκρατες, Δημόσθενες (232) ; so some other adjectives of the third declension (see 308), and δεσπότης, δέσποτα *master* (192).

d. The vocative of nouns in -τηρ (273), of compound proper names in -ων, e.g. Ἀγάμεμνον, Αὐτόμεδον (except Λακεδαῖμον), and of Ἀπόλλων, Ποσειδῶν (Hom. Ποσειδάων), σωτήρ *savior*, and Hom. δᾱήρ, *brother-in-law* — voc. Ἄπολλον, Πόσειδον (Hom. Ποσειδᾱον), σῶτερ, δᾶερ (see 223 *b*).

e. Ἑτοῖμος *ready* became ἕτοιμος in New Attic.

143. The last syllable of the genitive and dative of oxytones of the first and second declensions is circumflexed ; e.g. τῑμῆς, τῑμῇ, τῑμαῖν, τῑμῶν, τῑμαῖς, cases of τῑμή ; θεοῦ, θεῷ, θεῶν, θεοῖς, from θεός.

144. The genitive and dative of the *Attic* second declension (203) are exceptions ; as νεώς *temple*, gen. νεώ, dat. νεῴ.

145. In the first declension, -ων of the genitive plural (for -ᾱων, -έων) is circumflexed (184 *b*). But the feminine of adjectives and participles in -ος is written and accented like the masculine and neuter. E.g.

δικῶν, δοξῶν (from δίκη, δόξα), πολιτῶν (from πολίτης for πολῑτά-ων, πολῑτέ-ων) ; but ἀξίων, λεγομένων (fem. gen. plur. of ἄξιος, λεγόμενος, 296). For the genitive plural of other adjectives and participles, see 313. Cf. 165 *d*.

146. Three nouns of the first declension are paroxytone in the genitive plural : ἀφύη *anchovy*, ἀφύων ; χρήστης *creditor*, χρήστων ; ἐτησίαι *Etesian winds*, ἐτησίων. Contrast ἀφυῶν from ἀφυής *dull* ; χρηστῶν from χρηστός *useful, good*.

147. Most monosyllables of the third declension accent the last syllable in the genitive and dative of all numbers ; here -ων and -οιν are circumflexed. E.g. θής *servant*, θητός, θητί, θητοῖν, θητῶν, θησί.

148. Δᾴς *torch*, δμώς *slave*, οὖς *ear*, παῖς *child*, Τρώς *Trojan*, φῶς *light*, and a few others, violate the last rule in the genitive dual and plural; so πᾶς *all*, in both genitive and dative plural. E.g. παῖς, παιδός, παιδί, παισί, but παίδων ; πᾶς, παντός, παντί, but πάντων, πᾶσι.

149. The interrogative τίς, τίνος, τίνι, etc., always accents the first syllable. So do all monosyllabic participles ; e.g. ὤν, ὄντος, ὄντι, ὄντων, οὖσι ; βάς, βάντος.

Accent of Verbs

150. Verbs, simple or compound, generally have recessive accent (129 *d*). E.g.

βουλεύω, βουλεύομεν, ἐβούλευον; παρέχω, πάρεχε; ἀποδίδωμι, ἀπόδοτε; σύνοιδα (σύν and οἶδα); βουλεύονται, βουλεῦσαι (aor. opt. act.), but βούλευσαι (aor. imper. mid.). See 133.

151. The chief exceptions to this principle are these:

a. The imperatives εἰπέ *say*, ἐλθέ *come*, εὑρέ *find*, λαβέ *take*, ἰδέ *behold*, are oxytone, their plurals εἰπέτε, ἐλθέτε, etc., paroxytone. But their compounds are regular; e.g. ἄπελθε, κατάλαβε (cf. 136). Similarly the second aorist middle imperative, second person singular, of these and other verbs in -ω is perispomenon, which is due to contraction; e.g. λιποῦ for λιπέ-(σ)ο, λαβοῦ for λαβέ-(σ)ο, παραβαλοῦ *bring alongside*. For compounds like κατά-θου see 152 *c*.

b. The forms of the present indicative of φημί *say* and εἰμί *am*, except φής and εἶ, are oxytone when not enclitic. 159 *c*.

c. Contract verbs present only apparent exceptions to 150; e.g. indic. τιμῶ for τιμάω, φιλοῦσι for φιλέουσι; subjv. λυθῇ for λυθέ-η, φανῶ for φανέ-ω; opt. λυθεῖμεν for λυθέ-ῖ-μεν, ποιοῖμεν for ποιέο-ῖ-μεν. Similarly other forms which are due to contraction; e.g. second aor. act. infin. λαβεῖν, ἐλθεῖν, λιπεῖν for λαβέ-εν, ἐλθέ-εν, λιπέ-εν (8, 28); pres. and second aor. act. and mid. subjv. of most verbs in -μι; e.g. τιθῶ for τιθέω, θῶ for θέω, ἱστῶμαι, ἀποθῶμαι, also perf. κεκτῶμαι. Optatives of the -μι inflection or formed without thematic vowel regularly circumflex the penult; e.g. ἱσταῖμεν, ἱσταῖτο, διδοῖσθε (772), εἰδεῖτε, λυθεῖεν.

Note, however, that δύναμαι *am able*, ἐπίσταμαι *understand*, κρέμαμαι *hang*, ὀνίνημι *help*, and ἐπριάμην (761) *bought*, have recessive accent in subjv. and opt.; e.g. δύνωμαι, δύναιτο, ἐπίστωμαι, πρίαιτο.

d. The following forms accent the penult: the first aorist active infinitive, the second aorist middle infinitive (except πρίασθαι and ὄνασθαι), the perfect middle and passive infinitive, and all infinitives in -ναι or -μεν (except those in -μεναι); e.g. βουλεῦσαι, γενέσθαι, λελύσθαι, ἱστάναι, διδόναι, λελυκέναι, δόμεν but δόμεναι (both epic for δοῦναι).

e. The following participles are oxytone: the second aorist active masc. and neuter sing., and all of the third declension in -ς except the first aorist active; e.g. λιπών, λιπόν, λυθείς, λυθέν, διδούς, δεικνύς, λελυκώς, ἱστάς (pres.); but the first aorist active has recessive accent; e.g. λύσᾱς, τιμήσᾱς. So ἰών, present participle of εἶμι *go*.

But the perfect middle and passive participle is always paroxytone; e.g. λελυμένος, λελομένοι.

f. The verbal adjectives in -τός are oxytone; e.g. λυτός, τῑμητός. Those in -τέος are paroxytone; e.g. λυτέος, ποιητέος. This applies to verbals compounded with a preposition, if they have a gerundive force; e.g. ἐξαιρετός, -τή, -τόν *to be removed*. But if they are purely adjectival in sense, the accent is recessive; e.g. ἐξαίρετος, ἐξαίρετον *picked out, choice*. So all verbals in -τος not compounded with a preposition; e.g. ἄλυτος, ἄλυτον *indissoluble*, δημοποίητος, -τον *created by the people*.

g. The accent of infinitives, participles, and verbal adjectives may in general be traced to their quality as verbal nouns. Hence the case-forms of participles follow the accent of adjectives (141), and are not recessive; e.g. βουλεύων, βουλεύοντος, βουλεύουσα, βουλευούσης, βουλεῦον (not βούλευον), φιλέων, φιλῶν, neut. φιλέον, φιλοῦν (not φίλεον, φίλουν).

152. There are these exceptions to the recessive accent of compound verbs.

a. The accent cannot go farther back than the augment or reduplication, since the augment, at least, was originally an adverbial modifier, and therefore emphatic; e.g. παρ-εῖχον (not πάρειχον) *I provided*, παρ-ῆν (not πάρην) *was present*, from πάρειμι, ἀφ-ῖκται (not ἄφικται) *has arrived*, from ἀφικνοῦμαι.

So when the augment falls on a long vowel or a diphthong which is not changed by it; e.g. ὑπ-εῖκε (imperfect) *he was yielding*; but ὕπ-εικε (imperative) *yield!* **136.**

b. Compounds of δός, ἔς, θές, and σχές are paroxytone; e.g. ἀπόδος, πάρες, παράσχες (not ἄποδος etc.).

c. Monosyllabic second aorist middle imperatives in -ου have recessive accent when compounded with a *dissyllabic* preposition; e.g. κατά-θου *put down*, ἀπό-δου *sell*; otherwise they circumflex the ου (151 a); e.g. ἐν-θοῦ *put in*, but uncontracted ἔν-θεο.

d. Compounds of ἔσται *will be* do not have recessive accent; e.g. παρέσται *will be present*, but πάρεστι *is present*.

153. Final -αι and -οι are long in the optative (133); e.g. aor. opt. act. λῦσαι, but aor. inf. λῦσαι, aor. mid. imper. λῦσαι.

Proclitics

154. Some words have no accent, or merge their accent in the accent of adjoining words. If a word loses its accent in the *following* word, it is called a proclitic (προκλίνω *lean forward*). If a word loses its accent in the *preceding* word, it is called an enclitic (**158**).

a. Proclitics and enclitics are as common in English as in Greek. In the sentence *Give me the ápple*, *me* is enclitic, *the* is proclitic. In the Greek equivalent, δός μοι τὸ μῆλον, the pronoun μοι *me* is enclitic (**159 a**), τὸ *the* is virtually proclitic, since it is barytone (**129 c**), its accent being the grave, or equivalent to no accent (**134**).

b. The term proclitic is usually restricted to the monosyllables enumerated in 155. But prepositions, even when dissyllabic, and the nom. and acc. forms of the article are proclitics in effect, since they become barytone before the following word (134).

155. The proclitics are the articles ὁ, ἡ, οἱ, αἱ; the prepositions εἰς (ἐς), ἐξ (ἐκ), ἐν; the conjunctions εἰ and ὡς (so ὡς used as a preposition, but not when it is the adverb *thus, so*); and the negative οὐ (οὐκ, οὐχ, but not οὐχί).

156. If a word which is normally proclitic occurs in a position where its accent cannot be merged in the following word, it becomes orthotone (129 *e*, 136). The following cases should be noted:

a. Οὐ takes the acute at the end of a sentence; e.g. πῶς γὰρ οὔ *for why not?* So when it stands alone, e.g. Οὔ *No.*

b. Ὡς and sometimes ἐξ and εἰς take the acute when (in poetry) they follow their noun; e.g. κακῶν ἔξ *out of evils*; θεὸς ὥς *like a god* (cf. 135).

c. Ὡς is accented also when it means *thus*; e.g. ὣς εἶπεν *thus he spoke.* This use of ὥς is chiefly poetic; but καὶ ὣς *even so* and οὐδ' ὣς or μηδ' ὣς *not even so* sometimes occur in Attic prose.

d. A proclitic before an enclitic (158) receives an acute; e.g. εἴ τις, εἴ φησιν οὗτος, οὔ φημι.

157. When ὁ is used for the relative ὅς, it is accented (as in *Od.* 2, 262); and many editors accent all articles when they are demonstrative, e.g. *Il.* 1, 9, ὃ γὰρ βασιλῆι χολωθείς, and write ὃ μέν ... ὃ δέ, and οἳ μέν ... οἳ δέ, in Attic Greek. Cf. English: SOME, *to be sure,* ... *but* OTHERS ...

Enclitics

158. An enclitic (ἐγκλίνω *lean upon*) is a word which loses its own accent, and is pronounced as if it were part of the preceding word (154); as ἄνθρωποί τε, Latin hóminésque.

159. The enclitics are —

a. The personal pronouns μοῦ, μοί, μέ; σοῦ, σοί, σέ; οὗ, οἷ, ἕ, and (in poetry) σφίσι.

To these are added the dialectal and poetic forms μεῦ, σέο, σεῦ, τοί, τύ (accus. for σέ), ἕο, εὗ, ἕθεν, μίν, νίν, σφί, σφίν, σφέ, σφωέ, σφωῖν, σφέων, σφέας, σφάς, σφέα.

b. The indefinite pronoun τὶς, τὶ, in all its forms (except ἄττα); also the indefinite adverbs πού, ποθί, πῄ, ποί, ποθέν, ποτέ, πώ, πώς. These must be distinguished from the interrogatives τίς, τί, ποῦ, πόθι, πῇ, ποῖ, πόθεν, πότε, πῶ, πῶς.

c. The present indicative of εἰμί *am* and of φημί *say,* except the forms εἶ and φής (151 *b*); but epic ἐσσί and Ionic εἶς are enclitic.

d. The particles γέ, τέ, τοί, πέρ ; the inseparable -δε in ὅδε, τούσδε, etc. (not δέ *but*) ; and -θε and -χι in εἴθε and ναίχι (163). So also the poetic νύν (not νῦν), and the epic κέ (κέν), θήν, and ῥά.

160. The word before the enclitic always retains its own accent, and it never changes a final acute to the grave (134).

a. If this word is oxytone or perispomenon, it remains unchanged ; e.g. τῑμαί τε (134), τῑμῶν γε, σοφός τις, σοφοί τινες, σοφῶν τινες.

b. If it is proparoxytone or properispomenon, it receives an acute on the last syllable as a second accent. Thus ἄνθρωπός τις, ἄνθρωποί τινες, δεῖξόν μοι, παῖδές τινες, οὗτός ἐστιν.

c. If it is paroxytone, it receives no additional accent (to avoid two acutes on successive syllables). Here a dissyllabic enclitic keeps its accent (to avoid three successive unaccented syllables). E.g. λόγος τις (not λόγός τις), λόγοι τινές (not λόγοι τινες), λόγων τινῶν, οὕτω φησίν (but οὗτός φησιν by *b*). When the final vowel of a dissyllabic enclitic is elided, there is no change ; e.g. ἄνδρα τιν' ὁρῶ, but ἄνδρα τινὰ ὁρῶ. (Papyri and mediaeval MSS. show anomalies, e.g. τέκνά τε.)

161. Enclitics sometimes retain their accent :

a. For emphasis, when they begin a sentence or clause, e.g. τινὲς λέγουσι SOME *say*, or when pronouns express antithesis, e.g. οὐ τάρα Τρωσὶν ἀλλὰ σοὶ μαχούμεθα *not against Trojans, you may be sure, but against* YOU *shall we fight*, S. *Ph.* 1253.

b. Ἐστί at the beginning of a sentence, and when it signifies *existence* or *possibility*, becomes ἔστι ; so after οὐκ, μή, εἰ, the adverb ὡς, καί, ἀλλ' or ἀλλά, and τοῦτ' or τοῦτο, and in the circumlocutions ἔστιν οἵ *there be who*, *some*, ἔστιν ὅτε *sometimes*.

c. When the preceding syllable is elided ; e.g. πόλλ' ἐστίν (140).

d. After an accented preposition and ἕνεκα *on account of*, the personal pronouns, but not the indefinite pronoun τὶς, generally retain their accent ; e.g. ἐπὶ σοί (not ἐπί σοι), περὶ σέ, yet πρός με ; ἕνεκα σοῦ.

e. The forms οὗ, ἕ, σφίσιν are generally not written as enclitic when they are used as indirect reflexives (986).

f. A dissyllabic enclitic retains its accent after a paroxytone (160 *c*).

162. When several enclitics occur in succession, each takes an acute from the following, the last remaining without accent ; e.g. ἤ νύ σέ που θεός ἴσχει *surely now some god, I ween, possesses thee, Il.* 5, 812.

163. When an enclitic forms the last part of a compound word, the compound is accented as if the enclitic were a separate word. Thus οὗτινος, ᾧτινι, ὧντινων, ὥσπερ, ὥστε, οἵδε, τούσδε, εἴτε, οὔτε, μήτε, are only apparent exceptions to 126, 130, and 132.

SOME DIALECTAL VARIATIONS FROM ATTIC

164. Vowels. The Ionic dialect is marked by the use of η for original ᾱ, even after ε, ι, ρ (where the Attic has ᾱ); and the Doric and Aeolic by the use of original ᾱ where the Attic has η. E.g.

Ionic γενεή Attic γενεᾱ, Ionic ἰήσομαι Attic ἰᾱσομαι (from ἰᾱομαι, 593) ; Doric τῑμᾱσῶ Attic τῑμήσω (from τῑμάω) ; Aeolic and Doric λᾱθᾱ Attic λήθη.

But an Attic ᾱ caused by contraction (as in τῑμᾱ for τῑμαε) is never changed to η; and wherever η interchanges with ε, representing an original ē, it is never changed to ᾱ; e.g. φῑλήσω from φιλέω, τίθημι and τίθεμεν.

165. a. The loss of ϝ in Attic often left no trace; e.g. ξένος *stranger*, for ξένϝος; μόνος *alone*, for μονϝος. But in Ionic these became ξεῖνος, μοῦνος; cf. Ionic κοῦρος *boy* with Attic κόρη *girl* (originally κορϝος, κορϝη). See 32.

b. Ionic shows the original long diphthong in the combination ηι where Attic has ει; e.g. βασιλήιος *royal* (stem βασιληϝ-), Att. βασιλεῖος.

c. Ionic does not avoid successive vowels to the same extent as Attic; and it therefore often omits contraction (40). It uses εν for εο and εου; e.g. ποιεῦμεν, ποιεῦσι (from ποιέομεν, ποιέουσι), but Att. ποιοῦμεν, ποιοῦσι. New Ionic does not use ν movable (110), and some editors reject it from Homer. See also 102 and 660.

d. Doric contracts αε to η (e.g. ὁρῇ *he sees*, for ὁράει, Att. ὁρᾷ); ᾱε to ᾱ (e.g. ἅλιος *sun*, for ἀέλιος, Hom. ἠέλιος, Att. ἥλιος); ᾱων to ᾱν (e.g. χαλεπᾶν *hard*, where the fem. gen. plur. is distinguished from the masc. and neut.; cf. 145, 296).

e. Interchange of stem vowels often occurs; e.g. Dor. τράπω *turn*, Att. Ion. τρέπω; Ion. τέσσερες *four*, Att. τέτταρες; Aeol. ὄν *upon*, Att. ἀνά; Ion. ἔσσων *worse*, Att. ἥττων; Ion. μέζων *greater*, Att. μείζων; Ion. ἰστίη *hearth*, Att. ἑστίᾱ; Ep. πίσυρες *four*, Att. τέτταρες; Aeol. ὄνυμα *name*, Att. ὄνομα (but cf. ἀν-ώνυμος); Ion. Dor. ὦν *therefore*, Att. οὖν.

f. Metrical lengthening, to avoid a succession of short syllables, appears in Ep. οὐλόμενος *ruinous* for ὀλόμενος, εἰνάλιος *in the sea* for ἐνάλιος, ἠγάθεος *very holy* for ἀγάθεος, ἀθάνατος *deathless* for ἀθάνατος.

g. In compensative lengthening (32) Doric generally lengthens ε to η, o to ω; e.g. ξῆνος *stranger*, Att. ξένος (165 a); τώς *the*, Att. τούς (for τόνς, Cretan); ἠμί *am*, Att. εἰμί (for ἐσμι). Aeolic lengthens α to αι, ε to ει, o to ου; e.g. παῖσα *all*, Att. Dor. πᾶσα (for πανσα, παντ-ι̯α); τίθεις *placing*, Att. τιθείς (for τιθεντ-ς); μοῖσα *Muse*, Att. μοῦσα, Dor. μῶσα (for μοντ-ι̯α). But Aeolic often doubles a liquid or nasal instead of lengthening the vowel; e.g. ξέννος *stranger*; ἔννεκα *on account of*, Ion. εἵνεκα, Att. ἕνεκα; ἔμμι *am* (so Hom.) and ἔμμεναι *to be*; φθέρρω *destroy*, Att. φθείρω.

h. Shortening before a short vowel is common in Ionic; e.g. βασιλέος *of a king*, for βασιλῆος, Att. βασιλέως. The gen. plur. of the first declension, ending in -άων, was weakened to -εων; e.g. Boeot. δραχμάων *of drachmas*, Ion. δραχμέων, Att. δραχμῶν.

i. Aspiration is regularly dropped in Aeolic and often in New Ionic. This is called *psilosis* (ψίλωσις *a making bare*); e.g. ἀπίκετο *arrived*, Att. ἀφίκετο; Hom. Hdt. αὖτις *again*, Att. αὖθις; so ἀπ' οὗ *from which* (where the rough breathing is written in literary texts but not pronounced), Att. ἀφ' οὗ (**104**).

166. Consonants. *a.* Doric retains original τι (**578**), e.g. in ἔχοντι *they have*, Aeol. ἔχοισι, Ion. Att. ἔχουσι; so Dor. τύ *thou*, Lat. tū, Att. Ion. Aeol. σύ. Cf. **95** *b.*

b. Interchange of consonants is seen in New Ionic κότε, κοῦ, κῶς, κότερος, Att. πότε, ποῦ, πῶς, πότερος (**409**); Dor. ὄκα *when*, Att. ὅτε; Dor. ἐνθεῖν *go, come*, Att. ἐλθεῖν (but ἐνθεῖν and ἐλθεῖν may have come from different bases). Note also Hom. Ὀδυσσεύς *Odysseus*, colloquial Att. Ὀλυτεύς, Lat. Ulixes; Greek δάκρυον *tear*, Lat. lacrima.

c. In Aeolic the accent recedes at least one *mora* (the time of a short vowel). This is called *barytonesis* (βαρυτόνησις); e.g. αὖτος *self*, Ion. Att. αὐτός; τίθεις *placing*, Att. τιθείς; λίπειν *to leave*, Att. λιπεῖν; Ζεῦς (= Ζεύς, **137**) *Zeus*, Att. Ζεύς. This does not occur in prepositions or conjunctions; e.g. ἀπύ *from*, Att. ἀπό; yet the principle of **154** *b* obtains here also.

PUNCTUATION MARKS

167. *a.* Greek texts use the comma and the period, like the English. They also have a colon, a point above the line (·), which is equivalent to the English colon and semicolon; e.g. οὐκ ἔσθ' ὅ γ' εἶπον· οὐ γὰρ ὧδ' ἄφρων ἔφυν *that is not what I meant; for I am not so foolish*, S. *El.* 941.

b. The mark of interrogation (;) is the same as the English semicolon; e.g. πότε ἦλθεν; *when did he come?*

PART II

INFLECTION

168. Inflection is a change in the form of a word, made to express its relation to other words. It includes the *declension* of substantives, adjectives, participles, and pronouns, and the *conjugation* of verbs.

169. In the process of inflection various endings, or *suffixes*, are added to a *stem*, or *base*, which conveys the fundamental *idea* underlying the word. Thus the idea *bring, carry* is contained in the stem φερε, φερο, φορο, which with proper endings, and sometimes none at all, may become an intelligible word: φέρο-μεν *we bring*, φόρο-s *tribute*, φέρε *bring!* In φόρ-o-s and φέρ-o-μεν we detect a common suffix -o- and a root or base φερ-, φορ-, with vowel gradation (**34**). A stem becomes *nominal*, e.g. φόρο-s, or *verbal*, e.g. φέρε, according to its meaning. The original meaning of endings and suffixes is no longer obvious. Many bases were dissyllabic. The base *temē*, with varying accent and suffixes, appears in τέμ-ν-ω *cut*, τέμα-χ-os *slice*, τέ-τμη-κα *have cut*, τόμ-o-s *a cutting*. Further, vowel gradation may alter a stem within the same system of inflection. Thus, in the declension of μήτηρ *mother* the forms of the stem in different cases are μητηρ, μητερ-, μητρ-; in λείπω *leave* the imperfect is ἔλειπον, stem λειπο-, the aorist ἔλιπον, stem λιπο-, the perfect λέλοιπα, stem λοιπ-. Cf. **34**; **107**; **806**.

170. There are three **numbers**: singular, dual, and plural. The plural denotes more than one object and is often used for the dual, which denotes two objects, or a natural pair, e.g. τὼ χεῖρε *the two hands*.

171. There are three **genders**: masculine, feminine, and neuter.

172. The *grammatical* gender in Greek is very often different from the *natural* gender. Examples of natural gender are ὁ ἀνήρ *the man*, ἡ γυνή *the woman*, ἡ κόρη *the girl*. But many names of things are masculine or feminine, i.e. they must be modified by masculine or feminine forms of article, adjective, or pronoun, and some words denoting persons may be grammatically neuter; e.g. ὁ εὐρὺς ποταμός *the broad river* (masc.),

38

ἡ καλὴ οἰκίᾱ the beautiful house (fem.), τοῦτο τὸ πρᾶγμα this thing (neut.), τὸ γράδιον the little old woman (174 d).

173. Nouns which may be either masculine or feminine are said to be of the *common* gender; e.g. ὁ θεός god, ἡ θεός goddess; ὁ βοῦς ox, ἡ βοῦς cow. Names of animals which include both sexes, but have only one grammatical gender, are called *epicene* (ἐπίκοινος); e.g. ὁ ἀετός the eagle, ἡ ἀλώπηξ the fox, both including males and females. The masculine is used when a whole class is denoted; e.g. οἱ ἄνθρωποι mankind (all men and women, 948). It is also used when a woman speaks of herself in the plural; e.g. καὶ γὰρ ἠδικημένοι σιγησόμεσθα, κρεισσόνων νικώμενοι for even though I (Medea) am wronged, yet will I keep silent, overcome by my betters, E. Med. 314.

174. The gender must often be learned by observation. But

a. Names of males are generally masculine, and names of females feminine (172).

b. Names of *winds*, *months*, and most *rivers* are masculine; and most names of *countries*, *towns*, *trees*, and *islands* are feminine.

c. Most nouns denoting *qualities* or *conditions* are feminine; e.g. ἀρετή virtue, ἐλπίς hope.

d. Diminutive nouns are neuter even when they denote persons; e.g. παιδίον little child; γύναιον little woman; Σωκρατίδιον dear little Socrates. Neuter, also, a e τέκνον and τέκος child. Yet, in poetry, the grammatical gender is sometimes disregarded; e.g. φίλε τέκνον (not φίλον) dear child! κολλικοφάγε Βοιωτίδιον you little bun-eating Boeotian!

e. Indeclinable nouns, including infinitives, and words or expressions quoted, are neuter; e.g. τὸ λέγειν to speak, or the act of speaking, τὸ δέκα the number ten, τὸ λάμβδα the letter L, τὸ παρ' Ὁμήρῳ ζωρότερον the word in Homer meaning 'purer.'

175. There are five **cases**: nominative, genitive, dative, accusative, and vocative.

176. The cases have in general the same meaning as in Latin; but the genitive, besides denoting *of* or possession, often means *from*; the dative denotes *to* or *for*, but also *with*, *by*, *in*, *at*, *on*. The chief functions of the Latin ablative are divided in Greek between the genitive and dative, since the original forms of the instrumental, locative, and ablative have been lost. 1040.

177. *a.* The nominative and vocative plural are always alike.

b. In neuters, the nominative, accusative, and vocative are alike in all numbers; in the plural these end in ᾰ.

c. The nominative, accusative, and vocative dual are always alike; and the genitive and dative dual are always alike.

178. All the cases except the nominative and vocative are called *oblique* cases.

NOUNS

179. There are three declensions of nouns (substantives, adjectives, and participles), corresponding in general to the first three declensions in Latin:

First, or ᾱ declension, with stems in ᾱ.
Second, or ο declension, with stems in ο.
Third, or consonant declension, with stems in a consonant or in ι and υ, which sometimes become semivowels (26).

180.   CASE ENDINGS OF NOUNS

	VOWEL DECLENSION		CONSONANT DECLENSION	
SING.	*Masc. and Fem.*	*Neuter*	*Masc. and Fem.*	*Neuter*
Nom.	ς or none	ν	ς or none	none
Gen.	ς or ιο		ος	
Dat.	ι			ι
Acc.	ν		ν or ἄ	none
Voc.	none	ν	none or like Nom.	none
DUAL				
N.A.V.	none		ε	
G.D.	ιν		οιν	
PLUR.				
N.V.	ι	ἄ	ες	ἄ
Gen.	ων		ων	
Dat.	ις (ισι)		σι, σσι, εσσι	
Acc.	νς (ᾱς)	ἄ	νς, ᾰς	ἄ

For the laws governing changes in these endings, see 24, 27, 75, 85.

SUBSTANTIVES

FIRST DECLENSION

181. Stems of the first declension end originally in -ᾱ. This -ᾱ is often modified, so that the nominative singular of feminines ends in -η or -ᾰ as well as in -ᾱ; that of masculines ends in -ᾱς or -ης. There are no neuters.

182. The following table shows how the final ᾱ or η of the stem unites with the case endings (180), when any are added, to form the actual terminations:

	SINGULAR			PLURAL
	Feminine		*Masculine*	*Masc. and Fem.*
Nom.	ᾱ or ἄ	η	ᾱ-s	η-s	α-ι
Gen.	ᾱ-s or η-s	η-s	Hom. ᾱ-ο (for ᾱ-ιο)	ὣν (for ἐ-ων, ἀ-ων)
Dat.	ᾳ or ῃ	ῃ	ᾳ	ῃ	α-ις or α-ισι
Acc.	ᾱ-ν or ἄ-ν	η-ν	ᾱ-ν	η-ν	ᾱs (for α-νς)
Voc.	ᾱ or ἄ	η	ᾱ	ἄ or η	α-ι

DUAL

Masculine and Feminine

N.A.V.　　ᾱ
G.D.　　α-ιν

Feminines

183. The nouns (ἡ) χώρᾱ *land*, (ἡ) γνώμη *opinion*, (ἡ) τῑμή *honor*, (ἡ) πεῖρα *test*, (ἡ) γέφῡρα *bridge*, (ἡ) Μοῦσα *Muse*, are thus declined:

Stem　　(χωρᾱ-)　　(γνωμᾱ-)　　(τῑμᾱ-)　　(πειρᾱ-)　　(γεφῡρᾱ-)　　(Μουσᾱ-)

SINGULAR

Nom.	χώρᾱ	γνώμη	τῑμή	πεῖρα	γέφῡρα	Μοῦσα
Gen.	χώρᾱs	γνώμης	τῑμῆς	πείρᾱs	γεφύρᾱs	Μούσης
Dat.	χώρᾳ	γνώμῃ	τῑμῇ	πείρᾳ	γεφύρᾳ	Μούσῃ
Acc.	χώρᾱν	γνώμην	τῑμήν	πεῖραν	γέφῡραν	Μοῦσαν
Voc.	χώρᾱ	γνώμη	τῑμή	πεῖρα	γέφῡρα	Μοῦσα

DUAL

N.A.V.	χώρᾱ	γνώμᾱ	τῑμᾱ́	πείρᾱ	γεφύρᾱ	Μούσᾱ
G.D.	χώραιν	γνώμαιν	τῑμαῖν	πείραιν	γεφύραιν	Μούσαιν

PLURAL

Nom.	χῶραι	γνῶμαι	τῑμαί	πεῖραι	γέφῡραι	Μοῦσαι
Gen.	χωρῶν	γνωμῶν	τῑμῶν	πειρῶν	γεφῡρῶν	Μουσῶν
Dat.	χώραις	γνώμαις	τῑμαῖς	πείραις	γεφύραις	Μούσαις
Acc.	χώρᾱς	γνώμᾱς	τῑμᾱ́ς	πείρᾱς	γεφύρᾱς	Μούσᾱς
Voc.	χῶραι	γνῶμαι	τῑμαί	πεῖραι	γέφῡραι	Μοῦσαι

184. *a.* Final -αι (nom. and voc.) is always short (**133**).

b. The genitive plural regularly has the circumflex on the last syllable, being a contraction of -ἐ-ων from Hom. -ᾱ-ων (**145, 146, 165** *h*).

185. The stem retains ᾱ in the singular after ε, ι, or ρ, e.g. χώρᾱ, χώρᾱς *land*, οἰκίᾱ, οἰκίᾱς *house*, νέᾱ, νέᾱς *new*; otherwise ᾱ becomes η.

186. But nouns having σ, λλ, ττ (σσ), αιν, or a double consonant (19) before final ᾱ of the stem, have ᾰ in the nominative, accusative, and vocative singular, and η in the genitive and dative, like Μοῦσα. E.g. ἅμαξα *wagon*, ἁμάξης; δίψα *thirst*, δίψης; ῥίζα *root*, ῥίζης; ἅμιλλα *contest*, ἁμίλλης; θάλασσα (Attic θάλαττα) *sea*, θαλάσσης; λέαινα *lioness*, λεαίνης; τρίαινα *trident*, τριαίνης. So μέριμνα *care*, δέσποινα *mistress*; also τόλμα *daring*, δίαιτα *way of living*, ἄκανθα *thorn*, εὔθῡνα *scrutiny*.

187. The following have ᾰ in the nominative, accusative, and vocative, and ᾱ in the genitive and dative, singular (after ε, ι, or ρ):

a. Most nouns ending in -ρα preceded by a diphthong or by ῡ; e.g. μοῖρα *fate*, μοίρᾱς, μοῖραν; see γέφῡρα *bridge*, 183.

b. Most abstract nouns formed from adjectives in -ης or -οος; e.g. ἀλήθεια *truth* (ἀληθής *true*), ἀληθείᾱς; εὔνοια *kindness* (εὔνοος *kind*), εὐνοίᾱς.

c. Nouns in -εια and -τρια designating females; e.g. βασίλεια *queen* (but βασιλείᾱ *kingdom*), ψάλτρια *female harper*. So μυῖα *fly*, μυίᾱς, μυῖαν.

188. EXCEPTIONS. Δέρη *neck*, and κόρη *girl* (originally δέρϝη, κόρϝη), have η after ρ (185). Ἔρση *dew*, and κόρση (Attic κόρρη) *temple*, have η after σ (186). Some proper names have ᾱ irregularly; e.g. Λήδᾱ *Leda*, gen. Λήδᾱς. Both οᾱ and οη are allowed; e.g. βοή *cry*, στοά *porch*.

Masculines

189. The nouns (ὁ) ταμίᾱς *steward*, (ὁ) πολίτης *citizen*, (ὁ) κριτής *judge*, and (ὁ) Εὐρῑπίδης *Euripides*, are thus declined:

Stem	(ταμιᾱ-)	(πολῑτᾱ-)	(κριτᾱ-)	(Εὐρῑπῐδᾱ-)
		SINGULAR		
Nom.	ταμίᾱς	πολίτης	κριτής	Εὐρῑπίδης
Gen.	ταμίου	πολίτου	κριτοῦ	Εὐρῑπίδου
Dat.	ταμίᾳ	πολίτῃ	κριτῇ	Εὐρῑπίδῃ
Acc.	ταμίᾱν	πολίτην	κριτήν	Εὐρῑπίδην
Voc.	ταμίᾱ	πολῖτα	κριτά	Εὐρῑπίδη
		DUAL		
N.A.V.	ταμίᾱ	πολῑτᾱ	κριτᾱ	
G.D.	ταμίαιν	πολίταιν	κριταῖν	
		PLURAL		
Nom.	ταμίαι	πολῖται	κριταί	
Gen.	ταμιῶν	πολῑτῶν	κριτῶν	
Dat.	ταμίαις	πολίταις	κριταῖς	
Acc.	ταμίᾱς	πολίτᾱς	κριτάς	
Voc.	ταμίαι	πολῖται	κριταί	

190. The stem retains ᾱ in the singular after ε, ι, or ρ; otherwise ᾱ becomes η. But compounds of -μετρης have η, e.g. γεωμέτρης *land measurer*.

191. The genitive singular of masculines of the ᾱ declension ends in -ου on the analogy of nouns of the second or ο declension, most of which are masculine.

192. The vocative singular has ᾰ in nouns in -της, e.g. πολῖτα *citizen*, στρατιῶτα *soldier*; in national names, e.g. Πέρσα *Persian*; in compounds, e.g. γεωμέτρα *land measurer*. Δεσπότης *master* has voc. δέσποτᾰ, with recessive accent (**142** c).

Contracts of the First Declension

193. Most nouns in -αᾱ, -εᾱ, and -εᾱς are contracted (**39**) in all their cases.

Μνάᾱ, μνᾶ *mina*, σῡκέᾱ, σῡκῆ *fig tree*, and Ἑρμέᾱς, Ἑρμῆς *Hermes*, are thus declined:

Stem	(μνᾱ- for μναᾱ-)		(σῡκη- for σῡκεᾱ-)		('Ερμη- for 'Ερμεᾱ-)	
			SINGULAR			
Nom.	(μνάᾱ)	μνᾶ	(σῡκέᾱ)	σῡκῆ	('Ερμέᾱς)	'Ερμῆς
Gen.	(μνάᾱς)	μνᾶς	(σῡκέᾱς)	σῡκῆς	('Ερμέου)	'Ερμοῦ
Dat.	(μνάᾳ)	μνᾷ	(σῡκέᾳ)	σῡκῇ	('Ερμέᾳ)	'Ερμῇ
Acc.	(μνάᾱν)	μνᾶν	(σῡκέᾱν)	σῡκῆν	('Ερμέᾱν)	'Ερμῆν
Voc.	(μνάᾱ)	μνᾶ	(σῡκέᾱ)	σῡκῆ	('Ερμέᾱ)	'Ερμῆ
			DUAL			
N.A.V.	(μνάᾱ)	μνᾶ	(σῡκέᾱ)	σῡκᾶ	('Ερμέᾱ)	'Ερμᾶ
G.D.	(μνάαιν)	μναῖν	(σῡκέαιν)	σῡκαῖν	('Ερμέαιν)	'Ερμαῖν
			PLURAL			
N.V.	(μνάαι)	μναῖ	(σῡκέαι)	σῡκαῖ	('Ερμέαι)	'Ερμαῖ
Gen.	(μναῶν)	μνῶν	(σῡκεῶν)	σῡκῶν	('Ερμεῶν)	'Ερμῶν
Dat.	(μνάαις)	μναῖς	(σῡκέαις)	σῡκαῖς	('Ερμέαις)	'Ερμαῖς
Acc.	(μνάᾱς)	μνᾶς	(σῡκέᾱς)	σῡκᾶς	('Ερμέᾱς)	'Ερμᾶς

194. Βορέᾱς *North wind*, which appears uncontracted in fifth-century Attic, has also a contracted form Βορρᾶς, gen. Βορροῦ, dat. Βορρᾷ, acc. Βορρᾶν, voc. Βορρᾶ.

195. In the dual and the accusative plural ε before ᾱ is absorbed, the result being ᾱ, not η, on the analogy of uncontracted forms (σῡκᾶ, σῡκᾶς, like τῑμᾰ, τῑμᾱς). See **45** a.

First Declension in the Dialects

196. a. The Ionic has η for ā throughout the singular, even after ε, ι, or ρ; e.g. γενεή *race*, χώρη, ταμίης. So Ionic has η for ἄ, e.g. πρύμνη *stern*, Att. πρύμνα. But Homer has θεᾶ *goddess*, Ἑρμείᾱς *Hermes*, perhaps Aeolisms. Cf. Hom. voc. νύμφᾰ, nom. νύμφη *maiden*. The Ionic generally uses uncontracted forms of contract nouns, e.g. σῡκέη, μνέαι; and abstracts in -είη, -οίη, Att. -εια, -οια, e.g. ἀληθείη, εὐνοίη (**187** *b*). Hom. has Ἀθηναίη *Athena*, Att. Ἀθηναίᾱ and Ἀθηνᾶ. Doric and Aeolic have ā unchanged, e.g. νῑκᾱ *victory*, τόλμᾱ *daring* (Att. τόλμα), Ἑρμᾶς.

b. Nom. Sing. Hom. sometimes has -τᾰ for -της; e.g. ἱππότα for ἱππότης *horseman*, μητίετα (with recessive accent) *counsellor*. Cf. Latin poēta = ποιητής, nauta = ναύτης.

c. Gen. Sing. For -ου Homer has the earlier form -ᾱο for -ᾱ-ιο, e.g. Ἀτρεΐδᾱο; sometimes -ω after vowels, e.g. Βορέω (nom. Βορέᾱς). Hom. and Hdt. have -εω (always one syllable in Hom.) for -ηο (**33**), e.g. Ἀτρεΐδεω (**131**), Τήρεω (gen. of Τήρης). Doric and Aeolic contract -ᾱο to -ᾱ, e.g. Ἀτρεΐδᾱ.

d. Acc. Sing. Hdt. sometimes forms an acc. in -εα (for -ην) from proper nouns in -ης, e.g. Ξέρξης, acc. Ξέρξεα or Ξέρξην; so δεσπότεα for δεσπότην, from δεσπότης *master*.

e. Gen. Plur. Hom. -ᾱων, the original form, e.g. κλισιᾱων *of tents*; sometimes -ῶν. Hom. and Hdt. have Ionic -έων (one syllable in Hom.), e.g. πυλέων *of gates* (**54**). Doric and Aeolic have -ᾶν for -ᾱων; it occurs also in choral passages in the Attic drama.

f. Dat. Plur. Poetic -αισι (also Aeolic and Old Attic form); Ionic -ῃσι (Hom., Hdt., Old Attic), Hom. also -ῃς (rarely -αις).

g. Acc. Plur. Aeolic -αις, Doric -ανς, -ᾰς, -ᾱς (all for -α-νς).

SECOND DECLENSION

197. Stems of the second declension end in -*o*. The nominative singular regularly ends in -ος or -ον. Nouns in -ος are masculine, less commonly feminine; those in -ον are neuter.

198. The following table shows how the final *o* of the stem unites with the case endings, when any are added, to form the actual terminations:

	SINGULAR		DUAL		PLURAL	
	Masc. and Fem.	Neuter	Masc., Fem., and Neuter		Masc. and Fem.	Neuter
N.	o-ς	o-ν			N. o-ι	ἄ
G.	ου (for o-o)		N.A.V.	ω	G. ων	
D.		ῳ	G.D.	o-ιν	D. o-ις or o-ισι	
A.		o-ν			A. ους (for o-νς)	ἄ
V.	ε	o-ν			V. o-ι	ἄ

199. In the genitive singular the Homeric -o-ιο becomes -o-ι̯-o (**37**), then -oo, contracted to Att. Ion. -ου, and to -ω in Aeolic and some Doric dialects. In the dative singular the ending was originally -αι, with which -o of the stem contracts to -ῳ. In the vocative singular -o interchanges with -ε (cf. **169**); so also in a few adverbs, e.g. πανδημεί in a mass (πᾶς all, δῆμος people).

200. The nouns (ὁ) λόγος *word*, (ἡ) νῆσος *island*, (ὁ, ἡ) ἄνθρωπος *man* or *human being*, (ἡ) ὁδός *road*, (τὸ) δῶρον *gift*, are thus declined:

Stem	(λογο-)	(νησο-)	(ἀνθρωπο-)	(ὁδο-)	(δωρο-)
			SINGULAR		
Nom.	λόγος	νῆσος	ἄνθρωπος	ὁδός	δῶρον
Gen.	λόγου	νήσου	ἀνθρώπου	ὁδοῦ	δώρου
Dat.	λόγῳ	νήσῳ	ἀνθρώπῳ	ὁδῷ	δώρῳ
Acc.	λόγον	νῆσον	ἄνθρωπον	ὁδόν	δῶρον
Voc.	λόγε	νῆσε	ἄνθρωπε	ὁδέ	δῶρον
			DUAL		
N.A.V.	λόγω	νήσω	ἀνθρώπω	ὁδώ	δώρω
G.D.	λόγοιν	νήσοιν	ἀνθρώποιν	ὁδοῖν	δώροιν
			PLURAL		
Nom.	λόγοι	νῆσοι	ἄνθρωποι	ὁδοί	δῶρα
Gen.	λόγων	νήσων	ἀνθρώπων	ὁδῶν	δώρων
Dat.	λόγοις	νήσοις	ἀνθρώποις	ὁδοῖς	δώροις
Acc.	λόγους	νήσους	ἀνθρώπους	ὁδούς	δῶρα
Voc.	λόγοι	νῆσοι	ἄνθρωποι	ὁδοί	δῶρα

201. The chief feminine nouns of the second declension are the following:

a. Words meaning *way*: e.g. ὁδός *road, street*, μέθοδος *procedure*, κέλευθος *way* (poet.), ἁμαξιτός *wagon road*, ἀτραπός *path*.

b. Names of *countries, towns, trees*, and *islands*, which are regularly feminine (**174** *b*): e.g. Ἤπειρος *Epirus* also ἤπειρος *mainland*, Κόρινθος *Corinth*, Σέρῑφος *the island Seriphus* also σέρῑφος *wormwood*, νῆσος *island*; also a few names of females, e.g. νυός *daughter-in-law* (**174** *a*).

c. Various words: e.g. βάσανος *touchstone*, βίβλος *papyrus scroll*, γέρανος *crane*, γνάθος *jaw*, δοκός *beam*, δρόσος *dew*, κάμῑνος *oven*, κάρδοπος *kneading-trough*, κῑβωτός *chest*, νόσος *disease*, πλίνθος *brick*, ῥάβδος *rod*, σορός *coffin*, σποδός *ashes*, τάφρος *ditch*, ψάμμος *sand*, ψῆφος *pebble*.

202. The nominative in -ος is sometimes used for the vocative in -ε; e.g. ὦ φίλος. Θεός *god* always has θεός as vocative; ἀδελφός *brother* has vocative ἄδελφε, with recessive accent (cf. **142**).

Attic Declension

203. A few masculine and feminine nouns of this declension have stems apparently in -ω, which is seen in all the cases. These forms arise usually from transfer of quantity (33) and the shortening of a long vowel before a vowel (35). So νεώς *temple*, Hom. νηός, Dor. νᾱός. A few have -ως after a consonant. This is called the *Attic declension*, though it is not confined to Attic Greek. The noun (ὁ) νεώς *temple* is thus declined:

SINGULAR		DUAL		PLURAL	
Nom.	νεώς			Nom.	νεώ
Gen.	νεώ	N.A.V.	νεώ	Gen.	νεών
Dat.	νεῴ	G.D.	νεῴν	Dat.	νεῴς
Acc.	νεών			Acc.	νεώς
Voc.	νεώς			Voc.	νεώ

204. There are no neuter substantives of the Attic declension in good use. But the corresponding adjectives, e.g. ἵλεως *propitious*, εὔγεως *fertile*, have neuters in -ων, e.g. ἵλεων, εὔγεων. See 299.

205. The accent of these nouns in the nominative is due to the original form (Μενέλεως for Μενέλᾱος, ἵλεως for ἵλᾱος), and is retained in all the other cases.

206. Some nouns of this class may have -ω in the accusative singular; e.g. λαγώς *hare*, acc. λαγών or λαγώ. So Ἄθως, τὸν Ἄθων or Ἄθω; Κῶς, τὴν Κῶν or Κῶ; and Κέως, Τέως, Μίνως. Ἕως *dawn* has regularly ἕω.

207. Although most nouns of the Attic declension are formed by transfer of quantity (33), some come by contraction; e.g. λαγώς from λαγωός.

Contract Substantives of the Second Declension

208. *a.* Stems in -οο and -εο are contracted to form nominatives in -ους, -ουν (42; 43).

b. Νόος, νοῦς *mind*, περίπλοος, περίπλους *a sailing round*, and ὀστέον, ὀστοῦν *bone*, are thus declined:

	SINGULAR					
Nom.	(νόος)	νοῦς	(περίπλοος)	περίπλους	(ὀστέον)	ὀστοῦν
Gen.	(νόου)	νοῦ	(περιπλόου)	περίπλου	(ὀστέου)	ὀστοῦ
Dat.	(νόῳ)	νῷ	(περιπλόῳ)	περίπλῳ	(ὀστέῳ)	ὀστῷ
Acc.	(νόον)	νοῦν	(περίπλοον)	περίπλουν	(ὀστέον)	ὀστοῦν
Voc.	(νόε)	νοῦ	(περίπλοε)	περίπλου	(ὀστέον)	ὀστοῦν

DUAL

| N.A.V. | (νόω) | νώ | (περιπλόω) | περίπλω | (ὀστέω) | ὀστώ |
| G.D. | (νόοιν) | νοῖν | (περιπλόοιν) | περίπλοιν | (ὀστέοιν) | ὀστοῖν |

PLURAL

Nom.	(νόοι)	νοῖ	(περίπλοοι)	περίπλοι	(ὀστέα)	ὀστᾶ
Gen.	(νόων)	νῶν	(περιπλόων)	περίπλων	(ὀστέων)	ὀστῶν
Dat.	(νόοις)	νοῖς	(περιπλόοις)	περίπλοις	(ὀστέοις)!	ὀστοῖς
Acc.	(νόους)	νοῦς	(περιπλόους)	περίπλους	(ὀστέα)	ὀστᾶ
Voc.	(νόοι)	νοῖ	(περίπλοοι)	περίπλοι	(ὀστέα)	ὀστᾶ

209. The accent of some of these forms is irregular:

a. The dual contracts -έω and -όω into -ώ (not -ῶ).

b. Compounds in -οος accent all forms like the *contracted* nominative singular; e.g. περίπλοος, περίπλους *sailing round*, gen. περιπλόου, περίπλου. Κανοῦν *basket* (κάνεον) takes its accent from the genitive and dative κανοῦ, κανῷ.

210. For -εα contracted in the plural to -ᾱ, not -η, see **45** *a.*

Second Declension in the Dialects

211. *a. Gen. Sing.* Hom. -οιο, e.g. θεοῖο, ποταμοῖο; sometimes -οο, also -ου, e.g. οὐρανοῦ, as in Attic, Ionic, and some Doric dialects. Aeolic and Doric -ω; e.g. ὠράνω, μεγάλω. See **37**; **199.**

b. Gen. and Dat. Dual. Hom. -οιιν; e.g. ἵπποιιν.

c. Dat. Plur. Ionic and poetic -οισι; e.g. ἵπποισι; also Aeolic and Old Attic, found rarely even in Plato and other writers.

d. Acc. Plur. Doric variously -ονς, -ως, -ος, -ους; e.g. νόμως, τὼς λύκος; Aeolic -οις.

e. The Ionic generally omits contraction.

f. In the "Attic" declension Hom. has Ἀθόως *Athos,* Κόως *Cos* (**206**), γάλοως *sister-in-law*; but νηός *temple,* λᾱός *people,* κάλος *rope* (Att. κάλως), λαγωός *hare* (**207**). Hdt. has λαγός, Κέος *Ceos,* λεώς.

THIRD DECLENSION

212. This declension includes all nouns not belonging to either the first or the second. Stems end in a consonant or in ι and υ, which sometimes become semivowels (**26**). The genitive singular ends in -ος.

213. The stem of a noun of the third declension cannot always be determined by the nominative singular; but it is generally found by dropping -ος of the genitive.

Formation of Cases

NOMINATIVE SINGULAR

214. The numerous forms of the nominative singular of this declension must be learned partly by practice. The following are the general principles on which the nominative is formed from the stem:

a. Masculine and feminine stems, except those in ν, ρ, σ, and οντ (*b* and *c*), add ς, with phonetic results according to 69 and 70. E.g.

φύλαξ *guard*, φύλακ-ος; βήξ *cough*, βηχ-ός; γύψ *vulture*, γῦπ-ός; φλέψ *vein*, φλεβ-ός; ἐλπίς (for ἐλπιδς) *hope*, ἐλπίδ-ος; χάρις *grace*, χάριτ-ος; ὄρνῑς *bird*, ὄρνῑθ-ος; νύξ *night*, νυκτ-ός; μάστιξ *whip*, μάστῑγ-ος; σάλπιγξ *trumpet*, σάλπιγγ-ος. So Αἴᾱς *Ajax*, Αἴαντ-ος; λύσᾱς *having loosed*, λύσαντ-ος; πᾶς *all*, παντ-ός; τιθείς *placing*, τιθέντ-ος; χαρίεις *graceful*, χαρίεντ-ος; δεικνύς *showing*, δεικνύντ-ος. The *neuters* of the last five words, λῦσαν, πᾶν, τιθέν, χαρίεν, and δεικνύν, are given under *d*, below.

b. Masculine and feminine stems in ν, ρ, and σ merely lengthen the last vowel. E.g.

αἰών *age*, αἰῶν-ος; δαίμων *divinity*, δαίμον-ος; λιμήν *harbor*, λιμέν-ος; θήρ *beast*, θηρ-ός; ἀήρ *air*, ἀέρ-ος; Σωκράτης (Σωκρατεσ-) *Socrates*.

c. Masculine stems in οντ drop τ (**24**), and lengthen ο to ω. E.g.

λέων *lion*, λέοντ-ος; γέρων *old man*, γέροντ-ος; λέγων *saying*, λέγοντ-ος; ὤν *being*, ὄντ-ος.

d. In neuters, the nominative singular is generally the same as the stem. Final τ of the stem is dropped (**24**). E.g.

σῶμα *body*, σώματ-ος; μέλι *honey*, μέλιτ-ος; γάλα *milk*, γάλακτ-ος; μέλᾱν (neuter of μέλᾱς) *black*, μέλᾱν-ος; λῦσαν (neuter of λύσᾱς) *having loosed*, λύσαντ-ος; πᾶν *all*, παντ-ός; τιθέν *placing*, τιθέντ-ος; χαρίεν *graceful*, χαρίεντ-ος; διδόν *giving*, διδόντ-ος; λέγον *saying*, λέγοντ-ος; δεικνύν *showing*, δεικνύντ-ος. For the *masculine* nominatives of these adjectives and participles, see *a*, above.

215. EXCEPTIONS TO **214** *a–c*. *a.* In πούς *foot*, ποδ-ός, ου is irregular; we expect πώς. Δάμαρ *wife*, δάμαρτ-ος, does not add ς.

b. Stems in -ῑν add ς and have -ῑς (**75**) in the nominative; e.g. ῥίς *nose*, ῥῑν-ός. These also add ς: κτείς *comb*, κτεν-ός (**75**); εἷς *one*, ἐν-ός; δελφίς (later δελφίν) *dolphin*, δελφῖν-ος; and the adjectives μέλᾱς *black*, μέλαν-ος, and τάλᾱς *wretched*, τάλαν-ος.

c. The later form ὀδούς (New Ionic ὀδών) *tooth*, gen. ὀδόντ-ος, is properly a participle; cf. ἔδω *eat* (**217** *a*).

216. EXCEPTIONS TO **214** *d*. Some neuter stems in -ατ have -αρ in the nominative; e.g. ἧπαρ *liver*, gen. ἥπατ-ος (**228**). For nouns in -ας with double stems in -ατ (or -ᾱτ) and -ασ, e.g. κρέας, πέρας (228), and τέρας, see 231 b. Φῶς (for φάος) light has gen. φωτ-ός; but Homer has the uncontracted φάος (stem φαεσ-). For πῦρ fire, gen. πῦρ-ός, see 291.

217. PARTICIPLES. *a.* Masculine participles from verbs in -ωμι add s to -οντ and have nominatives in -ούς (70); e.g. διδούς giving, διδόντ-ος. Neuters in -οντ are regular (214 d).

Other masculine participles from stems in -οντ have nominatives in -ων, like substantives (214 c).

b. The perfect active participle, with stem in -οτ, forms its nominative in -ώς (masc.) and -ós (neut.); e.g. λελυκώς having loosed, neut. λελυκός, gen. λελυκότ-ος. See 329.

<h3 style="text-align:center">ACCUSATIVE SINGULAR</h3>

218. *a.* Most masculines and feminines with consonant stems add α to the stem in the accusative singular; e.g. φύλαξ (φυλακ-) watchman, φύλακα; λέων (λεοντ-) lion, λέοντα (27).

b. Those with vowel stems add ν; e.g. πόλις state, πόλιν; ἰχθῦς fish, ἰχθῦν; ναῦς ship, ναῦν; βοῦς ox, βοῦν.

c. Barytones in -ις and -υς with dental (τ, δ, θ) stems generally drop the dental and add ν; e.g. ἔρις (ἐριδ-) strife, ἔριν; χάρις (χαριτ-) grace, χάριν; ὄρνῑς (ὀρνῑθ-) bird, ὄρνῑν; εὔελπις (εὐελπιδ-) hopeful, εὔελπιν (but the oxytone ἐλπίς hope, has ἐλπίδα).

219. Homer, Herodotus, and the Attic poets make accusatives in -α of the nouns in 218 c; e.g. ἔριδα (Hom.), χάριτα (Hdt.), ὄρνῑθα (Aristoph.). Κλεῖς (κλειδ-) key, collar bone, has κλεῖν and κλεῖδα.

220. Ἀπόλλων and Ποσειδῶν (Ποσειδάων) have accusatives Ἀπόλλω and Ποσειδῶ, besides the forms in -ωνα.

<h3 style="text-align:center">VOCATIVE SINGULAR</h3>

221. The vocative singular of masculines and feminines is sometimes the same as the nominative, and sometimes the same as the stem.

222. It is the same as the nominative

a. In stems ending in a stop consonant; e.g. nom. and voc. φύλαξ (φυλακ-) watchman.

b. In oxytones with stems ending in a liquid or a nasal; e.g. nom. and voc. ἅλς (ἀλ-) salt, ποιμήν (ποιμεν-) shepherd.

But barytone stems in a liquid or nasal have the vocative like the stem; e.g. δαίμων (δαιμον-) divinity, voc. δαῖμον; ῥήτωρ (ῥητορ-) orator, voc. ῥῆτορ.

EEK GRAMMAR

ǝms in -ιδ, and *barytones* with stems in -ντ (but
ocative like the stem; e.g. ἐλπίς (ἐλπιδ-) *hope,*
(λεοντ-) *lion,* voc. λέον; γίγᾱς (γιγαντ-) *giant,*
) *loosing,* voc. λῦων. So Αἴᾱς (Αἰαντ-) *Ajax,* voc.
Αἴαν (Hom.), but Αἴας in Attic.

b. Σωτήρ (σωτηρ-) *preserver,* Ἀπόλλων (Ἀπολλων-), and Ποσειδῶν (Ποσειδων-
for Ποσειδᾱον-) show vowel gradation (**34**) in the vocative; thus voc.
σῶτερ, Ἄπολλον, Πόσειδον (Hom. Ποσείδᾱον). For the recessive accent here
and in similar forms, see 142 *d.*

224. All others have the vocative the same as the stem; e.g.
Σωκράτης (Σωκρατεσ-) *Socrates,* voc. Σώκρατες (**142** *c*); πόλις (πολι-)
city, voc. πόλι; παῖς (παιδ-) *boy,* voc. παῖ; γέρων (γεροντ-) *old
man,* voc. γέρον (**24**); πατήρ *father,* voc. πάτερ; ἀνήρ *man,* voc.
ἄνερ (**34, 142** *d*).

DATIVE PLURAL

225. The dative plural is formed by adding σι to the stem,
with phonetic results according to 69 and 70. E.g.

φύλαξ (φυλακ-), φύλαξι; ῥήτωρ (ῥητορ-), ῥήτορσι; ἐλπίς (ἐλπιδ-), ἐλπίσι;
πούς (ποδ-), ποσί; λέων (λεοντ-), λέουσι; δαίμων (δαιμον-), δαίμοσι (**76**);
φρήν (φρεν-), φρεσί (**76**); τιθείς (τιθεντ-), τιθεῖσι; χαρίεις (χαριεντ-),
χαρίεσι (**69**); ἱστάς (ισταντ-), ἱστᾶσι; δεικνύς (δεικνυντ-), δεικνῦσι; βασιλεύς
(βασιλευ-), βασιλεῦσι; βοῦς (βου-), βουσί; γραῦς (γραυ-), γραυσί.

ACCUSATIVE PLURAL

226. The original ending -νς becomes -ας according to **27**; e.g.
πόδ-ας (for ποδ-νς) *feet,* λέοντ-ας *lions.*

227. STEMS ENDING IN A PALATAL, LABIAL, OR DENTAL STOP

I. *Masculines and Feminines*

	(ὁ) φύλαξ	(ὁ) σάλπιγξ	(ἡ) θρίξ	(ἡ) φλέψ	(ὁ) λέων
	watchman	trumpet	hair	vein	lion
Stem	(φυλακ-)	(σαλπιγγ-)	(τριχ-, 105 *e*)	(φλεβ-)	(λεοντ-)

SINGULAR

Nom.	φύλαξ	σάλπιγξ	θρίξ	φλέψ	λέων
Gen.	φύλακος	σάλπιγγος	τριχός	φλεβός	λέοντος
Dat.	φύλακι	σάλπιγγι	τριχί	φλεβί	λέοντι
Acc.	φύλακα	σάλπιγγα	τρίχα	φλέβα	λέοντα
Voc.	φύλαξ	σάλπιγξ	θρίξ	φλέψ	λέον

DUAL

| N.A.V. | φύλακε | σάλπιγγε | τρίχε | φλέβε | λέοντε |
| G.D. | φυλάκοιν | σαλπίγγοιν | τριχοῖν | φλεβοῖν | λεόντοιν |

PLURAL

N.V.	φύλακες	σάλπιγγες	τρίχες	φλέβες	λέοντες
Gen.	φυλάκων	σαλπίγγων	τριχῶν	φλεβῶν	λεόντων
Dat.	φύλαξι	σάλπιγξι	θριξί	φλεψί	λέουσι
Acc.	φύλακας	σάλπιγγας	τρίχας	φλέβας	λέοντας

	(ὁ) γίγᾶς	(ὁ) θής	(ἡ) λαμπάς	(ὁ ἡ) ὄρνῑς	(ἡ) ἐλπίς
	giant	hired man	torch	bird	hope
Stem	(γιγαντ-)	(θητ-)	(λαμπαδ-)	(ὀρνῑθ-)	(ἐλπιδ-)

SINGULAR

Nom.	γίγᾶς	θής	λαμπάς	ὄρνῑς	ἐλπίς
Gen.	γίγαντος	θητός	λαμπάδος	ὄρνῑθος	ἐλπίδος
Dat.	γίγαντι	θητί	λαμπάδι	ὄρνῑθι	ἐλπίδι
Acc.	γίγαντα	θῆτα	λαμπάδα	ὄρνῑν	ἐλπίδα
Voc.	γίγαν	θής	λαμπάς	ὄρνῑς	ἐλπί

DUAL

| N.A.V. | γίγαντε | θῆτε | λαμπάδε | ὄρνῑθε | ἐλπίδε |
| G.D. | γιγάντοιν | θητοῖν | λαμπάδοιν | ὀρνίθοιν | ἐλπίδοιν |

PLURAL

N.V.	γίγαντες	θῆτες	λαμπάδες	ὄρνῑθες	ἐλπίδες
Gen.	γιγάντων	θητῶν	λαμπάδων	ὀρνίθων	ἐλπίδων
Dat.	γίγᾶσι	θησί	λαμπάσι	ὄρνῑσι	ἐλπίσι
Acc.	γίγαντας	θῆτας	λαμπάδας	ὄρνῑθας	ἐλπίδας

228.   II. *Neuters* (*Stems ending in* τ)

	(τὸ) σῶμα	(τὸ) πέρας	(τὸ) ἧπαρ
	body	end	liver
Stem	(σωματ-)	(περατ-)	(ἡπατ-)

SINGULAR

N.A.V.	σῶμα	πέρας	ἧπαρ
Gen.	σώματος	πέρατος	ἥπατος
Dat.	σώματι	πέρατι	ἥπατι

DUAL

| N.A.V. | σώματε | πέρατε | ἥπατε |
| G.D. | σωμάτοιν | περάτοιν | ἡπάτοιν |

PLURAL

N.A.V.	σώματα	πέρατα	ἥπατα
Gen.	σωμάτων	περάτων	ἡπάτων
Dat.	σώμασι	πέρασι	ἥπασι

229.　STEMS ENDING IN A NASAL OR LIQUID

	(ὁ) ποιμήν	(ἡ) φρήν‘	(ὁ) αἰών	(ὁ) ἡγεμών	(ὁ) δαίμων
	shepherd	mind	age	leader	divinity
Stem	(ποιμεν-)	(φρεν-)	(αἰων-)	(ἡγεμον-)	(δαιμον-)

SINGULAR

Nom.	ποιμήν	φρήν	αἰών	ἡγεμών	δαίμων
Gen.	ποιμένος	φρενός	αἰῶνος	ἡγεμόνος	δαίμονος
Dat.	ποιμένι	φρενί	αἰῶνι	ἡγεμόνι	δαίμονι
Acc.	ποιμένα	φρένα	αἰῶνα	ἡγεμόνα	δαίμονα
Voc.	ποιμήν	φρήν	αἰών	ἡγεμών	δαῖμον (222)

DUAL

N.A.V.	ποιμένε	φρένε	αἰῶνε	ἡγεμόνε	δαίμονε
G.D.	ποιμένοιν	φρενοῖν	αἰώνοιν	ἡγεμόνοιν	δαιμόνοιν

PLURAL

N.V.	ποιμένες	φρένες	αἰῶνες	ἡγεμόνες	δαίμονες
Gen.	ποιμένων	φρενῶν	αἰώνων	ἡγεμόνων	δαιμόνων
Dat.	ποιμέσι	φρεσί	αἰῶσι	ἡγεμόσι	δαίμοσι
Acc.	ποιμένας	φρένας	αἰῶνας	ἡγεμόνας	δαίμονας

	(ἡ) ῥίς	(ὁ) ῥήτωρ	(ὁ) σωτήρ	(ὁ) ἅλς	(ὁ) θήρ
	nose	orator	preserver	salt	beast
Stem	(ῥῑν-)	(ῥητορ-)	(σωτηρ-)	(ἁλ-)	(θηρ-)

SINGULAR

Nom.	ῥίς	ῥήτωρ	σωτήρ	ἅλς	θήρ
Gen.	ῥῑνός	ῥήτορος	σωτῆρος	ἁλός	θηρός
Dat.	ῥῑνί	ῥήτορι	σωτῆρι	ἁλί	θηρί
Acc.	ῥῖνα	ῥήτορα	σωτῆρα	ἅλα	θῆρα
Voc.	ῥίς	ῥῆτορ (222)	σῶτερ (223)	ἅλς	θήρ

DUAL

N.A.V.	ῥῖνε	ῥήτορε	σωτῆρε	ἅλε	θῆρε
G.D.	ῥῑνοῖν	ῥητόροιν	σωτῆροιν	ἁλοῖν	θηροῖν

PLURAL

N.V.	ῥῖνες	ῥήτορες	σωτῆρες	ἅλες	θῆρες
Gen.	ῥῑνῶν	ῥητόρων	σωτήρων	ἁλῶν	θηρῶν
Dat.	ῥῑσί	ῥήτορσι	σωτῆρσι	ἁλσί	θηρσί
Acc.	ῥῖνας	ῥήτορας	σωτῆρας	ἅλας	θῆρας

Stems ending in σ

230. The final σ of the stem appears only where there is no case ending, as in the nominative singular, being elsewhere dropped. (See 90.) Two vowels brought together by this omission of σ are generally contracted.

231. a. The substantive stems in -εσ are chiefly neuters, and have -os in the nominative, accusative, and vocative singular. Masculines in -εσ are proper names, with -ης (214 *b*) in the nominative. For the feminine τριήρης, see 238.

b. Stems in -ασ, all neuters, have the nominative, accusative, and vocative singular in -as. Some exhibit also a stem in -ατ or -ᾱτ.

232. Σωκράτης (Σωκρατεσ-) *Socrates*, (τὸ) γένος (γενεσ-) *race*, and (τὸ) γέρας (γερασ-) *prize*, are thus declined:

SINGULAR

Nom.		Σωκράτης		γένος		γέρας
Gen.	(Σωκράτε-os)	Σωκράτους	(γένε-os)	γένους	(γέρα-os)	γέρως
Dat.	(Σωκράτε-ι)	Σωκράτει	(γένε-ι)	γένει	(γέρα-ι)	γέραι
Acc.	(Σωκράτε-α)	Σωκράτη		γένος		γέρας
Voc.		Σώκρατες		γένος		γέρας

DUAL

N.A.V.	(γένε-ε)	γένει	(γέρα-ε)	γέρᾱ
G.D.	(γενέ-οιν)	γενοῖν	(γερά-οιν)	γερῷν

PLURAL

N.V.	(γένε-α)	γένη	(γέρα-α)	γέρᾱ
Gen.	(γενέ-ων)	γενῶν	(γερά-ων)	γερῶν
Dat.	(γένεσ-σι)	γένεσι	(γερασ-σι)	γέρασι
Acc.	(γένε-α)	γένη	(γέρα-α)	γέρᾱ

233. (Τὸ) κέρας (κερᾱτ-, κερασ-) *horn* is thus declined:

SINGULAR				DUAL			
N.A.V.			κέρας	N.A.V.	κέρᾱτε	(κέρα-ε)	κέρᾱ
Gen.	κέρᾱτος	(κέρα-os)	κέρως	G.D.	κερᾱτοιν	(κερά-οιν)	κερῷν
Dat.	κέρᾱτι	(κέρα-ι)	κέραι				

PLURAL

N.A.V.	κέρᾱτα	(κέρα-α)	κέρᾱ
Gen.	κερᾱτων	(κερά-ων)	κερῶν
Dat.	κέρᾱσι		

234. Τέρας *prodigy* is declined in Attic like πέρας (**228**). But in Homer the stem is in -ασ, e.g. τέραα (or τείρεα), τεράων, τεράεσσι. Hom. has κέρᾰσι and κεράεσσι, dat. plur. of κέρας *horn*. In Hdt. ᾰ is weakened to ε before a vowel, e.g. τέρεος, τέρεα (but also τέρατος, τέρατα), κέρεος, κέρει, κέρεα, κερέων; so Hom. οὖδας *ground*, οὔδεος, οὔδεϊ, and in Attic poetry βρέτας *image*, βρέτεος, βρέτη, βρετέων.

235. In the dative plural of all stems in σ, σσ is reduced in Attic to σ (**85**), e.g. γένεσι for Hom. γένεσ-σι.

236. The dative sing. of stems in -ασ ends in -ᾰι. But it is sometimes written -ᾳ, as in ᾱ stems (**183**).

237. Proper names in -ης, gen. -εος, -ους, besides the accusative in -η, have a form in -ην as of the first declension; e.g. Σωκράτην, Δημοσθένην, Πολυνείκην, Τισσαφέρνην; so acc. plur. Ἀριστοφάνᾱς, Plat. *Symp.* 218 a. For the recessive accent in the vocative of these nouns, see **142** *c*.

238. The adjective τριήρης *triply rowed* is used as a feminine substantive, (ἡ) τριήρης (sc. ναῦς) *trireme*, and is thus declined:

SINGULAR		DUAL		PLURAL	
Nom.	τριήρης	N.A.V. (τριήρε-ε)	τριήρει	N.V. (τριήρε-ες) τριήρεις	
Gen.	(τριήρε-ος) τριήρους		τριήρει	Gen. (τριηρέ-ων) τριήρων	
Dat.	(τριήρε-ι) τριήρει	G.D. (τριηρέ-οιν)	τριήροιν	Dat. (τριήρεσ-σι) τριήρεσι	
Acc.	(τριήρε-α) τριήρη		τριήροιν	Acc.	τριήρεις
Voc.	τριήρες				

239. The accent in the genitive dual and plural is influenced by that of the other cases.

240. In the plural, the accusative (for τριήρεας) takes the nominative ending.

241. Stems in -εσ preceded by ε are doubly contracted in some cases (**45** *f*). The masculines are proper names in -κλέης (κλέος *glory*). (Τὸ) δέος (δεεσ-) *fear* and Περικλέης, Περικλῆς (Περικλεεσ-) *Pericles* are thus declined:

Nom.	δέος	(Περικλέης)	Περικλῆς
Gen.	(δέε-ος) δέους	(Περικλέε-ος)	Περικλέους
Dat.	(δέε-ι) δέει	(Περικλέε-ι) (Περικλέει)	Περικλεῖ
Acc.	δέος	(Περικλέε-α)	Περικλέᾱ (poet. Περικλῆ)
Voc.	δέος	(Περίκλεες)	Περίκλεις

242. In proper names in -κλέης, the text of Homer has -κλῆος, -κλῆϊ, -κλῆα, though the uncontracted forms may be read. Herodotus has -κλέος, -κλέϊ, -κλέα. Attic poetry has the uncontracted forms often. In adjectives in -εης Homer sometimes contracts εε to ει; e.g. εὐκλής, acc. plur. εὐκλεῖας for εὐκλέεας (with recessive accent).

243. There is one Attic noun stem in -οσ, closely related to stems in -εσ. (Ἡ) αἰδώς (αἰδοσ-) *shame* (cf. αἰδέ-ομαι for αἰδεσ-ομαι *am ashamed*) is thus declined:

	SINGULAR	DUAL AND PLURAL
Nom.	αἰδώς	wanting
Gen.	(αἰδό-ος) αἰδοῦς	
Dat.	(αἰδό-ι) αἰδοῖ	
Acc.	(αἰδό-α) αἰδῶ	
Voc.	αἰδώς	

244. Ionic (ἡ) ἠώς *dawn* has stem ἠοσ- (105 *f*), and is declined like αἰδώς : gen. ἠοῦς, dat. ἠοῖ, acc. ἠῶ. In Homer the uncontracted forms αἰδόος, ἠόα should be read. Attic ἕως *dawn* is declined like νεώς (203) ; but see 206.

Stems in ωυ

245. A few stems in -ωυ (-ωϝ) lose υ (26) and form masculine nouns in -ως, which are often contracted in the dative and accusative singular and in the nominative and accusative plural.

246. The nouns (ὁ) ἥρως *hero*, (ὁ) Τρώς *Trojan*, and (ὁ) μήτρως *mother's brother*, are thus declined:

SINGULAR

Nom.	ἥρως	Τρώς	μήτρως
Gen.	ἥρωος	Τρωός	μήτρωος
Dat.	ἥρωι or ἥρῳ	Τρωί	μήτρωι or μήτρῳ
Acc.	ἥρωα or ἥρω	Τρῶα	μήτρωα
Voc.	ἥρως	Τρώς	μήτρως

DUAL

N.A.V.	ἥρωε	Τρῶε	μήτρωε
G.D.	ἡρώοιν	Τρώοιν (148)	μητρώοιν

PLURAL

N.V.	ἥρωες (rarely ἥρως)	Τρῶες	μήτρωες
Gen.	ἡρώων	Τρώων (148)	μητρώων
Dat.	ἥρωσι	Τρωσί	μήτρωσι
Acc.	ἥρωας (rarely ἥρως)	Τρῶας	μήτρωας

247 *a.* Nouns in -ως sometimes have forms of the "Attic" second declension (203) ; e.g. gen. ἥρω (like νεώ), acc. ἥρων ; gen. μήτρω, Μίνω (206).
b. Like μήτρως are declined also (ὁ) πάτρως *father's brother*, (ὁ) θώς *jackal*.
c. Distinguish Τρώς *man of Troy* (substantive) from Τρωϊκός and Τρώϊος *Trojan* (adjectives).

Stems in οι

248. A few stems in -οι lose ι (26) and form feminine nouns in -ώ, which are contracted in the oblique cases. (Ἡ) πειθώ (πειθοι-) *persuasion* and (ἡ) Σαπφώ (Σαπφοι-) *Sappho* are thus declined:

Nom.	πειθώ	Σαπφώ
Gen.	(πειθό-ος) πειθοῦς	(Σαπφό-ος) Σαπφοῦς
Dat.	(πειθό-ι) πειθοῖ	(Σαπφό-ι) Σαπφοῖ
Acc.	(πειθό-α) πειθώ	(Σαπφό-α) Σαπφώ
Voc.	πειθοῖ	Σαπφοῖ

No dual or plural forms of these nouns are found in this declension, but a few occur of the second; e.g. acc. plur. γοργούς from γοργώ *Gorgon*.

249. The vocative in -οῖ shows the pure stem in -οι, of which there was a stronger grade -ωι, seen in the older nominatives Λητώ, Σαπφώ.

250. Herodotus has an accusative singular in -οῦν; e.g. ʼΙοῦν (for ʼΙώ) from ʼΙώ *Io*, gen. ʼΙοῦς; Λητοῦν, from Λητώ *Leto* (cf. Lat. Latona).

251. A few feminines in -ών (with regular stems in -ον, 229) have occasional forms like those of nouns in -ώ; e.g. ἀηδών *nightingale*, gen. ἀηδοῦς, voc. ἀηδοῖ; εἰκών *image*, gen. εἰκοῦς acc. εἰκώ; χελιδών *swallow*, voc. χελῑδοῖ.

Stems ending in ι and υ

252. Most stems in -ι (with nominatives in -ις) and a few in -υ (with nominatives in -υς and -υ) have ε in place of their final ι or υ in all cases except the nominative, accusative, and vocative singular, and have -ως in place of -ος in the genitive singular. The dative singular, nominative and accusative dual, and nominative plural are contracted.

253. The nouns (ἡ) πόλις (πολι-) *state*, (ὁ) πῆχυς (πηχυ-) *cubit*, and (τό) ἄστυ (ἀστυ-) *city*, are thus declined:

SINGULAR

Nom.		πόλις		πῆχυς		ἄστυ
Gen.		πόλεως		πήχεως		ἄστεως
Dat.	(πόλε-ι)	πόλει	(πήχε-ι)	πήχει	(ἄστε-ι)	ἄστει
Acc.		πόλιν		πῆχυν		ἄστυ
Voc.		πόλι		πῆχυ		ἄστυ

DUAL

N.A.V.	(πόλε-ε)	πόλει	(πήχε-ε)	πήχει	(ἄστε-ε)	ἄστει
G.D.		πολέοιν		πηχέοιν		ἀστέοιν

PLURAL

N.V.	(πόλε-ες) πόλεις	(πήχε-ες) πήχεις	(ἄστε-α) ἄστη
Gen.	πόλεων	πήχεων	ἄστεων
Dat.	πόλεσι	πήχεσι	ἄστεσι
Acc.	πόλεις	πήχεις	(ἄστε-α) ἄστη

254. The accent of πόλεως (131) is explained by the earlier Homeric πόληος, from which it is derived by transfer of quantity (33). The gen. plur. πόλεων follows in accent the gen. singular. But in poetry and the dialects ἀστέων, πηχέων are accented according to rule.

255. The dual in εε uncontracted occurs rarely. The accusatives πόλεις and πήχεις are borrowed from the nominative (cf. 240).

256. No neuters in -ι, gen. -εως, were in common Attic use. The foreign words κόμμι *gum*, πέπερι *pepper*, have gen. κόμμεως, πεπέρεως, but πέπερι is generally treated as a dental stem (227).

257. The original ι of the stem of nouns in -ις (Attic gen. -εως) is retained in Ionic, Doric, and Aeolic. E.g. πόλις, πόλιος, (πόλιι) πόλῑ, πόλιν; plur. πόλιες, πολίων; Hom. πολίεσσι (Hdt. πόλισι), πόλιας (Hdt. also πόλῑς for πολι-νς). Homer has also πόλει (with πτόλεϊ) and πόλεσι in the dative. There are also epic forms πόληος, πόληϊ, πόληες, πόληας. The Attic poets have a genitive in -εος.

Ionic, Doric, and Aeolic have a genitive in -εος in ♫ouns in -υς of this class; also uncontracted forms πήχεες, ἄστεϊ, ἄστεα.

258. The inflections of 253 are explained by vowel gradation (34), in which the weaker grades ι and υ vary with the stronger ει and ευ. E.g. weak grade πόλι-ς, πόλι-ν, πῆχυ-ς, πῆχυν; strong grade πολει̯-ι, πολει̯-ες, πηχευ̯-ι, πηχευ̯-ες, which, after loss of ι and υ (26), contract to πόλει, πόλεις, πήχει, πήχεις.

259. Οἶς *sheep*, although an ι stem (οἰ- for ὀϝι-, cf. Lat. ovi-s), is thus declined: οἶς, οἰός, οἰΐ, οἶν or ὄϊν, οἶ; οἶε, οἰοῖν; οἶες, οἰῶν, οἰσί, οἶς (291).

260. Most nouns in -υς retain υ; e.g. (ὁ) ἰχθῦς (ἰχθυ-) *fish*, (ὁ) μῦς (μυ-) *mouse*, which are thus declined:

SINGULAR		DUAL		PLURAL	
Nom.	ἰχθύς μῦς	N.A.V.	ἰχθύε μύε	N.V.	ἰχθύες μύες
Gen.	ἰχθύος μυός	G.D.	ἰχθύοιν μυοῖν	Gen.	ἰχθύων μυῶν
Dat.	ἰχθύϊ μυΐ			Dat.	ἰχθύσι μυσί
Acc.	ἰχθύν μῦν			Acc.	ἰχθῦς μύας
Voc.	ἰχθύ μῦ				

261. The nominative plural and dual rarely have ῡς and ῡ; e.g. ἰχθῦς (like acc.) and ἰχθῦ (for ἰχθύε) in comedy.

262. Homer and Herodotus have both ἰχθύας and ἰχθῦς (for ἰχθυ-νς) in the accusative plural.

263. Oxytones and monosyllables have ῡ in the nominative, accusative, and vocative singular: ἰχθῦς, μῦς. The weak grade with ῠ appears in the other cases (**35**). Herodian accents as perispomenon, ἰχθῦς.

264. Ἔγχελυς eel, is declined like ἰχθῦς in the singular, like πῆχυς in the plural: gen. sing. ἐγχέλυ-ος, nom. plur. ἐγχέλεις.

Stems ending in ευ, αυ, ου

265. Nouns in -ευς, -αυς, -ους retain υ in the nominative and vocative singular and dative plural, but lose υ before a vowel (**37**); e.g. (ὁ) βασιλεύς (βασιλευ-) king, (ἡ) γραῦς (γραυ-) old woman, (ἡ) ναῦς (ναυ-) ship, (ὁ, ἡ) βοῦς (βου-) ox, cow, which are thus declined:

SINGULAR

Nom.	βασιλεύς	γραῦς	ναῦς	βοῦς
Gen.	βασιλέως	γρᾱός	νεώς	βοός
Dat. (βασιλέ-ι)	βασιλεῖ	γρᾱΐ	νηΐ	βοΐ
Acc.	βασιλέᾱ	γραῦν	ναῦν	βοῦν
Voc.	βασιλεῦ	γραῦ	ναῦ	βοῦ

DUAL

N.A.V.	βασιλῆ	γρᾶε	νῆε	βόε
G.D.	βασιλέοιν	γρᾱοῖν	νεοῖν	βοοῖν

PLURAL

N.V.	βασιλῆς	γρᾶες	νῆες	βόες
Gen.	βασιλέων	γρᾱῶν	νεῶν	βοῶν
Dat.	βασιλεῦσι	γραυσί	ναυσί	βουσί
Acc.	βασιλέᾱς	γραῦς	ναῦς	βοῦς

266. These nouns originally had a stronger grade in -ην, -ᾱν, -ων, still seen before vowels; e.g. in γρᾱ-ός, νη-ί (for γρᾱϝ-ος, νηϝ-ι, cf. Lat. nāv-is), and in the Homeric and Doric forms (**267, 270**). These long diphthongs are shortened before a consonant, giving βασιλεύς, ναῦς, βοῦς, βασιλεῦσι, ναυσί, βουσί; and η, after the loss of ϝ (υ), is shortened before the vowel of the case ending (**35**) in βασιλέως, νεῶν. Βοῦς, βοός (for βοϝ-ος, Lat. bov-is), has the weak grade throughout.

267. Homer has the long diphthong in βασιλῆ(ϝ)-ος, βασιλῆ(ϝ)-ι, βασι-λῆ(ϝ)-α, βασιλῆ(ϝ)-ας, and νη(ϝ)-ός (**270**), whence came the Attic βασιλέως etc., and νεώς, by transfer of quantity (**33**). In proper names Homer has e.g. Πηλῆος, Πηλέος, Πηλῆι, rarely contracted, as Πηλεῖ, Ἀχιλλεῖ.

268. Nominative plural in -ης, as βασιλῆς (for βασιλῆες), is the prevailing form until about 350 B.C.; after 324 B.C. βασιλεῖς is regular. Nom. dual βασιλῆ is for βασιλῆε. In Attic drama the accusative sometimes has -έᾰ, -έᾰς.

269. When a vowel precedes, -έως of the genitive singular may be contracted into -ῶς, and -έᾱ of the accusative singular into -ᾶ; rarely -έᾱς of the accusative plural into -ᾶς, and -έων of the genitive plural into -ῶν. E.g. Πειραιεύς *Peiraeus* has gen. Πειραιέως, Πειραιῶς, dat. Πειραιεῖ, Πειραιεῖ, acc. Πειραιέᾱ, Πειραιᾶ; Δωριεύς *a Dorian* has gen. plur. Δωριέων, Δωριῶν, acc. Δωριέᾱς, Δωριᾶς.

270. In Doric and Ionic ναῦς is thus declined:

	SINGULAR			PLURAL		
	Doric	Homer	Herodotus	Doric	Homer	Herodotus
Nom.	ναῦς	νηῦς	νηῦς	νᾶες	νῆες, νέες	νέες
Gen.	νᾱός	νηός, νεός	νεός	νᾱῶν	νηῶν, νεῶν	νεῶν
Dat.	νᾱΐ	νηΐ	νηΐ	ναυσί, νάεσσι	νηυσί, νήεσσι, νέεσσι	νηυσί
Acc.	ναῦν	νῆα, νέα	νέα	νᾶας	νῆας, νέας	νέας

271. Homer has γρηῦς (γρην-) for γραῦς, and βόας and βοῦς in the accusative plural of βοῦς.

272. Χοῦς *three-quart measure* is declined like βοῦς, except in the accusatives χόᾱ and χόας. See χοῦς in **291.**

Stems in ερ varying with ρ

273. In several words three vowel grades (**34**) appear: -τηρ, -τερ, -τρ. The middle grade is seen e.g. in the vocative singular, with recessive accent. The weak grade appears in the genitive and dative singular, which are oxytone; also in the dative plural, where ρ becomes ρα (**27**).

274. a. The nouns (ὁ) πατήρ (πατερ-) *father*, (ἡ) μήτηρ (μητερ-) *mother*, (ἡ) θυγάτηρ (θυγατερ-) *daughter*, are thus declined:

	SINGULAR		
Nom.	πατήρ	μήτηρ	θυγάτηρ
Gen.	πατρός	μητρός	θυγατρός
Dat.	πατρί	μητρί	θυγατρί
Acc.	πατέρα	μητέρα	θυγατέρα
Voc.	πάτερ	μῆτερ	θύγατερ

	DUAL		
N.A.V.	πατέρε	μητέρε	θυγατέρε
G.D.	πατέροιν	μητέροιν	θυγατέροιν

PLURAL

N.V.	πατέρες	μητέρες	θυγατέρες
Gen.	πατέρων	μητέρων	θυγατέρων
Dat.	πατράσι	μητράσι	θυγατράσι
Acc.	πατέρας	μητέρας	θυγατέρας

b. Γαστήρ *belly* is declined and accented like πατήρ. Μητρός, μητρί, θυγατρός, θυγατρί are accented like πατρός, πατρί. ᾿Αστήρ *star* has ἀστέρος, ἀστέρι, etc., but dative plural ἀστράσι.

275. These nouns are treated with great freedom by the poets, who have πατέρος, πατέρι, but πατρῶν; so also θυγατέρι, θύγατρα, θύγατρες, θυγατρῶν, θυγατέρεσσι, θύγατρας.

276. ᾿Ανήρ (ὁ) *man* has the weak grade in all cases except the nominative and vocative singular, and inserts δ between ν and ρ (109).

277. ᾿Ανήρ *man* and Δημήτηρ *Demeter* are thus declined:

	SINGULAR		DUAL		PLURAL	
Nom.	ἀνήρ	Δημήτηρ	N.A.V.	ἄνδρε	N.V.	ἄνδρες
Gen.	ἀνδρός	Δήμητρος	G.D.	ἀνδροῖν	Gen.	ἀνδρῶν
Dat.	ἀνδρί	Δήμητρι			Dat.	ἀνδράσι
Acc.	ἄνδρα	Δήμητρα			Acc.	ἄνδρας
Voc.	ἄνερ	Δήμητερ				

278. The poets have ἀνέρος, ἀνέρι, ἀνέρα, ἀνέρες, ἀνέρων, ἀνέρας; Δήμητρος and Δημήτερος. Homer has ἄνδρεσσι as well as ἀνδράσι in the dative plural.

Gender of the Third Declension

279. The gender in this declension must often be learned by observation. But some general rules may be given.

280. *a.* MASCULINE are stems in

ευ; e.g. βασιλεύς (βασιλευ-) *king.*

ρ (except those in ἄρ); e.g. κρᾱτήρ (κρᾱτηρ-) *mixing-bowl,* ψᾱ́ρ (ψᾱρ-) *starling.*

ν (except those in ῑν, γον, δον); e.g. κανών (κανον-) *rule.*

ντ; e.g. λέων (λεοντ-) *lion.*

ητ (except those in τητ); e.g. λέβης (λεβητ-) *kettle.*

ωτ; e.g. ἔρως (ἐρωτ-) *love.*

b. EXCEPTIONS. Feminine are γαστήρ *belly,* κήρ *fate,* χείρ *hand,* φρήν *mind,* ἀλκυών *halcyon,* εἰκών *image,* ἠιών *shore,* χθών *earth,* χιών *snow,* μήκων *poppy,* ἐσθής (ἐσθητ-) *dress.*

Neuter are πῦρ *fire* and φῶς (φωτ-, **216**) for φάος (**231**) *light.*

281. a. FEMININE are stems in

ι and υ, with nom. in ις and υς; e.g. πόλις (πολι-) *state,* ἰσχύς (ἰσχυ-) *strength.*

αυ; e.g. ναῦς (ναυ-) *ship.*

δ, θ, τητ; e.g. ἔρις (ἐριδ-) *strife,* ταχυτής (ταχυτητ-) *speed.*

ῑν, γον, δον; e.g. ἀκτῑς (ἀκτῑν-) *ray,* σταγών (σταγον-) *drop,* χελῑδών (χελῑδον-) *swallow.*

b. EXCEPTIONS. Masculine are ἔχι-ς *viper,* ὄφι-ς *serpent,* βότρυ-ς *cluster of grapes,* θρῆνυ-ς *footstool,* ἰχθύ-ς *fish,* μῦ-ς *mouse,* νέκυ-ς *corpse,* στάχυ-ς *ear of grain,* πέλεκυ-ς *axe,* πῆχυ-ς *cubit,* πούς (ποδ-) *foot,* δελφῑς (δελφῑν-) *dolphin.*

282. NEUTER are stems in

ι and υ with nom. in ι and υ; e.g. πέπερι *pepper,* ἄστυ *city.*

ας; e.g. γέρας *prize* (**231**).

ες, with nom. in ος; e.g. γένος (γενεσ-) *race* (**231**). So φάος, φῶς *light.*

αρ; e.g. νέκταρ *nectar.*

ατ; e.g. σῶμα (σωματ-) *body.*

283. Labial and palatal stems are either masculine or feminine.

284. Variations in gender sometimes occur in poetry; see, for example, αἰθήρ *sky,* and θίς *heap,* in the Lexicon. See also **288**.

Third Declension in the Dialects

285. a. *Gen. and Dat. Dual.* Homeric -οιιν for -οιν, e.g. ποδοῖιν *with both feet,* Σειρήνοιιν *Sirens.*

b. *Dat. Plur.* Homeric -σι, e.g. βέλεσ-σι *missiles,* δέπασ-σι *cups;* whence an ending -εσσι arises, e.g. πόδ-εσσι *feet,* ἄνδρ-εσσι *men;* so γένυ-σσι *jaws;* reduced to -εσι, e.g. ἀνάκτ-εσι *lords.* The ending -εσσι is sometimes read even in -σ stems, e.g. ἐπέ-εσσι *words,* properly ἔπεσ-σι. Aeolic and Attic tragedy also have -εσσι.

c. Most of the uncontracted forms in the paradigms, which are not used in Attic prose, are found in Homer or Herodotus; cf. Πατρόκλεες *Patroclus!* with Περίκλεις, **241**; some of them occur in the Attic poets.

Other dialect forms have been noted under the several paradigms.

IRREGULAR SUBSTANTIVES

286. a. Some substantives belong to more than one declension, and are called *heteroclitic.* Thus σκότος *darkness* is usually declined like λόγος (**200**), but sometimes like γένος (**232**). So Οἰδίπους *Oedipus* has genitive Οἰδίποδος or Οἰδίπου, dative Οἰδίποδι, accusative Οἰδίποδα or Οἰδίπουν.

See also γέλως, ἔρως, ἱδρώς, and others, in **291**.

b. For the double accusatives in -η and -ην of Σωκράτης, Δημοσθένης, etc., see **237**.

287. Nouns which in the oblique cases have different stems from that of the nominative are called *metaplastic*; e.g. πτυχή *fold*, acc. πτύχα; υἱός *son*, gen. υἱέος and υἱοῦ; Ἀπόλλων *Apollo*, acc. Ἀπόλλω and Ἀπόλλωνα.

288. Nouns which are of different genders in different numbers are called *heterogeneous*; e.g. ὁ σῖτος *grain*, plur. τὰ σῖτα; ὁ δεσμός *chain*, τὰ δεσμά *chains*, but οἱ δεσμοί *cases of imprisonment*.

289. *Defective* nouns have only certain cases; e.g. ὄναρ *dream*, ὄφελος *use* (only nom. and acc.); τὴν νίφα *snow* (only acc.). Some, generally from their meaning, have only one number; e.g. πειθώ *persuasion*, τὰ Ὀλύμπια *the Olympic games*. Ὀδόντες *teeth* occurs usually in the plural; the nom. sing. ὀδούς appears to be late (215 c).

290. *Indeclinable* nouns have one form for all cases. These are foreign words, e.g. Ἀδάμ, Ἰσραήλ; names of letters, ἄλφα, βῆτα; most of the cardinal numbers; the infinitive used as a noun, e.g. τὸ γράφειν *the act of writing*; some abbreviated forms, e.g. Hom. δῶ *house*, Att. δῶμα; τὸ χρεών *fate*.

291. The following are the most important substantives having peculiarities of inflection:

1. Ἅιδης *Hades*, gen. -ου, etc., regular. Hom. Ἀΐδης, gen. -āο or -εω, dat. -ῃ, acc. -ην; also Ἄϊδος, Ἄϊδι (from stem Ἀϊδ-).

2. Ἄρης *Ares*, Ἄρεως (poet. Ἄρεος), (Ἄρεΐ) Ἄρει, (Ἄρεα) Ἄρη or Ἄρην, Ἄρες (Hom. also Ἄρες). Hom. also Ἄρηος, Ἄρηι, Ἄρηα.

3. Stem ἀρν-, gen. (τοῦ or τῆς) ἀρνός *lamb*, ἀρνί, ἄρνα; plur. ἄρνες, ἀρνῶν, ἀρνάσι (Hom. ἄρνεσσι), ἄρνας. In the nom. sing. ἀμνός (2d decl.) is used.

4. γάλα (τό) *milk*, γάλακτος, γάλακτι, etc. (24).

5. γέλως (ὁ) *laughter*, γέλωτος, etc., regular; in Attic poets acc. γέλωτα or γέλων. In Hom. generally of second declension, dat. γέλῳ, acc. γέλω, γέλων (γέλον?). See 286 a.

6. γόνυ (τό) *knee*, γόνατος, γόνατι, etc. (from stem γονατ-); Ion. and poet. γούνατος, γούνατι, etc.; Hom. also gen. γουνός, dat. γουνί, plur. γοῦνα, γούνων, γούνεσσι (285 b), the stem of which is γονϝ- (165 a).

7. γυνή (ἡ) *woman*, γυναικός, γυναικί, γυναῖκα, γύναι (24); dual γυναῖκε, γυναικοῖν; plur. γυναῖκες, γυναικῶν, γυναιξί, γυναῖκας.

8. δάκρυον (τό) *tear*, δακρύου, etc., regular. But poet. δάκρυ, dat. plur. δάκρυσι.

9. δένδρον (τό) *tree*, δένδρου, regular (Ion. δένδρεον, δένδρος, Aeol. δένδριον); dat. sing. δένδρει; plur. δένδρη, δένδρεσι.

10. δόρυ (τό) *spear* (cf. γόνυ); (from stem δορατ-) δόρατος, δόρατι; plur. δόρατα, etc. Ion. and poet. δούρατος, etc.; Epic also gen. δουρός, dat. δουρί;

dual δοῦρε; plur. δοῦρα, δούρων, δούρεσσι (165 a). Poet. δόρει, poet. (and prose) δορός, δορί.

11. ἔρως (ὁ) love, ἔρωτος, etc. In poetry also ἔρος, ἔρῳ, ἔρον.

12. Ζεύς (Aeol. Δεύς) Zeus, Διός, Διΐ, Δία, Ζεῦ. Ion. and poet. Ζηνός, Ζηνί, Ζῆνα. Pindar has Δΐ for Διΐ.

13. θέμις (ἡ) justice (also as a proper name, Themis), gen. θέμιδος, etc., regular like ἔρις. Hom. θέμιστος, etc. Pind. θέμιτος, θέμιν, θέμιτες. Hdt. gen. θέμιος. In Attic prose, indeclinable in θέμις ἐστί fas est; e.g. θέμις εἶναι.

14. ἱδρώς (ὁ) sweat, ἱδρῶτος, etc. Hom. has dat. ἱδρῷ, acc. ἱδρῶ (246).

15. κάρᾱ (τό) head, poetic; in Attic only nom., acc., and voc. sing., with dat. κάρᾳ (tragic). Hom. κάρη, gen. κάρητος, καρήατος, κρᾶατος, κρᾱτός; dat. κάρητι, καρήατι, κρᾶατι, κρᾱτί; acc. (τὸν) κρᾶτα, (τὸ) κάρη or κάρ; plur. nom. κάρᾱ, καρήατα, κρᾶατα; gen. κρᾱτων; dat. κρᾱσί; acc. κάρᾱ with (τοὺς) κρᾶτας; nom. and acc. plur. also κάρηνα, gen. καρήνων. Soph. (τὸ) κρᾶτα.

16. κρίνον (τό) lily, κρίνου, etc. In plural also κρίνεα (Hdt.) and κρίνεσι (poetic). See 286 a.

17. κύων (ὁ, ἡ) dog, voc. κύον : the rest from stem κυν-, κυνός, κυνί, κύνα; plur. κύνες, κυνῶν, κυσί, κύνας.

18. λᾶς (ὁ) stone, Hom. λᾶας, poetic; gen. λᾶος (or λᾶου), dat. λᾶϊ, acc. λᾶαν, λᾶν, λᾶα; dual λᾶε; plur. λᾶες, λάων, λάεσσι or λάεσι.

19. λίπα (in Hom. always elided λίπ', generally with ἐλαίῳ oil) fat, oil; λίπα may be an instrumental (for λιπέσα) used as an adverb, copiously. Some understand Hom. λίπ' as dat. for λιπί.

20. μάρτυς (ὁ, ἡ) witness, gen. μάρτυρος, etc., dat. plur. μάρτυσι. Hom. nom. μάρτυρος (2d decl.), plur. μάρτυροι.

21. μάστιξ (ἡ) whip, gen. μάστιγος, etc.; Hom. dat. μάστῑ, acc. μάστιν.

22. Οἰδίπους (ὁ) Oedipus. See 286 a.

23. οἶς (ἡ) sheep, for declension in Attic see 259. Hom. ὄϊς, ὄϊος, ὄϊν, ὄϊες, ὀΐων, ὀΐεσσι (ὀΐεσι, ὄεσσι), ὄϊς.

24. ὄνειρος (ὁ), ὄνειρον (τό), dream, gen. -ου; also gen. ὀνείρατος, dat. ὀνείρατι; plur. ὀνείρατα, ὀνειράτων, ὀνείρασι; nom. acc. sing. also ὄναρ (τό).

25. ὄρνις (ὁ, ἡ) bird, see 227. Also poetic forms from stem ὀρνῑ-, nom. and acc. sing. ὄρνῑς, ὄρνῑν, plur. ὄρνεις, ὀρνέων, acc. ὄρνεις or ὄρνῑς. Hdt. acc. ὄρνῑθα. Luc. voc. ὄρνι. Doric gen. ὄρνῑχος, etc., from stem ὀρνῑχ-.

26. ὄσσε (τώ) eyes, dual, poetic; plur. gen. ὄσσων, dat. ὄσσοις or ὄσσοισι.

27. οὖς (τό) ear, ὠτός, ὠτί; plur. ὦτα, ὤτων (148), ὠσί. Hom. gen. οὔατος; plur. οὔατα, οὔασι and ὠσί. Doric ὦς. Attic and Doric are contractions for ὀ(υ)ατ, orig. οὔ(σ)ατ-.

28. Πνύξ (ἡ) Pnyx, Πυκνός, Πυκνί, Πύκνα (also Πυνκ-ός, etc.). See 106.

29. πρέσβυς elder (properly adj.), poetic, acc. πρέσβυν (as adj.), voc. πρέσβυ; plur. οἱ πρέσβεις chiefs, elders : the common word in this sense is πρεσβύτης, distinct from πρεσβευτής. Πρέσβυς (ὁ) ambassador, with gen. πρέσβεως, is rare and poetic in sing., but common in prose in plur., πρέσβεις, πρέσβεων, πρέσβεσι, πρέσβεις (like πῆχυς). Πρεσβευτής (ὁ) ambassador is common in sing., but rare in plural.

30. πῦρ (τό) *fire* (stem πῦρ-), πυρός, πυρί; plur. τὰ πυρά *watch-fires*, dat. πυροῖς.

31. ταώς or ταῶς, Attic ταῶς (ὁ), *peacock*, like νεώς (203); also dat. ταῶνι, ταῶσι, chiefly poetic.

32. τῦφῶς (ὁ) *whirlwind*; declined like νεώς (203). Also proper name Τῦφῶς, in poetry generally Τῦφῶνος, Τῦφῶνι, Τῦφῶνα. See 286 *a*.

33. ὕδωρ (τό) *water*, ὕδατος, ὕδατι, ὕδωρ; plur. ὕδατα, ὑδάτων, ὕδασι. Boeotian nom. οὔδωρ, Hesiod dat. ὕδει.

34. υἱός (ὁ) *son*, υἱοῦ, υἱῷ, etc.; also (from stem υἱυ-) υἱέος, υἱεῖ; dual υἱεῖ, υἱέοιν; plur. υἱεῖς, υἱέων, υἱέσι, υἱεῖς; also with υ for υι, e.g. ὑός, ὑοῦ, ὑέος, etc. Hom. also (from stem υἱ-) gen. υἷος, dat. υἷι, acc. υἷα; dual υἷε; plur. υἷες, υἱάσι, υἷας.

35. χείρ (ἡ) *hand*, χειρός, χειρί, χεῖρα; χεῖρε, χεροῖν; χεῖρες, χειρῶν, χερσί (Hom. χείρεσσι or χείρεσι), χεῖρας: poet. also χερός, χερί, dual χειροῖν.

36. (χόος) χοῦς (ὁ) *mound*, χοός, χοῖ, χοῦν (like βοῦς, 265).

37. χοῦς (ὁ) *three-quart measure*: see 272. Ionic and late nom. χοεύς, with gen. χοέως, χοῶς, etc., regularly like Πειραιεύς and Δωριεύς (269).

38. χρώς (ὁ) *skin*, χρωτός, χρωτί (χρῷ only in ἐν χρῷ *near*), χρῶτα; poet. also χροός, χροΐ, χρόα.

Epic -φι (-φιν), -θεν, -θι, -δε

292 *a*. In Homer the ending -φι or -φιν (cf. Lat. ti-bi and dat. plur. ending -bus) forms in both singular and plural a genitive or dative. Syntactically the meaning may be instrumental, locative, or ablative; e.g. instrumental βίηφι *with violence*, δακρυόφι *with tears*; locative κλισίηφι *in the hut*, ὄρεσφι *on the mountains*, παρὰ ναῦφι *by the ships*; ablative ἀπὸ νευρῆφι *from the string*. Stems in ᾱ form singulars, in ο both singulars and plurals, in consonants mostly plurals. All nominal stems, including participles, may have this ending; e.g. ἄμ' ἠόι φαινομένηφι *with the appearing of dawn*.

b. The suffixes -θεν, -θι, and -δε sometimes occur in the poets as case endings; e.g. Hom. οἶνον ἔνθεν (instead of οὗ) ἔπῑνον *the wine of which they drank*; ἐξ οὐρανόθεν *from the sky*; Ἰλιόθι πρό *in front of Ilios*; Aesch. σέθεν (instead of σοῦ, 369 *a*) ἐξ αἵματος *from thy blood*.

ADJECTIVES

FIRST AND SECOND DECLENSIONS

293. Adjectives of Three Endings. *a*. Most adjectives in -ος have three endings, -ος, -η (or -ᾱ), -ον. The masculine and neuter are of the second declension, and the feminine is of the first.

b. If ε, ι, or ρ precedes -ος, the feminine ends in ᾱ (164); e.g. ἄξιος, ἀξίᾱ, ἄξιον *worthy*.

294. Σοφός *wise,* ἄξιος *worthy,* and μακρός *long,* are thus declined:

SINGULAR

Nom.	σοφός	σοφή	σοφόν	ἄξιος	ἀξία	ἄξιον
Gen.	σοφοῦ	σοφῆς	σοφοῦ	ἀξίου	ἀξίας	ἀξίου
Dat.	σοφῷ	σοφῇ	σοφῷ	ἀξίῳ	ἀξίᾳ	ἀξίῳ
Acc.	σοφόν	σοφήν	σοφόν	ἄξιον	ἀξίαν	ἄξιον
Voc.	σοφέ	σοφή	σοφόν	ἄξιε	ἀξία	ἄξιον

Nom.	μακρός	μακρά	μακρόν
Gen.	μακροῦ	μακρᾶς	μακροῦ
Dat.	μακρῷ	μακρᾷ	μακρῷ
Acc.	μακρόν	μακράν	μακρόν
Voc.	μακρέ	μακρά	μακρόν

DUAL

N.A.V.	σοφώ	σοφά	σοφώ	ἀξίω	ἀξία	ἀξίω
G.D.	σοφοῖν	σοφαῖν	σοφοῖν	ἀξίοιν	ἀξίαιν	ἀξίοιν

N.A.V.	μακρώ	μακρά	μακρώ
G.D.	μακροῖν	μακραῖν	μακροῖν

PLURAL

N.V.	σοφοί	σοφαί	σοφά	ἄξιοι	ἄξιαι	ἄξια
Gen.	σοφῶν	σοφῶν	σοφῶν	ἀξίων	ἀξίων	ἀξίων
Dat.	σοφοῖς	σοφαῖς	σοφοῖς	ἀξίοις	ἀξίαις	ἀξίοις
Acc.	σοφούς	σοφάς	σοφά	ἀξίους	ἀξίας	ἄξια

N.V.	μακροί	μακραί	μακρά
Gen.	μακρῶν	μακρῶν	μακρῶν
Dat.	μακροῖς	μακραῖς	μακροῖς
Acc.	μακρούς	μακράς	μακρά

295. This is by far the largest class of adjectives. All participles in -ος and all superlatives (**346**) are declined like σοφός, and all comparatives in -τερος (**346**) are declined like μακρός (except in accent).

296. The nominative and genitive plural of adjectives and participles in -ος accent the feminine like the masculine: e.g. ἄξιος has ἄξιαι, ἀξίων (*not* ἀξίαι, ἀξιῶν; see **145**).

For feminines in ᾰ of the third and first declensions combined, see **313**.

297. The masculine dual forms in -ω and -οιν in all adjectives and participles may be used for the feminine forms in -ᾱ and -αιν.

298. Adjectives of Two Endings. Some adjectives in -ος, chiefly compounds, have only two endings, -ος and -ον, the feminine being the same as the masculine. They are declined like σοφός, omitting the feminine. There are also a few adjectives of the "Attic" second declension, ending in -ως and -ων (**203**).

299. Ἄλογος *irrational* and ἵλεως *gracious* are thus declined:

SINGULAR

	Masc. and Fem.	*Neut.*	*Masc. and Fem.*	*Neut.*
Nom.	ἄλογος	ἄλογον	ἵλεως	ἵλεων
Gen.	ἀλόγου	ἀλόγου	ἵλεω	ἵλεω
Dat.	ἀλόγῳ	ἀλόγῳ	ἵλεῳ	ἵλεῳ
Acc.	ἄλογον	ἄλογον	ἵλεων	ἵλεων
Voc.	ἄλογε	ἄλογον	ἵλεως	ἵλεων

DUAL

N.A.V.	ἀλόγω	ἀλόγω	ἵλεω	ἵλεω
G.D.	ἀλόγοιν	ἀλόγοιν	ἵλεῳν	ἵλεῳν

PLURAL

N.V.	ἄλογοι	ἄλογα	ἵλεῳ	ἵλεα
Gen.	ἀλόγων	ἀλόγων	ἵλεων	ἵλεων
Dat.	ἀλόγοις	ἀλόγοις	ἵλεῳς	ἵλεῳς
Acc.	ἀλόγους	ἄλογα	ἵλεως	ἵλεα

300. Some adjectives in -ος, though not compounds (298), may be declined with either two or three endings, especially in poetry. E.g. βίαιος *violent* has fem. βίαιος and βιαίᾱ; ἐλευθέριος *pertaining to a freeman*, fem. ἐλευθέριος or ἐλευθερίᾱ; φρόνιμος *prudent*, fem. φρόνιμος; fem. θαλάσσιος *of the sea*, E. *I.T.* 236; ἐπιθῡμίᾱς ματαίους *foolish desires*, Plat. *Rep.* 554 a.

301. Adjectives in -ως, -ων commonly have α in the neuter plural; but ἔκπλεω from ἔκπλεως occurs X. *C.* 1, 6, 7. For the accent, see 205.

302. Πλέως *full* has a feminine in α: πλέως, πλέᾱ, πλέων, plur. πλέῳ, πλέαι, πλέα; but its compounds (298) have two endings, e.g. ἔκπλεως, ἔκπλεως, ἔκπλεων. The defective σῶς *safe* has nom. σῶς, σῶν (also fem. σᾶ), acc. σῶν, neut. plur. σᾶ, acc. plur. σῶς. The Attic has σῶοι, σῶαι, σῶα in nom. plur. Homer has σόος, σόη, σόον.

303. Many adjectives in -εος and -οος are contracted. Χρύσεος *golden*, ἀργύρεος *of silver*, and ἁπλόος *simple*, are thus declined:

SINGULAR

Nom.	(χρύσεος)	χρῡσοῦς	(χρῡσέᾱ)	χρῡσῆ	(χρύσεον)	χρῡσοῦν
Gen.	(χρῡσέου)	χρῡσοῦ	(χρῡσέᾱς)	χρῡσῆς	(χρῡσέου)	χρῡσοῦ
Dat.	(χρῡσέῳ)	χρῡσῷ	(χρῡσέᾳ)	χρῡσῇ	(χρῡσέῳ)	χρῡσῷ
Acc.	(χρύσεον)	χρῡσοῦν	(χρῡσέᾱν)	χρῡσῆν	(χρύσεον)	χρῡσοῦν

DUAL

N.A.	(χρῡσέω)	χρῡσώ	(χρῡσέᾱ)	χρῡσᾶ	(χρῡσέω)	χρῡσώ
G.D.	(χρῡσέοιν)	χρῡσοῖν	(χρῡσέαιν)	χρῡσαῖν	(χρῡσέοιν)	χρῡσοῖν

PLURAL

Nom.	(χρύσεοι)	χρῡσοῖ	(χρύσεαι)	χρῡσαῖ	(χρύσεα)	χρῡσᾶ
Gen.	(χρῡσέων)	χρῡσῶν	(χρῡσέων)	χρῡσῶν	(χρῡσέων)	χρῡσῶν
Dat.	(χρῡσέοις)	χρῡσοῖς	(χρῡσέαις)	χρῡσαῖς	(χρῡσέοις)	χρῡσοῖς
Acc.	(χρῡσέους)	χρῡσοῦς	(χρῡσέᾱς)	χρῡσᾶς	(χρύσεα)	χρῡσᾶ

SINGULAR

Nom.	(ἀργύρεος)	ἀργυροῦς	(ἀργυρέᾱ)	ἀργυρᾶ	(ἀργύρεον)	ἀργυροῦν
Gen.	(ἀργυρέου)	ἀργυροῦ	(ἀργυρέᾱς)	ἀργυρᾶς	(ἀργυρέου)	ἀργυροῦ
Dat.	(ἀργυρέῳ)	ἀργυρῷ	(ἀργυρέᾳ)	ἀργυρᾷ	(ἀργυρέῳ)	ἀργυρῷ
Acc.	(ἀργύρεον)	ἀργυροῦν	(ἀργυρέᾱν)	ἀργυρᾶν	(ἀργύρεον)	ἀργυροῦν

DUAL

N.A.	(ἀργυρέω)	ἀργυρώ	(ἀργυρέᾱ)	ἀργυρᾶ	(ἀργυρέω)	ἀργυρώ
G.D.	(ἀργυρέοιν)	ἀργυροῖν	(ἀργυρέαιν)	ἀργυραῖν	(ἀργυρέοιν)	ἀργυροῖν

PLURAL

Nom.	(ἀργύρεοι)	ἀργυροῖ	(ἀργύρεαι)	ἀργυραῖ	(ἀργύρεα)	ἀργυρᾶ
Gen.	(ἀργυρέων)	ἀργυρῶν	(ἀργυρέων)	ἀργυρῶν	(ἀργυρέων)	ἀργυρῶν
Dat.	(ἀργυρέοις)	ἀργυροῖς	(ἀργυρέαις)	ἀργυραῖς	(ἀργυρέοις)	ἀργυροῖς
Acc.	(ἀργυρέους)	ἀργυροῦς	(ἀργυρέᾱς)	ἀργυρᾶς	(ἀργύρεα)	ἀργυρᾶ

SINGULAR

Nom.	(ἁπλόος)	ἁπλοῦς	(ἁπλέᾱ)	ἁπλῆ	(ἁπλόον)	ἁπλοῦν
Gen.	(ἁπλόου)	ἁπλοῦ	(ἁπλέᾱς)	ἁπλῆς	(ἁπλόου)	ἁπλοῦ
Dat.	(ἁπλόῳ)	ἁπλῷ	(ἁπλέᾳ)	ἁπλῇ	(ἁπλόῳ)	ἁπλῷ
Acc.	(ἁπλόον)	ἁπλοῦν	(ἁπλέᾱν)	ἁπλῆν	(ἁπλόον)	ἁπλοῦν

DUAL

N.A.	(ἁπλόω)	ἁπλώ	(ἁπλέᾱ)	ἁπλᾶ	(ἁπλόω)	ἁπλώ
G.D.	(ἁπλόοιν)	ἁπλοῖν	(ἁπλέαιν)	ἁπλαῖν	(ἁπλόοιν)	ἁπλοῖν

PLURAL

Nom.	(ἁπλόοι)	ἁπλοῖ	(ἁπλέαι)	ἁπλαῖ	(ἁπλόα)	ἁπλᾶ
Gen.	(ἁπλόων)	ἁπλῶν	(ἁπλέων)	ἁπλῶν	(ἁπλόων)	ἁπλῶν
Dat.	(ἁπλόοις)	ἁπλοῖς	(ἁπλέαις)	ἁπλαῖς	(ἁπλόοις)	ἁπλοῖς
Acc.	(ἁπλόους)	ἁπλοῦς	(ἁπλέᾱς)	ἁπλᾶς	(ἁπλόα)	ἁπλᾶ

304. a. All contract forms of these adjectives are *perispomena*, except -ώ for -έω and -όω in the dual (see 209 *a*). See also 209 *b* and 45 *a*. Compounds in -οος which have two endings (298) leave -οα in the neuter plural uncontracted; e.g. εὔνους (εὔνοος), εὔνουν *loyal*, gen. εὔνου (209 *b*), nom. plur. εὔνοι, εὔνοα. No distinct vocative forms occur.

b. The uncontracted dat. plur. fem. ἁπλόαις (with stem in -ο like the masc.) occurs in Pind. *N.* 8, 36.

305. A few adjectives in -εος and -οος are left uncontracted; e.g. νέος *young* (for νεfος, cf. Lat. novus), ἀργαλέος *painful*, ὄγδοος *eighth*; ἀθρόος *crowded* has uncontracted fem. ἀθρόα, ἀθρόᾱς, etc., neut. plur. ἀθρόα (Att. contracted masc. and neut. ἄθρους, ἄθρουν, etc.). 48.

THIRD DECLENSION

306. Adjectives belonging only to the third declension have two endings, the feminine being the same as the masculine. Most of these end in -ης and -ες (stems in -εσ), or in -ων and -ον (stems in -ον), and are compounds.

307. Ἀληθής *true* and εὐδαίμων *happy* are thus declined:

SINGULAR

	Masc. and Fem.	Neut.	Masc. and Fem.	Neut.
Nom.	ἀληθής	ἀληθές	εὐδαίμων	εὔδαιμον
Gen.	(ἀληθέος) ἀληθοῦς		εὐδαίμονος	
Dat.	(ἀληθέϊ) ἀληθεῖ		εὐδαίμονι	
Acc.	(ἀληθέα) ἀληθῆ	ἀληθές	εὐδαίμονα	εὔδαιμον
Voc.	ἀληθές		εὔδαιμον	

DUAL

N.A.V.	(ἀληθέε) ἀληθεῖ		εὐδαίμονε	
G.D.	(ἀληθέοιν) ἀληθοῖν		εὐδαιμόνοιν	

PLURAL

N.V.	(ἀληθέες) ἀληθεῖς	(ἀληθέα) ἀληθῆ	εὐδαίμονες	εὐδαίμονα
Gen.	(ἀληθέων) ἀληθῶν		εὐδαιμόνων	
Dat.	ἀληθέσι		εὐδαίμοσι	
Acc.	ἀληθεῖς	(ἀληθέα) ἀληθῆ	εὐδαίμονας	εὐδαίμονα

308. For the recessive accent of neuters like εὔδαιμον and of many barytone compounds in -ης (e.g. αὐτάρκης, αὔταρκες), see 142. So τριήρης *trireme*, gen. plur. τριήρων (239). But adjectives in -ώδης and -ήρης accent the neuter on the same syllable as the masculine; e.g. εὐώδης *fragrant*, neut. εὐῶδες; ποδήρης *reaching to the feet*, ποδῆρες. Ἀληθες *oh, really!* is proparoxytone.

309. In adjectives in -ης, εα is contracted to ᾱ after ε, and to ᾱ or η after ι or υ; e.g. εὐκλεής *glorious*, acc. (εὐκλέα) εὐκλεᾶ; ὑγιής *healthy*, (ὑγιέα) ὑγιᾱ and ὑγιῆ; εὐφυής *comely*, (εὐφυέα) εὐφυᾱ and εὐφυῆ. See 45 b.

310. The accusative plural ἀληθεῖς takes the form of the nominative. Cf. 240.

311. Adjectives compounded of nouns and a prefix are generally declined like those nouns; e.g. εὔελπις, εὔελπι (stem εὐελπιδ-) *hopeful*, gen.

εὐέλπιδος, acc. εὔελπιν (218 c), voc. εὔελπι; εὔχαρις, εὔχαρι *graceful*, gen. εὐχάριτος, acc. εὔχαριν, voc. εὔχαρι. But compounds of πατήρ and μήτηρ end in -τωρ (gen. -τορος), and those of πόλις in -ις (gen. -ιδος); e.g. ἀπάτωρ, ἄπατορ *fatherless*, gen. ἀπάτορος; ἄπολις, ἄπολι *without a country*, gen. ἀπόλιδος.

312. For the declension of comparatives in -ων (stem in -ον), see **355.**

FIRST AND THIRD DECLENSIONS COMBINED

313. Adjectives of this class have the masculine and neuter of the third declension and the feminine of the first. The feminine always has ă in the nominative and accusative singular (cf. **187**); in the genitive and dative singular it has ā after a vowel or diphthong, otherwise η.

The feminine genitive plural is circumflexed regularly (**145**). Cf. **296.**

For feminine dual forms the masculine may be used (cf. **297**).

314. *Stems in υ* (nom. -ύς, -εῖα, -ύ). The masculine and neuter are declined like πῆχυς and ἄστυ (**253**), except that the genitive singular ends in -ος (not -ως) and the neuter plural in -έα and the dual in -έε are not contracted.

315. Γλυκύς *sweet* is thus declined:

SINGULAR

Nom.		γλυκύς	γλυκεῖα		γλυκύ
Gen.		γλυκέος	γλυκείᾱς		γλυκέος
Dat.	(γλυκέϊ)	γλυκεῖ	γλυκείᾳ	(γλυκέϊ)	γλυκεῖ
Acc.		γλυκύν	γλυκεῖαν		γλυκύ
Voc.		γλυκύ	γλυκεῖα		γλυκύ

DUAL

N.A.V.		γλυκέε	γλυκείᾱ		γλυκέε
G.D.		γλυκέοιν	γλυκείαιν		γλυκέοιν

PLURAL

N.V.	(γλυκέες)	γλυκεῖς	γλυκεῖαι		γλυκέα
Gen.		γλυκέων	γλυκειῶν		γλυκέων
Dat.		γλυκέσι	γλυκείαις		γλυκέσι
Acc.		γλυκεῖς	γλυκείᾱς		γλυκέα

316. The feminine stem in -εια comes from the strong form of the stem, -εν (-εϝ), by adding -ια; e.g. γλυκεν-, γλυκ-εϝ-ια, γλυκε-ια, γλυκεῖα. See **34; 258.** Masculine and neuter have the weak form in -υ. The accusative plural γλυκεῖς takes the form of the nominative (cf. **240**).

317. The Ionic feminine of adjectives in -υς has -εα. Homer has εὐρέα (for εὐρύν) as masc. accusative of εὐρύς *wide*.

318. Adjectives in -υς are oxytone, except θῆλυς *female, fresh*, and ἥμισυς *half*. Compare also πρέσβυς old (291), and the Ep. fem. πρέσβα. Θῆλυς sometimes has only two terminations in poetry.

319. *Stems in* ν (nom. -ᾱς, -αινα, -αν; -ην, -εινα, -εν). The adjectives μέλᾱς (μελαν-), μέλαινα, μέλαν *black*, and τέρην (τερεν-), τέρεινα, τέρεν *tender* (Lat. tener), are thus declined:

		SINGULAR			
Nom.	μέλᾱς	μέλαινα	μέλαν	τέρην	τέρεινα	τέρεν
Gen.	μέλανος	μελαίνης	μέλανος	τέρενος	τερείνης	τέρενος
Dat.	μέλανι	μελαίνῃ	μέλανι	τέρενι	τερείνῃ	τέρενι
Acc.	μέλανα	μέλαιναν	μέλαν	τέρενα	τέρειναν	τέρεν
Voc.	μέλαν	μέλαινα	μέλαν	τέρεν	τέρεινα	τέρεν

		DUAL			
N.A.V.	μέλανε	μελαίνᾱ	μέλανε	τέρενε	τερείνᾱ	τέρενε
G.D.	μελάνοιν	μελαίναιν	μελάνοιν	τερένοιν	τερείναιν	τερένοιν

		PLURAL			
N.V.	μέλανες	μέλαιναι	μέλανα	τέρενες	τέρειναι	τέρενα
Gen.	μελάνων	μελαινῶν	μελάνων	τερένων	τερεινῶν	τερένων
Dat.	μέλασι	μελαίναις	μέλασι	τέρεσι	τερείναις	τέρεσι
Acc.	μέλανας	μελαίνᾱς	μέλανα	τέρενας	τερείνᾱς	τέρενα

320. The feminine forms μέλαινα and τέρεινα come from μελαν-ια and τερεν-ια (99). Μέλᾱς is for μελαν-ς (75, 32). Μέλᾱς and τάλᾱς *wretched* are the only adjectives in -ν having the nom. suffix ς. The dat. plur. μέλασι is for μελν-σι (76). The nominatives μέλᾱς and τέρην are generally used for the vocative.

321. Like the masculine and neuter of τέρην is declined ἄρρην, ἄρρεν (older ἄρσην, ἄρσεν) *male, masculine.*

322. *Stems in* ντ. Many participles and a few adjectives denoting fullness have stems in -ντ.

323. Χαρίεις *graceful* and πᾶς *all* are thus declined:

		SINGULAR			
Nom.	χαρίεις	χαρίεσσα	χαρίεν	πᾶς	πᾶσα	πᾶν
Gen.	χαρίεντος	χαριέσσης	χαρίεντος	παντός	πάσης	παντός
Dat.	χαρίεντι	χαριέσσῃ	χαρίεντι	παντί	πάσῃ	παντί
Acc.	χαρίεντα	χαρίεσσαν	χαρίεν	πάντα	πᾶσαν	πᾶν
Voc.	χαρίεν	χαρίεσσα	χαρίεν	πᾶς	πᾶσα	πᾶν

DUAL

| N.A.V. | χαρίεντε | χαριέσσᾱ | χαρίεντε |
| G.D. | χαριέντοιν | χαριέσσαιν | χαριέντοιν |

PLURAL

N.V.	χαρίεντες	χαρίεσσαι	χαρίεντα	πάντες	πᾶσαι	πάντα
Gen.	χαριέντων	χαριεσσῶν	χαριέντων	πάντων	πᾱσῶν	πάντων
Dat.	χαρίεσι	χαριέσσαις	χαρίεσι	πᾶσι	πάσαις	πᾶσι
Acc.	χαρίεντας	χαριέσσᾱς	χαρίεντα	πάντας	πάσᾱς	πάντα

324. *a.* The nominatives χαρίεις and χαρίεν are for χαριεντ-s and χαριεντ, and πᾶς and πᾶν for παντ-s and παντ (**70**; **24**). The ᾱ in πᾶν is due to the ᾱ of πᾶς; in compounds α is short, e.g. Hom. ἄπᾰν and πρόπᾰν. For the accent of πάντων and πᾶσι, see **148**. Πᾱσῶν is regular (**313**).

b. For the feminine χαρίεσσα (for χαριετ-ια from the weak stem χαριετ-), see **95**; and for dat. plur. χαρίεσι from the same stem, see **69**. Πᾶσα is for παντ-ια (**95** *b*).

325. Homer and Attic poetry have the uncontracted forms in -όεις, -όεσσα, -ήεις, -ήεσσα; e.g. σκιόεντα *shadowy*, τῑμήεντα *precious*. But the contracted τῑμῆς (for τῑμήεις) and τῑμῆντα occur. The Attic poets sometimes contract adjectives in -όεις; e.g. πλακοῦς, πλακοῦντος (for πλακόεις, πλακόεντος) *flat* (*cake*); πτεροῦντα (for πτερόεντα), πτεροῦσσα (for πτερόεσσα) *winged*; αἰθαλοῦσσα (for αἰθαλόεσσα) *flaming*; μελιτοῦττα (for μελιτόεσσα, **63** *c*) *honied* (*cake*). So names of places (properly adjectives); e.g. Ἐλαιοῦς, Ἐλαιοῦντος *Elaeus*, Ἐλαιοῦσσα (an island), from forms in -όεις, -όεσσα; Ῥαμνοῦς, Ῥαμνοῦντος *Rhamnus* (from -όεις). See **45** *e*.

Doric has forms in -άεις for -ήεις (**164**), sometimes contracted to -ᾶς, -ᾶντος, e.g. αἰγλᾶντα *radiant*. With forms in -όεις (-οεντ) cf. Lat. -ōsus (for -ōnsus).

326. A few other combinations occur of stems varying according to gender; e.g. ἑπτέτης, ἑπτέτους *seven years old*, fem. ἑπτέτις, ἑπτέτιδος, neut. ἑπτέτες; Σκύθης, Σκύθου a *Scythian*, fem. Σκύθις, Σκύθιδος, Σκύθιν Aeschin. 3, 172.

327. One adjective in -ων, ἑκών, ἑκοῦσα, ἑκόν *willing*, gen. ἑκόντος, used as a predicate in the sense of *willingly*, has three endings, and is declined like participles in -ων (**329**). So its compound ἄκων (ἀέκων) *unwillingly*, ἄκουσα, ἄκον, gen. ἄκοντος, etc.

Declension of Participles

328. All participles in the active voice (except the perfect)(**801**), and all aorist passive participles have stems in -ντ, and belong to the first and third declensions combined. Participles in the middle and passive,(except the aorist) are declined like σοφός (**294**).

329. The participles λύων *loosing,* ὤν *being,* τιθείς *placing,* διδούς *giving,* ἱστάς *setting,* λύσας *having loosed,* δεικνύς *showing,* δύς *having entered,* λελυκώς *having loosed,* and εἰδώς *knowing,* are thus declined :

SINGULAR

Nom.	λύων	λύουσα	λῦον	ὤν	οὖσα	ὄν
Gen.	λύοντος	λυούσης	λύοντος	ὄντος	οὔσης	ὄντος
Dat.	λύοντι	λυούσῃ	λύοντι	ὄντι	οὔσῃ	ὄντι
Acc.	λύοντα	λύουσαν	λῦον	ὄντα	οὖσαν	ὄν
Voc.	λύων	λύουσα	λῦον	ὤν	οὖσα	ὄν

DUAL

N.A.V.	λύοντε	λυούσᾱ	λύοντε	ὄντε	οὔσᾱ	ὄντε
G.D.	λυόντοιν	λυούσαιν	λυόντοιν	ὄντοιν	οὔσαιν	ὄντοιν

PLURAL

N.V.	λύοντες	λύουσαι	λύοντα	ὄντες	οὖσαι	ὄντα
Gen.	λυόντων	λυουσῶν	λυόντων	ὄντων	οὐσῶν	ὄντων
Dat.	λύουσι	λυούσαις	λύουσι	οὖσι	οὔσαις	οὖσι
Acc.	λύοντας	λυούσᾱς	λύοντα	ὄντας	οὔσᾱς	ὄντα

SINGULAR

Nom.	τιθείς	τιθεῖσα	τιθέν	διδούς	διδοῦσα	διδόν
Gen.	τιθέντος	τιθείσης	τιθέντος	διδόντος	διδούσης	διδόντος
Dat.	τιθέντι	τιθείσῃ	τιθέντι	διδόντι	διδούσῃ	διδόντι
Acc.	τιθέντα	τιθεῖσαν	τιθέν	διδόντα	διδοῦσαν	διδόν
Voc.	τιθείς	τιθεῖσα	τιθέν	διδούς	διδοῦσα	διδόν

DUAL

N.A.V.	τιθέντε	τιθείσᾱ	τιθέντε	διδόντε	διδούσᾱ	διδόντε
G.D.	τιθέντοιν	τιθείσαιν	τιθέντοιν	διδόντοιν	διδούσαιν	διδόντοιν

PLURAL

N.V.	τιθέντες	τιθεῖσαι	τιθέντα	διδόντες	διδοῦσαι	διδόντα
Gen.	τιθέντων	τιθεισῶν	τιθέντων	διδόντων	διδουσῶν	διδόντων
Dat.	τιθεῖσι	τιθείσαις	τιθεῖσι	διδοῦσι	διδούσαις	διδοῦσι
Acc.	τιθέντας	τιϑείσᾱς	τιθέντα	διδόντας	διδούσᾱς	διδόντα

SINGULAR

Nom.	ἱστάς	ἱστᾶσα	ἱστάν	λύσας	λύσᾱσα	λῦσαν
Gen.	ἱστάντος	ἱστάσης	ἱστάντος	λύσαντος	λυσάσης	λύσαντος
Dat.	ἱστάντι	ἱστάσῃ	ἱστάντι	λύσαντι	λυσάσῃ	λύσαντι
Acc.	ἱστάντα	ἱστᾶσαν	ἱστάν	λύσαντα	λύσᾱσαν	λῦσαν
Voc.	ἱστάς	ἱστᾶσα	ἱστάν	λύσας	λύσᾱσα	λῦσαν

DUAL

| N.A.V. | ἱστάντε | ἱστᾶσᾱ | ἱστάντε | λύσαντε | λῡσᾱσᾱ | λύσαντε |
| G.D. | ἱστάντοιν | ἱστάσαιν | ἱστάντοιν | λῡσάντοιν | λῡσᾱσαιν | λῡσάντοιν |

PLURAL

N.V.	ἱστάντες	ἱστᾶσαι	ἱστάντα	λύσαντες	λύσᾱσαι	λύσαντα
Gen.	ἱστάντων	ἱστᾱσῶν	ἱστάντων	λῡσάντων	λῡσᾱσῶν	λῡσάντων
Dat.	ἱστᾶσι	ἱστάσαις	ἱστᾶσι	λύσᾱσι	λῡσᾱσαις	λύσᾱσι
Acc.	ἱστάντας	ἱστάσᾱς	ἱστάντα	λύσαντας	λῡσᾱσᾱς	λύσαντα

SINGULAR

Nom.	δεικνύς	δεικνῦσα	δεικνύν	δύς	δῦσα	δύν
Gen.	δεικνύντος	δεικνύσης	δεικνύντος	δύντος	δύσης	δύντος
Dat.	δεικνύντι	δεικνύσῃ	δεικνύντι	δύντι	δύσῃ	δύντι
Acc.	δεικνύντα	δεικνῦσαν	δεικνύν	δύντα	δῦσαν	δύν
Voc.	δεικνύς	δεικνῦσα	δεικνύν	δύς	δῦσα	δύν

DUAL

| N.A.V. | δεικνύντε | δεικνῦσᾱ | δεικνύντε | δύντε | δύσᾱ | δύντε |
| G.D. | δεικνύντοιν | δεικνύσαιν | δεικνύντοιν | δύντοιν | δύσαιν | δύντοιν |

PLURAL

N.V.	δεικνύντες	δεικνῦσαι	δεικνύντα	δύντες	δῦσαι	δύντα
Gen.	δεικνύντων	δεικνῡσῶν	δεικνύντων	δύντων	δῡσῶν	δύντων
Dat.	δεικνῦσι	δεικνύσαις	δεικνῦσι	δῦσι	δύσαις	δῦσι
Acc.	δεικνύντας	δεικνύσᾱς	δεικνύντα	δύντας	δύσᾱς	δύντα

SINGULAR

Nom.	λελυκώς	λελυκυῖα	λελυκός	εἰδώς	εἰδυῖα	εἰδός
Gen.	λελυκότος	λελυκυίᾱς	λελυκότος	εἰδότος	εἰδυίᾱς	εἰδότος
Dat.	λελυκότι	λελυκυίᾳ	λελυκότι	εἰδότι	εἰδυίᾳ	εἰδότι
Acc.	λελυκότα	λελυκυῖαν	λελυκός	εἰδότα	εἰδυῖαν	εἰδός
Voc.	λελυκώς	λελυκυῖα	λελυκός	εἰδώς	εἰδυῖα	εἰδός

DUAL

| N.A.V. | λελυκότε | λελυκυίᾱ | λελυκότε | εἰδότε | εἰδυίᾱ | εἰδότε |
| G.D. | λελυκότοιν | λελυκυίαιν | λελυκότοιν | εἰδότοιν | εἰδυίαιν | εἰδότοιν |

PLURAL

N.V.	λελυκότες	λελυκυῖαι	λελυκότα	εἰδότες	εἰδυῖαι	εἰδότα
Gen.	λελυκότων	λελυκυιῶν	λελυκότων	εἰδότων	εἰδυιῶν	εἰδότων
Dat.	λελυκόσι	λελυκυίαις	λελυκόσι	εἰδόσι	εἰδυίαις	εἰδόσι
Acc.	λελυκότας	λελυκυίᾱς	λελυκότα	εἰδότας	εἰδυίᾱς	εἰδότα

330. Participles in -ων (stem -οντ) form the nom. sing. masc. without ς, like λέων (227). So in the second aorist active of ω verbs, e.g. εἰπών

having said, λιπών *having left*; these are accented like ὤν: εἰπών, εἰποῦσα, εἰπόν; λιπών, λιποῦσα, λιπόν.

331. Stems in -οντ forming present and second aorist participles of μι verbs take s in the nom. sing. masc., e.g. διδούς *giving*, δούς *having given* (for δο-ντ-s, 70, 32). So all stems in -αντ, -εντ, and -υντ. The dat. plur. also shows the loss of ντ before σ, with lengthening of the preceding vowel.

332. *a.* The feminines in -ουσα, -εισα, -ῦσα, and -ᾱσα are formed by adding ια to the stem; e.g. λῦουσα (λῦο-ντ-ια), οὖσα (ὀντ-ια), ἱστᾶσα (ἱστα-ντ-ια), τιθεῖσα (τιθε-ντ-ια), δῦσα (δυ-ντ-ια). 95 *b*.

b. In the perfect the stem ends in -υσ, to which ια is added; e.g. λελυκυῖα (for λελυκ-υσ-ια). 90.

333. The vocative is like the nominative. 223.

334. The full accent of polysyllabic barytone participles appears in βουλεύων, βουλεύουσα, βουλεῦον *planning*, and βουλεύσᾱς, βουλεύσᾱσα, βουλεῦσαν *having planned*. 151 *g*.

335. For the accent of the genitive and dative of monosyllabic participles, see 149 and the inflection of ὤν and δῦς above. E.g. θείς *having placed* has gen. θέντος, θέντων, etc.

336. Contract Participles. The present participle of verbs in -άω, -έω, -όω, the future participle of nasal and liquid verbs (491), and the participle of the Attic future (678) are contracted. Τῖμάων, τῖμῶν *honoring*, and φιλέων, φιλῶν *loving*, are declined as follows:

SINGULAR

N.	(τῖμάων)	τῖμῶν	(τῖμάουσα)	τῖμῶσα	(τῖμάον)	τῖμῶν
G.	(τῖμάοντος)	τῖμῶντος	(τῖμαούσης)	τῖμώσης	(τῖμάοντος)	τῖμῶντος
D.	(τῖμάοντι)	τῖμῶντι	(τῖμαούσῃ)	τῖμώσῃ	(τῖμάοντι)	τῖμῶντι
A.	(τῖμάοντα)	τῖμῶντα	(τῖμάουσαν)	τῖμῶσαν	(τῖμάον)	τῖμῶν
V.	(τῖμάων)	τῖμῶν	(τῖμάουσα)	τῖμῶσα	(τῖμάον)	τῖμῶν

DUAL

N.	(τῖμάοντε)	τῖμῶντε	(τῖμαούσᾱ)	τῖμώσᾱ	(τῖμάοντε)	τῖμῶντε
G.	(τῖμαόντοιν)	τῖμώντοιν	(τῖμαούσαιν)	τῖμώσαιν	(τῖμαόντοιν)	τῖμώντοιν

PLURAL

N.	(τῖμάοντες)	τῖμῶντες	(τῖμάουσαι)	τῖμῶσαι	(τῖμάοντα)	τῖμῶντα
G.	(τῖμαόντων)	τῖμώντων	(τῖμαουσῶν)	τῖμωσῶν	(τῖμαόντων)	τῖμώντων
D.	(τῖμάουσι)	τῖμῶσι	(τῖμαούσαις)	τῖμώσαις	(τῖμάουσι)	τῖμῶσι
A.	(τῖμάοντας)	τῖμῶντας	(τῖμαούσᾱς)	τῖμώσᾱς	(τῖμάοντα)	τῖμῶντα
V.	(τῖμάοντες)	τῖμῶντες	(τῖμάουσαι)	τῖμῶσαι	(τῖμάοντα)	τῖμῶντα

SINGULAR

N.	(φιλέων)	φιλῶν	(φιλέουσα)	φιλοῦσα	(φιλέον)	φιλοῦν
G.	(φιλέοντος)	φιλοῦντος	(φιλεούσης)	φιλούσης	(φιλέοντος)	φιλοῦντος
D.	(φιλέοντι)	φιλοῦντι	(φιλεούσῃ)	φιλούσῃ	(φιλέοντι)	φιλοῦντι
A.	(φιλέοντα)	φιλοῦντα	(φιλέουσαν)	φιλοῦσαν	(φιλέον)	φιλοῦν
V.	(φιλέων)	φιλῶν	(φιλέουσα)	φιλοῦσα	(φιλέον)	φιλοῦν

DUAL

| N. | (φιλέοντε) | φιλοῦντε | (φιλεούσᾱ) | φιλούσᾱ | (φιλέοντε) | φιλοῦντε |
| G. | (φιλεόντοιν) | φιλούντοιν | (φιλεούσαιν) | φιλούσαιν | (φιλεόντοιν) | φιλούντοιν |

PLURAL

N.	(φιλέοντες)	φιλοῦντες	(φιλέουσαι)	φιλοῦσαι	(φιλέοντα)	φιλοῦντα
G.	(φιλεόντων)	φιλούντων	(φιλεουσῶν)	φιλουσῶν	(φιλεόντων)	φιλούντων
D.	(φιλέουσι)	φιλοῦσι	(φιλεούσαις)	φιλούσαις	(φιλέουσι)	φιλοῦσι
A.	(φιλέοντας)	φιλοῦντας	(φιλεούσᾱς)	φιλούσᾱς	(φιλέοντα)	φιλοῦντα
V.	(φιλέοντες)	φιλοῦντες	(φιλέουσαι)	φιλοῦσαι	(φιλέοντα)	φιλοῦντα

337. Present participles of verbs in -όω (contracted -ῶ) are declined like φιλῶν; e.g. δηλῶν, δηλοῦσα, δηλοῦν *manifesting*; gen. δηλοῦντος, δηλούσης; dat. δηλοῦντι, δηλούσῃ, etc. No uncontracted forms of verbs in -όω are used. 483.

338. A few second perfect participles in -αώς have -ῶσα in the feminine by analogy with the masculine, and retain ω in the oblique cases. They are contracted in Attic; e.g. Hom. ἑσταώς, ἑσταῶσα, ἑσταός, Attic ἑστώς, ἑστῶσα, ἑστός *standing*, gen. ἑστῶτος (Hom. ἑσταότος), ἑστώης, ἑστῶτος, etc.; plur. ἑστῶτες, ἑστῶσαι, ἑστῶτα, gen. ἑστώτων, ἑστωσῶν. The neuter ἑστός is due to analogy with λελυκός and other perfect participles, but some texts give ἑστώς. Hdt. has ἑστεώς, ἑστεῶσα, ἑστεός, ἑστεῶτος, ἑστεώσης, etc. Like ἑσταώς is τεθνεώς, τεθνεῶσα, τεθνεός *dead*.

Adjectives with One Ending

339. Some adjectives of the third declension have only one ending, which is both masculine and feminine; e.g. φυγάς, φυγάδος *fugitive*; ἄπαις, ἄπαιδος *childless*; ἀγνώς, ἀγνῶτος *unknown*; ἄναλκις, ἀνάλκιδος *weak*. The oblique cases occasionally occur as neuter. Some of these adjectives are used as substantives; e.g. φυγάς *refugee*; πένης, πένητος *poor* and *pauper*; γυμνής, γυμνῆτος *stripped*, also *light-armed soldier*; ἐπήλυδα ἔθνεα *foreign nations*, cf. (ὁ, ἡ) ἔπηλυς *foreigner*; αὐτόχειρ *murderous* and *murderer*.

340. The poetic ἴδρις *knowing*, has acc. ἴδριν, voc. ἴδρι, nom. plur. ἴδριες.

341. A very few adjectives of one termination occur in the first declension, ending in -ᾱς or -ης; e.g. γεννάδᾱς *noble*, gen. γεννάδου.

IRREGULAR ADJECTIVES

342. The irregular adjectives, μέγας (μεγα-, μεγαλο-) *great*, πολύς (πολυ-, πολλο-) *much*, and πρᾷος (πρᾳο-, πρᾱϋ-) *mild*, are thus declined:

SINGULAR

Nom.	μέγας	μεγάλη	μέγα	πολύς	πολλή	πολύ
Gen.	μεγάλου	μεγάλης	μεγάλου	πολλοῦ	πολλῆς	πολλοῦ
Dat.	μεγάλῳ	μεγάλῃ	μεγάλῳ	πολλῷ	πολλῇ	πολλῷ
Acc.	μέγαν	μεγάλην	μέγα	πολύν	πολλήν	πολύ
Voc.	μεγάλε	μεγάλη	μέγα			

DUAL

N.A.V.	μεγάλω	μεγάλᾱ	μεγάλω
G.D.	μεγάλοιν	μεγάλαιν	μεγάλοιν

PLURAL

N.V.	μεγάλοι	μεγάλαι	μεγάλα	πολλοί	πολλαί	πολλά
Gen.	μεγάλων	μεγάλων	μεγάλων	πολλῶν	πολλῶν	πολλῶν
Dat.	μεγάλοις	μεγάλαις	μεγάλοις	πολλοῖς	πολλαῖς	πολλοῖς
Acc.	μεγάλους	μεγάλᾱς	μεγάλα	πολλούς	πολλάς	πολλά

SINGULAR

Nom.	πρᾷος	πρᾱεῖα	πρᾷον
Gen.	πρᾴου	πρᾱείᾱς	πρᾴου
Dat.	πρᾴῳ	πρᾱείᾳ	πρᾴῳ
Acc.	πρᾷον	πρᾱεῖαν	πρᾷον

DUAL

N.V.	πρᾴω	πρᾱείᾱ	πρᾴω
G.D.	πρᾴοιν	πρᾱείαιν	πρᾴοιν

PLURAL

N.V.	πρᾷοι or πρᾱεῖς	πρᾱεῖαι	πρᾷα or πρᾱέα
Gen.	πρᾴων or πρᾱέων	πρᾱειῶν	πρᾴων or πρᾱέων
Dat.	πρᾴοις or πρᾱέσι	πρᾱείαις	πρᾴοις or πρᾱέσι
Acc.	πρᾴους	πρᾱείᾱς	πρᾷα or πρᾱέα

343. Πολλός, -ή, -όν is found in Homer and Herodotus, declined regularly throughout. Homer has forms πολέος, πολέες, πολέων, πολέσσι, πολέσι, πολέσσι, πολέας, not to be confounded with epic forms of πόλις (257); also πουλύς, πουλύ. The stem of all forms was πολυ-, by assimilation πολλο- (63 b).

344. Πρᾷος has two stems, one πρᾳο-, from which the masculine and neuter are generally formed; and one πρᾱϋ-, from which the feminine and some other forms come. There is an epic form πρηΰς (lyric πρᾶϋς) coming from the latter stem. The forms belonging to the two stems differ in accent.

345. Some compounds of πούς (ποδ-) *foot* have -ουν in the nominative neuter and the accusative masculine; e.g. τρίπους, τρίπουν *three-footed*, like ἁπλοῦς, ἁπλοῦν (303); but τρίποδα *tripod*. Cf. 286 a.

COMPARISON OF ADJECTIVES

I. COMPARISON BY -τερος, -τατος

346. Most adjectives add -τερος (stem τερο-) to the masculine stem to form the comparative, and -τατος (stem τατο-) to form the superlative. Stems in -ο with a short penult lengthen ο to ω before -τερος and -τατος. Comparatives are inflected like μακρός, superlatives like σοφός (294), except in accent. E.g.

κοῦφος (κουφο-) *light*, κουφότερος (-ᾱ, -ον) *lighter*, κουφότατος (-η, -ον) *lightest*.
σοφός (σοφο-) *wise*, σοφώτερος *wiser*, σοφώτατος *wisest*.
ἄξιος (ἀξιο-) *worthy*, ἀξιώτερος, ἀξιώτατος.
σεμνός (σεμνο-) *august*, σεμνότερος, σεμνότατος.
πικρός (πικρο-) *bitter*, πικρότερος, πικρότατος.
ὀξύς (ὀξυ-) *sharp*, ὀξύτερος, ὀξύτατος.
μέλᾱς (μελαν-) *black*, μελάντερος, μελάντατος.
ἀληθής (ἀληθεσ-) *true*, ἀληθέστερος, ἀληθέστατος.

347. Stems in ο do not lengthen ο to ω if the penultimate vowel is followed by a stop and a liquid or nasal (121). See πικρός above (scanned πῑκρός in Homer). Likewise κενός *empty* (original stem κενϝο-) and στενός *narrow* (στενϝο-) make κενότερος, κενότατος; στενότερος, στενότατος. Compare Ionic κεινός, στεινός, and 165 a.

348. *a.* Φίλος *dear* drops ο of the stem, making φίλτερος, φίλτατος. So παλαιός *ancient*, παλαίτερος, παλαίτατος (cf. the adverb πάλαι *long ago*), and γεραιός *aged*, γεραίτερος, γεραίτατος.

b. Another ending -αίτερος, -αίτατος is thus formed, and used in the comparison of μέσος *middle* (μεσαίτερος, μεσαίτατος), ἥσυχος *quiet*, ἴσος *equal*, ὄρθριος *early*.

349. Similarly an ending -έστερος, -έστατος is developed by analogy with ἀληθέστερος, ἀληθέστατος (346). Thus some adjectives in -οος add -έστερος and -έστατος to the stem and contract: εὔνοος, εὔνους *loyal*, εὐνούστερος, εὐνούστατος (303). So adjectives in -ων (stem -ον, 307), e.g. σώφρων *sober*, σωφρονέστερος, σωφρονέστατος. But πέπων *ripe* has πεπαίτερος, πεπαίτατος; πίων *fat*, πῑότερος, πῑότατος; ἐπιλήσμων *forgetful*, ἐπιλησμονέστερος, but superlative ἐπιλησμότατος.

350. A few adjectives in -ος are thus compared: ἄφθονος *abundant*, ἀφθονέστερος, ἀφθονέστατος (beside ἀφθονώτερος, ἀφθονώτατος); ἄκρᾱτος *unmixed* (of strong wine), ἀκρᾱτέστερος, ἀκρᾱτέστατος (as if from ἀκρᾱτής *lacking* *in self-control*); ἐρρωμένος *strong* (properly participle, *strengthened*), ἐρρωμενέστερος, ἐρρωμενέστατος.

351. Adjectives in -εις add -τερος and -τατος to the weak stem in -ετ (**324 b**); e.g. χαρίεις *graceful* (χαριετ-), χαριέστερος, χαριέστατος for χαριετ-τερος, χαριετ-τατος (**66**). So πένης *poor* (πενητ-, weak stem πενετ-), πενέστερος, πενέστατος; cf. πενέστης *serf*.

352. An ending -ίστερος, -ίστατος appears in a few words; e.g. λάλος *talkative*, λαλίστερος; κλέπτης *thief* (**363**), κλεπτίστατος; ἅρπαξ *rapacious*, ἁρπαγίστατος.

353. Adjectives may be compared by prefixing μᾶλλον *more*, and μάλιστα *most*; e.g. μᾶλλον σοφός *more wise*, μάλιστα κακός *most bad*, μᾶλλον ἑκών *more willingly* (the only mode of comparison admissible for ἑκών).

II. COMPARISON BY -ίων, -ιστος

354. a. Some adjectives, chiefly in -ύς and -ρός, are compared by changing these endings to -ίων and -ιστος. E.g.

ἡδύς *sweet*, ἡδίων, ἥδιστος.
ταχύς *swift*, ταχίων (rare), commonly θάττων, θάσσων (**105 e, 94**), τάχιστος.
αἰσχρός *base*, αἰσχίων, αἴσχιστος.
ἐχθρός *hostile*, ἐχθίων, ἔχθιστος.
κῦδρός (poet.) *glorious*, κύδίων, κύδιστος.

b. The terminations -ίων and -ιστος are thus added to the base of the word (**169**), not to the adjective stem.

355. Comparatives in -ίων, neuter -ιον, are thus declined:

SINGULAR			PLURAL			
Nom.	ἡδίων	ἥδιον	N.V.	ἡδίονες ἡδίους	ἡδίονα ἡδίω
Gen.	ἡδίονος		Gen.	ἡδιόνων
Dat.	ἡδίονι		Dat.	ἡδίοσι
Acc.	ἡδίονα ἡδίω	ἥδιον	Acc.	ἡδίονας ἡδίους	ἡδίονα ἡδίω

DUAL
N.A.V. ἡδίονε
G.D. ἡδιόνοιν

356. a. The superlative forms in -ιστος are declined like σοφός (**294**). For the comparative, cf. εὐδαίμων (**307**). The shortened forms are from a stem in -ιοσ, cf. Lat. mel-ius, meliōris (for mel-iōs-is); hence ἡδίω for ἡδ-ίοσ-α, ἡδίους for ἡδ-ίοσ-ες (see **90** and page 15). The accusative plural in -ους follows the form of the nominative.

b. Doric poetry and Homer sometimes have comparatives in -ίων: φίλίων *dearer*, Od. 19, 351.

c. The vocative singular of these comparatives seems not to occur.
d. For the recessive accent in the neuter singular, see **142** *b.*

III. IRREGULAR COMPARISON

357. Sometimes several words are assigned to a single positive of related meaning. Others exhibit peculiarities of form due to phonetic change. The following are the most important cases of irregular comparison:

1. ἀγαθός *good*	. ἀμείνων		
	(ἀρείων)	.	ἄριστος
	. βελτίων	.	βέλτιστος
	(βέλτερος)		(βέλτατος)
	. κρείττων, κρείσσων	.	κράτιστος
	(κρέσσων)		(κάρτιστος)
	(φέρτερος)		(φέρτατος, φέριστος)
	λῴων (λωίων, λωίτερος)		λῷστος
2. κακός *bad*	κακίων (κακώτερος)		κάκιστος
	- χείρων (χερείων)	.	χείριστος
	(χειρότερος, χερειότερος)		
	. ἥττων, ἥσσων (for ἡκ-ι̯ων)		(ἥκιστος, rare)
	(ἕσσων)		adv. ἥκιστα
			least
3. καλός *beautiful*	καλλίων		κάλλιστος
4. μακρός *long*	μακρότερος		μακρότατος
	(μάσσων)		(μήκιστος)
5. μέγας *great*	. μείζων (μέζων)	.	μέγιστος
6. μῑκρός *small*	μῑκρότερος		μῑκρότατος
(Hom. ἐλάχεια, fem.			
of ἐλαχύς)	. ἐλάττων, ἐλάσσων	.	ἐλάχιστος
	. μείων		(μεῖστος, rare)
7. ὀλίγος *little,* pl. *few* .	ὀλείζων (in inscriptions; Hom. '	ὀλίγιστος	
	ὑπ-ολίζων *rather less*)		
8. πολύς *much*	. πλείων, πλέων, neut. πλέον, πλεῖν ·	πλεῖστος	
9. ῥᾴδιος *easy* (Ion. -	ῥᾴων (Ion. ῥηίων)	.	ῥᾷστος
ῥηίδιος)	(ῥηίτερος)		(ῥηίτατος, ῥήιστος)
10. φίλος *dear*	(φίλτερος)		φίλτατος
	φιλαίτερος (Xen., Alexandrian)	φιλαίτατος	
			(Xen., Alex.)
	(φιλίων, twice in Hom.)		

The forms in parentheses are Ionic or poetic. Those in *-ων* are declined like ἡδίων (**355**).

358. Ἀμείνων is for ἀμεν-ιων, χείρων for χερ-ιων (**100**, cf. **356** *b*), originally ἀμεν-ίων, χερ-ίων, cf. Hom. χερ-είων. Μείζων, Ion. μέζων, is for μεγ-ιων (**96**). For ἥττων (ἥκ-ιων) and ἐλάττων (ἐλαχ-ιων), see **94**. With κρείττων (for κρετ-ιων) compare Aeol. κρέτος *power*, Att. κράτος (seen in κράτιστος).

359. Κακίων is Lat. peior, χείρων Lat. deterior; χείρους sometimes means *rascals*.

360. Ἐλάττων and ἐλάχιστος in the plural are often used as comp. and superl. of ὀλίγοι *few*; ἐλάττων refers to number or quantity, μείων to size, ἥττων (*weaker, inferior*) to degree.

361. Other irregularities in comparison will be found in the Lexicon under the following words (see also **348**–**350**, **352**):

ἄχαρις, βαθύς, βλάξ, βραδύς, γλυκύς, ἐπίχαρις, ἴδιος, μάκαρ, νέος, παχύς, πλησίος, πρέσβυς, προὔργου (**51**), πρώιος, σπουδαῖος, σχολαῖος, ψευδής, ὠκύς.

362. Some comparatives and superlatives have no positive, but their stem generally appears in an adverb or preposition. E.g.

ἄνω *up*, ἀνώτερος *upper*, ἀνώτατος *uppermost*.
κάτω *down*, κατώτερος *lower*, κατώτατος *lowest*.
πρό *before*, πρότερος *former*, πρῶτος *first* (poet. πρώτιστος).
ὑπέρ *over*, ὑπέρτερος *higher, superior*, ὑπέρτατος *highest, supreme*.
ὕστερος *later, latter, last*.
ἐξ *out of*, ἔσχατος *farthest, last, extreme*.

Homer has ῥίγιον *more dreadful*, ῥίγιστος; κήδειος *dear*, κήδιστος; κερδαλέος *crafty*, κερδίων, κέρδιστος; ὁπλότερος *younger*, ὁπλότατος; ὑψίων *higher*, ὕψιστος; μέσσατος, μέσατος *midmost*; δεύτατος *last*, cf. δεύτερος *second*.

363. Comparatives and superlatives may be formed from substantives, and even from pronouns. E.g.

βασιλεύς *king*, βασιλεύτερος *more kingly*, βασιλεύτατος; κλέπτης *thief*, κλεπτίστερος, κλεπτίστατος (**352**); κύων *dog*, κύντερος *more impudent*, κύντατος. So αὐτός *self*, αὐτότατος *his very self*, Lat. ipsissimus. Other comparative forms are seen in ἑκάτερος *each* (of two), superlative ἕκαστος *each* (of many); ἕτερος *other*; ὁπότερος *which* (of two), πότερον *whether*.

PRONOUNS

Personal and Intensive Pronouns

364. The personal pronouns are ἐγώ *I*, σύ *thou*, and οὗ (genitive) *of him, of her, of it*. Αὐτός *self* is used as a personal pronoun for *him, her, it*, etc. in the oblique cases, but never in the nominative.

They are thus declined:

SINGULAR

Nom.	ἐγώ	σύ		αὐτός	αὐτή	αὐτό
Gen.	ἐμοῦ, μου	σοῦ, σου	οὗ, οὐ	αὐτοῦ	αὐτῆς	αὐτοῦ
Dat.	ἐμοί, μοι	σοί, σοι	οἷ, οἱ	αὐτῷ	αὐτῇ	αὐτῷ
Acc.	ἐμέ, με	σέ, σε	ἕ, ἑ	αὐτόν	αὐτήν	αὐτό

DUAL

N.A.	νώ	σφώ		αὐτώ	αὐτά	αὐτώ
G.D.	νῷν	σφῷν		αὐτοῖν	αὐταῖ	αὐτοῖν

PLURAL

Nom.	ἡμεῖς	ὑμεῖς	σφεῖς	αὐτοί	αὐταί	αὐτά
Gen.	ἡμῶν	ὑμῶν	σφῶν	αὐτῶν	αὐτῶν	αὐτῶν
Dat.	ἡμῖν	ὑμῖν	σφίσι	αὐτοῖς	αὐταῖς	αὐτοῖς
Acc.	ἡμᾶς	ὑμᾶς	σφᾶς	αὐτούς	αὐτάς	αὐτά

365. The stems of the personal pronouns in the first person are ἐμε- (cf. Lat. me), νω- (cf. nos), and ἠμε- (for ἀσμε-), ἐγώ being of distinct formation; in the second person, σε- (for τϝε-, cf. Dor. τύ, Lat. tu, te), σφω-, ὑμε- (for yusme-, 26); in the third person, ἑ- (for σϝε, cf. se) and σφ-.

366. The unaccented forms are enclitic and unemphatic (159 a; 161 a, d, e).

367. For the uses of οὗ, οἷ, etc., see 986; 987. In Attic prose οἷ, σφεῖς, σφῶν, σφίσι, σφᾶς are the only common forms, and when used are regularly indirect reflexives (direct reflexive σφίσι Thuc. 3, 7). The orators seldom use this pronoun at all. The tragedians use chiefly σφιν (not σφι) and σφε (369 a, 370). For the nominative of the pronoun in the third person, demonstrative pronouns are used, and for the oblique cases, αὐτός.

368. Αὐτός in all cases may be an intensive adjective pronoun, like Lat. ipse self (988 a), and is always such in the nominative except when preceded by the article (375, 988 b).

369. a. The following is the Homeric declension of ἐγώ, σύ, and οὗ. The forms with ἀμμ- and ὑμμ- are Aeolic.

SINGULAR

Nom.	ἐγώ, ἐγών	σύ, τύνη	
Gen.	ἐμεῖο, ἐμέο, ἐμεῦ, μευ, ἐμέθεν	σεῖο, σέο, σεο, σεῦ, σευ, σέθεν	εἷο, ἕο, ἑο, εὗ, εὐ, ἕθεν, ἕθεν
Dat.	ἐμοί, μοι	σοί, τοι, τεΐν	ἑοῖ, οἷ, οἱ
Acc.	ἐμέ, με	σέ, σε	ἑέ, ἕ, ἑ, μιν

DUAL

N.A.	νῶϊ, νώ	σφῶϊ, σφώ	σφωε
G.D.	νῶϊν	σφῶϊν, σφῷν	σφωϊν

PLURAL

Nom.	ἡμεῖς, ἄμμες	ὑμεῖς, ὕμμες	σφείων, σφέων,
Gen.	ἡμείων, ἡμέων	ὑμείων, ὑμέων	σφέων, σφῶν
Dat.	ἡμῖν, ἄμμι	ὑμῖν, ὕμμι	σφίσι, σφισι, σφιν
Acc.	ἡμέας, ἄμμε	ὑμέας, ὕμμε	σφέας, σφεας, σφε

b. Herodotus has the following inflection:

SINGULAR

Nom.	ἐγώ	σύ	
Gen.	ἐμέο, ἐμεῦ, μευ	σέο, σεῦ, σευ	εὑ
Dat.	ἐμοί, μοι	σοί, τοι	οἱ
Acc.	ἐμέ, με	σέ, σε	ἑ, μιν

PLURAL

Nom.	ἡμεῖς	ὑμεῖς	σφεῖς
Gen.	ἡμέων	ὑμέων	σφέων, σφεων
Dat.	ἡμῖν	ὑμῖν	σφίσι, σφισι
Acc.	ἡμέας	ὑμέας	σφέας, σφεας, neut. σφεα

370. The tragedians use σφε and σφιν (both enclitic) as personal pronouns, both masculine and feminine. They sometimes use σφε and rarely σφιν as singular. In Homer σφε may be used as accusative in all numbers and genders.

371. a. The tragedians use the Doric accusative νιν (enclitic) as a personal pronoun in all genders (the neuter rarely), and in both singular and plural.

b. The Ionic μιν is used in all genders, but only in the singular.

372. The penult of ἡμῶν, ἡμῖν, ἡμᾶς, ὑμῶν, ὑμῖν, and ὑμᾶς is sometimes accented in poetry, when they are not emphatic, and ῑν and ᾱς are shortened; e.g. ἥμων, ἥμιν, ἥμας, ὕμων, ὕμιν, ὕμας. If they are emphatic, they are sometimes written ἡμίν, ἡμάς, ὑμίν, ὑμάς. So σφάς is written for σφᾶς.

373. Herodotus has αὐτέων in the feminine for αὐτῶν (196 e). The Ionic contracts ὁ αὐτός into ωὑτός or ωὐτός, and τὸ αὐτό into τωὐτό.

374. The Doric has ἐγών; ἐμέος, ἐμοῦς, ἐμεῦς; ἐμίν; ἁμές, ἁμέων or ἁμῶν, ἁμίν or ἁμιν, ἁμέ; τύ, τύνη; τέος, τεοῦς, τεῦς, τέο, τεῦ, τεοῦ; τίν, τίνη; τέ, τυ, τιν; ὑμές; ὑμέων; ὑμίν, ὑμιν; ὑμέ; ἑοῦς, ἑοῦ; ϝίν; νιν; σφείων, ψέων; φίν, ψίν; σφέ, ψέ. Pindar has ἐγών, τύ, τοί, σφιν, τίν, νιν.

375. Αὐτός preceded by the article means *the same* (Lat. idem); e.g. ὁ αὐτὸς ἀνήρ *the same man*. See 988 b.

376. Αὐτός is often united by crasis (51) with the article; e.g. ταὐτοῦ for τοῦ αὐτοῦ; ταὐτῷ for τῷ αὐτῷ; ταὐτῇ for τῇ αὐτῇ (not to be confounded with ταύτῃ from οὗτος); αὐτή for ἡ αὐτή Lat. eadem, to be distinguished from αὐτή Lat. ipsa, and from αὕτη (388) Lat. haec. In the contracted form the neuter singular has ταὐτό or ταὐτόν.

Reflexive Pronouns

377. The reflexive pronouns are ἐμαυτοῦ, ἐμαυτῆς *of myself*; σεαυτοῦ, σεαυτῆς *of thyself*; and ἑαυτοῦ, ἑαυτῆς, ἑαυτοῦ *of himself, herself, itself*. They are thus declined:

SINGULAR

	Masc.	Fem.	Masc.	Fem.		Masc.	Fem.
Gen.	ἐμαυτοῦ	ἐμαυτῆς	σεαυτοῦ	σεαυτῆς		σαυτοῦ	σαυτῆς
Dat.	ἐμαυτῷ	ἐμαυτῇ	σεαυτῷ	σεαυτῇ	or	σαυτῷ	σαυτῇ
Acc.	ἐμαυτόν	ἐμαυτήν	σεαυτόν	σεαυτήν		σαυτόν	σαυτήν

PLURAL

	Masc.	Fem.	Masc.	Fem.
Gen.	ἡμῶν αὐτῶν		ὑμῶν αὐτῶν	
Dat.	ἡμῖν αὐτοῖς	ἡμῖν αὐταῖς	ὑμῖν αὐτοῖς	ὑμῖν αὐταῖς
Acc.	ἡμᾶς αὐτούς	ἡμᾶς αὐτάς	ὑμᾶς αὐτούς	ὑμᾶς αὐτάς

SINGULAR

	Masc.	Fem.	Neut.		Masc.	Fem.	Neut.
Gen.	ἑαυτοῦ	ἑαυτῆς	ἑαυτοῦ		αὐτοῦ	αὐτῆς	αὐτοῦ
Dat.	ἑαυτῷ	ἑαυτῇ	ἑαυτῷ	or	αὐτῷ	αὐτῇ	αὐτῷ
Acc.	ἑαυτόν	ἑαυτήν	ἑαυτό		αὐτόν	αὐτήν	αὐτό

PLURAL

	Masc.	Fem.	Neut.		Masc.	Fem.	Neut.
Gen.	ἑαυτῶν	ἑαυτῶν	ἑαυτῶν		αὐτῶν	αὐτῶν	αὐτῶν
Dat.	ἑαυτοῖς	ἑαυταῖς	ἑαυτοῖς	or	αὐτοῖς	αὐταῖς	αὐτοῖς
Acc.	ἑαυτούς	ἑαυτάς	ἑαυτά		αὐτούς	αὐτάς	αὐτά

also

Gen.	σφῶν αὐτῶν
Dat.	σφίσιν αὐτοῖς σφίσιν αὐταῖς
Acc.	σφᾶς αὐτούς σφᾶς αὐτάς

378. The reflexives are compounded of the stems of the personal pronouns (364) and the oblique cases of αὐτός. But in the plural the two pronouns are declined separately in the first and second persons, and often in the third; so, for emphasis, με . . . αὐτόν, Plat. *Ap.* 23 a.

379. In Homer the two pronouns are always separated in all persons and numbers; e.g. ἐμέθεν αὐτῆς, σοὶ αὐτῷ, οἷ αὐτῷ, ἓ αὐτήν. Herodotus has ἐμεωυτοῦ, σεωυτοῦ, ἑωυτοῦ, σφέων αὐτῶν, etc.

Possessive Pronouns

380. The possessive pronouns ἐμός *my*, σός *thy*, ἡμέτερος *our*, ὑμέτερος *your*, σφέτερος *their*, and the poetic ὅς *his*, are declined like adjectives in -ος (293).

381. Homer has dual possessives νωΐτερος *of us two*, σφωΐτερος *of you two*; also τεός (Doric and Aeolic, = Lat. tuus) for σός, ἑός for ὅς (89), ἁμός for ἡμέτερος, ὑμός for ὑμέτερος, σφός for σφέτερος. The Attic poets sometimes have ἁμός or ἁμός for ἐμός (often as *our*).

382. Ὅς is not used in Attic prose. *His, her, its* are there expressed by the genitive of αὐτός; e.g. ὁ πατὴρ αὐτοῦ *his father*.

Reciprocal Pronouns

383. The reciprocal pronoun is ἀλλήλων *of one another*, used only in the oblique cases of the dual and plural. It is thus declined:

	DUAL			PLURAL		
Gen.	ἀλλήλοιν	ἀλλήλαιν	ἀλλήλοιν	ἀλλήλων	ἀλλήλων	ἀλλήλων
Dat.	ἀλλήλοιν	ἀλλήλαιν	ἀλλήλοιν	ἀλλήλοις	ἀλλήλαις	ἀλλήλοις
Acc.	ἀλλήλω	ἀλλήλᾱ	ἀλλήλω	ἀλλήλους	ἀλλήλᾱς	ἄλληλα

384. The stem is ἀλληλο- (for ἀλλ-αλλο-), a doubling of ἄλλος *other*.

The Article

385. The definite article ὁ, ἡ, τό *the* (stems ὁ-, ἁ-, το-) is declined as follows:

	SINGULAR			DUAL				PLURAL		
Nom.	ὁ	ἡ	τό	N.A.	τώ	τώ	τώ	Nom.	οἱ	αἱ	τά
Gen.	τοῦ	τῆς	τοῦ	G.D.	τοῖν	τοῖν	τοῖν	Gen.	τῶν	τῶν	τῶν
Dat.	τῷ	τῇ	τῷ					Dat.	τοῖς	ταῖς	τοῖς
Acc.	τόν	τήν	τό					Acc.	τούς	τάς	τά

386. The feminine dual forms τᾱ́ and ταῖν (especially τᾱ́) are very rare, and τώ and τοῖν are generally used for all genders (**297**). Homer has gen. τοῖο, dual τοῖιν; nom. pl. τοί, ταί; gen. pl. fem. τᾱ́ων; dat. pl. masc. τοῖσι, fem. τῇσι, τῆς. Herodotus has dat. pl. τοῖσι, τῇσι; τοῖσι, ταῖσι occur in Attic poetry, so τοί less commonly. Doric: τῶ, τᾶς, τᾷ, τᾱ́ν, τοί, ταί, gen. pl. fem. τᾶν. Aeolic: τῶ, τᾶς, gen. pl. τᾶν, acc. pl. τοῖς, ταῖς.

387. There is no indefinite article; but the indefinite pronoun τις (**394**) may often be translated by *a* or *an*, e.g. ἄνθρωπός τις *a (certain) man*.

Demonstrative Pronouns

388. The demonstrative pronouns are οὗτος *this, that*, ὅδε *this* (*here*), and ἐκεῖνος *that* (*there*). They are thus declined:

	SINGULAR			PLURAL		
Nom.	οὗτος	αὕτη	τοῦτο	οὗτοι	αὗται	ταῦτα
Gen.	τούτου	ταύτης	τούτου	τούτων	τούτων	τούτων
Dat.	τούτῳ	ταύτῃ	τούτῳ	τούτοις	ταύταις	τούτοις
Acc.	τοῦτον	ταύτην	τοῦτο	τούτους	ταύτᾱς	ταῦτα

DUAL

N.A.	τούτω	τούτω	τούτω
G.D.	τούτοιν	τούτοιν	τούτοιν

SINGULAR

Nom.	ὅδε	ἥδε	τόδε	ἐκεῖνος	ἐκείνη	ἐκεῖνο
Gen.	τοῦδε	τῆσδε	τοῦδε	ἐκείνου	ἐκείνης	ἐκείνου
Dat.	τῷδε	τῇδε	τῷδε	ἐκείνῳ	ἐκείνῃ	ἐκείνῳ
Acc.	τόνδε	τήνδε	τόδε	ἐκεῖνον	ἐκείνην	ἐκεῖνο

DUAL

N.A.	τώδε	τώδε	τώδε	ἐκείνω	ἐκείνω	ἐκείνω
G.D.	τοῖνδε	τοῖνδε	τοῖνδε	ἐκείνοιν	ἐκείνοιν	ἐκείνοιν

PLURAL

Nom.	οἵδε	αἵδε	τάδε	ἐκεῖνοι	ἐκεῖναι	ἐκεῖνα
Gen.	τῶνδε	τῶνδε	τῶνδε	ἐκείνων	ἐκείνων	ἐκείνων
Dat.	τοῖσδε	ταῖσδε	τοῖσδε	ἐκείνοις	ἐκείναις	ἐκείνοις
Acc.	τούσδε	τάσδε	τάδε	ἐκείνους	ἐκείνᾱς	ἐκεῖνα

389. Feminine dual forms in -ᾱ and -αιν are very rare (297).

390. Ὅδε is formed of the article ὁ (originally a demonstrative) and the enclitic suffix -δε (159 d). For the accent of ἥδε, τήνδε, etc., see 160. For τοῖσδε Homer has τοῖσδεσσι or τοῖσδεσι.

391. Ἐκεῖνος appears as κεῖνος in Herodotus, in poetry, and sometimes in Attic prose. Dor. and Aeol. have κῆνος. Herodotus has gen. pl. fem. τουτέων (cf. 373). Dor. has τοῦτοι, ταῦται, gen. pl. fem. ταυτᾶν.

392. The demonstratives, including some adverbs, may be emphasized by adding the deictic suffix -ῑ́, before which a short vowel is dropped. E.g. οὑτοσῑ́, αὑτηῑ́, τουτῑ́ *this here*; ὁδῑ́, ἡδῑ́, τοδῑ́; τουτουῑ́, ταυτῑ́, τουτωνῑ́. So τοσουτοσῑ́, ὡδῑ́, οὑτωσῑ́. In comedy γέ, rarely δέ, may precede this -ῑ́, making -γῑ́ or -δῑ́; e.g. τουτογῑ́, τουτοδῑ́.

393. Other demonstrative pronouns are the following:

a. Referring to what has been described in the preceding context.

τοσοῦτος	τοσαύτη	τοσοῦτο(ν)	so much, so many, Lat. tantus
τοιοῦτος	τοιαύτη	τοιοῦτο(ν)	such (in quality), Lat. talis
τηλικοῦτος	τηλικαύτη	τηλικοῦτο(ν)	so old, so great

b. Referring to what is to follow.

τοσόσδε	τοσήδε	τοσόνδε	so much, so many
τοιόσδε	τοιάδε	τοιόνδε	such (in quality)
τηλικόσδε	τηλικήδε	τηλικόνδε	so old, so great

These are formed from τόσος, τοῖος, which seldom occur in prose, and τηλίκος, which is poetic. The forms τοιοῦτον, τοσοῦτον are commoner than τοιοῦτο, τοσοῦτο (24, 114).

Interrogative and Indefinite Pronouns

394. *a.* The interrogative pronoun τίς, τί who? which? what? always takes the acute on the first syllable (149).

b. The indefinite pronoun τὶς, τὶ any one, some one, is enclitic, and its proper accent belongs on the last syllable (134 *b*).

	Interrogative		Indefinite	
		SINGULAR		
Nom.	τίς	τί	τὶς	τὶ
Gen.	τίνος, τοῦ		τινός, του	
Dat.	τίνι, τῷ		τινί, τῳ	
Acc.	τίνα	τί	τινά	τὶ
		DUAL		
N.A.	τίνε		τινέ	
G.D.	τίνοιν		τινοῖν	
		PLURAL		
Nom.	τίνες	τίνα	τινές	τινά
Gen.	τίνων		τινῶν	
Dat.	τίσι		τισί	
Acc.	τίνας	τίνα	τινάς	τινά

395. *a.* For the neut. pl. indefinite τινά a form ἄττα (Hom. ἄσσα) occurs; ἄσσα and ἄττα arose from improper division of word-groups like ὀλίγα σσα (originally τι̯α) some few things, which became ὀλίγ' ἄσσα. Megarian has σά for τινά.

b. The Ionic has τέο and τεῦ for τοῦ, τέῳ for τῷ (but Hom. τῷ), τέων for τίνων, and τέοισι for τίσι; also these same forms, as indefinite and enclitic, for τον, τῳ, etc. Hdt. gen. pl. τεῶν.

396. Οὗτις and μήτις, poetic for οὐδείς and μηδείς *no one*, are declined like τίς.

397. Ἄλλος *other, another*, is declined like αὐτός (364): ἄλλος, ἄλλη, ἄλλο; ἄλλου, ἄλλης, ἄλλου, etc. For the form ἄλλος, Lat. alius, cf. 98; and for the neuters ἄλλο, τοῦτο, αὐτό, etc., 24.

398. *a.* The indefinite δεῖνα *so-and-so* is sometimes indeclinable, and is sometimes declined as follows:

	SINGULAR	PLURAL
	All Genders	*Masculine*
Nom.	δεῖνα	δεῖνες
Gen.	δεῖνος	δείνων
Dat.	δεῖνι	
Acc.	δεῖνα	δεῖνας

b. Δεῖνα in all its forms always has the article.

Relative Pronouns

399. The relative pronoun ὅς, ἥ, ὅ *who, which, that, what*, is thus declined:

SINGULAR			DUAL				PLURAL		
Nom.	ὅς	ἥ	ὅ	N.A.	ὥ	ὥ	ὥ	Nom.	οἵ	αἵ	ἅ
Gen.	οὗ	ἧς	οὗ	G.D.	οἷν	οἷν	οἷν	Gen.	ὧν	ὧν	ὧν
Dat.	ᾧ	ᾗ	ᾧ					Dat.	οἷς	αἷς	οἷς
Acc.	ὅν	ἥν	ὅ					Acc.	οὕς	ἅς	ἅ

400. Feminine dual forms ἅ and αἷν are very rare and doubtful (297).

401. For ὅς used as a demonstrative, especially in Homer, see **1023.** Homer often uses the forms ὁ, ἡ, τό (originally demonstratives, 390) as relatives (see **933** and **937**); the nom. pl. is τοί, ταί. Homer has ὅο (in some texts ὅου) and ἕης for οὗ and ἧς.

402. The enclitic -περ adds emphasis to the relative; e.g. ὅσπερ, ἥπερ, ὅπερ *precisely the one who, the very thing which*. The enclitic conjunction τε becomes attached to the relative in ὅστε, used by the poets and in Ion. prose; in Att. it is confined to the forms ἐφ' ᾧτε *on condition that*, and ἅτε *inasmuch as*.

403. The indefinite relative ὅστις, ἥτις, ὅ τι *whoever, whatever,* is thus declined:

SINGULAR

Nom.	ὅστις	ἥτις	ὅ τι
Gen.	οὗτινος, ὅτου	ἧστινος	οὗτινος, ὅτου
Dat.	ᾧτινι, ὅτῳ	ᾗτινι	ᾧτινι, ὅτῳ
Acc.	ὅντινα	ἥντινα	ὅ τι

DUAL

N.A.	ὥτινε	ὥτινε	ὥτινε
G.D.	οἷντινοιν	οἷντινοιν	οἷντινοιν

PLURAL

Nom.	οἵτινες	αἵτινες	ἅτινα, ἅττα
Gen.	ὧντινων, ὅτων	ὧντινων	ὧντινων, ὅτων
Dat.	οἷστισι, ὅτοις	αἷστισι	οἷστισι, ὅτοις
Acc.	οὕστινας	ἅστινας	ἅτινα, ἅττα

404. Ὅστις is compounded of the relative ὅς and the indefinite τις, each part being declined separately. For the accent, see **163**. The plural ἅττα (Ionic ἅσσα) for ἅτινα must not be confounded with ἅττα (**395** *a*). Ὅ τι is thus written (sometimes ὅ, τι) to distinguish it from the conjunction ὅτι *that, because*; but some texts, following the manuscripts, write ὅτι for both words.

405. The shorter forms ὅτου, ὅτῳ, ὅτων, and ὅτοις, which are rare in Attic prose authors, are used by the poets and in inscriptions to the exclusion of οὗτινος, etc.

406. *a.* The following are the peculiar Homeric forms of ὅστις:

	SINGULAR		PLURAL	
Nom.	ὅτις	ὅττι		ἅσσα
Gen.	ὅττεο, ὅττευ, ὅτευ		ὅτεων	
Dat.	ὅτεῳ		ὁτέοισι	
Acc.	ὅτινα	ὅττι	ὅτινας	ἅσσα

b. Herodotus has ὅτευ, ὅτεῳ, ὅτεων, ὁτέοισι, and ἅσσα (**404**).

407. The indefinite relatives are often indirect interrogatives, correlated with the direct interrogative τίς, τί (**408**).

PRONOMINAL ADJECTIVES

408. The demonstrative, interrogative, indefinite, and relative pronouns and many pronominal adjectives correspond to each other in form and meaning. The following are the most important:

INTERROG. (*Direct and Indirect*)	INDEFINITE (*Enclitic*)	DEMONSTR.	RELATIVE (*Also Exclamatory*)	INDEF. REL. (*Also Indirect Interrogative*)
τίς *who?* *which? what?* quis? qui?	τὶς *anybody,* *some one,* aliquis, quidam	(ὅς, ὁ) ὅδε *this,* hic; οὗτος *this,* ille, is, iste; ἐκεῖνος *that,* ille	ὅς *who, which,* qui	ὅστις *whoever,* *any one who,* quicumque, quisquis
πότερος *which (of two)?* uter?	πότερος or ποτερός *one of two* (rare)	ἕτερος *the one or the other of two,* alter	ὁπότερος *which of the two*	ὁπότερος *whichever of the two,* utercumque
πόσος *how much? how many?* quantus?	ποσός *of some quantity*	(τόσος) τοσόσδε, τοσοῦτος *so much, so many,* tantus	ὅσος *as much as, as many* as, quantus	ὁπόσος *of whatever size or number,* quantuscumque
ποῖος *of what kind?* qualis?	ποιός *of some kind*	(τοῖος) τοιόσδε, τοιοῦτος *such,* talis	οἷος *of which kind, such* as, qualis	ὁποῖος *of whatever kind,* qualiscumque
πηλίκος *how old? how large?*	πηλίκος *of some age, of some size* (rare)	(τηλίκος) τηλικόσδε, τηλικοῦτος *so old* (or *young*), *so large*	ἡλίκος *of which age or size, as old as, as large as*	ὁπηλίκος *of whatever age or size*

Forms in parentheses are poetic.

409. Homer has ππ (Aeolic) in ὁππότερος, ὁπποῖος; σσ in ὅσσος, τόσσος. Herodotus has κ for π: κότερος, κόσος, κοῖος, ὁκότερος, ὁκόσος, ὁκοῖος (**426**).

410. *a.* Τὶς added to οἷος, ὅσος, ὁπόσος, ὁποῖος, and ὁπότερος makes them more indefinite; e.g. ὁποῖος τις *of what kind soever*.

b. The particles οὖν, δή, δήποτε may be added to the indefinite relative to make the indefiniteness more general; e.g. ὁστισοῦν *anybody, no matter who*; ὁτιοῦν *anything whatever*; ὁποσουτινοσοῦν *at any price whatsoever*; ὁτουοῦν *whose ever*; so ἄλλοι δή *others, be they who they may*, Il. 1, 295. The function of a relative is here lost.

c. Rarely, especially in philosophic discourse, ὁπότερος means *either of two*, losing its relative force even without οὖν.

411. There are also negative pronominal adjectives; e.g. οὔτις, μήτις (poetic for οὐδείς, μηδείς) *no one*; οὐδέτερος, μηδέτερος *neither of two*, Lat. neuter. See **427**.

ADVERBS

412. Adverbs are old case forms of nouns (substantive and adjective) and pronouns. In many instances the stems are no longer in use as separate words, the adverbs being crystallized forms and not felt to be inflections. Some are made with suffixes the origin of which is unknown. E.g.

Genitive: ποῦ *where?* οὗ, ὅπου *where* (relative), αὐτοῦ *right here*, ἑξῆς *next*, ἐκποδών *out of the way* (ἐκ and ποδῶν *feet*), whence ἐμποδών *in the way*.

Dative-Instrumental: πῇ *how?* κοινῇ *in common, publicly*, λάθρᾱ *secretly*.

Accusative: πρῶτον *first* or *at first*, Lat. primum, πολύ *much*, πολλά *often*, μῑκρόν *a little*, ἄγᾱν, later ἄγαν *too much*, τήμερον *today*.

Locative: singular ending -ι, plural -σι, e.g. οἴκοι (**133**) *at home*, Πῦθοῖ *at Pytho* (Delphi), ποῖ *whither?* οἷ, ὅποι *to where* (relative), πάλαι *long ago*, ἐκεῖ *over there*, Πλαταιᾶσι *at Plataea*, Ὀλυμπίᾱσι *at Olympia*, θύρᾱσι *at the doors, outside*, Ἀθήνησι *at Athens*. Forms in -ᾱσι and -ησι occur as regular datives of nouns in early Attic inscriptions.

Ablative: ὡς *as*, οὕτως *so*, and all other adverbs in -ως (**418**). Possibly also ἄνω *above*, κάτω *below*, ὧδε *so*, οὔπω *not yet*.

413. Place *where* is denoted by the locative endings -ι and -σι (**412**), also by -θι and the genitive suffix -ου; place *whence* by -θεν; place *whither* by -δε (-ζε) or -σε. E.g.

οἴκοι (poetic οἴκοθι) *at home* (cf. οἶκος *house*), οἴκοθεν *from home*, οἴκαδε (poetic οἰκόνδε) *home, homeward* (from οἶκα, an old accusative); αὐτοῦ *right here*, αὐτόθεν *from right here*, αὐτόσε *to the very place*; ἀμφοτέρωθι *on both sides*, ἀμφοτέρωθεν *from both sides*; ἄλλοθι *elsewhere*, ἄλλοθεν *from elsewhere*, ἄλλοσε *in another direction*; Hom. οὐρανόθι *in heaven*, οὐρανόθεν *from the sky*; Ἀθήνησι *at Athens*, Ἀθήνηθεν *from Athens*, Ἀθήναζε (for Ἀθήνασδε **86** *d*) *to Athens*; πάντοσε *in every direction*.

414. The suffix -θεν often drops ν in poetry; e.g. πρόσθε *in front* (**113**). A suffix -θα appears in ἔνθα *there, where* (whence ἐνθάδε *here*).

415. In Homer, the forms in -θι and -θεν may be governed by a preposition as genitives; e.g. Ἰλιόθι πρό *before Ilios*, ἐξ ἀλόθεν *from the sea*. Homer uses the suffix -δε freely; e.g. ὅνδε δόμονδε *to his house*, πόλινδε *to the city*, ἄλαδε *to the sea* (**292**).

416. Some adverbs of place are related to prepositions (which were originally adverbs); e.g. ἔξω *outside* (ἐξ), ἔσω *inside* (ἐν, εἰς), κάτω *below* (κατά).

417. Adverbs denoting *manner* usually end in -ως and are freely formed from adjectives and pronouns, sometimes also from participles. E.g.

δίκαιος *just*, δικαίως *justly*; σοφός *wise*, σοφῶς *wisely*; ἁπλοῦς *simple*, ἁπλῶς *simply*, *without qualification*; ἡδύς *pleasant*, ἡδέως *gladly*; ἀληθής *true*, ἀληθῶς *truly*; σαφής *plain*, σαφῶς *plainly*; εὐδαίμων *happy*, εὐδαιμόνως *happily*; διαφέρων (pres. participle) *different*, διαφερόντως *differently*, *preëminently*; συντεταμένος (perf. pass. participle of συντείνω *strain*), συντεταμένως *with might and main*.

418. The adverb in *-ως* is readily determined by changing *ν* of the genitive plural masculine of the adjective to *s*; e.g. δίκαιος, δικαίων, δικαίως; ἡδύς, ἡδέων, ἡδέως. In origin the ending *-ως* is an ablative of *o* stems (412), whence it was applied to all.

419. The meaning of the adverb may not always be determined from the corresponding adjective; e.g. ἄλλος *other*, ἄλλως *in vain*; πᾶς *all*, πάντως *in any case*; ἴσος *equal*, ἴσως *perhaps*. Sometimes a variation in meaning is denoted by a change in accent; e.g. ἄτεχνος *without art*, ἀτέχνως *without art*, but ἀτεχνῶς *literally, absolutely*.

420. Various other terminations occur. E.g. **-α**: μάλα *very*, ἅμα *at the same time*, τάχα *quickly*; **-ακις**: πολλάκις *often*; **-δην**: ἄρδην *utterly*, συλλήβδην *in a word*; **-δον**: ἔνδον *within*, σχεδόν *pretty nearly*; **-τε**: ἄλλοτε *at another time*, ὅτε *when*; **-τι, -στι**: ἀμαχητί *without a battle*, Ἑλληνιστί *in Greek*.

421. Comparison of Adverbs. The neuter accusative singular of the comparative of an adjective forms the comparative of the adverb derived from it; the neuter accusative plural of the superlative forms the superlative of the adverb. E.g.

> σοφῶς (σοφός) *wisely*, σοφώτερον, σοφώτατα.
> ἀληθῶς (ἀληθής) *truly*, ἀληθέστερον, ἀληθέστατα.
> ἡδέως (ἡδύς) *gladly*, ἥδῑον, ἥδιστα.
> χαριέντως (χαρίεις) *gracefully*, χαριέστερον, χαριέστατα.
> σωφρόνως (σώφρων) *prudently*, σωφρονέστερον, σωφρονέστατα.
> μάλα *very*, μᾶλλον (98), μάλιστα.
> (εὖ) *well*, ἄμεινον (357), ἄριστα.
> (μῑκρόν) *little*, ἧττον *less* (357), ἥκιστα.

422. *a.* Adverbs in *-ω* generally form the comparative in *-τέρω*, the superlative in *-τάτω*; e.g. ἄνω *above*, ἀνωτέρω, ἀνωτάτω; πόρρω *far*, πορρωτέρω, πορρωτάτω. So ἐγγύς *near* has ἐγγύτερον and ἐγγυτέρω, ἐγγυτάτω and (rarely) ἐγγύτατα.

b. A few comparatives end in *-ως*, not *-ον*; e.g. βεβαιοτέρως *more firmly*, ἀσφαλεστέρως *more safely*, βελτῑόνως *better*.

423. Certain pronominal adverbs correspond to each other in form and meaning, like the adjectives given above (408). Such are shown on page 92.

INTERROG.	INDEFINITE	DEMONSTR.	RELATIVE	INDEF. REL.
(Direct and Indirect)	*(Enclitic)*			*(Also Indirect Interrogative)*
ποῦ *where?*	πού *somewhere*	(ἔνθα) ἐνθάδε *here*, ἐνταῦθα *there*, ἐκεῖ *over there*	οὗ *where*, ἔνθα *where*	ὅπου *where*, *wherever*
ποῖ *whither?*	ποί *to some place*	ἐκεῖσε *thither*, ἐνταῦθα *thither* (ἔνθα, ἐνθάδε *thither*)	οἷ *whither* (ἔνθα *whither*)	ὅποι *whither*, *to wherever*
πόθεν *whence?*	ποθέν *from some place*	(ἔνθεν) ἐνθένδε, ἐντεῦθεν *from here, from there*; ἐκεῖθεν *from there, thence*	ὅθεν *whence* (ἔνθεν *whence*)	ὁπόθεν *whence*, *from which*
πότε *when?*	ποτέ *some time, ever*	τότε *at that time, then*	ὅτε *when*	ὁπότε *when*, *whenever*
πηνίκα *at what time?*		(τηνίκα) τηνικάδε, τηνικαῦτα *at that time*	ἡνίκα *at which time, when*	ὁπηνίκα *at which time, when*
πῇ *which way? how?*	πή *some way, somehow*	(τῇ) τῇδε, ταύτῃ *this way, thus*	ᾗ *in which way, as*	ὅπῃ *in which way, as*
πῶς *how?*	πώς *in some way, somehow*	(τώς), (ὥς) ὧδε, οὕτως *thus, so, in this way*; ἐκείνως *in that way*	ὡς *as, how*	ὅπως *how*

Forms in parentheses are poetic or uncommon in prose.

424. Ἔνθα and ἔνθεν are relatives in prose, *where, whence*; as demonstratives they appear chiefly in a few expressions like ἔνθα καὶ ἔνθα *here and there*, ἔνθεν καὶ ἔνθεν *on both sides*. For ὥς *thus*, in Attic prose, see **156 c.** In this use it is sometimes accented ὧς.

425. *a.* The poets have κεῖθι, κεῖθεν, κεῖσε for ἐκεῖ, ἐκεῖθεν, and ἐκεῖσε, like κεῖνος for ἐκεῖνος (**391**).

b. Herodotus has ἐνθαῦτα, ἐνθεῦτεν for ἐνταῦθα, ἐντεῦθεν (**105 f**).

c. There are various poetic adverbs; e.g. πόθι, ποθί, ὅθι (for ποῦ, πού, οὗ), τόθι *there*, τόθεν *thence*, ᾗ *where*, ἧμος *when*, τῆμος *then*.

426. Homer has ππ (Aeolic) in ὅππως, ὁππότε. Herodotus has κοῦ, ὅκου, κότε; so οὔκω *not yet*, for οὔπω (**409**).

427. There are negative adverbs of *place, manner,* etc.; e.g. οὐδαμοῦ, μηδαμοῦ *nowhere,* οὐδαμῇ, μηδαμῇ *in no way,* οὐδαμῶς, μηδαμῶς *by no means.* Ποτέ is often added to negatives; e.g. οὔποτε *never,* οὐπώποτε *never yet.* So τίς ποτε *who in the world?* See 411.

428. Οὖν may be added to the indefinite relative adverbs, as in ὁπωσοῦν *in any way whatever,* to make the indefiniteness more general. Cf. 410 b.

NUMERALS

429. The numeral adjectives and adverbs are as follows:

	Sign	Cardinal	Ordinal	Adverb
1	α′	εἷς, μία, ἕν *one*	πρῶτος *first*	ἅπαξ *once*
2	β′	δύο *two*	δεύτερος *second*	δίς *twice*
3	γ′	τρεῖς, τρία *three*	τρίτος *third*	τρίς *thrice*
4	δ′	τέτταρες, τέτταρα	τέταρτος	τετράκις
5	ε′	πέντε	πέμπτος	πεντάκις
6	ϛ′	ἕξ	ἕκτος	ἑξάκις
7	ζ′	ἑπτά	ἕβδομος	ἑπτάκις
8	η′	ὀκτώ	ὄγδοος (305)	ὀκτάκις
9	θ′	ἐννέα (48)	ἔνατος	ἐνάκις
10	ι′	δέκα	δέκατος	δεκάκις
11	ια′	ἕνδεκα	ἑνδέκατος	ἑνδεκάκις
12	ιβ′	δώδεκα	δωδέκατος	δωδεκάκις
13	ιγ′	τρεῖς καὶ δέκα (or τρεισκαίδεκα)	τρίτος καὶ δέκατος	τρεισκαιδεκάκις
14	ιδ′	τέτταρες καὶ δέκα (or τετταρεσκαίδεκα)	τέταρτος καὶ δέκατος	τετταρεσκαιδεκάκις
15	ιε′	πεντεκαίδεκα	πέμπτος καὶ δέκατος	πεντεκαιδεκάκις
16	ιϛ′	ἑκκαίδεκα (83)	ἕκτος καὶ δέκατος	ἑκκαιδεκάκις
17	ιζ′	ἑπτακαίδεκα	ἕβδομος καὶ δέκατος	ἑπτακαιδεκάκις
18	ιη′	ὀκτωκαίδεκα	ὄγδοος καὶ δέκατος	ὀκτωκαιδεκάκις
19	ιθ′	ἐννεακαίδεκα	ἔνατος καὶ δέκατος	ἐννεακαιδεκάκις
20	κ′	εἴκοσι(ν)	εἰκοστός	εἰκοσάκις
21	κα′	εἷς καὶ εἴκοσι(ν) or εἴκοσι (καὶ) εἷς	πρῶτος καὶ εἰκοστός	εἰκοσάκις ἅπαξ
30	λ′	τριάκοντα	τριᾱκοστός	τριᾱκοντάκις
40	μ′	τετταράκοντα	τετταρακοστός	τετταρακοντάκις
50	ν′	πεντήκοντα	πεντηκοστός	πεντηκοντάκις
60	ξ′	ἑξήκοντα	ἑξηκοστός	ἑξηκοντάκις
70	ο′	ἑβδομήκοντα	ἑβδομηκοστός	ἑβδομηκοντάκις
80	π′	ὀγδοήκοντα	ὀγδοηκοστός	ὀγδοηκοντάκις
90	ϟ′	ἐνενήκοντα	ἐνενηκοστός	ἐνενηκοντάκις

100	ρ′	ἑκατόν	ἑκατοστός	ἑκατοντάκις
200	σ′	διᾱκόσιοι, -αι, -α	διᾱκοσιοστός	διᾱκοσιάκις
300	τ′	τριᾱκόσιοι	τριᾱκοσιοστός	τριᾱκοσιάκις
400	υ′	τετρακόσιοι	τετρακοσιοστός	τετρακοσιάκις
500	φ′	πεντακόσιοι	πεντακοσιοστός	πεντακοσιάκις
600	χ′	ἑξακόσιοι	ἑξακοσιοστός	ἑξακοσιάκις
700	ψ′	ἑπτακόσιοι	ἑπτακοσιοστός	ἑπτακοσιάκις
800	ω′	ὀκτακόσιοι	ὀκτακοσιοστός	ὀκτακοσιάκις
900	ϡ′	ἐνακόσιοι	ἐνακοσιοστός	ἐνακοσιάκις
1000	͵α	χίλιοι, -αι, -α	χῑλιοστός	χῑλιάκις
2000	͵β	δισχίλιοι	δισχῑλιοστός	δισχῑλιάκις
3000	͵γ	τρισχίλιοι	τρισχῑλιοστός	τρισχῑλιάκις
10000	͵ι	μύριοι, -αι, -α	μῡριοστός	μῡριάκις
20000	͵κ	δισμύριοι		δισμῡριάκις
100000	͵ρ	δεκακισμύριοι		δεκακισμῡριάκις

430. Above 10,000, δύο μῡριάδες 20,000, τρεῖς μῡριάδες 30,000, etc., may be used.

431. The dialects have the following peculiar forms:
1–4. See 435, 437.
5. Aeolic πέμπε for πέντε.
9. Hdt. εἴνατος for ἔνατος; also εἰνάκις, etc.
12. Doric and Ionic δυώδεκα; poetic δυοκαίδεκα.
20. Epic ἐείκοσι; Doric εἴκατι.
30, 80, 90, 200, 300. Ionic τριήκοντα, ὀγδώκοντα, ἐννήκοντα (Hom.), διηκόσιοι, τριηκόσιοι.
40. Hdt. τεσσεράκοντα.
Homer has τρίτατος, τέτρατος, ἑβδόματος, ὀγδόατος, εἴνατος, δυωδέκατος, ἑεικοστός, and also the Attic form of each.

432. The cardinal numbers from 1 to 4 are thus declined:

	1				2
Nom.	εἷς	μία	ἕν	N.A.	δύο
Gen.	ἑνός	μιᾶς	ἑνός	G.D.	δυοῖν, δυεῖν
Dat.	ἑνί	μιᾷ	ἑνί		
Acc.	ἕνα	μίαν	ἕν		

	3		4	
Nom.	τρεῖς	τρία	τέτταρες	τέτταρα
Gen.	τριῶν		τεττάρων	
Dat.	τρισί		τέτταρσι	
Acc.	τρεῖς	τρία	τέτταρας	τέτταρα

433. The stem of εἷς (for ἑμ-s, ἑν-s) was originally σεμ-, cf. Lat. sem-el, sin-guli. Ἔν is for ἑμ (24). The weak grade σμ- gives μία (for σμ-ια), ἅ-παξ *once*, ἁ-πλοῦς *single, simple* (88 and *a*, 27).

434. The compounds οὐδείς and μηδείς *no one, none*, are declined like εἷς. E.g. οὐδείς, οὐδεμία, οὐδέν; gen. οὐδενός, οὐδεμιᾶς; dat. οὐδενί, οὐδεμιᾷ; acc. οὐδένα, οὐδεμίαν, οὐδέν, etc. Plural forms sometimes occur; e.g. οὐδένες, οὐδένων, οὐδέσι,' οὐδένας, μηδένες, etc. When οὐδέ or μηδέ is written separately or is separated from εἷς (as by a preposition or by ἄν), the negative is more emphatic; e.g. ἐξ οὐδενός *from no one*; οὐδ' ἐξ ἑνός *from not even one*; οὐδὲ εἷς *not a man*.

435. Homer has fem. ἴα, ἰῆς, ἰῇ, ἴαν, for μία; and ἰῷ for ἑνί. Homer has δύο and δύω, both indeclinable; and δοιώ and δοιοί, declined regularly. Herodotus has δυῶν, δυοῖσι, as well as δύο undeclined; δυεῖν occurs in Attic after 329 B.C.

436. In Attic, as in Hom. and Hdt., δύο may be treated as indeclinable; e.g. δύο νεῶν *of two ships*, δύο ναυσί *with two ships*.

437. Homer, the tragedians, Thucydides, and late prose have τέσσαρες, τεσσαράκοντα, for τέτταρες, τετταράκοντα. Attic inscriptions of the fifth century B.C. have only the forms with ττ. Herodotus has τέσσερες. Homer has the Aeolic πίσυρες; Doric has τέτορες; Pindar, dat. pl. τέτρασιν. 165 *e*.

438. *Both* is expressed by ἄμφω, Lat. ambo, ἀμφοῖν; more commonly by ἀμφότερος, generally plural, ἀμφότεροι, -αι, -α.

439. The cardinal numbers from 5 to 199 (except 101 to 104) are indeclinable. The cardinal numbers from 200 and all the ordinals are declined regularly, like other adjectives in -ος. E.g.

τριᾱκόσιοι, τριᾱκόσιαι, τριᾱκόσια *300*; πρῶτος, πρώτη, πρῶτον *first*; ἑκατὸν καὶ μία *101* (fem.).

440. In τρεῖς (τρία) καὶ δέκα *13* and τέτταρες (τέτταρα) καὶ δέκα *14*, the first part is declined. In ordinals (*13th* to *19th*) the forms τρεισκαιδέκατος etc. are rarely found in the best Attic.

441. *a*. In compound expressions like 21, 22, etc., 31, 32, etc., the numbers can be connected by καί in either order; but if καί is omitted, the larger precedes. E.g. εἷς καὶ εἴκοσι *one and twenty*, or εἴκοσι καὶ εἷς *twenty-one*; but (without καί) only εἴκοσι εἷς *twenty-one*. But if the substantive precedes the number, the larger numbers are placed first; e.g. τάλαντα μύρια καὶ τετρακισχίλια καὶ πεντακόσια καὶ ἑξήκοντα *14,560 talents*.

b. In ordinals we have πρῶτος καὶ εἰκοστός *twenty-first*, and also εἰκοστὸς καὶ πρῶτος, etc., always with καί; also εἷς καὶ εἰκοστός *one and twentieth*.

c. The numbers 18 and 19, 28 and 29, 38 and 39, etc., are often expressed by δυοῖν (ἑνὸς) δέοντες εἴκοσι (τριάκοντα, τετταράκοντα, etc.); e.g. ἔτη ἑνὸς δέοντα τριάκοντα *30 years lacking one*.

442. *a*. With collective nouns in the singular, especially ἡ ἵππος *cavalry*, the numerals in -ιοι sometimes appear in the singular; e.g. τὴν διᾱκοσίᾱν ἵππον the (troop of) 200 cavalry (200 horse); ἀσπὶς μυρία καὶ τετρακοσίᾱ (X. An. 1. 7. 10) 10,400 shields (i.e. men with shields).

b. Μύριοι means ten thousand; μυρίοι innumerable. Μυρίος sometimes has the latter sense; e.g. μῦρίος χρόνος countless time; μῡρίᾱ πενίᾱ incalculable poverty.

443. Fractions are denoted in various ways: by μοῖρα or μέρος part, the denominator being understood as one unit larger than the numerator mentioned, e.g. τὰ πέντε μέρη $\frac{5}{6}$; or the denominator also may be mentioned, e.g. τῶν πέντε τὰς δύο μοίρᾱς $\frac{2}{5}$; or by ordinals, e.g. πέμπτον μέρος $\frac{1}{5}$, τριτημόριον $\frac{1}{3}$, ἐπίτριτος $1\frac{1}{3}$ (unity + $\frac{1}{3}$); or by ἥμισυς half or the prefix ἡμι-half, e.g. ὁ ἥμισυς τοῦ ἀριθμοῦ half the number, ἡμιτάλαντον $\frac{1}{2}$ talent, τρία ἡμιτάλαντα $1\frac{1}{2}$ talents. Note also ἐγὼ πέμπτος four others besides myself; e.g. οἱ τριάκοντα (μετεπέμψαντό) με πέμπτον αὐτὸν εἰς τὸν θόλον the Thirty sent for me to come to the Rotunda along with four others (lit. myself the fifth), Plat. Ap. 32 c.

444. a. There are no distributive numerals in Greek like Lat. singuli, bini, etc. For these the cardinals may be used; e.g. ἀνδρὶ ἑκάστῳ πέντε μνᾶς five minas (Lat. quinas minas) to each man. Or prepositions may be used; e.g. ἀνὰ δέκα by tens; ἀνὰ πέντε παρασάγγᾱς τῆς ἡμέρᾱς at the rate of five parasangs (fifteen miles) a day, X. An. 4. 6. 4; σύνδυο two each.

b. Multiplication is expressed by the numeral adverbs; e.g. τὰ δὶς πέντε δέκα ἐστίν twice five are ten. Cf. 430. The suffixes -πλοῦς and -πλάσιος form multiplicatives, e.g. διπλοῦς twofold, διπλάσιος twice as great, διπλάσιοι twice as many. Cf. also διττός twofold, double, Hdt. διξός.

445. a. Adjectives in -αῖος are formed from the ordinals to express time (referring to days); e.g. τριταῖος on the third day, two days after, τῇ δευτεραίᾳ ἀπῆλθε he departed the next day.

b. Several adverbs express division; e.g. δίχα, διχῇ in two parts, divided, πολλαχῇ in many ways, μοναχῇ in one way only (412).

c. Unity is expressed in Greek by several stems: εἷς (σεμ-, 433; cf. Eng. same), μόνος (μονο-) one only, alone, (poetic) οἶος alone (οἰϝο-), and οἴνη ace (οἰνᾱ-, cf. Old Lat. oinos for unus). Πρῶτος first is for πρό-ατος foremost (πρό in front); cf. μέσ-ατος, 362.

446. a. The signs used to denote numbers (429) include the otherwise obsolete letters ϛ (which occupies the place of ϝ in the alphabetic order), ϟ, and ϡ, for 6, 90, and 900. See **3.** In a numeral expression the last letter has an accent above. Thousands begin anew with ,α, with a stroke below. E.g. ,αωξη′ 1868, ,δκε′ 4025, ,βγ′ 2003, ρδ′ 104.

b. The signs used in inscriptions of the classical period are: I = 1 or 1 obol, ⊢ = 1 drachma, Τ = 1 talent, IIII = 4, Γ (the later π, πέντε) = 5, ΓΙ = 6, Δ (δέκα) = 10, ΔΔΔ = 30, Ͱ = 50, Η (ἑκατόν) = 100, ΗΗΗ = 300, Χ (χίλιοι) = 1000, ͵Ͱ = 5000. E.g. ΗΔΔΔΔΙͰΙΙ = 144 drachmas, ΗΓͰΔΓ = 165.

c. The letters of the ordinary Greek alphabet are used to number the books of the Iliad and Odyssey, each poem having twenty-four books. Α, Β, Γ, etc. are generally used for the Iliad, and α, β, γ, etc. for the Odyssey.

VERBS

447. Voices. The Greek verb has three voices: active, middle, and passive.

448. *a.* The middle generally signifies that the subject performs an action *on himself* or *for his own benefit* (1243); e.g. middle βουλεύομαι *I take counsel (with myself), deliberate,* but active συμβουλεύω *I advise*; λούεται *he takes a bath.*

b. The passive employs the same forms as the middle except in the future and aorist tenses.

449. Deponent verbs have no active forms, but are used in the middle (or the middle and passive) with an active, often intransitive, sense.

450. Some deponents have the aorist in a middle form, and are called *middle deponents*; e.g. πορίζομαι *I provide (for myself)*, ἐπορισάμην *I procured.* Others make their aorist from the passive, and are called *passive deponents*; e.g. δύναμαι *I can*, ἐδυνήθην *I could.* If a deponent has both a middle and a passive aorist, the passive has a passive meaning; e.g. βιάζομαι *force*, ἐβιασάμην *forced*, ἐβιάσθην *was forced.* Many active verbs have only middle forms in the future, e.g. μανθάνω *learn*, fut. μαθήσομαι *shall learn*, (πηδάω) πηδῶ *jump*, fut. πηδήσομαι *shall jump*, ἀκούω *hear*, fut. ἀκούσομαι *shall hear* (verbs of perception or of physical activity).

451. Moods. There are four moods (properly so called): the indicative, subjunctive, optative, and imperative. To these is added, in the conjugation of the verb, the infinitive. The four moods, in contrast with the infinitive, are called finite, because their endings determine the person.

452. Tenses. There are seven tenses in the indicative: the present, imperfect, future, aorist, perfect, pluperfect, and future perfect. The imperfect and pluperfect occur only in the indicative. There are three tenses in the subjunctive and imperative: present, aorist, and perfect. There are five in the optative and infinitive: present, future, aorist, perfect, and future perfect. The future perfect usually has a passive meaning.

453. The present, perfect, future, and future perfect indicative are called *primary* (or *principal*) tenses; the imperfect, pluperfect, and aorist indicative are called *secondary* (or *historical*) tenses.

454. Many verbs have tenses known as the *second* aorist (in all voices), the *second* perfect and pluperfect (active), and the *second* future (passive).

These tenses are generally of more simple formation than the *first* aorist, perfect, etc. Few verbs have both forms in any tense. If both forms occur, the two generally differ in meaning (for example, the first being transitive, the second intransitive), but not always; or one is used in prose, the other in poetry.

455. The aorist indicative denotes action at a point or at a single moment of past time, and corresponds generally to the indefinite or historical perfect in Latin.

456. Number and Person. There are three numbers: singular, dual, and plural. In each tense of the indicative, subjunctive, and optative, there are three persons, the first, second, and third; but in the dual the first person is wanting, except in rare poetic forms (**582 b**). In each tense of the imperative there are two persons, the second and third.

457. Verbal Nouns. Some verbal forms resemble nouns in origin or function, and are called verbal nouns. These include the infinitive, a substantive case form (dative); and participles and verbal adjectives, all of which are inflected like adjectives. Verbal adjectives end in -τός and -τέος. Those in -τός denote capability, e.g. λυτός, *capable of being loosed, soluble*, or have the force of a past participle, e.g. γραπτός *written*. Those in -τέος denote what is to be done, e.g. γραπτέος *to be written*. See **804.**

TENSE SYSTEMS AND TENSE STEMS

458. In the conjugation of a verb, certain endings are added to different stems to show the person, number, and voice in the finite moods.

459. a. The middle endings differ from the active, but are used also for the passive except in the aorist passive, which has active (secondary) endings. Primary and secondary tenses have distinct endings in both active and middle.

b. Primary endings are used for the subjunctive, secondary for the optative (except in some forms of the first person singular).

460. The tenses are divided into nine classes or *tense systems*, each with its own *tense stem*. The *tense stems* are derived from a *verb stem* which is common to all the tenses. The verb stem may be either a primary base or a base to which some suffix has been added; e.g. base ἡδ-, ἥδομαι *be glad*; derived verb stem ἀνδάν-ω *make glad*; tense stem of the aor. pass. ἡσ-θη- *was pleased*. To form the tense stem, the verb stem may be modified by prefixing a *reduplication syllable* (**543**), and by adding signs for mood (**573**) and for tense. In some systems verb stem and tense stem may be the same.

461. The tense systems are the following:

SYSTEMS	TENSES
I *Present*	including *present* and *imperfect*
II *Future*	including *future active* and *middle*
III *First aorist*	including *first aorist active* and *middle*
IV *Second aorist*	including *second aorist active* and *middle*
V *First perfect*	including *first perfect* and *first pluperfect active*
VI *Second perfect*	including *second perfect* and *second pluperfect active*
VII *Perfect middle*	including *perfect* and *pluperfect middle (passive)* and *future perfect passive (middle)*
VIII *First passive*	including *first aorist* and *first future passive*
IX *Second passive*	including *second aorist* and *second future passive*

462. Since few verbs have both the first and the second forms of any tense (**454**), most verbs have only six tense systems, and many have even fewer.

463. The *principal parts* of a Greek verb are the first person singular indicative of the present, future, first aorist, first (or second) perfect active; the perfect middle, and the first (or second) aorist passive; with the second aorist (active or middle) when it occurs. If there is no future active, the future middle is given (**450**). The principal parts generally represent all the tense systems which the verb uses. E.g.

λύω *loose*, λύσω, ἔλῦσα, λέλυκα, λέλυμαι, ἐλύθην.

λείπω *leave*, λείψω, λέλοιπα, λέλειμμαι, ἐλείφθην, 2 aor. ἔλιπον.

φαίνω *show*, φανῶ, ἔφηνα, πέφαγκα (2 perf. πέφηνα), πέφασμαι, 2 aor. pass. ἐφάνην.

πράττω *do*, πράξω, ἔπρᾱξα, 2 perf. πέπρᾱχα and πέπρᾱγα, πέπρᾱγμαι, ἐπρᾱχθην.

σκώπτω *jeer*, σκώψομαι, ἔσκωψα, ἐσκώφθην.

στέλλω *send*, στελῶ, ἔστειλα, ἔσταλκα, ἔσταλμαι, ἐστάλην.

464. In deponent verbs the principal parts are the present, future, perfect, and aorist (or aorists, **450**) indicative. E.g.

(ἡγέομαι) ἡγοῦμαι *lead*, ἡγήσομαι, ἡγησάμην, ἥγημαι, ἡγήθην (in composition).

βούλομαι *wish*, βουλήσομαι, βεβούλημαι, ἐβουλήθην.

γίγνομαι *become*, γενήσομαι, γεγένημαι, 2 aor. ἐγενόμην.

(αἰδέομαι) αἰδοῦμαι *respect*, αἰδέσομαι, ᾔδεσμαι, ᾐδέσθην.

ἐργάζομαι *work*, ἐργάσομαι, ἠργασάμην, εἴργασμαι, ἠργάσθην.

465. When a verb forms its tense stems directly from a root or base, it is called a *primitive* verb; e.g. λύ-ω *loose*, ἥδ-ομαι *be pleased*. When the tense stem is derived from a noun (substantive or adjective), the verb is called a *denominative*; e.g. βασιλεύ-ω *be king*, from βασιλεύς *king*; δηλό-ω *show*, from δῆλος *clear*.

466. Vowel Gradation. The verb stem often shows different grades in quantity or form (**31, 34**); e.g. present λῡ-ω, perfect λέ-λῠ-κα; singular τίθη-μι, plural τίθε-μεν; present λείπ-ω, 2 aorist ἔ-λιπ-ον, perfect λέ-λοιπ-α.

467. Thematic Vowel. The tense stem often ends in a vowel, o or ε (ω or η), called the *thematic* vowel, and written o/ε or ω/η; e.g. λέγο-μεν *we say,* λέγε-τε *you say,* subjv. λέγω-μεν, λέγη-τε. **169.**

468. A verb inflected by means of this thematic o/ε is said to belong to the *thematic* inflection. A verb in which this element is lacking is called *athematic.*

469. The thematic inflection includes those present, imperfect, and second aorist tenses which have the thematic vowel, and all future tenses. The endings are as follows:

a. Present and future singular indicative active end in -ω, -εις, -ει. The term ω *verb* is sometimes applied here.

b. Present and future third person plural indicative ended in -ντι, which became -νσι (**101**). This, with the thematic vowel, made -ονσι, which became -ουσι (**75**), the regular ending.

c. All past tenses in the third plural active end in -ν.

d. Middle endings -σαι and -σο lose σ except in the perfect and pluperfect, and then contract with the final vowel of the tense stem; e.g. λύε-(σ)αι, λύῃ (**90**). But contraction does not occur in the optative; e.g. λύοι-(σ)ο, λύοιο.

e. The imperative active second person singular has no personal ending except in the first aorist, e.g. λῦσο-ν.

f. The infinitive active ended in -εν, which (with the thematic vowel ε) gave -ειν (**42**). The perfect infinitive has -ναι, the aorist -αι.

470. The athematic inflection includes all present and imperfect tenses which lack o/ε, the endings being added directly to the tense stems. This is characteristic of μι *verbs.* The athematic inflection also includes all passive aorists (except in the subjunctive), all middle perfects and pluperfects, many second aorists, and a few second perfect and pluperfect forms.

471. Verb stems in ω verbs end in either a vowel or a consonant. The first are called *vowel* or *pure verbs*; e.g. λύ-ω. If the vowel is a, ε, or o, it contracts with the ending; e.g. φιλέ-ω *love,* φιλῶ. Consonant verbs either have a stop (or mute), e.g. λέγ-ω *say,* λείπ-ω *leave,* or a liquid or nasal, e.g. φέρ-ω *carry,* μέν-ω *stay,* φαίν-ω *show.*

CONJUGATION OF VERBS IN Ω

472. The following synopses include

a. All the tenses of λύω *loose,* an uncontracted vowel verb, representing tense systems I, II, III, V, VII, VIII. **461.**

b. Those tenses of λείπω *leave* — the second perfect and pluperfect active and the second aorist active and middle — which represent tense systems IV and VI.

c. The tenses of φαίνω *show* — the future and aorist active and middle of a verb the stem of which ends in a nasal or liquid; and the second aorist and second future passive — which represent tense systems II, III, and IX.

473. The paradigms include the simple and compound forms of the perfect imperative active, although it is hardly probable that the simple form occurred.

474. Each tense of λύω is translated in the synopsis of **475**, except forms like the future perfect infinitive and participle, and the tenses of the subjunctive and optative. The meaning of these last cannot be fully understood until the constructions are explained in the Syntax. But the following examples will make them clearer than any possible translation of the forms, some of which (e.g. the future optative) cannot be used in independent sentences.

Subjunctive: λύωμεν or λύσωμεν αὐτόν *let us loose him,* μὴ λύσῃς αὐτόν *do not loose him,* ἐὰν λύω or λύσω αὐτόν *if I loose him,* ἵνα αὐτὸν λύω or λύσω *that I may loose him.* **Optative:** εἴθε λύοιμι or λύσαιμι αὐτόν *O that I may loose him,* εἰ λύοιμι or λύσαιμι αὐτόν *if I should loose him,* ἵνα αὐτὸν λύοιμι or λύσαιμι *that I might loose him,* εἶπον ὅτι αὐτὸν λύοιμι *I said that I was loosing him,* εἶπον ὅτι αὐτὸν λύσαιμι *I said that I had loosed him,* εἶπον ὅτι αὐτὸν λύσοιμι *I said that I should loose him.*

475.

	I. PRESENT SYSTEM	II. FUTURE SYSTEM	III. FIRST AORIST SYSTEM
ACTIVE VOICE	*Present and Imperfect*	*Future*	*1 Aorist*
Indic.	λύω *I loose or am loosing*	λύσω *I shall loose*	
	ἔλῡον *I was loosing*		ἔλῡσα *I loosed*
Subj.	λύω		λύσω
Opt.	λύοιμι	λύσοιμι	λύσαιμι
Imper.	λῦε *loose*		λῦσον *loose*
Infin.	λύειν *to loose*	λύσειν *to be about to loose*	λῦσαι *to loose or to have loosed*
Part.	λύων *loosing*	λύσων *about to loose*	λύσᾱς *having loosed*
MIDDLE VOICE	*Present and Imperfect*	*Future*	*1 Aorist*
Indic.	λύομαι *I loose (for myself)*	λύσομαι *I shall loose (for myself)*	
	ἐλῡόμην *I was loosing (for myself)*		ἐλῡσάμην *I loosed (for myself)*
Subj.	λύωμαι		λύσωμαι
Opt.	λῡοίμην	λῡσοίμην	λῡσαίμην
Imper.	λύου *loose (for thyself)*		λῦσαι *loose(for thyself)*
Infin.	λύεσθαι *to loose (for one's self)*	λύσεσθαι *to be about to loose (for one's self)*	λύσασθαι *to loose or to have loosed (for one's self)*
Part.	λῡόμενος *loosing (for one's self)*	λῡσόμενος *about to loose (for one's self)*	λῡσάμενος *having loosed (for one's self)*

		VIII. FIRST PASSIVE SYSTEM	
PASSIVE VOICE	*Present and Imperfect*	*1 Future*	*1 Aorist*
Indic.	λύομαι *I am* ∫*(being)* ἐλῡόμην *I was* ⎱*loosed*	λυθήσομαι *I shall be loosed*	ἐλύθην *I was loosed* λυθῶ *(for λυθέω)*
Subj.			
Opt.	with same	λυθησοίμην	λυθείην
Imper.	forms as the		λύθητι *be loosed*
Infin.	Middle	λυθήσεσθαι *to be about to be loosed*	λυθῆναι *to be loosed or to have been loosed*
Part.		λυθησόμενος *about to be loosed*	λυθείς *having been loosed*

VERBAL ADJECTIVES : ∫ λυτός *that may be loosed, loosed*
⎱ λυτέος *that must be loosed, to be loosed*

λῦω (λῡ-, λῠ-) *loose*

V. FIRST PERFECT SYSTEM	VII. PERFECT MIDDLE SYSTEM	
1 *Perfect and Pluperfect* λέλυκα *I have loosed* ἐλελύκη *I had loosed* λελυκὼς ὦ or λελύκω λελυκὼς εἴην or λελύκοιμι λελυκὼς ἴσθι or [λέλυκε, 473] λελυκέναι *to have loosed* λελυκώς *having loosed*		
	Perfect and Pluperfect Middle λέλυμαι *I have loosed (for myself)* ἐλελύμην *I had loosed (for myself)* λελυμένος ὦ λελυμένος εἴην λέλυσο (750) λελύσθαι *to have loosed (for one's self)* λελυμένος *having loosed (for one's self)*	
	Perf. and Pluperf. Passive λέλυμαι *I have* ⎰ *been* ἐλελύμην *I had* ⎱ *loosed* with same forms as the Middle	*Future Perfect Passive* λελύσομαι *I shall have been loosed* λελῡσοίμην λελύσεσθαι λελῡσόμενος

476. The middle of λύω commonly means *to release for one's self, have someone released* (causative), hence *to ransom, deliver.*

477. SYNOPSIS OF λείπω (λειπ-, λοιπ-, λιπ-) *leave*

TENSE SYSTEM: I	II	IV	VI
ACTIVE VOICE	*Pres. and Impf.*	*Future*	*2 Aorist*	*2 Perf. and Plup.*

	Pres. and Impf.	*Future*	*2 Aorist*	*2 Perf. and Plup.*
ACTIVE VOICE				
Indic.	λείπω	λείψω		λέλοιπα
	ἔλειπον		ἔλιπον	ἐλελοίπη
Subj.	λείπω		λίπω	λελοιπὼς ὦ or λελοίπω
Opt.	λείποιμι	λείψοιμι	λίποιμι	λελοιπὼς εἴην or λελοίποιμι
Imper.	λεῖπε		λίπε	
Infin.	λείπειν	λείψειν	λιπεῖν	λελοιπέναι
Part.	λείπων	λείψων	λιπών	λελοιπώς

				VII
MIDDLE VOICE	*Pres. and Impf.*	*Future*	*2 Aorist*	*Perf. and Plup. Middle (Passive)*
Indic.	λείπομαι	λείψομαι		λέλειμμαι
	ἐλειπόμην		ἐλιπόμην	ἐλελείμμην
Subj.	λείπωμαι		λίπωμαι	λελειμμένος ὦ
Opt.	λειποίμην	λειψοίμην	λιποίμην	λελειμμένος εἴην
Imper.	λείπου		λιποῦ	λέλειψο
Infin.	λείπεσθαι	λείψεσθαι	λιπέσθαι	λελεῖφθαι
Part.	λειπόμενος	λειψόμενος	λιπόμενος	λελειμμένος

		VIII		
PASSIVE VOICE	*Pres. and Impf.*	*1 Future*	*1 Aorist*	*Future Perfect*
Indic.		λειφθήσομαι		λελείψομαι
			ἐλείφθην	
Subj.	same forms		λειφθῶ (for λειφθέω)	
Opt.	as the	λειφθησοίμην	λειφθείην	λελειψοίμην
Imper.	Middle		λείφθητι	
Infin.		λειφθήσεσθαι	λειφθῆναι	λελείψεσθαι
Part.		λειφθησόμενος	λειφθείς	λελειψόμενος

VERBAL ADJECTIVES: λειπτός, λειπτέος

478.

SYNOPSIS OF φαίνω (φαν-) *show*

ACTIVE VOICE

TENSE SYSTEM:	I	II	III	V	VI
	Pres. and Impf.	*Future*	*1 Aorist*	*1 Perf. and Plup.*	*2 Perf. and Plup.*
Indic.	φαίνω / ἔφαινον	(φανέω) φανῶ	ἔφηνα	πέφαγκα / ἐπεφάγκη	πέφηνα / ἐπεφήνη
Subj.	φαίνω		φήνω	πεφάγκὼς ὦ or πεφάγκω	πεφήνὼς ὦ or πεφήνω
Opt.	φαίνοιμι	(φανέοιμι) φανοῖμι or (φανεοίην) φανοίην	φήναιμι	πεφάγκὼς εἴην or πεφάγκοιμι	πεφηνὼς εἴην or πεφήνοιμι
Imper.	φαῖνε		φῆνον	[πέφαγκε]	[πέφηνε]
Infin.	φαίνειν	(φανέειν) φανεῖν	φῆναι	πεφαγκέναι	πεφηνέναι
Part.	φαίνων	(φανέων) φανῶν	φήνᾱς	πεφαγκώς	πεφηνώς

MIDDLE VOICE

TENSE SYSTEM:	I	II	III	VII
	Pres. and Impf.	*Future*	*1 Aorist*	*Perf. and Plup. Middle (Passive)*
Indic.	φαίνομαι / ἐφαινόμην	(φανέομαι) φανοῦμαι	ἐφηνάμην	πέφασμαι / ἐπεφάσμην
Subj.	φαίνωμαι		φήνωμαι	πεφασμένος ὦ
Opt.	φαινοίμην	(φανεοίμην) φανοίμην	φηναίμην	πεφασμένος εἴην
Imper.	φαίνου		φῆναι	[πέφανσο]
Infin.	φαίνεσθαι	(φανέεσθαι) φανεῖσθαι	φήνασθαι	πεφάνθαι
Part.	φαινόμενος	(φανεόμενος) φανούμενος	φηνάμενος	πεφασμένος

PASSIVE VOICE (IX)

TENSE SYSTEM:	I	II	III	VIII
	Pres. and Impf.	*2 Future*	*2 Aorist*	*1 Aorist*
Indic.	same forms as the Middle	φανήσομαι	ἐφάνην	ἐφάνθην
Subj.			φανῶ (for φανέω)	φανθῶ (for φανθέω)
Opt.		φανησοίμην	φανείην	φανθείην
Imper.			φάνηθι	φάνθητι
Infin.		φανήσεσθαι	φανῆναι	φανθῆναι
Part.		φανησόμενος	φανείς	φανθείς

1 Future Passive wanting

VERBAL ADJECTIVE: φαντός (in compound ἄφαντος *invisible*)

479. *a.* The first perfect πέφαγκα means *I have shown*; the second perfect πέφηνα means *I have appeared.*

b. The passive of φαίνω means properly *to be shown* or *made evident, transpire*; the middle, *to appear* (*show one's self*). The second future passive φανήσομαι, *I shall appear* or *be shown*, does not differ in sense from φανοῦμαι; but ἐφάνθην is generally passive, *I was shown*, while ἐφάνην is *I appeared.* The aorist middle ἐφηνάμην means *I showed*; the simple form is rare and poetic, but ἀπεφηνάμην *I declared* is common.

480. 1. ACTIVE VOICE OF λύω

			Present	Imperfect	Future
INDICATIVE	S.	1.	λύω	ἔλυον	λύσω
		2.	λύεις	ἔλυες	λύσεις
		3.	λύει	ἔλυε	λύσει
	D.	2.	λύετον	ἐλύετον	λύσετον
		3.	λύετον	ἐλυέτην	λύσετον
	P.	1.	λύομεν	ἐλύομεν	λύσομεν
		2.	λύετε	ἐλύετε	λύσετε
		3.	λύουσι	ἔλυον	λύσουσι
SUBJUNCTIVE	S.	1.	λύω		
		2.	λύῃς		
		3.	λύῃ		
	D.	2.	λύητον		
		3.	λύητον		
	P.	1.	λύωμεν		
		2.	λύητε		
		3.	λύωσι		
OPTATIVE	S.	1.	λύοιμι		λύσοιμι
		2.	λύοις		λύσοις
		3.	λύοι		λύσοι
	D.	2.	λύοιτον		λύσοιτον
		3.	λυοίτην		λυσοίτην
	P.	1.	λύοιμεν		λύσοιμεν
		2.	λύοιτε		λύσοιτε
		3.	λύοιεν		λύσοιεν
IMPERATIVE	S.	2.	λῦε		
		3.	λυέτω		
	D.	2.	λύετον		
		3.	λυέτων		
	P.	2.	λύετε		
		3.	λυόντων		

	Present	*Future*
INFINITIVE	λύειν	λύσειν
PARTICIPLE	λύων, λύουσα,	λύσων, λύσουσα,
	λῦον (329)	λῦσον (329)

	1 *Aorist*	1 *Perfect*	1 *Pluperfect*
INDIC. S.	1. ἔλῦσα	λέλυκα	ἐλελύκη
	2. ἔλῦσας	λέλυκας	ἐλελύκης
	3. ἔλῦσε	λέλυκε	ἐλελύκει
D.	2. ἐλύσατον	λελύκατον	ἐλελύκετον
	3. ἐλῡσάτην	λελύκατον	ἐλελυκέτην
P.	1. ἐλύσαμεν	λελύκαμεν	ἐλελύκεμεν
	2. ἐλύσατε	λελύκατε	ἐλελύκετε
	3. ἔλῦσαν	λελύκᾱσι	ἐλελύκεσαν
			(See 709)
SUBJ. S.	1. λύσω	λελυκὼς ὦ (752) or λελύκω	
	2. λύσῃς	λελυκὼς ᾖς or λελύκῃς	
	3. λύσῃ	λελυκὼς ᾖ or λελύκῃ	
D.	2. λύσητον	λελυκότε ἦτον or λελύκητον	
	3. λύσητον	λελυκότε ἦτον or λελύκητον	
P.	1. λύσωμεν	λελυκότες ὦμεν or λελύκωμεν	
	2. λύσητε	λελυκότες ἦτε or λελύκητε	
	3. λύσωσι	λελυκότες ὦσι or λελύκωσι	
OPT. S.	1. λύσαιμι	λελυκὼς εἴην (765) or λελύκοιμι, -οίην	
	2. λύσαις, λύσειας	λελυκὼς εἴης or λελύκοις, -οίης	
	3. λύσαι, λύσειε	λελυκὼς εἴη or λελύκοι, -οίη	
D.	2. λύσαιτον	λελυκότε εἴητον, εἶτον, or λελύκοιτον	
	3. λῡσαίτην	λελυκότε εἰήτην, εἴτην, or λελυκοίτην	
P.	1. λύσαιμεν	λελυκότες εἴημεν, εἶμεν, or λελύκοιμεν	
	2. λύσαιτε	λελυκότες εἴητε, εἶτε, or λελύκοιτε	
	3. λύσαιεν, λύσειαν	λελυκότες εἴησαν, εἶεν, or λελύκοιεν	
IMPER. S.	2. λυσον	λελυκὼς ἴσθι (473) or [λέλυκε	
	3. λῡσάτω	λελυκὼς ἔστω or λελυκέτω	
D.	2. λύσατον	λελυκότε ἔστον or λελύκετον	
	3. λῡσάτων	λελυκότε ἔστων or λελυκέτων	
P.	2. λύσατε	λελυκότες ἔστε or λελύκετε]	
	3. λῡσάντων	λελυκότες ὄντων	
INFIN.	λῦσαι	λελυκέναι	
PART.	λύσᾱς, λύσᾱσα,	λελυκώς, λελυκυῖα, λελυκός (329)	
	λῦσαν (329)		

2. MIDDLE VOICE OF λύω

			Present	Imperfect	Future
INDICATIVE	S.	1.	λύομαι	ἐλῡόμην	λύσομαι
		2.	λύῃ, λύει	ἐλύου	λύσῃ, λύσει
		3.	λύεται	ἐλύετο	λύσεται
	D.	2.	λύεσθον	ἐλύεσθον	λύσεσθον
		3.	λύεσθον	ἐλῡέσθην	λύσεσθον
	P.	1.	λῡόμεθα	ἐλῡόμεθα	λῡσόμεθα
		2.	λύεσθε	ἐλύεσθε	λύσεσθε
		3.	λύονται	ἐλύοντο	λύσονται
SUBJUNCTIVE	S.	1.	λύωμαι		
		2.	λύῃ		
		3.	λύηται		
	D.	2.	λύησθον		
		3.	λύησθον		
	P.	1.	λῡώμεθα		
		2.	λύησθε		
		3.	λύωνται		
OPTATIVE	S.	1.	λῡοίμην	λῡσοίμην	
		2.	λύοιο	λύσοιο	
		3.	λύοιτο	λύσοιτο	
	D.	2.	λύοισθον	λύσοισθον	
		3.	λῡοίσθην	λῡσοίσθην	
	P.	1.	λῡοίμεθα	λῡσοίμεθα	
		2.	λύοισθε	λύσοισθε	
		3.	λύοιντο	λύσοιντο	
IMPERATIVE	S.	2.	λύου		
		3.	λῡέσθω		
	D.	2.	λύεσθον		
		3.	λῡέσθων		
	P.	2.	λύεσθε		
		3.	λῡέσθων		
INFINITIVE			λύεσθαι		λύσεσθαι
PARTICIPLE			λῡόμενος, λῡομένη, λῡόμενον (295)		λῡσόμενος, -η, -ον (295)

		1 *Aorist*	*Perfect*	*Pluperfect*
INDICATIVE	S. 1.	ἐλῦσάμην	λέλυμαι	ἐλελύμην
	2.	ἐλύσω	λέλυσαι	ἐλέλυσο
	3.	ἐλύσατο	λέλυται	ἐλέλυτο
	D. 2.	ἐλύσασθον	λέλυσθον	ἐλέλυσθον
	3.	ἐλῡσάσθην	λέλυσθον	ἐλελύσθην
	P. 1.	ἐλῡσάμεθα	λελύμεθα	ἐλελύμεθα
	2.	ἐλύσασθε	λέλυσθε	ἐλέλυσθε
	3.	ἐλύσαντο	λέλυνται	ἐλέλυντο
SUBJUNCTIVE	S. 1.	λύσωμαι	λελυμένος ὦ	
	2.	λύσῃ	λελυμένος ᾖς	
	3.	λύσηται	λελυμένος ᾖ	
	D. 2.	λύσησθον	λελυμένω ητον	
	3.	λύσησθον	λελυμένω ᾖτον	
	P. 1.	λῡσώμεθα	λελυμένοι ὦμεν	
	2.	λύσησθε	λελυμένοι ᾖτε	
	3.	λύσωνται	λελυμένοι ὦσι	
OPTATIVE	S. 1.	λῡσαίμην	λελυμένος εἴην	
	2.	λύσαιο	λελυμένος εἴης	
	3.	λύσαιτο	λελυμένος εἴη	
	D. 2.	λύσαισθον	λελυμένω εἴητον or εἶτον	
	3.	λῡσαίσθην	λελυμένω εἰήτην or εἴτην	
	P. 1.	λῡσαίμεθα	λελυμένοι εἴημεν or εἶμεν	
	2.	λύσαισθε	λελυμένοι εἴητε or εἶτε	
	3.	λύσαιντο	λελυμένοι εἴησαν or εἶεν	
IMPERATIVE	S. 2.	λῦσαι	λέλυσο (782)	
	3.	λῡσάσθω	λελύσθω (781)	
	D. 2.	λύσασθον	λέλυσθον	
	3.	λῡσάσθων	λελύσθων	
	P. 2.	λύσασθε	λέλυσθε	
	3.	λῡσάσθων	λελύσθων	
INFINITIVE		λύσασθαι	λελύσθαι	
PARTICIPLE		λῡσάμενος, -η, -ον (295)	λελυμένος, -η, -ον (295)	

3. PASSIVE VOICE OF λύω

			Future Perfect	*1 Aorist*	*1 Future*
INDICATIVE	S.	1.	λελύσομαι	ἐλύθην	λυθήσομαι
		2.	λελύσῃ, λελύσει	ἐλύθης	λυθήσῃ, λυθήσει
		3.	λελύσεται	ἐλύθη	λυθήσεται
	D.	2.	λελύσεσθον	ἐλύθητον	λυθήσεσθον
		3.	λελύσεσθον	ἐλυθήτην	λυθήσεσθον
	P.	1.	λελῡσόμεθα	ἐλύθημεν	λυθησόμεθα
		2.	λελύσεσθε	ἐλύθητε	λυθήσεσθε
		3.	λελύσονται	ἐλύθησαν	λυθήσονται
SUBJUNCTIVE	S.	1.		λυθῶ (757)	
		2.		λυθῇς	
		3.		λυθῇ	
	D.	2.		λυθῆτον	
		3.		λυθῆτον	
	P.	1.		λυθῶμεν	
		2.		λυθῆτε	
		3.		λυθῶσι	
OPTATIVE	S.	1.	λελῡσοίμην	λυθείην	λυθησοίμην
		2.	λελύσοιο	λυθείης	λυθήσοιο
		3.	λελύσοιτο	λυθείη	λυθήσοιτο
	D.	2.	λελύσοισθον	λυθεῖτον or λυθείητον	λυθήσοισθον
		3.	λελῡσοίσθην	λυθείτην or λυθειήτην	λυθησοίσθην
	P.	1.	λελῡσοίμεθα	λυθεῖμεν or λυθείημεν	λυθησοίμεθα
		2.	λελύσοισθε	λυθεῖτε or λυθείητε	λυθήσοισθε
		3.	λελύσοιντο	λυθεῖεν or λυθείησαν	λυθήσοιντο
IMPERATIVE	S.	2.		λύθητι	
		3.		λυθήτω	
	D.	2.		λύθητον	
		3.		λυθήτων	
	P.	2.		λύθητε	
				λυθέντων	
INFINITIVE			λελύσεσθαι	λυθῆναι	λυθήσεσθαι
PARTICIPLE			λελῡσόμενος, -η, -ον (295)	λυθείς, λυθεῖσα, λυθέν (329)	λυθησόμενος, -η, -ον (295)

481. SECOND AORIST (ACTIVE AND MIDDLE) AND SECOND PERFECT
AND PLUPERFECT (ACTIVE) OF λείπω *leave.* SYSTEMS IV AND VI

			2 Aorist Active	2 Aorist Middle	2 Perfect	2 Pluperfect
IND.	S.	1.	ἔλιπον	ἐλιπόμην	λέλοιπα	ἐλελοίπη
		2.	ἔλιπες	ἐλίπου	λέλοιπας	ἐλελοίπης
		3.	ἔλιπε	ἐλίπετο	λέλοιπε	ἐλελοίπει
	D.	2.	ἐλίπετον	ἐλίπεσθον	λελοίπατον	ἐλελοίπετον
		3.	ἐλιπέτην	ἐλιπέσθην	λελοίπατον	ἐλελοιπέτην
	P.	1.	ἐλίπομεν	ἐλιπόμεθα	λελοίπαμεν	ἐλελοίπεμεν
		2.	ἐλίπετε	ἐλίπεσθε	λελοίπατε	ἐλελοίπετε
		3.	ἔλιπον	ἐλίποντο	λελοίπᾱσι	ἐλελοίπεσαν
SUBJ.	S.	1.	λίπω	λίπωμαι	λελοιπὼς ὦ or λελοίπω
		2.	λίπῃς	λίπῃ	λελοιπὼς ᾖς or λελοίπῃς
		3.	λίπῃ	λίπηται	λελοιπὼς ᾖ or λελοίπῃ
	D.	2.	λίπητον	λίπησθον	λελοιπότε ἦτον or λελοίπητον
		3.	λίπητον	λίπησθον	λελοιπότε ἦτον or λελοίπητον
	P.	1.	λίπωμεν	λιπώμεθα	λελοιπότες ὦμεν or λελοίπωμεν
		2.	λίπητε	λίπησθε	λελοιπότες ἦτε or λελοίπητε
		3.	λίπωσι	λίπωνται	λελοιπότες ὦσι or λελοίπωσι
OPT.	S.	1.	λίποιμι	λιποίμην	λελοιπὼς εἴην or λελοίποιμι
		2.	λίποις	λίποιο	λελοιπὼς εἴης or λελοίποις
		3.	λίποι	λίποιτο	λελοιπὼς εἴη or λελοίποι
	D.	2.	λίποιτον	λίποισθον	λελοιπότε εἴητον, εἶτον, or λελοίποιτον
		3.	λιποίτην	λιποίσθην	λελοιπότε εἰήτην, εἴτην, or λελοιποίτην
	P.	1.	λίποιμεν	λιποίμεθα	λελοιπότες εἴημεν, εἶμεν, or λελοίποιμεν
		2.	λίποιτε	λίποισθε	λελοιπότες εἴητε, εἶτε, or λελοίποιτε
		3.	λίποιεν	λίποιντο	λελοιπότες εἴησαν, εἶεν, or λελοίποιεν
IMP.	S.	2.	λίπε	λιποῦ	
		3.	λιπέτω	λιπέσθω	
	D.	2.	λίπετον	λίπεσθον	
		3.	λιπέτων	λιπέσθων	
	P.	2.	λίπετε	λίπεσθε	
		3.	λιπόντων	λιπέσθων	
INF.			λιπεῖν	λιπέσθαι	λελοιπέναι	
PART.			λιπών, λιποῦσα, λιπόν (329)	λιπόμενος, -η, -ον (295)	λελοιπώς, λελοιπυῖα, λελοιπός (329)	

CONTRACT VERBS

482. Vowel or pure verbs (471) with stems ending in α, ε, or ο are contracted in the present and imperfect. See 39–47.

The present and imperfect active and middle (passive) of τῑμά-ω *honor*, φιλέ-ω *love*, and δηλό-ω *manifest* are thus inflected:

ACTIVE

PRESENT INDICATIVE

S.	1. (τῑμάω)	τῑμῶ	(φιλέω)	φιλῶ	(δηλόω)	δηλῶ
	2. (τῑμάεις)	τῑμᾷς	(φιλέεις)	φιλεῖς	(δηλόεις)	δηλοῖς
	3. (τῑμάει)	τῑμᾷ	(φιλέει)	φιλεῖ	(δηλόει)	δηλοῖ
D.	2. (τῑμάετον)	τῑμᾶτον	(φιλέετον)	φιλεῖτον	(δηλόετον)	δηλοῦτον
	3. (τῑμάετον)	τῑμᾶτον	(φιλέετον)	φιλεῖτον	(δηλόετον)	δηλοῦτον
P.	1. (τῑμάομεν)	τῑμῶμεν	(φιλέομεν)	φιλοῦμεν	(δηλόομεν)	δηλοῦμεν
	2. (τῑμάετε)	τῑμᾶτε	(φιλέετε)	φιλεῖτε	(δηλόετε)	δηλοῦτε
	3. (τῑμάουσι)	τῑμῶσι	(φιλέουσι)	φιλοῦσι	(δηλόουσι)	δηλοῦσι

PRESENT SUBJUNCTIVE

S.	1. (τῑμάω)	τῑμῶ	(φιλέω)	φιλῶ	(δηλόω)	δηλῶ
	2. (τῑμάῃς)	τῑμᾷς	(φιλέῃς)	φιλῇς	(δηλόῃς)	δηλοῖς
	3. (τῑμάῃ)	τῑμᾷ	(φιλέῃ)	φιλῇ	(δηλόῃ)	δηλοῖ
D.	2. (τῑμάητον)	τῑμᾶτον	(φιλέητον)	φιλῆτον	(δηλόητον)	δηλῶτον
	3. (τῑμάητον)	τῑμᾶτον	(φιλέητον)	φιλῆτον	(δηλόητον)	δηλῶτον
P.	1. (τῑμάωμεν)	τῑμῶμεν	(φιλέωμεν)	φιλῶμεν	(δηλόωμεν)	δηλῶμεν
	2. (τῑμάητε)	τῑμᾶτε	(φιλέητε)	φιλῆτε	(δηλόητε)	δηλῶτε
	3. (τῑμάωσι)	τῑμῶσι	(φιλέωσι)	φιλῶσι	(δηλόωσι)	δηλῶσι

PRESENT OPTATIVE (see 769)

S.	1. (τῑμαοίην)	τῑμῴην	(φιλεοίην)	φιλοίην	(δηλοοίην)	δηλοίην
	2. (τῑμαοίης)	τῑμῴης	(φιλεοίης)	φιλοίης	(δηλοοίης)	δηλοίης
	3. (τῑμαοίη)	τῑμῴη	(φιλεοίη)	φιλοίη	(δηλοοίη)	δηλοίη
D.	2. (τῑμαοίητον)	τῑμῴητον	(φιλεοίητον)	φιλοίητον	(δηλοοίητον)	δηλοίητον
	3. (τῑμαοιήτην)	τῑμῳήτην	(φιλεοιήτην)	φιλοιήτην	(δηλοοιήτην)	δηλοιήτην
P.	1. (τῑμαοίημεν)	τῑμῴημεν	(φιλεοίημεν)	φιλοίημεν	(δηλοοίημεν)	δηλοίημεν
	2. (τῑμαοίητε)	τῑμῴητε	(φιλεοίητε)	φιλοίητε	(δηλοοίητε)	δηλοίητε
	3. (τῑμαοίησαν)	τῑμῴησαν	(φιλεοίησαν)	φιλοίησαν	(δηλοοίησαν)	δηλοίησαν
	or	or	or	or	or	or
S.	1. (τῑμάοιμι)	τῑμῷμι	(φιλέοιμι)	φιλοῖμι	(δηλόοιμι)	δηλοῖμι
	2. (τῑμάοις)	τῑμῷς	(φιλέοις)	φιλοῖς	(δηλόοις)	δηλοῖς
	3. (τῑμάοι)	τῑμῷ	(φιλέοι)	φιλοῖ	(δηλόοι)	δηλοῖ
D.	2. (τῑμάοιτον)	τῑμῷτον	(φιλέοιτον)	φιλοῖτον	(δηλόοιτον)	δηλοῖτον
	3. (τῑμαοίτην)	τῑμῴτην	(φιλεοίτην)	φιλοίτην	(δηλοοίτην)	δηλοίτην
P.	1. (τῑμάοιμεν)	τῑμῷμεν	(φιλέοιμεν)	φιλοῖμεν	(δηλόοιμεν)	δηλοῖμεν
	2. (τῑμάοιτε)	τῑμῷτε	(φιλέοιτε)	φιλοῖτε	(δηλόοιτε)	δηλοῖτε
	3. (τῑμάοιεν)	τῑμῷεν	(φιλέοιεν)	φιλοῖεν	(δηλόοιεν)	δηλοῖεν

PRESENT IMPERATIVE

S.	2. (τίμαε)	τίμᾱ	(φίλεε)	φίλει	(δήλοε)	δήλου
	3. (τιμαέτω)	τιμάτω	(φιλεέτω)	φιλείτω	(δηλοέτω)	δηλούτω
D.	2. (τῑμάετον)	τῑμᾶτον	(φιλέετον)	φιλεῖτον	(δηλόετον)	δηλοῦτον
	3. (τῑμαέτων)	τῑμᾱτων	(φιλεέτων)	φιλείτων	(δηλοέτων)	δηλούτων
P.	2. (τῑμάετε)	τῑμᾶτε	(φιλέετε)	φιλεῖτε	(δηλόετε)	δηλοῦτε
	3. (τῑμαόντων)	τῑμώντων	(φιλεόντων)	φιλούντων	(δηλοόντων)	δηλούντων

PRESENT INFINITIVE

(τῑμάειν) τῑμᾶν (φιλέειν) φιλεῖν (δηλόειν) δηλοῦν

PRESENT PARTICIPLE (see 336)

(τῑμάων) τῑμῶν (φιλέων) φιλῶν (δηλόων) δηλῶν

IMPERFECT

S.	1. (ἐτίμαον)	ἐτίμων	(ἐφίλεον)	ἐφίλουν	(ἐδήλοον)	ἐδήλουν
	2. (ἐτίμαες)	ἐτίμᾱς	(ἐφίλεες)	ἐφίλεις	(ἐδήλοες)	ἐδήλους
	3. (ἐτίμαε)	ἐτίμᾱ	(ἐφίλεε)	ἐφίλει	(ἐδήλοε)	ἐδήλου
D.	2. (ἐτῑμάετον)	ἐτῑμᾶτον	(ἐφιλέετον)	ἐφιλεῖτον	(ἐδηλόετον)	ἐδηλοῦτον
	3. (ἐτῑμαέτην)	ἐτῑμάτην	(ἐφιλεέτην)	ἐφιλείτην	(ἐδηλοέτην)	ἐδηλούτην
P.	1. (ἐτῑμάομεν)	ἐτῑμῶμεν	(ἐφιλέομεν)	ἐφιλοῦμεν	(ἐδηλόομεν)	ἐδηλοῦμεν
	2. (ἐτῑμάετε)	ἐτῑμᾶτε	(ἐφιλέετε)	ἐφιλεῖτε	(ἐδηλόετε)	ἐδηλοῦτε
	3. (ἐτίμαον)	ἐτίμων	(ἐφίλεον)	ἐφίλουν	(ἐδήλοον)	ἐδήλουν

MIDDLE AND PASSIVE

PRESENT INDICATIVE

S.	1. (τῑμάομαι)	τῑμῶμαι	(φιλέομαι)	φιλοῦμαι	(δηλόομαι)	δηλοῦμαι
	2. (τῑμάῃ, τῑμάει)	τῑμᾷ	(φιλέῃ, φιλέει)	φιλῇ, φιλεῖ	(δηλόῃ, δηλόει)	δηλοῖ
	3. (τῑμάεται)	τῑμᾶται	(φιλέεται)	φιλεῖται	(δηλόεται)	δηλοῦται
D.	2. (τῑμάεσθον)	τῑμᾶσθον	(φιλέεσθον)	φιλεῖσθον	(δηλόεσθον)	δηλοῦσθον
	3. (τῑμάεσθον)	τῑμᾶσθον	(φιλέεσθον)	φιλεῖσθον	(δηλόεσθον)	δηλοῦσθον
P.	1. (τῑμαόμεθα)	τῑμώμεθα	(φιλεόμεθα)	φιλούμεθα	(δηλοόμεθα)	δηλούμεθα
	2. (τῑμάεσθε)	τῑμᾶσθε	(φιλέεσθε)	φιλεῖσθε	(δηλόεσθε)	δηλοῦσθε
	3. (τῑμάονται)	τῑμῶνται	(φιλέονται)	φιλοῦνται	(δηλόονται)	δηλοῦνται

PRESENT SUBJUNCTIVE

S.	1. (τῑμάωμαι)	τῑμῶμαι	(φιλέωμαι)	φιλῶμαι	(δηλόωμαι)	δηλῶμαι
	2. (τῑμάῃ)	τῑμᾷ	(φιλέῃ)	φιλῇ	(δηλόῃ)	δηλοῖ
	3. (τῑμάηται)	τῑμᾶται	(φιλέηται)	φιλῆται	(δηλόηται)	δηλῶται
D.	2. (τῑμάησθον)	τῑμᾶσθον	(φιλέησθον)	φιλῆσθον	(δηλόησθον)	δηλῶσθον
	3. (τῑμάησθον)	τῑμᾶσθον	(φιλέησθον)	φιλῆσθον	(δηλόησθον)	δηλῶσθον
P.	1. (τῑμαώμεθα)	τῑμώμεθα	(φιλεώμεθα)	φιλώμεθα	(δηλοώμεθα)	δηλώμεθα
	2. (τῑμάησθε)	τῑμᾶσθε	(φιλέησθε)	φιλῆσθε	(δηλόησθε)	δηλῶσθε
	3. (τῑμάωνται)	τῑμῶνται	(φιλέωνται)	φιλῶνται	(δηλόωνται)	δηλῶνται

PRESENT OPTATIVE

S.	1.	(τῑμαοίμην)	τῑμῴμην	(φιλεοίμην)	φιλοίμην	(δηλοοίμην)	δηλοίμην
	2.	(τῑμάοιο)	τῑμῷο	(φιλέοιο)	φιλοῖο	(δηλόοιο)	δηλοῖο
	3.	(τῑμάοιτο)	τῑμῷτο	(φιλέοιτο)	φιλοῖτο	(δηλόοιτο)	δηλοῖτο
D.	2.	(τῑμάοισθον)	τῑμῷσθον	(φιλέοισθον)	φιλοῖσθον	(δηλόοισθον)	δηλοῖσθον
	3.	(τῑμαοίσθην)	τῑμῴσθην	(φιλεοίσθην)	φιλοίσθην	(δηλοοίσθην)	δηλοίσθην
P.	1.	(τῑμαοίμεθα)	τῑμῴμεθα	(φιλεοίμεθα)	φιλοίμεθα	(δηλοοίμεθα)	δηλοίμεθα
	2.	(τῑμάοισθε)	τῑμῷσθε	(φιλέοισθε)	φιλοῖσθε	(δηλόοισθε)	δηλοῖσθε
	3.	(τῑμάοιντο)	τῑμῷντο	(φιλέοιντο)	φιλοῖντο	(δηλόοιντο)	δηλοῖντο

PRESENT IMPERATIVE

S.	2.	(τῑμάου)	τῑμῶ	(φιλέου)	φιλοῦ	(δηλόου)	δηλοῦ
	3.	(τῑμαέσθω)	τῑμάσθω	(φιλεέσθω)	φιλείσθω	(δηλοέσθω)	δηλούσθω
D.	2.	(τῑμάεσθον)	τῑμᾶσθον	(φιλέεσθον)	φιλεῖσθον	(δηλόεσθον)	δηλοῦσθον
	3.	(τῑμαέσθων)	τῑμάσθων	(φιλεέσθων)	φιλείσθων	(δηλοέσθων)	δηλούσθων
P.	2.	(τῑμάεσθε)	τῑμᾶσθε	(φιλέεσθε)	φιλεῖσθε	(δηλόεσθε)	δηλοῦσθε
	3.	(τῑμαέσθων)	τῑμάσθων	(φιλεέσθων)	φιλείσθων	(δηλοέσθων)	δηλούσθων

PRESENT INFINITIVE

(τῑμάεσθαι) τῑμᾶσθαι (φιλέεσθαι) φιλεῖσθαι (δηλόεσθαι) δηλοῦσθαι

PRESENT PARTICIPLE

(τῑμαόμενος) τῑμώμενος (φιλεόμενος) φιλούμενος (δηλοόμενος) δηλούμενος

IMPERFECT

S.	1.	(ἐτῑμαόμην)	ἐτῑμώμην	(ἐφιλεόμην)	ἐφιλούμην	(ἐδηλοόμην)	ἐδηλούμην
	2.	(ἐτῑμάου)	ἐτῑμῶ	(ἐφιλέου)	ἐφιλοῦ	(ἐδηλόου)]	ἐδηλοῦ
	3.	(ἐτῑμάετο)	ἐτῑμᾶτο	(ἐφιλέετο)	ἐφιλεῖτο	(ἐδηλόετο)	ἐδηλοῦτο
D.	2.	(ἐτῑμάεσθον)	ἐτῑμᾶσθον	(ἐφιλέεσθον)	ἐφιλεῖσθον	(ἐδηλόεσθον)	ἐδηλοῦσθον
	3.	(ἐτῑμαέσθην)	ἐτῑμάσθην	(ἐφιλεέσθην)	ἐφιλείσθην	(ἐδηλοέσθην)	ἐδηλούσθην
P.	1.	(ἐτῑμαόμεθα)	ἐτῑμώμεθα	(ἐφιλεόμεθα)	ἐφιλούμεθα	(ἐδηλοόμεθα)	ἐδηλούμεθα
	2.	(ἐτῑμάεσθε)	ἐτῑμᾶσθε	(ἐφιλέεσθε)	ἐφιλεῖσθε	(ἐδηλόεσθε)	ἐδηλοῦσθε
	3.	(ἐτῑμάοντο)	ἐτῑμῶντο	(ἐφιλέοντο)	ἐφιλοῦντο	(ἐδηλόοντο)	ἐδηλοῦντο

483. The uncontracted forms of these tenses are not Attic except a few occurrences in poetry. Uncontracted verbs in αω sometimes occur in Homer, but most of them were later displaced by forms in οω (659); those in εω are common in Homer; in Herodotus ε + ο sounds (ο, ω, οι) are always uncontracted, but ε + e sounds (ε, ει, η) are contracted. Verbs in οω are never used in the uncontracted forms. For dialect forms of these verbs, see 659–661.

484. SYNOPSIS OF τῑμάω, φιλέω, δηλόω, AND θηράω *hunt*,
IN THE INDICATIVE OF ALL VOICES

ACTIVE

Pres.	τῑμῶ	φιλῶ	δηλῶ	θηρῶ
Impf.	ἐτίμων	ἐφίλουν	ἐδήλουν	ἐθήρων
Fut.	τῑμήσω	φιλήσω	δηλώσω	θηράσω
Aor.	ἐτίμησα	ἐφίλησα	ἐδήλωσα	ἐθήρᾱσα
Perf.	τετίμηκα	πεφίληκα	δεδήλωκα	τεθήρᾱκα
Plup.	ἐτετῑμήκη	ἐπεφιλήκη	ἐδεδηλώκη	ἐτεθηράκη

MIDDLE

Pres.	τῑμῶμαι	φιλοῦμαι	δηλοῦμαι	θηρῶμαι
Impf.	ἐτῑμώμην	ἐφιλούμην	ἐδηλούμην	ἐθηρώμην
Fut.	τῑμήσομαι	φιλήσομαι	δηλώσομαι	θηράσομαι
Aor.	ἐτῑμησάμην	ἐφιλησάμην	ἐδηλωσάμην	ἐθηρᾱσάμην
Perf.	τετίμημαι	πεφίλημαι	δεδήλωμαι	τεθήρᾱμαι
Plup.	ἐτετῑμήμην	ἐπεφιλήμην	ἐδεδηλώμην	ἐτεθηράμην

PASSIVE

Pres. and Impf.: same as Middle.

Fut.	τῑμηθήσομαι	φιληθήσομαι	δηλωθήσομαι	(θηρᾱθήσομαι)
Aor.	ἐτῑμήθην	ἐφιλήθην	ἐδηλώθην	ἐθηράθην

Perf. and Plup.: same as Middle.

Fut. Perf.	τετῑμήσομαι	πεφιλήσομαι	δεδηλώσομαι	(τεθηράσομαι)

485. *a.* Some dissyllabic verbs in εω contract only εε and εει. E.g. πλέω *sail* has pres. πλέω, πλεῖς, πλεῖ, πλεῖτον, πλέομεν, πλεῖτε, πλέουσι; imperf. ἔπλεον, ἔπλεις, ἔπλει, ἐπλεῖτον, ἐπλείτην, ἐπλέομεν, ἐπλεῖτε, ἔπλεον; subj. πλέω; opt. πλέοιμι; infin. πλεῖν; partic. πλέων, πλέουσα, πλέον. The stem originally ended in ϝ(ϝ), for which see **37**. So θέω *run*, πνέω *breathe*, ῥέω *flow*, χέω *pour*. Cf. **611**. Δέω *want*, for δεϝ(σ)ω, has δεῖς, δεῖ, δέομεν; subj. δέη; opt. δέοι; infin. δεῖν; neut. partic. δέον. Δέομαι *want*, *request*, has δέει (2d pers.), δεῖται, δεόμεθα.

b. Δέω *bind* (for δεϝω) is contracted in most forms; e.g. δοῦσι, δοῦμαι, δοῦνται, ἔδουν, neut. partic. δοῦν.

486. A few verbs in αω have η for ᾱ in the contracted forms, since the stem had η, not α; e.g. διψάω, διψῶ *thirst*, διψῇς, διψῇ, διψῆτε; imperf. ἐδίψων, ἐδίψης, ἐδίψη; infin. διψῆν. So ζάω *live*, κνάω *scrape*, νάω *spin*, πεινάω *hunger*, σμάω *wipe*, χράω *give oracles*, with χράομαι *use*, and ψάω *rub*. Ζάω and χράομαι are thus inflected:

	INDIC. AND SUBJ.		IMPERATIVE		IMPERFECT		INFINITIVE
S.	1. ζῶ	χρῶμαι			ἔζων	ἐχρώμην	ζῆν χρῆσθαι
	2. ζῇς	χρῇ	ζῆ	χρῶ	ἔζης	ἐχρῶ	
	3. ζῇ	χρῆται	ζήτω	χρήσθω	ἔζη	ἐχρῆτο	
D.	2. ζῆτον	χρῆσθον	ζῆτον	χρῆσθε	ἐζῆτον	ἐχρῆσθον	PARTICIPLE
	3. ζῆτον	χρῆσθον	ζήτων	χρήσθων	ἐζήτην	ἐχρήσθην	ζῶν χρώμενος

Indic. and Subj.	Imperative	Imperfect
P. $\begin{cases} \text{1. ζῶμεν χρώμεθα} \\ \text{2. ζῆτε χρῆσθε} \\ \text{3. ζῶσι χρῶνται} \end{cases}$	$\begin{matrix} \\ \text{ζῆτε} \quad \text{χρῆσθε} \\ \text{ζώντων χρήσθων} \end{matrix}$	$\begin{matrix} \text{ἐζῶμεν ἐχρώμεθα} \\ \text{ἐζῆτε ἐχρῆσθε} \\ \text{ἔζων ἐχρῶντο} \end{matrix}$

487. Herodotus uses a weak stem in a for η, e.g. χρᾶται, κνᾶν, σμᾶν. The strong form χρη- gave imper. χρῆο, partic. χρηόμενος, which in Herodotus become χρέω, χρεώμενος (33).

488. Ῥῑγόω shiver has infinitive ῥῑγῶν (with ῥῑγοῦν), and optative ῥῑγῴην. Ἱδρόω sweat has ἱδρῶσι, ἱδρῴη, ἱδρῶντι, etc. Λούω wash sometimes drops υ before a short vowel (37), and is then inflected like δηλόω; e.g. ἔλου for ἔλου-ε, λοῦμαι for λόυ-ομαι.

489. The third person singular of the imperfect active does not take ν movable in the contracted form; e.g. ἐφίλεε or ἐφίλεεν gives ἐφίλει (never ἐφίλειν). See 112.

490. For -ᾶν (not -ᾷν) and -οῦν in the infinitive, see 45 e.

CONSONANT VERBS

491. Stems ending in a consonant are in general inflected like pure verbs which do not contract. But in liquid and nasal verbs the future active and middle are inflected like contract verbs in έω.

492. FUTURE AND FIRST AORIST ACTIVE AND MIDDLE AND SECOND AORIST AND SECOND FUTURE PASSIVE OF φαίνω

		Future Active	Future Middle	1 Aorist Active
Indicative	S. $\begin{cases} 1. \\ 2. \\ 3. \end{cases}$	φανῶ φανεῖς φανεῖ	φανοῦμαι φανῇ, φανεῖ φανεῖται	ἔφηνα ἔφηνας ἔφηνε
	D. $\begin{cases} 2. \\ 3. \end{cases}$	φανεῖτον φανεῖτον	φανεῖσθον φανεῖσθον	ἐφήνατον ἐφηνάτην
	P. $\begin{cases} 1. \\ 2. \\ 3. \end{cases}$	φανοῦμεν φανεῖτε φανοῦσι	φανούμεθα φανεῖσθε φανοῦνται	ἐφήναμεν ἐφήνατε ἔφηναν
Subjunctive	S. $\begin{cases} 1. \\ 2. \\ 3. \end{cases}$			φήνω φήνῃς φήνῃ
	D. $\begin{cases} 2. \\ 3. \end{cases}$			φήνητον φήνητον
	P. $\begin{cases} 1. \\ 2. \\ 3. \end{cases}$			φήνωμεν φήνητε φήνωσι

		Future Active	*Future Middle*	*1 Aorist Active*
OPTATIVE	S. 1.	φανοίην or φανοῖμι	φανοίμην	φήναιμι
	2.	φανοίης or φανοῖς	φανοῖο	φήναις or φήνειας
	3.	φανοίη or φανοῖ	φανοῖτο	φήναι or φήνειε
	D. 2.	φανοῖτον	φανοῖσθον	φήναιτον
	3.	φανοίτην	φανοίσθην	φηναίτην
	P. 1.	φανοῖμεν	φανοίμεθα	φήναιμεν
	2.	φανοῖτε	φανοῖσθε	φήναιτε
	3.	φανοῖεν	φανοῖντο	φήναιεν or φήνειαν
IMPERATIVE	S. 2.			φῆνον
	3.			φηνάτω
	D. 2.			φήνατον
	3.			φηνάτων
	P. 2.			φήνατε
	3.			φηνάντων
INFINITIVE		φανεῖν	φανεῖσθαι	φῆναι
PARTICIPLE		φανών, φανοῦσα, φανοῦν (336)	φανούμενος, -η, -ον (295)	φήνᾱς, φήνᾱσα, φῆναν (329)

		1 Aor. Mid.	*2 Aor. Pass.*	*2 Fut. Pass.*
INDICATIVE	S. 1.	ἐφηνάμην	ἐφάνην	φανήσομαι
	2.	ἐφήνω	ἐφάνης	φανήσῃ, φανήσει
	3.	ἐφήνατο	ἐφάνη	φανήσεται
	D. 2.	ἐφήνασθον	ἐφάνητον	φανήσεσθον
	3.	ἐφηνάσθην	ἐφανήτην	φανήσεσθον
	P. 1.	ἐφηνάμεθα	ἐφάνημεν	φανησόμεθα
	2.	ἐφήνασθε	ἐφάνητε	φανήσεσθε
	3.	ἐφήναντο	ἐφάνησαν	φανήσονται
SUBJUNCTIVE	S. 1.	φήνωμαι	φανῶ	
	2.	φήνῃ	φανῇς	
	3.	φήνηται	φανῇ	
	D. 2.	φήνησθον	φανῆτον	
	3.	φήνησθον	φανῆτον	
	P. 1.	φηνώμεθα	φανῶμεν	
	2.	φήνησθε	φανῆτε	
	3.	φήνωνται	φανῶσι	

		1 Aor. Mid.	2 Aor. Pass.	2 Fut. Pass.
OPTATIVE	S. 1.	φηναίμην	φανείην	φανησοίμην
	2.	φήναιο	φανείης	φανήσοιο
	3.	φήναιτο	φανείη	φανήσοιτο
	D. 2.	φήναισθον	φανεῖτον or φανείητον	φανήσοισθον
	3.	φηναίσθην	φανείτην or φανειήτην	φανησοίσθην
	P. 1.	φηναίμεθα	φανεῖμεν or φανείημεν	φανησοίμεθα
	2.	φήναισθε	φανεῖτε or φανείητε	φανήσοισθε
	3.	φήναιντο	φανεῖεν or φανείησαν	φανήσοιντο
IMPERATIVE	S. 2.	φῆναι	φάνηθι	
	3.	φηνάσθω	φανήτω	
	D. 2.	φήνασθον	φάνητον	
	3.	φηνάσθων	φανήτων	
	P. 2.	φήνασθε	φάνητε	
	3.	φηνάσθων	φανέντων	
INFINITIVE		φήνασθαι	φανῆναι	φανήσεσθαι
PARTICIPLE		φηνάμενος, -η, -ον (295)	φανείς, φανεῖσα, φανέν (329)	φανησόμενος, -η, -ον (295)

493. The uncontracted forms (φανέω, φανέομαι, etc.) of the future active and middle of φαίνω (478) and of other liquid and nasal futures are not Attic, but are found in Homer and Herodotus. So with some of the uncontracted forms of the aorist subjunctive passive in έω, e.g. λυθέω, φανέῃς.

494. The tenses of λείπω and φαίνω which are not inflected above follow the corresponding tenses of λύω; except the perfect and pluperfect middle, for which see 496. Λέλειμ-μαι is inflected like τέτριμ-μαι (497 a), and πέφασ-μαι is inflected in 497 b.

495. Some of the dissyllabic forms of λύω do not show the accent so well as polysyllabic forms, e.g. these of κωλύω hinder:
  Pres. Imper. Act. κώλῦε, κωλῦέτω, κωλῦετε. Aor. Opt. Act. κωλύσαιμι, κωλύσειας (or κωλύσαις), κωλύσειε (or κωλύσαι). Aor. Imper. Act. κώλῦσον, κωλῦσάτω. Aor. Inf. Act. κωλῦσαι. Aor. Imper. Mid. κώλῦσαι, κωλῦσάσθω. See 150, 133, 151 d.

*Perfect and Pluperfect Middle and Passive of Verbs
with Consonant Stems*

496. *a.* In the perfect and pluperfect middle and passive, many
sound-changes (**499**) occur when a consonant of the tense stem
comes before μ, τ, σ, or θ of the ending.

b. When the stem ends in a consonant, the third person plural
of these tenses is formed by the perfect middle participle (masculine and feminine plural) with εἰσί *are*, and ἦσαν *were* (**509**).

497. *a.* These tenses of τρῑ́βω *rub*, πλέκω *weave*, πείθω *persuade*,
and στέλλω (σταλ-) *send*, are thus inflected:

PERFECT INDICATIVE

S.	1. τέτρῑμμαι	πέπλεγμαι	πέπεισμαι	ἔσταλμαι
	2. τέτρῑψαι	πέπλεξαι	πέπεισαι	ἔσταλσαι
	3. τέτρῑπται	πέπλεκται	πέπεισται	ἔσταλται
D.	2. τέτρῑφθον	πέπλεχθον	πέπεισθον	ἔσταλθον
	3. τέτρῑφθον	πέπλεχθον	πέπεισθον	ἔσταλθον
P.	1. τετρίμμεθα	πεπλέγμεθα	πεπείσμεθα	ἐστάλμεθα
	2. τέτρῑφθε	πέπλεχθε	πέπεισθε	ἔσταλθε
	3. τετρῑμμένοι	πεπλεγμένοι	πεπεισμένοι	ἐσταλμένοι
	εἰσί	εἰσί	εἰσί	εἰσί

PERFECT SUBJUNCTIVE AND OPTATIVE

SUBJ.	τετρῑμμένος ὦ	πεπλεγμένος ὦ	πεπεισμένος ὦ	ἐσταλμένος ὦ
OPT.	τετρῑμμένος	πεπλεγμένος	πεπεισμένος	ἐσταλμένος
	εἴην	εἴην	εἴην	εἴην

PERFECT IMPERATIVE

S.	2. τέτρῑψο	πέπλεξο	πέπεισο	ἔσταλσο
	3. τετρίφθω	πεπλέχθω	πεπείσθω	ἐστάλθω
D.	2. τέτρῑφθον	πέπλεχθον	πέπεισθον	ἔσταλθον
	3. τετρίφθων	πεπλέχθων	πεπείσθων	ἐστάλθων
P.	2. τέτρῑφθε	πέπλεχθε	πέπεισθε	ἔσταλθε
	3. τετρίφθων	πεπλέχθων	πεπείσθων	ἐστάλθων

PERFECT INFINITIVE AND PARTICIPLE

INF.	τετρῑ́φθαι	πεπλέχθαι	πεπεῖσθαι	ἐστάλθαι
PART.	τετρῑμμένος,	πεπλεγμένος,	πεπεισμένος,	ἐσταλμένος,
	-η, -ον	-η, -ον	-η, -ον	-η, -ον

PLUPERFECT INDICATIVE

S.	1.	ἐτετρίμμην	ἐπεπλέγμην	ἐπεπείσμην	ἐστάλμην
	2.	ἐτέτριψο	ἐπέπλεξο	ἐπέπεισο	ἔσταλσο
	3.	ἐτέτριπτο	ἐπέπλεκτο	ἐπέπειστο	ἔσταλτο
D.	2.	ἐτέτριφθον	ἐπέπλεχθον	ἐπέπεισθον	ἔσταλθον
	3.	ἐτετρίφθην	ἐπεπλέχθην	ἐπεπείσθην	ἐστάλθην
P.	1.	ἐτετρίμμεθα	ἐπεπλέγμεθα	ἐπεπείσμεθα	ἐστάλμεθα
	2.	ἐτέτριφθε	ἐπέπλεχθε	ἐπέπεισθε	ἔσταλθε
	3.	τετριμμένοι ἦσαν	πεπλεγμένοι ἦσαν	πεπεισμένοι ἦσαν	ἐσταλμένοι ἦσαν

b. The same tenses of (τελέω) τελῶ (original stem τελεσ-) *finish*, φαίνω (φαν-) *show*, ἀλλάττω (ἀλλαγ-) *change*, and ἐλέγχω (ἐλεγχ-) *test*, are thus inflected:

PERFECT INDICATIVE

S.	1.	τετέλεσμαι	πέφασμαι	ἤλλαγμαι	ἐλήλεγμαι
	2.	τετέλεσαι	[πέφανσαι, 499 *d*]	ἤλλαξαι	ἐλήλεγξαι
	3.	τετέλεσται	πέφανται	ἤλλακται	ἐλήλεγκται
D.	2.	τετέλεσθον	πέφανθον	ἤλλαχθον	ἐλήλεγχθον
	3.	τετέλεσθον	πέφανθον	ἤλλαχθον	ἐλήλεγχθον
P.	1.	τετελέσμεθα	πεφάσμεθα	ἠλλάγμεθα	ἐληλέγμεθα
	2.	τετέλεσθε	πέφανθε	ἤλλαχθε	ἐλήλεγχθε
	3.	τετελεσμένοι εἰσί	πεφασμένοι εἰσί	ἠλλαγμένοι εἰσί	ἐληλεγμένοι εἰσί

PERFECT SUBJUNCTIVE AND OPTATIVE

SUBJ.	τετελεσμένος ὦ	πεφασμένος ὦ	ἠλλαγμένος ὦ	ἐληλεγμένος ὦ
OPT.	τετελεσμένος εἴην	πεφασμένος εἴην	ἠλλαγμένος εἴην	ἐληλεγμένος εἴην

PERFECT IMPERATIVE

S.	2.	τετέλεσο	[πέφανσο]	ἤλλαξο	ἐλήλεγξο
	3.	τετελέσθω	πεφάνθω	ἠλλάχθω	ἐληλέγχθω
D.	2.	τετέλεσθον	πέφανθον	ἤλλαχθον	ἐλήλεγχθον
	3.	τετελέσθων	πεφάνθων	ἠλλάχθων	ἐληλέγχθων
P.	2.	τετέλεσθε	πέφανθε	ἤλλαχθε	ἐλήλεγχθε
	3.	τετελέσθων	πεφάνθων	ἠλλάχθων	ἐληλέγχθων

PERFECT INFINITIVE AND PARTICIPLE

INF.	τετελέσθαι	πεφάνθαι	ἠλλάχθαι	ἐληλέγχθαι
PART.	τετελεσμένος,	πεφασμένος,	ἠλλαγμένος,	ἐληλεγμένος,
	-η, -ον	-η, -ον	-η, -ον	-η, -ον

PLUPERFECT INDICATIVE

S.	1.	ἐτετελέσμην	ἐπεφάσμην	ἠλλάγμην	ἐληλέγμην
	2.	ἐτετέλεσο	[ἐπέφανσο]	ἤλλαξο	ἐλήλεγξο
	3.	ἐτετέλεστο	ἐπέφαντο	ἤλλακτο	ἐλήλεγκτο
D.	2.	ἐτετέλεσθον	ἐπέφανθον	ἤλλαχθον	ἐληλέγχθον
	3.	ἐτετελέσθην	ἐπεφάνθην	ἠλλάχθην	ἐληλέγχθην
P.	1.	ἐτετελέσμεθα	ἐπεφάσμεθα	ἠλλάγμεθα	ἐληλέγμεθα
	2.	ἐτετέλεσθε	ἐπέφανθε	ἤλλαχθε	ἐλήλεγχθε
	3.	τετελεσμένοι	πεφασμένοι	ἠλλαγμένοι	ἐληλεγμένοι
		ἦσαν	ἦσαν	ἦσαν	ἦσαν

498. The periphrastic form in the third plural is necessary because τετρῖβ-νται, ἐπεπλεκ-ντο, τετελεσ-νται could not be pronounced. Sometimes ν of the ending becomes α (27), e.g. τετρῖφαται, τετάχαται (733). But when final ν of a stem is dropped (602), the regular forms in -νται and -ντο are used; e.g. κλίνω *incline*, κέκλι-μαι, κέκλι-νται.

499. For the phonetic changes here, see 66–69, 74, 79, and 82.

a. **Labial Stems.** Τέτρῑμμαι is for τετρῖβ-μαι (79), τέτρῑψαι for τετρῖβ-σαι (69), τέτρῑπται for τετρῖβ-ται, τέτρῑφθον for τετρῖβ-σθον (83). So λείπω, λέλειμμαι, λέλειψαι; γράφω *write*, γέγραμμαι (79); ῥίπτω *throw*, ἔρρῑμμαι. But when μπ occurs at the end of a stem, π is dropped before μ of the ending (81), but retained before other consonants. E.g. πέμπ-ω *send*:

(πεπεμπ-μαι) **πέπεμμαι**   (πεπεμπ-μεθα) **πεπέμμεθα**
(πεπεμπ-σαι) **πέπεμψαι**   (πεπεμπ-σθε) **πέπεμφθε** (83)
(πεπεμπ-ται) **πέπεμπται**

So κάμπτω *bend*, κέκαμμαι. Compare πέττω *cook*, πέπεμμαι, πέπεψαι, πέπεπται.

b. **Palatal Stems.** Πέπλεγμαι is for πεπλεκ-μαι (79), πέπλεχθε for πεπλεκ-σθε (83); ἤλλακτο for ἤλλαγ-το (66); ἦχθε *you have been led* (ἀγ-) for ἤγ-σθε. So πράττω *do* (πρᾱγ-), πέπρᾱγμαι, πέπρᾱκται; φυλάττω *guard* (φυλακ-), πεφύλαγμαι. But when γχ occurs at the end of the stem before μ of the ending, χ becomes γ (79) and one γ is dropped (81), as in ἐλήλεγ-μαι for ἐληλεγγ-μαι; before other consonants the second palatal is retained, as in ἐλήλεγξαι for ἐληλεγχ-σαι, ἐλήλεγκ-ται, etc.

c. **Dental Stems.** Πέπεισται is for πεπειθ-ται (66), πέπεισαι for πεπειθ-σαι (69), πέπεισθε for πεπειθ-σθε (83). This σ is then used in πέπεισμαι, πεπείσμεθα

(82). So φράζω *tell* (φραδ-), πέφρασμαι, πέφρασαι, πέφρασται; ἐθίζω *accustom* (ἐθιδ-), εἴθισμαι, εἴθισαι, εἴθισται, εἴθισθε, pluperf. εἰθίσμην, εἴθισο; σπένδω *pour* (σπενδ-), ἔσπεισμαι (75), ἔσπεισαι, ἔσπεισται.

d. Liquid and Nasal Stems. Verb stems ending in λ or ρ are inflected like ἔσταλμαι; e.g. ἀγγέλλω *announce* (ἀγγελ-), ἤγγελμαι, ἤγγελσαι; αἴρω *raise* (ἀρ-), ἦρμαι; ἐγείρω *rouse* (ἐγερ-), ἐγήγερμαι; πείρω *pierce* (περ-), πέπαρμαι. Stems in ν which retain the nasal, like verbs in αἴνω and ὕνω, are inflected like πέφασμαι; e.g. ἡδύνω *sweeten*, ἤδυσμαι; σημαίνω *indicate*, σεσήμασμαι, 3d sing. σεσήμανται. For σ in the first person, see **74.** But some stems drop the nasal, and the tense is inflected like a vowel verb; e.g. κλίνω *incline*, κέκλιμαι, κέκλιται, like λέλυμαι. The bracketed forms of the second person, πέφανσαι etc., do not occur.

e. Stems in σ. The stem of τελέω, τελῶ was originally τελεσ-; cf. τέλος *end*. Hence τετέλεσ-μαι, τετέλεσ-ται are regular. The forms τετελεσ-σαι, τετελεσ-σθε drop one σ (85), giving τετέλεσαι, τετέλεσθε.

CONJUGATION OF VERBS IN MI

500. The peculiar inflection of verbs in μι affects only the present and second aorist systems, and in a few verbs the second perfect system. Most second aorists and perfects here included do not belong to presents in μι, but are forms of verbs in ω; e.g. ἔβην, second aorist of βαίνω *go*; ἔγνων (γιγνώσκω *know*), ἐπτάμην (πέτομαι *fly*), and τέθναμεν, τεθναίην, τεθνάναι (second perfect of θνήσκω *die*). In all μι forms the endings are added directly to the tense stem without the thematic vowel (ᵒ/ₑ, **467**), except in the subjunctive, in which ʷ/η is used in all verbs, and in the optative of verbs in νῦμι.

501. There are two classes of verbs in μι :

(1) Those in ημι (from stems in α or ε) and ωμι (from stems in ο). In this class the present stem is often reduplicated; but it may also be the same as the verb stem, which is a primary base or root. E.g. φη-, φα- gives φη-μί *I say*, φα-μέν *we say*; στη-, στα- gives ἵ-στη-μι *set* (for σι-στη-μι, **88**); θη-, θε- gives τί-θη-μι *place* (for θι-θη-μι, **105** *a*); δω-, δο- forms δίδωμι *give*.

(2) Those in νῦμι, which have the μι form only in the present and imperfect indicative; these add νν (νῡ), after a vowel ννυ (ννῡ), to the verb stem to form the present system. E.g. δείκ-νῦ-μι (δεικ-) *show*, ῥώ-ννῡ-μι (ῥω-) *strengthen*. For poetic verbs in νημι (with να added to the stem), see **642.**

502. No single verb exhibits all the possible μι forms. Τίθημι and δίδωμι are irregular and incomplete in the second aorist active; ἔσβην, from σβέννῦμι *extinguish*, is the only second aorist of a verb in νῡμι. Since ἵστημι (stem στᾱ-, στη-, στα-) wants the second aorist middle, ἐπριάμην *bought* (stem πρια- with no present) is given in the paradigm. Since δείκνῡμι wants the second aorist, ἔδῡν *entered* (formed as if from a present δῡ-μι) is added. A few poetic forms show an athematic aorist in υμην. See λῡω, πνέω, σεύω, χέω in the Catalogue of Verbs.

503. SYNOPSIS OF ἵστημι, τίθημι, δίδωμι, AND δείκνῡμι, IN THE PRESENT AND SECOND AORIST SYSTEMS

ACTIVE

	INDIC.	SUBJ.	OPT.	IMPER.	INFIN.	PART.
Pres. and Impf.	ἵστημι ἵστην	ἱστῶ	ἱσταίην	ἵστη	ἱστάναι	ἱστάς
	τίθημι ἐτίθην	τιθῶ	τιθείην	τίθει	τιθέναι	τιθείς
	δίδωμι ἐδίδουν	διδῶ	διδοίην	δίδου	διδόναι	διδούς
	δείκνῡμι ἐδείκνῡν	δεικνύω	δεικνύοιμι	δείκνῡ	δεικνύναι	δεικνύς
2 Aor.	ἔστην	στῶ	σταίην	στῆθι	στῆναι	στάς
	ἔθετον θῶ	θῶ	θείην	θές	θεῖναι	θείς
	dual (504)					
	ἔδοτον	δῶ	δοίην	δός	δοῦναι	δούς
	dual (504)					
	ἔδῡν (502)	δύω	———	δῦθι	δῦναι	δύς

PASSIVE AND MIDDLE

	INDIC.	SUBJ.	OPT.	IMPER.	INFIN.	PART.
Pres. and Impf.	ἵσταμαι ἱστάμην	ἱστῶμαι	ἱσταίμην	ἵστασο	ἵστασθαι	ἱστάμενος
	τίθεμαι ἐτιθέμην	τιθῶμαι	τιθείμην	τίθεσο	τίθεσθαι	τιθέμενος
	δίδομαι ἐδιδόμην	διδῶμαι	διδοίμην	δίδοσο	δίδοσθαι	διδόμενος
	δείκνυμαι ἐδεικνύμην	δεικνύωμαι	δεικνυοίμην	δείκνυσο	δείκνυσθαι	δεικνύμενος
2 Aor. Mid.	ἐπριάμην (502)	πρίωμαι	πριαίμην	πρίω	πρίασθαι	πριάμενος
	ἐθέμην	θῶμαι	θείμην	θοῦ	θέσθαι	θέμενος
	ἐδόμην	δῶμαι	δοίμην	δοῦ	δόσθαι	δόμενος

504. INFLECTION OF ἵστημι *set*, τίθημι *place*, δίδωμι *give*, AND δείκνῡμι *show*, IN THE PRESENT AND SECOND AORIST SYSTEMS; WITH ἔδῡν *entered* AND ἐπριάμην *bought* (502)

ACTIVE

PRESENT INDICATIVE

Sing.	1.	ἵστημι	τίθημι	δίδωμι	δείκνῡμι
	2.	ἵστης	τίθης	δίδως	δείκνῡς
	3.	ἵστησι	τίθησι	δίδωσι	δείκνῡσι
Dual	2.	ἵστατον	τίθετον	δίδοτον	δείκνυτον
	3.	ἵστατον	τίθετον	δίδοτον	δείκνυτον
Plur.	1.	ἵσταμεν	τίθεμεν	δίδομεν	δείκνυμεν
	2.	ἵστατε	τίθετε	δίδοτε	δείκνυτε
	3.	ἱστᾶσι	τιθέᾱσι	διδόᾱσι	δεικνύᾱσι

IMPERFECT

Sing.	1.	ἵστην	ἐτίθην	ἐδίδουν	ἐδείκνῡν
	2.	ἵστης	ἐτίθεις	ἐδίδους	ἐδείκνῡς
	3.	ἵστη	ἐτίθει	ἐδίδου	ἐδείκνῡ
Dual	2.	ἵστατον	ἐτίθετον	ἐδίδοτον	ἐδείκνυτον
	3.	ἱστάτην	ἐτιθέτην	ἐδιδότην	ἐδεικνύτην
Plur.	1.	ἵσταμεν	ἐτίθεμεν	ἐδίδομεν	ἐδείκνυμεν
	2.	ἵστατε	ἐτίθετε	ἐδίδοτε	ἐδείκνυτε
	3.	ἵστασαν	ἐτίθεσαν	ἐδίδοσαν	ἐδείκνυσαν

PRESENT SUBJUNCTIVE

Sing.	1.	ἱστῶ	τιθῶ	διδῶ	δεικνύω
	2.	ἱστῇς	τιθῇς	διδῷς	δεικνύῃς
	3.	ἱστῇ	τιθῇ	διδῷ	δεικνύῃ
Dual	2.	ἱστῆτον	τιθῆτον	διδῶτον	δεικνύητον
	3.	ἱστῆτον	τιθῆτον	διδῶτον	δεικνύητον
Plur.	1.	ἱστῶμεν	τιθῶμεν	διδῶμεν	δεικνύωμεν
	2.	ἱστῆτε	τιθῆτε	διδῶτε	δεικνύητε
	3.	ἱστῶσι	τιθῶσι	διδῶσι	δεικνύωσι

PRESENT OPTATIVE

Sing.	1.	ἱσταίην	τιθείην	διδοίην	δεικνύοιμι
	2.	ἱσταίης	τιθείης	διδοίης	δεικνύοις
	3.	ἱσταίη	τιθείη	διδοίη	δεικνύοι
Dual	2.	ἱσταῖτον	τιθεῖτον	διδοῖτον	
	3.	ἱσταίτην	τιθείτην	διδοίτην	

		ἱσταῖμεν	τιθεῖμεν	διδοῖμεν	
Plur.	1.	ἱσταῖμεν	τιθεῖμεν	διδοῖμεν	
	2.	ἱσταῖτε	τιθεῖτε	διδοῖτε	
	3.	ἱσταῖεν	τιθεῖεν	διδοῖεν	

		or	or	or	
Dual	2.	ἱσταίητον	τιθείητον	διδοίητον	δεικνύοιτον
	3.	ἱσταιήτην	τιθειήτην	διδοιήτην	δεικνυοίτην
Plur.	1.	ἱσταίημεν	τιθείημεν	διδοίημεν	δεικνύοιμεν
	2.	ἱσταίητε	τιθείητε	διδοίητε	δεικνύοιτε
	3.	ἱσταίησαν	τιθείησαν	διδοίησαν	δεικνύοιεν

PRESENT IMPERATIVE

Sing.	2.	ἵστη	τίθει	δίδου	δείκνῡ
	3.	ἱστάτω	τιθέτω	διδότω	δεικνύτω
Dual	2.	ἵστατον	τίθετον	δίδοτον	δείκνυτον
	3.	ἱστάτων	τιθέτων	διδότων	δεικνύτων
Plur.	2.	ἵστατε	τίθετε	δίδοτε	δείκνυτε
	3.	ἱστάντων	τιθέντων	διδόντων	δεικνύντων

PRESENT INFINITIVE

ἱστάναι	τιθέναι	διδόναι	δεικνύναι

PRESENT PARTICIPLE (329)

ἱστάς	τιθείς	διδούς	δεικνύς

SECOND AORIST INDICATIVE (685)

Sing.	1.	ἔστην	(ἔθηκα)	(ἔδωκα)	ἔδῡν
	2.	ἔστης	(ἔθηκας)	(ἔδωκας)	ἔδῡς
	3.	ἔστη	(ἔθηκε)	(ἔδωκε)	ἔδῡ
Dual	2.	ἔστητον	ἔθετον	ἔδοτον	ἔδῡτον
	3.	ἐστήτην	ἐθέτην	ἐδότην	ἐδύτην
Plur.	1.	ἔστημεν	ἔθεμεν	ἔδομεν	ἔδῡμεν
	2.	ἔστητε	ἔθετε	ἔδοτε	ἔδῡτε
	3.	ἔστησαν	ἔθεσαν	ἔδοσαν	ἔδῡσαν

SECOND AORIST SUBJUNCTIVE

Sing.	1.	στῶ	θῶ	δῶ	δύω
	2.	στῇς	θῇς	δῷς	δύῃς
	3.	στῇ	θῇ	δῷ	δύῃ
Dual	2.	στῆτον	θῆτον	δῶτον	δύητον
	3.	στῆτον	θῆτον	δῶτον	δύητον
Plur.	1.	στῶμεν	θῶμεν	δῶμεν	δύωμεν
	2.	στῆτε	θῆτε	δῶτε	δύητε
	3.	στῶσι	θῶσι	δῶσι	δύωσι

Second Aorist Optative

Sing.	1.	σταίην	θείην	δοίην	
	2.	σταίης	θείης	δοίης	
	3.	σταίη	θείη	δοίη	(See 776)
Dual	2.	σταῖτον	θεῖτον	δοῖτον	
	3.	σταίτην	θείτην	δοίτην	
Plur.	1.	σταῖμεν	θεῖμεν	δοῖμεν	
	2.	σταῖτε	θεῖτε	δοῖτε	
	3.	σταῖεν	θεῖεν	δοῖεν	
		or	or	or	
Dual	2.	σταίητον	θείητον	δοίητον	
	3.	σταιήτην	θειήτην	δοιήτην	
Plur.	1.	σταίημεν	θείημεν	δοίημεν	
	2.	σταίητε	θείητε	δοίητε	
	3.	σταίησαν	θείησαν	δοίησαν	

Second Aorist Imperative

Sing.	2.	στῆθι	θές	δός	δῦθι
	3.	στήτω	θέτω	δότω	δύτω
Dual	2.	στῆτον	θέτον	δότον	δῦτον
	3.	στήτων	θέτων	δότων	δύτων
Plur.	2.	στῆτε	θέτε	δότε	δῦτε
	3.	στάντων	θέντων	δόντων	δύντων

Second Aorist Infinitive

στῆναι	θεῖναι	δοῦναι	δῦναι

Second Aorist Participle (329)

στάς	θείς	δούς	δύς

Middle and Passive

Present Indicative

Sing.	1.	ἵσταμαι	τίθεμαι	δίδομαι	δείκνυμαι
	2.	ἵστασαι	τίθεσαι	δίδοσαι	δείκνυσαι
	3.	ἵσταται	τίθεται	δίδοται	δείκνυται
Dual	2.	ἵστασθον	τίθεσθον	δίδοσθον	δείκνυσθον
	3.	ἵστασθον	τίθεσθον	δίδοσθον	δείκνυσθον
Plur.	1.	ἱστάμεθα	τιθέμεθα	διδόμεθα	δεικνύμεθα
	2.	ἵστασθε	τίθεσθε	δίδοσθε	δείκνυσθε
	3.	ἵστανται	τίθενται	δίδονται	δείκνυνται

IMPERFECT

Sing.	1. ἱστάμην	ἐτιθέμην	ἐδιδόμην	ἐδεικνύμην
	2. ἵστασο	ἐτίθεσο	ἐδίδοσο	ἐδείκνυσο
	3. ἵστατο	ἐτίθετο	ἐδίδοτο	ἐδείκνυτο
Dual	2. ἵστασθον	ἐτίθεσθον	ἐδίδοσθον	ἐδείκνυσθον
	3. ἱστάσθην	ἐτιθέσθην	ἐδιδόσθην	ἐδεικνύσθην
Plur.	1. ἱστάμεθα	ἐτιθέμεθα	ἐδιδόμεθα	ἐδεικνύμεθα
	2. ἵστασθε	ἐτίθεσθε	ἐδίδοσθε	ἐδείκνυσθε
	3. ἵσταντο	ἐτίθεντο	ἐδίδοντο	ἐδείκνυντο

PRESENT SUBJUNCTIVE

Sing.	1. ἱστῶμαι	τιθῶμαι	διδῶμαι	δεικνύωμαι
	2. ἱστῇ	τιθῇ	διδῷ	δεικνύῃ
	3. ἱστῆται	τιθῆται	διδῶται	δεικνύηται
Dual	2. ἱστῆσθον	τιθῆσθον	διδῶσθον	δεικνύησθον
	3. ἱστῆσθον	τιθῆσθον	διδῶσθον	δεικνύησθον
Plur.	1. ἱστώμεθα	τιθώμεθα	διδώμεθα	δεικνυώμεθα
	2. ἱστῆσθε	τιθῆσθε	διδῶσθε	δεικνύησθε
	3. ἱστῶνται	τιθῶνται	διδῶνται	δεικνύωνται

PRESENT OPTATIVE

Sing.	1. ἱσταίμην	τιθείμην	διδοίμην	δεικνυοίμην
	2. ἱσταῖο	τιθεῖο	διδοῖο	δεικνύοιο
	3. ἱσταῖτο	τιθεῖτο	διδοῖτο	δεικνύοιτο
Dual	2. ἱσταῖσθον	τιθεῖσθον	διδοῖσθον	δεικνύοισθον
	3. ἱσταίσθην	τιθείσθην	διδοίσθην	δεικνυοίσθην
Plur.	1. ἱσταίμεθα	τιθείμεθα	διδοίμεθα	δεικνυοίμεθα
	2. ἱσταῖσθε	τιθεῖσθε	διδοῖσθε	δεικνύοισθε
	3. ἱσταῖντο	τιθεῖντο	διδοῖντο	δεικνύοιντο

PRESENT IMPERATIVE

Sing.	2. ἵστασο	τίθεσο	δίδοσο	δείκνυσο
	3. ἱστάσθω	τιθέσθω	διδόσθω	δεικνύσθω
Dual	2. ἵστασθον	τίθεσθον	δίδοσθον	δείκνυσθον
	3. ἱστάσθων	τιθέσθων	διδόσθων	δεικνύσθων
Plur.	2. ἵστασθε	τίθεσθε	δίδοσθε	δείκνυσθε
	3. ἱστάσθων	τιθέσθων	διδόσθων	δεικνύσθων

PRESENT INFINITIVE

ἵστασθαι   τίθεσθαι   δίδοσθαι   δείκνυσθαι

PRESENT PARTICIPLE (295)

ἱστάμενος   τιθέμενος   διδόμενος   δεικνύμενος

SECOND AORIST MIDDLE INDICATIVE (502)

Sing.	1.	ἐπριάμην	ἐθέμην	ἐδόμην
	2.	ἐπρίω	ἔθου	ἔδου
	3.	ἐπρίατο	ἔθετο	ἔδοτο
Dual	2.	ἐπρίασθον	ἔθεσθον	ἔδοσθον
	3.	ἐπριάσθην	ἐθέσθην	ἐδόσθην
Plur.	1.	ἐπριάμεθα	ἐθέμεθα	ἐδόμεθα
	2.	ἐπρίασθε	ἔθεσθε	ἔδοσθε
	3.	ἐπρίαντο	ἔθεντο	ἔδοντο

SECOND AORIST MIDDLE SUBJUNCTIVE

Sing.	1.	πρίωμαι	θῶμαι	δῶμαι
	2.	πρίῃ	θῇ	δῷ
	3.	πρίηται	θῆται	δῶται
Dual	2.	πρίησθον	θῆσθον	δῶσθον
	3.	πρίησθον	θῆσθον	δῶσθον
Plur.	1.	πριώμεθα	θώμεθα	δώμεθα
	2.	πρίησθε	θῆσθε	δῶσθε
	3.	πρίωνται	θῶνται	δῶνται

SECOND AORIST MIDDLE OPTATIVE

Sing.	1.	πριαίμην	θείμην	δοίμην
	2.	πρίαιο	θεῖο	δοῖο
	3.	πρίαιτο	θεῖτο, θοῖτο	δοῖτο
Dual	2.	πρίαισθον	θεῖσθον	δοῖσθον
	3.	πριαίσθην	θείσθην	δοίσθην
Plur.	1.	πριαίμεθα	θείμεθα, θοίμεθα	δοίμεθα
	2.	πρίαισθε	θεῖσθε, θοῖσθε	δοῖσθε
	3.	πρίαιντο	θεῖντο, θοῖντο	δοῖντο

SECOND AORIST MIDDLE IMPERATIVE

Sing.	2.	πρίω	θοῦ	δοῦ
	3.	πριάσθω	θέσθω	δόσθω

Dual { 2. πρίασθον   θέσθον   δόσθον
{ 3. πριάσθων   θέσθων   δόσθων

Plur. { 2. πρίασθε   θέσθε   δόσθε
{ 3. πριάσθων   θέσθων   δόσθων

SECOND AORIST MIDDLE INFINITIVE

πρίασθαι   θέσθαι   δόσθαι

SECOND AORIST MIDDLE PARTICIPLE (295)

πριάμενος   θέμενος   δόμενος

Second Perfect of Mι Verbs

505. Ἵστημι and a few other verbs have a second perfect and pluperfect of the μι form. These are never used in the *singular* of the indicative, where the first perfect and pluperfect are the regular forms. The optative and imperative are poetic.

506. These tenses of ἵστημι are thus inflected:

SECOND PERFECT

Sing. {
1. (ἕστηκα) *stand,*   ἑστῶ   ἑσταίην
    am standing
2. (ἕστηκας)   ἑστῇς   ἑσταίης   ἕσταθι
3. (ἕστηκε)   ἑστῇ   ἑσταίη   ἑστάτω

Dual {
2. ἕστατον   ἑστῆτον   ἑσταῖτον or ἑσταίητον   ἕστατον
3. ἕστατον   ἑστῆτον   ἑσταίτην or ἑσταιήτην   ἑστάτων

Plur. {
1. ἕσταμεν   ἑστῶμεν   ἑσταῖμεν or ἑσταίημεν
2. ἕστατε   ἑστῆτε   ἑσταῖτε or ἑσταίητε   ἕστατε
3. ἑστᾶσι   ἑστῶσι   ἑσταῖεν or ἑσταίησαν   ἑστάντων

Infinitive ἑστάναι   *Participle* ἑστώς, ἑστῶσα, ἑστός (338)

SECOND PLUPERFECT

S. {
1. (εἱστήκη) *stood, was standing*
2. (εἱστήκης)
3. (εἱστήκει)

D. {
2. ἕστατον
3. ἑστάτην

P. {
1. ἕσταμεν
2. ἕστατε
3. ἕστασαν

For an enumeration of these forms, see **727.**

507. FULL SYNOPSIS OF THE INDICATIVE OF ἵστημι, τίθημι, δίδωμι, AND δείκνῡμι, IN ALL THE VOICES

ACTIVE

Pres.	ἵστημι,	τίθημι,	δίδωμι,	δείκνῡμι,
	set	place	give	show
Imperf.	ἵστην	ἐτίθην	ἐδίδουν	ἐδείκνῡν
Fut.	στήσω	θήσω	δώσω	δείξω
1 Aor.	ἔστησα set	ἔθηκα	ἔδωκα	ἔδειξα
2 Aor.	ἔστην came	ἔθετον etc.	ἔδοτον etc.	
	to a stand	in dual and plur.	in dual and plur.	
1 Perf.	ἔστηκα	τέθηκα	δέδωκα	
2 Perf.	ἔστατον etc.			δέδειχα
	in dual and plur.			
	am standing			
1 Plupf.	εἱστήκη	ἐτεθήκη	ἐδεδώκη	
2 Plupf.	ἔστατον etc.			ἐδεδείχη
	in dual and plur.			
	was standing			
Fut. Perf.	ἑστήξω shall			
	stand (736)			

MIDDLE

Pres.	ἵσταμαι	τίθεμαι	δίδομαι	δείκνυμαι
Impf.	ἱστάμην	ἐτιθέμην	ἐδιδόμην	ἐδεικνύμην
Fut.	στήσομαι	θήσομαι	δώσομαι	δείξομαι
1 Aor.	ἐστησάμην	ἐθηκάμην (not Attic)		ἐδειξάμην
2 Aor.		ἐθέμην	ἐδόμην	
Perf.	ἔσταμαι	τέθειμαι	δέδομαι	δέδειγμαι
Plupf.	(?)	(?)	ἐδεδόμην	ἐδεδείγμην

PASSIVE

Present, Imperfect, Perfect, Pluperfect: as in Middle.

Aor.	ἐστάθην	ἐτέθην	ἐδόθην	ἐδείχθην
Fut.	σταθήσομαι	τεθήσομαι	δοθήσομαι	δειχθήσομαι
Fut. Perf.	ἑστήξομαι			(δεδείξομαι,
	shall stand			late)

Irregular Verbs of the Μι *Form*

508. The verbs εἰμί *am*, εἶμι *go*, ἵημι *send*, φημί *say*, ἦμαι *sit*, κεῖμαι *lie*, and the second perfect οἶδα *know*, are thus inflected.

509.   *a.* εἰμί (stem ἐσ-, Latin es-se) *am.*

PRESENT

	Indicative	Subjunctive	Optative	Imperative
Sing. 1.	εἰμί	ὦ	εἴην	
2.	εἶ	ᾖς	εἴης	ἴσθι
3.	ἐστί	ᾖ	εἴη	ἔστω
Dual 2.	ἐστόν	ἦτον	εἶτον or εἴητον	ἔστον
3.	ἐστόν	ἦτον	εἴτην or εἰήτην	ἔστων
Plur. 1.	ἐσμέν	ὦμεν	εἶμεν or εἴημεν	
2.	ἐστέ	ἦτε	εἶτε or εἴητε	ἔστε
3.	εἰσί	ὦσι	εἶεν or εἴησαν	ἔστων

Infin. εἶναι. *Partic.* ὤν, οὖσα, ὄν, gen. ὄντος, οὔσης, etc. (329).
Verbal Adjective ἐστέος (συν-εστέον *one must associate with*).

	IMPERFECT	FUTURE		
	Indicative	Indicative	Optative	Infinitive
Sing. 1.	ἦ or ἦν	ἔσομαι	ἐσοίμην	ἔσεσθαι
2.	ἦσθα	ἔσῃ, ἔσει	ἔσοιο	
3.	ἦν	ἔσται	ἔσοιτο	
Dual 2.	ἦστον	ἔσεσθον	ἔσοισθον	*Partic.*
3.	ἤστην	ἔσεσθον	ἐσοίσθην	ἐσόμενος, -η, -ον
Plur. 1.	ἦμεν	ἐσόμεθα	ἐσοίμεθα	
2.	ἦτε or ἦστε	ἔσεσθε	ἔσοισθε	
3.	ἦσαν	ἔσονται	ἔσοιντο	

b. Εἰμί is for ἐσ-μι (32), εἶ for ἐσι (originally ἐσ-σί, 510 *a*), ἐστί is regular with the original ending; εἰσί is for (σ)-εντι (weak grade of ἐσ-), cf. Lat. sunt; in ἐσ-μέν σ is retained before μ by analogy with ἐσ-τέ (86 *b*); ὦ is ἔω (ἐσ-ω), εἴην for ἐσ-ιη-ν, εἶμεν for ἐσ-ῑ-μεν, cf. sīmus; εἶναι for ἐσ-ναι, ὤν for ἐών (ἐσ-ων). The imperfect ἦ (Attic) is for ἔσ-η, which gave Homeric ἦα (27). Ἦς is rare for ἦσθα.

c. The longer optative forms εἴημεν, εἴησαν, are found only in prose. Εἶμεν is used in poetry and by Plato, εἶτε in poetry, εἶεν in prose and poetry; εἶεν is more common than εἴησαν. An imperative 3 plur. ἔστωσαν is used by Demosthenes and Plato. Plato and the inscriptions also have ὄντων.

d. For the accent, see **159** *c* and **161** *b*. The participle ὤν keeps its accent in composition, e.g. παρών, παροῦσα, παρόντος, etc.; so ἔσται, as παρέσται.

510. DIALECTS. *a. Present Indic.* Aeolic ἔμμι, the most primitive form, nearest to ἐσ-μι (509 *b*). Hom. 2 sing. ἐσσί and εἶς, 1 plur. εἰμέν, 3 plur. ἔασι. Hdt. εἶς and εἰμέν. Doric ἠμί and εἰμί, ἐσσί, 1 plur. ἠμές, εἰμές, εἰμέν, 3 plur. ἐντί.

b. Imperfect. Hom. ἦα, ἔα, ἔον; ἦσθα, ἔησθα; ἦεν, ἔην, ἤην, ἦν (rare); ἦσαν, ἔσαν. Hdt. ἔα, ἔας, ἔατε. Ionic (iterative) ἔσκον. Later ἦς for ἦσθα. Doric 3 sing. ἦς (for ἠσ-τ, 24), 1 plur. ἦμες.

c. Future. Hom. ἔσσομαι etc., with ἐσσεῖται and ἔσεται; Dor. ἐσσῇ, ἐσσεῖται, ἐσσοῦνται.

d. Subj. Ionic ἔω, ἔῃς, ἔῃ (ἔῃσι, ῇσι), etc., 3 plur. ἔωσι; Hom. also 1 sing. μετ-είω, with metrical lengthening.

e. Opt. Ionic ἔοις, ἔοι.

f. Imper. Hom. and Aeol. ἔσ-σο (a regular middle form).

g. Infin. Hom. ἔμμεναι, ἔμεναι, ἔμεν, ἔμμεν; Dor. ἦμεν or εἶμεν; lyric ἔμμεν.

h. Partic. Ionic and Doric ἐών.

511.   *a.* εἶμι (stem εἰ-, ἰ-, Latin i-re) *go.*

PRESENT

		Indicative	Subjunctive	Optative	Imperative
Sing.	1.	εἶμι	ἴω	ἴοιμι or ἰοίην	
	2.	εἶ	ἴῃς	ἴοις	ἴθι
	3.	εἶσι	ἴῃ	ἴοι	ἴτω
Dual	2.	ἴτον	ἴητον	ἴοιτον	ἴτον
	3.	ἴτον	ἴητον	ἰοίτην	ἴτων
Plur.	1.	ἴμεν	ἴωμεν	ἴοιμεν	
	2.	ἴτε	ἴητε	ἴοιτε	ἴτε
	3.	ἴᾱσι	ἴωσι	ἴοιεν	ἰόντων

Infin. ἰέναι. *Partic.* ἰών, ἰοῦσα, ἰόν, gen. ἰόντος, ἰούσης, etc.
Verbal Adjectives ἰτός (poetic), ἰτέος, ἰητέος.

IMPERFECT

	Singular	Dual	Plural
1.	ᾖα or ᾖειν		ᾖμεν
2.	ᾔεισθα or ᾔεις	ᾖτον	ᾖτε
3.	ᾔειν or ᾔει	ᾔτην	ᾖσαν or ᾔεσαν

b. In compounds the participle ἰών keeps the accent of the simple form; e.g. παριών, παριοῦσα, παριόντος, παριοῦσι.

c. The indicative and subjunctive of εἶμι generally (always in Attic) have a future sense, *shall go*, taking the place of a future of ἔρχομαι *I go* (present), whose future ἐλεύσομαι is rarely (or never) used in Attic prose. The opt., infin., and partic. may be either present or future (in indirect discourse especially).

512. In older prose the forms of the imperfect are usually ἦα, ἦεισθα, ἦειν. Later prose has ἦειν, ἦεις, ἦει; ἦεσαν seems to be preferred to ἦσαν.

513. DIALECTS. *Present Indic.* 2 sing. Hom. εἶσθα, Hesiod εἶς. *Imperf.* Hom. 1 sing. ἦια, ἦιον, 3 sing. ἦιε, ἦε, ἦει (ἦεν?), ἴε; dual ἴτην; plur. ἦομεν, 3 pers. ἦισαν, ἦσαν, ἴσαν, ἦιον. Hdt. ἦια, ἦιε, ἦισαν. *Subj.* Hom. ἴησθα and ἴης, ἴησιν and ἴῃ, ἴομεν and ἴομεν. *Opt.* ἰείη and ἴοι. *Infin.* ἴμεναι, ἴμεν, ἰέναι. *Future* εἴσομαι.

514.   *a.* ἴημι (stem ἡ-, ἑ-) *send.*

ACTIVE

PRESENT

	Indicative	Subjunctive	Optative	Imperative
Sing. 1.	ἵημι	ἱῶ	ἱείην	
2.	ἵης, ἱεῖς	ἱῇς	ἱείης	ἵει *Infin.*
3.	ἵησι	ἱῇ	ἱείη	ἱέτω ἱέναι
Dual 2.	ἵετον	ἱῆτον	ἱεῖτον or ἱείητον	ἱέτον
3.	ἵετον	ἱῆτον	ἱείτην or ἱειήτην	ἱέτων *Partic.*
Plur. 1.	ἵεμεν	ἱῶμεν	ἱεῖμεν or ἱείημεν	ἱείς,
2.	ἵετε	ἱῆτε	ἱεῖτε or ἱείητε	ἵετε ἱεῖσα, ἱέν
3.	ἱᾶσι	ἱῶσι	ἱεῖεν or ἱείησαν	ἱέντων

IMPERFECT

Sing. 1.	ἵην
2.	ἵεις
3.	ἵει

Dual 2. ἵετον   *Future* ἥσω, in prose only in composition, e.g.
3. ἱέτην   ἀφήσω *I shall let go.*

Plur. 1. ἵεμεν   *First Aorist* ἧκα, only in indic., and in prose usu-
2. ἵετε   ally in composition, e.g. ἀφῆκα *I let go.*
3. ἵεσαν   *Perfect* εἷκα, only in composition.

SECOND AORIST (in prose only in composition)

	Indicative	Subjunctive	Optative	Imperative
Sing. 1.	(ἧκα)	ὧ	εἵην	*Infin.*
2.	(ἧκας)	ᾗς	εἵης	ἕς εἷναι
3.	(ἧκε)	ᾗ	εἵη	ἕτω
Dual 2.	εἷτον	ἧτον	εἷτον or εἵητον	ἕτον *Partic.*
3.	εἵτην	ἧτον	εἵτην or εἰήτην	ἕτων εἵς, εἷσα,
Plur. 1.	εἷμεν	ὧμεν	εἷμεν or εἵημεν	ἕν
2.	εἷτε	ἧτε	εἷτε or εἵητε	ἕτε
3.	εἷσαν	ὧσι	εἷεν or εἵησαν	ἕντων See 701.

MIDDLE

PRESENT

		Indicative	Subjunctive	Optative	Imperative	
Sing.	1.	ἵεμαι	ἱῶμαι	ἱείμην		Infin.
	2.	ἵεσαι	ἱῇ	ἱεῖο	ἵεσο	ἵεσθαι
	3.	ἵεται	ἱῆται	ἱεῖτο	ἱέσθω	
Dual	2.	ἵεσθον	ἱῆσθον	ἱεῖσθον	ἵεσθον	
	3.	ἵεσθον	ἱῆσθον	ἱείσθην	ἱέσθων	Partic.
Plur.	1.	ἱέμεθα	ἱώμεθα	ἱείμεθα		ἱέμενος
	2.	ἵεσθε	ἱῆσθε	ἱεῖσθε	ἵεσθε	
	3.	ἵενται	ἱῶνται	ἱεῖντο	ἱέσθων	

IMPERFECT

Sing.	1.	ἱέμην
	2.	ἵεσο
	3.	ἵετο
Dual	2.	ἵεσθον
	3.	ἱέσθην
Plur.	1.	ἱέμεθα
	2.	ἵεσθε
	3.	ἵεντο

Future ἥσομαι, only in composition, e.g. οὐ μεθήσομαι *I shall not relax my hold.*

First Aorist ἡκάμην, only in indic. and in composition.

Perfect εἷμαι, *Imper.* εἷσθω, *Infin.* εἷσθαι, *Partic.* εἱμένος, only in composition.

SECOND AORIST (only in composition)

		Indicative	Subjunctive	Optative	Imperative	
Sing.	1.	εἵμην	ὦμαι	εἵμην		Infin.
	2.	εἷσο	ᾗ	εἷο	οὗ	ἔσθαι
	3.	εἷτο	ἧται	εἷτο	ἔσθω	
Dual	2.	εἷσθον	ἧσθον	εἷσθον	ἔσθον	
	3.	εἵσθην	ἧσθον	εἵσθην	ἔσθων	Partic.
Plur.	1.	εἵμεθα	ὥμεθα	εἵμεθα		ἕμενος
	2.	εἷσθε	ἧσθε	εἷσθε	ἔσθε	
	3.	εἷντο	ὧνται	εἷντο	ἔσθων	

Aorist Passive εἵθην, *Subj.* ἑθῶ, *Infin.* ἑθῆναι, *Partic.* ἑθείς, only in composition, e.g. ἀφεθῆναι *to be released.*

Future Passive (in composition) ἑθήσομαι.

Verbal Adjectives (in composition) ἑτός, ἑτέος.

b. The present and imperfect of ἵημι are reduplicated forms (**501, 561**), for σι-ση-μι, σι-ση-ν (**88, 90**).

c. The imperfect active of ἀφίημι is ἀφίην or ἠφίην (**567**). The optatives ἀφίοιτε and ἀφίοιεν, for ἀφιεῖτε and ἀφιεῖεν, and προοῖτο, προοῖσθε, and προοῖντο (also accented πρόοιτο, etc.), for προεῖτο, προεῖσθε, and προεῖντο, sometimes occur. See **668, 773**.

515. In the 2 aor. act. mid. and aor. pass. and in the perfect forms ει is for ε + ε; e.g. εἷμεν is for ἑ-ἑ-μεν, εἵμην for ἑ-ἑ-μην, εἵθην for ἑ-ἑ-θην, εἷκα and εἷμαι for ἑ-ἑ-κα, ἑ-ἑ-μαι, in which ἑ-ἑ is the reduplicated weak grade of the stem. The strong grade is seen in 1 aor. ἡ-κα. Subj. ἰῶ, ἰῇς are for ἱέω, ἱέῃς; ὧ, ᾗς for ἕ-ω, ἕ-ῃς.

516. DIALECTS. *a.* Hom. ἵημι (usually with initial ἱ̆); imperf. ἵειν, ἵεις, ἵει, 3 plur. ἵεν; 1 aor. ἕηκα and ἧκα, ἐν-ήκαμεν, ἧκαν; 2 aor. ἕσαν, ἕμην, ἕντο, by omission of augment, for εἷσαν, εἵμην, εἷντο; infin. pres. ἱέμεναι, ἱέμεν, aor. ἕμεν. In ἀνίημι, Hom. fut. ἀνέσω, aor. ἄνεσα. Subj. μεθείω, μεθήῃ, ἀφέῃ, μεθῶμεν.

b. Hdt. ἱεῖ (in composition), ἱεῖσι; perf. mid. ἀν-έωνται for ἀν-εῖνται, and perf. pass. partic. με-μετ-ι-μένος, for μεθ-ειμένος *summoned.*

c. Dor. perf. ἕωκα, ἕωμαι.

517. φημί (stem φη-, φα-, Latin fā-ri) *say, say yes, affirm.*

	Indic.	Subj.	Opt.	Imper.	Indic.

<table>
<tr><td></td><td colspan="3" style="text-align:center">PRESENT</td><td></td><td>IMPERFECT</td></tr>
<tr><td></td><td>Indic.</td><td>Subj.</td><td>Opt.</td><td>Imper.</td><td>Indic.</td></tr>
<tr><td rowspan="3">Sing.</td><td>1. φημί</td><td>φῶ</td><td>φαίην</td><td></td><td>ἔφην</td></tr>
<tr><td>2. φῄς</td><td>φῇς</td><td>φαίης</td><td>φαθί or φάθι</td><td>ἔφησθα or ἔφης</td></tr>
<tr><td>3. φησί</td><td>φῇ</td><td>φαίη</td><td>φάτω</td><td>ἔφη</td></tr>
<tr><td rowspan="2">Dual</td><td>2. φατόν</td><td>φῆτον</td><td></td><td>φάτον</td><td>ἔφατον</td></tr>
<tr><td>3. φατόν</td><td>φῆτον</td><td></td><td>φάτων</td><td>ἐφάτην</td></tr>
<tr><td rowspan="3">Plur.</td><td>1. φαμέν</td><td>φῶμεν</td><td>φαῖμεν or φαίημεν</td><td></td><td>ἔφαμεν</td></tr>
<tr><td>2. φατέ</td><td>φῆτε</td><td>φαίητε</td><td>φάτε</td><td>ἔφατε</td></tr>
<tr><td>3. φᾱσί</td><td>φῶσι</td><td>φαῖεν or φαίησαν</td><td>φάντων</td><td>ἔφασαν</td></tr>
</table>

Infin. φάναι.

Partic. poetic, φάς, φᾶσα, φάν. In Attic prose, φάσκων, φάσκουσα, φάσκον.

Future φήσω, φήσειν, φήσων.

Aorist ἔφησα, φήσω, φήσαιμι, φῆσαι, φήσᾱς.

Verbal Adjectives φατός, φατέος.

A perfect passive imperative (3 pers.) πεφάσθω occurs (**520 b**).

518. All pres. indic. forms are enclitic except φῄς (**159 c**).

519. Ἔφην and the pres. subj. and opt. forms are often aoristic in meaning. Ἔφην and ἐφάμην (**520 b**) do not differ in formation or meaning from an athematic aorist; cf. ἔβην *went,* 2 aor. of βαίνω, and ἐπριάμην *bought.*

520. DIALECTS. *a. Present Indic.* Doric φᾱμί, φᾱτί, φαντί; Hom. φῆσθα for φῄs. *Infin.* Doric and poet. φάμεν.

Imperfect. Hom. ἔφην, φῆν, φῆs or φῆσθα, φῆ, φαμέν, ἔφασαν, ἔφαν, φάν; Doric ἔφᾱ, φᾶ.

Future. Doric φᾱσῶ.

Aorist. Doric φᾶσε for ἔφησε.

b. Middle forms, not known in Attic (Plato has passive πεφάσθω), are common in Homer. *Pres. imper.* φάο, φάσθω, φάσθε; *infin.* φάσθαι; *partic.* φάμενοs; *imperf.* ἐφάμην or φάμην, ἔφατο or φάτο, ἔφαντο or φάντο. Pindar *fut.* φᾱσομαι. These all have an active sense.

521. ἧμαι (stem ἡσ-) *sit*

῏Ημαι in the simple form is used only in Homer, Herodotus, and tragedy. In Attic prose and in comedy κάθ-ημαι is used.

Present Indic. ἧμαι, ἧσαι, ἧσται; ἧσθον; ἥμεθα, ἧσθε, ἧνται. *Imper.* ἧσο, ἧσθω, etc. *Infin.* ἧσθαι. *Partic.* ἥμενοs.

Imperfect. ἥμην, ἧσο, ἧστο; ἧσθον, ἥσθην; ἥμεθα, ἧσθε, ἧντο.

The missing tenses are supplied by the appropriate forms of ἕζομαι, ἵζω, ἵζομαι.

522. Κάθημαι is thus inflected:

	PRESENT			IMPERFECT
Indic.	*Subj.*	*Opt.*	*Imper.*	*Indic.*
κάθημαι	καθῶμαι	καθοίμην		ἐκαθήμην or καθήμην
κάθησαι	καθῇ	καθοῖο	κάθησο	ἐκάθησο or καθῆσο
κάθηται	καθῆται	καθοῖτο	καθήσθω	ἐκάθητο or καθῆστο, καθῆτο
κάθησθον	καθῆσθον	καθοῖσθον	κάθησθον	ἐκάθησθον or καθῆσθον
κάθησθον	καθῆσθον	καθοίσθην	καθήσθων	ἐκαθήσθην or καθήσθην
καθήμεθα	καθώμεθα	καθοίμεθα		ἐκαθήμεθα or καθήμεθα
κάθησθε	καθῆσθε	καθοῖσθε	κάθησθε	ἐκάθησθε or καθῆσθε
κάθηνται	καθῶνται	καθοῖντο	καθήσθων	ἐκάθηντο or καθῆντο

Infin. καθῆσθαι   *Partic.* καθήμενοs, -η, -ον

The missing tenses are supplied by the appropriate forms of καθέζομαι, καθίζω, καθίζομαι.

523. In comedy the imperative κάθου occurs for κάθησο.

524. DIALECTS. Homer has εἵαται, rarely ἕαται, for ἧνται; and εἵατο, ἕατο (once), for ἧντο. These forms should probably be written ἥαται, ἥατο, shortened (**35**) to ἕαται, ἕατο. Hom. also has καθῆστο, plur. καθείατο (properly καθήατο). Hdt. has plur. κατέαται and κατέατο, sing. καθῆστο.

525. κεῖμαι (stem κει-) *lie, am laid* (often as passive of τίθημι).

		PRESENT				IMPERFECT
		Indic.	*Subj.*	*Opt.*	*Imper.*	*Indic.*
Sing.	1.	κεῖμαι				ἐκείμην
	2.	κεῖσαι			κεῖσο	ἔκεισο
	3.	κεῖται	κέηται	κέοιτο	κείσθω	ἔκειτο
Dual	2.	κεῖσθον			κεῖσθον	ἔκεισθον
	3.	κεῖσθον			κείσθων	ἐκείσθην
Plur.	1.	κείμεθα				ἐκείμεθα
	2.	κεῖσθε	κέησθε	κεῖσθε	κεῖσθε	ἔκεισθε
	3.	κεῖνται	κέωνται	κέοιντο	κείσθων	ἔκειντο

Infin. κεῖσθαι. *Partic.* κείμενος.
Future κείσομαι, κείσῃ or κείσει, κείσεται, etc.

526. The subj. and opt. plural occur only in composition. In these moods κει- is shortened to κε- before a vowel (35).

527. DIALECTS. Homer has κέαται, κείαται, and κέονται, for κεῖνται; iterative κέσκετο for ἔκειτο; κέατο and κείατο for ἔκειντο, also κεῖντο; subj. κῆται and κεῖται. Hdt. has κέεται and κεῖται, κεέσθω, κέεσθαι, and ἐκέετο, for κεῖται, etc.; and always κέαται and ἐκέατο for κεῖνται and ἔκειντο.

528. Χρή *need*, an indeclinable substantive, is used without ἐστί as an impersonal verb, 3 sing., *one ought*, Lat. oportet. Uniting by crasis with other forms of ἐστί, it has the following inflection:

Subj. χρῇ (χρὴ ᾖ), opt. χρείη (χρὴ εἴη), infin. χρῆναι (χρὴ εἶναι), indeclinable partic. χρεών (χρὴ ὄν), imperf. χρῆν (χρὴ ἦν) and ἐχρῆν, fut. χρῆσται (χρὴ 'σται). So ἀπόχρη *it is enough*, with plur. ἀποχρῶσι, partic. ἀποχρῶν, imperf. ἀπέχρη, fut. ἀποχρήσει, aor. ἀπέχρησε.

529. οἶδα (stem ϝοιδ-, ϝειδη-, ϝιδ-, cf. Latin video) *know*

Οἶδα is a second perfect in form, but has the meaning of a present.

SECOND PERFECT

		Indicative	*Subjunctive*	*Optative*	*Imperative*
Sing.	1.	οἶδα	εἰδῶ	εἰδείην	
	2.	οἶσθα	εἰδῇς	εἰδείης	ἴσθι
	3.	οἶδε	εἰδῇ	εἰδείη	ἴστω
Dual	2.	ἴστον	εἰδῆτον	εἰδεῖτον	ἴστον
	3.	ἴστον	εἰδῆτον	εἰδείτην	ἴστων
Plur.	1.	ἴσμεν	εἰδῶμεν	εἰδεῖμεν or εἰδείημεν	
	2.	ἴστε	εἰδῆτε	εἰδεῖτε or εἰδείητε	ἴστε
	3.	ἴσασι	εἰδῶσι	εἰδεῖεν or εἰδείησαν	ἴστων

SECOND PLUPERFECT

Singular	Dual	Plural
1. ἤδη or ἤδειν		ᾖσμεν or ᾔδεμεν
2. ἤδησθα or ᾔδεις	ᾖστον	ᾖστε or ᾔδετε
3. ᾔδει(ν)	ᾔστην	ᾖσαν or ᾔδεσαν

Infin. εἰδέναι. *Partic.* εἰδώς, εἰδυῖα, εἰδός, gen. εἰδότος, εἰδυίᾱς (329). *Future* εἴσομαι. *Verbal Adjective* ἰστέος.

530. DIALECTS. *a.* The Ionic and late Greek have οἶδας, οἴδαμεν, οἴδᾱσι, occasionally found also in manuscripts of Attic authors. Comedy has 2 pers. οἶσθας. Ionic also ἴδμεν for ἴσμεν. Ionic fut. εἰδήσω, infin. εἰδήσέμεν and εἰδήσειν.

b. Ionic ᾔδεα, ᾔδεε, ᾔδέατε, Hom. ἠείδης and ᾔδης, ᾔείδη, ἴσαν (for ἰδ-σαν) in the pluperfect. The Attic poets rarely have ᾔδεμεν and ᾔδετε.

c. Hom. subj. εἰδέω and ἰδέω (once, doubtful), and with short thematic vowel εἴδομεν, εἴδετε; infin. ἴδμεναι and ἴδμεν; partic. εἰδυῖα and ἰδυῖα.

d. Boeotian imperative ἴττω for ἴστω; Aeolic ϝοίδημι and οἶδα.

e. Doric ἴσᾱμι, plur. ἴσαμεν, ἴσαντι.

531. The pluperfect forms ᾔδειν, ᾔδεις occur in Demosthenes. Manuscripts of Plato have 2 pers. ᾔδεισθα. Late Greek has ᾔδειμεν, ᾔδειτε, ᾔδεισαν.

532. *a.* Οἶσθα is for ϝοιδ-θα (66), ἴστε for ϝιδ-τε. In ἴσμεν (Hom. ἴδμεν), σ is due to ἴστε (82). Ἴσᾱσι (Hom. ἴσσᾱσι) is made from ϝιδ- and -σαντι, in which -αντι (-ᾱσι) is the ending of the athematic present and σ is due to the pluperfect -σαν (Hom. ἴσαν). The pluperfect ᾔδη is contracted from ἠ-είδη, the augment being η (538), not ε.

b. The pluperfect shows a stem ϝειδη-, seen in Lat. vidē-re. This is shortened in the plural, as in τίθημι, τίθεμεν. So also in the subj. εἰδέω (Hom.), contracted to εἰδῶ, εἰδῇς, etc.

AUGMENT

533. In the secondary tenses of the indicative the verb receives an augment (*increase*) at the beginning, which marks these as past tenses. Augment is of two kinds, syllabic and temporal.

534. Syllabic Augment. Verbs beginning with a consonant prefix the syllable ε to the tense stem; e.g. λύω *loose*, imperfect ἔ-λῡον, aorist indicative ἔ-λῡσα, pluperfect ἐ-λελύκη; λείπω *leave*, second aorist ἔ-λιπον; γράφω *write*, ἔ-γραψα, ἐ-γράφην.

535. Verbs beginning with ρ double the ρ after the augment (64); e.g. ῥίπτω *throw*, ἔ-ρρῑπτον, ἐ-ρρίφην; ῥέω *flow*, ἐ-ρρύην; ῥήγνῡμι *break*, ἔ-ρρηξα. Assimilation of a lost consonant is here the cause: ἔ-ρρηξα is for ἔ-ϝρηξα, ἐ-ρρύην for ἐ-σρύην. So in Homer, ἔ-δδεισε *feared* for ἐ-δϝεισε, ἔ-λλαβε *took* for ἐ-σλαβε, ἔ-ννεον *swam* for ἐ-σνεον, ἐ-σσείοντο *were shaken* for ἐ-τϝειοντο.

536. Βούλομαι *wish*, δύναμαι *be able*, and μέλλω *intend* often have η for ε in the augment, especially in later Attic; e.g. ἐβουλόμην or ἠβουλόμην, ἐβουλήθην or ἠβουλήθην; ἐδυνάμην or ἠδυνάμην, ἐδυνήθην or ἠδυνήθην; ἔμελλον or ἤμελλον. These forms may be due to the influence of ἐθέλω *wish*, which also has a present θέλω. Hence ἠβουλόμην : βούλομαι :: ἤθελον : θέλω.

537. The syllabic augment is often found before a verb beginning with a vowel. Here an initial consonant, ϝ or σ, has been lost. E.g.

ἄγνῡμι *break* (ϝαγ-), aor. ἔ-āξα, ἐ-άγην.
ἁλίσκομαι *be caught* (ϝαλ-), aor. ἑάλων or ἥλων, but imperf. ἡλισκόμην.
ἀνοίγω *open* (ϝοιγ-), imperf. ἀν-έῳγον.
ἐάω *allow* (σεϝα-), imperf. εἴων for ἐ-σεϝαον, aor. εἴᾱσα.
ἕζομαι *sit* (σεδ-), εἱσάμην for ἐ-σεδσαμην.
ἐθίζω *accustom* (σϝεθ-), εἴθιζον for ἐ-σϝεθιζον, εἴθισα.
εἶδον *saw* (ϝιδ-), for ἐ-ϝιδον.
εἷλον *caught* (σελ-?) for ἐ-(σ)ελον.
ἐλίττω *roll* (ϝελικ-), εἵλιττον for ἐ-ϝελιττον.
ἕλκω, ἑλκύω *drag* (σἐλκ-), εἷλκον for ἐ-σελκον.
ἕπομαι *follow* (σεπ-), εἱπόμην for ἐ-σεπομην.
ἐργάζομαι *work* (ϝεργ-), εἰργαζόμην for ἐ-ϝεργαζομην, but also ἠργαζόμην (**539**).
ἕρπω *creep* (σερπ-), εἷρπον for ἐ-σερπον.
ἑστιάω *entertain* (ϝεστια-), εἱστίων for ἐ-ϝεστιαον.
ἔχω *have, hold* (σεχ-), εἶχον for ἐ-σεχον.
ἵημι *send* (ση-), εἷτον for ἐ-σετον, aor. pass. εἵθην for ἐ-σεθην (**514 b**).
ὁράω *see* (ϝορ-), ἑώρων.
ὠθέω *push* (ϝωθ-), ἐώθουν for ἐ-ϝωθεον, aor. ἔωσα, aor. pass. ἐώσθην.
ὠνέομαι *buy* (ϝων-), ἐωνούμην for ἐ-ϝωνεομην, aor. ἐωνήθην.

538. Some of these forms have a double augment, temporal (**539**) and syllabic; e.g. ἀν-έῳγον, ἑώρων, ἐάγην, ἑάλων. They have been (doubtfully) explained as due to an augment ἠ, as in Hom. ἠείδη (**532**), with transfer of quantity (**33**); e.g. -έῳγον for ἠ-ϝοιγον, ἑώρων for ἠ-ϝοραον, ἐάγην for ἠ-ϝάγην, ἑάλων for ἠ-ϝάλων.

539. Temporal Augment. Verbs beginning with a vowel or diphthong are augmented by lengthening the initial vowel; α and ε become η, and ι, ο, υ become ῑ, ω, ῡ. E.g.

ἄγω *lead*, imperf. ἦγον, plpf. ἦχη, aor. pass. ἤχθη.
ἀκολουθέω *accompany*, ἠκολούθησα.
ἐλαύνω *drive*, ἤλαυνον, ἤλασα.
ἱκετεύω *implore*, ἱκέτευον, ἱκέτευσα, plpf. ἱκετεύκη.
ὀνειδίζω *reproach*, ὠνείδιζον.
ὀρθόω *erect*, ὤρθωσα.
ὑβρίζω *insult*, ὕβριζον, ὕβρισα, ὑβρίσθην.

540. A diphthong takes the temporal augment on its first vowel; ᾳ and αι become ῃ, αυ becomes ηυ, ει η, ευ ηυ, οι ῳ. E.g.

> αἰτέω ask, ᾔτουν, ᾔτησα, ᾔτηκη, ᾐτήθην.
> ᾄδω sing, ᾖδον.
> αὐξάνω increase, ηὔξησα, ηὐξήθην.
> εἰκάζω liken, ᾔκασα.
> εὑρίσκω find, ηὗρον.
> οἰκέω dwell, ᾤκουν, ᾤκησα.

541. A long initial vowel is not changed except that ᾱ generally becomes η; e.g. ἀθλέω struggle, ἤθλησα; but ἵημι send, imperf. ἵην. Both ᾱ and η are found in ἀναλίσκω and ἀναλόω spend (549), e.g. ἀνάλωσα and ἀνήλωσα. Ἀίω (poetic) hear has imperf. ἄιον.

542. Augment Omitted. *a.* Homer and the lyric poets often omit both the syllabic and the temporal augment; e.g. δῶκε for ἔδωκε, ἔχον for εἶχον, ὁμίλεον for ὡμίλουν, βῆ for ἔβη.

b. Herodotus always omits the syllabic augment in iteratives (606) and occasionally in the pluperfect. He uses the temporal augment in the majority of cases, but omits it regularly in ἀγινέω, αἰνέω, ἀμείβομαι, ἀναισιμόω, ἀνοίγω, ἀρρωδέω, διαιτάομαι, ἐάω, ἐλευθερόω, ἐργάζομαι, ἐσσόομαι, ἑτοιμάζω, ὁρμάω, ὁρμέω, ὀρτάζω, and all verbs beginning with ευ and οι. In some verbs the augment is omitted only in certain forms, e.g. ἄχθη (ἤχθη). In others his usage varies, e.g. in ἀγγέλλω, ἀλίζω, ἀλλάσσω, ἐπείγομαι, ἐπίσταμαι. He never adds the temporal augment to the Attic reduplication (554).

c. The Attic tragedians sometimes omit the augment in choral passages, seldom in the dialogue.

d. Ει and ευ are often without augment; εἴκασα or ἤκασα likened, καθεῦδον or καθηῦδον slept, εὐξάμην or ηὐξάμην prayed; ου is not augmented.

e. Doric and Aeolic do not augment verbs beginning with αι and αυ. Α is augmented to ᾱ, e.g. ἆγον for ἦγον (164).

REDUPLICATION

543. The perfect, pluperfect, and future perfect, in all the moods and in the participle, have a *reduplication*, which is a doubling of the initial sound of the verb. It occurs sometimes in the present and second aorist.

PERFECT AND FUTURE PERFECT

544. Verbs beginning with a single consonant (except ρ) are reduplicated in the perfect and future perfect by prefixing that consonant followed by ε. E.g.

λύω, λέ-λυκα, λέ-λυμαι, λε-λυκέναι, λε-λυκώς, λε-λυμένος, λε-λύσομαι; λείπω, λέλοιπα, λέλειμμαι, λελείψομαι. So θύω *sacrifice*, τέ-θυκα; φαίνω (φαν-) *show*, πέ-φασμαι, πε-φάνθαι; χαίνω *gape*, κέ-χηνα. Here the initial aspirate (θ, φ, χ) is replaced by its corresponding smooth stop (105 a).

545. In verbs beginning with two or more consonants (except a stop with a nasal or liquid), with a double consonant (ζ, ξ, ψ), or with ρ, the reduplication is represented by a simple ε, having the same form as the syllabic augment. E.g.

στέλλω *send*, ἔσταλκα; ζητέω *seek*, ἐζήτηκα; ψεύδω *cheat*, ἔψευσμαι, ἐψευσμένος; ῥίπτω *throw*, ἔρριμμαι, ἐρρῖφθαι (64).

546. a. Most verbs beginning with a stop followed by a liquid or nasal have the full reduplication; e.g. γράφω *write*, γέγραφα, γέγραμμαι, γεγράφθαι, γεγραμμένος. So κέκληκα, κέκλημαι, κεκλημένος, from καλέω *call*.

b. But those beginning with γν, and occasionally a few in βλ or γλ, have ε; e.g. γνωρίζω *recognize*, perf. ἐγνώρικα; γιγνώσκω (γνω-) *know*, ἔγνωκα; γλύφω *carve*, ἔγλυφα; βλαστάνω *sprout*, βεβλάστηκα or ἐβλάστηκα.

547. Μιμνήσκω (reduplicated present, μι-μνη-) *remind* has μέμνημαι *remember* (Lat. memini); κτάομαι *acquire*, κέκτημαι and ἔκτημαι *possess*; πίπτω *fall* (reduplicated, πι-πτ-ω), πέπτωκα. See also Homeric perfect passive of ῥυπόω.

548. Verbs beginning with a short vowel lengthen the vowel, and those beginning with a diphthong lengthen its first vowel, in all forms of the perfect and future perfect, the reduplication thus having the form of the temporal augment. E.g.

ἄγω *lead*, ἦχα, ἦγμαι, ἠγμένος; ἀκολουθέω *follow*, ἠκολούθηκα, ἠκολουθηκέναι; ὀρθόω *erect*, ὤρθωμαι; ὁρίζω *bound*, ὥρικα, ὥρισμαι; αἱρέω *take*, ᾕρηκα, ᾕρημαι, ᾑρήσομαι; εἰκάζω *liken*, ᾔκασμαι; εὑρίσκω *find*, ηὕρηκα, ηὕρημαι (or εὕρηκα, εὕρημαι, 541).

549. If the verb originally began with ϝ or σ, the ε which was left when the ϝ or σ was lost often contracted with a vowel of the stem, e.g. εἷκα for σε-σε-κα (514, 537); or ε remained uncontracted, e.g. ἔοικα *resemble* for ϝε-ϝοικα, ἔᾱγα for ϝε-ϝᾶγα from ϝάγνυμι *break*, ἔστηκα *stand* for σε-στηκα, from ἵστημι (σι-στημι). So ἀνήλωκα or ἀνάλωκα for ἀνα-ϝε-ϝαλωκα, from ἀνᾱλίσκω (ἀνα-ϝαλισκω) *spend*. See 552.

PLUPERFECT

550. When the reduplicated perfect begins with a consonant, the pluperfect prefixes the syllabic augment ε to the reduplication. In other cases the pluperfect keeps the reduplication of the perfect without change. E.g.

λύω, λέλυκα, ἐ-λελύκη, λέλυμαι, ἐ-λελύμην; στέλλω, ἔσταλκα, ἐστάλκη, ἔσταλμαι, ἐστάλμην; λαμβάνω, εἴληφα, εἰλήφη; ἀγγέλλω, ἤγγελκα, ἠγγέλκη, ἤγγελμαι, ἠγγέλμην; αἱρέω, ᾕρηκα, ᾑρήκη; εὑρίσκω, ηὕρηκα, ηὑρήκη, ηὑρήμην.

551. From ἵστημι *set* we have both εἱστήκη (older form, for ἐ-σε-στηκη) and ἑστήκη (through perf. ἕστηκα). Verbs with initial ϝ or σ (549) generally follow the perfect, e.g. εἵμην, ἐάγη. But ἔοικα *resemble* has ἐῴκη.

552. a. Five verbs, beginning with a liquid or μ, have ει instead of the reduplication:

λαγχάνω (λαχ-) *obtain by lot*, εἴληχα, εἰλήχη, εἴληγμαι.
λαμβάνω (λαβ-) *take*, εἴληφα, εἰλήφη, εἴλημμαι.
λέγω *collect*, in composition, -είλοχα, -ειλόχη, -είλεγμαι, rarely -λέλεγμαι; διαλέγομαι *discuss* has δι-είλεγμαι.
μείρομαι (μερ-) *obtain part*, εἵμαρται *it is fated*, εἵμαρτο.
stem ἐρ-, ῥη-, εἴρηκα *have said*, εἴρηκη, εἴρημαι, fut. pf. εἰρήσομαι.

εἴληφα and εἵμαρται arose from a lost initial σ (32), εἴληφα for σε-σλη-φα (cf. 535), εἵμαρται for σε-σμαρται.

b. Homeric δείδοικα and δείδια *fear*, from stem δϝι-, δϝοι-, are due to metrical lengthening after the loss of ϝ.

553. In Homer the reduplication is rarely omitted, e.g. ἄνωγα *bid*, ἔσσαι (ἔννῡμι *clothe*), ἔρχαται (ἔργω *bar*). Δέχαται (δέχομαι *receive*) is sometimes explained thus. But see **652.**

Attic Reduplication

554. Some verbs beginning with a, ε, or o, followed by a single consonant, reduplicate the perfect and pluperfect by repeating the initial vowel and consonant and lengthening the vowel of the second syllable as in the temporal augment. E.g.

ἀρόω *plough*, ἀρ-ήρομαι; ἐμέω *vomit*, ἐμήμεκα; ἐλέγχω *prove*, ἐλήλεγμαι; ἐλαύνω (ἐλα-) *drive*, ἐλήλακα, ἐλήλαμαι; ἀκούω *hear*, ἀκήκοα for ἀκ-ηκοϝα; ὄλλυμι *lose, destroy*, ὄλ-ωλα; ὀ-ρύττω *dig*, ὀρ-ώρυχα, ὀρ-ώρυγμαι. For the pluperfect, see **558.**

555. Though this process is called the *Attic* reduplication by the ancient grammarians, it is more common in Ionic than in Attic.

556. Other verbs which have the Attic reduplication are ἀγείρω, ἀλείφω, ἀλέω, ἐγείρω, ἐρείδω, ἔρχομαι, ἐσθίω, ὄμνυμι, φέρω. See also, for Ionic or poetic forms, αἱρέω, ἀλάομαι, ἀλυκτέω, ἀραρίσκω, ἐρείπω, ἐρίζω, ἔχω, ἠμύω, (ὀδυ-) ὀδώδυσμαι, ὄζω, ὀράω (ὄπωπα), ὀρέγω, ὄρνῡμι (ὀρ-).

557. Ἐγείρω (ἐγερ-) *rouse* has 2 perf. ἐγρ-ήγορα for ἐγ-ηγορα, with ρ repeated in the reduplication; but perf. mid. ἐγ-ήγερμαι.

558. By strict Attic usage the pluperfect takes a temporal augment in addition to the Attic reduplication. E.g. ἀκούω *hear*, ἀκήκοα, plup.

ἠκηκόη; so ἀπ-ωλώλει (ἀπ-όλλῡμι, ἀπ-όλωλα), ὠμωμόκει (ὄμνῡμι, ὀμώμοκα), and δι-ωρώρυκτο (δι-ορύττω, δι-ορώρυγμαι) occur in Attic prose. See also Homeric pluperfects of ἐλαύνω and ἐρείδω. But verbs with initial ε omit the additional augment, e.g. ἐλ-ηλέγμην (ἐλέγχω, ἐλήλεγμαι), ἐν-ηνέγμην (stem ἐνεκ-, see φέρω bear), ἐλ-ηλύθη (ἐλυθ-, pf. ἐλ-ήλυθα, see ἔρχομαι go, come).

REDUPLICATED AORISTS

559. The second aorist active and middle in all the moods and the participle often has a reduplication in Homer; e.g. πέφραδον from φράζω tell; πέπιθον from πείθω (πιθ-) persuade; τεταρπόμην (587) from τέρπω delight; κεκλόμην and κεκλόμενος (586) from κέλομαι command; ἤραρον from ἀραρίσκω (ἀρ-) join (556); ὤρορον from ὄρνῡμι (ὀρ-) rouse; πεπαλών (partic.) from πάλλω (παλ-) shake; κεκάμω (subj.) from κάμνω (καμ-) labor, so λελάχω from λαγχάνω obtain a lot; πεφιδέσθαι, inf. from φείδομαι (φιδ-) spare, so λε-λαθέσθαι, λε-λαβέσθαι. From ἀλέξω ward off we have ἄλαλκον (ἀλ-αλκ-), from ἐνίπτω chide ἠνίπ-απ-ον, from ἐρύκω check ἠρύκακον. In the indicative the syllabic augment may be prefixed to the reduplication; e.g. ἐκεκλόμην, ἔπεφνον (from φεν-), ἐπέφραδον.

560. In Attic the 2 aorist of ἄγω is reduplicated and adds the temporal augment. E.g. ἤγ-αγ-ον (ἀγ-αγ-), subj. ἀγάγω, opt. ἀγάγοιμι, inf. ἀγαγεῖν, part. ἀγαγών; mid. ἠγαγόμην, ἀγάγωμαι, etc. Φέρω bear has aorists ἤνεγκα and ἤνεγκον (stem ἐν-εγκ-).

REDUPLICATED PRESENTS

561. A few verbs reduplicate in the present by prefixing the initial consonant with ι; e.g. γι-γνώσκω know, τί-θημι (for θι-θημι, 105) place, γί-γνομαι become, ἵστημι (for σι-στημι), δί-δωμι, πῑπτω fall (πι-πτ-ω), μι-μνήσκω remind, τίκτω give birth (for τι-τκ-ω, full stem τεκ-, 106). In πίμ-πλημι fill and πίμ-πρημι set fire to, μ is inserted. One verb, τε-τραίνω bore, has ε in the reduplicated present.
For these see 604 and 605, with 612.

AUGMENT AND REDUPLICATION OF COMPOUND VERBS

562. In compound verbs (868 a) the augment or reduplication follows the preposition. Prepositions (except περί and πρό) here drop a final vowel before ε. E.g.

προσ-γράφω add in writing, προσ-έγραφον, προσ-γέγραφα; εἰσ-άγω introduce, εἰσ-ῆγον (152 a); ἐκ-βάλλω eject, ἐξ-έβαλλον, ἐκ-βέβληκα (116); ἐμ-βάλλω throw in, ἐν-έβαλλον, ἐμ-βέβληκα; συλ-λέγω collect, ⌜συν-έλεγον; συμ-πλέκω weave together, συν-έπλεκον (72); συγ-χέω confound, συν-έχεον, συγ-κέχυκα;

συ-σκευάζω pack up, συν-εσκεύαζον (77 a); ἀπο-βάλλω throw away, ἀπ-έβαλλον; ἀνα-βαίνω go up, ἀν-έβην; but περί-έβαλλον and προ-έλεγον.

563. Πρό may be contracted with the augment; e.g. προύλεγον and προύβαινον, for προέλεγον and προέβαινον.

564. Ἐξ, ἐν, and σύν in composition before ε resume their proper forms if they have been changed in the present. See ἐξέβαλλον, ἐνέβαλλον, συνέλεγον, in 562.

565. Some denominative verbs (851), derived from substantives or adjectives compounded with prepositions, are augmented or reduplicated after the preposition, like compound verbs; e.g. ὑποπτεύω suspect (from ὕποπτος), ὑπώπτευον, as if the verb were from ὑπό and ὀπτεύω; ἐπιδημέω be in town (from ἐπίδημος), ἐπεδήμησα; ἀπολογέομαι defend one's self, ἀπελογησάμην; even ἐξεκλησίαζον, from ἐκκλησία assembly, and παρηνόμουν, from παρα-νομέω transgress law. Κατηγορέω accuse (from κατήγορος) has κατηγόρουν (not ἐκατηγόρουν). See διαιτάω and διᾱκονέω in the Catalogue of Verbs. Such verbs are called indirect compounds (868 b).

566. Other indirect compounds are augmented or reduplicated at the beginning; e.g. οἰκοδομέω build (from οἰκοδόμος house-builder), ᾠκοδόμουν, ᾠκοδόμησα, ᾠκοδόμηται; μυθολογέω tell stories (from μῦθολόγος), ἐμῦθολόγουν; ὁδοποιέω (from ὁδο-ποιός) make a road, ὡδοποίουν.

567. A few verbs usually found only in compound form in prose are treated as simple verbs and take the augment before the preposition, and others have both augments; e.g. καθέζομαι sit, ἐκαθέζετο; καθίζω, ἐκάθιζον; καθεύδω sleep, ἐκάθευδον and καθηῦδον (epic καθεῦδον); ἀνέχω, ἠνειχόμην, ἠνεσχόμην (or ἠνσχόμην); ἀφίημι, ἀφίην or ἠφίην. See also ἀμφιέννῦμι, ἀμφιγνοέω, ἀμπίσχομαι, ἐνοχλέω, and ἀμφισβητέω dispute, impf. ἠμφισβήτουν and ἠμφεσβήτουν.

568. a. Indirect compounds of δυσ- ill, and occasionally those of εὖ well, are augmented or reduplicated after the adverb, if the following part begins with a short vowel. E.g.

δυσαρεστέω be displeased, δυσηρέστουν; εὐεργετέω do good, εὐεργέτηκα or εὐηργέτηκα. But inscriptions allow only εὐεργέτηκα.

b. In other cases, compounds of δυσ- have the augment or reduplication at the beginning, e.g. δυστυχέω (from δυσ-τυχής unfortunate), ἐδυστύχουν, δεδυστύχηκα; and those of εὖ generally omit the augment (especially in the inscriptions).

TENSE STEMS AND MOOD SUFFIXES

569. Tense Stems are formed by modification of the verb through the addition of certain suffixes, such as the thematic vowel (571), and various other sound elements.

570. Simple tense stems without suffix are found

a. In the present, imperfect, and second aorist active and middle and the second perfect and pluperfect of μι verbs (except in the subjunctive, which has the thematic vowel); e.g. stem φη, φα, φη-μί, φα-μέν, ἔ-φα-τε, but subjv. φῶμεν (for φα-ω-μεν).

b. In the perfect and pluperfect middle of all verbs, both in ω and in μι; e.g. stem λῡ, reduplicated λελυ-, λέλυ-μαι, ἐ-λελύ-μην.

571. Thematic Vowel. *a.* In the present, imperfect, and second aorist active and middle of ω verbs, in all futures, and in the future perfect, the tense stem ends in a thematic, or variable, vowel (467), which is ο before μ and ν and in the optative (of the tenses just mentioned), and is elsewhere ε. This is written $^o/\epsilon$; e.g. λῡ$^o/\epsilon$, present stem of λύω; λιπ$^o/\epsilon$, second aorist stem of λείπω.

b. The subjunctive has a long thematic vowel $^\omega/\eta$ in both ω and μι verbs; e.g. λύω-μεν, λύσω-μεν, τιθῶ-μεν for τιθέ-ω-μεν, θῆτε for θέ-η-τε. But Homer has $^o/\epsilon$, e.g. ἴομεν *let us go* (655).

572. Tense Suffixes. The suffixes, when such are used, which form the various tense systems are as follows:

1. Present, $^o/\epsilon$, τ$^o/\epsilon$, ι̯$^o/\epsilon$, ν$^o/\epsilon$, αν$^o/\epsilon$, νε$^o/\epsilon$, να, νυ, ισκ$^o/\epsilon$. Cf. **570**.
2. Future, σ$^o/\epsilon$.
3. First aorist, σα.
4. Second aorist, $^o/\epsilon$, e.g. ἐ-λίπ-ο-μεν, ἐ-λίπ-ε-τε; or none, e.g. ἔ-δο-μεν, ἔ-δο-τε (**570**), where ο belongs to the verb stem.
5. First perfect, κα.
6. Second perfect, α.
7. Perfect middle, none (**570** *b*); but future perfect, σ$^o/\epsilon$.
8. First passive, aorist θη, θε, future θησ$^o/\epsilon$.
9. Second passive, aorist η, ε, future ησ$^o/\epsilon$.

573. Mood Suffixes. The optative mood is distinguished by the suffix ῑ or ιη, contracting with the final vowel of the stem; e.g. λύοιτε for λύο-ῑ-τε, ἱσταίην for ἱστα-ιη-ν. In the first person singular the ending is always μι after ῑ, ν after ιη; e.g. λύο-ι-μι, φιλοίην (for φιλεο-ίη-ν). Ιη is shortened to ιε in the third plural before ν, e.g. λύο-ιε-ν, λυ-θε-ῖε-ν.

574. The form ιη appears only before active endings (which are used also in the aorist passive). It is found

a. In the *singular* of μι verbs, present and 2 aorist; of athematic 2 aorists (i.e. 2 aorists of ω verbs inflected without thematic vowel); and of the aorist passive; e.g. *ἱστα-ίη-ν, στα-ίη-ν, βα-ίη-ν*

(2 aor. opt. of βαίνω), λυθε-ίη-ν. In the dual and plural of all these tenses ῑ is more common; e.g. ἱστα-ῖ-μεν, στα-ῖ-τε, λυθε-ῖ-τε. Verbs in -νῡμι make the optative like λύω, e.g. δεικνύοιμι.

  b. In the *singular* of contracted presents in -ῴην and -οίην, rarely in the dual and plural; e.g. τῑμαο-ίη-ν, τῑμῴην; φιλεο-ίη-ν, φιλοίην. So in the future active singular of nasal and liquid verbs, e.g. φανεο-ίη-ν, φανοίην. Dual and plural: φανεό-ῑ-τον, φανοῖτον; φανεό-ῑ-μεν, φανοῖμεν.

  c. The 2 aorist of ἔχω *have*, ἔσχον, has opt. σχοίην when not compounded; but κατάσχοιμι.

  575. Forms like λύσειας, λύσειε, λύσειαν are more common in prose (except Plato) than λύσαις, λύσαι, λύσαιεν (656, 764).

  576. Poetry uses the shorter forms in -ιμεν, -ιτε, -ιεν instead of the longer -ιημεν, -ιητε, -ιησαν. Prose uses both, but the shorter are commoner except in the second plural of uncontracted verbs, e.g. βαίητε, λυθείητε, δοίητε; but contracted φιλοῖτε. Cf. 509 c.

ENDINGS

  577. The verb is inflected by adding certain endings to the different tense stems. Those which mark the persons in the finite moods are called personal endings. There is one class of endings for the active voice, and another for the middle and passive; but the first and second passive aorists have the active endings.

  There is also one set of endings in each class for primary tenses, and one for secondary tenses.

  578. The personal endings of the indicative, subjunctive, optative, and imperative, which are most distinctly preserved in verbs in μι and other primitive forms, are as follows:

| | | ACTIVE | | MIDDLE AND PASSIVE | |
		INDICATIVE (*Primary Tenses*) AND SUBJUNCTIVE	INDICATIVE (*Secondary Tenses*) AND OPTATIVE	INDICATIVE (*Primary Tenses*) AND SUBJUNCTIVE	INDICATIVE (*Secondary Tenses*) AND OPTATIVE
Sing.	1.	μι	ν	μαι	μην
	2.	s (σι), θα (σθα)	s, σθα	σαι	σο
	3.	σι (τι)	—	ται	το

Dual	2.	τον	τον	σθον	σθον
	3.	τον	την	σθον	σθην
Plur.	1.	μεν (μες)	μεν (μες)	μεθα	μεθα
	2.	τε	τε	σθε	σθε
	3.	νσι (ντι)	ν, σαν	νται	ντο

<table>
<thead>
<tr><th colspan="4">ACTIVE</th><th colspan="3">MIDDLE AND PASSIVE</th></tr>
<tr><th></th><th colspan="3">IMPERATIVE</th><th></th><th></th><th></th></tr>
<tr><th>Sing.</th><th>Dual</th><th>Plur.</th><th></th><th>Sing.</th><th>Dual</th><th>Plur.</th></tr>
</thead>
<tbody>
<tr><td>2.</td><td>θι</td><td>τον</td><td>τε</td><td>σο</td><td>σθον</td><td>σθε</td></tr>
<tr><td>3.</td><td>τω</td><td>των</td><td>ντων (τωσαν)</td><td>σθω</td><td>σθων</td><td>σθων (σθωσαν)</td></tr>
</tbody>
</table>

579. The endings of the infinitive are as follows:

ACTIVE: **εν** (contracted with preceding ε to ειν), in present and 2 aorist of ω verbs and in future active, e.g. λύε-εν λύειν, λιπέ-εν λιπεῖν, φιλέε-εν φιλεῖν, λύσε-εν λύσειν, τῑμάε-εν τῑμᾶν (45 e).

αι, in first aorist active, e.g. λῦσ-αι, τῑμῆσ-αι, στῆσ-αι.

ναι, in first and second aorists passive, present and 2 perfect of μι verbs, and perfect active, e.g. λυθῆ-ναι, φανῆ-ναι, τιθέ-ναι, ἑστά-ναι, λελυκέ-ναι.

εναι (for ϝεναι) in the 2 aorist of μι verbs, e.g. θεῖναι (for θέ-ϝεναι), δοῦναι (for δό-ϝεναι).

MIDDLE AND PASSIVE: **σθαι**, e.g. λύε-σθαι, δίδο-σθαι, λελύ-σθαι.

580. The endings added to the tense stem to form participial stems are as follows:

ACTIVE: **ντ**, in all active tenses except the perfect, and in the aorists passive (329).

οτ, in perfect active (329).

MIDDLE AND PASSIVE: **μενο**.

581. The verbal adjectives have the endings τός and τέος, added to the verb stem of the 1 or 2 aorist passive; e.g. λυ-τός, λυ-τέος, πεισ-τέος (ἐπείσ-θην from πείθ-ω), τακτός, τακτέος (ἐτάχ-θην from τάττω), θρεπτός from τρέφ-ω (105 e), τατός from ἐτάθην (τείνω), σταλτός from ἐστάλην (στέλλω).

REMARKS ON THE ENDINGS

582. a. Only verbs in μι have the primary endings μι and σι in the indicative active. The ω of λύω, λύσω, etc. is the thematic vowel lengthened, without personal ending. In the perfect indicative the ending α is unexplained. The original σι of the second person singular is found only in the epic ἐσ-σί *thou art* (510 *a*). The *s* of other forms, e.g. τίθη-ς, is probably the secondary ending. Θα (originally perfect ending) appears in οἶσθα (for οἰδ-θα) from οἶδα (529) and in ἦσ-θα from εἰμί (509) ; whence (σ)θα in many Homeric forms (655 *d*, 669 *d*), and rarely in Attic (e.g. ἔφη-σθα). In the third person singular τι is Doric, e.g. τίθη-τι for τίθη-σι ; and it is preserved in Attic in ἐσ-τί *is*. The ending in λύει, φέρει, etc. cannot be explained with certainty.

b. A first person dual in μεθον is found three times in poetry : περιδώ-μεθον, subj. of περιδίδωμι, *Il.* 23, 485 ; λελείμμεθον, from λείπω, S. *El.* 950 ; ὁρμώμεθον, from ὁρμάω, S. *Ph.* 1079. Generally the first person plural is used also for the dual.

c. In Homer τον and σθον are used rarely for την and σθην in the third person dual of past tenses.

d. In the first person plural μες is Doric. The poets often have μεσθα for μεθα (654 *a*).

e. In the third person plural νσι always drops ν (75) and the preceding vowel is lengthened (32) ; e.g. λύουσι for λύο-νσι. Here Aeolic has λύοισι, τίμαισι, φίλεισι, etc. The more primitive ντι is seen in Doric φερό-ντι (Lat. fe r u n t) for φέρουσι. An ending αντι appears in τιθέ-ᾱσι (τιθέ-αντι), διδόᾱσι (διδό-αντι), ἱστᾶσι (ἱστά-αντι), whence the same accent was given to Homeric τιθεῖσι and διδοῦσι (Dor. τιθέ-ντι, διδό-ντι) ; ᾱσι also appears in the perfect, λελύκᾱσι, though here the ending was originally ἀσι, e.g. Hom. πεφύκασι, λελόγχᾱσι, implying an ending ἄτι for ντι (27). But Hom. has ᾱσι in ἔᾱσι (εἰσί), ἴᾱσι (*they go*), βεβάᾱσι, γεγάᾱσι (perfects of βαίνω and γίγνομαι).

f. The secondary ending ν (first person) is for μ (24), which becomes α after a consonant, e.g. ἔλῡσα for ἐλῡσμ (27). This is extended to the pluperfect, where ε-α contracts to η. N is used in the optative if the mood suffix is ιη, e.g. ἱσταίην ; otherwise μι, e.g. λύοιμι. T, the ending of the third singular, is dropped (24), e.g. ἔλῡε, ἐλύθη, λύοι. A throughout the first aorist is due to the first person (ἔλῡσα) ; ε in the third person is borrowed from the perfect, without personal ending. In the third plural ν is for ντ (24). Σαν arose in the first aorist (ἔλῡσαν), thence extended to the aorist passive (ἐλύθη-σαν), the imperfect and second aorist of μι verbs (ἵστα-σαν, ἔστη-σαν), the pluperfect (ἐλελύκε-σαν, ἔστα-σαν), and the optative if the mood suffix is ιη (σταίη-σαν).

g. In the middle σαι is retained in the perfect, also in the present indicative of μι verbs ; σο is retained in the pluperfect, and in the imperfect of μι verbs. Elsewhere σ is lost, and εαι (e.g. in Hom. βούλεαι) contracts to η, written ει from about 400 B.C. Βούλει (not βούλη), οἴει, and ὄψει are always written with ει. See 667, 678. Σο also loses σ between vowels, e.g. ἐλύσεο, Ion. ἐλύεο, Att. ἐλύου. Σ disappears in σθε, second person plural, between consonants (83). Σθε is not original, however, but extended from σ stems (e.g. τετέλεσ-θε) to other verbs. In the third plural νται and ντο are retained after vowels. After consonants they become αται, ατο (27, 654 *c*), e.g. τετάχαται (Attic τεταγμένοι εἰσί).

h. Θι seldom appears in the imperative, except in the second aorist active of μι forms (**787**), and in the aorist passive, which has the active forms (**577**).

In the third person plural of the imperative the endings ντων and σθων are used in the older Attic; τωσαν and σθωσαν appear in inscriptions of the Alexandrian age, but in earlier literature only in Euripides and Thucydides.

FORMATION AND INFLECTION OF TENSE SYSTEMS

583. To understand the inflection of the verb, we must know the relation of each tense stem to the verb stem, and also certain internal modifications which the verb stem undergoes in some of the tense systems. Some verbs retain the same primary stem throughout all, or nearly all, the tense systems; e.g. λέγ-ω *say*, λέξω, ἔλεξα, λέλεγμαι, ἐλέχθην, λεχθήσομαι. Here the present stem and the verb stem are identical.

584. Many verbs vary the quantity of the vowel in the verb stem, e.g. λῡ́ω, λῡ́σω, ἔλῡσα, λέλῠκα, λέλῠμαι, ἐλῠ́θην.

585. Vowel Gradation (**31, 34**) appears in many verb stems. The normal grade generally shows ε or ο, with a variety η or ω, the weak grade shows α, ι, υ. Ο and ω appear in the perfect; the weak grade in the second aorists, active, middle, and passive. Thus the series ε, ο, α appears in κλέπ-τ-ω *steal*, κλέψω, ἔκλεψα, κέ-κλοφ-α, ἐ-κλάπ-ην (**27**); τρέπ-ω *turn*, τρέψω, ἔτρεψα, ἐτραπ-όμην (**27**), τέ-τροφ-α, τέ-τραμμαι (**27**), ἐ-τρέφ-θην and ἐ-τράπ-ην. Η, ω, α (not common): ῥήγ-νῡμι *break*, ῥήξω, ἔρρηξα, ἔ-ρρωγ-α, ἐ-ρράγην; τήκω *melt*, τήξω, ἔτηξα, τέτηκα, ἐτήχθην and ἐτάκην. Cf. ἀρήγ-ω *help*, ἀρωγ-ός *helper*. Diphthongs ει, οι, ι: λείπ-ω, λείψω, λέ-λοιπ-α, ἔ-λιπ-ον. Ευ, ου, υ: φεύγ-ω *flee*, φεύξομαι, πέφευγ-α (perhaps for πε-φουγ-α), ἔ-φυγ-ον. Cf. σπεύδ-ω *hasten*, σπουδ-ή *haste*.

586. The weak grade shows the loss of ε through early conditions of accent, leaving (between consonants) α, or the ι and υ of diphthongs. But between vowels no α is necessary; hence present γί-γν-ο-μαι *become*, cf. γέν-ος *family*, γόν-ος *child*; πέτ-ομαι *fly*, ἐ-πτ-ό-μην *flew*, πῐ-πτ-ω *fall*; ἔχ-ω *have* (for σεχ-ω), ἕξω, ἔ-σχ-ο-ν.

587. Verb stems ending in a liquid or nasal are apt to show the weak grade α in the first perfect, perfect middle, and second aorist passive; rarely in the first aorist active. The second perfect has ο, the other tenses ε. E.g.

δέρ-ω *flay*, δερῶ, ἔδειρα, δέ-δαρ-μαι, ἐ-δάρ-ην (for ο cf. the noun δορ-ά *skin*); στέλλω *send* (στελ-), perf. ἔ-σταλ-κα, ἔ-σταλ-μαι, 2 aor. pass. ἐ-στάλ-ην; φθείρω *destroy* (φθερ-), 1 perf. ἔ-φθαρ-κα, 2 perf. ἔ-φθορ-α, ἔ-φθαρ-μαι, ἐ-φθάρ-ην; τείνω *stretch* (τεν-), perf. τέ-τα-κα (for τε-τν-κα, 27), τέ-τα-μαι, ἐ-τά-θην; κτείνω *kill* (κτεν-), perf. ἀπ-έ-κτον-α (in composition only), 2 aor. ἔ-κταν-ον (poetic). So some other verbs, not ending in a liquid or nasal, e.g. πλέκ-ω *weave*, 2 perf. πέπλοχα, ἐπλάκην; στρέφ-ω *turn*, ἔστροφα, ἔστραμμαι, ἐστράφην; τρέφ-ω *nourish*, τέτροφα, τέθραμμαι, ἐτράφην.

588. A lengthened grade ω sometimes appears in the series ε, ο, α, ω; cf. τρέπω *turn*, τέτροφα, ἐτράπην, and τρωπάω *turn*; στρέφω, στρωφάω, πέτομαι *fly*, πωτάομαι. These forms are suspected and are probably not original.

589. In some verbs α of the stem is lengthened to η or ᾱ in the second perfect. These are ἄγνῡμι (ϝαγ-) *break*, ἔᾱγα; θάλλω (θαλ-) *flourish*, τέθηλα; κράζω *shriek*, κέκρᾱγα; λάσκω *utter*, λέλᾱκα (Hom. partic. λελᾱκυῖα); μαίνομαι *rage*, μέμηνα; σαίρω *grin*, σέσηρα; φαίνω *show*, πέφηνα.

590. ε added to the Stem. *a.* The present stem is sometimes formed by adding ε to the verb stem; e.g. δοκέ-ω *seem* (δοκ-), δόξω, ἔδοξα; γαμέ-ω *marry* (γαμ-), γαμῶ, ἔγημ-α, γε-γάμη-κα; ὠθέ-ω *push* (ϝωθ-), ὤσω.

b. Some verbs in ε, many of them denominatives like φιλέω *love*, have alternative presents without ε; e.g. γεγωνέω and γεγώνω, γηθέω, κτυπέω, κυρέω, μαρτυρέω, ῥῑπτέω and ῥῑπτω; poetic δουπέω, εἰλέω, ἐπαυρέω, κελαδέω, κεντέω, πατέομαι, ῥῑγέω, στυγέω, τορέω, χραισμέω.

c. Other tense stems, but not the present, second aorist, or second perfect, sometimes have ε; e.g. βούλ-ομαι *wish*, fut. βουλή-σομαι (594); αἰσθ-άνομαι *perceive*, αἰσθή-σομαι, ἤσθη-μαι; μάχ-ομαι *fight*, μαχέ-σομαι, μαχοῦμαι (90), ἐ-μαχε-σάμην, με-μάχη-μαι. So also ἁμαρτάνω *err*, αὐξάνω *increase*, δέω *want*, ἐθέλω *wish*, εὑρίσκω *find*, ἕψω *boil*, μανθάνω *learn*, μέλλω *intend*, μέλει *it concerns*, οἴομαι *think*, οἴχομαι *am gone*.

d. A few have ε in special tenses only; e.g. μένω *remain*, perfect με-μένη-κα; ἔχω *have*, ἔ-σχη-κα; νέμω *distribute*, νε-νέμη-κα. So γενή-σομαι, γεγένη-μαι (γίγνομαι *become*), δραμοῦμαι, δε-δράμη-κα *run*, but aor. ἔδραμ-ον.

591. A few verbs, chiefly poetic, add α to the verb stem. See βρῡχάομαι, γοάω, δημιάω, μηκάομαι, μητιάω, μῡκάομαι (2 aor. μύκον).

592. In ὄμνῡμι *swear* the stem ὀμ- appears also as ὀμο- in aor. ὤμο-σα, perf. ὀμ-ώμο-κα (554). So ἁλίσκομαι *be captured* (ἁλ-), fut. ἁλώ-σομαι (694); οἴχομαι (οἰχ-) *be gone* (590), poet. perf. ᾤχω-κα.

593. Lengthening of Vowels. Most stems ending in a short vowel lengthen this vowel before the tense suffix in all tenses formed from them, except the present and imperfect. A and ε become η, and ο becomes ω; but α after ε, ι, or ρ becomes ᾱ (31). E.g.

τῑμάω (τῑμα-) *honor,* τῑμή-σω, ἐτίμη-σα, τετίμη-κα, τετίμη-μαι, ἐτῑμή-θην; φιλέω (φιλε-) *love,* φιλήσω, ἐφίλησα, πεφίληκα, πεφίλημαι, ἐφιλήθην; δηλόω (δηλο-) *show,* δηλώσω, ἐδήλωσα, δεδήλωκα; δακρύω *weep,* δακρύσω. But ἐάω *let,* ἐάσω; ἰάομαι *heal,* ἰάσομαι; δράω *do,* δράσω, ἔδρᾱσα, δέδρᾱκα.

594. This applies also to stems which become vowel stems by adding ε (590); e.g. βούλομαι (βουλ-, βουλε-) *wish,* βουλή-σομαι, βεβούλη-μαι, ἐβουλή-θην. So stems which were originally dissyllabic are lengthened when the vowel of the first syllable was suppressed; e.g. κάμ-νω *be weary* (καμ-, καμα-), perf. κέ-κμη-κα, cf. κάμα-τος *toil;* βάλλω *throw,* perf. βέβληκα, cf. βέλος (βελεσ-) *missile.* This occurs also in the present θνήσκω *die* (θαν-, θανα-), cf. θάνα-τος *death,* 2 aorist ἔ-θαν-ον and perfect τέ-θνη-κα; also in future πτή-σομαι, from πέτ-ομαι *fly* (πετα-, πετ-). 107.

595. Ἀκροάομαι *hear* has ἀκροάσομαι etc.; χράω *give oracles* has χρήσω etc. (486). So τρήσω and ἔτρησα from stem τρᾰ-; see τετραίνω *bore.*

596. Some vowel stems retain the short vowel, contrary to the general rule (593); e.g. γελάω *laugh,* γελάσομαι, ἐγέλᾰσα; ἀρκέω *suffice,* ἀρκέσω, ἤρκεσα; μάχομαι (μαχε-) *fight,* μαχέσομαι (Ion.), ἐμαχεσάμην.

(a) This occurs in the following verbs: ἄγαμαι, αἰδέομαι, ἀκέομαι, ἀλέω, ἀνύω, ἀρκέω, ἀρόω, ἀρύω, γελάω, ἐλκύω (see ἕλκω), ἐμέω, ἐράω, ζέω, θλάω, κλάω *break,* ξέω, πτύω, σπάω, τελέω, τρέω, φλάω, χαλάω; and epic ἀκηδέω, κοτέω, λοέω, νεικέω, and the stems ἀα- and ἀε-; also ἀρέσκω (ἀρε-), ἄχθομαι (ἀχθε-), ἐλαύνω (ἐλα-), ἱλάσκομαι (ἱλα-), μεθύσκω (μεθυ-); and all verbs in αννῡμι and εννῡμι, with ὄλλῡμι (ὀλε-) and ὄμνῡμι (ὀμο-).

(b) The final vowel of the stem is variable in quantity in different tenses in the following verbs: αἰνέω, αἱρέω, δέω *bind,* δύω (see δύνω), ἐρύω (epic), θύω *sacrifice,* καλέω, λύω, μύω, ποθέω, πονέω; also βαίνω (βα-), εὑρίσκω (εὑρ-, εὑρε-), μάχομαι (μαχε-), πίνω (πι-, πο-), φθάνω (φθα-), φθίνω (φθι-).

597. Most of the verbs retaining the short vowel have verb stems ending in σ, and are not vowel stems, as their Homeric forms show. Thus αἰδέομαι *be ashamed,* Hom. fut. αἰδέσ-σομαι, stem αἰδεσ-, cf. ἀν-αιδής *shameless* (306, 243); τελέω *finish,* Hom. aor. ἐ-τέλεσ-σα, cf. τέλος *end* (232). When σσ became σ, as in ἐτέλεσα (85), ε was retained.

598. Stems which retain the short vowel (596), and some others, have σ before all endings *not beginning with* σ in the perfect and pluperfect middle. The same verbs have σ before θη or θε in the first passive tense system. E.g.

τελέω *finish,* τετέλεσ-μαι, ἐτετέλεσ-μην, ἐτελέσ-θην, τελεσ-θήσομαι; but τε-τέλε-σαι, τετέλε-σθε; γελάω *laugh,* ἐγελάσ-θην, γελασθῆναι. So, by analogy, other verbs, not belonging under 596 or 597, have this σ: χράω *give oracles,* χρήσω, κέχρη-σ-μαι, ἐχρήσ-θην; γιγνώσκω *know,* ἔγνωσ-μαι, ἐγνώσ-θην; κελεύω *command,* κεκέλευσ-μαι, ἐκελεύσ-θην.

599. This σ does not appear in the perfect middle stem unless it occurs in the passive system, and even then it is sometimes lacking, e.g. ἐπ-αινέω *praise*, ἐπήνημαι, ἐπαινεσθήσομαι. It is proper to σ stems (597) e.g. τετέλεσμαι, and to dental stems before the dental of the third singular and second plural endings ται and θε (66), e.g. πείθ-ω *persuade*, πέπεισται, πέπεισθε; νομίζω *think* (νομιδ-), νενόμισται. Thence it extended to the other persons πέπεισμαι, νενόμισμαι, etc.

600. This σ occurs in all the verbs of 596 (*a*) except ἀρόω, so far as they form these tenses; and in the following: ἀκούω, δράω, θραύω, κελεύω, κλείω (κλήω), κνάω, κναίω, κρούω, κυλίω (or κυλίνδω), λεύω, νέω *heap*, ξύω, παίω, παλαίω, παύω, πλέω, πρίω, σείω, τίνω, ὕω, χόω, χράω, χρίω, and poetic ῥαίω. Some, however, have forms both with and without σ.

601. A suffix θ, of uncertain origin, is added to stems of some poetic verbs; e.g. πλή-θ-ω *be full*, cf. πίμ-πλη-μι *fill*; πύ-θ-ω *rot*, cf. πύ-ον *pus*; ἐδιώκαθον, διώκω *pursue*; ἔσχεθον, ἔχω *have*; φλεγέθω, φλέγω *burn*. From these special forms are derived, — sometimes presents, e.g. φλεγέθω; imperfects, e.g. ἐδιώκαθον; second aorists, e.g. ἔσχεθον; subjunctives and optatives, e.g. εἰκάθω, εἰκάθοιμι; imperatives, e.g. ἀμυνάθετε; infinitives, e.g. διωκάθειν, εἰκάθειν, σχεθεῖν; participles, e.g. εἰκάθων, σχεθών. Since many, aside from a few presents like φλεγέθω, have an aoristic meaning, many scholars regard ἐδιώκαθον, εἴργαθον, etc., as second aorists, and accent the infinitives and participles διωκαθεῖν, ἐργαθεῖν, εἰκαθών, etc.

602. ν **of stem dropped.** A few verbs in -νω drop ν of the stem in the perfect and first passive systems:

κρίνω (κριν-) *separate*, κέκρικα, κέκριμαι, ἐκρίθην; κλίνω (κλιν-) *incline*, κέκλικα, κέκλιμαι, ἐκλίθην; πλῡνω (πλυν-) *wash*, πέπλυμαι, ἐπλύθην. But τείνω (τεν-) *stretch*, τέτακα, τέταμαι, ἐτάθην, ἐκ-ταθήσομαι, and κτείνω *kill* in some poetic forms, e.g. ἐκτά-θην, ἐκτά-μην, belong under 587. For the regular Homeric ἐκλίνθην and ἐκρίνθην, see 740.

603. When final ν of a stem is not thus dropped, it becomes nasal γ before κα (72), and is generally replaced by σ before μαι (74); e.g. φαίνω (φαν-), πέφαγκα, πέφασμαι, ἐφάνθην. See 732.

604. The verb stem may appear in the weak grade (586):

(1) in the present, e.g. γίγνομαι (γεν-) *become*, for γι-γν-ομαι, γενή-σομαι, ἐ-γεν-όμην, γέ-γον-α; ἴσχω *hold*, for σι-σχ-ω, cf. ἔχω (σεχ-); τίκτω *bear* (106); without reduplication (605), βαίνω *go* (βα-, 629), fut. βή-σομαι; εὑρί-σκω *find* (base heurēi-), fut. εὑρή-σω; ἀλί-σκομαι *am caught* (base halōi-), fut. ἁλώ-σομαι; λαμβάνω *take* (λαβ-, 638), fut. λήψομαι.

(2) in the second aorist, e.g. ἐ-πτ-όμην, πέτ-ομαι *fly* (cf. 594); ἐ-δάρ-ην, pres. δέρ-ω (*flay*); ἐ-τράπ-ην, pres. τρέπ-ω *turn*; ἐτράφ-ην, pres. τρέφ-ω *nourish* (27).

(3) in the perfect, e.g. πέ-πτα-μαι, pres. πετά-ννυμι *expand* (640); δέ-δαρ-μαι, pres. δέρ-ω *flay*; λέ-λὔ-κα, pres. λὔ-ω *loose*.

605. Reduplication. The verb stem may be reduplicated in the present (561) and second aorist (559) as well as in the perfect (543):

(1) in the present, e.g. γι-γνώσκω *know*, γί-γνομαι, ἴσχω (604), μίμνω, πίπτω, τίκτω, and many verbs in μι and σκω.

(2) in the second aorist, e.g. πείθω *persuade*, πέ-πιθον (epic); so ἄγω, ἤγαγον (Attic). For other second aorists, see 559, 560.

606. Iteratives. Homer and Herodotus have forms in σκον and σκόμην, denoting customary or repeated action in the past, or occurrence step by step. They are formed from the imperfect and second aorist stems, in Homer also from the first aorist; e.g. ἔχω, ἔχε-σκον; ἐρύω, ἐρύσα-σκε; φεύγω, φύγε-σκον; ἵστημι (στα-), στά-σκε; δίδωμι (δο-), δόσκον; εἰμί (ἐσ-), ἔσκον for ἐσσκον; ζώννῡμι *gird*, ζωννύ-σκετο. Verbs in έω have εεσκον, in Hom. also εσκον; e.g. καλέ-εσκον, πωλέ-σκετο. Verbs in άω, rarely other verbs, have αασκον or ασκον, e.g. γοά-ασκε, νῑκά-σκομεν, κρύπτ-ασκε. Cf. 649.

These forms are inflected like imperfects, and are confined to the indicative. They generally (in Hdt. always) omit the augment.

FORMATION OF TENSE STEMS AND INFLECTION OF TENSE SYSTEMS IN THE INDICATIVE

I. *Present System*

607. The present stem is formed from the verb stem in various ways (572). Verbs are divided into four classes, with reference to the relation of the present stem to the verb stem. A fifth class consists of verbs of which the tense systems are made up of wholly differing and unrelated verb stems.

608. FIRST CLASS. Here the present stem is formed from the verb stem either with or without the thematic vowel.

609. With Thematic Vowel. Verbs of the First Class with thematic vowel add $^o/_\epsilon$ to form ω verbs. E.g.

λέγω *say* (λεγ-), present stem λεγ$^o/_\epsilon$, giving λέγο-μεν, λέγε-τε, λέγο-μαι, λέγε-ται, ἔ-λεγο-ν, ἐ-λέγε-σθε, etc.

610. When vowel gradation occurs in verbs of the First Class, the present has the normal full grade; e.g. λείπ-ω *leave*, φεύγ-ω *flee*, τήκ-ω *melt*.

611. In some verbs the diphthong ευ loses υ (ϝ) before the thematic vowel; e.g. θέω *run* (θευ-ω), but fut. θεύσομαι; νέω *swim*, perf. νέ-νευ-κα; πλέω *sail*, aor. ἔ-πλευ-σα; πνέω *breathe*, ἔ-πνευ-σα; ῥέω *flow*, ῥεύ-σομαι; χέω *pour* (stem χευ-, weak grade in κέ-χυ-μαι). See 37, 485.

612. Without Thematic Vowel. Verbs of the First Class without thematic vowel add the personal ending directly to the verb stem, which is sometimes reduplicated (605). E.g.

Not reduplicated: εἰμί *am* (ἐσ-), ἐσ-τί, εἶ-μι *go*, ἧμαι *sit* (ἡσ-), ἠ-μί *say*, κεῖ-μαι *lie*, φη-μί *say*, δύνα-μαι *can*, ἐπίστα-μαι *understand*, κρέμα-μαι *hang*, ἐ-πριά-μην *bought*. Reduplicated: ἴη-μι *send* (ση-, 514 *b*), ἵστη-μι (στη-) *set*, δίδω-μι *give*, ὀνίνη-μι *help* (ὀνη-).

613. πίμ-πλη-μι *fill* (πλη-) and πίμ-πρη-μι *set fire* (πρη-) may lose the inserted μ when compounded with ἐμ- ; e.g. ἐμπίπλημι, but ἐνεπίμπλην.

614. In the verbs of 612 the normal full grade appears in the singular, e.g. φη-μί, ἵστη-μι, τίθη-μι, δίδω-μι, εἶ-μι, εἰδ-ῶ (subjv.) ; the weak grade occurs in the dual and plural, e.g. φα-μέν, ἵστα-μεν, τίθε-μεν, δίδο-μεν, ἴ-μεν, ἴσ-μεν. Cf. 662, 728.

615. SECOND CLASS. *Iota Class.* In this class the present stem is formed by adding ι°/ε to the verb stem and making the phonetic changes which this occasions (93–100). The ι was a semivowel (26). There are five divisions.

616. I. *Verbs in ζω.* Presents in ζω may be formed from stems in δ, with futures in σω ; e.g. κομίζω *carry* (κομιδ-ι̯-ω, cf. κομιδ-ή), fut. κομίσω ; φράζω (φραδ-) *say*, fut. φράσω ; ἐλπίζω *hope* (ἐλπιδ-, cf. ἐλπίς (227)).

617. Presents in ζω may be formed from stems in γ (or γγ), with futures in ξω ; e.g. σφάζω *slay* (σφαγ-), fut. σφάξω ; ῥέζω (ϝρεγ-) *do* (poetic and Ionic), fut. ῥέξω ; κλάζω (κλαγγ-) *scream* (cf. Lat. clango), fut. κλάγξω ; ἁρπάζω *seize* (ἁρπαγ-ι̯-ω, cf. ἁρπαγ-ή) ; σαλπίζω *sound the trumpet* (σαλπιγγ-ή *trumpet*).

618. Some verbs in ζω have stems both in δ and in γ ; e.g. παίζω *play*, fut. παιξοῦμαι (679), aor. ἔπαισα. Cf. παιδ-ίον *child*, παίγ-νιον *toy*. See also poetic forms of ἁρπάζω *seize*. See 624.

619. Νίζω *wash*, fut. νίψω, also has two tems : an original base νειγυ-gave present νίζω ; νειγυ- became νειβ-, νιβ-, seen in Homeric νίπτομαι and later νίπτω. Cf. 622 *b*.

620. Most verbs in ζω, especially those in αζω, with futures in σω, are formed merely on the analogy of those with actual stems in δ or γ. E.g. νομίζω *think*, σῴζω *save* (stems σωι- and σω-), διπλασιάζω *double*.

621. II. *Verbs in πτω.* Some labial (π φ) verb stems add ι°/ε, and thus form the present in πτω ; e.g. κόπτ-ω (κοπ-) *cut* (present stem κοπτ°/ε-), θάπτ-ω (ταφ-) *bury*, ῥίπτ-ω (ῥῑφ-, ῥῐφ-) *throw* (66).

622. a. Here the exact form of the verb stem cannot be determined from the present. Thus, in the examples above given, the stem is to be found in the second aorists ἐκόπην, ἐτάφην, and ἐρρίφην.

b. In καλύπτω *cover* and βλάπτω *hurt* the original base was καλυβ- (cf. καλύβ-η *hut*) and μλακυ- (giving βλάβ-η *injury*, cf. Lat. mulco). See 94.

623. III. *Verbs in* ττω (σσω). Most presents in ττω, Ionic and later Attic σσω, come from palatal stems, in κ or χ. These have futures in ξω; e.g. μαλάττω *soften* (μαλακ-ι̯-ω, cf. μαλακ-ός *soft*), fut. μαλάξω; κηρύττω *proclaim* (κηρῡκ-ι̯-ω, cf. κῆρυξ *herald*), fut. κηρύξω; ταράττω *confuse* (ταραχ-ι̯-ω, cf. ταραχ-ή), fut. ταράξω.

624. Stems in γ with presents in ττω (σσω) are due to analogy, since γι normally becomes ζ (96, 617). E.g. σφάζω *slay* (σφαγ-), fut. σφάξω, developed a present σφάττω like ταράττω. Conversely ἁρπάζω (ἁρπαγ-) had a future ἁρπάσω as if it were a dental stem. By some such confusion arose πρᾱττω *do* (πρᾱγ-), πρᾱξω; τάττω *arrange* (ταγ-), τάξω; ἀλλάττω *change* (ἀλλαγ-); δράττομαι *clutch* (δραγ-); μάττω *knead* (μαγ-); πλήττω *strike* (πληγ-); σάττω *pack* (σαγ-); φράττω *fence in* (φραγ-). See 97, 618.

625. Some presents in ττω (σσω) are formed from dental stems, with futures in σω or aorists in σα. These also arose by analogy with stems in κ or χ; e.g. ἐρέσσω *row* (ἐρετ-, cf. ἐρέτ-ης *rower*), ἤρεσα; βλίττω *take honey from the hive* (μελιτ-, 108 a).

626. Πέττω *cook* makes its present as from a stem πεκ-; the other tenses, πέψω, ἔπεψα, etc., belong to stem πεπ- seen in later πέπτω.

627. IV. *Liquid and Nasal Stems.* Of these there are three subdivisions:

628. (1) Presents in λλω are formed from verb stems in λ with ι⁰/ε added, λι assimilating to λλ (98); e.g. στέλλω *send*, for στελ-ι̯ω; ἀγγέλλω *announce* (ἀγγελ-ι̯ω); σφάλλω *trip up* (σφαλ-ι̯ω).

629. (2) Presents in αινω and αιρω are formed from verb stems in αν and αρ with ι⁰/ε added. Here ι is transferred to the vowel of the verb stem, making it αι; e.g. φαίνω *show* (φαν-ι̯ω); χαίρω *rejoice* (χαρ-ι̯ω). See 99.

630. (3) Presents in εινω, ειρω, ῑνω, ῑρω, ῡνω, and ῡρω come from stems in εν, ερ, ἰν, ἰρ, ὐν, and ὐρ, with ι⁰/ε added.

Here ι disappears and the preceding ε, ι, or υ is lengthened to ει, ῑ, or ῡ (32); e.g. τείνω (τεν-) *stretch*, for τεν-ι̯-ω; κείρω (κερ-) *shear*, for κερ-ι̯-ω; κρίνω (κριν-) *judge*, for κριν-ι̯-ω; ἀμύνω (ἀμυν-) *ward off*, for ἀμυν-ι̯-ω; σύρω (συρ-) *draw*, for συρ-ι̯-ω. Οἰκτῑρω (οἰκτιρ-) *pity*, commonly written οἰκτείρω, is the only verb in ῑρω.

631. Ὀφείλω (ὀφελ-) *owe, ought*, follows the analogy of stems in εν, to avoid confusion with ὀφέλλω (ὀφελ-) *increase*; but in Homer it has the Aeolic present ὀφέλλω.

632. Verbs of this division (IV) regularly have futures and aorists active and middle of the liquid form (677). For exceptions in poetry, see 682.

633. Many verbs with liquid stems do not belong to this class; e.g. δέμω and δέρω in Class I; δέρω has a parallel form δείρω. For βαίνω etc. in Class III, see 643.

634. V. Presents in αω, εω, οω, and denominative verbs from stems in ι, υ, ω, originally had the suffix ι°/ε. So also stems originally ending in σ and ϝ, or in a long vowel; e.g. τῑμά-ω honor (τῑμα-ι̯ω), φιλέ-ω love (φιλε-ι̯ω), δηλό-ω show (δηλο-ι̯ω), μηνί-ω, also μηνῑ́-ω am angry (μηνι-ι̯ω), ἱππεύ-ω am a horseman (ἱππευ-ι̯ω), τελέω finish (τελεσ-ι̯ω). These verbs do not differ in appearance from those of Class I.

635. Here belong καίω burn (καιϝω, for καϝ-ι̯ω) and κλαίω weep (κλαιϝω, for κλαϝ-ι̯ω), with futures καύσω (καϝ-σω) and κλαύσομαι (κλαϝ-σ°/ε).

636. The poets form some other presents in this way; e.g. δαίω (δαϝ-) burn, ναίω (ναϝ-) swim. So from stems in ασ-, μαίομαι (μα(σ)-ι̯ο-μαι) seek, δαίομαι (δασ-) divide. Ὀπυίω marry has stem ὀπυ-, whence fut. ὀπύσω; φῑτύω beget is for φῑτῦ-ι̯ω.

637. THIRD CLASS. N Class. (1) Some verb stems are strengthened in the present by adding ν before the thematic vowel °/ε; e.g. φθάν-ω (φθα-) anticipate; φθίν-ω (φθι-) waste; δάκν-ω (δακ-) bite; κάμν-ω (καμ-) be weary; τέμν-ω (τεμ-) cut.

638. (2) (a) Some consonant stems add αν; ἁμαρτάν-ω (ἁμαρτ-) err; αἰσθάν-ομαι (αἰσθ-) perceive; βλαστάν-ω (βλαστ-) sprout.

(b) Here, if the last vowel of the stem is short, another nasal (μ before a labial, ν before a dental, γ before a palatal) is inserted after this vowel; e.g. λανθάν-ω (λαθ-, λανθ-) escape notice; λαμβάν-ω (λαβ-, λαμβ-) take; θιγ-γάνω (θιγ-, θιγγ-) touch.

639. (3) A few stems add νε: βῡνέ-ω (with βύ-ω) stop up, ἱκνέ-ομαι (with ἵκ-ω) come, κυνέ-ω (κυ-) kiss; also ἀμπ-ισχνέ-ομαι am dressed and ὑπ-ισχνέ-ομαι promise (cf. ἴσχ-ω hold).

640. (4) Some stems add νυ or (after a vowel) νννν; e.g. δείκνῡ-μι (δεικ-) show, κεράννῡ-μι (κερα-) mix, ὄλλῡμι destroy (for ὀλ-νῡμι), ἕννῡμι clothe (ἑσ-, 86 c), σβέννῡμι (σβεσ-) extinguish.

641. Ἐλαύνω (ἐλα-) drive is for ἐλα-νυ-ω. Some presents in νω are from νϝ°/ε for νυ°/ε; e.g. Hom. ἱκάνω come to (ἱκᾱ-νϝ-ω), τίνω pay (τι-νϝ-ω). Att. τίνω lost ϝ without trace.

642. (5) A few poetic verbs add να to the stem, forming presents in νημι (or deponents in ναμαι); most of these have presents in ναω; e.g. δάμνημι (δαμ-να-), also δαμνάω subdue.

643. Βαίνω (βα-, βαν-) go, and ὀσφραίνομαι (ὀσφρ-, ὀσφραν-) smell, not only add ν or αν, but also belong to the Iota Class (II). See also κερδαίνω *gain*, ῥαίνω *sprinkle*, τετραίνω *bore*, with Homeric ἀλιταίνομαι (ἀλιτ-, ἀλιταν-) *sin against*.

644. FOURTH CLASS. *Verbs in* σκω. These add σκᵒ/ε to the verb stem, if it ends in a vowel, to form the present stem ; if the verb stem ends in a consonant, they add ισκᵒ/ε ; e.g. γηρά-σκω (γηρα-) *grow old*, ἀρέ-σκω (ἀρε-) *please* ; εὑρ-ίσκω (εὑρ-) *find*, στερ-ίσκω (στερ-) *deprive*.

645. Ὀφλ-ισκάνω (ὀφλ-) *be condemned* has both ισκ and the nasal addition αν (**638**).

646. Many presents of this class are reduplicated (**561**) ; e.g. γι-γνώ-σκω (γνω-). See **605**. Ἀρ-αρ-ίσκω has a form of Attic reduplication (**554**).

647. Θνήσκω *die* and μιμνήσκω *remind* have ισκᵒ/ε after a vowel.

648. Three verbs, ἀλύ-σκω (ἀλυκ-) *avoid*, διδά-σκω (διδαχ-) *teach*, and λά-σκω (λακ-) *utter*, drop the palatal before σκω. So Homeric ἐίσκω or ἴσκω (ἐϊκ- or ἱκ-) *liken*, and τιτύσκομαι (τυχ-, τυκ-), for τι-τυκ-σκομαι, *prepare* ; πάσχω *suffer* is for παθ-σκω (**69, 105** ƒ). Μίσγω *mix* is probably reduplicated, for μι-μσγω.

649. These verbs are often called *inceptive* or *inchoative*, though few have any inceptive meaning ; cf. γηράσκω *grow old*. They denote acts or events viewed as occurring in successive steps. Cf. Lat. c r e s c o, and **606**.

650. FIFTH, OR MIXED, CLASS. This includes verbs which have two or more tense stems formed from verb stems essentially different from each other, like Eng. *go*, *went* ; *am*, *be*, *was*. E.g.

αἱρέω (αἱρε-, ἑλ-) *take*, fut. αἱρήσω, 2 aor. εἷλον.

εἶδον (ϝειδ-, ϝοιδ-, ϝιδ-) *saw*, Lat. v i d i, 2 aor.; 2 perf. οἶδα *know* (**529**). Mid. εἴδομαι (poet.). Εἶδον is used as 2 aor. of ὁράω (see below).

εἶπον (εἰπ-, ἐρ-, ῥε-) *spoke*, 2 aor.; fut. (ἐρέω) ἐρῶ, perf. εἴ-ρη-κα, εἴρημαι, aor. pass. ἐρρήθην. The stem ἐρ- (ῥε-) is for ϝερ- (ϝρε-), seen in Lat. v e r - b u m. Εἴρημαι is for ϝε-ϝρη-μαι (**552**). So ἐν-έπω.

ἔρχομαι (ἐρχ-, ἐλευθ-, ἐλυθ-, ἐλθ-) *go*, fut. ἐλεύσομαι (poet.), 2 perf. ἐλήλυθα, 2 aor. ἦλθον. The Attic future is εἶμι *shall go* (**511**). The imperfect and the dependent moods of the present use the forms of εἶμι.

ἐσθίω (ἐσθ-, ἐδ-, φαγ-) *eat*, fut. ἔδομαι (**681**), 2 aor. ἔφαγον.

ὁράω (ὁρα-, ὀπ-, ϝιδ-) *see*, fut. ὄψομαι, perf. ἑώρακα or ἑόρακα, ἑώραμαι or ὦμμαι (for ὠπ-μαι), ὤφθην, 2 aor. εἶδον (see εἶδον above).

πάσχω (πενθ-, πονθ-, παθ-) *suffer*, fut. πείσομαι, 2 perf. πέπονθα, 2 aor. ἔπαθον. See **648**.

πίνω (πι-, πο-) *drink* (**637**), fut. πίομαι (**681**), perf. πέπωκα, 2 aor. ἔπιον.

τρέχω (τρεχ-, δραμ-) *run*, fut. δραμοῦμαι, perf. δεδράμηκα, 2 aor. ἔδραμον. The stem τρεχ- is for θρεχ- (**105** e), and δραμε- for δραμ- is used in fut. and perf. (**590** d).

φέρω (φερ-, οἰ-, ἐνεκ-, by reduplication with weak grade ἐν-ενεκ-, ἐνεγκ-) *bear*,

Lat. fero; fut. οἴσω, aor. ἤνεγκα, 2 perf. ἐν-ήνοχ-α (585, 723), ἐν-ήνεγ-μαι, aor. pass. ἠνέχθην.
ὠνέομαι (ὠνε-, πρια-) buy, fut. ὠνήσομαι, aor. ἐπριάμην.
For full forms of these verbs, see the Catalogue.

INFLECTION OF THE PRESENT AND IMPERFECT INDICATIVE OF Ω VERBS

651. For the paradigms of ω verbs, see 480–499. For explanation of forms, see 582 ff.

652. Certain poetic forms of ω verbs are athematic. E.g. Hom. ἔδ-μεναι from ἔδ-ω eat, φέρ-τε from φέρ-ω bear, δέχ-αται (for δέχ-νται, 27), third plur. of δέχομαι receive, partic. δέγ-μενος, imperf. ἐ-δέγ-μην. Cf. οἶ-μαι and οἴ-ο-μαι think. So λέλυ-μαι, ἐλύ-θη-ν from λύ-ω, and ἔ-βη-ν, ἔ-φῦ-ν from βαίνω, φύω, are athematic forms of ω verbs.

653. The thematic vowel ᵒ/ε, subj. ω/η, is contracted with the final vowel in verbs with stems ending in α, ε, ο, originally αι, ει, οι. See 634; for the paradigms, 482–483. Some contracted verbs have stems in a long vowel; e.g. δράω, δρῶ do, for δρά-ω; χράο-μαι, χρῶμαι use, for χρη-ιομαι. See 486.

DIALECT AND POETIC FORMS OF VERBS IN Ω

654. a. The Doric has the personal endings τι (Ionic, Attic, Aeolic σι), μες (μεν), τᾶν (Ionic, Attic την), σθᾶν (σθην), μᾶν (μην), μεσθα, ντι (Ionic, Attic, Aeolic νσι).

b. When σ is dropped in σαι and σο of the second person (582 g), Homer often keeps the εαι, ηαι, αο, εο uncontracted. Herodotus has εαι and αο, but in the subj. generally ῃ for ηαι. In Hdt., sometimes in Homer, εο appears as ευ. In Homer σαι and σο sometimes drop σ in the perf. and pluperf.; e.g. μέμνηαι for μέμνησαι, ἔσσυο for ἔσσυσο. A dental sometimes becomes σ before σαι; e.g. κέκασσαι for κεκαδ-σαι (κέκασμαι).
For Ionic contract forms, see 660 b.

c. The Ionic has αται and ατο for νται and ντο in the third person plural of the perfect and pluperfect, and ατο for ντο in the optative. Before these endings π, β, κ, and γ are aspirated (φ, χ); e.g. κρύπτω (κρυβ-), κεκρύφ-αται; λέγω, λελέχ-αται, λελέχ-ατο. Hdt. shortens η to ε before αται and ατο; e.g. οἰκέ-αται (perf. of οἰκέω), Att. ᾤκη-νται; ἐτετῖμέ-ατο (pluperf. of τῖμάω), ¹Att. ἐτετῖμη-ντο. Hom. has -δαται and -δατο, as if from a dental stem, in ἐληλά-δ-αται, from ἐλαύνω drive, and ἐρρά-δ-ατο, from ῥαίνω sprinkle. The forms αται and ατο sometimes occur in Attic (733). Herodotus has them also in the present and imperfect of verbs in μι.

d. Herodotus has εα, εας, εε in the pluperfect active, e.g. ἐτεθήπεα; whence comes the older Attic η, ης, ει(ν). Homer has εα, ης, ει(ν), with εε in ᾔδεε (530 b), and rarely ον, ες, ε.

e. Homer and Herodotus generally have the uncontracted forms of the future (in εω and εομαι) of nasal stems; e.g. μενέω, Attic μενῶ. When they are contracted, they follow the analogy of verbs in εω (**492**).

f. The Doric has σέω, σέομαι (contracted σῶ, σοῦμαι or σεῦμαι) for σω, σομαι in the future. The Attic has σοῦμαι in the future middle of a few verbs (**679**).

g. In Homer σσ is often retained in the future and aorist of verbs in εσ-; e.g. τελέω *finish* (for τελεσ-ιω), τελέσσω, ἐτέλεσσα. So καλέω *call*, ἐκάλεσσα; κομίζω *take care of* (κομιδ-), ἐκόμισσα, ἐκομισσάμην (**597, 599**).

h. In Homer aorists with σ sometimes have the thematic vowel, as in second aorists; e.g. ἷξον, ἷξες, from ἱκνέομαι *come*; ἐβήσετο (more common than ἐβήσατο), from βαίνω *go*. These are called *mixed* aorists.

i. In the poets εν is often used in the aorist passive indicative instead of ησαν; e.g. ὤρμηθεν for ὡρμήθησαν, from ὁρμάω *urge*. So ἄν or εν for ησαν or εσαν in the active of verbs in μι (**669** *d*).

655. *Subjunctive.* *a.* In Homer the subjunctive (especially in the first aor. act. and mid.) often has the short thematic vowels ε and ο (Attic η and ω), yet never in the singular of the active voice nor in the third person plural; e.g. ἐρύσσομεν, ἀλγήσετε, μυθήσομαι, εὔξεαι, δηλήσεται, ἀμείψεται, ἐγείρομεν, ἱμείρεται. So sometimes in Pindar.

b. In both aorist passive subjunctives Herodotus generally has the uncontracted forms in εω, εωμεν, εωσι, but contracts εη and εη to η and η; e.g. ἀφαιρεθέω (Att. -θῶ), φανέωσι (Att. -ῶσι), but φανῇ and φανῆτε (as in Attic).

c. In the second aorist passive subjunctive of some verbs, Homer has forms in εω, ηης, ηῃ, ειομεν, ηετε (**655** *a*), as they are commonly written; e.g. δαμείω (from ἐδάμην, 2 aor. pass. of δαμνάω *subdue*), δαμήῃς, δαμήῃ, δαμήετε; τραπείομεν (from ἐτάρπην, 2 aor. pass. of τέρπω *delight*). This is more fully developed in the second aorist active of the μι form (see **670** *b*).

d. In the subjunctive active Homer often has ωμι, ῃσθα, ῃσι; e.g. ἐθέλωμι, ἐθέλῃσθα, ἐθέλῃσι.

656. *Optative.* *a.* The forms of the first aorist optative active in ειας, ειε, ειαν are the common forms in all dialects (**575, 764**).

b. Homer sometimes has οισθα (**582** *a*) in the second person for οις; e.g. κλαίοισθα, βάλοισθα. For ατο (for ντο), see **654** *c*.

657. *Infinitive.* *a.* Homer often has μεναι and μεν in the infinitive active; e.g. ἀμυνέμεναι, ἀμυνέμεν (Attic ἀμύνειν, **791**); ἐλθέμεναι, ἐλθέμεν (ἐλθεῖν); ἀξέμεναι, ἀξέμεν (ἄξειν). For the perfect (only of the μι form), see **673**: the perf. in ἐναι does not occur in Homer. So Hom. μεναι, Dor. μεν in the aorist passive; e.g. ὁμοιωθή-μεναι (ὁμοιωθῆ-ναι), δαή-μεναι (also δαῆ-ναι), Hom.; αἰσχυνθή-μεν (αἰσχυνθῆ-ναι), Pind. See **659** *f*.

b. The Doric has εν (**792**) and the Aeolic ην for ειν in the infin.; e.g. ἀείδεν and γάρυεν (Dor.) for ἀείδειν and γηρύειν; φέρην and ἔχην (Aeol.) for φέρειν and ἔχειν; εἴπην (Aeol.) for εἰπεῖν; μεθύσθην (Aeol.) for μεθυσθῆναι (pass.).

658. *Participle.* The Aeolic has οισα for ουσα, and αις, αισα for ᾱς, ᾱσα, in the participle; e.g. ἔχοισα, θρέψαις, θρέψαισα (75, 32).

DIALECT FORMS OF CONTRACT VERBS

659. *Verbs in αω.* *a.* In the MSS. of Homer verbs in αω are often contracted as in Attic. In a few cases they remain uncontracted; sometimes without change, e.g. ναιετάουσι, ναιετάων, from ναιετάω *dwell*, sometimes with ᾱ, e.g. πεινάω *hunger*, διψάω *thirst* (cf. 486); sometimes with εον for ἄον in the imperfect, e.g. μενοίνεον from μενοινάω *long for*.

b. (1) The MSS. of Homer often give peculiar forms of verbs in αω, by which the two vowels (or the vowel and diphthong) which elsewhere are contracted are said to be *assimilated*, so as to give a double A or a double O sound. The second syllable, if it is short by nature or has a diphthong with a short initial vowel, is generally prolonged; sometimes the former syllable; rarely both. We thus have αᾱ (sometimes ᾱα) for αε or αη (αᾳ for αει or αη), and οω (sometimes ωο or ωω) for αο or αω (οῳ for αοι) :

ὁράᾳς for ὁράεις	ὁρόω for ὁράω
ὁράᾳ for ὁράει or ὁράῃ	ὁρόωσι for ὁράουσι
ὁράασθε for ὁράεσθε	ὁρόωσα for ὁράουσα
ὁράασθαι for ὁράεσθαι	ὁρόῳεν for ὁράοιεν
μνάασθαι for μνάεσθαι	ὁρόωνται for ὁράονται
ὁράᾳν for ὁράειν	αἰτιόῳ for αἰτιάοιο

(2) The lengthening of the first vowel occurs only when the word could not otherwise stand in the Homeric verse; e.g. ἡβώοντες for ἡβάοντες, ἡβώοιμι for ἡβάοιμι, μνάασθαι for μνάεσθαι, μνώοντο for (ἐ)μνάοντο. In this case the second vowel or diphthong is not lengthened. But it may be long in a final syllable, e.g. μενοινάᾳ (for -αει), or when ωσα or ωσι comes from οντια or ονσι, e.g. ἡβώωσα, δρώωσι, for ἡβα-οντια, δρα-ονσι. The "assimilation" never occurs unless the second vowel is long either by nature or by position; e.g. ὁράομεν, ὁράετε, ὁράετω cannot become ὁρόωμεν, ὁράατε, ὁράατο. Yet μνωόμενος for μνάόμενος occurs by exception.

(3) These forms extend also to the so-called Attic futures in άσω, άω, ῶ (678 *b*); e.g. ἐλόω, ἐλόωσι, κρεμόω, δαμάᾳ, δαμόωσι, for ἐλάσω (ἐλάω), ἐλάουσι, etc., Att. ἐλῶ, ἐλῶσι, etc.

(4) These forms, occurring only in the literary dialect of the epic poets, are commonly explained in two ways. Either they represent an actual *phonetic* stage in the process of contraction, e.g. ὁρόω stands midway between ὁράω and ὁρῶ; or they arose from *metrical* necessity: e.g. after ὁράω had been mistakenly contracted to ὁρῶ, it was then "distracted" to ὁρόω in order to restore the required number of syllables to the verse.

c. The Doric contracts αε and αη to η, αει and αη to ῃ, αο and αω to ᾱ except in final syllables; e.g. ὁρῶ, ὁρῇς, ὁρῇ, ὁράμες, ὁρῆτε, ὁράντι; impv. ὅρη; infin. ὁρῆν.

d. In Homer contracted verbs sometimes have athematic forms in the third person dual, e.g. προσαυδήτην (from προσαυδάω), φοιτήτην (φοιτάω), συλήτην (συλάω). So Hom. ὄρηαι (or ὀρῆαι) for ὀράεαι (Attic ὁρᾷ) in the pres. indic. middle of ὁράω. See 660 *d.*

e. Herodotus sometimes changes αω, αο, and αου to εω, εο, and εου, especially in ὁράω, εἰρωτάω, and φοιτάω; e.g. ὁρέω, ὁρέοντες, ὁρέουσι, εἰρώτεον, ἐφοίτεον. These forms are generally uncontracted.
In other cases Herodotus contracts verbs in αω as in Attic.

f. Homer sometimes forms the present infinitive active of verbs in αω and εω without thematic vowel; e.g. γοήμεναι (γοάω), πεινήμεναι (πεινάω), φιλήμεναι (φιλέω). See 660 *d.*

660. *Verbs in* εω. *a.* Verbs in εω generally remain uncontracted in both Homer and Herodotus. But Homer sometimes contracts εε or εει to ει, e.g. τάρβει (τάρβεε). Hdt. has generally δεῖ *must*, and δεῖν, but imperf. ἔδεε. Both Homer and Herodotus sometimes have εν for εο, e.g. ἀγνοεῦντες, διανοεῦντο; so in the Attic futures from ισω, ισομαι (678 *c*), e.g. κομιεύμεθα (Hdt.). Forms in εν for εον, like οἰχνεῦσι, ποιεῦσι, τελεῦσι, are of very doubtful authority.

b. Homer sometimes drops ε in εαι and εο (for εσαι,· εσο, 654 *b*) after ε, thus changing έεαι and έεο to έαι and έο, e.g. μυθέαι for μυθέεαι (from μυθέομαι), ἀποαιρέο (for ἀποαιρέεο); and he also contracts έεαι and έεο to εῖαι and εῖο, e.g. μυθεῖαι, αἰδεῖο (for αἰδέεο). Herodotus sometimes drops the second ε in έεο; e.g. φοβέο, αἰτέο, ἐξηγέο.

c. Homer sometimes has a form in ειω for that in εω; e.g. νεικείω. So in ἐτελείετο from τελείω. These are the older forms, from εσ stems, νεικεσ-ιω, τελεσ-ιω. But θείω *run*, πλείω *sail*, and πνείω *breathe* are cases of metrical lengthening.

d. Athematic forms of εω verbs occur; e.g. φορήμεναι and φορῆναι, from φόρημι *bear*, Att. φορέω. Homer has a few dual imperfects like ὁμαρτήτην (ὁμαρτέω) and ἀπειλήτην (ἀπειλέω). See 659 *d* and *f.*

661. *Verbs in* οω. *a.* Verbs in οω are always contracted in Herodotus, and his MSS. sometimes have εν (for ου) from οο or οου, especially in δικαιόω *think just,* imperf. ἐδικαίευν.

b. They are always contracted in Homer, except in the few cases in which they have forms in οω or οῳ resembling those of verbs in αω (659 *b*); e.g. ἀρόωσι (from ἀρόω *plough*); δηιόῳεν and (imperf.) δηιόωντο (from δηιόω); also ὑπνώοντας (from ὑπνόω).

INFLECTION OF THE PRESENT AND IMPERFECT OF ΜΙ VERBS

662. In μι verbs the stem shows the normal grade η, ω, ῡ in the singular of the present and imperfect indicative active, and the weak grade α, ε, ο, υ in the dual and plural and in most other forms derived from the present stem. This is one of the most important distinctions between μι forms and ω forms. For the paradigms, see 503–532.

663. The ending of the third person plural of the imperfect active is σαν. The third person plural of the present active has the ending ᾱσι (582 e), which is always contracted with a, but not with ε, ο, or υ, of the stem; e.g. ἱστᾶσι (for ἱστα-ᾱσι), but τιθέ-ᾱσι, διδό-ᾱσι, δεικνύ-ᾱσι.

664. The only verbs in μι with consonant stems are εἰμί (ἐσ-) am and ἧμαι (ἧσ-) sit.

665. Some thematic forms occur. E.g. the imperfect ἐτίθεις, ἐτίθει (as if from τιθέω), and ἐδίδουν, ἐδίδους, ἐδίδου (as if from διδόω), are more common than the forms in ης, η and ων, ως, ω. So τιθεῖς for τίθης in the present. Some verbs in ῦμι have presents in νω; e.g. δεικνύω and δείκνῡμι.

666. The thematic inflection is used in the present subjunctive; e.g. τιθῶ, τιθῇς, τιθῇ, τιθῶμαι (for τιθέ-ω, τιθέ-ης, etc.). Ἱστῶμαι is probably for ἱστέ-ωμαι, since Homeric MSS. give στέωμεν (for στῆομεν, 33).

667. Δύναμαι can and ἐπίσταμαι understand often have ἐδύνω (or ἠδύνω) and ἠπίστω for ἐδύνασο (or ἠδύνασο) and ἠπίστασο in the imperfect, and occasionally δύνᾳ and ἐπίστᾳ for δύνασαι and ἐπίστασαι. See 582 g.

668. Thematic forms of τίθημι and ἵημι occur in 3 sing. and in the dual and plural of the present and aorist optative. The accent is uncertain. E.g. συνθοῖτο, ἐπιθοίμεθα, ἐπιθοῖντο (also written ἐπίθοιντο); προοῖτο, προοῖσθε, προοῖντο (or πρόοιτο, πρόοιντο). See 514 c.

DIALECT FORMS OF VERBS IN ΜΙ

669. *a.* Homer and Herodotus have many forms (some doubtful) in which verbs in ημι (with stems in ε) and ωμι have the thematic inflection of verbs in εω and οω; e.g. τιθεῖ, διδοῖς, διδοῖ. So in compounds of ἵημι, e.g. ἀνιεῖς (or ἀνίεις), μεθιεῖ (or μεθίει) in pres., and προΐειν, προΐεις, ἀνΐει, in imperf. Hom. has impv. καθ-ιστα (Attic καθίστη). Hdt. has ἱστᾷ (for ἵστησι), ὑπερ-ετίθεα in imperf., and προσθέοιτο (for -θεῖτο) etc. in opt. For ἐδίδουν etc. and ἐτίθεις, ἐτίθει (also Attic) see 665.

b. In the Aeolic dialect most verbs in αω, εω, and οω take the form in μι; e.g. φίλημι (with φίλεισθα, φίλει) in Sappho, for φιλέω, etc.; ὄρᾱμι (ὀράω), κάλημι (καλέω), αἴνημι (αἰνέω).

c. A few verbs in Hom. and Hdt. drop σ in σαι and σο of the second person after a vowel; e.g. impv. παρίστασο (for -ασο) and imperf. ἐμάρναο (Hom.); ἐξεπίστεαι (for -ασαι) with change of α to ε (Hdt.). So θέο, impv. for θέσο (Att. θοῦ), and ἔνθεο (Hom.).

d. The Doric has τι, ντι for σι, νσι. Homer sometimes has σθα (582 a) for σ in 2 pers. sing., e.g. δίδωσθα (δίδοισθα or διδοῖσθα), τίθησθα. The poets have ν for σαν (with preceding vowel short) in 3 pers. plur., e.g. ἔσταν (for ἔστησαν), ἵεν (for ἵεσαν), πρότιθεν (for προετίθεσαν); see 654 i.

e. Herodotus sometimes has αται, ατο for νται, ντο in the present and imperfect of verbs in μι, with preceding α changed to ε; e.g. προτιθέαται (for -ενται), ἐδυνέατο (for -αντο).

670. *a.* Herodotus sometimes leaves εω uncontracted in the subjunctive of verbs in ημι; e.g. θέωμεν (Att. θῶμεν), διαθέωνται (-θῶνται), ἀπ-ιέωσι (Att. ἀφ-ιῶσι, from ἀφ-ίημι). He forms the subj. with εω in the plural also from stems in α; e.g. ἀπο-στέ-ωσι (-στῶσι), ἐπιστέ-ωνται (Att. ἐπίστωνται). Homer sometimes has these forms with εω; e.g. θέωμεν, στέωμεν (**756** *a*).

b. Generally, when the second aorist subjunctive active is uncontracted in Homer, the final vowel of the stem is lengthened, ε (or α) to η or ει, ο to ω, while the short thematic vowels ε and ο are used in the dual and plural, except before σι (for νσι). Thus we find in the manuscripts of Homer:

Stems in α	θήῃς
βείω (Attic βῶ)	θήῃ, ἀν-ήῃ
στήῃς	θείομεν
στήῃ, βήῃ, βέῃ, φθήῃ	
στήετον	Stems in ω
στήομεν, στείομεν, στέωμεν	γνώω
στήωσι, στείωσι, φθέωσι	γνώῃς
Stems in ε	γνώῃ, δώῃ, δώῃσιν
θείω, ἐφ-είω	γνώομεν, δώομεν
	γνώωσι, δώωσι

Many editions of Homer retain ει of the manuscripts before ο and ω, although η may be the correct form in all persons (see **655** *c*).

c. A few cases of the middle inflected as in 670 *b* occur in Homer; e.g. βλή-εται (βάλλω), ἄλ-εται (ἄλλομαι), ἀπο-θείομαι, κατα-θείομαι; so κατα-θῆαι (Hesiod) for καταθέ-ηαι (Att. καταθῇ).

671. For Homeric optatives of δαίνῡμι, δύω, λύω, and φθίνω, — δαινῦτο, δύη and δύμεν, λελῦτο and λελῦντο, φθῖμην (for φθι-ιμην), — see these verbs in the Catalogue, with **766** *a*, **776**.

672. Homer sometimes retains θι in the present imperative, e.g δίδωθι, ὄμνυθι (**784**). Pindar often has δίδοι.

673. Homer has μεναι or μεν (the latter only after a short vowel) for ναι in the infinitive. The final vowel of the stem is seldom long in the present; e.g. ἱστά-μεναι, ἰέ-μεναι, μεθιέ-μεν, ὀρνύ-μεναι, ὀρνύ-μεν, τιθέ-μεν, but τιθή-μεναι. In the second aorist active the vowel is regularly long (**797** *b*), e.g. στή-μεναι, γνώ-μεναι; but τίθημι, δίδωμι, and ἵημι have θέμεναι and θέμεν, δόμεναι and δόμεν, and (ἔμεν) μεθ-έμεν. See **701.** In the perfect of the μι form we have ἑστά-μεναι, ἑστά-μεν, τεθνά-μεναι, τεθνά-μεν.

674. Homer rarely has ημενος in the participle, from an athematic present in ημι, where Attic uses thematic forms. Cf. **660** *d*, **669** *b*. For second perfect participles in ως (αως, εως, ηως), see **802**.

II. Future System

675. *Future Active and Middle.* Stems ending in a vowel or a stop consonant add σ⁰/ε to form the stem of the future active and middle. The indicative active thus ends in σω, and the middle in σομαι. Verb stems with a short vowel lengthen α to η (except after ε, ι, ρ), ε to η, ο to ω (593). They are inflected like the present (see 480). E.g.

τῑμάω *honor,* τῑμήσω (τῑμησ⁰/ε-); δράω *do,* δράσω; κόπτω (κοπ-) *cut,* κόψω; βλάπτω (βλαβ-) *hurt,* βλάψω, βλάψομαι (69) ; γράφω *write,* γράψω, γράψομαι; πλέκω *twine,* πλέξω ; πρᾱττω (πρᾱγ-) *do,* πρᾱξω, πρᾱξομαι ; ταράττω (ταραχ-) *confuse,* ταράξω, ταράξομαι; φράζω (φραδ-) *tell,* φράσω (69) ; πείθω *persuade,* πείσω (for πειθ-σω); λείπω *leave,* λείψω, λείψομαι. So σπένδω *pour,* σπείσω (for σπενδ-σω, 70, 32) ; τρέφω *nourish,* θρέψω, θρέψομαι (105 e) ; βούλομαι *wish,* βουλήσομαι (590 c).

676. Verbs whose stems mutate between normal and weak grades (585) have the normal grade in the future ; e.g. πείσω, τρέψω, ῥήξω, στήσω.

677. *Liquid and Nasal Stems.* Stems ending in λ, μ, ν, ρ add εσ⁰/ε to form the future stem ; σ is dropped (90), making forms in έω and έομαι, contracted to ῶ and οῦμαι, and inflected like φιλῶ and φιλοῦμαι (482). See 492. E.g.

φαίνω (φαν-) *show,* fut. φανῶ for φαν-έ(σ)ω, φανοῦμαι for φαν-έ(σ)ο-μαι ; στέλλω (στελ-) *send,* στελῶ for στελ-έ(σ)ω, στελοῦμαι for στελ-έ(σ)ο-μαι ; νέμω *divide,* νεμῶ ; κρῑνω (κριν-) *judge,* κρινῶ ; ὄμνῡμι (ὀμ-) *swear,* ὀμοῦμαι.

678. *Attic Future. a.* The futures of καλέω *call* and τελέω *finish,* καλέσω and τελέσω (596), drop σ of the future stem, and contract καλε- and τελε- with ω and ομαι, making καλῶ, καλοῦμαι, τελῶ and (poetic) τελοῦμαι. These futures have thus the same forms as the presents.

So ὄλλῡμι (ὀλ-, ὀλε-) *destroy* has future ὀλέσω (Hom.), ὀλέω (Hdt.), ὀλῶ (Attic) ; and μαχέσομαι (Hdt.), μαχήσομαι (Hom.), future of μάχομαι (μαχε-) *fight,* becomes μαχοῦμαι in Attic. Καθέζομαι (ἑδ-) *sit* has καθεδοῦμαι.

b. In like manner, futures in ασω from verbs in αννῡμι, some in εσω from verbs in εννῡμι, and some in ασω from verbs in αζω, drop σ and contract αω and εω to ῶ. E.g. σκεδάννῡμι (σκεδα-) *scatter,* fut. σκεδάσω, (σκεδάω) σκεδῶ ; στορέννῡμι (στορε-) *spread,* στορέσω, (στορέω) στορῶ ; βιβάζω *cause to go,* βιβάσω, (βιβάω) βιβῶ. So ἐλαύνω (ἐλα-) *drive* (641), future ἐλάσω, (ἐλάω) ἐλῶ. For future ἐλόω, ἐλόωσι, etc. in Homer, see 659 b (3).

c. Futures in ισω and ισομαι from verbs in ιζω of more than two syllables regularly drop σ and insert ε ; then ιέω and ιέομαι are contracted to ιῶ and ιοῦμαι ; e.g. κομίζω *carry,* κομίσω, (κομιέω) κομιῶ, κομίσομαι, (κομιέομαι) κομιοῦμαι, inflected like φιλῶ, φιλοῦμαι (482). See 660 a.

d. These forms of the future, occurring generally when the verb stem ends in α or ε or ιδ (αδ), are called *Attic*, because the purer Attic seldom uses any others in these tenses; but they are found also in other dialects and even in Homer.

679. *Doric Future. a.* These verbs form the stem of the future middle in σε°/ε, and contract σέομαι to σοῦμαι: πλέω *sail*, πλευσοῦμαι (611); πνέω *breathe*, πνευσοῦμαι; νέω *swim*, νευσοῦμαι; κλαίω *weep*, κλαυσοῦμαι (635); φεύγω *flee*, φευξοῦμαι; πίπτω *fall*, πεσοῦμαι. See also παίζω (618) and πυνθάνομαι.

The Attic has these and (except in πίπτω) the regular futures πλεύσομαι, πνεύσομαι, κλαύσομαι, φεύξομαι.

b. These are called *Doric* futures, because the Doric commonly forms futures in σέω, σῶ, and σέομαι, σοῦμαι. In Attic the futures of this class are in the middle, with active meaning.

680. Stems in ευ which drop υ in the present (611) generally retain υ in the future (and aorist); e.g. πλέω *sail*, πλεύσομαι or πλευσοῦμαι. But χέω *pour* (χευ-) has fut. χέω, χέομαι, aor. ἔχεα (Hom. ἔχευα).

681. Two verbs besides χέω have no sign for the future. They are ἔδομαι from ἐσθίω (ἐδ-) *eat* and πίομαι from πίνω (πι-) *drink* (650). These were originally aorist subjunctives with short thematic vowel (655 *a*) and future meaning. So Hom. βέομαι (? βίομαι) *shall live*, ἀλεύεται *will avoid*.

682. A few poetic liquid stems add σ; e.g. κέλλω (κελ-) *land*, κέλσω; κύρω *meet*, κύρσω; ὄρνῡμι (ὀρ-) *rouse*, ὄρσω. So θέρομαι *be warmed*, Hom. fut. θέρσομαι; φθείρω (φθερ-) *destroy*, Hom. fut. φθέρσω. For the corresponding aorists, see 689 *b*.

III. *First Aorist System*

683. ***First Aorist Active and Middle.*** Stems ending in a vowel or a stop consonant add σα to form the stem of the first aorist active and middle. For the paradigms, see 480. E.g.

τῑμάω, ἐτίμησα, ἐτῑμησάμην (593, cf. 675); δράω, ἔδρᾱσα; κόπτω, ἔκοψα, ἐκοψάμην; βλάπτω, ἔβλαψα; γράφω, ἔγραψα, ἐγραψάμην; πλέκω, ἔπλεξα, ἐπλεξάμην; πράττω, ἔπρᾱξα, ἐπρᾱξάμην; ταράττω, ἐτάραξα; φράζω, ἔφρασα (for ἐφραδ-σα); πείθω, ἔπεισα (69); σπένδω, ἔσπεισα (for ἐσπενδ-σα); τρέφω, ἔθρεψα, ἐθρεψάμην (105 *e*); τήκω *melt*, ἔτηξα; πλέω *sail*, ἔπλευσα (611).

684. Verbs whose stems mutate between normal and weak grades (585) have the normal grade in the first aorist; e.g. ἔπεισα, ἔτρεψα, ἔρρηξα, ἔστησα.

685. Three verbs in μι, δίδωμι *give*, ἵημι *send*, and τίθημι *place*, have κα for σα in the first aorist active, giving ἔδωκα, ἧκα, and ἔθηκα. These forms are used in the indicative, and are most common in the singular; in the dual and plural of the indicative, and throughout the other moods, the second aorists are used. See 701. The 3 plur. ἔδωκαν, less commonly the other persons, is sometimes found in Attic. The middle forms ἡκάμην and ἐθηκάμην occur, the latter not in Attic. In κα, the κ is not a part of the tense suffix, as is the σ in σα, but is a very old modification of the root, seen in Lat. iēc-i (= ἧκ-α) and fēc-i (= ἐ-θηκ-α).

686. Χέω *pour* has aorists ἔχεα (Hom. ἔχευα) and ἐχεάμην, corresponding to the futures χέω and χέομαι (**680**), representing original ἐ-χευσα and ἐ-χευσα-μην. Εἶπον *said* has also (rarely in Attic) first aorist εἶπα; and φέρω *bear* has ἤνεγκ-α (from stem ἐνεγκ-).

For Homeric aorists like ἐβήσετο, ἐδύσετο, ἷξον, etc., see **654** h.

687. *Liquid and Nasal Verbs.* Stems ending in λ, μ, ν, ρ drop σ in σα, leaving α, and lengthen their last vowel, α to η (after ι or ρ to ᾱ) and ε to ει (**71** a, 92). See **492.** E.g.

φαίνω (φαν-), ἔφην-α (for ἔφανσα); στέλλω (στελ-), ἔστειλ-α (for ἐστελ-σα), ἐστειλ-άμην; ἀγγέλλω (ἀγγελ-) *announce*, ἤγγειλα, ἠγγειλάμην; περαίνω (περαν-) *finish*, ἐπέρᾱνα; μιαίνω (μιαν-) *stain*, ἐμίᾱνα; νέμω *divide*, ἔνειμα, ἐνειμάμην; κρῑνω *judge*, ἔκρῑνα; ἀμῡνω *keep off*, ἤμῡνα, ἠμῡνάμην; φθείρω (φθερ-) *destroy*, ἔφθειρα. Compare the futures in **677.**

688. A few nasal stems lengthen αν to ᾱν instead of ην; e.g. κερδαίνω (κερδαν-) *gain*, ἐκέρδᾱνα. A few lengthen ραν to ρην; e.g. τεραίνω (τετραν-) *bore*, ἐτέτρηνα.

689. *a.* Αἴρω *raise* has a stem ἀρ- for ἀερ- seen in ἀείρω, whence aor. ἦρα, ἠράμην, ἄρω, ἆρον, ἄρᾱς, ἄρωμαι, ἀραίμην, ἀράμενος.

b. The poetic κέλλω, κύρω, and ὄρνῡμι have aorists ἔκελσα, ἔκυρσα, and ὦρσα. See the corresponding futures (**682**). But ὀκέλλω (in prose) has ὤκειλα (see **92**).

IV. Second Aorist System

690. *Second Aorist Active and Middle.* The stem of the second aorist active and middle is the simple verb stem with ᵒ/ε affixed. Verbs whose stems mutate between normal and weak grades (**585**) have the weak grade. Otherwise the inflection is like that of the imperfect in the indicative, of the present in the other moods, but with different accent. E.g.

λείπω, ἔλιπον, ἐλιπόμην (2 aor. stem λιπ ᵒ/ε); λαμβάνω (λαβ-) *take*, ἔλαβον, ἐλαβόμην (2 aor. stem λαβ ᵒ/ε). See **481.**

691. The normal grade occurs in τέμνω *cut*, ἔτεμον. But the Ionic and poetic form ἔταμον shows the weak grade (for stem τμ; cf. **586**). So τρέπω, poetic ἔτραπον.

692. Further examples of the weak grade, with total disappearance of the stem vowel, are seen in πέτομαι (πετ-) *fly*, ἐπτόμην; ἐγείρω (ἐγερ-) *rouse*, ἠγρόμην; ἔπομαι (σεπ-) *follow*, ἐσπόμην; ἔχω (σεχ-) *have*, ἔσχον. So Homeric ἐκεκλόμην or κεκλόμην, from κέλομαι *command*; ἄλαλκον from ἀλέξω (ἀλεκ-) *ward off*: for these and other reduplicated second aorists, see **559, 560.**

693. All these verbs have consonant stems. The only vowel stem forming a second aorist with the thematic inflection is πίνω *drink*, ἔπιον. A few other second aorists are assigned to vowel verbs with totally different stems (650) ; e.g. αἱρέω *seize*, εἷλον ; ἐσθίω *eat*, ἔφαγον ; ὁράω *see*, εἶδον.

694. Some vowel verbs in ω have second aorists of the athematic inflection, like μι verbs. They are the following :

ἀλίσκομαι (ἀλ-, ἀλο-) *be taken* : ἑάλων or ἥλων *was taken*, ἁλῶ, ἁλοίην, ἁλῶναι, ἁλούς. Cf. **695.** '

βαίνω (βα-) *go* : ἔβην, βῶ, βαίην, βῆθι (also βᾶ in comp., e.g. κατάβα *step down!*), βῆναι, βάς. Hom. βάτην for ἐβήτην.

βιόω (βιο-) *live* : ἐβίων, βιῶ, βιῴην, βιῶναι, βιούς. Hom. impv. βιώτω. See **695.**

γηράσκω (γηρα-) *grow old*, 2 aor. infin. γηρᾶναι (poet.), Hom. partic. γηράς.

γιγνώσκω (γνω-, γνο-) *know* : ἔγνων, γνῶ, γνοίην, γνῶθι, γνῶναι, γνούς. See **695.**

διδράσκω (δρā-) *run* (only in composition) : ἔδρᾱν, ἔδρᾱς, ἔδρā, etc., subj. δρῶ, δρᾷς, δρᾷ, etc., opt. δραίην, δρᾶναι, δράς. Hdt. ἔδρην, δρῆναι, δράς. See **697.**

δύω (δῡ-, δυ-) *enter* : ἔδῡν *entered* (504), δύω, (for opt., see 776), δῦθι, δῦναι, δύς (329).

κτείνω (κτεν-, κτα-) *kill* : act. ἔκτᾰν, ἔκτᾰς, ἔκτᾰ, ἔκτᾰμεν, Hom. 3 plur. ἔκτᾰν (669 d), subj. κτέωμεν, infin. κτάμεναι, κτάμεν, κτάς. Mid. (Hom.) ἐκτάμην *was killed*, κτάσθαι, κτάμενος. Only in poetry.

πέτομαι (πετα-, πετ-, πτā-) *fly* : act. ἔπτην, (πτῶ, late), πταίην, (πτῆθι, πτῆναι, late), πτάς. Mid. ἐπτάμην, πτάσθαι, πτάμενος. Only in poetry.

τλā- *endure*, in fut. τλήσομαι : ἔτλην, τλῶ, τλαίην, τλῆθι, τλῆναι, τλάς.

φθάνω (φθα-) *anticipate* : ἔφθην, φθῶ, φθαίην, φθῆναι, φθάς.

φύω (φῡ-, φυ-) *produce* : ἔφῡν *was produced, am*, φύω, φῦναι, φύς. Cf. ἔδῡν and the inflection of δύς, **329.**

Add to these the single forms ἀπο-σκλῆναι, of ἀποσκέλλω *dry up*, σχές, impv. of ἔχω *have* (aor. ἔσχον), πῖθι, impv. of πίνω *drink* (aor. ἔπιον), and epic forms of ξυμβάλλω (696 a) and of κιγχάνω (κιχάνω).

695. Ἔγνων *knew* is thus inflected : ἔγνων, ἔγνως, ἔγνω, ἔγνωτον, ἐγνώτην, ἔγνωμεν, ἔγνωτε, ἔγνωσαν. Subj. γνῶ, like δῶ (504). Opt. γνοίην, like δοίην. Impv. γνῶθι, γνώτω, γνῶτον, γνώτων, γνῶτε, γνόντων (787). Infin. γνῶναι. Partic. γνούς, like δούς ; cf. **329.**

696. a. Some poetic (chiefly Homeric) second aorists of the athematic inflection in ημην, ιμην, and υμην are formed from stems in α, ι, and υ belonging to verbs in ω. Cf. 707. E.g.

βάλλω (βαλ-, βλη-) *throw*, 2 aor. act. (ἔβλην) ξυμ-βλήτην (dual), mid. (ἐβλήμην) ἔβλητο ; φθίνω (φθι-) *waste*, 2 aor. mid. ἐφθίμην ; σεύω (συ-) *urge*, ἐσσύμην (in Attic poets ἔσυτο, σύμενος) ; χέω (χυ-) *pour*, ἐχύμην, χύμενος.

See these verbs in the Catalogue. For other Homeric aorists, see ἀπαυράω, ἄω, βιβρώσκω, κλύω, κτίζω, λύω, οὐτάω, πελάζω, πλώω, πνέω, πτήσσω.

b. Some are formed from consonant stems, with the simple ending μην. E.g.

ἄλλομαι (ἀλ-) *leap*, 2 aor. mid. (ἀλ-μην) ἄλσο, ἄλτο, with Aeolic smooth breathing; δέχομαι (δεχ-) *receive*, (ἐδέγ-μην) δέκτο; (ἐλέγ-μην) ἔλεκτο *laid himself to rest* (see stem λεχ-).

Besides these, see ἀραρίσκω, γέντο *grasped*, πάλλω, πέρθω.

c. The inflection is like that of the pluperfect middle (480). Cf. 707.

697. Second aorists in ην or αμην from stems in α are inflected like ἔστην or ἐπριάμην; but ἔδραν substitutes ᾱ (after ρ) for η. For ἔκτᾱν, see 669 *d* and 698.

698. These forms, although having the athematic inflection of μι verbs, differ from them in not preserving the distinction between strong and weak grades in the different numbers; cf. τίθημι, τίθεμεν. The strong form is maintained throughout; e.g. ἔβη, ἔβητον, ἔβημεν, ἔβησαν. Yet cf. Hom. ἐβάτην (dual), ἔκτᾱν, ἔχυτο.

699. Two aorists (first and second) of the same verb are not common; cf. εἶπα, εἶπον *said*; ἔφθασα, ἔφθην *anticipated*; ἤνεγκα, ἤνεγκον *carried*. Usually they belong to different dialects or periods; e.g. ἔπεισα *I persuaded*, poetic ἔπιθον; Att. ἐτάφην *was buried*, Ion. ἐθάφθην; Att. εἶπον, Ion. and late Att. εἶπα. Ἔστησα means *I caused to stand*, ἔστην *I came to a stand*.

700. Μι *Verbs*. The stem of the second aorist indicative of μι verbs is the simple verb stem without thematic vowel.

701. The weak grade of the stem (θε, ἑ, δο) appears in the second aorists of τίθημι, ἵημι, and δίδωμι, which in the indicative occur only in the dual and plural (685); e.g. ἔθετον, ἔθεμεν, εἶτον, εἶμεν, ἔδοτον, ἔδομεν (504). The weak grade is proper also to the middle, e.g. ἐθέμεθα, εἴμεθα (ἑ-ἑ-μεθα). In ἔστην, ἔστητον, ἔστημεν, ἔστησαν, the strong form is carried through from the singular. The other verbs use the κ aorists in the singular, ἔθηκα, ἧκα, ἔδωκα (685).

702. The second aorist middle of μι verbs regularly drops σ in σο in the second person singular after a short vowel and then contracts that vowel with ο; e.g. ἔθου for ἐ-θε-σο, ἑ-θε-ο. So in the imperative; e.g. θοῦ for θε-σο, δοῦ for δο-σο, πρίω for πρια-σο. Cf. 669 *c*.

703. In the subjunctive the stem vowel, which is regularly weak, contracts with the thematic vowel; e.g. θῶ, θῇς, for θέω, θέῃς; ὦ, ᾖς, for ἔω, ἔῃς, etc. In πρίωμαι from ἐπριάμην, α of the stem is disregarded, and the forms are accented as if from a stem πρι; e.g. πρίη, πρίηται, etc., like λύη, λύηται.

704. In the optative the weak stem vowel contracts with the mood suffix; e.g. θείην for θε-ιη-ν, θεῖμεν for θε-ῖ-μεν. In πρίαιο the accent is recessive, as in the subjunctive (703).

705. The second person singular of the imperative ends in s or θι; e.g. θές, ἕς, δός (cf. σχές, 694 end); στῆθι, γνῶθι (cf. πτῆθι, πῖθι, τλῆθι, 694).

706. Other stems in ε having second aorists are σβέ-ννῡμι *quench*, ἔσβην, inflected like ἔστην, and ἀπο-σκλῆναι *dry up* (σκέλλω, 694 end).

707. The second aorists ὠνήμην, later ὠνάμην, from ὀνίνημι *help*, and ἐπλήμην (poetic) from πίμπλημι *fill*, are inflected like the pluperfect middle (480). So also those in ημην, ιμην, and υμην (696 a).

708. Verbs in ῡμι form no Attic second aorists from the stem in υ.

V. *First Perfect System*

709. *First Perfect and Pluperfect Active.* The stem of the first perfect active is formed by adding κα to the reduplicated verb stem. In the pluperfect the suffix is κεα, contracted to κη. For the inflection, see 480. E.g. λύω *loose*, λέ-λυ-κα, ἐ-λε-λύ-κη; πείθω *persuade*, πέ-πει-κα; κομίζω *carry*, κε-κόμι-κα.

710. Herodotus has the original εα, εας, εε of the pluperfect in the singular (654 d).

711. Vowel verbs lengthen the final vowel if short; e.g. φιλέω *love*, πε-φίλη-κα; ἐάω *allow*, εἴᾱ-κα (537); τίθημι (θη-, θε-) *place*, τέ-θη-κα.

712. Verbs whose stems mutate in other tenses generally show in the κα perfect the same grade as the present; e.g. πείθ-ω *persuade*, 2 aor. ἔ-πιθ-ον, 2 perf. πέ-ποιθ-α, 1 perf. πέ-πει-κα. But δείδω *fear* has δέ-δοι-κα.

713. The perfect in κα belongs especially to vowel stems, and in Homer it is found only with these. For these Homer sometimes has the second perfect in α (716); e.g. πεφύᾱσι, Att. πεφύκᾱσι. The κα form was afterwards extended to liquid, nasal, and dental stems.

714. *Liquid and Nasal Verbs.* *a.* A few liquid and nasal stems add κα without change; e.g. ἀγγέλλω *announce* (ἀγγελ-), ἤγγελ-κα; φαίνω *show* (φαν-), πέ-φαγ-κα (72).

b. Monosyllabic stems show the weak grade in α (27, 586); e.g. φθείρω *destroy* (φθερ-, φθρ-), ἔ-φθαρ-κα; στέλλω *send* (στελ-, στλ-), ἔ-σταλ-κα; τείνω *stretch* (τεν-, τν-), τέ-τα-κα.

c. A few nasal stems drop ν; e.g. κρῑνω *judge* (κριν-), κέ-κρι-κα.

d. Many liquid and nasal stems, originally dissyllabic, lose the vowel of the first syllable and lengthen the second (107); e.g. βάλλω *throw* (βελε-, βαλ-, βλη-), βέ-βλη-κα; καλέω *call* (καλε-), κέ-κλη-κα; θνῄσκω *die* (θανα-, θνη-), τέ-θνη-κα; τέμνω *cut* (τεμ-, τεμα-, τμη-), τέ-τμη-κα.

715. Stems ending in a dental drop the τ, δ, or θ before κα; e.g. κομίζω *carry* (κομιδ-), κε-κόμι-κα; πείθω *persuade* (πειθ-), πέ-πει-κα.

VI. *Second Perfect System*

716. *Second Perfect Active.* The stem of the second perfect is formed by adding α to the reduplicated verb stem. In the pluperfect the suffix is εα, contracted to η. E.g. γράφ-ω *write*, γέ-γραφ-α, ἐ-γεγράφ-η; φεύγω *flee*, πέ-φευγ-α, ἐ-πεφεύγ-η.

717. Οἶδα *know* (stem ϝειδ-, ϝοιδ-) has no reduplication.

718. Vowel mutation (**34**) is apt to show ο in the second perfect; e.g. λείπω *leave*, λέ-λοιπ-α; πέμπω *send*, πέ-πομφ-α (**723**) ; πείθω *persuade*, πέ-ποιθ-α *believe*; epic 2 aor. ἤλυθ-ον *went*, epic perf. εἰλ-ήλουθ-α; λαγχάνω *obtain by lot*, Ion. 2 perf. λέ-λογχ-α. But often the present stem determines the form of the perfect; e.g. φεύγω *flee*, 2 aor. ἔφυγον, perf. πέ-φευγ-α (not πε-φουγ-α; see **585**). So Att. ἐλ-ήλυθ-α *have come* (not ἐλ-ήλουθ-α).

719. Ἔρρωγα from ῥήγνῡμι (ῥηγ-, ῥαγ-, ῥωγ-) *break* and εἴωθα *be accustomed* change η of the stem to ω (**34**) ; εἴωθα is for σε-σϝω-θα (cf. **552**).

720. Stems having vowel gradation have long vowels in the second perfect; e.g. θάλλω *flourish*, τέ-θηλ-α; κράζω *bawl*, κέ-κρᾱγ-α; μαίνομαι *rage*, μέ-μην-α; τήκω *melt*, τέ-τηκ-α; φαίνω *show* πέ-φην-α; λαγχάνω *obtain by lot* (λαχ-), εἴ-ληχ-α (**552**).

721. Vowel stems do not form second perfects; ἀκήκο-α, from ἀκού-ω *hear* (stem ἀκου-, ἀκοϝ-), is only an apparent exception.

722. Homer has many second perfects not found in Attic; e.g. προβέβουλα, cf. βούλομαι *wish*; μέμηλε from μέλει *concern*; ἔολπα from ἔλπω *hope*; δέδουπα from δουπέω (δουπ-) *resound*.

723. *Aspirated Second Perfects.* Most stems ending in π or β change these to φ, and most ending in κ or γ change these to χ. Those in φ and χ make no change. E.g.

βλάπτω *hurt* (βλαβ-), βέβλαφα; κόπτω *cut* (κοπ-), κέκοφα; ἀλλάττω *change* (ἀλλαγ-), ἤλλαχα; φυλάττω *guard* (φυλακ-), πεφύλαχα; ἄγω *lead*, ἦχα. But πλήττω *beat*, πέπληγα; φεύγω *flee*, πέφευγα; στέργω *love*, ἔστοργα; λάμπω *shine*, λέλαμπα.

724. The following verbs form aspirated second perfects: ἄγω, ἀλλάττω, ἀνοίγω, βλάπτω, δείκνῡμι, κηρῦττω, κλέπτω, κόπτω, λαμβάνω, λάπτω, λέγω (*collect*), μάττω, πέμπω, πρᾱττω, πτήττω, τάττω, τρέπω, τρίβω, φέρω, φυλάττω. Ἀνοίγω has both ἀνέῳγα and ἀνέῳχα, and πρᾱττω has both πέπρᾱχα *have done* and πέπρᾱγα *fare* (*well* or *ill*).

725. The aspirated perfect is not found in Homer; only τέτροφα (τρέπω) occurs in tragedy, and only πέπομφα in Herodotus and Thucydides. It is frequent in comedy and in the subsequent prose.

726. Μι *Forms.* A few verbs have second perfects and pluperfects in which the endings, in the dual and plural, are added directly to the verb stem as in the μι conjugation. They are never found in the singular of the indicative. See the 2 perf. and plup. of ἵστημι, **506**.

727. The following ω verbs have forms of this class:

βαίνω (βα-) *go*, poetic 2 perf. βέβᾱσι (Hom. βεβάᾱσι), subj. βεβῶσι, infin. βεβάναι (Hom. βεβάμεν), partic. βεβώς (Hom. βεβαώς, βεβαυῖα) ; 2 plup. Hom. βέβασαν.

γίγνομαι (γεν-, γον-, γα-, 27) *become*, 2 perf. γέγονα *am*; Hom. 2 perf. γεγάασι, 2 plup. dual γεγάτην, infin. γεγάμεν, partic. γεγαώς, γεγαυῖα, Att. γεγώς, γεγῶσα (poetic).

δείδω (δϝει-, δϝοι-, δϝι-) *fear*, epic present: Attic 2 perf. δέδια, δέδιας, δέδιε; δέδιτον; δέδιμεν, δέδιτε, δεδίασι; 2 plup. ἐδεδίη, ἐδεδίης, ἐδεδίει; ἐδέδιτον, ἐδεδίτην; ἐδέδιμεν, ἐδέδισαν; subj. δεδίῃ, δεδίωσι; opt. δεδιείη; impv. δέδιθι; infin. δεδιέναι; partic. δεδιώς, δεδιυῖα, δεδιός. The 1 perf. is common in these forms: δέδοικα, δέδοικας, δέδοικε, δεδοίκασι; ἐδεδοίκη, ἐδεδοίκης, ἐδεδοίκει, ἐδεδοίκεσαν; δεδοικέναι; δεδοικώς, δεδοικυῖα, δεδοικός.

ἔοικα (ϝε-ϝοικ-α, 549) *seem*, poetic ἔοιγ-μεν, Hom. dual ἔικτον, Hom. plup. dual ἔικτην, Att. εἴξασι. Synopsis: ἔοικα, ἐοίκω, ἐοίκοιμι, ἐοικέναι (poetic εἰκέναι), ἐοικώς (εἰκώς, neut. εἰκός), plup. ἐῴκη.

θνῄσκω (θαν-, θνη-) *die*, 2 perf. τέθνατον, τέθναμεν, τεθνᾶσι, opt. τεθναίην, impv. τέθναθι, τεθνάτω, infin. τεθνάναι (Hom. τεθνάμεναι), partic. τεθνεώς (802), τεθνεῶσα (Hom. τεθνηώς, τεθνηυίη), plup. ἐτέθνασαν.

κράζω (κραγ-) *bawl* has 2 perf. κέκρᾱγα, impv. κέκρᾱχθι, and a thematic form κεκράγετε.

728. Some of the forms listed in 727, especially those from Homer, illustrate the original conjugation of the perfect and pluperfect as it appears in οἶδα (529), with strong stems in the singular, weak stems in the dual and plural, and all without thematic vowel. E.g., πέποιθα was originally inflected πέποισ-θα, πέποιθε, πέπιθμεν, πέπιστε, πεπίθατι (for πε-πιθ-ντι, 27). Cf. above ἔοικα, ἔικτον; γέγονα, γεγάτην, γεγάμεν; and Hom. μέμαμεν (μέμονα), plup. ἐπέπιθμεν (πέποιθα), πέπισθε (πέπονθα). The participle had the strong form in masc. and neut., e.g. εἰδώς, the weak in the fem., e.g. Hom. ἰδυῖα, ἀράρυῖα (ἀρηρώς), τεθάλυῖα (τεθηλώς). In Attic εἰδυῖα this original distinction was lost through analogy, as in πεποίθαμεν, etc.

VII. *Perfect Middle System*

729. *Perfect and Pluperfect Middle.* The stem of the perfect and pluperfect middle (and passive) is the reduplicated verb stem, to which the endings are directly affixed. E.g.

λύω, λέλυ-μαι, λέλυ-σαι, etc., ἐλελύ-μην, ἐλελύ-μεθα, etc.; λείπω (λειπ-), λέλειμμαι (79), λέλειψαι, etc.

For the inflection, see 480.

730. The stem may be modified in general as in the first perfect active, by lengthening the final vowel if short (711), by the use of the weak grade in α in monosyllabic stems (714 b), by dropping ν in a few verbs (714 c), or by lengthening the second vowel of stems originally dissyllabic (714 d); e.g. φιλέ-ω, πεφίλη-μαι, ἐπεφιλή-μην; φθείρω (φθερ-, φθρ-, 27), ἔφθαρμαι; κρίνω (κριν-), κέκρι-μαι; βάλλω (βελε-, βαλ-, βλη-), βέβλη-μαι.

731. Verbs having vowel mutation in the several tenses normally show the weak grade in the perfect and pluperfect middle; cf. ἔφθαρμαι (730), τέταμαι (τείνω), πέπυσμαι (πυνθάνομαι, fut. πεύσομαι). But if the present has the strong grade, the perfect often follows with the same stem; e.g. κλέπ-τω steal, κέκλεμμαι; πέμπ-ω send, πέπεμμαι (499).

732. When ν is not dropped before μαι (602), it is generally replaced by σ (74), and it sometimes becomes μ (73); e.g. φαίνω (φαν-), πέφασ-μαι, ἐ-πεφάσ-μην; ὀξύνω (ὀξυν-) sharpen, ὤξυμ-μαι. Before endings not beginning with μ, the original ν reappears; e.g. πέφαν-ται, πέφαν-θε; but forms in ν-σαι and ν-σο (like πέφαν-σαι, ἐ-πέφαν-σο) seem not to occur (75); periphrastic forms, πεφασμένος εἶ or ἦσθα, were apparently used for these.

733. In the third person plural of the perfect and pluperfect middle, consonant stems are compelled to use the perfect participle with εἰσί and ἦσαν (496 b).

Here, however, the Ionic endings αται and ατο for νται and ντο (654 c) are occasionally used even in Attic prose; e.g. τετάχ-αται and ἐτετάχ-ατο (Thucyd.) for τεταγμένοι εἰσί and ἦσαν.

734. *Future Perfect.* The stem of the future perfect is formed by adding σ⁰/ε to the stem of the perfect middle. It ends in σομαι, and has the inflection of the future middle (675). A short final vowel is always lengthened before σομαι. E.g.

λύω, λε-λύ-, λελύ-σομαι; γράφ-ω, γε-γραφ-, γεγράψομαι (69); λείπω, λε-λειπ-, λελείψομαι; δέω bind, δέδεμαι (596), δεδή-σομαι; πράττω (πρᾱγ-), πε-πρᾱγ-, πεπρᾱ́ξομαι.

735. The future perfect in Greek is best understood by reference to the corresponding perfect, which denotes a permanent state; i.e., the Greek perfect, unlike the Latin and the English perfect, is not properly a past tense, but expresses a fixed condition in the present — the so-called perfective use (1250 c). The future perfect is generally passive in sense. But it has a middle meaning in μεμνήσομαι shall remember and πεπαύσομαι shall cease (once for all); and it is active in κεκτήσομαι shall possess, from the deponent κτάομαι acquire. The future perfect is found in only a small number of verbs, and forms other than the indicative are extremely rare.

736. Two verbs have a special form in Attic Greek for the future perfect] active; θνῄσκω die has τεθνήξω shall be dead, formed from the perfect stem τεθνηκ-; and ἵστημι set has ἑστήξω shall stand, from ἑστηκ-, stem of perfect ἕστηκα stand. In Homer we have κεχαρήσω and κεχαρήσομαι, from χαίρω (χαρ-) rejoice; also κεκαδήσω from χάζω (χαδ-) make yield, and πεφιδήσεται from φείδομαι spare, which are from reduplicated aorists (559).

737. In most verbs the future perfect active is expressed by the perfect participle and ἔσομαι (future of εἰμί be); e.g. ἐγνωκότες ἐσόμεθα we shall be fully aware (lit. have learnt). The future perfect passive may also be expressed in this way; e.g. ἀπηλλαγμένοι ἐσόμεθα we shall be rid of (once for all).

VIII. *First Passive System*

738. *First Aorist Passive.* The stem of the first aorist passive is formed by adding θη or θε to the stem as it appears in the perfect middle (omitting the reduplication). The indicative, imperative (except before ντ), and infinitive have θη, the subjunctive, optative, and imperative have θε. It has the secondary active endings(578), and its inflection in the indicative may be compared with that of the athematic second aorist active·forms in 694, cf. 1235. E.g.

λύω, λέλυ-μαι, ἐλύθην (λυθη-); λείπω, λέλειμ-μαι, ἐλείφθην (λειπ-θη-, 66); πράττω (πρᾱγ-), πέπρᾱγ-μαι, ἐπράχθην (πρᾱγ-θη-); πείθω, πέπεισ-μαι, ἐπείσθην; φιλέω, πεφίλη-μαι, ἐφιλήθην; πλέω (πλευ-), πέπλευσ-μαι, ἐπλεύσθην (600); τείνω (τεν-), τέτα-μαι, ἐτάθην (587); βάλλω (βαλ-, βλη-), βέβλη-μαι, ἐβλήθην (714 d); τελέω, τετέλεσ-μαι (598), ἐτελέσθην; ἀκούω, ἤκουσμαι, ἠκούσθην. See 480; and for resemblances to the perfect middle, 730.

739. Τρέπω has τέτραμμαι (587), but ἐτρέφθην (Ion. ἐτράφθην); τρέφω has τέθραμμαι, ἐθρέφθην; and στρέφω has ἔστραμμαι, with (rare) ἐστρέφθην (Ion. and Dor. ἐστράφθην). Φαίνω has πέφασμαι (732), but ἐφάνθην like πέφανται.

740. In Homer ν is added to some vowel stems before θ of the aorist passive; e.g. ἱδρύω *erect,* ἵδρῡμαι, ἱδρύν-θην, as if from a stem in υν (Attic ἱδρΰθην). So Hom. ἐκλίνθην and ἐκρίνθην (602), from original stems in ν.

For ἐτέθην from τίθημι (θε-), and ἐτύθην from θύω *sacrifice,* see 105 c. For ἐθρέφθην from τρέφω *nourish,* and other forms with interchangeable aspirates, see 105 e.

741. In Homer the original ending of the third plural (-ντ) is seen in ἐτέρφθεν (= ἐτέρφθησαν) from τέρπω *delight.*

742. *First Future Passive.* The stem of the first future passive adds σ°/ε to the stem (in θη) of the first aorist passive. It ends in θησομαι, and is inflected like the future middle (675). E.g.

λύω, ἐλύθην, λυθήσομαι (stem λυθησ°/ε-); λείπω, ἐλείφθην, λειφθήσομαι; πράττω (πρᾱγ-), ἐπράχθην, πρᾱχθήσομαι; πείθω, ἐπείσθην, πεισθήσομαι; τείνω, ἐτάθην, ταθήσομαι; πλέκω, ἐπλέχθην, πλεχθήσομαι; τῑμάω, ἐτῑμήθην, τῑμηθήσομαι; τελέω, ἐτελέσθην, τελεσθήσομαι; κλῑνω, ἐκλίθην, κλιθήσομαι.

743. The first passive system rarely appears in verbs with monosyllabic liquid stems (587). But τείνω (τεν-) *stretch* has ἐτάθην and ταθήσομαι.

IX. *Second Passive System*

744. *Second Aorist Passive.* The stem of the second aorist passive is formed by adding η or ε to the verb stem. In the indicative, infinitive, and imperative, except before ντ (738), η is used. For the inflection, see 492. E.g.

βλάπτω (βλαβ-) *hurt*, ἐβλάβην; γράφω (γραφ-) *write*, ἐγράφην; ῥίπτω (ῥιφ-) *throw*, ἐρρίφην; φαίνω (φαν-) ἐφάνην; στρέφω *turn*, ἐστράφην (745); τέρπω *delight*, ἐτάρπην; στέλλω (στελ-) *send*, ἐστάλην.

745. Verbs whose stems mutate with ε, ο, α, or η, ω, α, generally have the weak grade with α (587). See στρέφω and τέρπω in 744. E.g. τήκω *melt*, ἐτάκην; ῥήγνῦμι *break*, ἐρράγην. But πλήττω (πληγ-) *strike* has ἐπλήγην, except in composition, ἐξ-επλάγην and κατ-επλάγην (from stem πλαγ-).

746. Some verbs have both passive aorists; e.g. βλάπτω (βλαβ-) *hurt*, ἐβλάφθην and ἐβλάβην; στρέφω *turn*, ἐστρέφθην (rare) and ἐστράφην. Τρέπω *turn* has all the six aorists: ἔτρεψα, ἐτρεψάμην, ἔτραπον (epic and lyric), ἐτραπόμην, ἐτρέφθην, ἐτράπην.

747. Homer has a third plural in -ν, e.g. ἐπάγεν *were fixed* = ἐπάγησαν. Cf. 741.

748. *Second Future Passive.* The stem of the second future passive adds σ⁰/ε to the stem (in η) of the second aorist passive. It ends in ησομαι and is inflected like the first future (742). E.g.

βλάπτω (βλαβ-), ἐβλάβην, βλαβή-σομαι; γράφω, ἐγράφην, γραφή-σομαι; φαίνω (φαν-), ἐφάνην, φανή-σομαι; στέλλω (στελ-), ἐστάλην, σταλή-σομαι; στρέφω, ἐστράφην, στραφή-σομαι.

749. The following table shows the nine tense stems (so far as they exist) of λύω, λείπω, πράττω (πρᾱγ-), φαίνω (φαν-), and στέλλω (στελ-), with their subdivisions.

Tense System

Present.	λῦ⁰/ε-	λειπ⁰/ε-	πρᾱττ⁰/ε-	φαιν⁰/ε-	στελλ⁰/ε-
Future.	λῦσ⁰/ε-	λειψ⁰/ε-	πρᾱξ⁰/ε-	φανε⁰/ε-	στελε⁰/ε-
1 Aorist.	λῦσα-		πρᾱξα-	φηνα-	στειλα-
2 Aorist.		λιπ⁰/ε-			
1 Perfect.	λελυκα-			πεφαγκα-	ἐσταλκα-
2 Perfect.		λελοιπα-	πεπρᾱγα- / πεπρᾱχα-	πεφηνα-	
Perf. { Perf.	λελυ-	λελειπ-	πεπρᾱγ-	πεφαν-	ἐσταλ-
Mid. { Fut. P.	λελῦσ⁰/ε-	λελειψ⁰/ε-	πεπρᾱξ⁰/ε-		
1 Pass. { Aor.	λυθε(η)-	λειφθε(η)-	πρᾱχθε(η)-	φανθε(η)-	
{ Fut.	λυθησ⁰/ε-	λειφθησ⁰/ε-	πρᾱχθησ⁰/ε-	φανθησ⁰/ε-	
2 Pass. { Aor.				φανε(η)-	σταλε(η)-
{ Fut.				φανησ⁰/ε-	σταλησ⁰/ε-

FORMATION OF THE DEPENDENT MOODS AND THE PARTICIPLE

Subjunctive

750. The subjunctive has the primary endings (578) in all its tenses. In all forms (even in verbs in μι) it has the long thematic vowel ω/η (571 *b*).

751. Ω *Verbs.* In ω verbs the present and second aorist tense stems change °/ε to ω/η, and the first aorist tense stem changes final α to ω/η. All have ω, ῃς, ῃ in the singular, and ωσι for ωνσι (75) in the third person plural, of the active. E.g.

λείπω, pres. subj. λείπω, λείπωμαι, 2 aor. λίπω, λίπωμαι; λύω, 1 aor. λύσω, λύσωμαι.

752. A perfect subjunctive active is rarely formed, on the analogy of the present, by changing final α of the tense stem to ω/η; e.g. λέλυκα, λελύκω; εἴληφα, εἰλήφω. See 763. But the more common form of the tense is the perfect active participle with ὦ (subjunctive of εἰμί *be*); e.g. λελυκὼς ὦ, εἰληφὼς ὦ.

753. The perfect subjunctive middle is almost always expressed by the perfect middle participle and ὦ; e.g. λελυμένος ὦ, ῇς, ῇ, etc.

754. A few verbs with vowel stems form a perfect subjunctive middle directly, by adding ω/η to the tense stem; e.g. κτά-ομαι *acquire*, perf. κέκτημαι *possess*, subj. κεκτῶμαι (for κε-κτη-ωμαι, shortened to κε-κτε-ωμαι), κεκτῇ, κεκτῆται; μιμνήσκω *remind*, μέμνημαι *remember* (Lat. memini), subj. μεμνῶμαι, μεμνώμεθα (Hdt. μεμνεώμεθα). These follow the analogy of ἱστῶμαι, -ῇ, -ῆται etc. (756). For a similar optative, see 766.

755. Μι *Verbs.* In all μι forms, including both passive aorists, the final vowel of the stem is contracted with the thematic vowel (ω or η), so that the subjunctive ends in ῶ or ῶμαι.

756. *a.* Verbs in ημι (with stems in ε and α) have ῶ, ῇς, ῇ, ῶμαι, ῇ, ῆται, etc., in the subjunctive, as if all had stems in ε. E.g. ἵστημι (στα-) has ἱστῆς, ἱστῇ, ἱστῆται, στῆς, στῇ, etc., as if the uncontracted form were ἱστε-ω, not ἱστα-ω. These verbs have Ionic stems in ε (see 670 *a*).

b. The inflection is that of the subjunctives φιλῶ and φιλῶμαι (482).

757. For the inflection of the aorist passive subjunctive, with ε of the tense stem contracted with ω or η, e.g. λυθῶ (for λυθέ-ω), λυθῶμεν (for λυθέ-ωμεν), etc., φανῶ (for φανέ-ω), etc., see 480, 3.

758. For a few subjunctives of the weak perfect of the μι form, e.g. ἑστῶ (for ἑστα-ω), βεβῶσι (for βεβα-ωσι), see 506.

759. Verbs in ωμι (with stem in o) have by contraction ῶ, ῷς, ῷ, etc., ῶμαι, ῷ, ῶται, etc. (for o-ω, o-ης, o-η, o-ωμαι, etc.) ; e.g. δίδωμι, subj. διδῶ, διδῷς, διδῷ ; διδῶμαι, διδῷ, διδῶται, etc.

760. Verbs in νῦμι form the subjunctive (as the optative, **775**) like verbs in ω ; e.g. δείκνῦμι, subj. δεικνύ-ω, δεικνύ-ωμαι.

761. Δύναμαι *can*, ἐπίσταμαι *understand*, κρέμαμαι *hang*, and the second aorist ἐπριάμην *bought* accent the subjunctive (as the optative, **774**) as if there were no contraction ; e.g. δύνωμαι, ἐπίστωμαι, κρέμωμαι, πρίωμαι (contrast τιθῶμαι).

Optative

762. The optative has the secondary endings (except after ι in the first person singular), preceded by the mood suffix (**573**) ι or ιη (ιε). See **574**.

763. Ω *Verbs.* Verbs in ω have the ending μι (for ν) in the first person singular in all tenses of the active voice. In the present, future, and second aorist systems, the thematic vowel (always o) is contracted with ι to οι, giving οιμι, οις, οι, etc., οιμην, οιο, οιτο, etc. In the first aorist system, final α of the tense stem is contracted with ι, giving αιμι, αις, αι, etc. (but see **764**), αιμην, αιο, αιτο, etc. The rare perfect active (like the subjunctive, **752**) follows the analogy of the present. E.g.

λέγοιμι (for λεγο-ῑ-μι), λέγοις (for λεγο-ῑ-ς), λέγοι (for λεγο-ῑ-τ (**24**)), λέγοιτε (for λεγο-ῑ-τε), λέγοιεν (for λεγο-ιε-ντ) ; λείπω, 2 aor. λίποιμι (for λιπο-ῑ-μι), λίποιεν (for λιπο-ιε-ντ) ; λύσαιμι (for λῦσα-ῑ-μι), λύσαιμεν (for λῦσα-ῑ-μεν), λυσαίμην (for λῦσα-ῑ-μην), λύσαισθε (for λῦσα-ῑ-σθε) ; perf. εἴληφα, opt. εἰλήφοιμι, etc.

764. Homer and Attic generally (but not in the inscriptions) use the terminations ειας, ειε, and ειαν, for αις, αι, αιεν, in the aorist active; e.g. λύσειας, λύσειε, λύσειαν. See λύσαιμι and φήναιμι in **480, 1**, and **492, 575, 656.**

765. The perfect middle is almost always expressed by the perfect middle participle and εἴην ; e.g. λελυμένος εἴην (see **480, 2**). The perfect active is more frequently expressed by the perfect active participle and εἴην than by the form in οιμι given in the paradigms; e.g. λελυκὼς εἴην. See **752, 753.**

766. a. A few verbs with vowel stems form a perfect optative middle (like the subjunctive, **754**) directly, by adding ῑ-μην or o-ῑ-μην to the tense stem; e.g. κτάομαι, perf. κέκτη-μαι, opt. κεκτήμην, κεκτῇο, κεκτῇτο (for κεκτη-ῑ-μην, κεκτη-ῑ-ο, κεκτη-ῑ-το), etc.; also κεκτῴμην, κεκτῷο, κεκτῷτο (for κεκτη-ο-ῑ-μην, etc.) ; so μιμνήσκω, μέμνημαι, opt. μεμνῇμην or μεμνῴμην (doubt-

OPTATIVE 177

ful); καλέω, κέκλημαι, opt. κεκλήμην, κεκλῇο, κεκλήμεθα ; and βάλλω, βέβλημαι, opt. δια-βεβλῇσθε. So Hom. λελῦτο and λελῦντο (for λελυ-ῖ-το and λελυ-ῖ-ντο), perf. opt. of λύω. Cf. δαινῦτο, pres. opt. of δαίνῡμι.

b. The forms in ῳμην belong to the thematic form of inflection; those in ημην etc. and ῦτο are athematic (772).

767. A few verbs have οιην (769) in the second perfect optative; e.g. ἐκπέφευγα, ἐκπεφευγοίην.

The second aorist optative of ἔχω *have* is σχοίην, but the regular σχοῖμι is used in composition (574 c).

768. A very few relics remain of an older active optative with ν for μι in the first person singular; e.g. τρέφοι-ν for τρέφοι-μι, ἁμάρτοι-ν for ἁμάρτοι-μι (from ἁμαρτάνω).

769. *Contract Verbs.* In the present active of contract verbs, forms in ιη-ν, ιη-s, ιη, etc., contracted with the thematic vowel o to οιην, οιηs, οιη, etc., are much more common in the singular than the regular forms in οιμι, οιs, οι, but they seldom occur in the dual and plural. Both the forms in οιην and those in οιμι are again contracted with an α of the verb stem to ῳην and ῳμι, and with an ε or o to οιην and οιμι (574 b). E.g.

τῑμα-ο-ιη-ν, τῑμα-οίην, τῑμῴην ; φιλε-ο-ιη-ν, φιλε-οίην, φιλοίην ; δηλο-ο-ιη-ν, δηλο-οίην, δηλοίην ; τῑμα-ο-ῖ-μι, τῑμά-οιμι, τῑμῷμι ; φιλε-ο-ῖ-μι, φιλέ-οιμι, φιλοῖμι ; δηλο-ο-ῖ-μι, δηλό-οιμι, δηλοῖμι. See the inflection in 482.

770. For the optative ῥῑγῴην, from ῥῑγόω *shiver*, see 488.

771. Μι *Verbs.* a. The present and second aorist active of the μι form, and both aorists passive in all verbs, have the suffix ιη, and in the first person singular the ending ν. Here α, ε, or o of the stem is contracted with ιη to αιη, ειη, or οιη ; e.g. ἱστα-ιη-ν, ἱσταίην ; στα-ιη-μεν, σταίημεν ; λυθε-ιη-ν, λυθείην ; δο-ιη-ν, δοίην.

b. In the dual and plural, forms with ῑ, and with ιε-ν in the third person plural, are much more common than the longer forms with ιη ; e.g. σταῖμεν, σταῖτε, σταῖεν (better than σταίημεν, σταίητε, σταίησαν). See 504, 574 a.

772. In the present and second aorist middle of verbs in ημι and ωμι, final α, ε, or o of the stem is contracted with ι into αι, ει, or οι, to which the simple endings μην etc. are added. E.g.

ἱσταίμην (for ἱστα-ῖ-μην), ἱσταῖο, ἱσταῖτο ; θείμην (θε-ῖ-μην), θεῖο (θε-ῖ-σο, θε-ῖ-ο), θεῖτο ; δοίμην (δο-ῖ-μην). See the inflection in 504. See also the cases of perfect optative middle in ημην and ῦτο in 766.

773. The optatives τιθοίμην, τιθοῖο, τιθοῖτο, etc. (also accented τίθοιο, τίθοιτο, etc.) and (in composition) θοίμην, θοῖο, θοῖτο, etc. (also accented σύν-θοιτο, πρόσ-θοισθε, etc.), as if formed from τιθέω (or τίθω), are found, as well as the regular τιθείμην, θείμην, etc., **668.** See also πρόοιτο and other forms of ἵημι, **514** c.

774. Δύναμαι, ἐπίσταμαι, κρέμαμαι, and the second aorists ἐπριάμην (**504**) and ὠνήμην (from ὀνίνημι *help*), accent the optative as if there were no contraction; δυναίμην, δύναιο, δύναιτο; ἐπίσταιτο, ἐπίσταισθε, κρέμαιο, πρίαιο, πρίαιντο, ὄναισθε. For the similar subjunctive, see **761.**

775. Verbs in νῦμι form the optative (as the subjunctive, **760**) like verbs in ω; e.g. δείκνυμι, opt. δεικνύοιμι, δεικνυοίμην (inflected like λύοιμι, λυοίμην).

776. Second aorists from stems in υ of the μι form (e.g. ἔδῦν) have no optative in Attic (see **504, 708**). But Homer has a few forms like δύη, δῦμεν (for δυ-ιη, δυ-ι-μεν), from ἔδῦν.

777. A few second perfect optatives of the μι form are made by adding ιη-ν to stems in α; e.g. τεθναίην (for τεθνα-ιη-ν), ἑσταίην (**506**). See the enumeration of μι forms, **727.**

Imperative

778. Ω *Verbs.* The present and the second aorist active and middle of ω verbs have the thematic vowel ε (ο before ντων), to which the imperative endings (**578**) are affixed. But the second person singular in the active has no ending; in the middle it drops σ in σο and contracts ε-ο to ου. E.g.

λεῖπε, λειπέ-τω, λείπε-τον, λειπέ-των, λείπε-τε, λειπό-ντων; λείπου, λειπέ-σθω, λείπε-σθον, λειπέ-σθων, λείπε-σθε, λειπέ-σθων. So λῖπε and λιποῦ.

779. The first aorist active and middle have the endings ον and αι in the second person singular, the origin of which is unknown. In other persons the regular endings are added to the stem in σα (or α). E.g.

λῦσον, λῦσά-τω, λῦσα-τον, λῦσά-των, λῦσα-τε, λῦσά-ντων; λῦσαι, λῦσά-σθω, λῦσα-σθε, λῦσά-σθων; φῆνον, φηνά-τω, etc.; φῆναι, φηνά-σθω, φῆνα-σθε, φηνά-σθων.

780. The perfect active is very rare, except in a few cases of the μι form (**506**) with a present meaning. But Aristophanes has κεκράγετε *keep on shrieking* from κράζω (κραγ-), and κεχήνετε *gape* from χάσκω (χαν-).

781. The third person singular of the perfect passive is the only form of perfect imperative in common use; for this see **1276.**

782. The second person singular of the middle occasionally occurs as an emphatic form; e.g. πέπαυσο *stop!*

783. The perfect imperative in all voices can be expressed by the perfect participle and ἴσθι, ἔστω, etc. (imperative of εἰμί *be*); e.g. εἰρημένον ἔστω

for εἰρήσθω *let it have been said* (i.e. *let what has been said stand*), πεπεισμένοι ἔστων *suppose them to have been persuaded*.

784. Μι Verbs. The present imperative of the μι form retains θι in the
second person singular active only in a few primitive verbs; e.g. φα-θί
from φημί (φη-, φα-) *say*, ἴ-θι from εἶμι (εἰ-, ἰ-) *go*, ἴσ-θι from εἰμί (ἐσ-) *be*
and from οἶδα (ϝιδ-) *know*. See **509, 511, 517, 529**.

For Homeric forms in θι see **672**.

785. The present active commonly omits θι in the second person, and lengthens the preceding vowel of the stem (α, ε, ο, or υ)
to η, ει, ου, or ῡ; e.g. ἵστη, τίθει, δίδου, and δείκνῡ. The other
persons add the regular endings (**578**) to the weak stem; e.g.
ἱστά-τω, ἵστα-τε, ἱστά-ντων; τιθέ-τω; δίδο-τε; δεικνύ-ντων.

786. The present middle of verbs in ημι and ωμι has the regular form
in σο, and also poetic forms in ω (for ασο) and ου (for εσο and οσο), in
the second person singular; e.g. ἵστασο or ἵστω, τίθεσο or τίθου, δίδοσο or
δίδου. Cf. **582 g.** But verbs in ῡμι always retain υσο; e.g. δείκνῡμι, δείκνυσο.
In the other persons the inflection is regular: see the paradigms (**504**).

787. a. In the second aorist active the stem vowel is regularly
long (η, ω, ῡ), except before ντων (**578**), and θι is retained in the
second person singular. E.g.

στῆ-θι (στα-), στή-τω, στῆ-τε, στά-ντων; βῆ-θι (βα-), βή-τω, βῆ-τε, βά-ντων;
γνῶ-θι, γνώ-τω, γνῶ-τε, γνό-ντων; δῦ-θι, δύ-τω, δῦ-τε, δύ-ντων. See **695** and
797 b.

b. But we have ς instead of θι in θές (from τίθημι), δός (from δίδωμι), ἕς
(from ἵημι), and σχές (from ἔσχον, 2 aor. of ἔχω). These verbs have the
short vowel in all persons; e.g. θές, θέ-τω, θέ-τε, θέ-ντων; δός, δό-τω, δό-τε,
δό-ντων.

c. Στῆθι and βῆθι have poetic forms στᾱ and βᾱ, used only in composition; e.g. κατά-βᾱ *come down*, παρά-στᾱ *stand near*.

788. a. In the second aorist middle, σο drops σ in the second
person singular after a short vowel, and contracts that vowel
with ο (**702**). E.g.

ἐπριάμην, πρίασο (poet.), πρίω (for πρια-ο); ἐθέμην, θοῦ (for θε-σο, θε-ο); ἐδόμην,
δοῦ (for δο-σο, δο-ο). So epic δέξο (δεχ-σο), λέξο (λεχ-σο).

b. The other persons have the regular endings (**578**); e.g. πριά-σθω;
θέ-σθω, θέ-σθων; δό-σθω, δό-σθε, δό-σθων.

789. a. The first aorist passive adds the ordinary active endings
(θι, τω, etc.) directly to θε- (θη-) of the tense stem (**738**), after
which θι becomes τι (**105 b**); e.g. λύθη-τι, λυθή-τω, etc.

b. The second aorist passive adds the same terminations to ε-(η-) of the tense stem (744), θι being retained; e.g. φάνη-θι, φανή-τω; στάλη-θι, σταλή-τω, etc.

c. Both aorists have ε-ντων in the third person plural; e.g. λυθέ-ντων, φανέ-ντων, σταλέ-ντων.

790. A few second perfects of the μι form have imperatives in θι: see θνήσκω, τέθναθι, and δείδω, δέδιθι, in 727.

Infinitive

791. Ω *Verbs.* The present, second aorist, and future active add εν to the tense stem, the thematic vowel (here always ε) being contracted with εν to ειν; e.g. λέγειν (for λεγ-ε-εν), ἰδεῖν (for ἰδ-έ-εν), λιπεῖν (for λιπέ-εν), λέξειν (for λεξ-ε-εν).

792. The ending ν instead of εν appears in Doric and Aeolic; e.g. γᾱρύε-ν in Pindar (Attic γηρύειν).

793. For contract presents in ᾶν (not ᾷν) for ά-εν (instead of άειν), and οῦν for ό-εν (instead of όειν), in which the spurious diphthongs ει and ου were treated as ε and ο, see 45 *e.*

794. The first aorist active has αι; e.g. λῦσαι, φῆναι.

795. The perfect active adds ναι to the tense stem; e.g. λελυκ-έ-ναι, γεγραφ-έ-ναι, πεφην-έ-ναι, λελοιπ-έ-ναι.

796. *a.* The infinitive middle adds σθαι to the tense stem in the present, future, and first and second aorists. E.g.

λέγε-σθαι, λέξε-σθαι, φαίνε-σθαι, φανεῖ-σθαι (for φανέε-σθαι), φήνα-σθαι, λύσα-σθαι, λιπέ-σθαι.

b. Both passive futures likewise add σθαι. E.g.

λυθήσε-σθαι, λειφθήσε-σθαι, φανήσε-σθαι, σταλήσε-σθαι.

797. Μι *Verbs.* *a.* The present, second aorist, and second perfect active of the μι form, and both passive aorists, add ναι to the tense stem in the infinitive. E.g.

ἱστά-ναι, τιθέ-ναι, διδό-ναι, δεικνύ-ναι, στῆ-ναι, γνῶ-ναι, δῦ-ναι, τεθνά-ναι, λυθῆ-ναι (738), φανῆ-ναι (744).

b. In the second aorist active the final vowel of the stem is regularly long (698, 787 *a*); e.g. ἵστημι (στα-), στῆ-ναι; ἔβην (βα-), βῆ-ναι.

798. Some μι forms have the more primitive ending εναι (for ϝεναι) in the infinitive active. Such are δοῦναι (from old δο-ϝεναι, δο-εναι); θεῖναι (for θε-ϝεναι); εἶναι, 2 aor. of ἵημι (for ἑ-ϝεναι); 2 perf. δεδιέναι (for δε-δϝι-ϝεναι). See **579**.

799. In all the simple forms of the middle voice (the present and second aorist of the μι form, and all perfects), vowel stems add σθαι directly to the tense stem. Consonant stems drop the σ (**83**). E.g.

ἵστα-σθαι, τίθε-σθαι, δίδο-σθαι, θέ-σθαι, δό-σθαι, ἵε-σθαι (from ἵημι); λελύ-σθαι, τετῑμῆ-σθαι, δεδηλῶ-σθαι, δεδό-σθαι, πτά-σθαι (from πέτο-μαι, πτα-), ἐστάλ-θαι, λελεῖφ-θαι, πεπλέχ-θαι, τετρῖφ-θαι, πεφάν-θαι, ἦσ-θαι (stem ἠσ-).

Participles and Verbals in τος and τεος

800. All active tenses (except the perfect) and both aorists passive add ντ to their tense stem to form the stem of the participle. Stems in οντ of ω verbs have nominatives in ων; those of μι verbs have nominatives in ους. See **580, 329**.

801. The perfect active participle adds the suffix οτ to the tense stem to form the masculine and neuter, and the suffix υια to form the feminine. See **580, 329, 727, 728**.

802. Homer has many varieties of the second perfect participle of the μι form; in αώς, gen. αῶτος (sometimes αότος), fem. αυῖα, e.g. γεγαώς, βεβαώς; in ηώς, gen. ηῶτος or ηότος, fem. ηυῖα, e.g. τεθνηώς, τεθνηῶτος or -ότος, τεθνηυῖα (**727**). Herodotus has εώς, εῶσα, εός, gen. εῶτος, εώσης, e.g. ἐστεώς etc., some forms of which (e.g. ἐστεῶτα, τεθνεῶτι) occur in Homer. The Attic contracts αώς, αῶσα, αός, to ώς, ῶσα, ός (or ώς), gen. ῶτος, ώσης, etc., but leaves τεθνεώς (2 perf. of θνῄσκω) uncontracted. See **338**.

803. All tenses of the middle voice add μενο to the tense stem to form the stem of the participle. See **580, 295**.

804. The stem of the verbals in τος and τεος is formed by adding το or τεο to the verb stem, which generally has the same form as in the first aorist passive (with the change of φ and χ to π and κ, **66**). See **581**.

PART III

FORMATION OF WORDS

805. The Greek language, like most others in the Indo-European family, has a highly developed and flexible system of word formation, in which bases or stems are modified by various prefixes, suffixes, and inflectional endings to form new words or to determine the relation of words in a sentence. E.g., the base γραφ, with or without the suffix °/ε, may give γράφω *I write*, γράφε-τε *you write*, λογο-γράφο-s *speech-writer*, γραφ-ίς *stilus*, γράμμα *document*, γραμματ-ικό-s *scholar*, γραφ-εύ-s *scribe*, ἄ-γραφο-s *unwritten*; so Modern Greek τηλέ-γραφο-s *far-written*.

806. A root or base is the ultimate part of a word remaining after its formative elements are removed. It gives the meaning or abstract idea apart from its relations. It is not necessarily a monosyllable. E.g. in ἐ-γεν-όμην *became*, the removal of the augment — an adverbial prefix signifying past time (**533**) — and the personal ending μην leaves γεν°/ε, which appears in γέν-os *race*, γένε-σις *birth*, γενή-σομαι (**593**) *shall become*, with which should be compared γνή-σιos *well-born*, γόν-os *offspring*.

807. *Simple and Compound Words.* A *simple* word is formed from a single stem; e.g. λόγos (base λεγ-, λογ-, stem λογο-) *speech*, γράφω (base γραφ-, stem γραφ°/ε-) *write*. A *compound* word is formed by combining two or more stems; e.g. λογο-γράφο-s (λογο-, γραφ°/ε-) *speech-writer*, voc. λογο-γράφε.

FORMATION OF SIMPLE WORDS

808. *Primitives and Denominatives.* Substantives or adjectives formed directly from a root (**169**) or from a stem found in a verb are called *primitives*; e.g.

δίκ-η *retribution* (stem δικᾱ-), from the root δικ-; ἀρχή (stem ἀρχᾱ-) *beginning*, from ἀρχ-, stem of ἄρχω; γραφεύs (γραφευ-) *writer*, γραμμή (γραμμᾱ-

for γραφ-μᾱ-) line (813), γραφικός (γραφικο-) able to write, all from γραφ-, stem of γράφω write; ποιη-τής poet (maker), ποίη-σις poesy, ποίη-μα poem, ποιη-τικός able to make, from ποιε-, stem of ποιέω make (815 a).

809. Substantives, adjectives, and verbs formed from the stems of nouns or adjectives are called *denominatives*; e.g. βασιλείᾱ *kingdom*, from βασιλε(υ)- (265); ἀρχαῖος *ancient*, from ἀρχᾱ- (stem of ἀρχή); δικαιοσύνη *justice*, from δικαιο-; τῑμά-ω *honor*, from τῑμᾱ-, stem of the noun τῑμή.

810. *Suffixes.* Roots or stems are developed into new stems by the addition of syllables called *suffixes*. (a) They may specify or determine more exactly the meaning of the root, e.g. γράμμα (for γραφ-ματ-) *document*, suffix ματ-, γραμμή (γραφ-μᾱ-) *line*, suffix μᾱ-. (b) They may denote or characterize the root as noun, verb, or pronoun, e.g. γραφ-ίς (suffix ιδ-) *writing instrument*, γραφ-ικό-s (suffix ικο-) *able to write*, γραπ-τό-s (suffix το-) *written*.

811. Although a suffix thus determines the meaning or application of a root, its own meaning can be seen in only a few cases. Nor is the division between stem (or root) and suffix always certain. E.g., in λόγ-ο-s *word* (root λογ-) the suffix seems to be -ο-; but comparing the vocative λόγε we apparently have a base λογ°/ε not different in kind from that seen in λέγο-μεν, λέγε-τε, impv. λέγε. So γένος *race*, gen. γένε(σ)-ος, has a suffix εσ-, which, however, is seen to be arbitrarily divided from the root γεν- when γένε-σι-s *birth* and γενέ-σθαι are compared.

812. Rarely a noun stem has no suffix other than the case ending, and is identical with the verb stem; e.g. φύλαξ *guard*, from stem φυλακ-, seen also in φυλάττω *I guard* (623); φλόξ (φλογ-) *flame*, from same stem as φλέγ-ω (816).

813. The final consonant of a stem is subject to the same phonetic changes before a suffix as before an ending; e.g. γράμ-μα for γραφ-μα, λέξις for λεγ-σις, δικασ-τής for δικαδ-της. See 66, 69, 79.

814. *a.* A final vowel of the stem may be contracted with a vowel of the suffix; e.g. ἀρχαῖος *ancient*, from ἀρχᾱ- and ιο-s (842). But such a vowel is sometimes dropped; e.g. οὐράν-ιος *heavenly*, from οὐρανο- and ιο-s, βασιλ-ικός *kingly*, from βασιλε(υ)- and ικο-s; εὔνο-ια *good-will*, from εὐνοο- and ια (826).

b. Mutation of ο and ε (cf. 811) occurs in many denominatives; e.g. οἰκέ-ω *dwell* (οἶκο-s *house*), οἰκέ-της *house-servant*, and οἰκεῖος (οἰκε-ιος) *domestic*; apparently (825) also ᾱ and ω interchange, e.g. στρατιώ-της *soldier* (στρατιᾱ-), Σικελιώ-της *Sicilian Greek* (Σικελιᾱ-). Ionic and Attic have η for ᾱ, e.g ὑλή-εις *woody*, from ὕλη (ὑλᾱ-).

815. *a.* Many vowel stems (especially verb stems) lengthen their final vowel before a consonant of the suffix, as in verbs (593); e.g. ποίη-μα, ποίη-σις, ποιη-τικός, ποιη-τής, from ποιε-.

b. Many add σ before μ and τ of a suffix, as in the perfect and aorist passive

(598); e.g. κελευ-σ-τής *boatswain*, κέλευ-σ-μα *command*, from κελευ- (κελεύω), κεκέλευ-σ-μαι.

c. Others add θ, e.g. στα-θ-μός *station*, from στα- (ἵστημι); πλῆ-θ-ος *crowd*, from πλη- (πίμπλημι). See 601.

d. A few add τ, e.g. ἐρε-τ-μό-ν *oar*, cf. Lat. rē-mus, ἐρέττω *row* (for ἐρε-τ-ιω).

e. A few are made by reduplication, e.g. ἐδ-ωδ-ή *food*, cf. ἔδ-ω *eat*. So some proper names used by children, Γορ-γώ *Gorgo*, Μορ-μώ *Mormo*.

f. Others drop a final consonant, e.g. σωφρο-σύνη *self-control*, from σωφρον-.

816. Vowel mutation (34) occurs in many nouns and adjectives, especially those in ος and η. A change of ε to ο (ει and ευ to οι and ου) is especially common. E.g. λήθη *forgetfulness*, from λαθ- (cf. λανθάνω, λέληθα); γόνος *offspring*, from γεν- (cf. γέγονα); λοιπός *remaining*, from λειπ- (cf. λέλοιπα); στοργή *affection*, cf. στέργ-ω, perf. ἔστοργα; πομπή *sending*, cf. πέμπ-ω, perf. πέπομφα; τρόπος, τροπή, *turn*, cf. τρέπ-ω; φλόξ *flame*, gen. φλογός, cf. φλέγ-ω; σπουδή *haste*, cf. σπεύδ-ω. So also in adverbs, e.g. συλ-λήβ-δην (λαβ-): see 420.

FORMATION OF NOUNS

Primitive Nouns

817. The simplest and most common suffixes in nouns are ο (nom. ος or ον) and ᾱ (nom. α or η). Nouns thus formed have a great variety of meanings. The change of ε to ο (816) is here regular. E.g.

λόγο-s (λογ-ο-) *speech*, cf. λεγ-, stem of λέγω; στόλος *expedition* and στολή *equipment*, cf. στελ-, stem of στέλλω *send*; μάχ-η (μαχ-ᾱ-) *battle*.

818. *Agent.* a. The following suffixes denote the masculine agent:

ευ (nom. εύς): γραφ-εύ-s *writer* (γράφ-ω *write*); γον-εύ-s *parent* (cf. γέν-ος *race*, γέ-γον-α *am by birth*).

τηρ (nom. τήρ): σω-τήρ *savior* (cf. σῴζω *save*, 620); δο-τήρ *giver* (cf. δί-δο-μεν).

τορ (nom. τωρ): ῥή-τωρ *orator* (cf. εἴ-ρη-κα *have spoken*, 650).

τρο (nom. τρός): ἰᾱ-τρός *physician* (cf. ἰά-ομαι *heal*).

τᾱ (nom. της): ποιη-τής *poet*, from ποιε- (ποιέω); ὀρχη-σ-τής *dancer*, from ὀρχε- (ὀρχέομαι *dance*). See 815 a, b.

b. To these correspond the following feminine suffixes:

τειρᾱ (nom. τειρᾰ): σώτειρα, fem. of σωτήρ; δό-τειρα, fem. of δοτήρ.

τριᾱ (nom. τριᾰ): ποιήτρια *poetess*; ὀρχήστρια *dancing-girl*.

τριδ (nom. τρίς): ὀρχηστρίς *dancing-girl*, gen. -ίδος.

τιδ (nom. τις): προφῆτις *prophetess*; οἰκέτις *female servant*.

c. Verbals in τηρ and τρις are oxytone: those in τωρ, τρια, and τειρα have recessive accent (129 d).

819. *Action.* These suffixes denote *action* or *process* in the abstract, but the words they form are often used concretely:

τι (nom. τις, fem.): πίσ-τις *belief* (πείθω *persuade*, πειθ-, ποιθ-, πιθ-).

σι (nom. σις, fem.): λύ-σις *loosing*, from λυ- (λύω); ποίη-σις *poetry* (abstract or concrete); βά-σις *step* (cf. βαίνω).

σιᾱ (nom. σιᾱ, fem.) : δοκιμα-σίᾱ *testing* (δοκιμάζω *test*).

μο (nom. μός, masc.) : ὀδυρ-μός *wailing* (ὀδύρ-ομαι *wail*) ; σπα-σ-μός *spasm* (σπά-ω *draw*, 815 *b*) ; ῥυθμός (815 *c*) *rhythm* (ῥέω *flow*, stem ῥευ-, ῥυ-).

μᾱ (nom. μη, fem., μᾱ, fem.) : γνώ-μη *knowledge* (γι-γνώ-σκω *know*) ; ὀδ-μή *odor* (ὄζω *smell*) ; τόλ-μᾱ *daring* (cf. τάλᾱ-s *enduring, wretched*, τλῆ-ναι *endure*, 694).

ιᾱ (nom. ίᾱ) : πεν-ίᾱ *poverty* (πέν-ομαι *be poor*) ; μαν-ίᾱ *madness* (μαίνομαι *rage*).

820. From stems in ευ (εϝ) with suffix ιᾱ come nouns in είᾱ denoting action; e.g. βασιλείᾱ *kingly power, kingdom* (for βασιλευ-ια, 37), παιδείᾱ *education*. These are denominatives (809).

For feminines in ειᾰ of nouns in ευs, see 825.

821. *Result.* These suffixes denote the *result* of an action:

ματ (nom. μα, neut.) : πρᾱγ-μα *thing, act,* from πρᾱγ- (πράττω *do*) ; ῥῆμα *saying (thing said)*, cf. ἐρρή-θην *was said* ; τμῆ-μα *section,* gen. τμήματος, cf. τέ-τμη-κα, τέμ-νω *cut.*

εσ (nom. os, neut.) : λάχος (λαχεσ-) *lot,* from λαχ- (λαγχάνω *gain by lot*) ; ἔθος (ἐθεσ-) *custom,* from ἐθ- (εἴωθα *am accustomed,* 719) ; ἦθος (ἠθεσ-) *character* ; γένος (γενεσ-) *race,* from γεν-, cf. ἐ-γεν-όμην and 816 ; τέμα-χ-ος *slice,* cf. τέμ-νω, τέ-τμη-κα.

In some primitives this suffix εσ- denotes *quality* ; e.g. βάθος (βαθεσ-) *depth* (from root βαθ-) ; βάρος (βαρεσ-) *weight* (from root βαρ-) ; θάλπος (θαλπεσ-) *heat* (θάλπ-ω *warm*).

822. *Means* or *Instrument.* This is denoted by

τρο (nom. τρον) : ἄρο-τρον *plough,* Lat. arātrum (ἀρό-ω *plough*) ; λύ-τρον *ransom,* from λυ- (λύω) ; λοῦ-τρον *bath* (λού-ω *wash*).

τρᾱ (nom. τρᾱ) : χύ-τρᾱ *pot,* from χυ- (χέω *pour*) ; ξύ-σ-τρᾱ *scraper* (ξύ-ω *scrape*), 815 *b.*

θ-ρο (nom. θρον) : βά-θ-ρο-ν *step* (βαίνω *go*). 815 *c.*

823. A few words with adjectival suffixes denote an *instrument*; e.g. πο-τήρ-ιο-ν *cup* (πίνω *drink,* 650) ; πτε-ρό-ν *feather* (cf. πέτ-ομαι, ἐ-πτ-όμην *fly*).

824. Some primitives are formed from stems in

ανο, e.g. στέφ-ανο-s *crown* (στέφ-ω *crown*).

ονᾱ, e.g. ἡδ-ονή *pleasure* (ἥδ-ομαι *be pleased*).

ον or ων, e.g. εἰκ-ών *image,* from εἰκ- (ἔοικα *resemble*) ; κλύδ-ων *wave,* from κλυδ- (κλύζω *dash*) ; θεράπ-ων *attendant.*

Denominative Nouns

825. *Person Concerned.* A person concerned with anything may be denoted by the following suffixes :

ευ, masc. (nom. εύs), sometimes ειᾰ (for εϝ-ια), fem. (nom. ειᾰ) : ἱερ-εύs *priest* (ἱερό-s *sacred*), fem. ἱέρ-εια *priestess* ; βασιλ-εύs *king,* fem. βασίλ-εια *queen* ; πορθμ-εύs *ferryman,* from πορθμό-s *ferry* (cf. πόρ-ο-s *way through,* and 815 *c,* 819).

τᾱ, masc. (nom. της), τιδ, fem. (nom. τις) : πολῑ́-της *citizen*, from πόλι-s *city*, fem. πολῑ̂-τις *female citizen* ; οἰκέ-της *house-servant*, from οἶκο-s *house*, fem. οἰκέ-τις *housemaid* ; δεσμώ-της *prisoner*, from δεσμό-s *imprisonment* ; στρατιώ-της *soldier*, from στρατιά *army* (814 *b*) ; Σικελιώτης, a *Greek living in Sicily*, from Σικελία *Sicily*.

826. *Quality.* Substantives denoting *quality* are formed from adjective stems by these suffixes :

τητ (nom. της, fem.) : νεό-της, gen. νεότητ-ος, *youth*, from νέο-s *young* ; ἰσό-της (ἰσοτητ-) *equality*, from ἴσο-s *equal* (cf. Lat. vēritās, gen. vēritāt-is, and virtūs, gen. virtūt-is).

συνᾱ (nom. σύνη, fem.) : δικαιο-σύνη *justice*, from δίκαιο-s *just* ; σωφρο-σύνη *self-control*, from σώφρων (σωφρον-) *sober*.

ῑᾱ (nom. ιᾱ or ιᾰ, fem.) : σοφ-ίᾱ *wisdom* (σοφό-s), κακίᾱ *vice* (κακό-s), ἀλήθεια *truth*, for ἀληθεσ-ια (ἀληθής *true*, 90), εὔνοια *kindness*, for εὐνο-ια (εὔνοο-s, εὔνους *kind*) ; ἀτυχ-ίᾱ *misfortune* is made like κακίᾱ, though the related adjective is ἀ-τυχ-ής (like ἀληθής).

827. The suffix ιᾱ is added to the weak stem of substantives in ων (824) to form corresponding feminines ; e.g. θεράπαινα *handmaid*, for θεραπ-ν-ια (27, 99), cf. θεράπων ; λέαινα *lioness*, for λε-ν-ια, 27, cf. λέων *lion*. Added to stems in κ or τ (94) the suffix ιᾱ gives ττᾱ, Ion. σσᾱ, e.g. Φοίνιττα, Φοίνισσα (Φοινικ-) *Phoenician woman* ; Κρῆττα, Κρῆσσα (Κρητ-) *Cretan woman* ; μέλιττα, μέλισσα *bee* (μέλιτ-ος *of honey*).

828. The suffix αδ (nom. άς, fem.) expresses a numerical group (430) ; e.g. δυάς *dyad*, μῡριάς *myriad*.

829. *Place.* This is denoted by these suffixes :

ιο (nom. ιον, neut.) : Ἀρτεμίσ-ιο-ν (sc. ἱερόν) *precinct of Artemis* ; κουρε-ῖον *barber-shop* (for κουρευ-ιο-ν, 37), from κουρεύ-s *barber* ; χαλκε-ῖο-ν *smithy*, from χαλκεύ-s *blacksmith*. Hence arose an ending εῖο-ν ; e.g. λογ-εῖον (λόγο-s) *speaking-place*, Μουσ-εῖον (Μοῦσα) *haunt of the Muses*, Ἀσκληπι-εῖον *precinct of Asclepius*.

τηρ-ιο, from nouns in -τήρ : δικασ-τήρ-ιο-ν *court-room*, from δικαστήρ (Babrius) *juror*, Att. δικαστής ; δεσμωτήρ-ιο-ν *prison*, cf. δεσμώτης *prisoner*.

ων (nom. ών, masc.) : ἀνδρών *men's apartment*, from ἀνήρ *man*, gen. ἀνδρ-ός ; ἀμπελών *vineyard*, from ἄμπελο-s *vine*.

ῑτιδ (nom. ῖτις, fem.) : ἀνδρων-ῖτις *men's apartment*.

τρᾱ (nom. τρᾱ, fem.) : παλαί-σ-τρᾱ (815 *b*) *wrestling-school* ; ὀρχή-σ-τρᾱ *dancing-ground*.

830. *Diminutives.* These are formed from noun stems by the following suffixes :

ιο (nom. ιον, neut.) : παιδ-ίον *little child*, from παιδ- (παῖς *child*) ; κηπ-ίον *little garden* (κῆπος). Sometimes also ιδιο-, αριο-, υδριο-, υλλιο- (all with nom. in ιον) ; οἰκ-ίδιον *little house* (οἶκος) ; παιδ-άριον *little child* ; μελ-ύδριον *little song* (μέλος) ; ἐπ-ύλλιον *little verse*, versicle (ἔπος).

ισκο- (nom. ίσκος, masc.) and ισκᾱ- (nom. ίσκη, fem.) : παιδ-ίσκος *young boy*, παιδ-ίσκη *young girl*.

831. Diminutives sometimes express *endearment*, and sometimes *contempt*; e.g. πατρίδιον *daddy* (πατήρ *father*), Σωκρατίδιον, Εὐρῑπίδιον; so νεᾱνίσκος is sometimes contemptuous or ironical (νεᾱνίᾱ-s *young man*). Cf. the Eng. suffix -*ish*.

832. Many diminutive forms are not diminutive in meaning; e.g. βιβλ-ίο-ν *book*, θηρ-ίο-ν *animal*, πεδ-ίο-ν *plain*. This is especially exemplified in Modern Greek.

833. *Patronymics.* These denote *descent* from a parent or ancestor (generally a father), and are formed from proper names by the suffixes **δᾱ** (nom. δης, masc. paroxytone) and **δ** (nom. s for δs, fem. oxytone); after a consonant ιδᾱ and ιδ (nom. ίδης and ίs).

a. Stems (in ᾱ-) of the first declension shorten α and add **δᾱ** and **δ**; e.g. Βορεά-δης *son of Boreas*, and Βορεά-s, gen. Βορεά-δος, *daughter of Boreas*, from Βορέᾱς *Boreas*. In Δημάδης *Demades* (properly *son of* Δημέᾱς) contraction has taken place.

b. Stems of the second declension drop the final ο and add ιδᾱ and ιδ; e.g. Πριαμ-ίδης *son of Priam*, Πριαμ-ίs, gen. Πριαμίδος, *daughter of Priam*, from Πρίαμο-s. Except those in ιο-, which change ο to α, making nominatives in ιάδης and ιάs (as in α); e.g. Θεστιάδης and Θεστιάs *son* and *daughter of Thestius* (Θέστιο-s).

c. Stems of the third declension add ιδᾱ and ιδ, those in ευ dropping ν before ι; e.g. Κεκροπ-ίδης *son* (or *descendant*) *of Cecrops*, Κεκροπ-ίs, gen. Κεκροπίδος, *daughter of Cecrops*, from Κέκροψ, gen. Κέκροπ-ος; 'Ατρείδης (Hom. 'Ατρεΐδης) *son of Atreus*, from 'Ατρεύ-s, gen. 'Ατρέ-ως; Πηλείδης (Hom. Πηλεΐδης) *son of Peleus*, from Πηλεύ-s, gen. Πηλέ-ως, Hom. also Πηληιάδης (as if from a form Πηλήιος).

834. Occasionally patronymics are formed by the suffix ῑον or ῑων (nom. ῑων); e.g. Κρονίων, gen. Κρονΐωνος or Κρονίονος (to suit the metre), *son of Cronos* (Κρόνο-s).

835. The suffix νδᾱs is used in the dialects, especially the Boeotian; e.g. 'Επαμεινώνδᾱς *son of* 'Επαμείνων. The adjective suffixes ιο and ειο are often used by the poets as patronymics; e.g. Τανταλεῖος παῖς *son of Tantalus*.

836. Rarely the suffix ιδᾱ (833) denotes maternal descent: Μολῑον-ίδαι *sons of Molione*, Δανα-ΐδης *son of Danae*.

837. The father is sometimes included when the patronymic is in the plural; e.g. Πεισιστρατ-ίδαι *Peisistratus and his sons*.

838. The dual in Homer sometimes refers to two brothers; e.g. Αἴαντε *Ajax and his brother* (Teucer).

839. The suffixes ιδεο (nom. ιδοῦς, masc.) and ιδεᾱ (nom. ιδῆ, fem.) denote indirect relationship; e.g. ἀδελφ-ιδοῦς *nephew*, ἀδελφ-ιδῆ *niece* (ἀδελφό-s *brother*).

840. Gentiles. *a.* These designate a person as belonging to some *country* or *town*, and are formed by the following suffixes:

ευ (nom. *εύς*, masc.) : 'Ερετρι-εύς *Eretrian* ('Ερέτρια); Μεγαρεύς *Megarian* (Μέγαρα, plur.) ; Κολωνεύς *of Colonos* (Κολωνό-s) ; Παιανιεύς *of the deme Paiania.*

τᾱ (nom. *της*, masc. paroxytone) : Τεγεᾱ-της *of Tegea* (Τεγέᾱ), 'Ηπειρώ-της *of Epirus* ('Ήπειρος), Σικελιώ-της *Sicilian Greek* (Σικελίᾱ, 814, 825).

b. Feminine stems in ιδ (nom. *ίς*, gen. *ίδος*) correspond to masculines in ευ, e.g. Μεγαρίς *Megarian woman*; and feminine in τιδ (nom. *τις*, gen. *τιδος*), to masculines in τᾱ, e.g. Σικελιῶ-τις *Sicilian Greek woman.*

Adjectives

841. *a.* The simplest suffixes by which primitive adjectives (like nouns) are formed from roots or stems are **o** and **ᾱ** (nom. masc. *os* ; fem. *η, ᾱ,* or *os* ; neut. *ον*) : σοφ-ό-s, σοφή, σοφό-ν *wise*; κακ-ό-s *bad*; λοιπ-ό-s *remaining* (λειπ-, λοιπ-, **816**).

b. Some have **υ** (nom. *ύς, εῖα, ύ*), added only to roots : ἡδ-ύ-s *sweet*, from ἡδ- (ἥδομαι *be pleased*) ; βαρ-ύ-s *heavy* (cf. βάρ-os *weight*) ; ταχ-ύ-s *swift* (cf. τάχ-os *swiftness*).

c. Some have **εσ** (nom. *ης, ες*) : ψευδ-ής (ψευδεσ-) *false* (ψεύδομαι *lie*) ; σαφ-ής (σαφεσ-) *plain* (root σαφ-).

Most adjectives in *ης* are compounds (**867**).

d. Some expressing *inclination* or *tendency* have **μον** (nom. *μων, μον*) : μνή-μων *mindful*, from μνᾱ- (μέ-μνη-μαι) ; τλή-μων *suffering*, from τλᾱ (τλῆ-ναι, **694**) ; ἐπι-λήσ-μων *forgetful*, from λαθ- (λανθάνω, **813**).

842. Adjectives signifying *belonging* or *related* in any way *to* a person or thing are formed from noun stems by the suffix **ιο** (nom. *ιος*) : οὐράν-ιος *heavenly* (οὐρανό-s), οἰκεῖος *domestic* (οἰκο-s, see 814 *b*) ; δίκαιος *just* (δικᾱ-), 'Αθηναῖος *Athenian* ('Αθῆναι, stem 'Αθηνᾱ-).

843. *a.* Denominatives formed by **κο, ικο,** and **ακο** denote *relation*, like adjectives in *ιος* (**842**), sometimes *fitness* or *ability* : φυσι-κός *natural* (φύσι-s *nature*) ; by analogy with *ι* stems, ἀρχ-ικός *fit to rule* (ἀρχ-ή *rule*) ; πολεμικός *warlike, of war* (πόλε-μο-s *war*) ; βασιλ-ικός *kingly* (βασιλεύ-s *king*) ; 'Ολυμπια-κός *Olympic* ('Ολυμπί-ᾱ) ; Πελοποννησι-ακός *Peloponnesian* (Πελοπον-νήσ-ιο-s from Πελοπόννησος).

b. Similar adjectives are formed directly from verb stems by **τικο** (nom. *τικος*) : πρᾱκ-τικός *fit for action, practical,* from πρᾱγ- (πρᾱττω, verbal πρᾱκ-τό-s) ; αἰσθη-τικός *capable of feeling* (αἰσθάνομαι, verbal αἰσθη-τό-s).

844. Other adjectives with various meanings are formed by various suffixes besides the simple **o**; e.g. **νο, λο, ρο, μο, ιμο,** or **τηριο,** all with nom. in *os* : δει-νός (δει- for δϝει-) *terrible*, δει-λός *timid*, φθονε-ρός *envious* (φθόνος *envy*), ἱππάσ-ιμος *fit for riding* (ἱππάζο-μαι), μάχ-ιμος *warlike*, χρήσι-μος *useful*, σωτήρ-ιο-s *preserving* (σωτήρ), whence πεισ-τήριος *persuasive* (πείθ-ω).

Verbals in λός are active, those in νός are passive; those in ρός are generally active but sometimes passive, e.g. φοβε-ρός, both *frightful* and *afraid*. Most adjectives in νος, λος, and ρος are oxytone.

845. Adjectives denoting *material* are formed by ινο (nom. ινος proparoxytone), e.g. λίθ-ινος *of stone* (λίθος). εο (nom. εος, contr. οῦς), e.g. χρύσεος, χρῦσοῦς *golden* (χρῡσός). **303.**

846. Adjectives in ινός (oxytone) denote time, e.g. ἐαρ-ινός *vernal* (ἔαρ *spring*), νυκτερ-ινός *by night* (νύξ *night*, νύκτερος *by night*).

847. Those denoting *fulness* (chiefly poetic) are formed by εντ (nom. εις, εσσα, εν); χαρίεις *graceful* (χάρι-ς), gen. χαρί-εντος; ὑλή-εις (814 b) *woody*; cf. **858.** Lat. grātiōsus, silvōsus.

848. All participles are primitive (verbal) adjectives: so the verbals in τός and τέος.

849. Comparatives and superlatives in τερος and τατος are denominatives; but those in ιων and ιστος are primitives, adding these terminations directly to the base (**354 b**).

Adverbs and Prepositions

850. Adverbs are crystallized case forms of substantives, adjectives, and pronouns. For their formation, see 412–428. For prepositions, originally adverbs of place, see 1197.

II. DENOMINATIVE VERBS

851. A verb whose stem is derived from the stem of a substantive or adjective is called a *denominative* (**809**). The following are the principal terminations of such verbs in the present indicative active. They belong to the Second Class, with original stems in ι⁰/ε (615 ff.).

1. **αω** (original stem in ᾱ, shortened to α): τῑμάω *honor*, from noun τῑμή (τῑμᾱ-) *honor*. Thence from other stems by analogy: ἀριστάω *breakfast*, from ἄριστον.

2. **εω** (ε-): ἀριθμέω *count*, from ἀριθμό-s *number* (814 b); thence εὐτυχέω *be fortunate*, from εὐτυχ-ής (stem in-εσ), εὐδαιμονέω *be happy*, from εὐδαίμων.

3. **οω** (ο-): μισθόω *let for hire*, from μισθό-s *pay*; by analogy, ζημιόω *punish*, from ζημίᾱ *damage*.

4. **ευω** (ευ-): βασιλεύω *be king*, from βασιλεύ-s *king*; by analogy, βουλεύω *take counsel*, from βουλή; ἀληθεύω *be truthful*, from ἀληθής.

5. **αζω** (αδ-): ἁρπάζω *seize*, cf. ἁρπαγή *forcible seizure*; by analogy, δικάζω *judge*, from δίκη (δικᾱ-) *justice* (**620**).

6. **ιζω** (ιδ-): ἐλπίζω *hope*, from ἐλπίς (ἐλπιδ-) *hope* (**852**); by analogy, νομίζω *think*.

7. αινω (αν-): εὐφραίνω *gladden,* cf. εὔφρων *glad,* φρήν *heart,* dat. plur. φρεσί (for φρα-σί, see **76**); ποιμαίνω *tend flocks,* cf. ποιμήν *shepherd*; thence from other stems without a nasal: σημαίνω *signify,* from σῆμα (σηματ-) *sign.*

8. ῦνω (υν-): ἡδῦνω *sweeten,* from ἡδύ-s *sweet.*

852. Verbs in αζω were formed originally from stems in γ (**617**), those in ιζω from stems in δ (**616**). Some denominatives end in λλω, αιρω, ειρω, and ῦρω; e.g. ἀγγέλλω (ἄγγελο-s) *announce,* καθαίρω (καθαρό-s) *purify,* ἱμείρω (ἵμερο-s) *long for,* μαρτύρομαι (μάρτυς, stem μαρτυρ-) *call to witness.*

853. Verbs formed from the same noun stem with different endings sometimes have different meanings; e.g. πολεμέω and (poetic) πολεμίζω *make war,* πολεμόω *make hostile,* both from πόλεμο-s *war*; δουλόω *enslave,* δουλεύω *be a slave,* from δοῦλο-s *slave.*

854. Verbs in ιζω and ιαζω often denote imitation of the person indicated by the verb; e.g. ἑλληνίζω *speak Greek,* from Ἕλλην; Βοιωτιάζω *speak with a Boeotian accent,* cf. Βοιωτιᾶ; σοφίζω *affect wisdom,* cf. σοφός *wise,* but σοφιστής *professor of wisdom*; μηδίζω *side with the Medes* (be a traitor to the Greek cause).

855. *Desideratives.* *a.* Verbs expressing a *desire* to do anything are sometimes formed from other verbs and from nouns by the ending σειω, sometimes αω or ιαω; e.g. δρᾱ-σείω *desire to do* (δρά-ω); γελα-σείω *desire to laugh* (γελά-ω); φον-άω *be bloodthirsty* (φόνος); κλαυ-σ-ιάω *desire to weep* (κλαίω, stem κλαυ-).

b. Some verbs in ιαω denote a bodily condition; e.g. ὀφθαλμιάω *have diseased eyes,* ὠχριάω *be pale,* ἐρυθριάω *blush.*

FORMATION OF COMPOUND WORDS

856. In a compound word we have to consider (1) the first part of the compound, (2) the last part, and (3) the meaning of the whole.

I. First Part of a Compound Word

857. *a.* When the first part of a compound is a substantive or adjective, only its stem appears in the compound.

b. Before a consonant, stems of the first declension generally change final ᾱ to ο; those of the second declension retain ο; and those of the third add ο. Before a vowel, stems of the first and second declensions drop ᾱ or ο. E.g.

θαλασσο-κράτωρ (θαλασσᾱ-) *ruler of the sea,* χορο-διδάσκαλος (χορο-) *chorus-teacher,* παιδο-τρίβης (παιδ-) *trainer of boys,* κεφαλ-αλγής (κεφαλᾱ-) *causing headache,* χορ-ηγός (χορο-) *chorus-manager*; so ἰχθυο-φάγος (ἰχθυ-) *fish-*

eater, φυσιο-λόγος *inquiring into nature*. The analogy of the second (or ο-) declension prevails throughout. But see 866.

858. There are many exceptions. Rarely final ᾱ or η of the first declension is retained before a consonant; e.g. ἀγορᾱ-νόμος (ἀγορᾷ *market*) *market commissioner*, χοη-φόρος (χοή *libation*) *bringer of libations*. So, from an ο stem, ἐλαφη-βόλος (ἔλαφο-s) *deer-slayer*; and from a consonant stem, λαμπαδ-η-δρομίᾱ (λαμπαδ-) *torch race*. Stems in εσ (**230**) often change εσ to ο; e.g. τειχο-μαχία (τειχεσ-) *fight at the wall*. The stems of ναῦς *ship* and βοῦς *ox* generally appear without change (ναυ- and βου-); e.g. ναυ-μαχία *sea-fight*, βου-κόλος *herdsman*. Sometimes a noun appears in one of its cases, as if it were a distinct word; e.g. νεώσ-οικος *ship-house*, ναυσί-πορος *traversed by ships*.

859. Compounds of which the first part is the stem of a verb are chiefly poetic.

a. Here the verbal stem sometimes appears without change before a vowel, and with ε, ι, or ο added before a consonant. E.g.

πείθ-αρχος *obedient to authority*; μεν-ε-πτόλεμος *steadfast in battle*; ἀρχι-τέκτων *master-builder*; λιπ-ο-ταξία *deserting one's post*.

b. Sometimes σι (before a vowel σ) is added to the verb stem. E.g.

λῡσί-πονος *toil-relieving*; στρεψί-δικος (στρεφ-) *justice-twisting*; τερψί-νοος (τερπ-) *soul-delighting*; πλήξ-ιππος (πληγ-) *horse-lashing*.

860. *a.* A preposition or an adverb may be the first part of a compound word; e.g. προ-βάλλω *throw before* (**868** *a*), ἀει-λογίᾱ *continual talking*, εὐ-γενής *well-born*.

b. Here no change of form occurs, except when a final vowel is elided, or when πρό contracts ο with a following ε or ο into ου, e.g. προύχω (πρό, ἔχω) *hold before*, προύργου (πρό, ἔργου) *forward*, φροῦδος (πρό, ὁδοῦ) *gone* (**51**).

c. Phonetic changes occur here as usual; e.g. ἐγχώριος (ἐν and χώρα) *native*; see **72**.

861. The following *inseparable* prefixes are never used alone:

a. ἀν- (ἀ- before a consonant), called *alpha privative*, with a negative force like the cognate English *un-*, Latin in-. It is prefixed to substantive, adjective, and verb stems, to form adjectives; e.g. ἀν-ελεύθερος *unfree*, ἀν-αιδής *shameless*, ἀν-όμοιος *unlike*, ἄ-παις *childless*, ἄ-γραφος *unwritten*, ἄ-θεος *godless*, ἄ-(ϝ)οινος *wineless*. From such adjectives, substantives and verbs may be formed; e.g. ἀνελευθερίᾱ *meanness*, ἀναίδεια *shamelessness*, ἀνομοιόω *make unlike*.

b. δυσ- *ill* (opposed to εὖ *well*, increasing the bad sense of a word or taking away its good sense), denoting *difficulty* or *trouble*; e.g. δύσ-πορος *hard to pass* (opposed to εὔ-πορος); δυσ-τυχής *unfortunate* (opposed to εὐ-τυχής).

c. νη- (Lat. nē), a poetic *negative* prefix; e.g. νή-ποινος *unavenged*; νη-μερτής *unerring* (for νη-αμερτής).

d. ἡμι- (Lat. semi-) *half*; e.g. ἡμί-θεος *demigod*.

e. ἀ- or ἀ- *copulative*, denoting *union* or *intensity*; e.g. ἄ-λοχος (λέχος *couch*) *bedfellow*; ἀ-θρόος *crowded*; ἀ-τενής *intense*; ἄ-πᾶς *each and every*.

862. A few intensive prefixes are found in poetry, — ἀρι-, ἐρι-, δα-, ζα-, e.g. ἀρί-γνωτος *well-known*; δα-φοινός *bloody*.

II. LAST PART OF A COMPOUND WORD

863. At the beginning of the last part of a compound noun or adjective, *a*, *ε*, or *o* (unless it is long by position) is very often lengthened to *η* or *ω*. E.g.

στρατ-ηγός (στρατό-s, ἄγω) *general*; ὑπ-ήκοος (ὑπό, ἀκούω) *obedient*; κατ-ηρεφής (κατά, ἐρέφω) *covered*; ἐπ-ώνυμος (ἐπί, ὄνομα) *naming* or *named for*; κατ-ήγορος (κατά, ἀγορ-) *accuser*; but ἄν-ολβος *unblest*. Λοχ-ᾱγός (λόχος *company*) *captain* is probably Doric in origin.

864. The last part of a compound noun or adjective is often changed in form before the suffix. This takes place especially in compound adjectives, and when an abstract noun forms the last part of a compound noun. E.g.

φιλό-τῑμος (τῑμή) *honor-loving*; εὔ-φρων (φρήν) *joyous*; πολυ-πρᾱγμων (πρᾶγμα) *meddlesome*; λιθο-βολίᾱ (λίθος, βολή) *stone-throwing*, ναυ-μαχίᾱ (ναῦς, μάχη) *sea-fight*; εὐ-πρᾱξίᾱ (πρᾶξις) *success (doing well)*.

865. An abstract noun compounded with a preposition may retain its form; e.g. προ-βουλή *forethought*. Compounds of which the first part is not a preposition and the last part is unchanged are rare; e.g. μισθο-φορά *taking wages*.

866. When the second part originally began with ϝ, the vowel of the first part may be retained (contrary to **857**) or contracted with the vowel of the second part; e.g. τῑμᾱ-ϝορος *guarding honor*, τῑμωρός; κακο-ϝεργός *working evil*, κακοῦργος. Compounds of ἔχω (originally σεχω) contract; e.g. κληροῦχος (κλῆρος, ὀχο-) *lot-holder*, whence πολι-οῦχος *protecting the city*.

867. Compound adjectives in *ης* (**841** *c*) are especially frequent.

a. The last part may be a noun, generally a neuter in *os* (stem in *εσ-*); e.g. εὐ-γενής (γένος) *well-born*, δεκα-ετής (ἔτος) *of ten years*, εὐ-τυχής (τύχη) *fortunate*.

b. The last part may be formed from a verb stem; e.g. ἀ-φαν-ής (φαν-) *unseen*, ἡμι-θαν-ής (θαν-) *half-dead*.

868. *a.* A compound verb can be formed *directly* only by prefixing a preposition to a verb; e.g. προσ-άγω *bring to*.

b. Indirect compounds (denominatives) are formed from compound substantives or adjectives. E.g.

λιθοβολέω *throw stones*, denom. from λιθο-βόλος *stone-thrower*; νομοθετέω *make laws*, from νομοθέτης *lawmaker*; ἀπειθέω *disobey*, from ἀπειθής *disobedient*; κατηγορέω *accuse*, from κατ-ήγορος (**863**) *accuser*. See **565**.

III. MEANING OF COMPOUNDS

869. Compound nouns (including adjectives) are of three classes, distinguished by the relation of the parts of the compound to each other and to the whole.

870. (1) *Objective* compounds are those composed of a noun and a verb, adjective, or preposition, in which the noun (as first or second part) stands to the other part in some relation (commonly that of object) which could be expressed by an oblique case of the noun. E.g.

λογο-γράφος *speech-writer* (λόγους γράφων); μισ-άνθρωπος *man-hating* (μισῶν ἀνθρώπους); λῦσί-πονος *toil-relieving*; στρατ-ηγός *general* (*army-leading*, στρατὸν ἄγων); ἀξιό-λογος *worthy of mention* (ἄξιος λόγου); ἁμαρτ-ί-νοος (**859 a**) *erring in mind* (ἁμαρτὼν νοῦ); ἰσό-θεος *godlike* (ἴσος θεῷ); τερπ-ι-κέραυνος (**859 a**) *delighting in thunder* (τερπόμενος κεραυνῷ); διο-τρεφής *reared by Zeus* (cf. δι-πετής *fallen* or *sent from Zeus*, and Διι-τρεφής, a proper name). So with a preposition: ἐγ-χώριος *native* (ἐν χώρᾳ); ἐφ-ίππιος *belonging on a horse* (ἐφ' ἵππῳ); ἐφ-έστιος *on the hearth* (ἐφ' ἑστίᾳ). Cf. Eng. *bookbinder, sightseeing, catchfly*.

871. When the last part of an objective compound is a *transitive* verbal in ος formed by the suffix ο (**817**), it generally accents the penult if this is *short*, otherwise the last syllable. But if the last part is intransitive or passive (in sense), the accent is recessive. E.g. λογο-γράφος *speech-writer*; στρατ-ηγός *general*; λογο-ποιός *story-maker*; λιθο-βόλος *thrower of stones*, but λιθό-βολος *pelted with stones*; μητρο-κτόνος *matricide, matricidal*, but μητρό-κτονος *killed by a mother*.

872. (2) *Determinative* compounds are nouns or adjectives in which the first part, generally as adjective or adverb, qualifies (or *determines*) the second part. E.g.

ἀκρό-πολις *citadel* (ἀκρὰ πόλις); μεσ-ημβρία (μέση ἡμέρα, **108**) *mid-day*; ψευδό-μαντις *false prophet*; ὁμό-δουλος *fellow-slave* (ὁμοῦ δουλεύων); δυσ-μαθής *learning with difficulty*; ὠκυ-πέτης *swift-flying*; προ-βουλή *forethought*; ἀμφι-θέατρον *amphitheatre* (*theatre extending all round*); ἄ-γραφος *unwritten*. Here belong adjectives like μελι-ηδής (ἡδύς) *honey-sweet*, 'Αρηί-θοος *swift as Ares* (*Ares-swift*). Cf. Eng. *hidebound, footloose, sportsman.*

873. Here belong a few compounds sometimes called *copulative*, made of two nouns or two adjectives, and signifying a combination of the two things or qualities. Strictly, the first part limits the last, like an adjective or adverb.

Such are ἰᾱτρό-μαντις *physician-prophet* (a *prophet* who is also a *physician*); ξιφο-μάχαιρα *sword-sabre*; ἀνδρό-παις *man-child*; γλυκύ-πικρος *bitter-sweet*; θεό-ταυρος *god-bull* (of Zeus changed to a bull).

874. (3) *Possessive* or *attributive* compounds are adjectives in which the first part qualifies the second (as in determinatives) and the whole denotes a quality or attribute belonging to some person or thing. E.g.

ἀργυρό-τοξος *with silver bow* (ἀργυροῦν τόξον ἔχων); κακο-δαίμων *ill-fated* (κακὸν δαίμονα ἔχων); πικρό-γαμος *wretchedly married* (πικρὸν γάμον ἔχων); ὁμό-νομος *having the same laws*; ἑκατογ-κέφαλος *hundred-headed*; δεκα-ετής *of ten years* (duration); ἀγαθο-ειδής *having the appearance* (εἶδος) *of good*; ἔν-θεος *inspired* (*having a god within*); ὠκύ-πους *swift-footed* (ὠκεῖς πόδας ἔχων), — but ποδ-ώκης (πόδας ὠκύς) *foot-swift* is a determinative. Cf. Eng. *bright-eyed, redskin*.

875. In compound verbs, the original verb remains the fundamental part, modified more or less in meaning by the preposition prefixed (**868 a**). Other compounds than those here mentioned present no difficulties in respect to meaning.

PART IV

SYNTAX

DEFINITIONS

876. A sentence expresses a thought in words. Syntax treats of the relation of these words to one another. A sentence may contain a declaration (affirmative or negative), a question, a command (imperative or optative), or an exclamation.

877. *Subject and Predicate.* Every sentence must contain two parts, a *subject* and a *predicate*. The subject is that of which something is stated. The predicate is that which is stated of the subject. E.g., in the sentence Δαρεῖος βασιλεύει τῶν Περσῶν *Darius is king of the Persians*, Δαρεῖος is the subject and βασιλεύει τῶν Περσῶν is the predicate.

878. *a.* A Greek verb, with its personal endings (577), makes the simplest form of sentence; e.g. εἰ-μί *I am*, ἔφα-τε *you said*.

b. A *simple* sentence contains only one clause. A *complex* sentence has a main clause, on which one or more subordinate clauses depend.

879. *a.* When any part of εἰμί *am* connects the subject with a following noun or adjective, the verb is called the *copula* (i.e. *means of coupling*), and what follows is called the predicate; e.g. Δαρεῖός ἐστι βασιλεύς *Darius is king*, Σόλων ἐστὶ σοφός *Solon is wise*, where ἐστί is the copula. The copulas ἐστί and εἰσί are often omitted, especially in proverbial sayings, e.g. χαλεπὰ τὰ καλά *good things are hard*, Plat. *Rep.* 435 c, with nouns like ἀνάγκη *necessity*, ὥρα *time*, and with the impersonal verbal in -τέον. The omission of other forms of εἰμί is rare. For copulative verbs, see 896.

b. Εἰμί can form a complete predicate, as in εἰσὶ θεοί *there are gods*.

880. *Object.* That upon which the action of a verb is exerted is called the *object*. The object may be either *direct* or *indirect*: e.g., in ἔδωκε τὰ χρήματα τῷ ἀνδρί *he gave the money to the man* χρήματα is the direct object and ἀνδρί is the indirect object.

881. Verbs which can have a direct object are called *transitive*; those which cannot are called *intransitive*.

195

SUBJECT AND PREDICATE

Subject

882. The subject of a finite verb (451) is in the nominative; e.g. ὁ ἀνὴρ ἦλθεν *the man came.*

883. *a.* The subject of the infinitive is in the accusative; e.g. φησὶ τοὺς ἄνδρας ἀπελθεῖν *he says that the men went away.*

b. But the subject of the infinitive is generally omitted when it is the same as the subject or the object (direct or indirect) of the leading verb; e.g. βούλεται ἀπελθεῖν *he wishes to go away*; φησὶ γράφειν *he says that he is writing*; παραινοῦμέν σοι μένειν *we advise you to remain.* See 923.

c. So when it is the same with any important adjunct of the leading verb; e.g. κακούργου ἐστὶ κριθέντ' ἀποθανεῖν *it is proper for a malefactor to die by sentence of the law* (924 *b*), Dem. 4, 47.

884. The subject of the leading verb is expressed again with the infinitive for emphasis or contrast; e.g. ηὐξάμην ἐμέ τε τυγχάνειν διδάσκοντα καὶ ἐκείνην μανθάνουσαν *I prayed that I might succeed in teaching and she in learning,* X. *Oec.* 7, 8; ἡγησάμενος ἐμαυτὸν ἐπιεικέστερον εἶναι *having come to the conclusion that I was too respectable,* Plat. *Ap.* 36 c. So when the speaker includes others besides himself, e.g. ἔφη σφᾶς ἂν τὸ αὐτὸ ὑποσχεῖν *he said that he and his men could offer the same thing,* Thuc. 7, 21; here the predicate modifiers are sometimes in the nominative, e.g. ἐνόμιζε λαθεῖν ἂν τοῦτο ποιοῦντες *he thought they could do this* (1588) *without getting caught,* Thuc. 7, 48.

885. The subject nominative of the first or second person is omitted, except when special emphasis is required. Pronominal subjects are expressed when a contrast is suggested; e.g. κἀγὼ δέ, εἰ μὲν ὑμεῖς ἐθέλετε ἐξορμᾶν ἐπὶ ταῦτα, ἕπεσθαι ὑμῖν βούλομαι *and I for one, if you want to start on this enterprise, am ready to follow your lead,* X. *An.* 3, 1, 25. **984.**

886. The nominative of the third person is omitted,

a. When it is expressed or implied in the context; e.g. ὁ Κῦρος πράττει ἃ βούλεται *Cyrus does what he* (Cyrus) *pleases.*

b. When it is a general word for *persons*; e.g. λέγουσι *they say, it is said.*

c. When it is indefinite; e.g. ὀψὲ ἦν *it was late*; καλῶς ἔχει *it is well*; δηλοῖ *it is evident* (*the case shows*); so in the impersonal construction with the verbal in τέον, e.g. τῷ νόμῳ πειστέον (ἐστὶ) *we must obey the law* (1599).

d. When the verb implies its own subject, e.g. κηρύττει *the herald* (κῆρυξ) *proclaims,* ἐσάλπιγξε *the trumpeter sounded the trumpet,* κωλύει *a hindrance occurs.* In passive expressions like παρεσκεύασταί μοι *preparation has been made by me* (*I am prepared*), the subject is really the idea of *preparation* etc. contained in the verb. See 1241.

e. With verbs like ὕει *it rains,* ἀστράπτει *it lightens,* σείει *there is an earth-quake (it shakes),* where, however, some subject like Ζεύς or θεός was understood. In poetry (Homer always) this subject is often expressed.

887. Many verbs in the third person singular have an infinitive or a sentence as their subject. These are often called *impersonal* verbs. Such are πρέπει and προσήκει *it is proper,* ἔνεστι and ἔξεστι *it is possible,* δοκεῖ *it seems good,* συμβαίνει *it happens,* and the like ; e.g. ἔξεστιν ὑμῖν τοῦτο ποιεῖν *it is in your power to do this (to do this is possible for you).* So also δεῖ and χρή *it is required, we ought* ; e.g. δεῖ ἡμᾶς ἀπελθεῖν *we must go away.*

The name *impersonal* is applied with greater propriety (though less frequently) to the verbs of **886** *c* and *d*.

Subject Nominative and Verb

888. *a.* A finite verb agrees with its subject nominative in number and person ; e.g. ἐγὼ λέγω *I say,* οὗτος λέγει *this man says,* οἱ ἄνδρες λέγουσιν *the men say.*

b. But a nominative in the *neuter plural* is regarded as a collective, and regularly takes a singular verb ; e.g. ταῦτα ἐγένετο *these things happened,* πάντα ἐσέκειτο *everything was placed on board,* Thuc. 6, 32. So ἀδύνατά ἐστι (or ἀδύνατόν ἐστι) *it is impossible.*

889. Exceptions occur, especially in Homer, and with nouns denoting persons. Several are found in Xenophon ; e.g. *An.* 1, 7, 17. So τέκνα μὴ θάνωσ' Ἡρακλέους *that Heracles's children may not die,* E. *Her.* 47. A plural verb may be used when there is a notion of variety or distribution.

890. A singular collective noun denoting persons *may* take a plural verb ; e.g. τὸ πλῆθος ἐψηφίσαντο πολεμεῖν *the majority voted for war,* Thuc. 1, 125.

891. When several subjects are connected by *and,* they generally have a plural verb. But the verb may agree with one of the subjects (generally the nearest) and be understood with the rest. The latter generally happens when they are connected by *or* or *nor.* E.g.

σοφοὶ ἐγώ τε καὶ σὺ ἦμεν *you and I were wise,* Plat. *Th.* 154 d ; μαχούμεθα κοινῇ ἐγώ τε καὶ σύ *you and I will join forces,* Plat. *Rep.* 335 e ; οὐ σὺ μόνος οὐδὲ οἱ σοὶ φίλοι πρῶτον ταύτην δόξαν ἔσχετε *it was not you alone nor your friends who first took up this notion,* Plat. *Lg.* 888 b ; ἐμοὶ καὶ Πείσωνι ἐπιτυγχάνει Μηλόβιός τε καὶ Μνησιθείδης ἐκ τοῦ ἐργαστηρίου ἀπιόντες, καὶ καταλαμβάνουσι πρὸς αὐταῖς ταῖς θύραις *Melobius and Mnesithides meet Piso and me as they come out of the shop and catch us right at the door,* Lys. 12, 12 ; ἐμὲ οὔτε καιρὸς οὔτ' ἐλπὶς οὔτε φόβος οὔτ' ἄλλο οὐδὲν ἐπῆρεν *as for me, neither opportunity nor hope nor fear nor anything else incited me,* Dem. 18, 298.

892. If the subjects are of different persons, the verb is in the first person rather than the second or third, and in the second rather than the third. See examples under 891.

893. *a.* A verb in the dual may follow two subjects in the singular, or even a plural subject denoting two persons or things. But even a subject in the dual may have a verb in the plural. See *Il.* 4, 453; 5, 10, 275; 16, 218.

b. A copulative verb (897) is often attracted to the number of the predicate substantive; e.g. (singular predicate) αἱ δὲ εἰσφοραὶ καὶ χορηγίαι εὐδαιμονίας ἱκανὸν σημεῖόν ἐστιν *his taxes and payments for choruses are a sufficient sign of prosperity*, Antiphon 2, γ, 8; (plural predicate) τὸ χωρίον ὅπερ Ἐννέα Ὁδοὶ ἐκαλοῦντο *the place which used to be called Nine Corners*, Thuc. 4, 102.

c. If the copula is a participle, it may be attracted to the gender as well as the number of the predicate; e.g. τὰς θυγατέρας παιδία ὄντα *their daughters, who were little children*, Dem. 194, 1. See 915.

894. Sometimes a singular verb has a masculine or feminine subject in the plural; e.g. ἔστι δὲ ἑπτὰ στάδιοι ἐξ Ἀβύδου ἐς τὴν ἀπαντίον *and it is seven stadia from Abydos to the opposite coast*, Hdt. 7, 34. In such cases the plural form often seems to have arisen from an afterthought, especially when the subject follows the verb. This construction was miscalled Pindaric, σχῆμα Πινδαρικόν.

See also the phrases ἔστιν οἵ etc., 1028.

895. A preposition with a numeral may represent the subject of a verb; e.g. ἀπέθανον αὐτῶν περὶ τριακοσίους *about three hundred of them were killed*, X. *H.* 4, 6, 11.

Predicate Substantive and Adjective

896. With verbs signifying *to be, to become, to appear, to be named, chosen, made, thought* or *regarded*, and the like, a substantive or adjective in the predicate is in the same case as the subject. E.g.

οὗτός ἐστι βασιλεύς *this man is king*; Ἀλέξανδρος θεὸς ὠνομάζετο *Alexander was named a god*; ᾑρέθη στρατηγός *he was chosen general*; ἡ πόλις φρούριον κατέστη *the city became a fortress*, Thuc. 7, 28; οὗτός ἐστιν εὐδαίμων *this man is happy*; ἡ πόλις μεγάλη ἐγένετο *the city became great*; ηὔξηται μέγας *he has grown (to be) great*; νομίζεται σοφός *he is thought wise*.

897. The verbs which are here included with the copula εἰμί (879) are called *copulative* verbs. The predicate nominative with the passive verbs of this class represents the predicate accusative of the active construction (1075).

898. The predicate *adjective* with these verbs agrees with the subject in gender and number, as well as in case. See 916.

899. The predicate of an infinitive with its subject accusative expressed (**883 a**) is in the accusative; e.g. βούλεται τὸν υἱὸν εἶναι σοφόν *he wishes his son to be wise.* So when the participle is used like the infinitive in indirect discourse (**1590**); e.g. ᾔδεσαν τὸν Κῦρον βασιλέα γενόμενον *they knew that Cyrus had become king.*

For such a predicate with the subject omitted, see **923** and **924**.

APPOSITION

900. A substantive annexed to another substantive to describe it, and denoting the same person or thing, agrees with it in case. This is called *apposition,* and the noun thus used is called an *appositive.* E.g.

Δαρεῖος ὁ βασιλεύς *Darius the king.* Ἀθῆναι, μεγάλη πόλις *Athens, a great city.* Ὑμᾶς τοὺς σοφούς *you wise ones.* Ἡμῶν τῶν Ἀθηναίων *of us Athenians.* Θεμιστοκλῆς ἥκω (sc. ἐγώ) παρὰ σέ *I, Themistocles, am come to you,* Thuc. 1, 137. Φιλήσιος καὶ Λύκων οἱ Ἀχαιοί *Philesius and Lycon the Achaeans,* X. *An.* 5, 6, 27.

901. A noun in apposition with two or more nouns is generally plural (or dual); e.g. ὕπνος πόνος τε, κύριοι ξυνωμόται *sleep and toil, imperious conspirators,* Aesch. *Eu.* 127; θάρρος καὶ φόβον, ἄφρονε ξυμβούλω *rashness and fear, two senseless counsellors,* Plat. *Ti.* 69 d.

902. An adjective may have a genitive in apposition with a genitive which it implies; e.g. Ἀθηναῖος ὤν, πόλεως τῆς μεγίστης *an Athenian, citizen of the greatest city in the world,* Plat. *Ap.* 29 d.

For a genitive in apposition with the genitive implied in a possessive pronoun, see **1001.**

903. A noun which might stand in the *partitive* genitive (**1088**) sometimes takes the case of the words denoting its parts, especially when the latter include the *whole* of the former; e.g. οἰκίαι αἱ μὲν πολλαὶ πεπτώκεσαν, ὀλίγαι δὲ περιῆσαν *most of the houses were in ruins, but a few remained* (where we might have τῶν οἰκιῶν), Thuc. 1, 89. So οὗτοι ἄλλος ἄλλα λέγει *these men all say different things,* X. *An.* 2, 1, 15; ὅταν πάντες τὸ ἐφ᾽ ἑαυτὸν ἕκαστος σπεύδῃ *when all devote themselves to their individual interests,* Thuc. 1, 141. This is called *partitive* apposition.

904. A noun may be in apposition with a whole sentence, being in the nominative when it is closely connected in thought with the subject of the sentence, elsewhere in the accusative; e.g. κεῖνται πεσόντες, πίστις οὐ σμικρὰ πόλει *they lie prostrate, — no small (cause of) confidence to the city,* E. *Rh.* 415. Ἑλένην κτάνωμεν, Μενελέῳ λύπην πικράν *let us kill Helen, — which will be a bitter grief to Menelaus,* E. *Or.* 1105.

905. A noun may be in apposition with the subject or the object of a sentence, where we use *as* or a *like* word; e.g. ἵπποι ἤγοντο θῦμα τῷ Ἡλίῳ *horses were brought as an offering to the Sun* (in active, ἵππους ἄγειν θῦμα *to bring horses as an offering*), X. C. 8, 3, 12; ἔξεστιν ὑμῖν ἡμᾶς λαβεῖν ξυμμάχους *you can gain us as allies*, X. An. 5, 4, 6. So τυχεῖν τινος φίλου *to gain one as a friend*; χρῶμαι τούτῳ φίλῳ *I treat him as a friend*; also τίνος διδάσκαλοι ἥκετε *as teachers of what are you come?* Plat. Euthyd. 287 a. See 1078.

906. Homer often adds an appositive denoting a *part* to a noun or pronoun denoting a person; e.g. Δηιοπίτην οὔτασεν ὦμον *he wounded D. in the shoulder*, Il. 11, 420; ἀλλ᾽ οὐκ Ἀτρεΐδῃ Ἀγαμέμνονι ἥνδανε θυμῷ *but it pleased not the heart of Agamemnon, son of Atreus* (lit. *to A., his heart*), Il. 1, 24. Cf. 1058.

For ὁ δέ in Homer followed by a noun in apposition, see 935 a.

907. A substantive in apposition with another substantive may have the force of an attributive adjective; e.g. ἀνὴρ βασιλεύς *a king*, ἀνὴρ βουκόλος *a herdsman*. So ἄνδρες as a term of respect in ἄνδρες στρατιῶται *soldiers!* ἄνδρες δικασταί *gentlemen of the court!* ἄνδρες ἀδελφοί *brethren!* Acts 23, 1, but ἀδελφοί *brothers!* (informal), Acts 23, 5. But ἀνήρ in this construction may sometimes have a derogatory force; e.g. φηλήτης ἀνήρ *a cheat*, Aesch. Cho. 1001.

908. Names of cities are sometimes plural, e.g. Θῆβαι (Hom. Θήβη) *Thebes*, Πλαταιαί *Plataea*. The masculine plural originally referred to the inhabitants; e.g. Δελφοί *Delphi*, Λεοντῖνοι *Leontini*.

909. The predicate with such substantives may conform to sense rather than to grammar; e.g. Μυκῆναι μικρὸν ἦν *Mycenae was small* (a small place), Thuc. 1, 10. On the other hand αὐταῖς *her* refers to τῶν Ἀθηνῶν *Athens* in Thuc. 1, 36.

910. The plural may be used by a speaker in modest reference to himself. In tragedy it is often interchanged with the singular; e.g. παριέμεσθα, καί φαμεν κακῶς φρονεῖν τότ᾽, ἀλλ᾽ ἄμεινον νῦν βεβούλευμαι *I ask your pardon, and admit that I was foolish before, but now have come to a better resolve*, E. Med. 892. When women thus use the plural, a modifying adjective or participle is either masculine plural or feminine singular; e.g. τήνδε δὲ χθόνα ἐᾶτέ μ᾽ οἰκεῖν· καὶ γὰρ ἠδικημένοι σιγησόμεσθα *let me live in this land; for even though I am wronged, yet will I be silent*, E. Med. 314; ἠγριώμεθα δοκοῦσ᾽ Ὀρέστην μηκέθ᾽ ἥλιον βλέπειν *I was embittered, thinking that Orestes no longer looked upon the light of day*, E. I. T. 348. So Med. 579, Ion 1250, I. A. 985. Cf. 173.

911. The plural may be used by a speaker of another person in a general or allusive way; e.g. ὑβρισμένους ὑφ᾽ ὧν ἥκιστα ἐχρῆν *outraged by one who ought least* (to have treated them so), Lys. 32, 10; δεσποτῶν θανάτοισι *since the death of my lord*, Aesch. Cho. 53.

912. The plural often denotes parts, quantities, or instances of a single object or abstract idea; e.g. ἄρτοι *loaves of bread* or *different kinds of bread*, κρέα *pieces of meat*, πυροί *supplies of wheat*, ἐν κοπρίῃσι *in heaps of filth*, Semonid. 7, 6. So ταῦτα for τοῦτο, e.g. ταῦτ' ἀκούσας *when he heard this.*

913. Names of festivals are in the plural, e.g. τὰ Διονύσια *the festival of Dionysus*, τὰ Θεσμοφόρια *the Thesmophoria*, τὰ 'Ολύμπια *the Olympic games.*

914. The dual, frequent in Homer and more common in Attic than in the other dialects, is used to denote natural pairs, e.g. τὼ ὀφθαλμώ *the two eyes.* Yet αἱ χεῖρες *the hands* is preferred to τὼ χεῖρε, and ἄμφω and δύο regularly occur with the plural; e.g. εὖρος δύο πλέθρων (**1082** *e*) *of two plethra in breadth*, X. *An.* 1, 2, 23.

AGREEMENT OF ADJECTIVES

915. Adjectives agree with their substantives in gender, number, and case. This applies also to the article and to adjective pronouns and participles. E.g.

ὁ σοφὸς ἀνήρ *the wise man*; τοῦ σοφοῦ ἀνδρός, τῷ σοφῷ ἀνδρί, τὸν σοφὸν ἄνδρα, τῶν σοφῶν ἀνδρῶν, etc. Οὗτος ὁ ἀνήρ *this man*; τούτου τοῦ ἀνδρός, τούτων τῶν ἀνδρῶν. Αἱ πρὸ τοῦ στόματος νῆες ναυμαχοῦσαι *the ships engaged in battle before the mouth (of the harbor)*, Thuc. 7, 23.

This includes predicate adjectives with copulative verbs, the *case* of which has already been considered (**896**); e.g. αἱ ἄρισται δοκοῦσαι εἶναι φύσεις *the natures which are deemed to be best*, X. *M.* 4, 1, 3.

916. The adjective may be either *attributive* or *predicate*. An attributive adjective simply qualifies the noun, without making an assertion about it; e.g. σοφὸς ἀνήρ *a wise man*, ὁ σοφὸς ἀνήρ *the wise man.* The predicate adjective may be connected with its substantive by the copula (**879**) or by a copulative verb (**897**), becoming a part of the predicate or assertion which is made of the subject; e.g. ὁ ἀνὴρ ἀγαθός ἐστιν *the man is good*; καλεῖται ἀγαθός *he is called good.* It may stand to its noun in any relation which implies some part of εἰμί; e.g. πτηνὰς διώκεις τὰς ἐλπίδας *you are pursuing hopes which are winged*, E. frag. 273; ἀθάνατον τὴν μνήμην καταλείψουσιν *immortal is the memory they will leave behind them*, Isoc. 9, 3; ποιεῖ τοὺς Μήδους ἀσθενεῖς *he makes the Medes (to be) weak.* Every adjective which is not attributive is classed as a predicate.

A predicate adjective is often recognized by its position with respect to the article; see **970**, and the examples.

917. A collective noun in the singular denoting persons may take a plural participle; e.g. Τροίαν ἐλόντες 'Αργείων στόλος *the Argives' army, having taken Troy*, Aesch. *Ag.* 577. Cf. **890.**

918. An adjective may conform to the *real* rather than the *grammatical* gender of a noun denoting a person; e.g. φίλε τέκνον *dear child!* (**174** *d*).

919. An *attributive* adjective belonging to several nouns generally agrees with the nearest or the most prominent one, and is understood with the rest; e.g. τὸν καλὸν κἀγαθὸν ἄνδρα καὶ γυναῖκα *the cultivated man and woman,* Plat. *G.* 470 e; παντὶ καὶ λόγῳ καὶ μηχανῇ *by every word and device.*

920. a. A *predicate* adjective (like a verb, 891) is regularly plural if it belongs to several singular nouns, or dual if it belongs to two. If the nouns are of different genders, the adjective is commonly masculine if one of the nouns denotes a male *person,* and commonly neuter if all denote things. E.g. εἶδε πατέρα τε καὶ μητέρα καὶ ἀδελφοὺς καὶ τὴν ἑαυτοῦ γυναῖκα αἰχμαλώτους γεγενημένους *he saw that both his father and his mother, his brothers, and his own wife had been made captives,* X. *C.* 3, 1, 7; δόξα δὴ καὶ ἐπιμέλεια καὶ νοῦς καὶ τέχνη καὶ νόμος σκληρῶν καὶ μαλακῶν πρότερα ἂν εἴη, *opinion, therefore, and attention, reason, and art must be prior to things hard and soft,* Plat. *Lg.* 892 b. Persons, even when female, may be referred to generically by the masculine; e.g. συνεληλύθασιν ἀδελφαί τε καὶ ἀδελφιδαῖ καὶ ἀνεψιαὶ τοσαῦται, ὥστε εἶναι ἐν τῇ οἰκίᾳ τέσσαρας καὶ δέκα τοὺς ἐλευθέρους *so many sisters, nieces, and cousins have collected that there are in the house fourteen that are gentlefolk,* X. *M.* 2, 7, 2.

b. But a predicate adjective may agree in both gender and number with the nearest or most prominent noun; e.g. πρόρριζος αὐτός, ἡ γυνή, τὰ παιδία, κάκιστ᾽ ἀπολοίμην *may I perish miserably root and branch, myself, my wife, my children,* Ar. *R.* 587.

921. A masculine or feminine noun, denoting a class rather than an individual, may have a neuter predicate adjective; e.g. καλὸν ἡ ἀλήθεια *a beautiful thing is truth,* Plat. *Lg.* 663 e; ἀθάνατον ἄρα ἡ ψυχή; *is the soul then immortal (an immortal thing)?* Plat. *Ph.* 105 c; γυναῖκές ἐσμεν ἀθλιώτατον φυτόν *we women are most unhappy creatures,* E. *Med.* 231.

922. A predicate adjective is often used where the English has an adverb or adverbial phrase; e.g. ἑκόντες ἦλθον *they came willingly* or *were glad to come;* ὅρκιος δέ σοι λέγω *I say it to you on my oath,* S. *Ant.* 305; κατέβαινον εἰς τὰς κώμας σκοταῖοι *it was dark when they began the descent to the villages,* X. *A.* 4, 1, 10. So ἄσμενος *gladly,* and πολύς, e.g. φέρονται οἱ λίθοι πολλοὶ *the stones are hurled in great numbers;* πολὺς ἐνέκειτο λέγων *he was very insistent in his speech,* Hdt. 7, 158. There is often, however, a great distinction between the adjective and the adverb; e.g. πρῶτος αὐτοὺς εἶδον *I was the first to see them;* πρώτους αὐτοὺς εἶδον *they were the first whom I saw;* πρῶτον (adv.) αὐτοὺς εἶδον *first (of all that I did) I saw them.*

Adjectives Belonging to an Omitted Subject

923. When the subject of an infinitive is omitted because it is the same as the subject nominative of the leading verb (883 *b*), adjective words and nouns which would agree with the omitted subject are assimilated to the preceding nominative. E.g.

βούλεται σοφὸς εἶναι he wishes to be wise; Πέρσης ἔφη εἶναι he said he was a
Persian, X. An. 4, 4, 17; οὐχ ὁμολογήσω ἄκλητος ἥκειν I shall not admit
that I am come unbidden, Plat. Symp. 174 d; οὐκ ἔφη αὐτὸς ἀλλ' ἐκεῖνον
στρατηγεῖν he (Cleon) said that not (he) himself, but he (Nicias) was
general; he said οὐκ (ἐγὼ) αὐτὸς (στρατηγῶ) ἀλλ' ἐκεῖνος (στρατηγεῖ), αὐτός
being adjective (988 a) and ἐκεῖνος substantive; Thuc. 4, 28. Such adjective words or nouns may be in the predicate with copulative verbs
(896) or in other constructions. See X. Oec. 7, 8; Symp. 1, 6.

924. But when the subject of an infinitive is omitted because
it is the same as the object or other adjunct (**883 c**) of the leading verb, —

a. If this adjunct is a dative, adjective words and nouns may
either be assimilated to the dative, or stand in the accusative in
agreement with the omitted subject of the infinitive. E.g.

πρέπει σοι εἶναι προθύμῳ (or προθύμον) it becomes you to be zealous; νῦν σοι
ἔξεστιν ἀνδρὶ γενέσθαι now it is in your power to show yourself a man,
X. An. 7, 1, 21; παντὶ προσήκει ἄρχοντι φρονίμῳ εἶναι it becomes every ruler
to be prudent, X. Hipp. 7, 1; συμφέρει αὐτοῖς φίλους εἶναι it is for their
interest to be friends, X. Oec. 11, 23; ἔδοξεν αὐτοῖς συσκευασαμένοις ἃ
εἶχον καὶ ἐξοπλισαμένοις προιέναι they decided to pack up what they had
and arm themselves completely and advance, X. An. 2, 1, 2; but ἔδοξεν
αὐτοῖς προφυλακὰς καταστήσαντας συγκαλεῖν τοὺς στρατιώτας they decided
to station pickets and to assemble the soldiers (ib. 3, 2, 1); in 1, 2, 1 we
find two datives and an accusative.

b. If the adjunct is a genitive, *predicate* adjectives are generally
assimilated to it; but other adjective words and all substantives
stand in the accusative. E.g.

Κύρου ἐδέοντο ὡς προθυμοτάτου γενέσθαι they asked Cyrus to be as devoted to
them as possible, X. H. 1, 5, 2; but (with a substantive) Ἀθηναίων
ἐδεήθησαν σφίσι βοηθοὺς γενέσθαι they asked the Athenians to become their
helpers, Hdt. 6, 100; κακούργου ἐστὶ κριθέντ' ἀποθανεῖν, στρατηγοῦ δὲ
μαχόμενον τοῖς πολεμίοις it is proper for a malefactor to die by the sentence of a court, but for a general (to die) fighting the enemy, Dem. 4, 47;
δέομαι ὑμῶν μεμνημένους τῶν εἰρημένων τὰ δίκαια ψηφίσασθαι I beg of you
to remember what has been said, and to vote what is just, Isoc. 19, 51.

925. Words in the construction of **924** which refer to a preceding accusative are of course in the accusative; e.g. ἄλλους πέπεικα συμμαθητάς μοι
φοιτᾶν I have induced others to go as my fellow-pupils, Plat. Euthyd. 272 c.

926. The principles of **923** and **924** apply also to a predicate with ὤν
or with the participle of a copulative verb; e.g. ᾔδεσαν σοφοὶ ὄντες they
knew that they were wise (but ᾔδεσαν τούτους σοφοὺς ὄντας they knew that these
men were wise). **1590.**

927. When an infinitive depends on a participle which supplies its omitted subject, predicate words take the case of the participle; e.g. ἦλθον ἐπί τινα τῶν δοκούντων εἶναι σοφῶν *I accosted one who had the reputation of being wise*, Plat. *Ap.* 21 b; τῶν προσποιουμένων εἶναι σοφιστῶν τινας *some of those who profess to be sophists*, Isoc. 15, 221. So τοῖς δοκοῦσιν εἶναι σοφοῖς *to those who are reputed to be wise*.

928. When the subject of an infinitive is general or indefinite it is often omitted; e.g. σιγᾶν κελεύω (sc. πάντας) *I command silence*, S. *Ph.* 865. Here a predicate modifier is in the accusative; e.g. ῥᾷον ἔχοντας φυλάττειν ἢ κτήσασθαι πάντα πέφυκεν *it is naturally easier to keep anything when you have it than to acquire it*, Dem. 2, 26.

Adjective Used as a Substantive

929. *a.* An attributive adjective or participle, generally with the article, may be used as a substantive. E.g.

ὁ δίκαιος *the just man*; ὁ ἐχθρός *the enemy*; φίλος *a friend*; κακή *a base woman*; τὸ μέσον or μέσον *the middle*; οἱ κακοί *the bad*; τοῖς ἀγαθοῖς *to the good*; κακά *evils*; τὰ θνητά *things mortal*; οἱ γραψάμενοι Σωκράτην *the accusers of Socrates*.

b. In some cases, a noun is distinctly implied; e.g. τῇ ὑστεραίᾳ (sc. ἡμέρᾳ) *on the next day*; ἡ δεξιά (sc. χείρ) *the right hand*; ἡ εὐθεῖα (sc. ὁδός) *the straight road*; ὁ ἄκρατος (sc. οἶνος) *unmixed wine*. So with other attributive words, e.g. ἐς τὴν ἑαυτῶν (sc. γῆν) *into their own land*; εἰς τοῦ ἀδελφοῦ *to my brother's* (for εἰς τὴν τοῦ ἀδελφοῦ οἰκίαν).

930. Sometimes the omitted substantive is not easy to supply; e.g. ἐξ ἐναντίας *from the opposite quarter, over against*; ἐξ ἴσου *on an equal basis, equal*; ἐν ἀσφαλεῖ *in safety* (= ἀσφαλές, *safe*).

931. The neuter singular of an adjective with the article is often used as an abstract noun; e.g. τὸ καλόν *beauty* (= κάλλος), τὸ δίκαιον *justice* (= δικαιοσύνη).

932. The participle, which is a verbal adjective, is occasionally thus used; e.g. τὸ δεδιός *fear* (= τὸ δεδιέναι), Thuc. 1, 36; ἐν τῷ μὴ μελετῶντι *in the want of practice* (*in the not practising*) (= ἐν τῷ μὴ μελετᾶν), Thuc. 1, 142. So in Latin, opus est maturato *there is need of haste*.

THE ARTICLE

Homeric Use of the Article

933. In Homer the article appears generally as a demonstrative pronoun, which was its original function. If used as a substantive, it may serve as a personal pronoun of the third person or (in the forms beginning with τ) as a relative, when the antecedent is definite. E.g.

τὴν δ' ἐγὼ οὐ λύσω but her I will not free, Il. 1, 29 ; τοῦ δὲ κλύε Φοῖβος 'Απόλλων and Phoebus Apollo heard him, Il. 1, 43 ; ὁ γὰρ ἦλθε θοὰς ἐπὶ νῆας 'Αχαιῶν for he came to the swift ships of the Achaeans, Il. 1, 12. As relative, πυρὰ πολλὰ τὰ καίετο many fires which were burning, Il. 10, 12 ; δῶρα τά οἱ ξεῖνος δῶκε gifts which a stranger gave him, Od. 21, 13.

934. Even in Homer, adjectives and participles used as substantives (929 a) sometimes have the article, as in Attic Greek ; e.g. οἱ γὰρ ἄριστοι ἐν νηυσὶν κέαται for the bravest lie in the ships, Il. 11, 658 ; οἱ ἄλλοι the (those) others ; τά τ' ἐόντα τά τ' ἐσσόμενα both things that are and things that are to be, Il. 1, 70.

935. a. When ὁ, ἡ, τό are used before a noun in Homer, they are generally pronouns (especially ὁ δέ), and the substantive is in apposition with them ; e.g. ὁ δ' ἔβραχε χάλκεος "Αρης and he, brazen Ares, roared, Il. 5, 859 ; ἡ δ' ἀέκουσ' ἅμα τοῖσι γυνὴ κίεν and she, the woman, went with them unwillingly, Il. 1, 348.

b. Nearer the Attic use of the article are examples like these : αὐτὰρ ὁ τοῖσι γέρων ὁδὸν ἡγεμόνευεν but he, the old man, showed them the way, Od. 24, 225 ; τὸν δ' οἶον πατέρ' εὗρον and him, the father, they found alone, ib. 226.

c. Hardly, if at all, to be distinguished from the Attic article is that found in examples like these : ὅτε δὴ τὴν νῆσον ἀφικόμεθ' when now we had come to the island, Od. 9, 543 ; τό τε σθένος 'Ωαρίωνος and the might of Orion, Il. 18, 486 ; αἱ δὲ γυναῖκες ἱστάμεναι θαύμαζον and the women stood and wondered, Il. 18, 495.

d. It is therefore often difficult to decide the exact force of an article in early Greek. The examples above show a gradual transition, even in Homer, from the original pronoun to the true definite article.

936. The examples in 935 c are exceptional ; in such cases the nouns usually stand without the article in Homer, as in Latin. E.g. δεινὴ δὲ κλαγγὴ γένετ' ἀργυρέοιο βιοῖο and terrible came the clang from the silver bow, Il. 1, 49, would in Attic Greek require ἡ κλαγγή and τοῦ βιοῦ.

937. Herodotus generally uses the forms of the article beginning with τ in the place of the ordinary relative, of which he uses only the forms ὅς, ἥ, οἵ, and αἵ, except after prepositions. E.g. ἄλλος ὄρνις ἱρὸς, τῷ οὔνομα Φοῖνιξ another sacred bird, whose name is Phoenix, 2, 73. In other respects he uses the article as it is used in Attic prose.

938. The lyric poets follow the Homeric usage with respect to the article more closely than Herodotus ; and the tragic poets, especially in the lyric chorus, admit the article in the τ forms as a relative or a personal pronoun to avoid hiatus, to make a syllable long by position, or to mark special emphasis. The article is often omitted in Attic poetry where it would be required in prose (936). The dialogue of comedy, being more colloquial, uses it oftener than that of tragedy.

Attic Use of the Article

939. In Attic Greek the article generally corresponds to our article *the*; e.g. ὁ ἀνήρ *the man*, τῶν πόλεων *of the cities*; τοῖς Ἕλλησιν *to the Greeks*, τὰ δέκα ἔτη *the* (well known) *ten years* (at Troy), Thuc. 1, 11.

940. The Greek may use the article in certain cases in which the English omits it. Such are the following (941–949):

941. Proper names may take the article; e.g. ὁ Σωκράτης or Σωκράτης *Socrates*.

942. Abstract substantives often take the article; e.g. ἡ ἀρετή *virtue*, ἡ δικαιοσύνη *justice*; ἡ εὐλάβεια *caution*. But ἀρετή etc. are also used in the same sense, and words like εὖρος *width*, μέγεθος *size*, ὄνομα *name*, commonly omit the article.

943. *a.* Substantives qualified by a demonstrative pronoun regularly take the article; e.g. οὗτος ὁ ἀνήρ *this man*; ἐν ταῖσδε ταῖς πόλεσιν *in these cities*. For the position see 972.

b. But this article may be omitted with proper names, e.g. οὗτος Νεοπτόλεμος *this Neoptolemus*, Dem. 18, 114; also when the substantive is in the predicate, or where the demonstrative is equivalent to *here* or *there*, e.g. ὁρῶμεν ὀλίγους τούτους ἀνθρώπους *we see few men here*, X. *An.* 4, 7, 5; αὕτη ἔστω ἱκανὴ ἀπολογία *let this be a sufficient answer*, Plat. *Ap.* 24 b. So οὑτοσὶ ἀνήρ *this man here*, and οὗτος ἀνήρ used familiarly or contemptuously; see also νῆες ἐκεῖναι ἐπιπλέουσι *ships are sailing up yonder*, Thuc. 1, 51.

c. The tragedians often omit this article with demonstratives.

944. *a.* Substantives with a possessive pronoun take the article when they refer to definite individuals, but not otherwise; e.g. ὁ ἐμὸς πατήρ *my father*, ὁ σὸς κοινωνός *your partner*, Dem. 18, 21 (998); but σὸς κοινωνός would mean *a partner of yours*. For predicates see 954.

b. So also with substantives on which a possessive genitive of a personal, demonstrative, or reflexive pronoun depends; e.g. ὁ πατήρ μου *my father*; ὁ ἐμαυτοῦ πατήρ *my own father*; ὁ τούτων πατήρ *their father*; ἡ ἑαυτῶν γῆ *their own land*, but παῖς ἑαυτοῦ *a child of his own*.

945. Τοιοῦτος, τοσοῦτος, τοιόσδε, τοσόσδε, and τηλικοῦτος, standing in the attributive position (959), may take the article; e.g. τὸν τοιοῦτον ἄνδρα *such a man as he*. It is always used with δεῖνα (398), e.g. ὁ δεῖνα *What's-his-name*.

946. A numeral may have the article to distinguish a part of a number (443); to express a round number, especially with ἀμφί, περί, ὑπέρ, or εἰς; to express merely a number in the abstract. E.g. τῶν πέντε τὰς δύο μοίρας νέμονται *they hold two parts out of five*, or *two fifths*, Thuc. 1, 10; οἱ μὲν τέτταρες οὐδὲν ἔφασαν εἰδέναι τοῦ πράγματος *four of them* (out of the total of five) *said they knew nothing of the affair*, Lys. 22, 8; ἔμειναν ἡμέρας ἀμφὶ τὰς τριάκοντα *they remained about thirty days*, X. *An.* 4, 8, 22; ὅπως μὴ ἐρεῖς ὅτι ἐστὶ τὰ δώδεκα δὶς ἔξ *don't say that twelve is twice six,* Plat. *Rep.* 337 b; τὸ ἕν *the number one, unity,* A. *Met.* 986 a 15.

947. The article is often used, where we use a possessive pronoun, to mark something as belonging to a person or thing mentioned in the sentence; e.g. ἔρχεται αὐτή τε ἡ Μανδάνη πρὸς τὸν πατέρα καὶ τὸν Κῦρον τὸν υἱὸν ἔχουσα *Mandane comes to her father* (lit. *to the father) herself, and with her son Cyrus,* X. *C.* 1, 3, 1.

948. The article may have a generic force, marking an object as the representative of a class; e.g. ὁ ἄνθρωπος *man* (in general); οἱ ἄνθρωποι *mankind* (opposed to gods or the lower animals); οἱ γέροντες *the aged* (as a class).

949. The article sometimes has a distributive force, where we should use *each* or *a*; e.g. ὑπισχνεῖται δώσειν τρία ἡμιδαρεικὰ τοῦ μηνὸς τῷ στρατιώτῃ *he promises to give three half-darics a month to each soldier,* X. *An.* 1, 3, 21. See **444 a, 1136.**

950. *a.* An adverb, a preposition with its case, or any similar expression, may be used with the article to qualify a substantive, like an attributive adjective; e.g. οἱ τότε ἄνθρωποι *the men of that time;* τοῦ πάλαι Κάδμου *of ancient Cadmus,* S. *O.T.* 1; οἱ ἐν ἄστει Ἀθηναῖοι *the Athenians in the city;* ὁ πρὸς τοὺς Λακεδαιμονίους πόλεμος *the Peloponnesian War.*

b. Here a substantive denoting *men* or *things* is often omitted; e.g. οἱ ἐν ἄστει *the city party* (of 403 B.C.); τοῖς τότε *to the men of that time;* οἱ ἀμφὶ Πλάτωνα *Plato and his school,* or (in later Greek) simply *Plato.*

951. The substantives γῆ *land,* πράγματα *things* or *affairs,* υἱός *son,* and sometimes others readily suggested by the context, may be omitted after the article, when a qualifying adjective or genitive is added; e.g. εἰς τὴν ἑαυτῶν (sc. γῆν) *to their own land;* ἐκ τῆς περιοικίδος *from the neighboring country;* τὰ τῆς πόλεως *the affairs of the state, politics;* τὰ τῶν πολεμίων *the enemy's cause;* Περικλῆς ὁ Ξανθίππου (sc. υἱός) *Pericles son of Xanthippus;* τὴν ταχίστην (sc. ὁδόν) *the quickest way.* Expressions like τὰ (or τὸ) τῆς τύχης, τὰ τῆς ὀργῆς, with no definite nouns understood, sometimes do not differ from τύχη *fortune* and ὀργή *wrath.* Cf. **929 b.**

952. Instead of repeating a substantive with new adjuncts in the same sentence, it may be sufficient to repeat its article; e.g. οἱ τῶν πολιτῶν παῖδες καὶ οἱ τῶν ἄλλων *the children of citizens and those of the other inhabitants.*

953. *a.* The infinitive, as a verbal noun (**1520**), may take a neuter article; e.g. τὸ εἰδέναι *the knowledge;* σοὶ τὸ μὴ σιγῆσαι λοιπὸν ἦν *it remained for you not to be silent,* Dem. 18, 23.

b. In like manner, a neuter article may precede a whole clause considered as a substantive; e.g. τὸ γνῶθι σαυτὸν πανταχοῦ 'στι χρήσιμον *the saying "know thyself" is everywhere useful.*

954. A predicate noun seldom has the article; e.g. νὺξ ἡ ἡμέρη ἐγένετο *the day became night,* Hdt. 1, 103; καλεῖται ἡ ἀκρόπολις ἔτι ὑπ' Ἀθηναίων πόλις *the citadel is still called "city" by the Athenians*, Thuc. 2, 15. So when it has a possessive pronoun; e.g. οὗτος ἐμὸς ἑταῖρος ἦν *he was a chum of mine*, Plat. *Ap.* 21 a.

But when the predicate refers definitely to distinct persons or things, it may have the article; e.g. εἰσὶ δ' οὗτοι οἱ εἰδότες τἀληθές; *and are they the ones* (whom I mean) *who know the truth?* Plat. *H. Maj.* 284 e; οὗτοι οἱ δεινοί εἰσί μου κατήγοροι *these are my really formidable accusers*, Plat. *Ap.* 18 c.

955. Βασιλεύς is generally used without the article to designate the king of Persia; e.g. τούτους ἀποπέμπει βασιλεῖ *these he sends to the King*, Thuc. 1, 128. But the article is sometimes found: compare Isoc. 4, 166 and 179. So sometimes μέγας βασιλεύς; e.g. μεγάλου βασιλέως βασίλεια *a palace of the Great King*, X. *An.* 1, 2, 8. The article is omitted in official records of personal names, and in formal use; e.g. Τολμίδης Ἠλεῖος *Tolmides of Elis*, X. *An.* 2, 2, 20.

956. The article is often omitted in some familiar expressions of time and place, which are probably older than the Attic use of the article; e.g. ἅμα ἕῳ *at daybreak*; νυκτός *by night*; ἅμα ἦρι *at the opening of spring*; ἐν ἀγορᾷ *in the market-place*; κατ' ἀγρούς *in the country*; κατὰ γῆν *by land*; κατὰ θάλατταν *by sea*; ἐκ δεξιᾶς *from the right*.

957. The article is generally used with the name of a god and an epithet denoting his cult, or when the name depends upon a substantive which has the article; e.g. ὁ Ζεὺς ὁ Μειλίχιος *Zeus, requirer of propitiatory offerings*, X. *An.* 7, 8, 4; τῆς Ἀρτέμιδος τῆς Ἐφεσίας *of Ephesian Artemis*, X. *An.* 5, 3, 6; τὸ ἱερὸν τοῦ Ἀπόλλωνος *the sanctuary of Apollo*, Thuc. 1, 29. The article is necessary in oaths except with the name of Zeus, e.g. νὴ Δία *by Zeus*, νὴ τὸν Ἡρακλέα *by Heracles*, μὰ τοὺς θεοὺς *no, by the gods*. Without the article θεός is often used to mean *divinity, God* (with no implication of monotheism).

958. The article must be used in ἡ Ἀσία *Asia*, ἡ Ἑλλάς *Hellas*, ἡ Εὐρώπη *Europe*, and with many adjectival names; e.g. ἡ Ἀττική *Attica* (sc. γῆ, 951); yet κατὰ Θετταλίαν *in Thessaly*.

Position of the Article

959. *Attributive Position.* *a.* An attributive adjective which qualifies a substantive with the article commonly stands between the article and the substantive, and is said to be in the *attributive* position; e.g. ὁ σοφὸς ἀνήρ *the wise man*, τῶν μεγάλων πόλεων *of the great cities.* See **916.**

b. The noun with the article may be followed by the adjective with the article repeated. The first article is sometimes omitted. In these cases the noun has greater emphasis than in the preceding form (*a*). E.g.

ὁ ἀνὴρ ὁ σοφός, sometimes ἀνὴρ ὁ σοφός *the wise man* (but *not* ὁ ἀνὴρ σοφός, see **970**) ; αἱ πόλεις αἱ δημοκρατούμεναι *the states which are under democracies* ; ἄνθρωποι οἱ ἀδικώτατοι *men who are the most unjust* ; πῶς ἡ ἄκρατος δικαιοσύνη πρὸς ἀδικίαν τὴν ἄκρατον ἔχει (the question) *how pure justice is related to pure injustice,* Plat. *Rep.* 545 a.

960. This applies to possessive pronouns and all expressions which have the force of attributive adjectives, when they are preceded by the article (**950** *a*), and to dependent genitives (except *partitives* and the genitive of the *personal* pronoun) ; e.g. ὁ ἐμὸς πατήρ *my father* ; ἡ σὴ μήτηρ *thy mother* ; ὁ ἐμαυτοῦ πατήρ *my own father* (but ὁ πατήρ μου *my father,* see **975** *a*) ; οἱ ἐν ἄστει ἄνθρωποι or οἱ ἄνθρωποι οἱ ἐν ἄστει *the men in the city* ; οὐδεὶς τῶν τότε Ἑλλήνων *none of the Greeks of that time* ; τὸ τῷ ὄντι ψεῦδος *the real falsehood* ; εἰς τὴν ἐκείνων πόλιν *into their city* ; οἱ τῶν Θηβαίων στρατηγοί *the generals of the Thebans* ; τὸν δῆμον τὸν Ἀθηναίων *the people of Athens* ; ἐν τῇ ἀναβάσει τῇ μετὰ Κύρου *in the upward march with Cyrus,* X. *An.* 5, 1, 1. For participles see **968.**

961. Two or even three articles may thus stand together ; e.g. τὰ γὰρ τῆς τῶν πολλῶν ψυχῆς ὄμματα *the eyes of the soul of the multitude,* Plat. *So.* 254 a.

962. Of the three attributive positions, the first (e.g. ὁ σοφὸς ἀνήρ) is the most common and the most simple and natural ; the second (ὁ ἀνὴρ ὁ σοφός) is rather formal ; the third (ἀνὴρ ὁ σοφός) is the least common except in poetry, the attributive being added as an afterthought or correction.

963. The article at the beginning of a clause may be separated from its substantive by the postpositive words μέν, δέ, τὲ, γὲ, γάρ, δή, οὖν, οἶμαι, τοὶ, τοίνυν, and by τὶς in Herodotus.

964. The *partitive* genitive (**1088**) rarely stands in either of the attributive positions, but either precedes or follows the governing noun and its article ; ˙e.g. οἱ κακοὶ τῶν πολιτῶν, or τῶν πολιτῶν οἱ κακοί *the bad among the citizens* (rarely οἱ τῶν πολιτῶν κακοί).

Even the other uses of the adnominal genitive occasionally have this position, e.g. διὰ τὸν ὄλεθρον τῶν συστρατιωτῶν ὀργιζόμενοι *angered by the death of their fellow soldiers,* X. *An.* 1, 2, 26.

965. a. Ὁ ἄλλος in the singular generally means *the rest,* seldom *the other* ; οἱ ἄλλοι means *the others* : e.g. ἡ ἄλλη πόλις *the rest of the state* (but ἄλλη πόλις *another state*) ; οἱ ἄλλοι Ἕλληνες *the other Greeks* ; περὶ τῶν ἄλλων ἀπάντων ζῴων *in the case of all other animals,* Plat. *Ap.* 25 b.

b. Both ὁ ἄλλος and ἄλλος (rarely ἕτερος) may have the meaning of *besides* ; e.g. εὐδαιμονιζόμενος ὑπὸ τῶν πολιτῶν καὶ τῶν ἄλλων ξένων *congratulated by the citizens and the foreigners besides,* Plat. *G.* 473 c ; οὐ γὰρ ἦν χόρτος οὐδὲ ἄλλο οὐδὲν δένδρον *for there was no grass, nor any tree either* (lit. *nor any other tree*), X. *An.* 1, 5, 5. Hence ὁ ἄλλος is used in summing up, and may mean *in general* ; e.g. τὸν ἄλλον τὸν ἐμὸν βίον *my means of livelihood in general,* Lys. 24, 5.

966. Πολύς with the article generally (though not always) means the *greater part*, especially in οἱ πολλοί *the multitude, the majority, the rabble*, and τὸ πολύ *the greater part*. E.g. οἱ πλείονες *the majority*, τὸ πλέον *the greater part*, οἱ πλεῖστοι and τὸ πλεῖστον *the greatest number or part*; ὀλίγοι *few, only a few*, οἱ ὀλίγοι *the aristocracy*.

967. When a noun has two or more qualifying words, each of them may take an article and stand in either attributive position (959), or all may stand between one article and its noun; e.g. κατὰ τὴν ᾿Αττικὴν τὴν παλαιὰν φωνήν *according to the old Attic dialect*, Plat. *Crat.* 398 d; τὰ τείχη τὰ ἑαυτῶν τὰ μακρά *their own long walls*, Thuc. 1, 108; πέμποντες εἰς τὰς ἄλλας ᾿Αρκαδικὰς πόλεις *sending to the other Arcadian cities*, X. *H.* 7, 4, 38; τὴν ὑπ᾿ ᾿Αρετῆς ῾Ηρακλέους παίδευσιν *the instruction of Heracles by Virtue*, X. *M.* 2, 1, 34. Occasionally one stands between the article and the noun, while another follows the noun without an article; e.g. οἱ ἀπὸ τῶν ἐν τῇ ᾿Ασίᾳ πόλεων ῾Ελληνίδων *the men from the Greek cities in Asia*, X. *H.* 4, 3, 15.

968. When an attributive participle (916) with dependent words qualifies a substantive with the article, either the participle or the dependent words may follow the substantive; e.g. τὸν ῥέοντα ποταμὸν διὰ τῆς πόλεως *the river which runs through the city*, X. *H.* 5, 2, 4; τὸν ἐφεστηκότα κίνδυνον τῇ πόλει *the danger impending over the city*, Dem. 18, 176; ἡ ἐν τῷ ᾿Ισθμῷ ἐπιμονὴ γενομένη *the delay which occurred at the Isthmus*, Thuc. 2, 18. But such expressions may also take either of the attributive positions (959 a or b).

969. The Greeks commonly said *the Euphrates river*, τὸν Εὐφράτην ποταμόν, etc., rather than *the river Euphrates*. So sometimes with names of mountains, e.g. τὸ Πήλιον (ὄρος) *Mt. Pelion*; and seas, e.g. ὁ ῾Ελλήσποντος, ὁ ᾿Ιόνιος κόλπος. With names of cities and islands the article is often omitted. It may be omitted also with names of inhabitants, e.g. Θηβαῖοι, ῞Ελληνες (except when opposed to οἱ βάρβαροι), and with names of months and winds, e.g. ᾿Ελαφηβολιῶνος (μηνός), νότος, βορέας.

970. *Predicate Position.* When an adjective either precedes the article, or follows directly a noun which has an article, it is always a predicate adjective, and is said to be in the *predicate position* (see 916). E.g.

ὁ ἀνὴρ σοφός or σοφὸς ὁ ἀνήρ (sc. ἐστίν) *the man is wise, or wise is the man*; πολλοὶ οἱ πανοῦργοι *many are the evil-doers*; ἐφημέρους γε τὰς τύχας κεκτήμεθα *we possess our fortunes only for a day*, Gnom.; ψιλὴν ἔχων τὴν κεφαλήν *having his head bare*, X. *An.* 1, 8, 6.

971. The predicate force of such adjectives must often be rendered by a periphrasis; e.g. πτηνὰς διώκεις τὰς ἐλπίδας *the hopes you are pursuing are winged*, lit. *you are pursuing hopes (which are) winged*, E. frag. 273; ἡγούμενοι αὐτονόμων τῶν ξυμμάχων *being leaders of allies who were independent*, Thuc. 1, 97. So πόσον ἄγει τὸ στράτευμα; *how large is the army he is bringing?*

972. A noun qualified by a demonstrative pronoun (οὗτος, ὅδε, ἐκεῖνος) regularly takes the article, and the pronoun stands in the predicate position (970). See 943 a–c. E.g.

οὗτος ὁ ἀνήρ *this man* or ὁ ἀνὴρ οὗτος (never ὁ οὗτος ἀνήρ); περὶ τούτων τῶν πόλεων *about these cities.*

973. But if an adjective or other qualifying word is added, the demonstrative may stand between this and its noun; e.g. ἡ στενὴ αὕτη ὁδός *this narrow road*, X. *An.* 4, 2, 6; τῷ ἀφικομένῳ τούτῳ ξένῳ *to this stranger who has come*, Plat. *Prot.* 313 b. See 975 *b.*

974. Ἕκαστος, ἑκάτερος, ἄμφω, and ἀμφότερος have the predicate position like a demonstrative, e.g. ἑκάστη ἡ ἡμέρα *each day*; but with ἕκαστος the article may be omitted. Τοιοῦτος, τοσοῦτος, τοιόσδε, τοσόσδε, and τηλικοῦτος, when they take the article, usually have the first attributive position (959 a).

975. a. A dependent genitive of the *personal* pronoun (whether partitive or not) has the predicate position (970, 998 b), while the genitive of other pronouns (unless it is partitive) has the first attributive position (959 a); e.g. ἡμῶν ἡ πόλις or ἡ πόλις ἡμῶν *our city*; ἡ τούτων πόλις *these men's city*; μετεπέμψατο 'Αστυάγης τὴν ἑαυτοῦ θυγατέρα καὶ τὸν παῖδα αὐτῆς *Astyages sent for his (own) daughter and her son*, X. *C.* 1, 3, 1.

b. But if a qualifying word is added, the personal pronoun may stand between this and the noun; e.g. ἡ δοκοῦσα ἡμῶν πρότερον σωφροσύνη *what previously seemed to be our modesty*, Thuc. 1, 32; ἡ πάλαι ἡμῶν φύσις *our old nature*, Plat. *Symp.* 189 d. See 973.

976. a. The adjectives ἄκρος, μέσος, and ἔσχατος, when they are in the predicate position (970), mean *the top* (or *extremity*), *the middle, the last*, of the thing which their substantives denote; e.g. ἡ ἀγορὰ μέση or μέση ἡ ἀγορά *the middle of the market* (while ἡ μέση ἀγορά would mean *the middle market*); ἄκρα ἡ χείρ *the extremity of the hand.* But they may also be used (like the corresponding words in English) with dependent genitive; e.g. μέση ἡμέρα or μέσον ἡμέρας *mid-day*; τὸ ἄκρον τοῦ ὄρους *the top of the mountain.*

b. When no article is used, as in the older poetry, the context must decide the meaning. Compare summus, medius, extremus, and ultimus in Latin.

977. Πᾶς and σύμπας *all* and ὅλος *whole* generally have the predicate position; e.g. πάντες οἱ ἄνδρες or οἱ ἄνδρες πάντες *all the men*; ὅλη ἡ πόλις or ἡ πόλις ὅλη *all the city.* But they are preceded by the article when they denote the sum total; e.g. ἡ πᾶσα Σικελία *the whole of Sicily*, τὸ ὅλον γένος *the entire race.*

The distinction here was probably no greater than that between *all the city* and *the whole city* in English. We find even οἱ πάντες ἄνθρωποι *all mankind*, X. *An.* 5, 6, 7.

978. Αὐτός as an intensive pronoun, ipse (988 *a*), has the predicate position; e.g. αὐτὸς ὁ ἀνήρ *the man himself.* But ὁ αὐτὸς ἀνήρ *the same man.*

Pronominal Article in Attic Greek

979. In Attic prose the article retains its original demonstrative force chiefly in the expression ὁ μέν . . . ὁ δέ *the one . . . the other.* E.g.

οἱ μὲν αὐτῶν ἐτόξευον, οἱ δ' ἐσφενδόνων *some of them shot with bows, and others used slings,* X. *An.* 3, 3, 7; δεῖ τοὺς μὲν εἶναι δυστυχεῖς, τοὺς δ' εὐτυχεῖς *some must be unfortunate, while others are (must be) fortunate,* E. frag. 207; τῶν πόλεων αἱ μὲν τυραννοῦνται, αἱ δὲ δημοκρατοῦνται, αἱ δὲ ἀριστοκρατοῦνται *some states are governed by tyrants, others by democracies, and others by aristocracies,* Plat. *Rep.* 338 d.

980. Some authorities accent the demonstrative article, ὅ, ἥ, οἵ, αἵ. See **157.**

981. The neuter τὸ μέν . . . τὸ δέ, τὰ μέν . . . τὰ δέ, may be used adverbially, *partly . . . partly.* For τοῦτο μέν . . . τοῦτο δέ in this sense, see **1010.**

982. *a.* Ὁ δέ etc., indicating a change of subject, mean *and he, but he, but the other,* etc., even when no ὁ μέν precedes; e.g. Ἰνάρως Ἀθηναίους ἐπηγάγετο · οἱ δὲ ἦλθον *Inaros called in the Athenians; and they came,* Thuc. 1, 104.

b. With prepositions these expressions are generally inverted; e.g. πολλὰ μέν . . . ἐν δὲ τοῖς, Plat. *Euthyd.* 303 c; παρὰ μὲν τοῦ ξύλα, παρὰ δὲ τοῦ σίδηρος, [X.] *Rep. A.* 2, 11.

983. A few other relics of the demonstrative meaning of the article are found in Attic, chiefly the following :

τὸν καὶ τόν *this man and that;* τὸ καὶ τό *this and that;* τὰ καὶ τά *these and those;* e.g. ἔδει γὰρ τὸ καὶ τὸ ποιῆσαι, καὶ τὸ μὴ ποιῆσαι *for we ought to have done this thing and that, and not to have done the other,* Dem. 9, 68. πρὸ τοῦ (or προτοῦ) *before this, formerly.* καὶ τόν or καὶ τήν, before an infinitive ; e.g. καὶ τὸν κελεῦσαι δοῦναι (sc. λέγεται) *and (it is said) he commanded him to give (it),* X. *C.* 1, 3, 9. So occasionally τῷ *therefore,* which is common in Homer.

PRONOUNS

Personal and Intensive Pronouns

984. The nominatives of the personal pronouns are usually omitted except when emphasis or contrast is required. See **885.**

985. The forms ἐμοῦ, ἐμοί, and ἐμέ are more emphatic than the enclitics μοῦ, μοί, μέ. The latter seldom occur after prepositions, except in πρός με.

986. Of the personal pronouns of the third person, οὗ, οἷ, etc. **(364),** only οἷ and the plural forms in σφ- are used in Attic prose. There they are generally *indirect reflexives*, that is, in a dependent clause (or joined with an infinitive or participle in the leading clause) they refer to the subject of the leading verb. E.g.

ἔλεξαν ὅτι πέμψειε σφᾶς ὁ Ἰνδῶν βασιλεύς *they said that the king of the Hindus had sent them,* X. C. 2, 4, 7; ἐπρεσβεύοντο ἐγκλήματα ποιούμενοι, ὅπως σφίσιν ὅτι μεγίστη πρόφασις εἴη τοῦ πολεμεῖν *they sent embassies, making charges, that they might have the strongest possible ground for war,* Thuc. 1, 126; λέγων ὅτι πλείους ἔτι αἱ λοιπαί εἰσι νῆες χρήσιμαι σφίσιν (= ἑαυτοῖς) ἢ τοῖς πολεμίοις *saying that they themselves had more seaworthy ships remaining than the enemy,* Thuc. 7, 72; ἐνταῦθα λέγεται Ἀπόλλων ἐκδεῖραι Μαρσύαν νικήσας ἐρίζοντά οἱ περὶ σοφίας *here Apollo is said to have flayed Marsyas, having beaten him in a contest (with himself,* οἷ*) in skill,* X. An. 1, 2, 8.

For the restricted use of these pronouns in Attic Greek, see also **367**. For σφέ, σφίν, νίν, and μίν, see **370** and **371**.

987. In Homer and Herodotus, and when they occur in the Attic poets, all these pronouns are generally personal pronouns, though sometimes (direct or indirect) reflexives. E.g.

ἐκ γάρ σφεων (= αὐτῶν) φρένας εἵλετο Παλλὰς Ἀθήνη *for Pallas Athena bereft them of their senses,* Il. 18, 311; τὸν κριὸν ἀπὸ ἕο (= ἑαυτοῦ) πέμπε θύραζε *he sent the ram forth from himself through the door,* Od. 9, 461; αὐτίκα δέ οἱ (= αὐτῷ) εὕδοντι ἐπέστη ὄνειρος *and soon a dream came to him in his sleep,* Hdt. 1, 34; οὐδαμοῖσι τῶν νῦν σφεας περιοικεόντων εἰσὶ ὁμόγλωσσοι *they have not the same speech as any of their present neighbors,* Hdt. 1, 57; τίνι τρόπῳ θανεῖν σφε φής; *in what manner do you say she died?* S. Tr. 878.

988. Αὐτός has three uses:

a. In all its cases it may be an intensive adjectival pronoun, *himself, herself, itself, themselves* (like Lat. ipse). E.g.

αὐτὸς ὁ στρατηγός *the general himself;* ἐπ᾽ αὐτοῖς τοῖς αἰγιαλοῖς *on the very coasts,* Thuc. 1, 7; ὑπὸ λόφον αὐτόν *right under the crest,* Il. 13, 615; αὐτὴ δικαιοσύνη *pure justice;* τὸ δίκαιον αὐτό *justice in the abstract.*

b. Αὐτός in all its cases, when preceded by the article, means *the same* (idem). E.g.

ὁ αὐτὸς ἀνήρ *the same man;* τὸν αὐτὸν πόλεμον *the same war;* ταὐτά *the same things* (**49**), to be distinguished from ταῦτα *these things.*

c. The *oblique cases* of αὐτός are the ordinary personal pronouns of the third person, *him, her, it, them.* E.g.

στρατηγὸν αὐτὸν ἀπέδειξε *he appointed him as general.* See four other examples in X. An. 1, 1, 2 and 3.

The *nominative* of αὐτός is always emphatic, and even the oblique cases may have an intensive meaning if placed in an emphatic position.

989. A pronoun with which αὐτός intensive agrees is often omitted; e.g. ταῦτα ἐποιεῖτε αὐτοί (sc. ὑμεῖς) *you did this yourselves;* πλευστέον εἰς ταύτας αὐτοῖς ἐμβᾶσιν (sc. ὑμῖν) *you must sail, embarking on these ships in person,* Dem. 4, 16. Hence, used absolutely by slave or pupil, it may mean *master,* e.g. αὐτὸς ἔφη (ipse dixit) *the master said it.* So in the sense of *by oneself;* e.g. αὐτοὶ γάρ ἐσμεν *we are all alone by ourselves,* Ar. *Ach.* 504. For the meaning *and all* with the dative, see **1187.**

990. Αὐτός with an ordinal numeral (**429**) may designate a person as making one of a given number; e.g. ᾑρέθη πρεσβευτὴς δέκατος αὐτός *he was chosen ambassador with nine others,* X. *H.* 2, 2, 17; μεταπεμψάμενοί με πέμπτον αὐτόν *sending for me and four others,* Plat. *Ap.* 32 c (**443**).

991. The oblique cases of αὐτός are often used where the indirect reflexives (**986**) might stand, and sometimes even where the direct reflexives (**993**) would be allowed; e.g. ἁπλῶς τὴν ἑαυτοῦ γνώμην ἀπεφαίνετο Σωκράτης πρὸς τοὺς ὁμιλοῦντας αὐτῷ *Socrates used to declare his own opinion plainly to those who associated with him,* X. *M.* 4, 7, 1, where οἷ might have been used; but in *M.* 1, 2, 3, we have ἐλπίζειν ἐποίει τοὺς συνδιατρίβοντας ἑαυτῷ *he inspired hope in those who associated with him.* The union of an intensive and a personal pronoun in αὐτός explains this freedom of usage.

992. In Homer αὐτός may mean *same* without the article; e.g. ἵπποι δ' αὐταὶ ἔασι παροίτεραι αἳ τὸ πάρος περ *the same mares are leading that led before,* *Il.* 23, 480. Generally αὐτός emphasizes the chief person or thing in contrast to a subordinate person or thing; e.g. αὐτῶν καὶ τεκέων *themselves and their children,* *Il.* 3, 301.

Reflexive Pronouns

993. The reflexive pronouns (**377**) refer to the subject of the clause in which they stand. Sometimes in a dependent clause they refer to the subject of the leading verb — that is, they are *indirect* reflexives (**986**). E.g.

γνῶθι σεαυτόν *know thyself;* δίδωμί σοι ἐμαυτὸν δοῦλον *I give myself to you as a slave,* X. *C.* 4, 6, 2; οἱ ἡττώμενοι ἑαυτούς τε καὶ τὰ ἑαυτῶν πάντα ἀποβάλλουσιν *the vanquished lose themselves as well as all that belongs to them,* X. *C.* 3, 3, 45; ἔπεισεν Ἀθηναίους ἑαυτὸν κατάγειν *he persuaded the Athenians to restore him (from exile),* Thuc. 1, 111.

994. Occasionally a reflexive refers to some emphatic word which is neither the leading nor a dependent subject; e.g. ἀπὸ σαυτοῦ 'γώ σε διδάξω *I will teach you from your own case (from yourself),* Ar. *N.* 385. In fact, these pronouns correspond almost exactly in their use to the English reflexives *myself, thyself, himself,* etc.

995. The third person of the reflexive is sometimes used for the first or second; e.g. δεῖ ἡμᾶς ἐρέσθαι ἑαυτούς *we must ask ourselves,* Plat. *Ph.* 78 b;

οὐ γὰρ μόνον ἡμῖν παρεῖναι οὐκ ἐξῆν, ἀλλ' οὐδὲ παρ' αὐτοῖς εἶναι so far from being allowed to be present (at their meetings), we could not even be present in our own homes, Lys. 12, 33.

996. The reflexive is sometimes used for the reciprocal (**383**) ; ἡμῖν αὐτοῖς διαλεξόμεθα we will discourse with one another (i.e. among ourselves), Dem. 48, 6.

997. A reflexive may be strengthened by a preceding αὐτός ; e.g. οἷός τε αὐτὸς αὐτῷ βοηθεῖν able (himself) to help himself, Plat. G. 483 b ; τὸ γιγνώσκειν αὐτὸν ἑαυτόν for one (himself) to know himself, Plat. Ch. 165 b.

For the personal pronouns οὗ, οἷ, etc. as direct and indirect reflexives, see **986** and **987**.

Possessive Pronouns

998. a. The possessive pronouns (**380**) are generally equivalent to the possessive genitive (**1082 a**) of the personal pronouns. Thus ὁ σὸς πατήρ = ὁ πατήρ σου, your father.

For the article with possessives, see **944 a**.

b. For ἐμός and σός here the enclitic forms μοῦ (not ἐμοῦ) and σοῦ may be used ; ἡμῶν and ὑμῶν for ἡμέτερος and ὑμέτερος are less frequent. These genitives have the predicate position (**975**).

999. The possessive is occasionally equivalent to the objective genitive of the personal pronoun ; e.g. ἡ ἐμὴ εὔνοια, which commonly means my good-will (towards others), may mean good-will (felt) to me ; e.g. εὐνοίᾳ γὰρ ἐρῶ τῇ σῇ for I shall speak out of good-will to you, Plat. G. 486 a ; ἐπὶ τῇ ὑμετέρᾳ παρακελεύσει for your exhortation, to exhort you, Plat. Ap. 36 d. See **1082 c**.

1000. Σφέτερος their, and (poetic) ὅς his, her, its, are regularly reflexive (direct or indirect).

1001. An adjective or an appositive in the genitive may refer to the genitive implied in a possessive ; e.g. τἀμὰ δυστήνου κακά the woes of me, unhappy one, S. O. C. 344 ; τὴν ὑμετέραν τῶν σοφιστῶν τέχνην the art of you Sophists, Plat. H. Maj. 281 d. See **902**.

1002. By the possessive pronouns and the possessive genitive, the words my father can be expressed in Greek in five forms : ὁ ἐμὸς πατήρ, ὁ πατὴρ ὁ ἐμός, πατὴρ ὁ ἐμός, ὁ πατήρ μου, and (after another word) μου ὁ πατήρ (e.g. ἔφη μου ὁ πατήρ). So ὁ σὸς πατήρ, etc. The article is necessary in all these forms. See **944 a**.

1003. a. Our own, your own (plural), and their own are expressed by ἡμέτερος, ὑμέτερος, and σφέτερος, usually strengthened by αὐτῶν (**988 a**) in agreement with the ἡμῶν, ὑμῶν, or σφῶν implied in the possessive ; e.g. τὸν ἡμέτερον αὐτῶν πατέρα our own father ; τῇ ὑμετέρᾳ αὐτῶν μητρί to your own mother ; τοὺς σφετέρους αὐτῶν παῖδας their own children. For the third person plural ἑαυτῶν can be used ; e.g. τοὺς ἑαυτῶν παῖδας more common than τοὺς σφετέρους αὐτῶν παῖδας (also σφῶν αὐτῶν παῖδας without the article); but we seldom find ἡμῶν (or ὑμῶν) αὐτῶν.

b. Expressions like τὸν ἐμὸν αὐτοῦ πατέρα for τὸν ἐμαυτοῦ πατέρα, etc., with singular possessives, are poetic. In prose the genitive of the reflexive (ἐμαυτοῦ, σεαυτοῦ, or ἑαυτοῦ), in the attributive position (959), is the regular form; e.g. μετεπέμψατο τὴν ἑαυτοῦ θυγατέρα he sent for his (own) daughter, X. C. 1, 3, 1.

Demonstrative Pronouns

1004. Οὗτος *this, that* and ὅδε *this* generally refer to what is near in place, time, or thought; ἐκεῖνος *that* refers to what is more remote. They may be used as substantives or adjectives.

1005. The distinction between οὗτος and ὅδε, both of which correspond to our *this*, must be learned by practice. In the historians οὗτος (with τοιοῦτος, τοσοῦτος, and οὕτως) frequently refers to a speech just made, while ὅδε (with τοιόσδε, τοσόσδε, and ὧδε) refers to one about to be made; e.g. τάδε εἶπεν *he spoke as follows*, but ταῦτα εἶπεν *thus he spoke* or *that is what he said* (said after the speech): see Thuc. 1, 72, and 79, 85, and 87. In the orators οὗτος refers to one's opponent. Elsewhere οὗτος (especially in the neuter) often refers to something that follows; e.g. ῥᾷον γὰρ τούτων προειρημένων μαθήσει *for you will more easily understand it when this* (the following) *is premised,* Plat. *Rep.* 510 b. So ἐκεῖνος and its derivatives may refer to what follows as being unfamiliar and therefore remote until it has been presented; e.g. πολὺ ἂν δικαιότερον ἐκείνοις τοῖς γράμμασιν ἢ τούτοις πιστεύοιτε *it would be much fairer for you to trust these documents* (to be cited) *than the others* (already presented), Lys. 16, 7. Here the common translation of ἐκεῖνος *former,* οὗτος *latter,* would be wholly wrong. So ἐκεῖθεν εἴσεσθε, ὅτι, etc. *you will realize* (it) *from the following circumstance, viz. that,* etc., Dem. 45, 48. Conversely, ὅδε may sometimes refer to what precedes; e.g. οἵδε μὲν τῷ Ἰονίῳ κόλπῳ ὁριζόμενοι *the foregoing are bounded by the Ionian gulf,* Thuc. 7, 57.

1006. Οὗτος is sometimes exclamatory, e.g. οὗτος, τί ποιεῖς *you there! what are you doing?* Ar. *R.* 198.

1007. The unemphatic demonstrative which is often used in English as the antecedent of a relative (*I saw those who were present*) is not expressed in Greek. Here a participle with the article is generally used; e.g. εἶδον τοὺς παρόντας. If a demonstrative is used (οἱ παρῆσαν τούτους εἶδον *I saw these men who were present*), it has special emphasis (1029). A relative with omitted antecedent sometimes expresses the sense required; e.g. εἶδον οὓς ἔλαβεν *I saw* (those) *whom he took* (1026).

1008. The demonstratives, especially ὅδε, may call attention to the presence or approach of an object, in the sense of *here* or *there*; ὅδε γὰρ δὴ βασιλεὺς χώρας *for here now is the king of the land,* S. *Ant.* 155; σῶμα μὲν ἐν κόλποις κατέχει τόδε γαῖα Πλάτωνος here lies Plato's body, held in the lap of Earth, Speusippus; for νῆες ἐκεῖναι (Thuc. 1, 51) see 943 b. In colloquial language ὅδε is often equivalent to the first personal pronoun (= I or your humble servant).

1009. Οὗτος sometimes repeats a preceding description for emphasis in a single word; e.g. ὁ γὰρ τὸ σπέρμα παρασχών, οὗτος τῶν φύντων αἴτιος for he who supplied the seed — he is responsible for the harvest, Dem. 18, 159.

1010. Τοῦτο μέν ... τοῦτο δέ first ... secondly, partly ... partly, is used nearly in the sense of τὸ μέν ... τὸ δέ (981), especially by Herodotus (1059). For οὑτοσί, ὁδί, ἐκεινοσί, οὑτωσί, ὡδί, etc., see 392.

Interrogative Pronoun

1011. The interrogative τίς who? what? may be either substantive or adjective; e.g. τίνας εἶδον whom did I see? or τίνας ἄνδρας εἶδον what men did I see?

1012. Τίς may be used both in direct and in indirect questions; e.g. τί βούλεται; what does he want? ἐρωτᾷ τί βούλεσθε he asks what you want. In indirect questions the relative forms ὅστις, ὁποῖος, ὁπόσος are more common than τίς, ποῖος, πόσος; e.g. ἐρωτᾷ ὅ τι βούλεσθε (1601).

1013. The article may be used with an interrogative; e.g. ἄγε δὴ ταχέως τουτὶ ξυνάρπασον come now, catch this quickly; τὸ τί catch what? Ar. Nub. 775; τόνδε τίνα καλεῖς τὸν δημιουργόν; what do you call this artist? τὸν ποῖον; which one? Plat. Rep. 596 c.

1014. The same principles apply to the pronominal adjectives πόσος, ποῖος, etc. (408).

Indefinite Pronoun

1015. a. The indefinite τις (enclitic) generally means some, any, and may be either substantive or adjective; e.g. τοῦτο λέγει τις somebody says this, ἄνθρωπός τις some man.

b. It is sometimes nearly equivalent to the English a or an; e.g. εἶδον ἄνθρωπόν τινα I saw a certain man, or I saw a man; ἔστι τις Σωκράτης there is a man named Socrates, Plat. Ap. 18 b.

1016. Τίς sometimes implies that the word to which it is joined is not to be taken in its strict meaning; e.g. κλέπτης τις ἀναπέφανται he now turns out to be a sort of thief, Plat. Rep. 334 a; μέγας τις rather large; τριάκοντά τινας ἀπέκτειναν they killed some thirty men, Thuc. 8, 73.

So often with the adverbial τι (1059); e.g. σχέδον τι very nearly, Thuc. 3, 68.

1017. Occasionally τὶς means *everyone*, like πᾶς τις; e.g. εὖ μέν τις δόρυ θηξάσθω *let everyone sharpen well his spear*, *Il.* 2, 382; φοβεῖται δέ τις *everyone is afraid*, Aesch. *Cho.* 56.

1018. In a half-ironical way, τὶς, τὶ may mean *something important*; e.g. οἴονταί τι εἶναι, ὄντες οὐδενὸς ἄξιοι *they think they are something, when they are worth nothing*, Plat. *Ap.* 41 e; λέγειν τι *to say something (worth while)*, opposed to οὐδὲν λέγειν *to talk nonsense*.

Relative Pronouns

1019. A relative agrees with its antecedent in gender and number; but its case depends on the construction of the clause in which it stands. E.g.

εἶδον τοὺς ἄνδρας οἳ ἦλθον *I saw the men who came*; οἱ ἄνδρες οὓς εἶδες ἀπῆλθον *the men whom you saw went away*.

1020. The relative follows the person of the antecedent; e.g. ὑμεῖς οἳ τοῦτο ποιεῖτε *you who do this*; ἐγὼ ὃς τοῦτο ἐποίησα *I, the one who did this*; οὗτος σύ, Μενέλαον εἶπον, ὃς πεπύργωσαι θράσει, *you there, Menelaus I mean, who exalt yourself in boldness*, E. *Or.* 1567. For this the construction of 1562 may be used.

1021. *a.* A relative referring to several antecedents follows the rule given for predicate adjectives (920); e.g. περὶ πολέμου καὶ εἰρήνης, ἃ μεγίστην ἔχει δύναμιν ἐν τῷ βίῳ τῶν ἀνθρώπων *about war and peace, which have a very great influence in the lives of men*, Isoc. 8, 2; ἀπαλλαγέντες πολέμων καὶ κινδύνων καὶ ταραχῆς, εἰς ἣν νῦν πρὸς ἀλλήλους καθέσταμεν *freed from wars, dangers, and confusion, in which we are now involved with one another*, Isoc. 8, 20.

b. The relative may be plural if it refers to a collective noun (890); e.g. πλήθει οἵπερ δικάσουσιν *to the multitude who are to judge*, Plat. *Phdr.* 260 a.

c. On the other hand, ὅστις *whoever* may have a plural antecedent; e.g. πάντα ὅ τι βούλονται *everything, whatsoever they want*.

1022. A neuter relative may refer to a masculine or feminine antecedent denoting a thing; e.g. διὰ τὴν πλεονεξίαν, ὃ πᾶσα φύσις διώκειν πέφυκεν *for gain, which every nature naturally follows*, Plat. *Rep.* 359 c. See 921.

1023. *a.* In Homer the original demonstrative force of ὅς is still sometimes apparent (cf. 933); e.g. ὃς γὰρ δεύτατος ἦλθεν *for he came second*, *Od.* 1, 286; ὃ γὰρ γέρας ἐστὶ θανόντων *for this is the right of the dead*, *Il.* 23, 9.

b. A few similar expressions occur in Attic prose, especially the Platonic ἦ δ' ὅς *said he* (where ἦ is imperfect of ἠμί *say*). So καὶ ὅς *and he*, καὶ οἳ *and they*, and (in Hdt.) ὃς καὶ ὅς *this man and that*. (Cf. τὸν καὶ τόν, **983**.) So also ὃς μέν . . . ὃς δέ, in the oblique cases, are occasionally used for ὁ μέν . . . ὁ δέ; e.g. πόλεις Ἑλληνίδας, ἃς μὲν ἀναιρῶν, εἰς ἃς δὲ τοὺς φυγάδας κατάγων *as for cities in Greece — he is destroying some, into others bringing back their exiles*, Dem. 18, 71.

1024. *a.* In the epic and lyric poets τὲ — originally a sign of parataxis or coördination — is often appended to relative words without affecting their meaning; e.g. οὐκ ἄεις ἅ τέ φησι θεά; *dost thou not hear what the goddess says? Il.* 15, 130. Sometimes it makes the relative more indefinite, cf. Lat. quicumque.

b. But οἷός τε in Attic Greek means *able, capable*, like δυνατός. Cf. οὐ γὰρ ἦν ὥρα οἵα ἄρδειν *it was not the proper season for watering*, X. *An.* 2, 3, 13, and τί οἷοί τε ἔσεσθε ἡμῖν συμπρᾶξαι *what will you be able to do to help us?* X. *An.* 5, 4, 9, τὲ having had originally a generic force.

1025. *Preposition omitted.* When the relative and its antecedent would properly have the same preposition, it is usually expressed only with the antecedent; e.g. ἀπὸ τῆς αὐτῆς ἀγνοίας ἧσπερ πολλὰ προίεσθε τῶν κοινῶν *by the same want of sense by which* (for ἀφ᾽ ἧσπερ) *you sacrifice many of your public interests*, Dem. 18, 134.

OMISSION OF THE ANTECEDENT

1026. The antecedent of a relative may be omitted when it can easily be supplied from the context, especially if it is indefinite (**1438**). E.g.

ἔλαβεν ἃ ἐβούλετο *he took what he wanted*; ἔπειθεν ὁπόσους ἐδύνατο *he persuaded as many as he could*; ἃ μὴ οἶδα οὐδὲ οἴομαι εἰδέναι *what I do not know I do not even think I know*, Plat. *Ap.* 21 d; ἐγὼ καὶ ὧν ἐγὼ κρατῶ μενοῦμεν παρὰ σοί *I and those whom I control will remain with you*, X. *C.* 5, 1, 26.

1027. In such cases it is a mistake to say that ταῦτα, ἐκεῖνοι, etc. are *understood*; see **1029**. The relative clause here really becomes a substantive, and contains its antecedent within itself. Such a relative clause, as a substantive, may even have the article: e.g. ἔχουσα τὴν ἐπωνυμίαν τὴν τοῦ ὅ ἔστιν *having the name of the absolutely existent* (*of the "what is"*), Plat. *Ph.* 92 d; ἐκείνου ὀρέγεται τοῦ ὅ ἔστιν ἴσον *they aim at that absolute equality* (*at the "what is equal"*), ibid. 75 b; τῷ σμικρῷ μέρει, τῷ ὅ ἦρχε ἐν αὐτῷ *through the small element which was shown to be the ruling power within him* (*the "what ruled"*), Plat. *Rep.* 442 c. Here it must not be thought that τοῦ and τῷ are antecedents, or pronouns at all. ↙.3

1028. The following expressions belong here: — ἔστιν ὧν, ἔστιν οἷς, ἔστιν οὕς *some* (**894**; in the nominative εἰσὶν οἵ is more common than ἔστιν οἵ, cf. Lat. sunt qui = aliqui); ἔστιν οἵτινες (especially in questions); ἔνιοι (from ἔνι = ἔνεστι or ἔνεισι, and οἵ) *some*; ἐνίοτε (ἔνι and ὅτε) *sometimes*; ἔστιν οὗ *somewhere*; ἔστιν ᾗ *in some way*; ἔστιν ὅπως *somehow*. Other copulative verbs (**897**) are sometimes used in this way; e.g. φανεῖται ἃ τῶν ὑμετέρων οὐκ ἐλάσσω ἡμῖν πρόσεισι *just as many of your allies, so it will turn out, will join us*, Thuc. 1, 40.

1029. When a clause containing a relative with omitted antecedent precedes the leading clause, the latter often contains a demonstrative referring back with emphasis to the omitted antecedent; e.g. ἃ ἐβούλετο ταῦτα ἔλαβεν *what he wanted, that he took*, entirely different from ταῦτα ἃ ἐβούλετο ἔλαβεν *he took these* (definite) *things, which he wanted*; ταῦτ' ἔχω ὅσσ' ἔμαθον *I have* (*only*) *that which I have learned*, Chrysippus; ἃ ποιεῖν αἰσχρόν, ταῦτα νόμιζε μηδὲ λέγειν εἶναι καλόν *what it is base to do, this deem not good even to say*, Isoc. 1, 15 (here ταῦτα is not the *antecedent* of ἅ, which is indefinite and is not expressed). See **1007**.

ASSIMILATION AND ATTRACTION

1030. When a relative would naturally be in the accusative as the object of a verb, it is generally *assimilated* to the case of its antecedent if this is a genitive or dative. E.g.

ἐκ τῶν πόλεων ὧν ἔχει *from the cities which he holds* (for ἃς ἔχει); τοῖς ἀγαθοῖς οἷς ἔχομεν *with the good things which we have* (for ἃ ἔχομεν); ἄξιοι τῆς ἐλευθερίας ἧς κέκτησθε *worthy of the freedom which you possess*, X. *An.* 1, 7, 3; εἰ τῷ ἡγεμόνι πιστεύσομεν ᾧ ἂν Κῦρος διδῷ *if we shall trust the guide whom Cyrus may give us*, X. *An.* 1, 3, 16. This assimilation is also called *attraction*.

1031. When an antecedent is omitted which (if expressed) would have been a genitive or dative, the assimilation still takes place; and a preposition which would have belonged to the antecedent passes over to the relative; e.g. ἐδήλωσε τοῦτο οἷς ἔπραττε *he showed this by what he did* (like ἐκείνοις ἅ); σὺν οἷς μάλιστα φιλεῖς *with those men whom you most love* (σὺν ἐκείνοις οὕς), X. *An.* 1, 9, 25; ἀμελήσας ὧν με δεῖ πράττειν *having neglected what* (ἐκείνων ἅ) *I ought to do*, X. *C.* 5, 1, 8; οἷς ηὐτυχήκεσαν ἐν Λεύκτροις οὐ μετρίως ἐκέχρηντο *they had not used moderately the successes which they had gained at Leuctra* (τοῖς εὐτυχήμασιν ἃ ηὐτυχήκεσαν, see 1052), Dem. 18, 18.

1032. A relative is seldom assimilated *from* any other construction than that of the object accusative, or *into* any other case than the genitive or dative. Yet exceptions occur; e.g. παρ' ὧν βοηθεῖς οὐκ ἀπολήψει χάριν *you will get no thanks from those whom* (παρ' ἐκείνων οἷς) *you help*, Aeschin. 2, 117. Even the nominative is (very rarely) assimilated; e.g. βλάπτεσθαι ἀφ' ὧν ἡμῖν παρεσκεύασται *to be injured as a result of our preparations* (like ἀπ' ἐκείνων ἅ), Thuc. 7, 67.

1033. A like assimilation takes place in relative adverbs; e.g. διεκομίζοντο εὐθὺς ὅθεν ὑπεξέθεντο παῖδας καὶ γυναῖκας *they immediately brought over their children and women from the places to which they had carried them for safety* (where ὅθεν *from which* stands for ἐκεῖθεν οἷ *from the places whither*), Thuc. 1, 89.

1034. The antecedent occasionally is assimilated to the case of the relative, when this immediately follows; e.g. ἔλεγον ὅτι πάντων ὧν δέονται πεπραγότες εἶεν *they said that they had carried out everything which* (πάντα ὧν) *they needed*, X. *H*. 1, 4, 2 ; τὴν οὐσίαν ἣν κατέλιπε οὐ πλείονος ἀξία ἐστὶν ἢ τεττάρων καὶ δέκα ταλάντων *the estate which he left is not worth more than fourteen talents*, Lys. 19, 47 ; πλοῦτον δ' ὃν μὲν δῶσι θεοὶ παραγίγνεται ἔμπεδος *wealth which the gods give abides steadfast*, Solon 12, 9. Cf. *urbem quam* statuo vestra est, Verg. *Aen*. 1, 573.

This *inverted assimilation* takes place in οὐδεὶς ὅστις οὐ *everybody*, in which οὐδείς follows the case of the relative ; e.g. οὐδενὶ ὅτῳ οὐκ ἀποκρινόμενος (for οὐδείς ἐστιν ὅτῳ) *replying to everybody*, Plat. *Men*. 70 c.

1035. A peculiar assimilation occurs in certain expressions with οἷος and ὅσος ; e.g. χαριζόμενον οἵῳ σοι ἀνδρί *pleasing a man like you* (for τοιούτῳ οἷος σύ), X. *M*. 2, 9, 3 ; πρὸς ἄνδρας τολμηροὺς οἵους καὶ 'Αθηναίους *against bold men like the Athenians*, Thuc. 7, 21 ; ὄντος πάγου οἵου δεινοτάτου *there being a most awful frost* (for τοιούτου οἷος δεινότατος), Plat. *Symp*. 220 b ; ἠμφιεσμένων θαυμαστὰ ὅσα *clad in a marvelous quantity of wraps* (for θαυμαστόν ἐστιν ὅσα (1068), Plat. *Symp*. 220 b.

1036. The antecedent is often *attracted* into the relative clause, and agrees with the relative. E.g.

μὴ ἀφέλησθε ὑμῶν αὐτῶν ἣν διὰ παντὸς ἀεὶ τοῦ χρόνου δόξαν κέκτησθε καλήν *do not rob yourselves of the good reputation which* (*what good reputation*) *you have always had through all time* (for τὴν καλὴν δόξαν ἣν κέκτησθε), Dem. 20, 142. The article is sometimes allowed even here ; e.g. ἃς σὺ λέγεις τὰς σκέψεις, μὴ σκέμματα ᾖ τῶν ῥᾳδίως ἀποκτιννύντων *as for the considerations you urge, I rather suspect they may prove to be* (**1349**) *the considerations of persons who so rashly kill*, Plat. *Crito* 48 c.

1037. This *attraction* may be joined with assimilation (**1030**) ; e.g. ἀμαθέστατοί ἐστε ὧν ἐγὼ οἶδα 'Ελλήνων *you are the most ignorant of the Greeks whom I know* (for τῶν 'Ελλήνων οὓς οἶδα), Thuc. 6, 40 ; ἐξ ἧς τὸ πρῶτον ἔσχε γυναικός *from the wife whom he married first*, Dem. 57, 37 ; ἐπορεύετο σὺν ᾗ εἶχε δυνάμει *he marched with the force which he had* (for σὺν τῇ δυνάμει ἣν εἶχεν), X. *H*. 4, 1, 23.

RELATIVE IN EXCLAMATIONS

1038. Οἷος, ὅσος, and ὡς are used in exclamations ; e.g. ὅσα πράγματα ἔχεις *how much trouble you have!* X. *C*. 1, 3, 4 ; ὡς ἀστεῖος *how witty!* οἷα ποιεῖτε *how you are behaving!* Plat. *Ph*. 117 d.

RELATIVE NOT REPEATED

1039. A relative is seldom repeated *in a new case* in the same sentence. Either it is omitted and understood in the latter part of the sentence, or a personal or demonstrative pronoun takes its place. E.g.

ἐκεῖνοι τοίνυν, οἷς οὐκ ἐχαρίζονθ᾽ οἱ λέγοντες οὐδ᾽ ἐφίλουν αὐτοὺς ὥσπερ ὑμᾶς οὗτοι νῦν *those men, then, whom the orators did not try to gratify, and whom they did not love as these now love you* (lit. *and they did not love them as* etc.), Dem. 3, 24. Here αὐτούς is used to avoid repeating the relative in a new case, οὕς. ᾿Αριαῖος δὲ, ὃν ἡμεῖς ἠθέλομεν βασιλέα καθιστάναι, καὶ ἐδώκαμεν καὶ ἐλάβομεν πιστά and *Ariaeus, whom we wished to make king, and (to whom) we gave and (from whom) we received pledges*, etc., X. *An.* 3, 2, 5; τί αὐτὸν οἴεσθε πεποιηκέναι περὶ ὧν οὐδεὶς αὐτῷ σύνοιδεν, ἀλλ᾽ αὐτὸς μόνος διεχείριζεν, ὃς ἃ δι᾽ ἑτέρων ἐπράχθη καὶ οὐ χαλεπὸν ἦν περὶ τούτων πυθέσθαι, ἐτόλμησε τέτταρσι καὶ εἴκοσι μναῖς τοὺς αὑτοῦ θυγατριδοῦς ζημιῶσαι *what do you suppose he has done (in matters) about which nobody shares his knowledge, but (which) he managed all alone, seeing that in matters which were transacted through other persons, and about which it was easy to learn the facts, he has gone so far as to cause a loss of four and twenty minas to his own grandchildren?* Lys. 32, 27. Here both the omission and the substitution of a demonstrative pronoun are illustrated.

THE CASES

1040. The Greek is descended from a language which had *eight* cases: an *ablative*, a *locative*, and an *instrumental*, besides the five found in Greek. In *form* these cases reappear in a few words in Greek. In *syntax* the functions of the ablative were absorbed by the genitive; those of the instrumental (including the notion of accompaniment) and of the locative, by the dative.

NOMINATIVE AND VOCATIVE

1041. The nominative is used chiefly as the subject of a finite verb (882), or in the predicate after verbs signifying *to be* etc. in agreement with the subject (896).

1042. The vocative, with or without ὦ, is used in addressing a person or thing; e.g. ὦ ἄνδρες ᾿Αθηναῖοι *men of Athens!* ἀκούεις, Αἰσχίνη; *do you hear, Aeschines?*

1043. The nominative is sometimes used in exclamations, and even in other expressions, when characterization is intended; e.g. ὤμοι ἐγὼ δειλός *woe is me, wretch that I am!* ὦ πόλις, πόλις *O my city!* λῆρος *what nonsense!* So ἡ Πρόκνη ἔκβαινε *Procne, come out!* Ar. *Av.* 665. For the genitive, see 1124.

ACCUSATIVE

1044. The primary purpose of the accusative is to denote the nearer or *direct* object of a verb, as opposed to the remoter or *indirect* object denoted by the dative (880). It thus bears the same relation to a verb that the objective genitive (1082 c) bears to a noun. The object denoted by the accusative may be the external object of the action of a transitive verb, or the internal (cognate) object which is often implied in the meaning of even an intransitive verb. But the accusative has also assumed other functions, as will be seen, which cannot be brought under this or any other single category.

Accusative of Direct (External) Object

1045. The direct object of the action of a transitive verb is put in the accusative; e.g. τοῦτο σῴζει ἡμᾶς this preserves us; ταῦτα ποιοῦμεν we do these things.

1046. Many verbs which are transitive in English, and govern the objective case, take either a genitive or a dative in Greek. See **1099, 1160, 1183.**

1047. Many verbs which are transitive in Greek are intransitive in English; e.g. ὀμοῦμαι τοὺς θεούς I will swear by the gods; πάντας ἔλαθεν he escaped the notice of all; αἰσχύνεται τὸν πατέρα he feels shame before his father; σιγᾷ (or σιωπᾷ) τι he keeps silent about something.

1048. Verbal adjectives and even verbal nouns occasionally take an object accusative instead of the regular objective genitive (1142, 1082 c), e.g. ἐπιστήμονες ἦσαν τὰ προσήκοντα they were acquainted with what was proper, X. C. 3, 3, 9; τὰ μετέωρα φροντιστής a student of celestial matters (like φροντίζων), Plat. Ap. 18 b; χοὰς προπομπός escorting libations (like προπέμπουσα), Aesch. Ch. 23. Cf. **1056.**

Cognate Accusative (Internal Object)

1049. Any verb whose meaning permits it may take an accusative of kindred signification. This accusative repeats the idea already contained in the verb, and may follow intransitive as well as transitive verbs. E.g.

πάσας ἡδονὰς ἥδεσθαι to enjoy all pleasures, Plat. Phil. 63 a; ηὐτύχησαν τοῦτο τὸ εὐτύχημα they enjoyed this good fortune, X. An. 6, 3, 6. So πεσεῖν πτώματα to suffer (to fall) falls, Aesch. Pr. 919; νόσον νοσεῖν or νόσον ἀσθενεῖν or νόσον κάμνειν to suffer with a disease; ἁμάρτημα ἁμαρτάνειν to commit an error (to sin a sin); δουλείαν δουλεύειν to be subject to slavery; ἀρχὴν ἄρχειν to hold an office; ἀγῶνα ἀγωνίζεσθαι to contend in a trial or in the games; γραφὴν γράφεσθαι to bring an indictment; γραφὴν διώκειν to prosecute an indictment; δίκην ὀφλεῖν to lose a lawsuit; νίκην νικᾶν to gain a victory; μάχην νικᾶν to win a battle; πομπὴν πέμπειν to form or conduct a procession; πληγὴν τύπτειν to strike a blow; ἐξῆλθον ἐξόδους they went out on expeditions, X. H. 1, 2, 17.

224   GREEK GRAMMAR

1050. It will be seen that this construction is far more extensive in Greek than in English. It includes not only accusatives of kindred formation and meaning, e.g. νίκην νικᾶν *to gain a victory*, but also those of merely kindred meaning, e.g. μάχην νικᾶν *to win a battle*. Cf. τιμωρίαν πολὺ χαλεπωτέραν ἢ οἵαν ἐμὲ ἀπεκτόνατε *vengeance far more severe than that which you have inflicted by killing me*, Plat. *Ap.* 39 c. The accusative may also limit the meaning of the verb to one of many applications; e.g. Ὀλύμπια νικᾶν *to gain an Olympic victory*, Thuc. 1, 126; ἑστιᾶν γάμους *to give a wedding feast*, Ar. *Av.* 132; ψήφισμα νικᾷ *he carries a decree (gains a victory with a decree)*, Aeschin. 3, 68; Βοηδρόμια πέμπειν *to celebrate the Boedromia by a procession*, Dem. 3, 31. So also (in poetry) βαίνειν (or ἐλθεῖν) πόδα *to take a step* or *to set foot*; see E. *Alc.* 1153.

For the cognate accusative becoming the subject of a passive verb, see **1241.**

1051. The cognate accusative may follow adjectives or even substantives. E.g.

κακοὶ πᾶσαν κακίαν *bad in every kind of badness*, Plat. *Rep.* 490 d; δοῦλος τὰς μεγίστας δουλείας *a slave to the direst slavery*, ibid. 579 d.

1052. A neuter adjective sometimes represents a cognate accusative, its noun being implied in the verb. E.g.

μεγάλα ἁμαρτάνειν (sc. ἁμαρτήματα) *to commit great faults*; ταὐτὰ λυπεῖσθαι καὶ ταὐτὰ χαίρειν *to have the same griefs and the same joys*, Dem. 18, 292. So τί χρήσομαι τούτῳ (= τίνα χρείαν χρήσομαι) *what use shall I make of this?* and οὐδὲν χρήσομαι τούτῳ *I shall make no use of this* (**1183**). So χρήσιμος οὐδέν *good for nothing* (**1051**). See **1059.**

1053. *a.* Here belongs the accusative of *effect*; this expresses a result beyond the action of the verb, which is effected by that action. E.g.

πρεσβεύειν τὴν εἰρήνην *to negotiate a peace* (as ambassadors, πρέσβεις), Dem. 19, 134; but πρεσβεύειν πρεσβείαν *to go on an embassy*; ἕλκος οὐτάσαι *to wound with a thrust*, *Il.* 5, 361 (lit. *thrust a wound*). Cf. the English *breaking a hole*, as opposed to *breaking a stick*. See **1079.**

b. So after verbs of *looking*; e.g. Ἄρη δεδορκέναι *to look war (Ares)*, cf. Aesch. *Sev.* 53; ἡ βουλὴ ἔβλεψεν ἆπυ *the Council looked mustard*, Ar. *Eq.* 631. This idiom, occurring first in poetry, is frequent in colloquial speech.

1054. For verbs which take a cognate accusative and an ordinary object accusative at the same time, see **1074.**

1055. Connected with the cognate accusative is the accusative used with verbs of motion to express the particular ground over which the motion passes; e.g. ὁδὸν ἰέναι (ἐλθεῖν, πορεύεσθαι, etc.) *to go over a road*; ὄρος καταβαίνειν *to descend a mountain*; πλεῖν θάλατταν *to sail the sea*. These verbs thus acquire a transitive meaning. Cf. **1047.**

Accusative of Specification — Adverbial Accusative

1056. The accusative of *specification* may be joined with a verb, adjective, noun, or even a whole sentence, to denote a *part, character, or quality* to which the expression refers. E.g.

τυφλὸς τὰ ὄμματ᾽ εἶ *you are blind in your eyes,* S. O. T. 371; καλὸς τὸ εἶδος *beautiful in form*; ἄπειροι τὸ πλῆθος *infinite in number*; δίκαιος τὸν τρόπον *just in his character*; δεινοὶ μάχην *mighty in battle*; κάμνω τὴν κεφαλήν *I have a pain in my head*; τὰς φρένας ὑγιαίνειν *to be sound in mind*; διαφέρει τὴν φύσιν *he differs in nature*; ποταμὸς, Κύδνος ὄνομα, εὖρος δύο πλέθρων *a river, Cydnus by name, of two plethra in breadth,* X. *An.* 1, 2, 23; Ἕλληνές εἰσι τὸ γένος *they are Greeks by race*; γένεσθε τὴν διάνοιαν μὴ ἐν τῷ δικαστηρίῳ, ἀλλ᾽ ἐν τῷ θεάτρῳ *imagine yourselves (become in thought) not in court, but in the theatre,* Aeschin. 3, 153; ἐπίστασθέ (με) οὐ μόνον τὰ μεγάλα ἀλλὰ καὶ τὰ μικρὰ πειρώμενον ἀεὶ ἀπὸ θεῶν ὁρμᾶσθαι *you know that not only in great things but even in small I try to begin with the gods,* X. *C.* 1, 5, 14.

1057. This is sometimes called the accusative by *synecdoche*, or the *limiting* accusative. It most frequently denotes a *part*; but it may refer to any circumstance to which the meaning of the expression is restricted. This construction sometimes resembles that of 1240, with which it must not be confounded. For the dative of respect, see 1182.

1058. Accusative of the Whole and of the Part. In poetry, especially Homer, it is common to find an accusative denoting a person with another accusative denoting the part especially affected. Both are direct objects of the verb, but when the construction becomes passive the person becomes the subject, the part remains as an accusative of specification; e.g. αἰεί μιν φρένας ἀμφὶ κακαὶ τείρουσι μέριμναι *ever do harsh cares wear out his spirit,* Mimn. 1, 7; ϝὲ (= ἑ) βάλε κνήμην *him he smote on the shin,* *Il.* 21, 591; in the passive construction, βλῆτο κνήμην *he was smitten on the shin,* *Il.* 4, 518. Cf. 906.

1059. An accusative in certain expressions has the force of an adverb. E.g.

τοῦτον τὸν τρόπον *in this way, thus*; τὴν ταχίστην (sc. ὁδόν) *in the quickest way*; (τὴν) ἀρχήν *at first*; τὴν ἀρχὴν οὐ *not at all*; τέλος *finally*; προῖκα *as a gift,* gratis; χάριν *for the sake of*; δίκην *in the manner of*; κυνὸς δίκην *like a dog*; τὸ πρῶτον or πρῶτον *at first*; τὸ λοιπόν *for the rest*; πάντα *in all things*; τἄλλα *in other respects*; οὐδέν *in nothing, not at all*; τί *in what, why?* τί *in any respect, at all*; ταῦτα *in respect to this, therefore.* So τοῦτο μέν . . . τοῦτο δέ (1010).

1060. Several of these (1059) are to be explained by 1056, e.g. τἄλλα, τί *why?* ταῦτα, τοῦτο (with μέν and δέ), and sometimes οὐδέν and τί. Some are to be explained as cognate accusatives (see 1051 and 1052).

Accusative of Extent

1061. The accusative may denote *extent* of time or space. E.g.

αἱ σπονδαὶ ἐνιαυτὸν ἔσονται *the truce is to be for a year*, Thuc. 4, 118; ἔμεινεν ἡμέρας πέντε *he remained five days*; ἀπέχει ἡ Πλάταια τῶν Θηβῶν σταδίους ἑβδομήκοντα *Plataea is seventy stadia distant from Thebes*, Thuc. 2, 5; ἀπέχοντα Συρακουσῶν οὔτε πλοῦν πολὺν οὔτε ὁδόν (*Megara*) *not a long sail or land-journey distant from Syracuse*, Thuc. 6, 49.

1062. This accusative with an *ordinal* number denotes *how long since* (including the date of the event); e.g. ἑβδόμην ἡμέραν τῆς θυγατρὸς αὐτῷ τετελευτηκυίας *when his daughter had been dead* (*only*) *six days* (lit. *for the seventh day*), Aeschin. 3, 77.

1063. A peculiar idiom is found in expressions like τρίτον ἔτος τουτί (*this the third year*), i.e. *two years ago*; e.g. ἀπηγγέλθη Φίλιππος τρίτον ἢ τέταρτον ἔτος τουτὶ Ἡραῖον τεῖχος πολιορκῶν *two or three years ago* (lit. *this is the third or fourth year since*) *Philip was reported to be besieging Fort Heraion*, Dem. 3, 4.

Terminal Accusative (Poetic)

1064. In poetry, the accusative without a preposition may denote the place or object *toward which* motion is directed. E.g.

μνηστῆρας ἀφίκετο *she came to the suitors*, Od. 1, 332; ἀνέβη μέγαν οὐρανὸν Οὔλυμπόν τε *she ascended to mighty heaven and Olympus*, Il. 1, 497; τὸ κοῖλον Ἄργος βὰς φυγάς *going as an exile to the hollow Argos*, S.O.C. 378.

In prose a preposition would be used here.

Accusative in Oaths with νή and μά

1065. The accusative follows the adverbs of swearing νή and μά *by*. Cf. **1047**.

1066. An oath introduced by νή is affirmative; one introduced by μά (unless ναί *yes* precedes) is negative; e.g. νὴ τὸν Δία *yes, by Zeus*; μὰ τὸν Δία *no, by Zeus*; but ναί, μὰ Δία *yes, by Zeus*.

1067. Μά is sometimes omitted when a negative precedes; e.g. οὔ, τόνδ' Ὄλυμπον, *no, by yonder Olympus*, S. Ant. 758.

Two Accusatives with One Verb

1068. Verbs signifying *to ask, to demand, to teach, to remind, to clothe* or *unclothe, to conceal, to deprive*, and *to take away*, may take two object accusatives. E.g.

οὐ τοῦτ' ἐρωτῶ σε *that is not what I am asking you*, Ar. *Nub*. 641; οὐδένα τῆς συνουσίας ἀργύριον πράττει *you exact no fee for your teaching from any one*, X. *M*. 1, 6, 11; πόθεν ἤρξατό σε διδάσκειν τὴν στρατηγίαν *how did he begin to teach you strategy?* ibid. 3, 1, 5; τὴν ξυμμαχίαν ἀναμιμνῄσκοντες τοὺς Ἀθηναίους *reminding the Athenians of the alliance*, Thuc. 6, 6; τὸν μὲν ἑαυτοῦ (χιτῶνα) ἐκεῖνον ἠμφίεσε *he put his own (tunic) on the other boy*, X. *C*. 1, 3, 17; ἐκδύων ἐμὲ χρηστηρίαν ἐσθῆτα *stripping me of my oracular garb*, Aesch. *Ag*. 1269; τὴν θυγατέρα ἔκρυπτε τὸν θάνατον τοῦ ἀνδρός *he concealed from his daughter her husband's death*, Lys. 32, 7; τούτων τὴν τιμὴν ἀποστερεῖ με *he cheats me out of the price of these*, Dem. 28, 13; τὸν πάντα δ' ὄλβον ἦμαρ ἔν μ' ἀφείλετο *but one day deprived me of all my happiness*, E. *Hec*. 285.

1069. In poetry some other verbs have this construction; thus χρόα νίζετο ἄλμην *he washed the dried spray from his skin*, *Od*. 6, 224; so τιμωρεῖσθαί τινα αἷμα *to punish one for blood (shed)*, see E. *Alc*. 733.

1070. Verbs of this class sometimes have other constructions. For verbs of *depriving* and *taking away*, see **1118**. For the accusative and genitive with verbs of *reminding*, see **1107**.

1071. Verbs signifying *to do anything to* or *to say anything of* a person or thing take two accusatives. E.g.

ταυτί με ποιοῦσιν *they do these things to me*; τί μ' εἰργάσω; *what didst thou do to me?* κακὰ πολλὰ ἔοργεν Τρῶας *many evils has he wrought to the Trojans*, *Il*. 16, 424; ἐκεῖνόν τε καὶ τοὺς Κορινθίους πολλά τε καὶ κακὰ ἔλεγε *of him and the Corinthians he said much that was bad*, Hdt. 8, 61; οὐ φροντιστέον τί ἐροῦσιν οἱ πολλοὶ ἡμᾶς *we must not consider what the multitude will say of us*, Plat. *Crito* 48 a.

1072. These verbs often take εὖ or καλῶς *well*, or κακῶς *ill*, instead of the accusative of a thing; τούτους εὖ ποιεῖ *he does them good*; ὑμᾶς κακῶς ποιεῖ *he injures you*; κακῶς ἡμᾶς λέγει *he abuses us*.

The passive of these expressions is εὖ πάσχετε, εὖ ἀκούομεν. See **1242**.

1073. A verb and an accusative depending upon it may together be treated as a single word having another accusative as its object; e.g. τίνα τάκεις οἰμωγὰν τὸν ἐκ δολερᾶς ματρὸς ἀλόντα; *why art thou dissolved in lamentation for him who was overthrown by a deceitful mother?* S. *E*. 122 (= τί οἰμώζεις *grieve for*). So with τίθεμαι, ποιοῦμαι, etc.; e.g. σκεύη καὶ ἀνδράποδα ἁρπαγὴν ποιησάμενος (= ἁρπάσας) *seizing (as booty) equipment and slaves*, Thuc. 8, 62.

1074. A transitive verb may have a cognate accusative (**1049**) and an ordinary object accusative at the same time. E.g.

Μέλητός με ἐγράψατο τὴν γραφὴν ταύτην *Meletus brought this indictment against me*, Plat. *Ap*. 19 b; Μιλτιάδης ὁ τὴν ἐν Μαραθῶνι μάχην τοὺς βαρβάρους νικήσας *Miltiades, who won the battle at Marathon over the barbarians*, Aeschin. 3,

181; ὤρκωσαν πάντας τοὺς στρατιώτας τοὺς μεγίστους ὅρκους *they made all the soldiers swear the strongest oaths*, Thuc. 8, 75.

On this principle verbs of *dividing* may take two accusatives; e.g. τὸ στράτευμα κατένειμε δώδεκα μέρη *he made twelve divisions of the army*, X. C. 7, 5, 13.

1075. Verbs signifying *to name, to choose* or *appoint, to make, to think* or *regard*, and the like, may take a predicate accusative besides the object accusative. E.g.

τί τὴν πόλιν προσαγορεύεις; *what do you call the state?* τὴν τοιαύτην δύναμιν ἀνδρείαν ἔγωγε καλῶ *such a power as this I call courage*, Plat. *Rep.* 430 b; στρατηγὸν αὐτὸν ἀπέδειξε *he appointed him general*, X. *An.* 1, 1, 2; εὐεργέτην τὸν Φίλιππον ἡγοῦντο *they thought Philip a benefactor*, Dem. 18, 43; πάντων δεσπότην ἑαυτὸν πεποίηκεν *he has made himself master of everything*, X. C. 1, 3, 18.

1076. This is the active construction corresponding to that of the passive copulative verbs (**897**), in which the object accusative becomes the subject nominative (**1236**) and the predicate accusative becomes a predicate nominative (**896**). Like the latter, it includes also predicate adjectives; e.g. τοὺς συμμάχους προθύμους ποιεῖσθαι *to make the allies eager*; τὰς ἁμαρτίας μεγάλας ἦγεν *he thought the faults great*.

1077. With verbs of *naming* the infinitive εἶναι may connect the two accusatives; e.g. σοφιστὴν ὀνομάζουσι τὸν ἄνδρα εἶναι *they call the man a sophist*, Plat. *Prot.* 311 e.

1078. Many other transitive verbs may take a predicate accusative in apposition with the object accusative; e.g. ἔλαβε τοῦτο δῶρον *he took this as a gift*; θάνατόν νύ τοι ὅρκι' ἔταμνον *death to thee, then, are the oaths I have sworn*, *Il.* 4, 155 (see **905**). Especially an interrogative pronoun may be so used; e.g. τίνας τούτους ὁρῶ; *who are these whom I see?* or *whom do I see here?* See **916, 971.**

1079. A predicate accusative may denote the *effect* of the action of the verb upon its direct object; e.g. παιδεύειν τινὰ σοφόν *to train one (to be) wise*. See **1053.**

For one of two accusatives retained with the passive, see **1240.**

For the accusative absolute, see **1571.**

GENITIVE

1080. As the chief use of the accusative is to limit the meaning of a verb, so the chief use of the genitive is to limit the meaning of a noun (substantive, adjective, sometimes adverb). When the genitive is used as the object of a verb, it seems to depend on the nominal idea which belongs to the verb: βασιλεύει τῆς χώρας involves the idea βασιλεύς ἐστι τῆς χώρας *he is king of the country*. The Greek is somewhat arbitrary in deciding when it will allow either idea to preponderate in the construction, and with some verbs it allows both the accusative and the genitive. In the same general sense the genitive follows verbal adjectives. Besides this genitive, there is the genitive used in constructions which originally belonged to the ablative. Most uses of the genitive may be traced either to the *partitive* idea or to the idea of *separation* (including *source*). See 1040.

Genitive with Substantives (*Attributive Genitive*)

1081. A substantive in the genitive may limit the meaning of another substantive, to express various relations, most of which are denoted by *of* or by the possessive case in English.

1082. The genitive thus depending on a substantive is called *attributive* (916) or *adnominal*. Its most important relations are the following:

a. POSSESSION or other close relation: e.g. ἡ τοῦ πατρὸς οἰκία *the father's house*, ἡ πατρὶς ἡμῶν *our country*, τὸ τῶν ἀνδρῶν γένος *the lineage of the men*. So ἡ τοῦ Διός *the daughter of Zeus*, τὰ τῶν θεῶν religion, τὰ τῆς πόλεως *the interests of the state, politics* (951). **The Possessive Genitive.**

b. The SUBJECT of an action or feeling: e.g. ἡ τοῦ δήμου εὔνοια *the good-will of the people* (i.e. *which the people feel*). **The Subjective Genitive.**

c. The OBJECT of an action or feeling: e.g. διὰ τὸ Παυσανίου μῖσος *owing to the hatred of* (i.e. *felt against*) *Pausanias*, Thuc. 1, 96; πρὸς τὰς τοῦ χειμῶνος καρτερήσεις *as regards his endurance of the winter*, Plat. *Symp.* 220 a. So οἱ θεῶν ὅρκοι *the oaths (sworn) in the name of the gods* (cf. θεοὺς ὀμνύναι, 1047), X. *An.* 2, 5, 7. **The Objective Genitive.**

d. MATERIAL or CONTENTS, including that of which anything consists: e.g. βοῶν ἀγέλη *a herd of cattle*; ἄλσος ἡμέρων δένδρων *a grove of cultivated trees*, X. *An.* 5, 3, 12; κρήνη ἡδέος ὕδατος *a spring of fresh water*, X. *An.* 6, 4, 4; δύο χοίνικες ἀλφίτων *two quarts of meal*. **Genitive of Material.**

e. MEASURE, of space, time, or value: e.g. τριῶν ἡμερῶν ὁδός *a three days' journey*; ὀκτὼ σταδίων τεῖχος *a wall of eight stadia (in length)*; τριάκοντα ταλάντων οὐσία *an estate of thirty talents*; μισθὸς τεττάρων μηνῶν *pay for four months*; πράγματα πολλῶν ταλάντων *affairs of* (i.e. *involving*) *many talents*, Ar. *Nub.* 472. **Genitive of Measure.**

f. CAUSE or ORIGIN : μεγάλων ἀδικημάτων ὀργή *anger at great offences,* γραφὴ ἀσεβείας *an indictment for impiety.* **The Causal Genitive.**

g. THE WHOLE, with substantives denoting a part : e.g. πολλοὶ τῶν ῥητόρων *many of the orators,* ἀνὴρ τῶν ἐλευθέρων *a man* (i.e. *one*) *of the freemen.* **The Partitive Genitive.** See also **1088.**

These seven classes are not exhaustive ; but they will give a general idea of these relations, many of which it is difficult to classify. The range is extended, especially in poetry. See **1083–1086.**

1083. Examples like πόλις ᾿Αργους *city of Argos,* Ar. *Eq.* 813, Τροίης πτολίεθρον *the city of Troy, Od.* 1, 2, in which the genitive is used instead of apposition, are poetic.

1084. Poetry often has a periphrasis of a substantive and dependent genitive, instead of a qualifying adjective ; e.g. μένος ᾿Ατρεῖδαο *the mighty son of Atreus, Il.* 11, 268 ; ἀμφὶ βίην Διομήδεος *round the mighty Diomed, Il.* 5, 781. Here an adjective or participle sometimes agrees in sense rather than in grammar ; e.g. φίλτατ᾿ Αἰγίσθου βία *dearest Aegisthus,* Aesch. *Ch.* 893. Such expressions denote majesty, courtesy, or affection. Cf. ᾿Ιοκάστης κάρα *dear Iocasta,* S. *O. T.* 950.

1085. Quality may be expressed by the genitive, especially in poetry ; e.g. λευκῆς χιόνος πτέρυγι *with snow-white pinion,* S. *Ant.* 114.

1086. Two genitives denoting different relations may depend on one noun ; e.g. ἵππου δρόμον ἡμέρας *within a day's run for a horse,* Dem. 19, 273 ; διὰ τὴν τοῦ ἀνέμου ἄπωσιν αὐτῶν ἐς τὸ πέλαγος *by the wind's driving them (the wrecks) out to sea,* Thuc. 7, 34.

1087. Certain substantives on which the genitive depends may be omitted, if easily understood ; e.g. Δημοσθένης Δημοσθένους (sc. υἱός) *Demosthenes son of Demosthenes ;* εἰς τοῦ ἀδελφοῦ (sc. οἰκίαν) *to my brother's ;* εἰς κουρέως (sc. κουρεῖον) *to the barber's ;* εἰς ᾿Αΐδαο *to the house of Hades.*

1088. *Partitive Genitive (Genitive of the Whole).* The partitive genitive (**1082 g**) may follow all substantives, adjectives (especially superlatives), pronouns, participles with the article, and adverbs, which denote a part. E.g.

οἱ ἀγαθοὶ τῶν ἀνθρώπων *the good among (the) men,* or *men who are good ;* ὁ ἥμισυς τοῦ ἀριθμοῦ *the half of the number ;* ἄνδρα οἶδα τοῦ δήμου *I know of a man belonging to the people ;* τοῖς θρανίταις τῶν ναυτῶν *to the upper benches of the sailors,* Thuc. 6, 31 ; οὐδεὶς τῶν παίδων *no one of the children ;* πάντων τῶν ῥητόρων δεινότατος *most eloquent of all the orators ;* ὁ βουλόμενος καὶ ἀστῶν καὶ ξένων *any one who pleases, citizens or strangers,* Thuc. 2, 34 ; δῖα γυναικῶν *divine among women, Od.* 4, 305 ; ποῦ γῆς ; ubi terrarum? *where on earth?* τίς τῶν πολιτῶν *who of the citizens?* δὶς τῆς ἡμέρας *twice a day*; εἰς τοῦτο ἀνοίας *to this pitch of folly*; ἐπὶ μέγα δυνάμεως *to a great degree of power*, Thuc. 1, 118; ἐν τούτῳ παρασκευῆς *in this state of preparation*; ἃ μὲν διώκει τοῦ ψηφίσματος ταῦτ' ἐστὶν *what he attacks in the decree is this* (lit. *what parts of the decree he prosecutes*, etc.), Dem. 18, 56; εὐφημότατ' ἀνθρώπων *in the most plausible way possible* (*most plausibly of men*), Dem. 19, 50; ὅτε δεινότατος σαυτοῦ ταῦτα ἦσθα *when you were at the top of your form in these matters*, X. *M.* 1, 2, 46; σαφέστατα ἀνθρώπων *more clearly than anybody else in the world*, Lys. 24, 9; ἐν παντὶ κακοῦ *in utter distress*, Plat. *Rep.* 579 b. See **964**.

1089. The partitive genitive has the predicate position as regards the article (**970**), while other attributive genitives (except *personal* pronouns, **975**) have the attributive position (**959**). It is often separated from the word on which it depends by other words and phrases, and often begins a sentence or clause as the logical topic.

1090. An adjective or participle generally agrees in gender with a dependent partitive genitive. But sometimes, especially when it is singular, it is neuter, agreeing with μέρος *part* understood; e.g. τῶν πολεμίων τὸ πολύ (for οἱ πολλοί) *the greater part of the enemy*. On the other hand, adjectives denoting size or quantity sometimes agree in gender with the genitive; e.g. τῆς μαρίλης συχνήν *a lot of coal dust*, Ar. *Ach.* 350.

1091. A partitive genitive sometimes depends on τὶς or μέρος understood; e.g. ἔφασαν ἐπιμειγνύναι σφῶν τε πρὸς ἐκείνους καὶ ἐκείνων πρὸς ἑαυτούς *they said that some of their own men had mixed with them, and some of them with their own men* (τινάς being understood with σφῶν and ἐκείνων), X. *An.* 3, 5, 16. Cf. **1098**.

1092. Similar to such phrases as ποῦ γῆς; εἰς τοῦτο ἀνοίας, etc. is the use of ἔχω and an adverb with the genitive; e.g. πῶς ἔχεις δόξης; *in what state of opinion are you?* Plat. *Rep.* 456 d; εὖ σώματος ἔχειν *to be in a good condition of body*, ibid. 404 d; ὡς εἶχε τάχους *as fast as he could* (lit. *in the condition of speed in which he was*), Thuc. 2, 90; so ὡς ποδῶν εἶχον, Hdt. 6, 116; εὖ ἔχειν φρενῶν *to be in his right mind* (see E. *Hipp.* 462).

Genitive with Verbs

PREDICATE GENITIVE

1093. As the attributive genitive (**1082**) stands in the relation of an attributive adjective to its leading substantive, so a genitive may stand in the relation of a predicate adjective (**896**) to a verb.

1094. Verbs signifying *to be* or *to become* and other copulative verbs may have a predicate genitive expressing any of the relations of the attributive genitive (**1082**). E.g.

a. **Possessive.** Ὁ νόμος ἐστὶν οὗτος Δράκοντος *this law is Draco's*, Dem. 23, 51; πενίαν φέρειν οὐ παντός, ἀλλ' ἀνδρὸς σοφοῦ *bearing poverty is not in the power of every one, but only of a wise man*, Men. *Mon.* 463; τοῦ θεῶν νομίζεται (ὁ χῶρος); *to what god is the place held sacred?* S. *O. C.* 38.

b. **Subjective.** Οἶμαι αὐτὸ (τὸ ῥῆμα) Περιάνδρου εἶναι *I think it (the saying) is Periander's*, Plat. *Rep.* 336 a.

c. **Objective.** Οὐ τῶν κακούργων οἶκτος, ἀλλὰ τῆς δίκης *pity is not for evildoers, but for the right*, E. *frag.* 272.

d. **Material.** Ἔρυμα λίθων πεποιημένον *a wall built of stones*, Thuc. 4, 31; οἱ θεμέλιοι παντοίων λίθων ὑπόκεινται *the foundations are laid (consisting) of all kinds of stones*, Thuc. 1, 93.

e. **Measure.** (Τὰ τείχη) σταδίων ἦν ὀκτώ *the walls were eight stadia (in length)*, Thuc. 4, 66; ἐπειδὰν ἐτῶν ᾖ τις τριάκοντα *when one is thirty years old*, Plat. *Lg.* 721 a.

f. **Origin.** Τοιούτων ἐστὲ προγόνων *from such ancestors are you sprung*, X. *An.* 3, 2, 14.

g. **Partitive.** Τούτων γενοῦ μοι *become one of these for my sake*, Ar. *Nub.* 107; Σόλων τῶν ἑπτὰ σοφιστῶν ἐκλήθη *Solon was called one of the Seven Wise Men*, Isoc. 15, 235.

1095. Verbs signifying *to name, to choose* or *appoint, to make, to think* or *regard*, and the like, which take two accusatives referring to the same person or thing (**1075**), may take a possessive or partitive genitive in place of the predicate accusative. E.g.

τὴν Ἀσίαν ἑαυτῶν ποιοῦνται *they make Asia their own*, X. *Ag.* 1, 33; ἐμὲ θὲς τῶν πεπεισμένων *put me down as (one) of those who are persuaded*, Plat. *Rep.* 424 c; (τοῦτο) τῆς ἡμετέρας ἀμελείας ἄν τις θείη δικαίως *anyone might rightfully charge this to our neglect*, Dem. 1, 10.

1096. These verbs (**1095**) in the passive are among the copulative verbs of **896**, and they still retain the genitive; e.g. τῆς πρώτης (sc. τάξεως) τεταγμένος *posted in (so as to be of) the front rank*, Lys. 16, 15. See also the last example under **1094 g.**

Genitive expressing a Part

1097. *a.* Any verb may take a partitive genitive if its action affects the object *only in part*. E.g.

πέμπει τῶν Λυδῶν *he sends some of the Lydians* (but πέμπει τοὺς Λυδούς *he sends the Lydians*); πίνει τοῦ οἴνου *he drinks some of the wine*; τῆς γῆς ἔτεμον *they ravaged (some) of the land*, Thuc. 1, 30.

b. This principle applies especially to verbs signifying *to share* (i.e. to give or take *a part*) or *to enjoy*. E.g.

μετεῖχον τῆς λείας *they shared in the booty*, and so often μεταποιεῖσθαί τινος *to claim a share of anything* (cf. **1099**); ἀπολαύομεν τῶν ἀγαθῶν *we enjoy* *the blessings* (i.e. *our share of them*) ; οὕτως ὄναισθε τούτων *thus may you enjoy these*, Dem. 28, 20. So οὐ προσήκει μοι τῆς ἀρχῆς *I have no concern in the government*; μέτεστί μοι τούτου *I have a share in this* (1161).

1098. Many of these verbs also take an accusative, when they refer to the whole object. Thus ἔλαχε τούτου means *he obtained a share of this by lot*, but ἔλαχε τοῦτο *he obtained this by lot*. Μετέχω and similar verbs may regularly take an accusative like μέρος *part*; e.g. τῶν κινδύνων πλεῖστον μέρος μεθέξουσιν *they will have the greatest share of the dangers*, Isoc. 6, 3 (where μέρους would mean that they have only *a part of a share*). This use of μέρος shows the nature of the genitive with these verbs. Cf. 1091.

In συντρίβειν τῆς κεφαλῆς *to bruise his head* and κατεαγέναι τῆς κεφαλῆς *to have his head broken* the genitive is probably partitive. See Ar. *Ach.* 1180, *Pax* 71 ; Isoc. 18, 52. These verbs take also the accusative.

GENITIVE WITH VARIOUS VERBS

1099. The partitive genitive is used with verbs signifying *to take hold of, to touch, to claim, to aim at, to hit, to attain, to miss, to make trial of, to begin*. E.g.

ἐλάβετο τῆς χειρὸς αὐτοῦ *he grasped his hand*, X. *H.* 4, 1, 38 ; πυρὸς ἔστι θιγόντα μὴ εὐθὺς καίεσθαι *it is possible to touch fire and not be burned immediately*, X. *C.* 5, 1, 16 ; τῆς ξυνέσεως μεταποιεῖσθαι *to lay claim to sagacity*, Thuc. 1, 140 ; ἥκιστα τῶν ἀλλοτρίων ὀρέγονται *they are least of all eager for what is another's*, X. *Symp.* 4, 42 ; οὐδὲ μὴν ἄλλου στοχαζόμενος ἔτυχε τούτου *nor did he aim at another man and hit this one*, Antiphon 2, α, 4 ; τῆς ἀρετῆς ἐφικέσθαι *to attain to virtue*, Isoc. 1, 5 ; ὁδοῦ εὐπόρου τυχεῖν *to find a passable road*, X. *H.* 6, 5, 52 ; πολλῶν καὶ χαλεπῶν χωρίων ἐπελάβοντο *they took possession of many rough places*, ibid. ; πειράσαντες τοῦ χωρίου *having made an attempt on the place*, Thuc. 1, 61.

1100. With verbs meaning *to miss* and *to begin* the genitive may be ablatival (denoting separation, 1117) or partitive ; e.g. ταύτης ἀποσφαλέντα τῆς ἐλπίδος *disappointed in this hope*, Hdt. 6, 5 (ablatival) ; σφαλεὶς τῆς ἀληθείας *having missed the truth*, Plat. *Rep.* 451 a ; τὸ ψεύδεσθαι τῆς ἀληθείας *to be cheated out of the truth*; τῶν στρατειῶν οὐδεμιᾶς ἀπελείφθην πώποτε *I never yet missed a single campaign*, Lys. 16, 18 ; εἰκὸς ἄρχειν με λόγου *it is proper that I should speak first*, X. *C.* 6, 1, 6 (partitive) ; τοῦ λόγου ἤρχετο ὧδε *he began his speech as follows*, X. *An.* 3, 2, 7 ; Διὸς ἀρχόμεναι *beginning with Zeus*, Pind. *N.* 5, 25 (ablatival) ; πόθεν ἄρξωμαι; *where am I to begin?* (lit. *from what?* 292), Aesch. *Ch.* 855. Here a preposition is more common in prose ; e.g. ἐκ παιδὸς ἀρξάμενον *beginning with boyhood*, Plat. *Ap.* 31 d.

1101. Verbs of *taking hold* may have an object accusative, with a genitive of the part taken hold of ; e.g. ἔλαβον τῆς ζώνης τὸν Ὀρόνταν *they seized Orontas by his girdle*, X. *An.* 1, 6, 10.

1102. *a.* The poets extend the construction of verbs of *taking hold* to those of *pulling, dragging, leading*, and the like; e.g. ἄλλον μὲν χλαίνης ἐρύων ἄλλον δὲ χιτῶνος *pulling one by the cloak, another by the tunic, Il.* 22,493; βοῦν ἀγέτην κεράων *the two led the heifer by the horns, Od.* 3, 439. *b.* So even in prose: τὰ νήπια παιδία δέουσι τοῦ ποδὸς σπάρτῳ *they tie the infants by the foot with a cord*, Hdt. 5, 16; μήποτε ἄγειν τῆς ἡνίας τὸν ἵππον *never to lead the horse by the bridle*, X. *Eq.* 6, 9. *c.* Under this head is usually placed the poetic genitive with verbs of *imploring*, denoting the part grasped by the suppliant; e.g. ἐμὲ λισσέσκετο γούνων *she implored me by* (i.e. *clasping*) *my knees, Il.* 9, 451. The explanation is less simple in λίσσομαι Ζηνὸς ᾽Ολυμπίου *I implore by Olympian Zeus, Od.* 2, 68: cf. νῦν δέ σε πρὸς πατρὸς γουνάζομαι *and now I implore thee by thy father, Od.* 13, 324.

1103. The partitive genitive is used with verbs signifying *to taste, to smell, to hear, to perceive, to comprehend, to remember, to forget, to desire, to care for, to spare, to neglect, to wonder at, to admire, to despise.* E.g.

ἐλευθερίης γευσάμενοι *having tasted of freedom*, Hdt. 6, 5; κρομμύων ὀσφραίνομαι *I smell onions*, Ar. *R.* 654; φωνῆς ἀκούειν μοι δοκῶ *methinks I hear a voice*, Ar. *Pax* 61; αἰσθάνεσθαι, μεμνῆσθαι, or ἐπιλανθάνεσθαι τούτων *to perceive, remember,* or *forget this*; ὅσοι ἀλλήλων ξυνίεσαν *all who comprehended each other's speech*, Thuc. 1, 3 **(1105)**; τούτων τῶν μαθημάτων ἐπιθυμῶ *I long for this learning*, X. *M.* 2, 6, 30; χρημάτων φείδεσθαι *to be sparing of money*, ibid. 1, 2, 22; τῆς ἀρετῆς ἀμελεῖν *to neglect virtue*, Isoc. 1, 48; εἰ ἄγασαι τοῦ πατρός *if you admire your father*, X. *C.* 3, 1, 15; μηδενὸς οὖν ὀλιγωρεῖτε μηδὲ καταφρονεῖτε τῶν προστεταγμένων *do not then neglect or despise any of my injunctions*, Isoc. 3, 48; τῶν κατηγόρων θαυμάζω *I am astonished at my accusers*, Lys. 25, 1.

For a causal genitive with verbs like θαυμάζω, see **1121.**

1104. Verbs of *hearing, learning*, etc. may take an accusative of the thing heard etc. and a genitive of the person heard from; e.g. τούτων τοιούτους ἀκούω λόγους *I hear such sayings from these men*; πυθέσθαι τοῦτο ὑμῶν *to learn this from you.* The genitive here belongs under **1125.** A sentence may take the place of the accusative; e.g. τούτων ἄκουε ὅ τι λέγουσιν *hear from these men what they say.* See also ἀποδέχομαι *accept (a statement) from*, in the Lexicon.

1105. Verbs of *understanding*, e.g. ἐπίσταμαι, have the accusative. Συνίημι, quoted above with the genitive **(1103)**, usually takes the accusative of a thing. Μέμνημαι means *to remember about, be reminded of, mention*, when it has the genitive; with accusative it means *keep in remembrance.*

1106. The impersonals μέλει and μεταμέλει take the genitive of a thing with the dative of a person **(1161)**; e.g. μέλει μοι τούτου *I am interested in this*, μεταμέλει σοι τούτου *you are sorry for this*; προσήκει *it concerns* has the same construction.

1107. Causative verbs of this class take the accusative of a person and the genitive of a thing; e.g. μή μ' ἀναμνήσῃς κακῶν *do not remind me of evils* (i.e. *cause me to remember them*), E. *Alc.* 1045; τοὺς παῖδας γευστέον αἵματος *we must make the children taste blood*, Plat. *Rep.* 537 a.

But verbs of *reminding* also take two accusatives (**1068**).

1108. Ὄζω *smell of* has a genitive, probably partitive; e.g. ὄζουσ' ἀμβροσίας καὶ νέκταρος *they smell of ambrosia and nectar*, Ar. *Ach.* 196. A second genitive may be added to designate the source of the odor; e.g. εἰ τῆς κεφαλῆς ὄζω μύρου *if my head smells of perfume*, Ar. *Eccl.* 524.

1109. The partitive genitive is used with verbs signifying *to rule, to lead,* or *to direct.* E.g.

Ἔρως τῶν θεῶν βασιλεύει *Love is king of the gods*, Plat. *Symp.* 195 c; Πολυκράτης Σάμου τυραννῶν *Polycrates, while he was tyrant of Samos*, Thuc. 1, 13; Μίνως τῆς νῦν Ἑλληνικῆς θαλάσσης ἐκράτησε καὶ τῶν Κυκλάδων νήσων ἦρξε *Minos became master of what is now the Greek sea, and ruler of the Cyclades*, Thuc. 1, 4; τῶν ἡδονῶν ἐκράτει *he was master over his pleasures*, X. *M.* 1, 5, 6; ἡγούμενοι αὐτονόμων τῶν ξυμμάχων *leading their allies on a basis of independence* (**971**), Thuc. 1, 97.

1110. Some verbs meaning *to rule* may have the accusative when the idea of *conquering* is uppermost; e.g. τοὺς Θρᾷκας κρατήσαντες *having beaten the Thracians*, X. *An.* 7, 6, 32 (*having got them in hand*).

1111. For other cases with many of the verbs of **1099, 1102,** and **1109,** see the Lexicon. For the dative in poetry with ἡγέομαι and ἀνάσσω, see **1164.**

1112. Verbs signifying *fulness* and *want* take the genitive of material (**1082 d**). E.g.

χρημάτων εὐπόρει *he had plenty of money*, Dem. 18, 235; σεσαγμένος πλούτου τὴν ψυχὴν ἔσομαι *I shall have my soul loaded with wealth*, X. *Symp.* 4, 64; οὐκ ἂν ἀποροῖ παραδειγμάτων *he would be at no loss for examples*, Plat. *Rep.* 557 d; οὐδὲν δεήσει πολλῶν γραμμάτων *there will be no need of many documents*, Isoc. 4, 78.

1113. Verbs signifying *to fill* take the accusative of the thing filled and the genitive of material. E.g. δακρύων ἔπλησεν ἐμέ *he filled me with tears*, E. *Or.* 368.

1114. Δέομαι *I want* may have a cognate accusative of the thing desired; e.g. δεήσομαι ὑμῶν μετρίαν δέησιν *I will make of you a moderate request*, Aeschin. 3, 61; τοῦτο ὑμῶν δέομαι *I beg this of you*, Plat. *Ap.* 17 c; cf. **1074.**

1115. Δεῖ *there is need* may take a dative (sometimes in poetry an accusative) of the person besides the genitive; e.g. δεῖ μοι τούτου *I need this*, αὐτὸν γάρ σε δεῖ προμηθέως *for thou thyself needest a counsellor*, Aesch. *Pr.* 86.

1116. *a.* Besides the common phrases πολλοῦ δεῖ *far from it,* ὀλίγου δεῖ *almost,* in which the main idea is expressed in the infinitive clause subject of δεῖ (**1521**), Demosthenes has ironically οὐδὲ πολλοῦ δεῖ *one may not even say that it is far from it,* i.e. *it lacks everything of being.*

b. By an ellipsis of δεῖν (**1538**), ὀλίγου and μικροῦ come to mean *almost*; e.g. ὀλίγου πάντες *almost all,* Plat. *Rep.* 552 d.

GENITIVE OF SEPARATION AND COMPARISON

1117. The genitive (as ablative) may denote that from which anything is *separated* or *distinguished.* On this principle the genitive is used with verbs denoting *to remove, to restrain, to release, to cease, to fail, to give up,* and the like. E.g.

ἡ νῆσος οὐ πολὺ διέχει τῆς ἠπείρου *the island is not far distant from the mainland*; ἐπιστήμη χωριζομένη δικαιοσύνης *knowledge separated from justice,* Plat. *Menex.* 246 e; λῦσόν με δεσμῶν *release me from chains*; ἐπίσχες τοῦ δρόμου *stop your running,* Ar. Av. 1200; τούτους οὐ παύσω τῆς ἀρχῆς *I will not depose them from their authority,* X. C. 8, 6, 3; οὐ παύεσθε τῆς μοχθηρίας *you do not cease from your rascality*; οὐκ ἐψεύσθη τῆς ἐλπίδος *he was not disappointed in his hope,* X. H. 7, 5, 24 (**1100**); τῆς ἐλευθερίας παραχωρῆσαι Φιλίππῳ *to surrender freedom to Philip,* Dem. 18, 68; ἡ ἐπιστολὴ ἣν οὗτος ἔγραψεν ἀπολειφθεὶς ἡμῶν *the letter which this man wrote without our knowledge* (lit. *separated from us*), Dem. 19, 36.

Transitive verbs of this class may take also an accusative if the sense requires it; e.g. λύσω δεσμὰ παιδός; *shall I take the shackles off the child?* E. *Her.* 1123. See **1118, 1125.**

1118. Verbs of *depriving* may take a genitive in place of the accusative of a thing, and those of *taking away* a genitive in place of the accusative of a person (**1068, 1070**); e.g. ἐμὲ τῶν πατρῴων ἀπεστέρηκε *he has robbed me of my patrimony,* Dem. 29, 3; τῶν ἄλλων ἀφαιρούμενοι χρήματα *taking away property from the others,* X. *M.* 1, 5, 3; πόσων ἀπεστέρησθε *of how much have you been bereft!* Dem. 8, 63.

1119. The poets use this genitive with verbs of *motion*; e.g. Οὐλύμποιο κατήλθομεν *we descended from Olympus, Il.* 20, 125; Πυθῶνος ἔβας *thou didst come from Pytho,* S. *O. T.* 152. Here a preposition would be used in prose.

1120. The genitive is used with verbs signifying *to surpass, to be inferior, to differ,* and all others which imply comparison. E.g.

(ἄνθρωπος) ξυνέσει ὑπερέχει τῶν ἄλλων *man surpasses the others in sagacity,* P. *Menex.* 237 d; ἐπιδείξαντες τὴν ἀρετὴν τοῦ πλήθους περιγιγνομένην *showing that bravery proves superior to numbers,* Isoc. 4, 91; ὁρῶν ὑστερίζουσαν τὴν πόλιν τῶν καιρῶν *seeing the city too late for its opportunities,* Dem. 18, 102; ἐμπειρίᾳ πολὺ προέχετε τῶν ἄλλων *in experience you far excel the others,* X. *H.* 7, 1, 4; οὐδὲν πλήθει γε ἡμῶν λειφθέντες *when they were not at all inferior to (left behind by) us in numbers*, X. *An.* 7, 7, 31; εἶπον (αὐτῷ) τοῦ κήρυκος μὴ λείπεσθαι *they told him not to be left behind the herald* (i.e. *to follow him closely*), Thuc. 1, 131; οὐδὲν διοίσεις Χαιρεφῶντος *you will not differ from Chaerephon at all*, Ar. *Nub.* 503. So τῶν ἐχθρῶν νικᾶσθαι (or ἡττᾶσθαι), *to be overcome by one's enemies*; but these two verbs take also the genitive with ὑπό (**1236**). So τῶν ἐχθρῶν κρατεῖν *to prevail over one's enemies*, and τῆς θαλάσσης κρατεῖν *to be master of the sea*. Compare the examples under **1109**.

Genitive of Cause and Source

1121. The ablatival genitive often denotes a *cause*, especially with verbs expressing emotions, e.g. *admiration, wonder, affection, hatred, pity, anger, envy*, or *revenge*. E.g.

(τούτους) τῆς μὲν τόλμης οὐ θαυμάζω, τῆς δὲ ἀξυνεσίας *I wonder not at their boldness, but at their folly*, Thuc. 6, 36; πολλάκις σε ηὐδαιμόνισα τοῦ τρόπου *often have I thought you happy because of your disposition*, Plat. *Crito* 43 b; ζηλῶ σε τοῦ νοῦ, τῆς δὲ δειλίας στυγῶ *I envy you for your mind, but loathe you for your cowardice*, S. *El.* 1027; μή μοι φθονήσῃς τοῦ μαθήματος *don't grudge me the knowledge*, Plat. *Euthyd.* 297 b; συγγιγνώσκειν αὐτοῖς χρὴ τῆς ἐπιθυμίας *we must forgive them for their desire*, ibid. 306 c; καὶ σφεας τιμωρήσομαι τῆς ἐνθάδε ἀπίξιος *and I shall punish them for coming hither*, Hdt. 3, 145; τούτους οἰκτίρω τῆς νόσου *I pity them for their disease*, X. *Symp.* 4, 37; τῶν ἀδικημάτων ὀργίζεσθαι *to be angry at the offences*, Lys. 31, 11.

Most of these verbs may take also an accusative or dative of the person.

1122. The genitive sometimes denotes a *purpose* or *motive* (where ἕνεκα is generally expressed); e.g. τῆς τῶν Ἑλλήνων ἐλευθερίας *for the liberty of the Greeks*, Dem. 18, 100; so 19, 76. See **1551**.

1123. Verbs of *disputing* take a causal genitive; e.g. οὐ βασιλεῖ ἀντιποιούμεθα τῆς ἀρχῆς *we do not dispute with the King the title to his dominion*, X. *An.* 2, 3, 23; Εὔμολπος ἠμφισβήτησεν Ἐρεχθεῖ τῆς πόλεως *Eumolpus disputed with Erechtheus for the city* (i.e. *disputed its possession with him*), Isoc. 12, 193.

1124. The genitive is sometimes used in *exclamations*, to give the cause of the astonishment. E.g.

Ὦ Πόσειδον, τῆς τέχνης *O Poseidon, what a trade!* Ar. *Eq.* 144; Ὦ Ζεῦ βασιλεῦ, τῆς λεπτότητος τῶν φρενῶν! *O King Zeus! what subtlety of intellect!* Ar. *Nub.* 153. For the nominative, see **1043**.

1125. a. The genitive sometimes denotes the *source*. E.g.

μάθε μου τάδε *learn this from me*, X. *C.* 1, 6, 44. Add the examples given under **1104**.

b. So with γίγνομαι, in the sense *to be born*; e.g. Δαρείου καὶ Παρυσάτιδος γίγνονται παῖδες δύο *of Darius and Parysatis are born two sons*, X. *An.* 1, 1, 1.

1126. In poetry the genitive occasionally denotes the *agent* or *instrument*; e.g. ἐν Ἀίδα κεῖσαι, σᾶς ἀλόχου σφαγεὶς Αἰγίσθου τε *thou liest in the house of Hades, slain by thy wife and Aegisthus*, E. *El.* 122; πρῆσαι πυρὸς δηίοιο θύρετρα *to burn the gates with ravening fire*, *Il.* 2, 415.

Genitive with Verbs of Judicial Action

1127. Verbs signifying *to accuse, to prosecute, to convict, to acquit,* and *to condemn* take a genitive denoting the *crime*, with an accusative of the person. E.g.

αἰτιῶμαι αὐτὸν τοῦ φόνου *I charge him with the murder*; ἐγράψατο αὐτὸν παρανόμων *he indicted him for an illegal proposition*; διώκει με δώρων *he prosecutes me for bribery*; Κλέωνα δώρων ἐλόντες καὶ κλοπῆς *having convicted Cleon of bribery and theft*, Ar. *Nub.* 591; ἔφευγε προδοσίας *he was brought to trial for treachery*, but ἀπέφυγε προδοσίας *he was acquitted of treachery*; ψευδομαρτυριῶν ἁλώσεσθαι προσδοκῶν *expecting to be convicted of false-witness*, Dem. 39, 18.

1128. Ὀφλισκάνω *lose a suit* has the construction of a passive of this class (**1236**); e.g. ὦφλε κλοπῆς *he was convicted of theft*. It may also have a cognate accusative; e.g. ὦφλε κλοπῆς δίκην *he was convicted of theft* (**1049**). For other accusatives with ὀφλισκάνω, e.g. μωρίαν *folly*, αἰσχύνην *shame*, χρήματα *money* (*fine*), see the Lexicon.

1129. Compounds of κατά of this class, including κατηγορῶ (**868 b**), commonly take a genitive of the *person*, which depends on the κατά. They may take also an object accusative denoting the crime or punishment. E.g.

οὐδεὶς αὐτὸς αὐτοῦ κατηγόρησε πώποτε *no man ever accused himself*, Dem. 38, 26; κατεβόων τῶν Ἀθηναίων *they decried the Athenians*, Thuc. 1, 67; θάνατον κατέγνωσαν αὐτοῦ *they condemned him to death*, Thuc. 6, 61; ὑμῶν δέομαι μὴ καταγνῶναι δωροδοκίαν ἐμοῦ *I beg you not to declare me guilty of taking bribes*, Lys. 21, 21; τὰ πλεῖστα κατεψεύσατό μου *he mostly lied about (against) me*, Dem. 18, 9; λέγω πρὸς τοὺς ἐμοῦ καταψηφισαμένους θάνατον *I am speaking to those who voted to condemn me to death*, Plat. *Ap.* 38 d.

1130. Verbs of *condemning* which are compounds of κατά may take three cases; e.g. πολλῶν οἱ πατέρες ἡμῶν μηδισμοῦ θάνατον κατέγνωσαν *our fathers condemned many to death for Medism*, Isoc. 4, 157.

For a genitive (of *value*) denoting the penalty, see **1133**.

1131. The verbs of **1127** often have a cognate accusative (**1049**) on which the genitive depends; e.g. γραφὴν γράφεσθαι ὕβρεως *to bring an indictment for outrage*; γραφὴν (or δίκην) ὑπέχειν, φεύγειν, διώκειν, ὀφλεῖν, ἀλῶναι.

Genitive with Compound Verbs

1132. The genitive often depends on a preposition included in a compound verb. E.g.

πρόκειται τῆς χώρας ἡμῶν ὄρη μεγάλα *high mountains lie in front of our land,* X. M. 3, 5, 25; ὑπερεφάνησαν τοῦ λόφου *they appeared above the hill,* Thuc. 4, 93; οὕτως ὑμῶν ὑπεραλγῶ *I grieve so for you,* Ar. Av. 466; ἀποτρέπει με τούτου *it turns me from this,* Plat. Ap. 31 d; τῷ ἐπιβάντι πρώτῳ τοῦ τείχους *to him who should first mount the wall,* Thuc. 4, 116; οὐκ ἀνθρώπων ὑπερεφρόνει *he did not despise men,* X. Ages. 11, 2.

For the genitive with verbs of *accusing* and *condemning*, compounds of κατά, see **1129.**

Genitive of Price or Value

1133. The genitive may denote the *price* or *value* of a thing. E.g.

τεύχε' ἄμειβε χρύσεα χαλκείων, ἑκατόμβοι' ἐννεαβοίων *he gave gold armor for bronze, armor worth a hundred oxen for armor worth nine,* Il. 6, 235; δόξα χρημάτων οὐκ ὠνητή (sc. ἐστίν) *glory is not to be bought with money,* Isoc. 2, 32; πόσου διδάσκει; *what does he charge for his lessons?* πέντε μνῶν *five minas,* Plat. Ap. 20 b; οὐκ ἂν ἀπεδόμην πολλοῦ τὰς ἐλπίδας *I would not have sold my hopes for a great deal,* Plat. Ph. 98 b; μείζονος αὐτὰ τιμῶνται *they value them more,* X. C. 2, 1, 13. But with ποιοῦμαι and other verbs of *valuing* or *rating* περί with the genitive is more common; e.g. περὶ πλείστου ποιεῖσθαι *to deem of the utmost importance.*

In judicial language, τιμᾶν τινί τινος is said of the court's judgment in estimating the penalty, *to fix the penalty;* τιμᾶσθαί τινί τινος of either party to the suit, *to propose* a penalty; e.g. ἀλλὰ δὴ φυγῆς τιμήσωμαι; *ἴσως γὰρ ἄν μοι τούτου τιμήσαιτε but shall I then propose exile as my punishment? — you (the court) might perhaps fix my penalty at this,* Plat. Ap. 37 c. So τιμᾶται δ' οὖν μοι ὁ ἀνὴρ θανάτου *anyhow, the man proposes death as my punishment,* Plat. Ap. 36 b. So also Σφοδρίαν ὑπῆγον θανάτου *they impeached Sphodrias on a capital charge* (cf. **1130**), X. H. 5, 4, 24.

1134. The thing bought sometimes stands in the genitive, either by analogy to the genitive of price, or in a causal sense (**1121**); e.g. τοῦ δώδεκα μνᾶς Πασίᾳ (sc. ὀφείλω); *for what (do I owe) twelve minas to Pasias?* Ar. Nub. 22; οὐδένα τῆς συνουσίας ἀργύριον πράττει *you exact no money for your teaching from anybody,* X. M. 1, 6, 11.

1135. The genitive depending on ἄξιος *worth, worthy,* and its compounds, or on ἀξιόω *think worthy,* is the genitive of *price* or *value;* e.g. ἄξιός ἐστι θανάτου *he deserves death;* οὐ Θεμιστοκλέα τῶν μεγίστων δωρεῶν ἠξίωσαν; *did they not think Themistocles worthy of the highest gifts?* Isoc. 4, 154. So sometimes ἄτιμος and ἀτιμάζω take the genitive. See **1140.**

Genitive of Time and Place

1136. The genitive may denote the *period of time within which* anything takes place. E.g.

ταῦτα τῆς ἡμέρας ἐγένετο *this happened during the day*, X. *An.* 7, 4, 14 (τὴν ἡμέραν would mean *through the whole day*, 1061); ποίου χρόνου δὲ καὶ πεπόρθηται πόλις; *and how long since (within what time) has the city really lain in ruins* (1250 c)? Aesch. *Ag.* 290; τοῦ ἐπιγιγνομένου χειμῶνος *in the following winter*, Thuc. 8, 29; δέκα ἐτῶν οὐχ ἥξουσι *they will not come within ten years*, Plat. *Lg.* 642 e. So δραχμὴν ἐλάμβανε τῆς ἡμέρας *he received a drachma a day* (949), Thuc. 3, 17.

1137. A similar genitive of the place *within which* or *at which* is found in poetry. E.g.

ἦ οὐκ Ἄργεος ἦεν Ἀχαιικοῦ *was he not in Achaean Argos?* *Od.* 3, 251; οἵη νῦν οὐκ ἔστι γυνὴ κατ' Ἀχαιίδα γαῖαν, οὔτε Πύλου ἱερῆς οὔτ' Ἄργεος οὔτε Μυκήνης *a woman whose like there is not in the Achaean land, nor at sacred Pylos, nor at Argos, nor at Mycenae, Od.* 21, 107. So in the Homeric πεδίοιο θέειν *to run over the plain* (i.e. *within its limits*), *Il.* 22, 23, λούεσθαι ποταμοῖο *to bathe in the river, Il.* 6, 508, and similar expressions. So ἀριστερῆς χειρός *on the left hand*, even in Hdt. (5, 77).

1138. A genitive denoting *place* occurs in Attic prose in a few such expressions as ἰέναι τοῦ πρόσω *to go forward*, X. *An.* 1, 3, 1, and ἐπετάχυνον τῆς ὁδοῦ τοὺς σχολαίτερον προσιόντας *they hurried over the road those who came up more slowly*, Thuc. 4, 47.

Genitive with Adjectives

1139. The *objective* genitive follows many verbal adjectives.

1140. These adjectives are chiefly kindred (in meaning or derivation) to verbs which take the genitive. E.g.

μέτοχος σοφίας *partaking of wisdom*, Plat. *Lg.* 689 d; ἰσόμοιροι τῶν πατρῴων *sharing equally their father's estate*, Isae. 6, 25. (1097 b)
ἐπιστήμης ἐπήβολοι *having attained knowledge*, Plat. *Euthyd.* 289 b; θαλάσσης ἐμπειρότατοι *most familiar with the sea* (*experienced in navigation*), Thuc. 1, 80. (1099)
ὑπήκοος τῶν γονέων *obedient (hearkening) to his parents*, Plat. *Rep.* 463 d; ἀμνήμων τῶν κινδύνων *unmindful of the dangers*, Antiphon 2, a, 7; ἄγευστος κακῶν *without a taste of evils*, S. *Ant.* 582; ἐπιμελὴς ἀγαθῶν, ἀμελὴς κακῶν *caring for the good, neglectful of the bad*; φειδωλοὶ χρημάτων *sparing of money*, Plat. *Rep.* 548 b. (1103)
τῶν ἡδονῶν πασῶν ἐγκρατέστατος *perfect master of all pleasures*, X. *M.* 1, 2, 14; νεὼς ἀρχικός *fit to command a ship*, Plat. *Rep.* 488 d; ἑαυτοῦ ὢν ἀκράτωρ *not being master of himself*, ibid. 579 c. (1109)

μεστὸς κακῶν *full of evils*; ἐπιστήμης κενός *void of knowledge*, Plat. *Rep*. 486 c; λήθης ὢν πλέως *being full of forgetfulness*, ibid.; πλείστων ἐνδεέστατος *most wanting in most things*, ibid. 579 e; ἡ ψυχὴ γυμνὴ τοῦ σώματος *the soul stript of the body*, Plat. *Crat*. 403 b; καθαρὰ πάντων τῶν περὶ τὸ σῶμα κακῶν *free (pure) from all the evils that belong to the body*, ibid. 403 e; τοιούτων ἀνδρῶν ὀρφανή *bereft of such men*, Lys. 2, 60; ἐπιστήμη ἐπιστήμης διάφορος *knowledge distinct from knowledge*, Plat. *Phil*. 61 d; ἕτερον τὸ ἡδὺ τοῦ ἀγαθοῦ *the pleasant (is) distinct from the good*, Plat. *G*. 500 d. (1112, 1117)
ἔνοχος δειλίας *chargeable with cowardice*, Lys. 14, 5; τούτων αἴτιος *responsible for this*, Plat. *G*. 447 a. (1127)
ἄξιος πολλῶν *worth much*, genitive of value. (1135)

1141. Compounds of *alpha privative* (**861**) sometimes take a genitive of kindred meaning, which depends on the idea of *separation* (**1117**) implied in them; e.g. ἄπαις ἀρρένων παίδων *destitute (childless) of male children*, X. *C*. 4, 6, 2; τιμῆς ἄτιμος *destitute of all honor*, Plat. *Lg*. 774 b; χρημάτων ἀδωρότατος *most free from taking bribes*, Thuc. 2, 65; ἀνήνεμον πάντων χειμώνων *free from the blast of every storm*, S. *O. C*. 677; ἀψόφητος ὀξέων κωκυμάτων *without the sound of shrill wailings*, S. *Aj*. 321.

1142. Some of these adjectives (**1139**) are kindred to verbs which take the accusative. E.g.

ἐπιστήμων τῆς τέχνης *understanding the art*, Plat. *G*. 448 b (**1103**); ἐπιτήδευμα πόλεως ἀνατρεπτικόν *a practice subversive of a state*, Plat. *Rep*. 389 d; κακοῦργος μὲν τῶν ἄλλων, ἑαυτοῦ δὲ πολὺ κακουργότερος *harmful to others, but far more harmful to himself*, X. *M*. 1, 5, 3; συγγνώμων τῶν ἀνθρωπίνων ἁμαρτημάτων *considerate of human faults*, X. *C*. 6, 1, 37; σύμψηφός σοι εἰμι τούτου τοῦ νόμου *I vote with you for this law*, Plat. *Rep*. 380 c.

1143. The possessive genitive sometimes follows adjectives denoting *possession*. E.g.

οἱ κίνδυνοι τῶν ἐφεστηκότων ἴδιοι *the risks belong especially to the men in authority*, Dem. 2, 28; ἱερὸς ὁ χῶρος τῆς Ἀρτέμιδος *the place is sacred to Artemis*, X. *An*. 5, 3, 13; κοινὸν πάντων *common to all*, Plat. *Symp*. 205 a.

For the dative with such adjectives, see **1175**.

1144. a. Such a genitive sometimes denotes mere *connection*; e.g. συγγενὴς αὐτοῦ *a relative of his*, X. *C*. 4, 1, 22; Σωκράτους ὁμώνυμος *a namesake of Socrates*, Plat. *Soph*. 218 b.
The adjective is here really used as a substantive. Such adjectives naturally take the dative (**1176**).

b. Here probably belongs ἐναγὴς τοῦ Ἀπόλλωνος *accursed (in the sight) of Apollo*, Aeschin. 3, 110; also ἐναγεῖς καὶ ἀλιτήριοι τῆς θεοῦ *accursed of the goddess*, Thuc. 1, 126, and ἐκ τῶν ἀλιτηρίων τῶν τῆς θεοῦ Ar. *Eq*. 445; — ἐναγής etc. being really substantives.

1145. After some adjectives the genitive can be best explained as depending on the substantive implied in them; e.g. τῆς ἀρχῆς ὑπεύθυνος *responsible for the office*, i.e. *liable to εὔθυναι for it*, Dem. 18, 117 (see δέδωκά γε εὐθύνας ἐκείνων, in the same section); παρθένοι γάμων ὡραῖαι *maidens ripe for marriage*, i.e. *having reached the age (ὥρα) for marriage*, Hdt. 1, 196 (see ἐς γάμου ὥρην ἀπικομένην, Hdt. 6, 61); φόρου ὑποτελεῖς *subject to the payment (τέλος) of tribute*, Thuc. 1, 19.

1146. Some adjectives of place, like ἐναντίος *opposite*, may take the genitive instead of the regular dative (1175), but chiefly in poetry; e.g. ἐναντίοι ἔσταν Ἀχαιῶν *they stood opposite the Achaeans*, *Il.* 17, 343; τοῦ Πόντου ἐπικάρσιαι *at an angle with the Pontus*, Hdt. 7, 36.

Genitive with Comparatives

1147. Adjectives and adverbs of the comparative degree may have the genitive of separation or distinction (1117) instead of the conjunction ἤ *than* and another case.

κρείττων ἐστὶ τούτων *he is better than they* (= κρείττων ἢ οὗτοι sc. εἰσί); νέοις τὸ σιγᾶν κρεῖττόν ἐστι τοῦ λαλεῖν *for the young silence is better than too much talk* (= ἢ τὸ λαλεῖν, 1545), Men. *Mon.* 387; πονηρία θᾶττον θανάτου θεῖ *wickedness runs faster than death*, Plat. *Ap.* 39 a.

1148. All adjectives and adverbs which *imply* a comparison may take a genitive: e.g. ἕτεροι τούτων *others than these*, ὕστεροι τῆς μάχης *too late for (later than) the battle*, τῇ ὑστεραίᾳ τῆς μάχης *on the day after the battle*. So τριπλάσιον ἡμῶν *thrice as much as we*.

1149. The genitive is less common than ἤ when, if ἤ were used, it would be followed by any other case than the nominative or the accusative without a preposition. Thus, for ἔξεστι δ' ἡμῖν μᾶλλον ἑτέρων *and we can (do this) better than others* (Thuc. 1, 85) μᾶλλον ἢ ἑτέροις would be more common. See X. *M.* 3, 5, 16 in 1159.

1150. After πλέον (πλεῖν) *more*, or ἔλαττον *less*, ἤ is occasionally omitted before a numeral without affecting the case; e.g. πέμψω ὄρνῑς ἐπ' αὐτόν, πλεῖν ἐξακοσίους τὸν ἀριθμόν *I will send birds against him, more than six hundred in number*, Ar. *Av.* 1251.

Genitive with Adverbs

1151. The genitive is used with adverbs derived from adjectives and participles which take the genitive. E.g.

οἱ ἐμπείρως αὐτοῦ ἔχοντες *they who are acquainted with him*; ἀναξίως τῆς πόλεως *in a way unworthy of the state*; τῶν ἄλλων Ἀθηναίων ἁπάντων διαφερόντως *beyond all the other Athenians*, Plat. *Crito* 52 b; ἐμάχοντο ἀξίως λόγου *they fought in a manner worthy of note*, Hdt. 6, 112. So ἐναντίον (1146).

1152. The genitive follows many adverbs of place. E.g.

εἴσω τοῦ ἐρύματος *within the fortress*; ἔξω τοῦ τείχους *outside of the wall*; ἐκτὸς τῶν ὅρων *beyond the boundaries*; χωρὶς τοῦ σώματος *apart from the body*; πέραν τοῦ ποταμοῦ *across the river*, Thuc. 6, 101; πρόσθεν τοῦ στρατοπέδου *in front of the camp*, X. H. 4, 1, 22; ἀμφοτέρωθεν τῆς ὁδοῦ *on both sides of the road*, ibid. 5, 2, 6; εὐθὺ τῆς Φασήλιδος *straight towards Phasēlis*, Thuc. 8, 88.

1153. Such adverbs, besides those given above, are chiefly ἐντός *within*; δίχα *apart from*; ἐγγύς, ἄγχι, πέλας, and πλησίον *near*; πόρρω (πρόσω) *far from*; ὄπισθεν and κατόπιν *behind*; and a few others of similar meaning. The genitive with most of them can be explained as a *partitive* genitive or as a genitive of *separation*; with εὐθύ, for example, it is partitive (**1099**), with δίχα, ablative (**1117**). For the dative in poetry, see **1190**.

1154. Λάθρᾳ (Ionic λάθρῃ) and κρύφα, *without the knowledge of*, sometimes take the genitive; e.g. λάθρῃ Λαομέδοντος *without the knowledge of Laomedon*, Il. 5, 269; κρύφα τῶν Ἀθηναίων, Thuc. 1, 101.

1155. Ἄνευ and ἄτερ *without*, ἄχρι and μέχρι *until*, ἕνεκα (εἵνεκα, οὕνεκα) *on account of*, μεταξύ *between*, and πλήν *except*, take the genitive like prepositions. See **1227**.

Genitive Absolute

1156. A noun or pronoun and a participle not grammatically connected with the main construction of the sentence may stand by themselves in the genitive. This is called the *genitive absolute*. E.g.

ταῦτ' ἐπράχθη Κόνωνος στρατηγοῦντος *this was done when Conon was general*, Isoc. 9, 56; οὐδὲν τῶν δεόντων ποιούντων ὑμῶν κακῶς τὰ πράγματα ἔχει *while you do nothing that you ought to do, affairs are in a bad state*, Dem. 4, 2; θεῶν διδόντων οὐκ ἂν ἐκφύγοι κακά *if the gods should grant (it to be so), he could not escape evils*, Aesch. Sev. 719; ὄντος γε ψεύδους ἔστιν ἀπάτη *when there is falsehood, there is deceit*, Plat. Soph. 260 c.

See **1571** and **1566**.

DATIVE

1157. The primary use of the *dative* case is to denote that *to* or *for* which anything is or is done: this includes the dative of the remote or indirect object, and the dative of *advantage* or *disadvantage*. The dative also denotes that *by* which or *with* which, and the time (sometimes the place) *in* which, anything takes place, — i.e. it is not merely a *dative*, but also an *instrumental* and a *locative* case. Most datives may be resolved into *datives of interest*. Cf. **1040**.

Dative Expressing *to* or *for*

DATIVE OF THE INDIRECT OBJECT

1158. The *indirect object* of the action of a transitive verb is put in the dative. This object is generally introduced in English by *to*. E.g.

δίδωσι μισθὸν τῷ στρατεύματι *he gives pay to the army*; ὑπισχνεῖταί σοι δέκα τάλαντα *he promises you ten talents*; ἔλεξαν τῷ βασιλεῖ τὰ γεγενημένα *they told the king what had happened*; βοήθειαν πέμψομεν τοῖς συμμάχοις *we will send aid to our allies* (here the dative is not the end of the motion, but denotes the persons interested in the sending).

1159. Certain intransitive verbs take the dative, many of which in English may have a direct object without *to*. E.g.

τοῖς θεοῖς εὔχομαι *I pray (to) the gods*, Dem. 18, 1; λυσιτελοῦν τῷ ἔχοντι *advantageous to the possessor*, Plat. *Rep.* 392 c; εἴκουσ' ἀνάγκῃ τῇδε *yielding to this necessity*, Aesch. *Ag.* 1071; τοῖς νόμοις πείθονται *they are obedient to the laws (they obey the laws)*, X. *M.* 4, 4, 15; βοηθεῖν δικαιοσύνῃ *to vindicate justice*, Plat. *Rep.* 427 e; εἰ τοῖς πλέοσιν ἀρέσκοντές ἐσμεν, τοῖσδ' ἂν μόνοις οὐκ ὀρθῶς ἀπαρέσκοιμεν *if we are pleasing to the majority, it cannot be right that we should be displeasing to these alone*, Thuc. 1, 38; ἐπίστευον αὐτῷ αἱ πόλεις *the cities trusted him*, X. *An.* 1, 9, 8; τοῖς Ἀθηναίοις παρῄνει *he used to advise the Athenians*, Thuc. 1, 93; τὸν μάλιστα ἐπιτιμῶντα τοῖς πεπραγμένοις ἡδέως ἂν ἐροίμην *I should like to ask the man who censures most severely what has been done*, Dem. 18, 64; τί ἐγκαλῶν ἡμῖν ἐπιχειρεῖς ἡμᾶς ἀπολλύναι; *what fault do you find with us that you try to destroy us?* Plat. *Crito* 50 d; τούτοις μέμφει τι; *have you anything to blame them for?* ibid.; ἐπηρεάζουσιν ἀλλήλοις καὶ φθονοῦσιν ἑαυτοῖς μᾶλλον ἢ τοῖς ἄλλοις ἀνθρώποις *they revile one another, and are more malicious to themselves than to other men*, X. *M.* 3, 5, 16; ἐχαλέπαινον τοῖς στρατηγοῖς *they were angry with the generals*, X. *An.* 1, 4, 12; ἐμοὶ ὀργίζονται *they are angry with me*, Plat. *Ap.* 23 c. So πρέπει μοι λέγειν *it is becoming to me to speak*, προσήκει μοι *it belongs to me*, δοκεῖ μοι *it seems to me*, δοκῶ μοι *methinks*.

1160. The verbs of this class which are not translated with *to* in English are chiefly those signifying *to benefit, serve, obey, defend, assist, please, trust, satisfy, advise, exhort*, or any of their opposites; also those expressing *friendliness, hostility, blame, abuse, reproach, envy, anger, threats*.

1161. The impersonals δεῖ, μέτεστι, μέλει, μεταμέλει, and προσήκει take the dative of a *person* with the genitive of a *thing*; e.g. δεῖ μοι τούτου *I have need of this*, μέτεστί μοι τούτου *I have a share in this*, μέλει μοι τούτου *I am interested in this*, μεταμελήσει αὐτῷ τούτων *he will be sorry for that*, προσήκει μοι τούτου *I am concerned in this.* For the genitive, see 1097 *b*, 1106, 1115. ἔξεστι *it is possible* takes the dative alone.

1162. Δεῖ and χρή take the accusative when an infinitive follows. For δεῖ (in poetry) with the accusative and the genitive, see 1115.

1163. Some verbs of this class (1160) may take the accusative; e.g. οὐδεὶς αὐτοὺς ἐμέμφετο *no one blamed them,* X. *An.* 2, 6, 30. Others, whose meaning would place them here (e.g. μισέω *hate*), take only the accusative. Λοιδορέω *revile* has the accusative, but λοιδορέομαι (middle) has the dative. ᾿Ονειδίζω *reproach* and ἐπιτιμῶ *censure* have the accusative as well as the dative; we have also ὀνειδίζειν (ἐπιτιμᾶν) τί τινι to cast a reproach (or censure) on one. Τιμωρεῖν τινι means regularly to avenge one (*to take vengeance for him*), τιμωρεῖσθαι (rarely τιμωρεῖν) τινα to punish one (*to avenge oneself on him*): see X. *C.* 4, 6, 8, τιμωρήσειν σοι τοῦ παιδὸς τὸν φονέα ὑπισχνοῦμαι *I promise to avenge you on the murderer of your son* (or *for your son,* 1121). Βοηθεῖν *come to the aid of* has the dative; but ὠφελεῖν *help* more often has the accusative.

1164. *a.* Verbs of *ruling*, which take the genitive in prose (1109), have also the dative in poetry, especially in Homer; e.g. πολλῇσιν νήσοισι καὶ ῎Αργεῖ παντὶ ἀνάσσειν *to be lord over many islands and all Argos,* Il. 2, 108; δαρὸν οὐκ ἄρξει θεοῖς *he will not rule the gods long,* Aesch. *Pr.* 940. Κελεύω *command,* which in Attic Greek has only the accusative (generally with the infinitive), has the dative in Homer; see *Il.* 2, 50.

b. ῾Ηγέομαι in the sense of *guide* or *direct* takes the dative even in prose; e.g. οὐκέτι ἡμῖν ἡγήσεται *he will no longer be our guide,* X. *An.* 3, 2, 20.

DATIVE OF ADVANTAGE OR DISADVANTAGE

1165. The person or thing for whose *advantage* or *disadvantage* anything is or is done is put in the dative (dativus commodi et incommodi). This dative is generally introduced in English by *for*. E.g.

πᾶς ἀνὴρ αὐτῷ πονεῖ *every man labors for himself,* S. *Aj.* 1366; Σόλων ᾿Αθηναίοις νόμους ἔθηκε *Solon made laws for the Athenians;* καιροὶ προεῖνται τῇ πόλει *opportunities have been let slip to* (*the detriment of*) *the state,* Dem. 19, 8; ἡγεῖτο αὐτῶν ἕκαστος οὐχὶ τῷ πατρὶ καὶ τῇ μητρὶ μόνον γεγενῆσθαι, ἀλλὰ καὶ τῇ πατρίδι *each one of them believed that he was born not merely for his father and mother, but for his country also,* Dem. 18, 205.

1166. A peculiar use of this dative is found in statements of time; e.g. τῷ ἤδη δύο γενεαὶ ἐφθίατο *two generations had already passed away for him* (i.e. *he had seen them pass away*), Il. 1, 250; ἡμέραι μάλιστα ἦσαν τῇ Μυτιλήνῃ ἑαλωκυίᾳ ἑπτά *it was about seven days since the capture of Mitylene* (lit. *for Mitylene captured,* 1564 *b*), Thuc. 3, 29; ἦν ἡμέρα πέμπτη ἐπιπλέουσι τοῖς ᾿Αθηναίοις *it was the fifth day since the Athenians began to come on in their ships,* X. *H.* 2, 1, 27. See 1172 *b*.

1167. Here belong such Homeric expressions as τοῖσι δ' ἀνέστη *and he rose up for them* (i.e. *to address them*), *Il.* 1, 68; τοῖσι μύθων ἦρχεν *he began to speak* (1099) *before them* (*for them*), *Od.* 1, 28. Cf. 1178.

1168. In Homer, verbs signifying *to ward off* take an accusative of the thing and a dative of the person; e.g. Δαναοῖσι λοιγὸν ἄμυνον *ward off destruction from the Danai* (lit. *for the Danai*), *Il.* 1, 456. Here the accusative may be omitted, so that Δαναοῖσι ἀμύνειν means *to defend the Danai.* For other constructions of ἀμύνω see the Lexicon, and cf. τιμωρεῖν, **1163.**

1169. Δέχομαι *receive* takes a dative by a similar idiom; e.g. δέξατό οἱ σκῆπτρον *he took his sceptre from him* (lit. *for him*), *Il.* 2, 186.

1170. Sometimes this dative has a force which seems to approach that of the possessive genitive; e.g. γλῶσσα δέ οἱ δέδεται *and his tongue is tied* (lit. *for him*), Theognis 178; οἱ ἵπποι αὐτοῖς δέδενται *they have their horses tied* (lit. *the horses are tied for them*), X. *An.* 3, 4, 35. The dative here is the dativus incommodi (**1165**).

1171. Here belongs the so-called *ethical dative*, in which the personal pronouns have the force of *for my sake* etc. Sometimes it has emotional effect; e.g. τί σοι μαθήσομαι; *what am I to learn, please you?* Ar. *Nub.* 111; τούτῳ πάνυ μοι προσέχετε τὸν νοῦν *to this, I beg you, give your close attention,* Dem. 18, 178.

For a dative with the dative of βουλόμενος etc., see **1586.**

DATIVE OF RELATION

1172. a. The dative may denote a person to whose case a statement is limited, — often belonging to the whole sentence rather than to any special word. E.g.

ἅπαντα τῷ φοβουμένῳ ψοφεῖ *everything sounds to one who is afraid,* S. *frag.* 58; σφῷν μὲν ἐντολὴ Διὸς ἔχει τέλος *as regards you two, the order of Zeus is fully executed,* Aesch. *Pr.* 12; ὑπολαμβάνειν δεῖ τῷ τοιούτῳ ὅτι εὐήθης τις ἄνθρωπος *with regard to such a one we must suppose that he is a simple person,* Plat. *Rep.* 598 d; τέθνηχ' ὑμῖν πάλαι *I have long been dead to you* (*in your eyes* or *as you thought*), S. *Ph.* 1030; πᾶσι νικᾶν τοῖς κριταῖς *to be the best in the opinion of all the judges,* Ar. *Av.* 445.

b. So in such general expressions as these: ἐν δεξιᾷ ἐσπλέοντι *on the right as you sail in* (*with respect to one sailing in*), Thuc. 1, 24; συνελόντι or ὡς συνελόντι εἰπεῖν *concisely* or *to speak concisely* (lit. *for one who has made the matter concise*). So ὡς ἐμοί *in my opinion.* See **1166.**

DATIVE OF POSSESSION

1173. The dative with εἰμί, γίγνομαι, and similar verbs may denote the *possessor.* E.g.

εἰσὶν ἐμοὶ ἐκεῖ ξένοι *I have* (sunt mihi) *friends there*, Plat. *Crito* 45 c; τίς ξύμμαχος γενήσεταί μοι; *what ally shall I find?* Ar. *Eq.* 222; ἄλλοις μὲν χρήματά ἐστι πολλά, ἡμῖν δὲ ξύμμαχοι ἀγαθοί *others have plenty of money, but we have good allies*, Thuc. 1, 86.

Dative of Agent

1174. *a.* The dative, denoting the person interested, may appear as the *agent* with the perfect and pluperfect passive, rarely with other passive tenses (**1236**). E.g.

ἐξετάσαι τί πέπρακται τοῖς ἄλλοις *to ask what has been done by the others*, Dem. 2, 27; ἐπειδὴ αὐτοῖς παρεσκεύαστο *when preparation had been made by them* (*when they had their preparations made*), Thuc. 1, 46; πολλαὶ θεραπεῖαι τοῖς ἰατροῖς ηὕρηνται *many cures have been discovered by physicians*, Isoc. 8, 39; τοῖς Κερκυραίοις οὐχ ἑωρῶντο (αἱ νῆες) *the ships were not visible to the Corcyraeans*, Thuc. 1, 51.

b. With the verbal adjective in -τέος, in its personal construction (**1597**), the agent is expressed by the dative; in its impersonal construction (**1599**), by the dative or the accusative.

Dative with Adjectives, Adverbs, and Substantives

1175. The dative follows many adjectives, adverbs, and substantives of kindred meaning with the verbs of **1160** and **1165**. E.g.

δυσμενὴς φίλοις *hostile to friends*, E. *Med.* 1151; ὕποχος τοῖς νόμοις *subject to the laws*; ἐπικίνδυνον τῇ πόλει *dangerous to the state*; βλαβερὸν τῷ σώματι *hurtful to the body*; εὔνους ἑαυτῷ *kind to himself*; ἐναντίος αὐτῷ *opposed to him* (cf. **1146**); τοῖσδ' ἅπασι κοινόν *common to all these*, Aesch. *Ag.* 523; συμφερόντως αὐτῷ *profitably to himself*; ἐμποδὼν ἐμοί *in my way*; τὰ παρ' ἡμῶν δῶρα τοῖς θεοῖς *the gifts (given) by us to the gods*, Plat. *Euthyph.* 15 a. So with an objective genitive and a dative; e.g. ἐπὶ καταδουλώσει τῶν Ἑλλήνων Ἀθηναίοις *for the subjugation of the Greeks to the Athenians*, Thuc. 3, 10.

1176. The dative is thus used with all words implying *likeness* or *unlikeness*. Here it is not always possible to distinguish it from the instrumental dative. E.g.

σκιαῖς ἐοικότες *like shadows*; τὸ ὁμοιοῦν ἑαυτὸν ἄλλῳ *the making oneself like another*, Plat. *Rep.* 393 c; τούτοις ὁμοιότατον *most like these*, Plat. *G.* 513 b; ὡπλισμένοι τοῖς αὐτοῖς Κύρῳ ὅπλοις *armed with the same arms as Cyrus*, X. *C.* 7, 1, 2; ἢ ὁμοίου ὄντος τούτοις ἢ ἀνομοίου *being either like or unlike these*, Plat. *Ph.* 74 c; ὁμοίως δίκαιον ἀδίκῳ βλάψειν *that he will punish a just and an unjust man alike*, Plat. *Rep.* 364 c; ἰέναι ἀλλήλοις ἀνομοίως to move unlike one another, Plat. Tim. 36 d; τὸν ὁμώνυμον ἐμαυτῷ my namesake, Dem. 3, 21; οὔτε ἑαυτοῖς οὔτε ἀλλήλοις ὁμολογοῦσιν they agree neither with themselves nor with one another, Plat. Phdr. 237 c; ἦν αὐτῷ ὁμογνώμων he was of the same mind with him, Thuc. 8, 92; ἄτοπος ἡ ὁμοιότης τούτων ἐκείνοις remarkable is the likeness of these to the others, Plat. Th. 158 c.

1177. After adjectives of *likeness* an abridged form of expression (brachylogy) may be used; e.g. κόμαι Χαρίτεσσιν ὁμοῖαι hair like (that of) the Graces, Il. 17, 51; τὰς ἴσας πληγὰς ἐμοί the same number of blows that I receive, Ar. R. 636. Cf. "an eye like Mars."

Dative with Compound Verbs

1178. The dative with many compound verbs must be interpreted from the context. E.g. Ἥρῃ δ' ἀνέστη Ἄρτεμις Artemis opposed Hera (**1175**), Il. 20, 70; χώρᾳ πύργος ἀνέστα he arose as a tower (of strength) to the land, S. O. T. 1201.

1179. The dative is used with verbs compounded with σύν and many compounded with ἐν or ἐπί, and with some compounded with πρός, παρά, περί, and ὑπό. E.g.

τοῖς ὅρκοις ἐμμένει ὁ δῆμος the people abide by the oaths, X. H. 2, 4, 43; αἱ ... ἡδοναὶ ψυχῇ ἐπιστήμην οὐδεμίαν ἐμποιοῦσιν (such) pleasures produce no knowledge in the soul, X. M. 2, 1, 20; ἐνέκειντο τῷ Περικλεῖ they attacked Pericles, Thuc. 2, 59; ἐμαυτῷ συνῄδη οὐδὲν ἐπισταμένῳ I was conscious (lit. shared with myself the knowledge) that I knew nothing, Plat. Ap. 22 d; ἤδη ποτέ σοι ἐπῆλθεν; did it ever occur to you? X. M. 4, 3, 3; προσέβαλλον τῷ τειχίσματι they attacked the fortification, Thuc. 4, 11; ἀδελφὸς ἀνδρὶ παρείη let a brother stand by a man (i.e. let a man's brother stand by him), Plat. Rep. 362 d; τοῖς κακοῖς περιπίπτουσιν they are involved in evils, X. M. 4, 2, 27; ὑπόκειται τὸ πεδίον τῷ ἱερῷ the plain lies below the temple, Aeschin. 3, 118.

Instrumental Dative

INSTRUMENTAL PROPER

1180. The instrumental dative, representing the lost instrumental case (**1040**), may denote the means, manner, or cause (instrument proper), or association and accompaniment (sociative or comitative dative).

1181. The dative is used to denote *cause, manner,* and *means* or *instrument.* E.g.

CAUSE: νόσῳ ἀποθανών having died of disease, Thuc. 8, 84; οὐ γὰρ κακονοίᾳ τοῦτο ποιεῖ, ἀλλ' ἀγνοίᾳ for he does not do this from ill-will, but from *ignorance*, X. *C.* 3, 1, 38; βιαζόμενοι τοῦ πιεῖν ἐπιθυμίᾳ *forced by a desire to drink*, Thuc. 7, 84; αἰσχύνομαί τοι ταῖς πρότερον ἁμαρτίαις *I am ashamed of* (*because of*) *my former faults*, Ar. *Nub.* 1355. MANNER: δρόμῳ ἵεντο ἐς τοὺς βαρβάρους *they rushed upon the barbarians in double time*, Hdt. 6, 112; κραυγῇ πολλῇ ἐπίασιν *they will advance with a loud shout*, X. *An.* 1, 7, 4; τῇ ἀληθείᾳ *in truth*; τῷ ὄντι *in reality*; βίᾳ *forcibly*; ταύτῃ *in this manner, thus*; λόγῳ *in word*; ἔργῳ *in deed*; τῇ ἐμῇ γνώμῃ *in my judgment*; ἰδίᾳ *privately*; δημοσίᾳ *publicly*; κοινῇ *in common*. MEANS or INSTRUMENT: ὁρῶμεν τοῖς ὀφθαλμοῖς *we see with our eyes*; γνωσθέντες τῇ σκευῇ τῶν ὅπλων *recognized by the fashion of their arms*, Thuc. 1, 8; κακοῖς ἰᾶσθαι κακά *to cure evils by evils*, S. *frag.* 75; οὐδεὶς ἔπαινον ἡδοναῖς ἐκτήσατο *no one gains praise by* (*indulging in*) *pleasures*, Stob. 29, 31.

1182. The dative of *respect* is a form of the dative of *manner*; e.g. τοῖς σώμασιν ἀδύνατοι, . . . ταῖς ψυχαῖς ἀνόητοι *incapable in their bodies*, . . . *senseless in their minds*, X. *M.* 2, 1, 31; ὕστερον ὃν τῇ τάξει, πρότερον τῇ δυνάμει καὶ κρεῖττόν ἐστιν *although it is later in order, it is prior and superior in power*, Dem. 3, 15. So πόλις, Θάψακος ὀνόματι *a city, Thapsacus by name*, X. *An.* 1, 4, 11. Cf. **1056.**

1183. Χράομαι *to use* (*to serve one's self by*) has the instrumental dative; e.g. χρῶνται ἀργυρίῳ *they use money*. A neuter pronoun (e.g. τί, τι, ὅ τι, or τοῦτο) may be added as a cognate accusative (**1049**); e.g. τί χρήσεταί ποτ' αὐτῷ; *what will he ever do with him?* (lit. *what use will he make of him?*), Ar. *Ach.* 935. So occasionally νομίζω; e.g. ἀγῶσι καὶ θυσίαις διετησίοις νομίζοντες *holding games and yearly festivals*, Thuc. 2, 38.

1184. The dative of *manner* is used with comparatives to denote the *degree of difference*. E.g.

πολλῷ κρεῖττόν ἐστιν *it is much better* (*better by much*); ἐὰν τῇ κεφαλῇ μείζονά τινα φῇς εἶναι καὶ ἐλάττω *if you say that anyone is a head taller or shorter* (lit. *by the head*), Plat. *Ph.* 101 a; πόλι λογίμῳ ἡ Ἑλλὰς γέγονε ἀσθενεστέρη *Greece has become weaker by one illustrious city*, Hdt. 6, 106; τοσούτῳ ἥδιον ζῶ *I live so much the more happily*, X. *C.* 8, 3, 40; τέχνη δ' ἀνάγκης ἀσθενεστέρα μακρῷ *and art is weaker than necessity by far*, Aesch. *Pr.* 514.

1185. So sometimes with superlatives, and even with other expressions which imply comparison; e.g. ὀρθότατα μακρῷ *most correctly by far*, Plat. *Lg.* 768 c; σχεδὸν δέκα ἔτεσι πρὸ τῆς ἐν Σαλαμῖνι ναυμαχίας *about ten years before the sea-fight at Salamis*, ibid. 698 c. But the neuter pronouns οὐδέν (μηδέν), τί, and τι are in the accusative with a comparative; e.g. οὐδὲν ἧττον *none the less, just as much*.

DATIVE OF ACCOMPANIMENT

1186. The dative is used to denote that by which any person or thing is *accompanied* (sociative dative). E.g.

τῷ στίβῳ τῶν ἵππων ἕπεσθαι to follow the horses' tracks, X. An. 7, 3, 43; ἐλθόντων Περσῶν˙παμπληθεῖ στόλῳ when the Persians came with an army in full force, X. An. 3, 2, 11; ἡμεῖς καὶ ἵπποις τοῖς δυνατωτάτοις καὶ ἀνδράσι πορευώμεθα let us march with the strongest horses and men, X. C. 5, 3, 35; οἱ Λακεδαιμόνιοι τῷ τε κατὰ γῆν στρατῷ προσέβαλλον τῷ τειχίσματι καὶ ταῖς ναυσίν the Lacedaemonians attacked the wall both with their land forces and with their ships, Thuc. 4, 11.

1187. This dative sometimes takes the dative of αὐτός for emphasis; e.g. μίαν (ναῦν) αὐτοῖς ἀνδράσιν εἷλον they took one (ship), men and all, Thuc. 2, 90; χαμαὶ βάλε δένδρεα μακρὰ αὐτῇσιν ῥίζῃσι καὶ αὐτοῖς ἄνθεσι μήλων he threw to the ground tall trees, with their very roots and their fruit-blossoms, Il. 9, 541.

1188. The dative is used with words implying *agreement* or *disagreement*, *union* or *approach*. E.g.

ἀμφισβητοῦσιν οἱ φίλοι τοῖς φίλοις, ἐρίζουσι δὲ οἱ ἐχθροὶ ἀλλήλοις friends dispute with friends, but enemies quarrel with one another, Plat. Prot. 337 b; τοῖς πονηροῖς διαφέρεσθαι to be at variance with the bad, X. M. 2, 9, 8; κακοῖς ὁμιλῶν associating with bad men, Men. Mon. 274; τοῖς φρονιμωτάτοις πλησίαζε draw near to the wisest, Isoc. 2, 13; ἄλλοις κοινωνεῖν to share with others, Plat. Rep. 369 e; τὸ ἑαυτοῦ ἔργον ἅπασι κοινὸν κατατιθέναι to make his work common to all, ibid.; δεόμενοι τοὺς φεύγοντας ξυναλλάξαι σφισί asking to bring the exiles to terms with them, Thuc. 1, 24; βούλομαί σε αὐτῷ διαλέγεσθαι I want you to converse with him, Plat. Lys. 211 c; προσβολὰς ποιούμενοι τῷ τείχει making assaults upon the wall, Thuc. 4, 23; ἐπανάστασις μέρους τινὸς τῷ ὅλῳ τῆς ψυχῆς a rebellion of one part of the soul against the whole, Plat. Rep. 444 b.

1189. To this class belong μάχομαι *fight*, πολεμέω *make war*, and similar expressions; e.g. μάχεσθαι τοῖς Θηβαίοις to fight against the Thebans, πολεμοῦσιν ἡμῖν they are at war with us. So ἐς χεῖρας ἐλθεῖν τινι or ἐς λόγους ἐλθεῖν τινι to come to a conflict (or a conference) with any one, διὰ φιλίας ἰέναι τινί to be on friendly terms with one. See Thuc. 7, 44; 8, 48. X. An. 3, 2, 8.

1190. The dative thus depends on adverbs of *place* and *time*; e.g. ἅμα τῇ ἡμέρᾳ at daybreak; ὕδωρ ὁμοῦ τῷ πηλῷ ᾑματωμένον water stained with blood together with the mud, Thuc. 7, 84; τὰ τούτοις ἐφεξῆς what comes next to this, Plat. Tim. 30 c; τοῖσδ' ἐγγύς nigh unto these, E. Her. 37 (ἐγγύς usually has the genitive, 1153).

Locative Dative

1191. The dative frequently represents the lost locative case (1040); e.g. Μαραθῶνι at Marathon, κύκλῳ in a circle, τῇδε this way, here. The locative dative may denote *place* or *date*.

The true locative survives only in adverbial forms; e.g. ἐκεῖ *there*, εἰ *if* (lit. *where*), Dor. πεῖ *where*, τηνεῖ *there*.

DATIVE OF PLACE

1192. In poetry, the dative without a preposition often denotes the place *where*. E.g.

Ἑλλάδι οἰκία ναίων *inhabiting dwellings in Hellas*, Il. 16, 595; αἰθέρι ναίων *dwelling in heaven*, Il. 4, 166; οὔρεσι *on the mountains*, Il. 13, 390; τόξ' ὤμοισιν ἔχων *having his bow on his shoulders*, Il. 1, 45; μίμνει ἀγρῷ *he remains in the country*, Od. 11, 188; ἧσθαι δόμοις *to sit at home*, Aesch. Ag. 862; νῦν ἀγροῖσι τυγχάνει (sc. ὤν) *now he happens to be in the country*, S. El. 313; σθένος ὦρσε ἑκάστῳ καρδίῃ *she roused strength in each man's heart*, Il. 11, 11 (yet for this cf. 906).

1193. In prose, the dative of place is chiefly used of Attic demes and a few other proper names; e.g. ἡ Μαραθῶνι μάχη *the battle of Marathon*, Πυθοῖ *at Pytho (Delphi)*. Ordinarily a preposition is used; e.g. ἐν Ἀθήναις *in Athens* (place *where*), εἰς Ἀθήνας *to Athens* (place *whither*).

DATIVE OF TIME

1194. The dative without a preposition often denotes time *when*. This is confined chiefly to words which express definitely a date, such as the *day, night, month*, or *year*, and names of *festivals*. E.g.

τῇ αὐτῇ ἡμέρᾳ ἀπέθανεν *he died on the same day*; (Ἑρμαῖ) μιᾷ νυκτὶ οἱ πλεῖστοι περιεκόπησαν *the most of the Hermae were mutilated in one night*, Thuc. 6, 27; οἱ Σάμιοι ἐξεπολιορκήθησαν ἐν ἄτῳ μηνί *the Samians were taken by siege in the ninth month*, Thuc. 1, 117; δεκάτῳ ἔτει ξυνέβησαν *they came to terms in the tenth year*, Thuc. 1, 103; ὡσπερεὶ Θεσμοφορίοις νηστεύομεν *we fast as if it were (on) the Thesmophoria*, Ar. Av. 1519. So τῇ ὑστεραίᾳ (sc. ἡμέρᾳ) *on the following day*, and δευτέρᾳ, τρίτῃ, *on the second, third*, etc., in giving the day of the month.

1195. Even the words mentioned, except names of festivals, generally take ἐν when no modifying word is joined with them. Thus ἐν νυκτί *at night* (rarely, in poetry, νυκτί), but μιᾷ νυκτί *in one night*; τῷ αὐτῷ χειμῶνι *in the same winter*, but more often ἐν τῷ αὐτῷ χειμῶνι, Thuc. 2, 34. Titles of books are often thus given in citation: Εὐριπίδης Ἀλκήστιδι *in Euripides, Alcestis*.

1196. A few expressions occur like ὑστέρῳ χρόνῳ *in after time*, χειμῶνος ὥρᾳ *in the winter season*, νουμηνίᾳ *(new-moon day) on the first of the month*, and others in poetry.

PREPOSITIONS

1197. The prepositions were originally adverbs, and as such they appear in composition with verbs (see **868 a**). They are used also as independent words, to connect substantives with other parts of the sentence.

1198. Homer often shows the original adverbial use of the preposition, e.g. ἀπὸ πατρὶ φίλῳ δόμεναι κούρην *back to her dear father to give the maiden*, *Il.* 1, 98, which gradually became πατρὶ ἀποδοῦναι *to restore to her father*, in which the adverb becomes part of the verb. In other instances it is connected more closely with the substantive, e.g. ἐξ ὀχέων σὺν τεύχεσιν ἆλτο *forth from the chariot he leapt with all his arms*, *Il.* 4, 419, so that the preposition is felt to govern the substantive.

1199. *Tmesis* (τμῆσις *cutting*, from τέμνω *cut*) is a term applied to the artificial separation of a preposition from its verb in poetry after Homer, especially by the interposition of enclitics and particles; e.g. πρό γε στενάξεις *too soon you mourn*, Aesch. *Pr.* 696.

1200. In general, the meaning proper to a case when used alone is retained when the case follows a preposition. The accusative denotes that *toward* which, *over* which, *along* which, or *upon* which motion is directed; the genitive, that *from* which anything proceeds (ablatival), or *connection* of any kind; the dative, that *in* which, *near* which, or *with* which (instrumental) anything is done. Thus παρά *near, by the side of*, is modified in meaning by the case following it; e.g. παρὰ τοῦ βασιλέως *from (the side of) the king*, παρὰ τῷ βασιλεῖ *beside the king* (or *at the court*), παρὰ τὸν βασιλέα *into the king's presence* (**1220**).

1201. The original adverbial use of the prepositions sometimes appears when they are used without a case; this occurs especially in the older Greek, seldom in Attic prose. Thus περί *round about* or *exceedingly*, in Homer; and πρὸς δέ or καὶ πρός *and besides* (occasionally in Attic prose), ἐν δέ *and among them*, ἐπὶ δέ *and upon this*, μετὰ δέ *and next*, in Herodotus.

1202. Position. *a.* A preposition sometimes follows its case, or a verb to which it belongs; e.g. νεῶν ἄπο; ὀλέσας ἄπο, *Od.* 9, 534. For the accent (*anastrophe*), see **135, 136**. Attic prose admits this only with περί; e.g. ὧν ἐγὼ οὐδὲν πέρι ἐπαΐω *which I don't profess any knowledge about*, Plat. *Ap.* 19 c.

b. A preposition may be separated from its case by particles, such as μέν, δέ, γε, τε, γάρ, οὖν; by the parenthetical οἶμαι *I think*; by attributives modifying the noun.

c. In poetry a preposition often stands between a noun and its attributive; e.g. ἡμετέρῳ ἐνὶ οἴκῳ *in our house*, *Il.* 1, 30. This order, very common in Latin, is rare in Attic prose.

1203. A few prepositions are used adverbially, with a verb (generally ἐστί) understood; e.g. πάρα for πάρεστι, ἔπι and μέτα (in Homer) for ἔπεστι and μέτεστι. So ἔνι for ἔνεστι, and poetic ἄνα up! for ἀνάστα (ἀνάστηθι). For the accent, see **135 b**.

1204. a. Sometimes εἰς with the accusative, and ἐκ or ἀπό with the genitive, are used in expressions which themselves imply no motion, with reference to some motion implied or expressed in the context; e.g. αἱ ξύνοδοι ἐς τὸ ἱερὸν ἐγίγνοντο the synods were held in the temple (lit. into the temple, involving the idea of going into the temple to hold the synods), Thuc. 1, 96; τοῖς ἐκ Πύλου ληφθεῖσι (ἐοικότες) like the men captured (in Pylos, and brought home) from Pylos, i.e. the captives from Pylos, Ar. Nub. 186; διήρπαστο καὶ αὐτὰ τὰ ἀπὸ τῶν οἰκιῶν ξύλα even the very timbers in the houses (lit. from the houses) had been stolen, X. An. 2, 2, 16; οἱ ἐκ τῆς ἀγορᾶς καταλιπόντες τὰ ὤνια ἔφυγον the people in the market-place abandoned their wares and fled, X. An. 1, 2, 18; οὐχ οἷοί τ' ἔφασαν εἶναι τοὺς ἐκ τῆς θαλάττης ἀνελέσθαι they said that they were unable to pick up the men in the water, Lys. 12, 36. See Plat. Ap. 32 b, where τοὺς ἐκ τῆς ναυμαχίας is used of the same event.

b. So ἐν with the dative sometimes occurs with verbs of motion, referring to rest which follows the motion; e.g. ἐν τῷ ποταμῷ ἔπεσον they fell (into and remained) in the river, X. Ages. 1, 32; ἐν γούνασι πῖπτε Διώνης she fell in Dione's lap, Il. 5, 370: see S. El. 1476.

These (a and b) are instances of the so-called constructio praegnans.

c. Source or starting-point often determines the choice of a preposition; e.g. ἀπὸ παιδίων ἀρξάμενοι beginning with boyhood, Hdt. 3, 11. Especially with verbs of tying; e.g. ἐξ ἀξίου τοῦ ξύλου (ἀπάγξασθαι) to hang oneself on a proper beam, Ar. R. 736; καταδήσας ἀπὸ δένδρων τοὺς ἵππους tying his horses to trees, X. H. 4, 4, 10.

1205. Adverbs of place are sometimes interchanged in the same way (**1204**); e.g. ὅποι καθέσταμεν where we are standing (lit. whither we have set ourselves, **1250 c**), S. O. C. 23; τίς ἀγνοεῖ τὸν ἐκεῖθεν πόλεμον δεῦρο ἥξοντα; who does not know that the war that is there will come hither? Dem. 1, 15.

So ἔνθεν καὶ ἔνθεν on this side and on that, like ἐκ δεξιᾶς (a dextra) on the right. Cf. **1204 c**.

1206. A preposition is often followed by its own case when it is part of a compound verb. E.g.

παρεκομίζοντο τὴν Ἰταλίαν they sailed along the coast of Italy, Thuc. 6, 44; ἐσῆλθέ με it occurred to me, Hdt. 7, 46; ἐξελθέτω τις δωμάτων let some one come forth from the house, Aesch. Ch. 663; ξυνέπρασσον αὐτῷ Ἀμφισσῆς the Amphisseans assisted him, Thuc. 3, 101. For other examples of the genitive, see **1132**; for those of the dative, see **1179**.

1207. a. Four prepositions take the genitive only: ἀντί, ἀπό, ἐξ (ἐκ), πρό.
b. Two take the dative only: ἐν, σύν.

c. Two take the accusative only: ἀνά, εἰς (ἐς).

d. Five take the genitive and accusative: ἀμφί, διά, κατά, μετά, ὑπέρ.

e. Five take the genitive, dative, and accusative: ἐπί, παρά, περί, πρός, ὑπό.

These are the uses in prose. For ἀνά and μετά with the dative in poetry, see 1210, 1219; for ἀμφί with the dative in poetry and Hdt., see 1209. For the improper prepositions, see 1227.

1208. The genitive (of source) is used with different prepositions to express the *agent*. With ὑπό *by*, the regular preposition in prose with a passive verb, the genitive denotes persons or things personified; with παρά *from* the idea of source is uppermost; with διά *through*, the intermediary; with ἀπό *from*, the starting-point, denoting *in consequence of* (often in Thucydides); ἐξ *from* denoting source is common in Hdt. and in poetry; πρός *in the presence of*, and therefore *with the connivance of*, especially in Hdt. and in poetry.

LIST OF PREPOSITIONS

1209. ἀμφί (Lat. amb-, cf. ἄμφω *both*), originally *on both sides of*; hence *about*. Chiefly poetic and Ionic. In Attic prose chiefly with the accusative, but περί is more common.

a. With the GENITIVE (very rare in prose), *about, concerning*: ἀμφὶ γυναικός *about a woman*, Aesch. *Ag.* 62.

b. With the DATIVE (only poetic and Ionic), *about, concerning, on account of*: ἀμφ' ὤμοισι *about his shoulders*, *Il.* 11, 527; ἀμφὶ τῷ νόμῳ τούτῳ *concerning this law*, Hdt. 1, 140; ἀμφὶ φόβῳ *through fear*, E. *Or.* 825.

c. With the ACCUSATIVE, *about, near*, of place, time, number, etc.: ἀμφ' ἅλα *by the sea*, *Il.* 1, 409; ἀμφὶ δείλην *towards evening*, X. *C.* 5, 4, 16; ἀμφὶ Πλειάδων δύσιν *about (the time of) the Pleiads' setting*, Aesch. *Ag.* 826. So ἀμφὶ δεῖπνον εἶχεν *he was at dinner*, X. *C.* 5, 5, 44. οἱ ἀμφὶ Κῦρον *Cyrus and his staff* (*those in the entourage of Cyrus*); οἱ ἀμφὶ Πλάτωνα *Plato and his school* (in later Greek *Platonists* or simply *Plato*, **950** *b*).

In COMP.: *about, on both sides, in two ways* (cf. ἀμφίβολος *ambiguous*).

1210. ἀνά (cf. adv. ἄνω *above*), originally *up* (opposed to κατά).

a. With the DATIVE (only epic and lyric), *up on*: ἀνὰ σκήπτρῳ *on a staff*, *Il.* 1, 15.

b. With the ACCUSATIVE, *up along*; and of motion *over, through, among* (cf. κατά):

(1) of PLACE: ἀνὰ τὸν ποταμόν *up the river*, Hdt. 2, 96; ἀνὰ στρατόν *throughout the host*, *Il.* 1, 10; οἰκεῖν ἀνὰ τὰ ὄρη *to dwell on the tops of the hills*, X. *An.* 3, 5, 16.

(2) of TIME: ἀνὰ τὸν πόλεμον *through the war*, Hdt. 8, 123; ἀνὰ χρόνον *in course of time*, Hdt. 5, 27.

(3) in DISTRIBUTIVE expressions: ἀνὰ ἑκατόν *by hundreds*, X. *An.* 5, 4, 12; ἀνὰ πᾶσαν ἡμέρην *every day*, Hdt. 2, 37 (so X. *C.* 1, 2, 8).

In COMP.: *up* (cf. ἀναβαίνω *go up*), *back* (cf. ἀναχωρέω *retire*), *again* (cf. ἀναπάλλω *swing back and forth*).

1211. ἀντί, with GENITIVE only, *instead of, for*: ἀντὶ πολέμου εἰρήνην ἐλώμεθα *in place of war let us choose peace*, Thuc. 4, 20; ἀνθ᾽ ὧν *wherefore*, Aesch. *Pr.* 31; ἀντ᾽ ἀδελφοῦ *for a brother's sake*, S. *El.* 537. Original meaning, *over against, against*.

In COMP.: *against, in opposition, in return, instead*.

1212. ἀπό (Lat. ab), with GENITIVE only, *from, off from, away from*; originally (as opposed to ἐξ) denoting *separation* or *departure* from something:

(1) of PLACE: ἀφ᾽ ἵππων ἆλτο *he leaped from the car* (*horses*), *Il.* 16, 733; ἀπὸ θαλάσσης *at a distance from the sea*, Thuc. 1, 7.

(2) of TIME: ἀπὸ τούτου τοῦ χρόνου *from this time*, X. *An.* 7, 5, 8.

(3) of CAUSE or ORIGIN: ἀπὸ τούτου τοῦ τολμήματος ἐπῃνέθη *for this bold act he was praised*, Thuc. 2, 25; τὸ ζῆν ἀπὸ πολέμου *to live by war*, Hdt. 5, 6; ἀπ᾽ οὗ ἡμεῖς γεγόναμεν *from whom we are sprung*, Hdt. 7, 150; sometimes the agent (**1208**): ἐπράχθη ἀπ᾽ αὐτῶν οὐδέν *nothing was done by them*, Thuc. 1, 17.

In COMP.: *from, away, off, in return, back* (cf. ἀποδίδωμι *give what is due*). Also negative (ἀπαγορεύω *forbid*) and intensive (ἀποφαίνω *show forth*).

1213. διά *through*.

a. With the GENITIVE:

(1) of PLACE: διὰ ἀσπίδος ἦλθε *it went through the shield*, *Il.* 7, 251.

(2) of TIME: διὰ νυκτός *through the night*, X. *An.* 4, 6, 22.

(3) of INTERVALS of time or place: διὰ πολλοῦ χρόνου *after a long time*, Ar. *Pl.* 1045; διὰ τρίτης ἡμέρης *every other day*, Hdt. 2, 37; διὰ ταχέων *soon after*, Plat. *Ap.* 32 e.

(4) of MEANS: ἔλεγε δι᾽ ἑρμηνέως *he spoke through an interpreter*, X. *An.* 2, 3, 17.

(5) in various phrases like δι᾽ οἴκτου ἔχειν *to pity*; διὰ φιλίας ἰέναι, *to be on friendly terms* (**1189**).

b. With the ACCUSATIVE:

(1) of CAUSE or AGENCY, *on account of, by help of, by reason of*: διὰ τοῦτο *on this account*; δι᾽ Ἀθήνην *by help of Athena*, *Od.* 8, 520; οὐ δι᾽ ἐμέ *not owing to me*, Dem. 18, 18; εἰ μὴ δι᾽ ἄνδρας ἀγαθούς *had it not been for some brave men*, Lys. 12, 60 (**1424**).

(2) of PLACE or TIME, *through, during* (poetic): διὰ δώματα *through the halls*, *Il.* 1, 600; διὰ νύκτα *through the night*, *Od.* 19, 66.

In COMP. (Lat. di-, dis-): *through* (διαβαίνω *cross*, διαμάχομαι *fight it out*); *apart, throughly*, i.e. *thoroughly* (διαρπάζω *tear in pieces*, διαφθείρω *destroy utterly*); *severally* (διαδίδωμι *distribute*, διαλέγομαι *converse*).

1214. εἰς or ἐς, with ACCUSATIVE only, *into, to,* originally (as opposed to ἐξ) *to within* (Lat. in with the accusative): εἰς always in Attic prose, except in Thucydides, who has ἐς. Both εἰς and ἐς are for ἐνς ; see also ἐν.

(1) of PLACE: διέβησαν ἐς Σικελίαν *they crossed over into Sicily,* Thuc. 6, 2 ; εἰς Πέρσας ἐπορεύετο *he departed for Persia (the Persians),* X. C. 8, 5, 20 ; τὸ ἐς Παλλήνην τεῖχος *the wall toward (looking to) Pallene,* Thuc. 1, 56.

(2) of TIME: ἐς ἠῶ *until dawn,* Od. 11, 375 ; so of a time *looked forward to:* προεῖπε τοῖς ἑαυτοῦ εἰς τρίτην ἡμέραν παρεῖναι *he gave notice to his men to be present the next day but one,* X. C. 3, 1, 42. So ἔτος εἰς ἔτος *from year to year,* S. Ant. 340 ; εἰς ἐνιαυτόν *year in, year out,* Solon 12, 47. So ἐς ὅ *until,* εἰς τὸν ἅπαντα χρόνον *for all time.*

(3) of NUMBER and MEASURE : εἰς διακοσίους *(amounting) to two hundred,* εἰς δύναμιν *to (the extent of) one's power.*

(4) of PURPOSE or REFERENCE : παιδεύειν εἰς τὴν ἀρετήν *to train for virtue,* Plat. G. 519 e ; εἰς πάντα πρῶτον εἶναι *to be first for everything,* Plat. Ch. 158 a ; χρήσιμον εἴς τι *useful for anything.*

In COMP.: *into, in, to.*

1215. ἐν, with DATIVE only, *in* (Hom. ἐνί), equivalent to Lat. in with the ablative ;

(1) of PLACE: ἐν Σπάρτῃ *in Sparta;* — with words implying a number of people, *among*: ἐν γυναιξὶ ἄλκιμος *brave among women,* E. Or. 754 ; ἐν πᾶσι *in the presence of all*; ἐν δικασταῖς *before* (coram) *a court*; ἐν τοῖς τριάκοντα *at meetings of the Thirty,* Lys. 12, 6.

(2) of TIME: ἐν τούτῳ τῷ ἔτει *in the course of this year*; ἐν χειμῶνι *in winter*; ἐν ἔτεσι πεντήκοντα *within fifty years,* Thuc. 1, 118.

(3) of other relations: figuratively, τὸν Περικλέα ἐν ὀργῇ εἶχον *they were angry with P. (held him in anger),* Thuc. 2, 21 ; ἐν πολλῇ ἀπορίᾳ ἦσαν *they were in great perplexity,* X. An. 3, 1, 2. CAUSE and DEPENDENCE : ἐν τῷ θεῷ τὸ τούτου τέλος ἦν, οὐκ ἐν ἐμοί *the issue of this was with (in the power of) God, not with me,* Dem. 18, 193 ; ἐν δορὶ μέν μοι μᾶζα *my staff of life is my spear (depends on it),* Archil. 2. INSTRUMENT: ἐν ξέναισι χερσὶ κηδευθείς *tended in death by strangers' hands,* S. El. 1141.

As ἐν was the form out of which εἰς and ἐς were developed, ἐν allowed the accusative (like Latin in) in some dialects, especially Aeolic ; e.g. ἐν πάντα νόμον *in every kind of government,* Pind. P. 2, 86.

In COMP.: *in, on, at.*

1216. ἐξ or ἐκ, with GENITIVE only (Lat. ex, e), *from, out of*; originally (as contrasted with ἀπό) *from within* (cf. εἰς).

(1) of PLACE: ἐκ Σπάρτης φεύγει *he is banished from Sparta.*

(2) of TIME: ἐκ παλαιοτάτου *from the most ancient time,* Thuc. 1, 18.

(3) of ORIGIN : ὄναρ ἐκ Διός ἐστιν *the dream comes from Zeus,* Il. 1, 63.

So also with passive verbs: ἐκ Φοίβου δαμείς *destroyed by Phoebus*, S. *Ph.* 335 (the agent viewed as the source), seldom in Attic prose. See 1208.

(4) of GROUND for a judgment: ἐβουλεύοντο ἐκ τῶν παρόντων *they took counsel with a view to (starting from) the present state of things*, Thuc. 3, 29; ἐκ τούτων σκοπεῖν *to consider in (the light of) these facts*.

In COMP.: *out, from, away, off, thoroughly* (ἔξοιδα *know all*).

1217. ἐπί *on, upon.*

a. With the GENITIVE:

(1) of PLACE: ἐπὶ πύργου ἔστη *he stood on a tower, Il.* 16, 700; sometimes *towards*: πλεύσαντες ἐπὶ Σάμου *having sailed towards Samos*, Thuc. 1, 116; so ἐπὶ τῆς τοιαύτης γενέσθαι γνώμης *to adopt (go over to) such an opinion*, Dem. 4, 6.

(2) of TIME: ἐφ' ἡμῶν *in our time*, ἐπ' εἰρήνης *in time of peace, Il.* 2, 797.

(3) of RELATION or REFERENCE to an object: τοὺς ἐπὶ τῶν πραγμάτων *those in charge of (public) affairs*, Dem. 18, 247; ἐπὶ Λιβύης ἔχειν τὸ ὄνομα *to be named for Libya*, Hdt. 4, 45; ἐπί τινος λέγων *speaking with reference to a person*, see Plat. *Ch.* 155 d; so ἐπὶ σχολῆς *at leisure*; ἐπ' ἴσας (sc. μοίρας) *in equal measure*, S. *El.* 1061.

b. With the DATIVE:

(1) of PLACE: ἧντ' ἐπὶ πύργῳ *they sat on a tower, Il.* 3, 153; πόλις ἐπὶ τῇ θαλάττῃ οἰκουμένη *a city situated upon (by) the sea*, X. *An.* 1, 4, 1.

(2) of TIME (of immediate succession): ἐπὶ τούτοις *thereupon*, X. *C.* 5, 5, 21.

(3) of CAUSE, PURPOSE, CONDITIONS: ἐπὶ παιδεύσει μέγα φρονοῦντες *proud of their education*, Plat. *Prot.* 342 d; ἐπ' ἐξαγωγῇ *for exportation*, Hdt. 7, 156; ἐπὶ τοῖσδε *on these conditions*, Ar. *Av.* 1602; ἐπὶ τῇ ἴσῃ καὶ ὁμοίᾳ *on fair and equal terms*, Thuc. 1, 27. So ἐφ' ᾧ and ἐφ' ᾧτε (1477).

(4) Likewise *over, for, at, in addition to, in the power of*: ἐπὶ τῷ σίτῳ ὄψον *a relish with bread*, X. *M.* 3, 14, 2; τὸ ἐπὶ τῷδε *after this*, E. *Hipp.* 855; ἐπὶ τῷ ἀδελφῷ *in his brother's power*, X. *An.* 1, 1, 4.

c. With the ACCUSATIVE:

(1) of PLACE: *to, up to, towards, against*: ἀναβὰς ἐπὶ τὸν ἵππον *mounting his horse*, X. *An.* 1, 8, 3; ἐπὶ δεξιά *to the right, on the right hand*, X. *An.* 6, 4, 1; ἐπὶ βασιλέα ἰέναι *to march against the King*, X. *An.* 1, 3, 1; ἐλθεῖν ἐπί τινα *to accost one*.

(2) of TIME or SPACE, denoting *extension*: ἐπὶ δέκα ἔτη *for ten years*, Thuc. 3, 68; ἐπ' ἐννέα κεῖτο πέλεθρα *he covered (lay over) nine plethra*, Od. 11, 577; so ἐπὶ πολύ *widely*; τὸ ἐπὶ πολύ *for the most part*; ἐκ τοῦ ἐπὶ πλεῖστον *from the remotest period*, Thuc. 1, 2.

(3) of an OBJECT sought: κατῆλθον ἐπὶ ποιητήν *I came down for a poet*, Ar. *R.* 1418; τρέχω ἐπ' ἀφύας *I run to get anchovies*, Ar. *Av.* 77.

In COMP.: *upon, over, after, toward, to, for, at, against, besides.*

1218. κατά (cf. adverb κάτω *below*), originally *down* (opposed to ἀνά).

a. With the GENITIVE:

(1) *down from:* ἀλάμενοι κατὰ τῆς πέτρας *by leaping down from the rock,* X. *An.* 4, 2, 17.

(2) *down upon:* μύρον κατὰ τῆς κεφαλῆς καταχέαντες *pouring perfume on his head,* Plat. *Rep.* 398 a.

(3) *beneath:* κατὰ χθονὸς ἔκρυψε *he buried beneath the earth,* S. *Ant.* 24; οἱ κατὰ χθονὸς θεοί *the gods below,* Aesch. *Pers.* 689.

(4) *against:* λέγων καθ' ἡμῶν *recounting against me* (*us*), S. *Ph.* 65; in lawsuits, Αἰσχίνης κατὰ Κτησιφῶντος *Aeschines against Ctesiphon.*

b. With the ACCUSATIVE, *down along:* of motion *over, through, among, into, against;* also *according to, concerning, opposite, dividing.*

(1) of PLACE: κατὰ ῥοῦν *down stream;* κατὰ γῆν καὶ κατὰ θάλατταν *by land and by sea,* X. *An.* 3, 2, 13; κατὰ Σινώπην πόλιν *opposite the city of Sinope,* Hdt. 1, 76.

(2) of TIME: κατὰ τὸν πόλεμον *during* (*at the time of*) *the war,* Hdt. 7, 137; κατὰ Ἄμασιν *about the time of Amasis,* Hdt. 2, 134.

(3) DISTRIBUTIVELY: κατὰ τρεῖς *by threes, three by three;* καθ' ἡμέραν or καθ' ἑκάστην ἡμέραν *day by day, daily.*

(4) *according to, concerning:* κατὰ τοὺς νόμους *according to law,* Dem. 8, 2; τὸ κατ' ἐμέ *as regards myself,* Dem. 18, 247; μεῖζω ἢ κατ' ἄνθρωπον σοφίαν *a greater than human wisdom,* Plat. *Ap.* 20 d; so κατὰ πάντα *in all respects,* κατὰ φύσιν *according to nature, naturally;* τὰ κατὰ πόλεμον *military matters.*

In COMP.: *down, against;* often denoting intensity or completeness (καταλείπω *leave behind, abandon, bequeath;* καταπίνω *gulp down, drink up*).

1219. μετά *with, amid, among.* See σύν.

a. With the GENITIVE:

(1) *with, in company with:* μετ' ἄλλων λέξο ἑταίρων *lie down with the rest of thy companions,* Od. 10, 320; μετὰ ζώντων *among the living,* S. *Ph.* 1312.

(2) *in union with, with the coöperation of:* μετὰ Μαντινέων ξυνεπολέμουν *they fought in alliance with the Mantineans,* Thuc. 6, 105; οἵδε μετ' αὐτοῦ ἦσαν *these were on his side,* Thuc. 3, 56; Ὑπέρβολον ἀποκτείνουσι μετὰ Χαρμίνου *they put Hyperbolus to death by the aid of Charminus,* Thuc. 8, 73; οἱ μετὰ Κύρου βάρβαροι *the Persians under Cyrus,* X. *An.* 1, 7, 10; μετὰ τοῦ νόμου *on the side of the law,* Plat. *Ap.* 32 c.

b. With the DATIVE (poetic, chiefly epic), *among:* μετὰ δὲ τριτάτοισιν ἄνασσεν *and he was reigning in the third generation,* Il. 1, 252.

c. With the ACCUSATIVE:

(1) *into* (*the midst of*), *after* (*in quest of*) poetic: μετὰ στρατὸν ἤλασ' Ἀχαιῶν *he drove into the host of the Achaeans,* Il. 5, 589; πλέων μετὰ χαλκόν *sailing after* (*in quest of*) *copper,* Od. 1, 184.

(2) generally *after, next to:* μετὰ τὸν πόλεμον *after the war;* μέγιστος μετὰ Ἴστρον *the largest* (*river*) *next to the Ister,* Hdt. 4, 53.

In COMP.: *with* (of sharing, e.g. μετέχω *have a share*), *among, after* (*in quest of*): it also denotes *change* (μετανοέω *change one's mind, repent*).

1220. παρά (Hom. also παραί), *by, near, alongside of* (see 1200).

a. With the GENITIVE, *from beside, from*: παρὰ νηῶν ἀπονοστήσειν *to return from the ships, Il.* 12, 114; παρ' ἡμῶν ἀπάγγελλε τάδε *take this message from us,* X. *An.* 2, 1, 20.

b. With the DATIVE, *with, beside, near*: παρὰ Πριάμοιο θύρῃσιν *at Priam's gates, Il.* 7, 346; παρὰ σοὶ κατέλυον *they lodged with you (were your guests),* Dem. 18, 82; παρ' αὐτοῖς *in our own homes,* Lys. 12, 33.

c. With the ACCUSATIVE, *to (a place) near, to*; also *by the side of, beyond* or *beside, except, along with, because of.*

(1) of PLACE: τρέψας πὰρ ποταμόν *turning to the (bank of the) river, Il.* 21, 603; ἐσιόντες παρὰ τοὺς φίλους *going in to (visit) their friends,* Thuc. 2, 51.

(2) of TIME: παρὰ πάντα τὸν χρόνον *throughout the whole time,* Dem. 18, 10.

(3) of CAUSE: παρὰ τὴν ἡμετέραν ἀμέλειαν *on account of our neglect,* Dem. 4, 11.

(4) of COMPARISON: παρὰ τἄλλα ζῷα *compared with (by the side of) other animals,* X. *M.* 1, 4, 14.

(5) with idea of *beyond* or *beside,* and *except*: οὐκ ἔστι παρὰ ταῦτ' ἄλλα *there are no others besides these,* Ar. *Nub.* 698; παρὰ τὸν νόμον *contrary to the law* (properly *beyond* it).

In COMP.: *beside, along by, hitherward, wrongly* (*beside the mark,* παράγω *mislead*), *over* (as in *overstep,* παροράω *overlook*).

1221. περί *around* (on all sides), *about* (cf. ἀμφί).

a. With the GENITIVE, *about, concerning* (Lat. d e): περὶ πατρὸς ἐρέσθαι *to inquire about his father, Od.* 3, 77; περὶ τοῦ στεφάνου (oration) *On the Crown,* Lat. d e C o r o n a; δεδιὼς περὶ αὐτοῦ *fearing for him,* Plat. *Prot.* 320 a. Poetic (chiefly epic) *above, surpassing*: κρατερὸς περὶ πάντων *mighty above all, Il.* 21, 566.

b. With the DATIVE, *about, around, concerning,* of PLACE or CAUSE (chiefly poetic): ἔνδυνε περὶ στήθεσσι χιτῶνα *he put on his tunic about his breast, Il.* 10, 21; ἔδδεισεν περὶ Μενελάῳ *he feared for Menelaus, Il.* 10, 240; δείσαντες περὶ τῇ χώρᾳ *through fear for our land,* Thuc. 1, 74.

c. With the ACCUSATIVE (nearly the same as ἀμφί), *about, near*: ἑστάμεναι περὶ τοῖχον *to stand round the wall, Il.* 18, 374; περὶ Ἑλλήσποντον *about (near) the Hellespont,* Dem. 8, 3; περὶ τούτους τοὺς χρόνους *about these times,* Thuc. 3, 89; ὢν περὶ ταῦτα *being about (engaged in) this,* Thuc. 7, 31.

In COMP.: *around, about, over* (περιοράω *overlook, permit*; περιγίγνομαι *get the better of*; also in arithmetic, *remain over*); *exceedingly* (περιχαρής *overjoyed*).

1222. πρό (Lat. p r o), with the GENITIVE only, *before*:

(1) of PLACE: πρὸ θυρῶν *before the door,* S. *El.* 109.

(2) of TIME: πρὸ δείπνου *before dinner,* X. *C.* 5, 5, 39.

(3) of DEFENCE: μάχεσθαι πρὸ παίδων *to fight for their children, Il.* 8, 57; διακινδυνεύειν πρὸ βασιλέως *to run risk in behalf of the king,* X. *C.* 8, 8, 4.

(4) of CHOICE or PREFERENCE: κέρδος αἰνῆσαι πρὸ δίκας δόλιον *to approve wily gain before justice*, Pind. *P.* 4, 140; πρὸ τούτου τεθνάναι ἂν ἕλοιτο *in preference to this he would choose death*, Plat. *Symp.* 179 a.

In COMP.: *before, in defence of, forward.*

1223. πρός (Hom. also προτί or ποτί), *at* or *by* (in front of).

a. With the GENITIVE:

(1) *in front of, looking towards*: κεῖται πρὸς Θρᾴκης *it lies over against Thrace*, Dem. 23, 182. In swearing: πρὸς θεῶν *before (by) the gods*. Sometimes *pertaining to* (as character): ἦ κάρτα πρὸς γυναικός *surely it is very like a woman*, Aesch. *Ag.* 592; πρὸς Κύρου *characteristic of Cyrus.*

(2) *from (on the part of)*: τιμὴν πρὸς Ζηνὸς ἔχοντες *having honor from Zeus*, *Od.* 11, 302. Sometimes with passive verbs, especially Ionic (1208): ἀτιμάζεσθαι πρὸς Πεισιστράτου *to be dishonored by Pisistratus*, Hdt. 1, 61; ἀδοξοῦνται πρὸς τῶν πόλεων *they are held in contempt by states*, X. *Oec.* 4, 2.

b. With the DATIVE:

(1) *at*: ἐπεὶ πρὸς Βαβυλῶνι ἦν ὁ Κῦρος *when Cyrus was at Babylon*, X. *C.* 7, 5, 1.

(2) *in addition to*: πρὸς τούτοις *besides this*; πρὸς τοῖς ἄλλοις *besides all the rest*, Thuc. 2, 61.

c. With the ACCUSATIVE:

(1) *to*: εἶμ' αὐτὴ πρὸς Ὄλυμπον *I am going myself to Olympus*, Il. 1, 420.

(2) *towards*: πρὸς Βορρᾶν *towards the North*, Thuc. 6, 2; *in relation to* (of persons): πρὸς ἀλλήλους ἡσυχίαν εἶχον *they kept the peace towards one another*, Isoc. 7, 51; πρὸς τοὺς ἄλλους ἅπαντας οὕτως βεβίωκα ὥστε μοι μηδὲ πρὸς ἕνα μηδὲν ἔγκλημα γενέσθαι *in my relations with all other persons I have so lived that no complaint has arisen against me on the part of a single individual*, Lys. 16, 10.

(3) *with a view to, according to, with reference to*: πρὸς τί με ταῦτ' ἐρωτᾷς; *what are you driving at* (lit. *to what does your question refer)*? X. *M.* 3, 7, 2; πρὸς τὴν παροῦσαν δύναμιν *according to their power at the time*, Dem 15, 28; πρὸς ταῦτα *in view of this*, especially with the imperative, Lat. proinde.

In COMP.: *to, toward, against, besides.*

1224. σύν, older Attic ξύν (Lat. cum), with DATIVE only, *with, in company with*, or *by aid of*. Σύν is chiefly poetic; it seldom occurs in Attic prose except in Xenophon, μετά with the genitive taking its place. The dative with σύν is instrumental.

(1) *in company with*: ἦλθε σὺν Μενελάῳ *he came with Menelaus*, Il. 3, 206 (in prose συνῆλθε τῷ Μενελάῳ, **1179**).

(2) *by aid of*: σὺν θεῷ *with God's help*, Il. 9, 49.

(3) *in accordance with*: σὺν δίκᾳ *with justice*, Pind. *P.* 9, 96.

(4) INSTRUMENT (like simple dative): μέγαν πλοῦτον ἐκτήσω ξὺν αἰχμῇ *thou didst gain great wealth by (with) thy spear*, Aesch. *Pers.* 755.

In COMP.: *with, together, altogether.*

1225. ὑπέρ (Hom. also ὑπείρ) *over* (Lat. super).

a. With the GENITIVE:

(1) of PLACE: στῆ ὑπὲρ κεφαλῆς *it stood over* (*his*) *head*, *Il.* 2, 20; of motion *over*: ὑπὲρ θαλάσσης καὶ χθονὸς ποτωμένοις (sc. ἡμῖν) *as we flit over sea and land*, Aesch. *Ag.* 576.

(2) *for, in behalf of* (opposed to κατά): θυόμενα ὑπὲρ τῆς πόλεως *sacrificed in behalf of the state*, X. *M.* 2, 2, 13; ὑπὲρ πάντων ἀγών *a struggle for our all*, Aesch. *Pers.* 405. Sometimes with τοῦ and infin., like ἵνα with subj.: ὑπὲρ τοῦ τὰ συνήθη μὴ γίγνεσθαι *to prevent the regular methods from being followed*, Aeschin. 3, 1.

(3) chiefly in the orators, *concerning* (like περί): τὴν ὑπὲρ τοῦ πολέμου γνώμην ἔχοντας *having such an opinion about the war*, Dem. 2, 1.

b. With the ACCUSATIVE, *over, beyond, exceeding*: ὑπὲρ οὐδὸν ἐβήσετο δώματος *he stepped over the threshold of the house*, *Od.* 7, 135; ὑπεὶρ ἅλα *over the sea*, *Od.* 3, 73; ὑπὲρ τὸ βέλτιστον *beyond what is best*, Aesch. *Ag.* 378; ὑπὲρ δύναμιν *beyond its power*, Thuc. 6, 16.

In COMP.: *over, above, beyond, in defence of, for the sake of.*

1226. ὑπό (Hom. also ὑπαί) *under* (Lat. sub), *by.*

a. With the GENITIVE:

(1) of PLACE: τὰ ὑπὸ γῆς *things under the earth*, Plat. *Ap.* 18 b. Sometimes *from under* (chiefly poetic): οὓς ὑπὸ χθονὸς ἧκε φάοσδε *whom he sent to light from beneath the earth*, Hes. *Th.* 669.

(2) to denote the AGENT with passive verbs: εἴ τις ἐτιμᾶτο ὑπὸ τοῦ δήμου (1208) *if anyone was honored by the people*, X. *H.* 2, 3, 15. When the agent is a thing and not a person, ὑπό personifies it: ἠνάγκασμαι ὑπὸ τῶν γεγενημένων τούτου κατηγορεῖν *I am forced by what has happened to accuse this man*, Lys. 12, 3. Hence

(3) of CAUSE: ὑπὸ δέους *through fear*; ὑφ' ἡδονῆς *through pleasure*; ὑπ' ἀπλοίας *by detention in port*, Thuc. 2, 85.

b. With the DATIVE (especially poetic): τῶν ὑπὸ ποσσί *beneath their feet*, *Il.* 2, 784; τῶν θανόντων ὑπ' Ἰλίῳ *of those who fell at* (*under the walls of*) *Ilium*, E. *Hec.* 764; ὑπὸ τῇ ἀκροπόλι *below the acropolis*, Hdt. 6, 105; οἱ ὑπὸ βασιλεῖ ὄντες *those who are under the king*, X. *C.* 8, 1, 6; ὑπὸ φειδωλῷ πατρὶ τεθραμμένος *brought up under the domination of a stingy father*, Plat. *Rep.* 572 c.

c. With the ACCUSATIVE:

(1) of PLACE, *under*, properly *to* (*a place*) *under*: ὑπὸ σπέος ἤλασε μῆλα *he drives* (*drove*) *the sheep into* (*under*) *a cave*, *Il.* 4, 279; ἦλθεθ' ὑπὸ Τροίην *you came to Troy* (i.e. *to besiege it*), *Od.* 4, 146; τάδε πάντα ὑπὸ σφᾶς ποιεῖσθαι *to bring all these under their sway*, Thuc. 4, 60.

(2) of TIME, *toward* (*entering into*): ὑπὸ νύκτα *at nightfall* (Lat. sub noctem) Thuc. 1, 115. Sometimes *at the time of, during*: ὑπὸ τὸν σεισμόν *at the time of the earthquake*, Thuc. 2, 27.

In COMP.: *under* (in place or rank), *underhand, slightly, gradually* (like sub).

Improper Prepositions

1227. These are adverbs which can never be used in composition with verbs. Most of them take the genitive.

  1. ἄνευ *without, except, apart from*: ἄνευ ἀκολούθου *without an attendant,* Plat. *Symp.* 217 a; ἄνευ τοῦ καλὴν δόξαν ἐνεγκεῖν *apart from (besides) bringing a good reputation,* Dem. 18, 89. So ἅμα *with,* 1190.

  2. ἄτερ *without, apart from* (poetic): ἄτερ Ζηνός *without (the help of) Zeus, Il.* 15, 292.

  3. ἄχρι *until, as far as*: ἄχρι τῆς τελευτῆς *until the end,* Dem. 18, 179.

  4. δίχα *apart from, unlike* (poetic): πυρὸς δίχα *without the aid of fire,* Aesch. *Sev.* 25; δίχα ἄλλων *different from others,* Aesch. *Ag.* 757.

  5. ἐγγύς *near* (with dative in poetry, 1190): θανάτου ἐγγύς *near death,* Plat. *Ap.* 38 c (1153).

  6. εἴσω (ἔσω) *inside, within*: εἴσω πυλῶν *within the gates,* Aesch. *Sev.* 557.

  7. ἐκτός *outside, without*: ἐκτὸς ἐλπίδος *beyond hope,* S. *Ant.* 330.

  8. ἔμπροσθεν *in front of*: ἔμπροσθε αὐτῆς *in front of it,* Hdt. 8, 87.

  9. ἐναντίον *against*: Ἀχιλῆος ἐναντίον *against Achilles, Il.* 20, 97; confronting, ἐναντίον τῶν δικαστῶν *before the judges* (i.e. *at the bar*).

  10. ἕνεκα or ἕνεκεν (Ionic εἵνεκα, εἵνεκεν) *on account of, for the sake of* (generally after its noun): ὕβριος εἵνεκα τῆσδε *on account of this outrage, Il.* 1, 214; μηδένα κολακεύειν ἕνεκα μισθοῦ *to flatter no one for a reward,* X. *H.* 5, 1, 17. Also οὕνεκα (οὗ ἕνεκα) for ἕνεκα, chiefly in the dramatists.

  11. ἐντός *within*: στέρνων ἐντός *within the breast,* Aesch. *Ag.* 77.

  12. ἔξω *out of, beyond*: ἔξω βελῶν *out of the range of missiles,* X. *C.* 3, 3, 69.

  13. εὐθύ *straight to*: εὐθὺ Πελλήνης *straight to Pellene,* Ar. *Av.* 1421.

  14. μεταξύ *between*: μεταξὺ σοφίας καὶ ἀμαθίας *between wisdom and folly,* Plat. *Symp.* 202 a.

  15. μέχρι *until, as far as*: μέχρι τῆς πόλεως *as far as the city,* Thuc. 6, 96.

  16. ὄπισθεν *behind*: ὄπισθε τῆς θύρης *behind the door,* Hdt. 1, 9.

  17. πλήν *except*: πλὴν γ᾽ ἐμοῦ καὶ σοῦ *except myself and you,* S. *El.* 909.

  18. πλησίον *near* (sometimes with dative, 1190): πλησίον πατρός *near your father,* S. *Tr.* 1076 (1153).

  19. χωρίς *separate from*: χωρὶς τῆς δόξης *apart from* (the question of) *honor,* Plat. *Ap.* 35 b.

  20. ὡς *to,* with the accusative, but only with *personal* objects: ἀφίκετο ὡς Περδίκκαν καὶ ἐς τὴν Χαλκιδικήν *he came to Perdiccas and into Chalcidice,* Thuc. 4, 79.

ADVERBS

1228. Adverbs qualify verbs, adjectives, and other adverbs. E.g.

οὕτως εἶπεν *thus he spoke*; ὡς δύναμαι *as I am able*; πρῶτον ἀπῆλθε *first he went away*; τὸ ἀληθῶς κακόν *that which is truly evil*; αὗταί σ᾽ ὁδηγήσουσι καὶ μάλ᾽ ἀσμένως *these will guide you even most gladly,* Aesch. *Pr.* 728.

1229. For adjectives used as adverbs, see **922.** For adverbs preceded by the article, and qualifying a noun like adjectives, see **950.** For adverbs with the genitive or dative, see **1088, 1092, 1152, 1175, 1176, 1190.**

THE VERB

VOICES

Active

1230. In the active voice the subject is represented as acting; e.g. τρέπω τοὺς ὀφθαλμούς *I turn my eyes*; ὁ πατὴρ φιλεῖ τὸν παῖδα *the father loves his child*; ὁ ἵππος τρέχει *the horse runs*.

1231. The form of the active voice includes most intransitive verbs; e.g. τρέχω *I run*. On the other hand, the form of the middle voice includes many deponent verbs which are active and transitive in meaning; e.g. τοῦτο τεκμαίρομαι *I infer this*. Some transitive verbs have certain intransitive tenses, which generally have the meaning of the middle voice, e.g. ἕστηκα *I stand*, ἔστην *I stood* or *came to a stop*, from ἵστημι *set*; other intransitive tenses have a passive force, e.g. ἀνέστησαν ὑπ' αὐτοῦ *they were driven out by him*, Thuc. 1, 8.

1232. The same verb may be both transitive and intransitive: e.g. ἐλαύνω *drive* (trans. or intrans.) or *march*; ἔχω *have*, sometimes *hold* or *stay* (e.g. ἔχε δή *stay now*, Plat. *Prot.* 349 d); with adverbs, *be*, e.g. εὖ ἔχει *it is well*, bene se habet. So πράττω *do*, εὖ (or κακῶς) πράττω *I am well* (or *badly*) *off*, *I do well* (or *badly*). The intransitive use sometimes arose from the omission of a familiar object; e.g. ἐλαύνειν (ἵππον or ἅρμα) *ride* or *drive*, τελευτᾶν (τὸν βίον) *end* (*life*) or *die*. Cf. the English verbs *drive, turn, move, increase, gather*.

1233. When a verb has both the first and the second aorist, or first and second perfect, the first aorist and perfect are generally transitive or causative, the second aorist and perfect generally intransitive (**479 a**). In such verbs the future active is transitive. Thus βαίνω *go*, βήσω *shall cause to go*, βήσομαι *shall go*, ἔβησα *caused to go*, ἔβην *went*; δύω *enter*, ἐνέδυσα *put on* (*another*), ἐνέδυν *entered, put on one's self*; ἵστημι *set*, ἔστησα *set*, ἔστην *stood*, 1 and 2 perf. both intrans. ἕστηκα, ἕστατον *stand*; κατάγνυμι *break*, κατέαγα *be broken*; μαίνω *madden*, ἔμηνα *maddened*, μέμηνα *be mad*; ὄλλυμι *destroy, lose*, ὀλώλεκα *have destroyed, lost*, ὄλωλα *am ruined*; φύω *make grow*, ἔφυσα *produced*, ἔφυν *grew, is*, πέφυκα *am by nature*.

Passive

1234. In the passive voice the subject is represented as acted upon; e.g. ὁ παῖς ὑπὸ τοῦ πατρὸς φιλεῖται *the child is loved by his father*.

1235. The passive is later in origin than the middle, and is the result of using middle forms and certain intransitive active forms in a passive sense. Thus the middle λύομαι, ἐλυόμην, λέλυμαι served also as passive forms, and there is no essential difference in form between ἔστην (aorist active intransitive) and ἐφάνην (aorist passive). The future middle may always be used as a passive in Homer (cf. 1248), but a special form (φανήσομαι, λυθήσομαι) was developed early from the aorists in -ην and -θην. Even the second aorist middle may have a passive sense in Homer and occasionally in Attic (especially κατέσχετο was seized).

1236. The *object* of the active becomes the subject of the passive. The *subject* of the active, the personal agent, is generally expressed by ὑπό with the genitive in the passive construction (1208).

1237. The dative here, as elsewhere, generally expresses the inanimate instrument; e.g. βάλλονται λίθοις *they are pelted with stones.*

1238. Even a genitive or dative depending on a verb in the active voice can become the subject of the passive; e.g. καταφρονεῖται ὑπ' ἐμοῦ *he is despised by me* (active, καταφρονῶ αὐτοῦ, 1103); πιστεύεται ὑπὸ τῶν ἀρχομένων *he is trusted by his subjects* (active, πιστεύουσιν αὐτῷ, 1160); ἄρχονται ὑπὸ βασιλέων *they are ruled by kings* (active, βασιλεῖς ἄρχουσιν αὐτῶν); ὑπὸ ἀλλοφύλων μᾶλλον ἐπεβουλεύοντο *they were plotted against to a greater degree by men of other races*, Thuc. 1, 2 (active, ἐπεβούλευον αὐτοῖς).

1239. *a.* The perfect and pluperfect passive may have the *dative* of the agent (1174).

b. The personal verbal in -τέος takes the dative (1598), the impersonal in -τέον the dative or accusative, of the agent (1599).

1240. When the active is followed by two accusatives, or by an accusative of a thing and a dative of a person, the case denoting a *person* is generally made the subject of the passive, and the other (an accusative) remains unchanged. E.g.

οὐδὲν ἄλλο διδάσκεται ἄνθρωπος *a man is taught nothing else* (in the active, οὐδὲν ἄλλο διδάσκουσιν ἄνθρωπον), Plat. *Meno* 87 c; ἄλλο τι μεῖζον ἐπιταχθήσεσθε *you will have some other greater command imposed on you* (active, ἄλλο τι μεῖζον ὑμῖν ἐπιτάξουσιν *they will impose some other greater command on you*), Thuc. 1, 140; οἱ ἐπιτετραμμένοι τὴν φυλακήν *those to whom the guard has been intrusted* (active, ἐπιτρέπειν τὴν φυλακὴν τούτοις), Thuc. 1, 126; διφθέραν ἐνημμένος *clad in a leather jerkin* (active, ἐνάπτειν τί τινι *to fit a thing on one*), Ar. *Nub.* 72; so ἐκκόπτεσθαι τὸν ὀφθαλμόν *to have his eye knocked out*, and ἀποτέμνεσθαι τὴν κεφαλήν *to have his head cut off*, etc., from possible active constructions ἐκκόπτειν τί τινι, and ἀποτέμνειν τί τινι. This construction has nothing to do with that of 1056.

In this construction the accusative of the *thing* (which is sometimes cognate, 1049) is retained with the passive, whereas the accusative or dative of the *person* is made the subject.

1241. *a.* A cognate accusative (1049) of the active form, or a neuter pronoun or adjective representing such an accusative, may become the subject of the passive. E.g.

ὁ κίνδυνος κινδυνεύεται *the risk is encountered* (active, τὸν κίνδυνον κινδυνεύει *he runs the risk*), see Plat. *Lach.* 187 b; εἰ οὐδὲν ἡμάρτηταί μοι *granting that no fault has been committed by me* (active, οὐδὲν ἡμάρτηκα), Andoc. 1, 33.

b. The passive may also be used impersonally, the cognate subject being implied in the verb itself; e.g. ἐπειδὴ αὐτοῖς παρεσκεύαστο *when preparation had been made by them*, Thuc. 1, 46; οὔτε ἠσέβηται οὔτε ὡμολόγηται (sc. ἐμοί) *no sacrilege has been committed and no confession has been made* (*by me*), Andoc. 1, 17.

c. This use occurs chiefly in such neuter participial expressions as τὰ σοὶ κἀμοὶ β ε β ι ω μ έ ν α *what you and I have done in our lives* (βιόω *live*), Dem. 18, 265; αἱ τῶν π ε π ο λ ι τ ε υ μ έ ν ω ν εὔθυναι *the accounts of their public acts*, Dem. 1, 28; so τ ὰ ἠ σ ε β η μ έ ν α *the impious acts which have been done*; τ ὰ κ ι ν δ υ ν ε υ θ έ ν τ α *the risks which were run*; τ ὰ ἡ μ α ρ τ η μ έ ν α *the errors which have been committed*. Even an intransitive verb may thus have a passive voice.

1242. Some intransitive active forms are used as passives of other verbs. Thus εὖ ποιεῖν *benefit*, εὖ πάσχειν *be benefited*; εὖ λέγειν *praise*, εὖ ἀκούειν (poet. κλύειν) *be praised*; αἱρεῖν *capture*, ἁλῶναι *be captured*; ἀποκτείνειν *kill*, ἀποθνήσκειν *be killed*; ἐκβάλλειν *cast out*, ἐκπίπτειν *be cast out*; διώκειν *prosecute*, φεύγειν *be prosecuted* (*be a defendant*); ἀπολύω *acquit*, ἀποφεύγω *be acquitted*; αἰτιᾶσθαι (deponent) *accuse*, αἰτίαν ἔχειν *be accused*; τιθέναι *place*, κεῖσθαι *be placed*; εὖ διατιθείς *putting in a good frame of mind*, εὖ διακείμενος *having a good disposition* (or *being in a favorable situation*).

Middle

1243. In the middle voice the subject is represented as acting upon himself, or in some manner which concerns himself.

a. As acting *on himself*. E.g.

ἐτράποντο πρὸς λῃστείαν *they betook (turned) themselves to piracy*, Thuc. 1, 5. So παύομαι *cease* (*stop one's self*), πείθεσθαι *trust* (*persuade one's self*), φαίνομαι *appear* (*show one's self*). This reflexive use of the middle is the least common.

b. As acting *for himself* or *with reference to himself*. E.g.

ὁ δῆμος τίθεται νόμους *the people make laws for themselves*, whereas τίθησι νόμους would properly be said of a lawgiver; τοῦτον μεταπέμπομαι *I send for him* (*to come to me*); ἀπεπέμπετο αὐτούς *he dismissed them*; προβάλλεται τὴν ἀσπίδα *he holds his shield to protect himself.* So αἱροῦμαι *choose,* ἀμύνομαι *defend one's self (ward off from one's self),* τιθέμενοι τὰ ὅπλα (technical in military language) *taking up their position.*

c. As acting on an object *belonging to himself.* E.g.

ἦλθε λυσόμενος θύγατρα *he came to ransom his (own) daughter, Il.* 1, 13.

1244. Often the middle expresses no more than is *implied* in the active ; e.g. τρόπαιον ἵστασθαι *to raise a trophy for themselves,* or τρόπαιον ἱστάναι *to raise a trophy.* The middle sometimes appears not to differ at all from the active in meaning, and has given way to it in some forms ; e.g. Hom. and poetic ὁράομαι, regular Attic ὁρῶ, *see* ; Hom. ἀκούομαι, Att. ἀκούω, *hear* (but always fut. ἀκούσομαι).

1245. On the other hand, the distinction between active and middle is often important ; e.g. εἰρήνην ποιοῦμαι *conclude peace,* εἰρήνην ποιῶ *bring about a peace* (of the mediator) ; αἱρῶ *take,* αἱροῦμαι *choose* ; ἀποδίδωμι *give back,* ἀποδίδομαι *sell* ; ἅπτω *fasten,* ἅπτομαι *cling to* ; ἄρχω *rule, be first,* ἄρχομαι *begin* ; γαμῶ *marry* (of the man), γαμοῦμαι *be married* (of the woman) ; δανείζω *lend,* δανείζομαι *borrow* ; δικάζω *sit in judgment,* δικάζομαι *go to law* ; ἔχω *have, hold,* ἔχομαι *cling to, be next to* ; φυλάττω *watch,* φυλάττομαι *be on one's guard against* ; γράφω νόμον *propose a vote,* γράφομαι *indict* ; τιμωρῶ τινα *avenge one,* τιμωροῦμαι *punish.* See also νόμον τιθέναι in **1243** *b,* and **1246.**

1246. The middle sometimes has a *causative* meaning ; e.g. ἐδιδαξάμην σε *I had you taught,* Ar. *Nub.* 1338 ; Ἀργεῖοι δὲ σφεων εἰκόνας ἐποιήσαντο *the Argives caused statues of them (Cleobis and Biton) to be made,* Hdt. 1, 31 (ἐποίησε would have been used of the artist).

1247. The passive of some of these verbs is used as a passive to both active and middle ; e.g. ἐγράφην can mean either *be written* or *be indicted,* ᾑρέθην either *be taken* or *be chosen.*

1248. The future middle of some verbs has a passive sense even in Attic ; e.g. ἀδικῶ *I do wrong,* ἀδικήσομαι *I shall be wronged* ; ἀριθμῶ *I count,* ἀριθμήσει *you will be numbered,* E. *Bacch.* 1318 ; so occasionally the second aorist middle (**1235**).

TENSES

1249. The tenses may express two relations. They may designate the time of an action as *present, past,* or *future* ; and also its character as *going on continuously* or *repeatedly,* as simply *taking place* or *occurring,* or as *finished* with a permanent result. Thus the present and the imperfect express action *in a line,* or extended ; the aorist denotes action *at a point* (**1261**). See the parts of ἵστημι in **507.** The character of an action appears in all the moods and in the infinitive and participle ; the relation of time appears always in the indicative, and to a certain extent (hereafter to be explained) in some of the dependent moods and in the participle.

I. *Tenses of the Indicative*

1250. The tenses of the indicative express time and character of action as follows:

a. PRESENT, action going on in present time: γράφω *I am writing,* δέω *I am binding.*

b. IMPERFECT, action going on in past time: ἔγραφον *I was writing,* ἔδεον *I was binding.*

c. PERFECT, action finished in present time and so denoting an accomplished state: γέγραφα *I have written,* δέδεμαι *I am in prison.*

d. PLUPERFECT, action finished in past time: ἐγεγράφη *I had written,* ἐδεδέμην *I was in prison.*

e. AORIST, action simply taking place in past time: ἔγραψα *I wrote,* ἔδησα *I bound.*

f. FUTURE, future action (either in its *progress* or in its mere *occurrence*): γράψω *I shall write* or *I shall be writing;* ἕξω *I shall have,* σχήσω *I shall get.*

g. FUTURE PERFECT, action to be finished in future time and so denoting a future state: γεγράψεται *it will have been written, it will stand written;* δεδήσομαι *I shall lie in prison;* τεθνήξει *he will be dead.*

1251. This is shown in the following table:

	Present Time	*Past Time*	*Future Time*
Action going on	PRESENT	IMPERFECT	FUTURE
Action simply taking place		AORIST	FUTURE
Action finished	PERFECT	PLUPERFECT	FUT. PERFECT

For the present and the aorist expressing a general truth (*gnomic*), see **1292, 1293.**

1252. In narration the present is sometimes used vividly for the aorist. E.g.

κελεύει πέμψαι ἄνδρας · ἀποστέλλουσιν οὖν, καὶ περὶ αὐτῶν ὁ Θεμιστοκλῆς κρύφα πέμπει *he bids them send men: accordingly they dispatch them, and Themistocles sends secretly concerning them,* Thuc. 1, 91. This is called the Historical Present. It does not occur in Homer.

1253. *a.* The present often expresses a customary or repeated action in present time; e.g. οὗτος μὲν ὕδωρ, ἐγὼ δὲ οἶνον πίνω *he drinks water, but I drink wine,* Dem. 19, 46. See **1292.**

b. The imperfect likewise may express customary or repeated past action; e.g. Σωκράτης ὥσπερ ἐγίγνωσκεν οὕτως ἔλεγε *as Socrates thought, so he used to speak,* X. *M.* 1, 1, 4.

1254. The present μέλλω, with the present or future (seldom the aorist) infinitive, forms a periphrastic future, which sometimes denotes intention or expectation; e.g. εἰ μέλλει ἡ πολιτεία σῴζεσθαι *if the constitution is to be saved,* Plat. *Rep.* 412 a; τὰ μέλλοντα ἔσεσθαι *the future.*

1255. The present and the imperfect, since they cannot denote the completion of an act, often express an *attempted* action; e.g. πείθουσιν ὑμᾶς *they are trying to persuade you,* Isae. 1, 26; Ἁλόννησον ἐδίδου *he offered (tried to give) Halonnesus,* Aeschin. 3, 83; ἃ ἐπράσσετο οὐκ ἐγένετο *what was attempted did not happen,* Thuc. 6, 74.

1256. *a.* The presents ἥκω *I am come* and οἴχομαι *I am gone* have the force of perfects, the imperfects having the force of pluperfects.

b. The present of a few other verbs may often be translated best by the perfect; e.g. ἀδικῶ (= ἄδικός εἰμι) *I have done wrong (am in the wrong),* νικῶμεν *we have won.*

1257. The present εἶμι *I am going,* with its compounds, usually has a future sense, and is used as a future of ἔρχομαι, ἐλεύσομαι not being in good use in Attic prose (**511** c). In Homer εἶμι is also present in sense.

1258. *a.* The present with πάλαι or any other expression of past time denotes an action begun in the past and continued in the present, and is translated by the perfect; e.g. κεῖνον ἰχνεύω πάλαι *I have been tracking him a long time,* S. *Aj.* 20.

b. Even without an adverb referring to the past, the present may be rendered by the English perfect if the action is not completed; e.g. ὅπερ λέγω *as I have been saying,* Plat. *Ap.* 21 a; ἐξ ὧν ἀκούω *from what I have heard,* X. *An.* 1, 9, 28. So other verbs of perception, such as μανθάνω *learn,* πυνθάνομαι *hear,* αἰσθάνομαι *perceive.*

1259. The imperfect of repeated action (**1253** b) with a negative may denote insistence, resistance, or refusal; e.g. οὐκ εἴα ὑπείκειν *he would not permit them to give in,* i.e. *he urged them not to give in,* Thuc. 1, 127.

1260. *a.* The imperfect of εἰμί, generally with ἄρα, may express a fact which is just recognized, having previously been denied or overlooked; e.g. οὐ σὺ μόνος ἄρ' ἦσθ' ἔποψ; *so you are not the only hoopoe, after all?* Ar. *Av.* 280.

b. Similarly, the imperfect may express something which is the result of a previous discussion, with reference to which the past tense is used; e.g. οἱ αὐτοὶ πολέμιοι ἡμῖν ἦσαν *the same men are, as we saw, hostile to us,* Thuc. 1, 35; ὃ τῷ μὲν δικαίῳ βέλτιον ἐγίγνετο, τῷ δὲ ἀδίκῳ ἀπώλλυτο *that which, as we proved, becomes better by justice but is ruined by injustice,* Plat. *Crito* 47 d.

1261. *a.* The *aorist* takes its name (ἀόριστος *unlimited, unqualified*) from its denoting a simple past *occurrence,* with none of the limitations (ὅροι) as to *completion, continuance, repetition,* etc. which belong to the other past tenses. It corresponds to the ordinary preterite in English, whereas the Greek imperfect corresponds to the forms *I was doing,* etc. E.g. ἐποίει τοῦτο *he was doing this* or *he did this habitually,* πεποίηκε τοῦτο *he has already done this,* ἐπεποιήκει τοῦτο *he had already (at some past time) done this,* but ἐποίησε τοῦτο is simply *he did this* without qualification of any kind. The aorist is therefore commonly used in rapid narration, the imperfect in detailed description. The aorist is more common in negative sentences (except in the case noted in 1259).

b. As it is not always important to distinguish between the progress of an action and its mere occurrence, it is occasionally indifferent whether the imperfect or the aorist is used; cf. ἔλεγον in Thuc. 1, 72 (end) with εἶπον, ἔλεξαν, and ἔλεξε in 1, 79. The two tenses show different views (both natural views) of the same act.

1262. The aorist of verbs which denote a *state* or *condition* may express the *entrance into* that state or condition; e.g. πλουτῶ *I am rich,* ἐπλούτουν *I was rich,* ἐπλούτησα *I became rich.* So ἐβασίλευσε *he became king,* ἦρξε *he took office* (also *he held office*), εἶχον *I had,* ἔσχον *I acquired.* This is called the Inceptive or Ingressive Aorist.

1263. With ἐπεί and ἐπειδή *after* the aorist is generally to be translated by our pluperfect; e.g. ἐπειδὴ ἀπῆλθον *after they had departed.* Cf. postquam venit.

1264. The aorist (sometimes the perfect) participle with ἔχω may form a periphrastic perfect, especially in Attic poetry; e.g. θαυμάσας ἔχω τόδε *I have wondered at this,* S. *Ph.* 1362. In prose, ἔχω with a participle generally has its common force; e.g. τὴν προῖκα ἔχει λαβών *he has received and has the dowry* (not simply *he has taken it*), Dem. 27, 17.

1265. Since the perfect denotes a present state, it is often translated by the present; e.g. ἀποθνῄσκειν *die,* τεθνηκέναι *be dead;* γίγνεσθαι *become,* γεγονέναι *be;* μιμνήσκειν *remind,* μεμνῆσθαι *remember;* καλεῖν *call,* κεκλῆσθαι *be called;* κτᾶσθαι *acquire,* κεκτῆσθαι *possess.* So οἶδα *I know* (novi) and many others. For further remarks on the perfect, see **735.**

In such verbs the pluperfect has the force of an imperfect; e.g. ᾔδη *I knew.*

1266. The perfect sometimes refers vividly to the future; e.g. εἴ με αἰσθήσεται, ὄλωλα *if he shall perceive me, I am ruined* (perii), S. *Ph.* 75.

So sometimes the present, e.g. ἀπόλλυμαι I am lost, Lys. 12, 14; and even the aorist may (through the context) imply a future action, e.g. ἀπωλόμην εἴ με λείψεις I am undone if you leave me, E. Alc. 386 (1415).

1267. The second person of the future may express a *permission*, or even a *command*; e.g. πράξεις οἷον ἂν θέλῃς you may act as you please, S. O. C. 956; πάντως δὲ τοῦτο δράσεις and in any case do this (you shall do this), Ar. Nub. 1352. So in imprecations; e.g. ἀπολεῖσθε to destruction with you! (lit. you shall perish). For μέλλω and the infinitive, see 1254.

1268. The future perfect denotes that a future act will be *immediate, decisive*, or *permanent*; e.g. φράζε, καὶ πεπράξεται speak, and it shall be (no sooner said than) done, Ar. Pl. 1027; οὐ Κρέοντος προστάτου γεγράψομαι I shall not be enrolled under the patronage of Creon, S. O. T. 411; τεθνήξει he will be dead. Cf. the similar use of the perfect infinitive, 1277. See 735.

1269. a. The division of the tenses of the indicative into *primary* (or *principal*) and *secondary* (or *historical*) is explained in 453.

b. In dependent clauses, when the construction allows both subjunctive and optative, or both indicative and optative, the subjunctive or indicative regularly follows primary tenses, and the optative follows secondary tenses. E.g.

πράττουσιν ἃ ἂν βούλωνται they do whatever they please, ἔπραττον ἃ βούλοιντο they did whatever they pleased, λέγουσιν ὅτι τοῦτο ποιοῦσιν they say that they are doing this, ἔλεξαν ὅτι τοῦτο ποιοῖεν they said that they were doing this. See 1442, 1502.

1270. The gnomic aorist is a primary tense, as it refers to present time (1293); and the historical present is secondary, as it refers to past time (1252).

1271. An exception to the principle of 1269 b occurs in indirect discourse, where the form of the direct discourse may always be retained, even after secondary tenses; so also in final and object clauses. See 1378, 1382, 1496 b.

1272. a. The distinction of primary and secondary tenses extends to the dependent moods only where the tenses there keep the same distinction of time which they have in the indicative, as in the optative and infinitive of indirect discourse (1282).

b. An optative of future time generally assimilates a dependent conditional relative clause or protasis to the optative when it might otherwise be in the subjunctive: thus we should generally have πράττοιεν ἂν ἃ βούλοιντο they would do whatever they pleased. See 1451. Such an optative seldom assimilates the subjunctive or indicative of a final or object clause (1371) in prose; but oftener in poetry. It very rarely assimilates an *indicative* of indirect discourse, although it may assimilate an interrogative *subjunctive* (1367).

II. *Tenses of the Dependent Moods*

A. Not in Indirect Discourse

1273. In the subjunctive and imperative, and also in the optative and infinitive when they are *not in indirect discourse* (**1281**), the tenses chiefly used are the present and aorist.

1274. *a.* These tenses here differ only in this, that the present expresses an action in its duration, that is, as *going on* or *repeated*, while the aorist expresses simply its *occurrence*, the time of both being otherwise precisely the same. E.g.

ἐὰν τοῦτο ποιῇ *if he shall be doing this,* or *if he shall do this (habitually),* ἐὰν τοῦτο ποιήσῃ (simply) *if he shall do this;* εἰ τοῦτο ποιοίη *if he should be doing this,* or *if he should do this (habitually),* εἰ τοῦτο ποιήσειε (simply) *if he should do this;* τοῦτο ποίει *do this (habitually),* τοῦτο ποίησον (simply) *do this;* οὕτω νικήσαιμί τ' ἐγὼ καὶ νομιζοίμην σοφός *on this condition may I gain the victory* (aor.) *and be thought* (pres.) *wise.* Ar. *Nub.* 520; βούλεται τοῦτο ποιεῖν *he wishes to be doing this* or *to do this (habitually),* βούλεται τοῦτο ποιῆσαι (simply) *he wishes to do this.*

b. This is a distinction entirely unknown to the Latin, which has (e.g.) only one form, si faciat, corresponding to εἰ ποιοίη and εἰ ποιήσειεν.

c. When, however, the aorist subjunctive is introduced by ἐπειδάν and similar conjunctions meaning *after,* or by ἕως ἄν, πρὶν ἄν, *until,* the aorist denotes a time preceding the action of the main verb, and may be translated by the perfect or the future perfect; e.g. ταῦτα, ἐπειδὰν περὶ τοῦ γένους εἴπω, ἐρῶ *when I shall have spoken (after I have spoken) about my birth, I will speak of these matters,* Dem. 57, 16; ἕως ἂν ἐκμάθῃς, ἔχ' ἐλπίδα *until you have learnt all, have hope,* S. *O. T.* 834.

1275. The perfect, which seldom occurs in these constructions, represents an action as *finished* at the time at which the present would represent it as *going on.* Frequently it denotes a present *state.* E.g.

δέδοικα μὴ λήθην πεποιήκῃ *I fear that it may have caused forgetfulness* (μὴ ποιῇ would mean *that it may cause*), Dem. 19, 3; μηδενὶ βοηθεῖν ὃς ἂν μὴ πρότερος βεβοηθηκὼς ὑμῖν ᾖ *to help no one who shall not previously have helped you* (ὃς ἂν μὴ ... βοηθῇ would mean *who shall not previously help you*), Dem. 19, 16. οὐκ ἂν διὰ τοῦτό γ' εἶεν οὐκ εὐθὺς δεδωκότες *it would not prove (on inquiry) that this was why they had failed to pay immediately* (with οὐ διδοῖεν this would mean *they failed to pay*), Dem. 30, 10; οὐ βουλεύεσθαι ἔτι ὥρα, ἀλλὰ βεβουλεῦσθαι *it is no longer time to be deliberating, but to make a decision* (lit. *to have finished deliberating*), Plat. *Crito* 46 a.

1276. The perfect *imperative* generally expresses a command that something shall be *decisive* and *permanent*; e.g. ταῦτα εἰρήσθω *let this have been said* (i.e. *let what has been said be final*), or *let this (which follows) be said once for all*; γραμμὴ AB γεγράφθω *let a line AB be drawn (and assumed throughout the demonstration)*; μέχρι τοῦδε ὡρίσθω ὑμῶν ἡ βραδυτής *at this point let the limit of your sluggishness be fixed*, Thuc. 1, 71. This is confined to the third person singular passive, the rare second person singular middle being merely emphatic. The *active* is used only when the perfect has a present meaning (1265).

1277. The perfect *infinitive* expresses *decisive* action or *permanent* state; e.g. εἶπον τὴν θύραν κεκλεῖσθαι *they ordered the gate to be shut (and kept so)*, X. H. 5, 4, 7. ἤλαυνεν ἐπὶ τοὺς Μένωνος, ὥστ᾽ ἐκείνους ἐκπεπλῆχθαι καὶ τρέχειν ἐπὶ τὰ ὅπλα *so that they were in deadly terror (thoroughly frightened) and ran to get their arms*, X. An. 1, 5, 13. So ἀπηλλάχθαι κακῶν *to be rid of trouble once for all*. The regular meaning of this tense, when it is not in indirect discourse, is that given in 1275.

1278. The future infinitive is regularly used only to represent the future indicative in *indirect discourse* (1282).

1279. It occurs occasionally in other constructions, in place of the regular present or aorist, to make more emphatic a future idea which the infinitive receives from the context, or to express a present intention of doing something in the future. E.g.

ἐδεήθησαν τῶν Μεγαρέων ναυσὶ σφᾶς ξυμπροπέμψειν *they asked the Megarians to escort them with ships*, Thuc. 1, 27; οὐκ ἀποκωλύσειν δυνατοὶ ὄντες *not being able to prevent*, Thuc. 3, 28; πολλοῦ δέω ἐμαυτόν γ᾽ ἀδικήσειν *I am far from* (1116) *intending to injure myself*, Plat. Ap. 37 b. In all such cases the future is rather exceptional (see 1273).

1280. One regular exception to the principle just stated is found in the periphrastic future (1254).

B. IN INDIRECT DISCOURSE

1281. The term *indirect discourse* includes all clauses depending on a verb of *saying* or *thinking* which contain the thoughts or words of any person stated *indirectly*, i.e. incorporated into the general structure of the sentence. It includes of course all *indirect* quotations and questions.

1282. When the optative and infinitive stand in indirect discourse, each tense represents the *corresponding tense* of the same verb in the direct discourse. E.g.

ἔλεξεν ὅτι γράφοι *he said that he was writing* (he said γράφω *I am writing*); ἔλεξεν ὅτι γράψοι *he said that he should write* (he said γράψω *I shall write*); ἔλεξεν ὅτι γράψειεν *he said that he had written* (he said ἔγραψα); ἔλεξεν ὅτι γεγραφὼς εἴη *he said that he had already written* (he said γέγραφα); ἤρετο εἴ τις ἐμοῦ εἴη σοφώτερος *he asked whether any one was wiser than I* (he asked ἔστι τις;), Plat. *Ap.* 21 a.

φησὶ γράφειν *he says that he is writing* (he says γράφω); ἔφη γράφειν *he said that he was writing* (γράφω); φησὶ γράψειν *he says that he will write* (γράψω); φησὶ γράψαι *he says that he wrote* (ἔγραψα); ἔφη γράψαι *he said that he had written* (ἔγραψα); φησὶ γεγραφέναι *he says that he has written* (γέγραφα); ἔφασαν τεθνάναι τὸν ἄνδρα *they said that the man was dead* (they said τέθνηκεν ὁ ἀνήρ, 1265), Antiphon 5, 29.

εἶπεν ὅτι ἄνδρα ἄγοι ὃν εἴρξαι δέοι *he said that he was bringing a man whom they must lock up* (he said ἄνδρα ἄγω ὃν εἶρξαι δεῖ), X. *H.* 5, 4, 8; ἐλογίζοντο ὡς, εἰ μὴ μάχοιντο, ἀποστήσοιντο αἱ πόλεις *they considered that, if they should not fight, the cities would revolt* (they thought ἐὰν μὴ μαχώμεθα, ἀποστήσονται *if we do not fight, they will revolt*), ibid. 6, 4, 6.

1283. These constructions are explained in 1502, 1509, and 1512. Here they merely show the force of the *tenses* in indirect discourse. Contrast especially the difference between φησὶ γράφειν and φησὶ γράψαι above with that between βούλεται ποιεῖν and βούλεται ποιῆσαι under 1274. Notice also the same distinction in the present and aorist optative. See 1510.

1284. The construction of 1282 is the strictly proper use of the future infinitive (1278, 1279).

1285. The future perfect infinitive is used here to express future completion with permanent effect (cf. 1277); e.g. νομίζετε ἐν τῇδε τῇ ἡμέρᾳ ἐμὲ κατακεκόψεσθαι *believe that on that day I shall have been already* (i.e. *shall be the same as*) *cut in pieces*, X. *An.* 1, 5, 16.

1286. *a.* The present infinitive may represent the *imperfect* as well as the present indicative; e.g. τίνας εὐχὰς ὑπολαμβάνετ' εὔχεσθαι τὸν Φίλιππον ὅτ' ἔσπενδεν *what prayers do you suppose Philip made when he was pouring libations?* (i.e. τίνας ηὔχετο), Dem. 19, 130. The perfect infinitive likewise represents both perfect and pluperfect. In such cases the time of the infinitive must always be shown by the context (as above by ὅτ' ἔσπενδεν).

b. For the present optative representing the imperfect, see 1503.

1287. Verbs of *hoping, expecting, promising, swearing,* and a few others, form an intermediate class between verbs which take the infinitive in indirect discourse and those which do not (see 1281); and though they regularly have the future infinitive (in indirect discourse, 1282), the present and aorist infinitive (not in indirect discourse, 1274) are allowed. E.g.

ἤλπιζον μάχην ἔσεσθαι *they expected that there would be a battle*, Thuc. 4, 71; but ἃ οὔποτε ἤλπισεν παθεῖν *what he never expected to suffer*, E. *Her.* 746; ὑπέσχετο μηχανὴν παρέξειν *he promised that he would provide an engine*, X. *C.* 6, 1, 21; περὶ τούτων ὑπέσχετο βουλεύσασθαι *he promised to take this matter under consideration*, X. *An.* 2, 3, 19; ὀμόσαντες ταύταις ἐμμενεῖν *having sworn to* (or *that they would*) *abide by these*, X. *H.* 5, 3,

26; ὀμόσαι εἶναι μὲν τὴν ἀρχὴν κοινήν. πάντας δ' ὑμῖν ἀποδοῦναι τὴν χώραν *to swear that the government should be (shared in) common, but that all should give up the land to you*, Dem. 23, 170.

1288. The future optative is never used except as the representative of the future indicative, either in indirect discourse (**1282**) or in the construction of **1382** (which is governed by the principles of indirect discourse). Even in these the future indicative is generally retained. See also **1518**.

III. Tenses of the Participle

1289. The tenses of the participle generally express the same time as those of the indicative; but they are present, past, or future *relatively* to the time of the verb with which they are connected. E.g.

ἁμαρτάνει τοῦτο ποιῶν *he errs in doing this*, ἡμάρτανε τοῦτο ποιῶν *he erred in doing this*, ἁμαρτήσεται τοῦτο ποιῶν *he will err in doing this*. Here ποιῶν is first present, then past, then future, absolutely; but always *present* to the verb of the sentence. So in indirect discourse: οἶδα τοῦτον γράφοντα (γράψαντα, γράψοντα, or γεγραφότα) *I know that he is writing (that he wrote, will write, or has written)*. οὐ πολλοὶ φαίνονται ἐλθόντες *it is plain that not many went (on the expedition)*, Thuc. 1, 10. For other examples see **1590**.

ταῦτα εἰπόντες ἀπῆλθον *when they had said this they departed*, ἐπῄνεσαν τοὺς εἰρηκότας *they praised those who had (already) spoken*, τοῦτο ποιήσων ἔρχεται *he is coming to do this*, τοῦτο ποιήσων ἦλθεν *he came to do this*, ἄπελθε ταῦτα λαβών *take this and be off* (λαβών being past to ἄπελθε, but absolutely future).

1290. *a.* The present may here also represent the imperfect; e.g.

οἶδα κἀκείνω σωφρονοῦντε, ἔστε Σωκράτει συνήστην *I know that even those two men were temperate as long as they associated with Socrates* (i.e. ἐσωφρονείτην), X. M. 1, 2, 18. See **1286**.

b. The (rare) future perfect participle is used to express future completion with permanent effect (cf. **1277**); e.g. ὡς διαπεπολεμησόμενον (accusative absolute, **1571**) *since the war would be at an end*, Thuc. 7, 25.

1291. The aorist participle in certain constructions (generally with a verb in the aorist) does not denote time past with reference to the leading verb, but expresses time coincident with that of the verb when the action of the verb and of the participle is practically one. See examples in **1566 h, 1587, 1588**, and *Greek Moods and Tenses*, §§ 144–150.

IV. Gnomic and Iterative Tenses

1292. The present is the tense commonly used in Greek, as in English, to denote a general truth or an habitual action. E.g.

τίκτει τοι κόρος ὕβριν, ὅταν κακῷ ὄλβος ἕπηται *satiety begets insolence, whenever prosperity attends the wicked*, Theognis 153.

1293. In animated language the aorist is used in this sense. This is called the *gnomic aorist*, and is generally translated by the English present. E.g.

ἤν τις τούτων τι παραβαίνῃ, ζημίαν αὐτοῖς ἐπέθεσαν *they impose a penalty on all who transgress*, X. C. 1, 2, 2; μί᾽ ἡμέρα τὸν μὲν καθεῖλεν ὑψόθεν, τὸν δ᾽ ἦρ᾽ ἄνω *one day (often) brings down one man from a height and raises another high*, E. *frag.* 424.

1294. Here one case in past time is vividly used to represent all possible cases. Examples containing such adverbs as πολλάκις *often*, ἤδη *already*, οὔπω *never yet* illustrate the construction; e.g. ἀθυμοῦντες ἄνδρες οὔπω τρόπαιον ἔστησαν *disheartened men never yet raised* (i.e. *never raise*) *a trophy*, Plat. *Critias* 108 c. Cf. "Faint heart never *won* fair lady."

1295. An aorist resembling the gnomic is found in Homeric similes; e.g. ἤριπε δ᾽ ὡς ὅτε τις δρῦς ἤριπεν *and he fell, as when some oak falls* (lit. *as when an oak once fell*), Il. 13, 389.

1296. The perfect is sometimes gnomic, like the aorist. E.g.

τὸ δὲ μὴ ἐμποδὼν ἀνανταγωνίστῳ εὐνοίᾳ τετίμηται *but those who are not before men's eyes are held in honor with a good will which has no rivalry*, Thuc. 2, 45.

1297. The imperfect and aorist are sometimes used with the adverb ἄν to denote a *customary* action. E.g.

διηρώτων ἂν αὐτοὺς τί λέγοιεν *I used to ask them (I would often ask them) what they meant*, Plat. *Ap.* 22 b; πολλάκις ἠκούσαμεν ἂν ὑμᾶς *we used often to hear you*, Ar. *Lys.* 511. This iterative usage, which involves no condition (1304), may have been colloquial.

1298. The Ionic has iterative forms in -σκον and -σκόμην in both imperfect and aorist. See 606. Herodotus uses these also with ἄν, as above (1297).

THE ADVERB ἄν

1299. The adverb ἄν (epic enclitic κέν, κέ, Doric κά) has two distinct uses.

a. It may be joined to all the secondary tenses of the indicative (in Homer also to the future indicative), and to the optative, infinitive, or participle, to denote that the action of the verb is dependent on some circumstances or condition, expressed or implied. Here it belongs strictly to the verb.

b. It is joined regularly to εἰ *if*, to all relative and temporal words, and sometimes to the final conjunctions ὡς, ὅπως, and ὄφρα, when these are followed by the subjunctive. Here, although as an adverb it qualifies the verb, it is always closely attached to the particle or relative, with which it often forms one word, as in ἐάν, ὅταν, ἐπειδάν (1311).

1300. There is no English word which can translate ἄν. In its first use it is expressed in the *would* or *should* of the verb (βούλοιτο ἄν *he would wish*; ἐλοίμην ἄν *I should choose*). In its second use it generally has no force which can be made apparent in English.

1301. Ἄν never begins a sentence or clause, but it may be separated from its verb and attached to a negative or interrogative word, to an adverb, or to a verb of *saying* or *thinking*; e.g. οὐκ ἄν μοι δοκεῖ τὸ τοιοῦτο ξυμβῆναι γενέσθαι *I do not think that such a thing could by any chance have happened,* Thuc. 3, 89; οὓς νομίζω ἂν σὺν τῇ παρούσῃ δυνάμει ταπεινοὺς ὑμῖν παρασχεῖν *whom I think I could, with the force at hand, bring under submission to you,* X. *An.* 2, 5, 13; τάχιστ' ἄν τε πόλιν οἱ τοιοῦτοι ἑτέρους πείσαντες ἀπολέσειαν *further, such men as these, if they should win others over, would very soon destroy a state,* Thuc. 2, 63. See 1310.

1302. The present and perfect indicative never take ἄν.

1303. The future indicative sometimes takes ἄν (or κέ) in the early poets, especially Homer; very rarely in Attic Greek. E.g. καί κέ τις ὧδ' ἐρέει *and some one will* (or *may*) *speak thus, Il.* 4, 176; ἄλλοι οἵ κέ με τιμήσουσι *others who will (perchance) honor me, Il.* 1, 174. The future with ἄν seems to be an intermediate construction between the simple future, *will honor,* and the optative with ἄν, *would honor.* The few examples in Attic prose are suspected. In Plat. *Ap.* 29 c ἤδη ἄν is separated by a long interval from the verb διαφθαρήσονται (anacoluthon).

1304. *a.* The past tenses of the indicative (generally the imperfect or aorist) are used with ἄν in a potential sense (1334), or in the apodosis of an unfulfilled condition (1407). E.g. οὐδὲν ἂν κακὸν ἐποίησαν *they could* (or *would*) *have done no harm;* ἦλθεν ἂν εἰ ἐκέλευσα *he would have come if I had commanded him.*

b. The imperfect and aorist indicative with ἄν may also have an iterative sense. See 1297.

1305. *a.* In Attic Greek the subjunctive is used with ἄν only in the dependent constructions mentioned in 1299 *b,* where ἄν is attached to the introductory particle or relative word.

See 1376, 1387, 1393, 1440.

b. In epic poetry, where the independent subjunctive often has the sense of the future indicative (1364), it may take κέ or ἄν, like the future (1303). E.g.

εἰ δέ κε μὴ δώῃσιν, ἐγὼ δέ κεν αὐτὸς ἕλωμαι *and if he does not give her up, then I will take her myself, Il.* 1, 324 (**1432**).

1306. The optative with ἄν has a potential sense (**1326**), and it often forms the apodosis of a condition expressed by the optative with εἰ, denoting what *would happen* if the condition should be fulfilled (**1418**).

1307. The *future* optative is never used with ἄν, since it could represent only the future indicative with ἄν (**1288**). Similarly the future infinitive and future participle with ἄν are excluded. In Plat. *Ap.* 30 b read ἂν ποιήσαντος, not ποιήσοντος. Cf. Plat. *Crito* 53 c, where some MSS. omit it.

1308. *a.* The present and aorist (rarely the perfect) infinitive and participle with ἄν represent the indicative or optative with ἄν; each tense being equivalent to the *corresponding tense* of one of these moods with ἄν, — the present representing also the imperfect, and the perfect also the pluperfect (**1286, 1290**).

b. Thus the present infinitive or participle with ἄν may represent either an imperfect indicative or a present optative with ἄν; *future?* the aorist, either an aorist indicative or an aorist optative with ἄν; the perfect, either a pluperfect indicative or a perfect optative with ἄν. E.g.

PRESENT. φησὶν αὐτοὺς ἐλευθέρους ἂν εἶναι, εἰ τοῦτο ἔπραξαν *he says that they would (now) be free* (ἦσαν ἄν) *if they had done this*; φησὶν αὐτοὺς ἐλευθέρους ἂν εἶναι, εἰ τοῦτο πράξειαν *he says that they would (hereafter) be free* (εἶεν ἄν) *if they should do this*; οἶδα αὐτοὺς ἐλευθέρους ἂν ὄντας, εἰ τοῦτο ἔπραξαν *I know that they would (now) be free* (ἦσαν ἄν) *if they had done this*; οἶδα αὐτοὺς ἐλευθέρους ἂν ὄντας, εἰ ταῦτα πράξειαν *I know that they would (hereafter) be free* (εἶεν ἄν) *if they should do this*; πόλλ' ἂν ἔχων ἕτερ' εἰπεῖν *although I might* (= ἔχοιμι ἄν) *say many other things,* Dem. 18, 258.

AORIST. φασὶν αὐτὸν ἐλθεῖν ἄν (or οἶδα αὐτὸν ἐλθόντα ἄν), εἰ τοῦτο ἐγένετο *they say (or I know) that he would have come* (ἦλθεν ἄν) *if this had happened*; φασὶν αὐτὸν ἐλθεῖν ἄν (or οἶδα αὐτὸν ἐλθόντα ἄν), εἰ τοῦτο γένοιτο *they say (or I know) that he would come* (ἔλθοι ἄν) *if this should happen*; ῥᾳδίως ἂν ἀφεθείς, προείλετο ἀποθανεῖν *although he might easily have been acquitted* (ἀφείθη ἄν) *he preferred to die,* X. *M.* 4, 4, 4.

PERFECT. εἰ μὴ τὰς ἀρετὰς ἐκείνας παρέσχοντο, πάντα ταῦθ' ὑπὸ τῶν βαρβάρων ἂν ἐαλωκέναι (φήσειεν ἄν τις) *had they not exhibited those exploits of valor, (one might say that) all this would now be in the hands of* (lit. *would have been captured by,* **1265**) *the barbarians* (ἐαλώκει ἄν), Dem. 19, 312; οὐκ ἂν ἡγοῦμαι αὐτοὺς δίκην ἀξίαν δεδωκέναι, εἰ αὐτῶν καταψηφίσαισθε *I do not think that, if you should condemn them, they would (thereby,* in the future, *prove to) have suffered proper punishment* (δεδωκότες ἂν εἶεν), Lys. 27, 9.

The context must decide in each case whether we have the equivalent of the indicative or of the optative with ἄν. In the examples given, the form of the protasis generally settles the question.

1309. The infinitive with ἄν is used chiefly in indirect discourse (1509); but the participle with ἄν is more common in other constructions (see examples above).

1310. When ἄν is used with the subjunctive (as in 1299 b), it may be separated from the introductory word only by monosyllabic particles like μέν, δέ, τέ, γάρ, etc. Cf. 1301.

1311. When ἄν is used with the subjunctive, it is combined with the introductory conjunction if crasis (49) is possible. Thus arise the forms ἐάν (ἤν, ἄν), ἐπήν (ἐπάν), ἐπειδάν, ὅταν, ὁπόταν, from εἰ if, ἐπεί, ἐπειδή when, ὅτε, ὁπότε when, + ἄν; also ἄν for ἂ ἄν, κἄν for καὶ ἄν (or ἐάν), but ἕως ἄν, πρὶν ἄν.

1312. In a long apodosis ἄν may be used twice or even three times with the same verb. E.g.

οὐκ ἂν ἡγεῖσθ' αὐτὸν κἂν ἐ π ι δ ρ α μ ε ῖ ν; *do you not think that he would even have rushed thither?* Dem. 27, 56. In Thuc. 2, 41, ἄν is used three times with παρέχεσθαι; in Plat. *Ap.* 40 d, three times with εὑρεῖν; cf. E. *I. T.* 245, 627.

1313. Ἄν may be used elliptically with a verb understood. E.g.

οἱ οἰκέται ῥέγκουσιν · ἀλλ' οὐκ ἂν πρὸ τοῦ (sc. ἔρρεγκον) *my servants are snoring; but in old times they wouldn't have,* Ar. *Nub.* 5. So in φοβούμενος ὥσπερ ἂν εἰ παῖς *scared as a child* (ὥσπερ ἂν ἐφοβεῖτο εἰ παῖς ἦν), Plat. *G.* 479 a.

1314. When an apodosis consists of several coördinate verbs, ἄν generally stands only with the first. E.g.

οὐδὲν ἂν διάφορον τοῦ ἑτέρου π ο ι ο ῖ, ἀλλ' ἐπὶ ταὐτὸν ἴ ο ι ε ν ἀμφότεροι *he would do nothing different from the other man, but both would make for* (go to get) *the same object* (ἄν belongs also with ἴοιεν), Plat. *Rep.* 360 c.

1315. The adverb τάχα *quickly, soon, readily* is often prefixed to ἄν, in which case τάχ' ἄν is nearly equivalent to ἴσως *perhaps.* The ἄν here always belongs in its regular sense (1299 a) to the verb of the sentence; e.g. τάχ' ἂν ἔλθοι *perhaps he would come,* τάχ' ἂν ἦλθεν *perhaps he would* (or *might*) *have come.* A redundant ἴσως may follow τάχ' ἄν.

THE MOODS

1316. The indicative is used in simple, absolute assertions or negations, and in questions or exclamations which include or concern such assertions; e.g. γράφει *he writes,* οὐκ ἔγραψεν *he did not write,* γράψει *he will write,* γέγραφεν *he has written,* τί ἐγράψατε; *what did you write?* ἔγραψε τοῦτο; *did he write this?* οἷα ποιεῖτε *how you behave!*

1317. The indicative has a tense to express every variety of time which is recognized by the Greek verb, and thus it can state a supposition as well as make an assertion in the past, present, or future. It also expresses certain other relations which in other languages (e.g. Latin) are generally expressed by a different mood. The following examples will illustrate these uses:

εἰ τοῦτο ἀληθές ἐστι, χαίρω *if this is true, I am glad* (**1400**), εἰ ἔγραψεν, ἦλθον ἄν *if he had written, I should have come* (**1407**), εἰ τοῦτο ποιήσεις, μεταμελήσει σοι *if you do that you will be sorry* (**1415**), ἐπιμελεῖται ὅπως τοῦτο γενήσεται *he takes care that this shall happen* (**1382**), λέγει ὅτι τοῦτο ποιεῖ *he says that he is doing this*; sometimes εἶπεν ὅτι τοῦτο ποιεῖ *he said that he was doing this* (he said ποιῶ, **1502**), εἴθε με ἔκτεινας, ὡς μήποτε τοῦτο ἐποίησα *O that thou hadst killed me, that I might never have done this!* (**1359, 1381**), εἴθε τοῦτο ἀληθὲς ἦν *O that this were true!* (**1359**).

1318. These constructions are explained in the sections referred to. Their variety shows the impossibility of including all the actual uses even of the indicative under any single fundamental idea.

1319. The various uses of the subjunctive are shown by the following examples:

ἴωμεν *let us go* (**1343**), μὴ θαυμάσητε *do not wonder* (**1345**), τί εἴπω; *what am I to say?* (**1367**), οὐ μὴ τοῦτο γένηται *this (surely) will not happen* (**1369**), οὐδὲ ἴδωμαι (Homeric) *nor shall I see* (**1364**).

ἔρχεται ἵνα τοῦτο ἴδῃ *he is coming that he may see this* (**1374**), φοβεῖται μὴ τοῦτο γένηται *he fears that this may happen* (**1389**), ἐὰν ἔλθῃ, τοῦτο ποιήσω *if he comes (or if he shall come), I shall do this* (**1413**), ἐάν τις ἔλθῃ, τοῦτο ποιῶ *if any one (ever) comes, I (always) do this* (**1403 a**), ὅταν ἔλθῃ, τοῦτο ποιήσω *when he comes (or when he shall come), I shall do this* (**1445**), ὅταν τις ἔλθῃ, τοῦτο ποιῶ *when any one comes, I (always) do this* (**1442 a**).

1320. The subjunctive, in its simplest and apparently most primitive use, expresses simple futurity (negative οὐ); this is seen in the Homeric independent construction, ἴδωμαι *I shall see*, εἴπησί τις *one will say*. In commands it is still future (negative μή); e.g. ἴωμεν *let us go*, μὴ ποιήσητε τοῦτο *do not do this*. In final and object clauses it expresses a future purpose or a future object of fear. In conditional and conditional relative sentences it expresses a future supposition; except in *general* conditions, where it is indefinite (but never strictly present) in its time.

1321. The various uses of the optative are shown by the following examples:

εὐτυχοίης *may you have good luck*; μὴ γένοιτο *may it not happen*; εἴθε μὴ ἀπόλοιντο *O that they may not be lost* (**1355**); ἔλθοι ἄν *he may go* or *he might go* (**1326**).

ἦλθεν ἵνα τοῦτο ἴδοι *he came that he might see this* (**1374**); ἐφοβεῖτο μὴ τοῦτο γένοιτο *he feared that this might happen* (**1389**); εἰ ἔλθοι, τοῦτ' ἂν ποιήσαιμι *if he should come, I should do this* (**1418**); εἴ τις ἔλθοι, τοῦτ' ἐποίουν *if anyone (ever) came, I (always) did this* (**1403** *b*); ὅτε ἔλθοι, τοῦτ' ἂν ποιήσαιμι *whenever he should come (at any time when he should come), I should do this* (**1447**); ὅτε τις ἔλθοι, τοῦτ' ἐποίουν *whenever anyone came, I (always) did this* (**1442** *b*); ἐπεμελεῖτο ὅπως τοῦτο γενήσοιτο *he took care that this should happen* (**1382**); εἶπεν ὅτι τοῦτο ποιοίη (ποιήσοι or ποιήσειε) *he said that he was doing (would do or had done) this* (**1502**).

1322. The optative in many of its uses is a vaguer and less distinct form of expression than the subjunctive, indicative, or imperative, in constructions of the same general character. This appears especially in its independent uses; e.g. the Homeric Ἑλένην ἄγοιτο *he may take Helen away*, *Il.* 4, 19 (see γυναῖκα ἀγέσθω, *Il.* 3, 72, referring to the same thing, and καί ποτέ τις εἴπησιν and *sometime one will say*, **1320**); ἴοιμεν *may we go* (cf. ἴωμεν *let us go*); μὴ γένοιτο *may it not happen* (cf. μὴ γένηται *let it not happen*); ἕλοιτο ἄν (Hom. sometimes ἕλοιτο alone) *he would take* (cf. Hom. ἕληται, sometimes with κέ, *he will take*). So in future conditions; e.g. εἰ γένοιτο *if it should happen* (cf. ἐὰν γένηται *if it shall happen*). In other dependent clauses it is generally a correlative of the subjunctive, sometimes of the indicative; here it represents a dependent subjunctive or indicative in its *changed relation* when the verb on which it depends is changed from present or future to past time. The same change in relation is expressed in English by a change from *shall, will, may, do, is*, etc. to *should, would, might, did, was*, etc. To illustrate these last relations, compare ἔρχεται ἵνα ἴδῃ, φοβεῖται μὴ γένηται, ἐάν τις ἔλθῃ τοῦτο ποιῶ, ἐπιμελεῖται ὅπως τοῦτο γενήσεται, and λέγει ὅτι τοῦτο ποιεῖ, with the corresponding forms after past leading verbs given in **1321**.

For a discussion of the whole relation of the optative to the subjunctive and the other moods, and of the original meaning of the subjunctive and optative, see *Moods and Tenses*, pp. 371–389.

1323. The imperative is used to express commands and prohibitions; e.g. τοῦτο ποίει *do this*; μή φεύγετε *do not fly*.

1324. The infinitive, which is a verbal noun, and the participle and the verbal in -τέος, which are verbal adjectives, are closely connected with the moods of the verb in many constructions.

1325. The following sections (**1326–1519**) treat of all constructions which require any other form of the finite verb than the indicative in simple assertions and questions (**1316**). The infinitive and participle are included here so far as either of them is used in indirect discourse, in protasis or apodosis, or after ὥστε (ὡς, ἐφ' ᾧ or ἐφ' ᾧτε) and πρίν. These constructions are divided as follows:

I. Potential Optative and Indicative with ἄν

Potential Optative

1326. The optative with ἄν expresses a future action as dependent on circumstances or conditions. Thus ἔλθοι ἄν is *he may go, he might (could or would) go*, or *he would be likely to go*, as opposed to an absolute statement like *he will go*. But the translation *he will go* as a future in assertions often quite positive, or *he must go*, in inferences, is frequently appropriate. E.g.

ἔτι γάρ κεν ἀλύξαιμεν κακὸν ἦμαρ *for (perhaps) we may still escape the evil day*, Od. 10, 269 ; πᾶν γὰρ ἂν πύθοιό μου *for you can learn anything you please from me*, Aesch. *Pr.* 617 ; τί τόνδ' ἂν εἴποις ἄλλο; *what else could you say of this man?* S. *Ant.* 646 ; οὐκ ἂν λειφθείην *I would not be left behind (in any case)*, Hdt. 4, 97 ; δὶς ἐς τὸν αὐτὸν ποταμὸν οὐκ ἂν ἐμβαίης *you cannot (could not) step twice into the same river*, Plat. *Crat.* 402 a ; οὐδ' ἄλλο οὐδὲν τἀγαθὸν ἂν εἴη *the chief good cannot be anything else, either*, Aristot. *Nic. Eth.* 1172 b 32 ; ἡδέως ἂν ἐροίμην Λεπτίνην *I would gladly ask (I should like to ask) Leptines*, Dem. 20, 129 ; ποῖ οὖν τραποίμεθ' ἂν ἔτι; *in what other direction can we (could we) possibly turn?* Plat. *Euthyd.* 290 a ; οὐ γὰρ ἂν ἀπέλθοιμ', ἀλλὰ κόψω τὴν θύραν *I will not go away, but I'll knock at the door*, Ar. *Ach.* 403 ; οὐκοῦν ἐν μέσῳ τις ἂν εἴη ἀριστοκρατίας τε καὶ ὀλιγαρχίας αὕτη ἡ πολιτεία; *must not this form of government, then, be something midway between aristocracy and oligarchy?* Plat. *Rep.* 547 c. So βουλοίμην ἄν, velim, *I should like*; cf. ἐβουλόμην ἄν, vellem (**1338**).

1327. This optative is usually called *potential*, and corresponds generally to the English potential forms with *may, can, might, could, would,* etc. It is equivalent to the Latin potential subjunctive, e.g. dicas, credas, cernas, putes, etc. *you may say, believe, perceive, think,* etc. The limiting condition is generally too indefinite to be distinctly present to the mind, and can be expressed only by words like *perhaps, possibly,* or *probably,* or by such vague forms as *if he pleased, if he should try, if he could, if there should be an opportunity,* etc. Sometimes a general condition, like *in any possible case,* is felt to be implied, so that the optative with ἄν hardly differs from an absolute future; e.g. οὐκ ἄν μεθείμην τοῦ θρόνου *I will not (would never) give up the throne,* Ar. *R.* 830. See the examples in **1329**. Cf. **1335**.

1328. The potential optative can express every degree of potentiality from the almost absolute future of the last example to the apodosis of a future condition expressed by the optative with εἰ (**1418**), where the form of the condition is assimilated to that of the conclusion. The intermediate steps may be seen in the following examples:

οὐκ ἄν δικαίως ἐς κακὸν πέσοιμί τι *I could not justly fall into any trouble,* S. *Ant.* 240, where δικαίως points to the condition *if justice should be done;* οὔτε ἐσθίουσι πλείω ἢ δύνανται φέρειν · διαρραγεῖεν γὰρ ἄν *nor do they eat more than they can carry, for (if they did) they would burst,* X. *C.* 8, 2, 21, where εἰ ἐσθίοιεν is implied by the former clause.

1329. The potential optative of the second person may express a mild command or exhortation; e.g. χωροῖς ἄν εἴσω *you may go in,* or *go in,* S. *Ph.* 674; κλύοις ἄν ἤδη *hear me now,* S. *El.* 637. See **1327, 1358**.

1330. The potential optative may express what may hereafter prove to be true or to have been true; e.g. ἡ ἐμὴ (σοφία) φαύλη τις ἄν εἴη *my wisdom may turn out to be of a trivial sort,* Plat. *Symp.* 175 e; ποῦ δῆτ᾽ ἄν εἶεν οἱ ξένοι *where may the strangers be?* i.e. *where is it likely to prove that they are?* S. *El.* 1450; εἴησαν δ᾽ ἄν οὗτοι Κρῆτες *and these would probably be* (or *must have been*) *Cretans,* Hdt. 1, 2; αὗται δὲ οὐκ ἄν πολλαὶ εἴησαν *and these* (the islands) *cannot have been "many,"* Thuc. 1, 9; οὗτοι δὲ τάχ᾽ ἄν μείζω τινὰ ἢ κατ᾽ ἄνθρωπον σοφίαν σοφοὶ εἶεν *but these men may perhaps (prove to) be wise in a kind of superhuman wisdom,* Plat. *Ap.* 20 d.

1331. Occasionally ἄν is omitted with the potential optative, chiefly in Homer; e.g. οὔ τι κακώτερον ἄλλο πάθοιμι *I could suffer nothing else that is worse,* *Il.* 19, 321. See Gildersleeve *S. C. G.* 450.

1332. The Attic poets sometimes omit ἄν after such indefinite expressions as ἔστιν ὅστις, ἔστιν ὅπως, ἔστιν ὅποι, etc.; e.g. ἔστ᾽ οὖν ὅπως Ἄλκηστις ἐς γῆρας μόλοι; *is it possible then that Alcestis can come to old age?* E. *Alc.* 52; so 113, and Aesch. *Pr.* 292.

1333. For the potential optative in Homer referring to past time, see **1409**.

Potential Indicative

1334. The past tenses of the indicative with ἄν express a past action as dependent on past circumstances or conditions. Thus, while ἦλθεν means *he went*, ἦλθεν ἄν means *he would have gone (under some past circumstances)*.

1335. This is called the potential indicative; and it probably arose as a past form of the potential optative, so that, while ἔλθοι ἄν meant originally *he may go* or *he would be likely to go*, ἦλθεν ἄν meant *he may have gone* or *he would have been likely to go*. It is the equivalent of the Latin forms like diceres *you would have said*, crederes *you would have believed*, cerneres, putares, etc., which are past potential forms corresponding to dicas, credas, cernas, putes, etc. (1327). E.g. putet and putaret are equivalent to οἴοιτο ἄν *he would be likely to think*, and ᾤετο ἄν *he would have been likely to think*.

1336. The potential indicative sometimes expresses (in its original force) what *would have been likely* to happen, i.e. *might have* happened (and perhaps *did* happen) with no reference to any definite condition. E.g.

ὑπό κεν ταλασίφρονά περ δέος εἷλεν *fear might have seized* (i.e. *would have been likely to seize*) *even a man of stout heart, Il.* 4, 421; ἦλθε τοῦτο τοὔνειδος τάχ' ἂν ὀργῇ βιασθέν *this reproach may perhaps have come from violence of wrath*, S. O. T. 523; ἐν ταύτῃ τῇ ἡλικίᾳ λέγοντες πρὸς ὑμᾶς ἐν ᾗ ἂν μάλιστα ἐπιστεύσατε *talking to you at that age at which you would have been most likely to put trust in them*, Plat. Ap. 18 c.

1337. Generally, however, the potential indicative implies a reference to some circumstances different from the real ones, so that ἦλθεν ἄν commonly means *he would have gone (if something had not been as it was)*. The unreal past condition here may be as vague and indefinite as the future condition to which the potential optative refers (1327). E.g.

οὐ γάρ κεν δυνάμεσθα (impf.) θυράων ἀπώσασθαι λίθον *for we could not have moved the stone from the doorway, Od.* 9, 304; cf. οὐδὲν ἂν κακὸν ποιήσειαν *they could do no harm (if they should try)*, with οὐδὲν ἂν κακὸν ἐποίησαν *they could have done no harm (if they had tried)*; τούτου τίς ἂν σοι τἀνδρὸς ἀμείνων ηὑρέθη; *who could have been found better than this man?* S. Aj. 119; ὀψὲ ἦν, καὶ τὰς χεῖρας οὐκ ἂν καθεώρων *it was late, and they would not have seen the show of hands*, X. H. 1, 7, 7; ποίων ἂν ἔργων ἀπέστησαν; *from what labors would they have shrunk?* Isoc. 4, 83.

1338. When no definite condition is understood with the potential indicative, the imperfect with ἄν is regularly past, as it always is in Homer (1408). See the examples in **1337**.

The imperfect with ἄν referring to present time, which is common in apodosis after Homer (1407), seldom appears in purely potential expressions, chiefly in ἐβουλόμην ἄν vellem, *I should wish, I should like* (which can mean also *I should have wished*) ; e.g. ἐβουλόμην ἂν αὐτοὺς ἀληθῆ λέγειν *I could wish that they spoke the truth*, Lys. 12, 22.

1339. The potential indicative may express every degree of potentiality from that seen in **1336** to that of the apodosis of an unfulfilled condition actually expressed. (Cf. the potential optative, **1328.**) Here, after Homer, the imperfect with ἄν may express present time (see **1407**). The intermediate steps to the complete apodosis may be seen in the following examples:

ἦγετε τὴν εἰρήνην ὅμως · οὐ γὰρ ἦν ὅ τι ἂν ἐποιεῖτε *still you kept the peace; for there was nothing which you could have done (if you had not)*, Dem. 18, 43. πολλοῦ γὰρ ἂν τὰ ὄργανα ἦν ἄξια *for the tools would be worth much (if they had this power)*, Plat. *Rep.* 374 d.

For the full conditional sentences, see **1407**.

1340. For a peculiar potential expression formed by imperfects denoting *obligation* etc., like ἔδει, χρῆν, etc., with the infinitive, see **1410**.

II. Commands, Exhortations, Prohibitions

1341. The imperative expresses a command, exhortation, or entreaty ; e.g. λέγε *speak!* φεῦγε *begone!* ἐλθέτω *let him come,* χαιρόντων *let them rejoice.* For the optative with ἄν, see **1329**.

1342. A combination of command and question is found in such phrases as οἶσθ' ὃ δρᾶσον; *dost thou know what to do?* Ar. *Av.* 54, where the imperative is the verb of the relative clause. So οἶσθα νῦν ἅ μοι γενέσθω; *do you know what must be done for me?* E. *I. T.* 1203.

1343. The *first person* of the subjunctive (generally *plural*) is used in exhortations. Its negative is μή. E.g. ἴωμεν *let us go,* ἴδωμεν *let us see,* μὴ τοῦτο ποιῶμεν *let us not do this.* This supplies the want of a first person of the imperative.

1344. Both subjunctive and imperative may be preceded by ἄγε (ἄγετε), φέρε, or ἴθι *come!* These words are used without regard to the number or person of the verb which follows. A hortatory ἀλλά often precedes the imperative; e.g. ἀλλ' ἄγε μίμνετε πάντες αὐτόθι *nay come, stay ye all here, Il.* 2, 331.

1345. In prohibitions, in the second and third persons, the *present imperative* or the *aorist subjunctive* is used with μή and its compounds. E.g.

μὴ ποίει τοῦτο *do not do this* (habitually, **1274**) or *do not go on doing this* or *abstain from doing this*; μὴ ποιήσῃς τοῦτο (simply) *do not do this*; μὴ κατὰ τοὺς νόμους δικάσητε · μὴ βοηθήσητε τῷ πεπονθότι δεινά · μὴ εὐορκεῖτε *do not judge according to the laws; do not help him who has suffered outrages; do not abide by your oaths,* Dem. 21, 211.

1346. The *third* person of the aorist imperative sometimes occurs in prohibitions; the *second* person very rarely.

1347. In Homer the independent subjunctive with μή (generally in the third person) may express fear or anxiety, with a desire to avert the object of the fear. E.g.

μὴ δὴ νῆας ἕλωσι *may they not seize the ships (as I fear they may),* Il. 16, 128; μή τι χολωσάμενος ῥέξῃ κακὸν υἷας 'Αχαιῶν *may he not (as I fear he may) in his wrath do any harm to the sons of the Achaeans,* Il. 2, 195.

1348. This usage occurs sometimes in Euripides and Plato; e.g. μή σοὺς διαφθείρῃ γάμους *my fear is that you may be sullied for a proper marriage,* E. Alc. 315; μή τις οἴηται *I fear that one may think,* Plat. Legg. 861 e. See *Moods and Tenses,* §§ 261–264.

1349. An independent present subjunctive with μή may express a cautious assertion, or a suspicion that something *may be* true; and with μὴ οὐ a cautious negation, or a suspicion that something *may not be* true. This is a favorite usage with Plato. E.g.

μὴ ἀγροικότερον ᾖ τὸ ἀληθὲς εἰπεῖν *I suspect that it may be rather boorish to tell the truth,* Plat. G. 462 e; ἀλλὰ μὴ οὐ τοῦτ' ᾖ χαλεπόν *but I rather think that this may not be a difficult thing,* Plat. Ap. 39 a.

1350. The indicative may be thus used (1349) with μή or μὴ οὐ, referring to present or past time. E.g.

ἀλλὰ μὴ τοῦτο οὐ καλῶς ὡμολογήσαμεν *but perhaps we did not do well in assenting to this,* Plat. Meno 89 c. Hence μήποτε *perhaps* in Aristotle and later Greek.

1351. In Attic Greek ὅπως and ὅπως μή are used colloquially with the future indicative in commands and prohibitions. E.g.

νῦν οὖν ὅπως σώσεις με *so now save me,* Ar. Nub. 1177; κατάθου τὰ σκεύη, χὤπως ἐρεῖς ἐνταῦθα μηδὲν ψεῦδος *put down the packs, and tell no lies here,* Ar. R. 627; ὅπως οὖν ἔσεσθε ἄξιοι τῆς ἐλευθερίας *(see that you) prove yourselves worthy of freedom,* X. An. 1, 7, 3; ὅπως μοι μὴ ἐρεῖς ὅτι ἔστι τὰ δώδεκα δὶς ἕξ *see that you do not tell me that twelve is twice six,* Plat. Rep. 337 b.

1352. The construction of **1351** is often explained by an ellipsis of σκόπει or σκοπεῖτε (see **1382**).

1353. The subjunctive occasionally occurs here with ὅπως μή, but not with ὅπως alone; e.g. ὅπως μὴ ᾖ τοῦτο *maybe this will prove true,* Plat. Crat. 430 d.

1354. The future indicative with οὐ, put as a question, may express a command; e.g. οὗτος, οὐ μενεῖς; *you there, stop!* Ar. Av. 1055.

III. Expression of a Wish

1355. When a wish refers to the future, it is expressed by the optative, either with or without εἴθε or εἰ γάρ (εἰ alone in poetry, in Homer also αἴθε, αἰ γάρ) *O that, O if.* The negative is μή, which can stand alone with the optative. E.g.

ὑμῖν θεοὶ δοῖεν ἐκπέρσαι Πριάμοιο πόλιν *may the gods grant to you to destroy Priam's city, Il.* 1, 18; αἲ γὰρ ἐμοὶ τοσσήνδε θεοὶ δύναμιν περιθεῖεν *O that the gods would clothe me with so much strength, Od.* 3, 205; τὸ μὲν νῦν ταῦτα πρήσσοις τάπερ ἐν χερσὶ ἔχεις *for the present may you carry out these things which you have now in hand,* Hdt. 7, 5; εἴθε φίλος ἡμῖν γένοιο *O that you may become our friend,* X. H. 4, 1, 38; μηκέτι ζῴην ἐγώ *may I no longer live,* Ar. Nub. 1255; εἴ μοι γένοιτο φθόγγος ἐν βραχίοσιν *O that I might find a voice in my arms,* E. Hec. 836.

The force of the tenses here is the same as in protasis (see **1274**).

1356. In poetry πῶς ἄν may introduce a wish in the form of a question; e.g. πῶς ἄν μ᾽ ἀδελφῆς χεὶρ περιστείλειεν; *would that a sister's hand might compose my body!* E. I. T. 627.

1357. The poets, especially Homer, sometimes prefix ὡς (probably exclamatory) to the optative in wishes; e.g. ὡς ἀπόλοιτο καὶ ἄλλος ὅτις τοιαῦτά γε ῥέζοι *likewise perish any other who may do the like! Od.* 1, 47.

1358. In poetry, especially in Homer, the optative alone sometimes expresses a *concession* or *permission,* sometimes a *command* or *exhortation;* e.g. αὖτις Ἀργείην Ἑλένην Μενέλαος ἄγοιτο *Menelaus may take back Argive Helen, Il.* 4, 19; τεθναίης, ὦ Προῖτ᾽, ἢ κάκτανε Βελλεροφόντην *either die, O Proetus, or kill Bellerophon, Il.* 6, 164; κεινὸς εἴην *set me down an empty fool,* Pind. O. 3, 45. Here, and in wishes without εἰ, εἰ γάρ, etc., we probably have an original independent use of the optative; whereas wishes introduced by any form of εἰ are probably elliptical protases.

See **1329** and Appendix I in *Greek Moods and Tenses,* pp. 371–389.

1359. When a wish refers to the present or the past, and it is implied that its object *is not* or *was not attained,* it is expressed in Attic Greek by a secondary tense of the indicative with εἴθε or εἰ γάρ, which here cannot be omitted. The negative is μή. The imperfect and aorist are distinguished here as in protasis (**1407**). E.g.

εἴθε τοῦτο ἐποίει *O that he were doing this,* or *O that he had done this;* εἴθε τοῦτο ἐποίησεν *O that he had done this;* εἴθ᾽ εἶχες βελτίους φρένας *O that thou hadst a better understanding,* E. El. 1061; εἰ γὰρ τοσαύτην δύναμιν εἶχον *O that I had so great power,* E. Alc. 1072; εἴθε σοι τότε συνεγενόμην *I wish I had met you at that time,* X. M. 1, 2, 46.

1360. The aorist ὤφελον *ought* of ὀφείλω *owe* (Lat. debeo), and in Homer sometimes the imperfect ὤφελλον, are used with the infinitive, chiefly in poetry, to express a present or past unattained wish (1412 *b*). E.g.

ὤφελε τοῦτο ποιεῖν *would that he were doing this* (lit. *he ought to be doing this*), or *would that he had done this* (*habitually*); ὤφελε τοῦτο ποιῆσαι *would that he had done this.* For the distinction made by the different tenses of the infinitive, see 1410 *b*. Τὴν ὄφελ' ἐν νήεσσι κατακτάμεν Ἄρτεμις *would that Artemis had slain her at the ships, Il.* 19, 59.

1361. Ὤφελον with the infinitive is negatived by μή (not οὐ), and it may even be preceded by εἴθε, εἰ γάρ, or ὡς; e.g. μή ποτ' ὤφελον λιπεῖν τὴν Σκῦρον *O that I had never left Scyros,* S. *Ph.* 969; εἰ γὰρ ὤφελον οἷοί τε εἶναι *would that they were able,* Plat. *Crito* 44 d; ὡς ὤφελες ὀλέσθαι *would that you had perished, Il.* 3, 428 (**1357**)

1362. In Homer the present optative (generally with εἴθε or εἰ γάρ) may express an unattained wish in *present* time; e.g. εἴθ' ὡς ἡβώοιμι βίη δέ μοι ἔμπεδος εἴη *would that I were again as young and my strength were firm, Il.* 11, 670.

This corresponds to the Homeric use of the optative in unreal conditions and their apodoses (**1408**). In both constructions the present optative is commonly future in Homer, as in other Greek.

1363. Homer never uses the indicative (**1359**) in wishes. He always expresses a past wish by the construction with ὤφελον (**1360**), and a present wish sometimes by ὤφελον and sometimes by the present optative (**1362**). For the infinitive, see **1541**.

IV. Homeric Subjunctive like Future Indicative — Interrogative Subjunctive

1364. In Homer the subjunctive in independent sentences sometimes has the force of a future indicative. E.g.

οὐ γάρ πω τοίους ἴδον ἀνέρας, οὐδὲ ἴδωμαι *for I never yet saw nor shall I ever see such men, Il.* 1, 262; καί ποτέ τις εἴπῃσιν *and one will* (or *may*) *some time say, Il.* 6, 459.

1365. This subjunctive may, like the future indicative, take κέ or ἄν in the potential sense. See **1305** *b*, **1320**.

1366. The question τί πάθω; *what will become of me?* or *what harm will it do me?* carries this use even into Attic Greek. E.g.

ὤ μοι ἐγώ, τί πάθω; *Od.* 5, 465; τί πάθω τλήμων; *what will become of me, wretch that I am?* Aesch. *Pr.* 912; τὸ μέλλον, εἰ χρή, πείσομαι · τί γὰρ πάθω; *I shall suffer what is to come, if it must be; for what harm can it do me?* E. *Ph.* 895.

1367. The first person of the subjunctive may be used in questions of appeal, where a person asks himself or another *what he is to do*. The negative is μή. It is often accompanied by a parenthetical βούλει or βούλεσθε (in poetry θέλεις or θέλετε). E.g.

εἴπω ταῦτα; *am I to say this?* or βούλει εἴπω ταῦτα; *do you wish me to say this?* ποῖ τράπωμαι; ποῖ πορευθῶ; *whither shall I turn? whither shall I go?* E. *Hec.* 1099 ; ποῦ δὴ βούλει καθιζόμενοι ἀναγνῶμεν; *where now wilt thou that we sit down and read?* Plat. *Phdr.* 228 e.

1368. The third person is sometimes found in these questions, chiefly when τὶs has the force of *we*; e.g. τί τις εἶναι τοῦτο φῇ; *what are we (is one) to say this is?* Dem. 19, 88.

V. Οὐ μή with Subjunctive and Future Indicative

1369. The subjunctive (generally the aorist) and sometimes the future indicative are used with the double negative οὐ μή in the sense of an emphatic future indicative with οὐ. E.g.

οὐ μὴ πίθηται *he will not obey*, S. *Ph.* 103 ; οὔτε γὰρ γίγνεται οὔτε γέγονεν, οὐδὲ οὖν μὴ γένηται *for there is not, nor has there been, nor will there ever be*, etc., Plat. *Rep.* 492 e ; οὔ ποτ' ἐξ ἐμοῦ γε μὴ πάθῃς τόδε *you never shall suffer this at my hands*, S. *El.* 1029 ; οὔ τοι μήποτέ σε . . . ἄκοντά τις ἄξει *no one shall ever take you against your will*, S. *O. C.* 176.

1370. In the dramatic poets, the second person singular of the future indicative (occasionally of the aorist subjunctive) with οὐ μή may express a strong prohibition. E.g.

οὐ μὴ καταβήσει *don't come down (you shall not come down)*, Ar. *V.* 397 ; οὐ μὴ τάδε γηρύσει *do not speak out in this way*, E. *Hipp.* 213 ; οὐ μὴ σκώψῃς *do not jeer*, Ar. *Nub.* 296.

This construction is not interrogative.

VI. Final and Object Clauses with ἵνα, ὡς, ὅπως, ὄφρα, and μή

1371. The final particles are ἵνα, ὡς, ὅπως, and (epic and lyric) ὄφρα *that, in order that*. To these must be added μή *lest* or *that*, which became in use a negative final particle. The clauses which are introduced by these particles may be divided into three classes :

a. Pure *final* clauses, expressing a purpose or motive ; e.g. ἔρχεται ἵνα τοῦτο ἴδῃ *he is coming that he may see this*. Here any of the final particles may be used (see **1377**).

b. Object clauses with ὅπως and verbs signifying *to strive for, to care for, to effect*; e.g. σκόπει ὅπως τοῦτο γενήσεται *see to it that this is done*.

c. Clauses with μή and verbs of *fear* or *caution*; e.g. φοβεῖται μὴ τοῦτο γένηται *he fears that this may happen*.

1372. The first two classes are to be specially distinguished. The object clauses in *b* are the *direct object* of the leading verb, and can even stand in apposition to an object accusative like τοῦτο; e.g. σκόπει τοῦτο, ὅπως μή σε ὄψεται *see to this, that he does not see you*, But a final clause could stand in apposition only to τούτου ἕνεκα *for the sake of this*, or διὰ τοῦτο *to this end*; e.g. ἔρχεται τούτου ἕνεκα, ἵνα ἡμᾶς ἴδῃ *he is coming for this purpose, that he may see us*.

For the origin of the clauses in *c*, which are objects of a verb of fear, and the development of final clauses, see *Moods and Tenses*, §§ 307–316.

1373. The negative in all these clauses is μή, except after μή *lest*, where οὐ is used; e.g. κατερρώδησαν μὴ οὐ δυνατοὶ γένωνται ὑπερβαλέσθαι *they feared that they should not be able to overcome them*, Hdt. 6, 9.

I. *Pure Final Clauses*

1374. Final clauses, expressing the purpose of the action denoted in the main clause, take the subjunctive after primary tenses, and the optative after secondary tenses. E.g.

δοκεῖ μοι κατακαῦσαι τὰς ἁμάξας, ἵνα μὴ τὰ ζεύγη ἡμῶν στρατηγῇ *I think we should burn our wagons, that our cattle may not be our commanders*, X. *An.* 3, 2, 27; εἴπω τι δῆτα κἄλλ', ἵν' ὀργίσῃ πλέον; *shall I speak still further, that you may be the more angry?* S. *O. T.* 364; παρακαλεῖς ἰατροὺς, ὅπως μὴ ἀποθάνῃ *you call in physicians, that he may not die*, X. *M.* 2, 10, 2; λυσιτελεῖ ἐᾶσαι ἐν τῷ παρόντι, μὴ καὶ τοῦτον πολέμιον προσθώμεθα *it is expedient to allow it for a time, lest we add him to the number of our enemies*, X. *C.* 2, 4, 12; φίλος ἐβούλετο εἶναι τοῖς μέγιστα δυναμένοις, ἵνα ἀδικῶν μὴ διδοίη δίκην *he wished to be a friend to men high in power, that he might do wrong and not be punished*, X. *An.* 2, 6, 21; τούτου ἕνεκα φίλων ᾤετο δεῖσθαι, ὡς συνεργοὺς ἔχοι *what he thought he needed friends for was that he might have helpers*, X. *An.* 1, 9, 21; ἀφικόμην ὅπως σοῦ δόμους ἐλθόντος εὖ πράξαιμί τι *I came that I might gain some good by your return home*, S. *O. T.* 1005.

κεφαλῇ κατανεύσομαι, ὄφρα πεποίθῃς *I will nod my assent, that you may trust me*, Il. 1, 522; ἔνθα κατέσχετ', ὄφρ' ἕταρον θάπτοι *there he tarried that he might bury his companion*, Od. 3, 284.

1375. The future indicative is rarely found in final clauses with ὅπως, ὄφρα, ὡς, and μή. This is almost entirely confined to poetry. See *Od.* 1, 56; 4, 163; *Il.* 20, 301; Ar. *Eccl.* 495.

1376. The adverb ἄν (κέ) is sometimes joined with ὡς, ὅπως, and ὄφρα (never with ἵνα) before the subjunctive in final clauses; e.g. ὡς ἂν μάθῃς, ἀντάκουσον *hear the other side, that you may learn*, X. *An.* 2, 5, 16. For this use, see *Moods and Tenses*, §§ 325–328. The final optative with ἄν is probably always potential (**1326**).

1377. Ὄφρα is the most common final particle in Homer, ὡς in tragedy, and ἵνα in comedy and prose. But ὅπως exceeds ἵνα in Thucydides and Xenophon. Ὡς was never in good use in prose, except in Xenophon.

1378. As final clauses express the purpose or motive of *some person*, they admit the double construction of indirect discourse (**1496, 1517**). Hence instead of the optative after past tenses we can have the mood and tense which would be used when a person conceived the purpose; that is, we can say either ἦλθεν ἵνα ἴδοι *he came that he might see* (**1374**), or ἦλθεν ἵνα ἴδῃ because the person himself would have said ἔρχομαι ἵνα ἴδω *I come that I may see.* E.g.

ξυνεβούλευε τοῖς ἄλλοις ἐκπλεῦσαι, ὅπως ἐπὶ πλέον ὁ σῖτος ἀντίσχῃ *he advised the rest to sail away, that the provisions might hold out longer*, Thuc. 1, 65; τὰ πλοῖα κατέκαυσεν, ἵνα μὴ Κῦρος διαβῇ *he burned the vessels, that Cyrus might not pass over*, X. *An.* 1, 4, 18; καὶ ἐπίτηδές σε οὐκ ἤγειρον ἵνα ὡς ἥδιστα διάγῃς *in fact I did not wake you up on purpose, for I wanted you to pass your time as happily as possible*, Plat. *Crito* 43 b.

1379. The subjunctive is even more common than the optative after past tenses in certain authors, e.g. Thucydides and Herodotus; but much less so in others, e.g. Homer and Xenophon.

1380. Purpose is often implied or suggested in a condition; e.g. πειράσομαι ἐὰν δύνωμαι τῶνδέ σ' ἐκλῦσαι πόνων *I will make trial if so be that I may release thee from these toils*, Aesch. *Pr.* 327. This occurs especially when the condition is introduced by εἴ πως, ἐάν πως, εἰ ἄρα *if haply*; e.g. ἰδὼν συκῆν ἦλθεν εἰ ἄρα τι εὑρήσει ἐν αὐτῇ *seeing a fig tree he came, if haply he might find anything thereon*, Mark 11, 13. See **1430**.

1381. The past tenses of the indicative are used in final clauses with ἵνα, sometimes with ὅπως or ὡς, to denote that the purpose is dependent on some act which does not or did not take place (as on some unfulfilled condition or some unaccomplished wish), and therefore *is not* or *was not attained.* E.g.

τί μ' οὐ λαβὼν ἔκτεινας εὐθύς, ὡς ἔδειξα μήποτε, κ.τ.λ. *why did you not take me and kill me at once, that I might never have shown (as I have done)*, etc.? S. *O. T.* 1391; φεῦ, φεῦ, τὸ μὴ τὰ πράγματ' ἀνθρώποις ἔχειν φωνήν, ἵν' ἦσαν μηδὲν οἱ δεινοὶ λόγοι *alas! alas! that the facts have no voice for men, so that words of eloquence might be as nothing*, E. *frag.* 442.

II. *Object Clauses with ὅπως after Verbs of Striving, etc.*

1382. Object clauses, which take the place of a substantive object of the main verb, depend on verbs signifying *to strive for, to care for, to effect,* and take the future indicative with ὅπως or ὅπως μή after both primary and secondary tenses.

The future optative *may* be used after secondary tenses, as the correlative of the future indicative, but commonly the indicative is retained on the principle of **1378**. E.g.

φρόντιζ' ὅπως μηδὲν ἀνάξιον τῆς τιμῆς ταύτης πράξεις *take heed that you do nothing unworthy of this honor,* Isoc. 2, 37; ἐπεμελεῖτο ὅπως μὴ ἄσιτοί ποτε ἔσοιντο *he took care that they should never be without food,* X. C. 8, 1, 43 (here ἔσονται would be more common); ἔπρασσον ὅπως τις βοήθεια ἥξει *they were trying to bring about the arrival of some assistance,* Thuc. 3, 4.

For ὅπως and ὅπως μή with the future indicative in commands and prohibitions, often explained by an ellipsis of σκόπει or σκοπεῖτε in this construction, see **1351.**

1383. When the main verb is in the passive, the substantive clause is of course subject, not object; e.g. ἐπράττετο ὅπως μὴ περιμενεῖτε τοὺς πρέσβεις, ἵνα ἰδίᾳ ποιήσησθε τὴν εἰρήνην *it was contrived that you should not wait for the envoys, in order that you might make a separate peace,* Aeschin. 3, 64.

1384. The future indicative with ὅπως sometimes follows verbs of *exhorting, entreating, commanding,* and *forbidding,* which commonly take an infinitive of the object; e.g. διακελεύονται ὅπως τιμωρήσεται πάντας τοὺς τοιούτους *they exhort him to take vengeance on all such,* Plat. *Rep.* 549 e.

1385. *a.* Sometimes the present or aorist subjunctive or optative is used in object clauses as in those expressing purpose. E.g.

ἄλλου του ἐπιμελήσει ἢ ὅπως ὅ τι βέλτιστοι πολῖται ὦμεν; *will you care for anything except that we may be the best possible citizens?* Plat. *G.* 515 b; ἐπεμέλετο αὐτῶν, ὅπως ἀεὶ ἀνδράποδα διατελοῖεν *he took care that they should always remain slaves,* X. C. 8, 1, 44.

b. Xenophon allows ὡς with the subjunctive or optative here.

1386. Μή *lest* may be used for ὅπως μή with the subjunctive.

1387. Ἄν or κέ can be used here, as in final clauses (**1376**), with ὅπως or ὡς and the subjunctive. So (rarely) in a construction corresponding to that of **1384**; e.g. παραγγέλλουσιν ὅπως ἂν τῇδε τῇ ἡμέρᾳ τελευτᾷ *they notify him that he is to die that day,* Plat. *Phaedo* 59 e.

1388. In Homer the construction of **1382** with ὅπως and the future is not found; but verbs signifying *to plan, consider,* and *try* take ὅπως or ὡς and the subjunctive or optative. E.g.

φραξώμεθ' ὅπως ὄχ' ἄριστα γένηται *let us consider how the very best may be done*, *Od.* 13, 365; φράσσεται ὥς κε νέηται *he will plan for his return*, *Od.* 1, 205; βούλευον ὅπως ὄχ' ἄριστα γένοιτο *they deliberated that the very best might be done*, *Od.* 9, 420. So rarely with λίσσομαι *entreat* (see **1384**).

III. *Clauses with* μή *after Verbs of Fearing, etc.*

1389. With verbs denoting *fear, caution*, or *danger*, μή *that* or *lest* takes the subjunctive after primary tenses, and the optative after secondary tenses. The subjunctive may also follow secondary tenses, to retain the mood in which the fear originally occurred to the mind. The negative form is μὴ οὐ (**1373**). E.g.

φοβοῦμαι μὴ τοῦτο γένηται (vereor *ne* accidat) *I fear that this may happen*; φοβοῦμαι μὴ οὐ τοῦτο γένηται (vereor *ut* accidat) *I fear that this may not happen*; φροντίζω μὴ κράτιστον ᾖ μοι σιγᾶν *I am anxious lest it may be best for me to be silent*, X. *M.* 4, 2, 39; οὐκέτι ἐπετίθεντο, δεδιότες μὴ ἀποτμηθείησαν *they no longer made attacks, fearing that they would be cut off*, X. *An.* 3, 4, 29; ἐφοβοῦντο μή τι πάθῃ *they feared that something might happen to him* (**1378**), X. *Symp.* 2, 11.

1390. The future indicative is very rarely used after μή in this construction. But ὅπως μή is sometimes used here, as in the object clauses of **1382**, with both future indicative and subjunctive; e.g. δέδοικα ὅπως μὴ ἀνάγκη γενήσεται *I fear that there may come a necessity*, Dem. 9, 75; ὅπως μή here is the equivalent of μή, *that* or *lest*, in the ordinary construction.

1391. Verbs of *fearing* may refer to objects of fear which are *present* or *past*. Here μή takes the present and past tenses of the indicative. E.g.

δέδοικα μὴ πληγῶν δέει *I fear that you need a whipping*, Ar. *Nub.* 493; φοβούμεθα μὴ ἀμφοτέρων ἅμα ἡμαρτήκαμεν *we fear that we have missed both at once*, Thuc. 3, 53; δείδω μὴ δὴ πάντα θεὰ νημερτέα εἶπεν *I fear that all which the goddess said was true*, *Od.* 5, 300; ὅρα μὴ παίζων ἔλεγεν *beware lest he was speaking in jest*, Plat. *Th.* 145 b. For the infinitive, see **1523**.

VII. Conditional Sentences

1392. In conditional sentences the clause containing the condition is called the protasis, and that containing the conclusion is called the apodosis. The protasis is introduced by some form of εἰ *if*.

1393. The adverb ἄν (epic κέ or κέν) is regularly joined to εἰ (epic αἰ) in the *protasis* when the verb is in the subjunctive; εἰ with ἄν forming ἐάν, ἄν, or ἤν. See **1299 b, 1311.** The simple εἰ is used with the indicative and optative. The same adverb ἄν is used in the *apodosis* with the optative, and also with the past tenses of the indicative when it is implied that the condition is not fulfilled.

1394. a. The negative adverb of the protasis is regularly μή, that of the apodosis is οὐ.

b. When οὐ stands in a protasis, it generally belongs to some particular word (e.g. οὐ πολλοί *few,* οὔ φημι *I deny,* **1612**), and not to the protasis as a whole; e.g. ἐάν τε σὺ καὶ Ἄνυτος οὐ φῆτε ἐάν τε φῆτε *whether you and Anytus deny it or admit it,* Plat. *Ap.* 25 b. See **1241 a,** second example.

1395. a. The supposition contained in a protasis may be either *particular* or *general.* A particular supposition refers to a definite act or to several definite acts, supposed to occur at some definite time or times; e.g. *if he (now) has this, he will give it; if he had it, he gave it; if he had had the power, he would have helped me; if he shall receive it* (or *if he receives it*), *he will give it; if he should receive it, he would give it.* A general supposition refers indefinitely to any act or acts of a given class, which may be supposed to occur or to have occurred at any time; e.g. *if ever he receives anything, he (always) gives it; if ever he received anything, he (always) gave it; if (on any occasion) he had had the power, he would (always) have helped me; if ever any one shall* (or *should*) *wish to go, he will* (or *would*) *always be permitted.*

b. Although this distinction is seen in all classes of conditions (as the examples show), it is only in the present and past conditions which do not imply non-fulfilment, i.e. in those of class I (**1398**), that the distinction affects the *construction.*

Classification of Conditional Sentences

1396. The classification of conditional sentences is based partly on the time to which the supposition refers, partly on what is implied with regard to the fulfilment of the condition, and partly on the distinction between particular and general suppositions explained in **1395.**

1397. Conditional sentences have *four* classes, two (I and II) containing present and past suppositions, and two (III and IV) containing future suppositions. Class I has two forms, one (*a*) with chiefly particular suppositions (present and past), the other (*b*) with only general suppositions (1 present, 2 past).

1398. We have thus the following forms:

I. Present and past suppositions implying nothing as to the truth or untruth of the protasis:

(a) **Chiefly Particular:**

(*protasis*) εἰ with indicative; (*apodosis*) any form of the verb. Εἰ τοῦτο ποιεῖ, καλῶς ἔχει *if he is doing this, it is well*; εἰ τοῦτο ἐποίησε, καλῶς ἔχει *if he did this, it is well.* See **1400.** In Latin: si hoc facit, bene est.

(b) **General:**

a. (*prot.*) ἐάν with subjunctive; (*apod.*) present indicative. Ἐάν τις κλέπτῃ, κολάζεται *if anyone (ever) steals, he is (always) punished.* See **1403 a.**

b. (*prot.*) εἰ with optative; (*apod.*) imperfect indicative. Εἴ τις κλέπτοι, ἐκολάζετο *if anyone ever stole, he was (always) punished.* See **1403 b.** For the Latin, see **1399.**

II. Present and past suppositions implying that the protasis is not true and that the condition is not fulfilled:

(*prot.*) εἰ with past tense of indicative; (*apod.*) past tense of indicative with ἄν. Εἰ τοῦτο ἐποίησε, καλῶς ἂν ἔσχεν *if he had done this, it would have been well*; εἰ τοῦτο ἐποίει, καλῶς ἂν εἶχεν *if he were doing this, it would (now) be well*, or *if he had done this, it would have been well.* See **1407.**

In Latin: si hoc faceret, bene esset (present); si hoc fecisset, bene fuisset (past).

III. Future suppositions in more vivid form:

(*prot.*) ἐάν with subjunctive (sometimes εἰ with future indicative); (*apod.*) any future form. Ἐὰν τοῦτο ποιῇ (or ποιήσῃ), καλῶς ἕξει *if he shall do this* (or *if he does this*), *it will be well* (**1413**). For εἰ τοῦτο ποιήσει see **1415.**

In Latin: si hoc faciet (or fecerit), bene erit.

IV. Future suppositions in less vivid form:

(*prot.*) εἰ with optative; (*apod.*) optative with ἄν. Εἰ τοῦτο ποιοίη (or ποιήσειε), καλῶς ἂν ἔχοι *if he should do this, it would be well.* See **1418.**

In Latin: si hoc faciat, bene sit.

1399. Latin commonly agrees with English in not marking the distinction between the general and the particular present and past conditions by different forms, and uses the indicative in both alike. See **1405.**

I. *Present and Past Conditions*

A. Simple Suppositions, Chiefly Particular

1400. When the protasis *simply states* a particular supposition, implying nothing as to the fulfilment of the condition, it has the indicative with εἰ. The apodosis may have any form of the verb required by the sense. E.g.

εἰ ἡσυχίαν Φίλιππος ἄγει, οὐκέτι δεῖ λέγειν *if Philip is keeping peace (with us), we need talk no longer*, Dem. 8, 5; εἰ ἐγὼ Φαῖδρον ἀγνοῶ, καὶ ἐμαυτοῦ ἐπιλέλησμαι · ἀλλὰ γὰρ οὐδέτερά ἐστι τούτων *if I don't know Phaedrus, I have forgotten who I am myself; but neither of these two things is so*, Plat. *Phdr.* 228 a; εἰ θεοῦ ἦν, οὐκ ἦν αἰσχροκερδής *granting that he was the son of a god, he was not avaricious*, Plat. *Rep.* 408 c; ἀλλ' εἰ δοκεῖ, πλέωμεν *but if it pleases you, let us sail*, S. *Ph.* 526; κάκιστ' ἀπολοίμην, Ξανθίαν εἰ μὴ φιλῶ *perdition catch me if I don't love Xanthias*, Ar. *R.* 579; εἰ δέ τι ἄλλο βέλτιον ἢ ταύτῃ, τολμάτω καὶ ὁ ἰδιώτης διδάσκειν *but if any other way is better than this, let even the private soldier venture to tell us*, X. *An.* 3, 2, 32; τότε τὸν Ὑπερείδην, εἴπερ ἀληθῆ μου νῦν κατηγορεῖ, μᾶλλον ἂν εἰκότως ἢ τόνδ' ἐδίωκεν *granting that what he now charges against me is true, it would have been more reasonable for him to prosecute Hyperides at that time than my client*, Dem. 18, 223.

1401. Even the future indicative may stand in a protasis of this class if it expresses merely a *present* intention or necessity that something shall hereafter be done; e.g. αἶρε πλῆκτρον, εἰ μαχεῖ *raise your spur, if you are going to fight*, Ar. *Av.* 759. Here εἰ μέλλεις μάχεσθαι would be the more common expression in prose (**1254**).

1402. For present or past conditions containing a potential indicative or optative (with ἄν), see **1431 c**.

B. PRESENT AND PAST GENERAL SUPPOSITIONS

1403. In general suppositions, the apodosis expresses a *customary* or *repeated* action or a *general truth* in present or past time, and the protasis refers in a general way to any of a class of acts.

a. Present general suppositions have ἐάν with the subjunctive in the protasis, and the present indicative (or some other present form denoting repetition) in the apodosis. E.g.

ἢν ἐγγὺς ἔλθῃ θάνατος, οὐδεὶς βούλεται θνήσκειν *if death comes near, no one is (ever) willing to die*, E. *Alc.* 671; ἅπας λόγος, ἂν ἀπῇ τὰ πράγματα, μάταιόν τι φαίνεται καὶ κενόν *all speech, if deeds are wanting, is plainly a vain and empty thing*, Dem. 2, 12.

b. Past general suppositions have εἰ with the optative in the protasis, and the imperfect indicative (or some other form denoting past repetition) in the apodosis. E.g.

εἴ τινας θορυβουμένους αἴσθοιτο, κατασβεννύναι τὴν ταραχὴν ἐπειρᾶτο *if he saw any falling into disorder (or whenever he saw, etc.), he (always) tried to quiet the confusion*, X. *C.* 5, 3, 55; εἴ τις ἀντείποι, εὐθὺς ἐτεθνήκει *if any one objected, he was immediately put to death*, Thuc. 8, 66. This construction occurs only once in Homer, *Il.* 24, 768.

1404. The gnomic aorist, which is a primary tense (1270), can always be used here in the apodosis with a dependent subjunctive; e.g. ἤν τις παραβαίνῃ, ζημίαν αὐτοῖς ἐπέθεσαν *if anyone transgresses, they (always) impose a penalty on him,* X. C. 1, 2, 2.

1405. The indicative is occasionally used in the place of the subjunctive or optative in general suppositions; that is, these sentences may follow the construction of ordinary present and past suppositions (1400), as in Latin and English; e.g. εἰ τις δύο ἢ καί τι πλείους ἡμέρας λογίζεται, μάταιός ἐστιν *if anyone counts on two or haply more days he is a fool,* S. Tr. 944.

1406. Here, as in future conditions (1416), εἰ (without ἄν) is sometimes used with the subjunctive in poetry. In Homer this is the more frequent form in *general* conditions.

II. *Present and Past Conditions with Supposition Contrary to Fact*

1407. When the protasis states a present or past supposition, implying that the condition *is not* or *was not fulfilled*, the secondary tenses of the indicative are used in both protasis and apodosis. The apodosis has the adverb ἄν.

The imperfect here refers to present time or to an act as going on or repeated in past time, the aorist to a simple occurrence in past time, and the (rare) pluperfect to an act completed in past or present time. E.g.

ταῦτα οὐκ ἂν ἐδύναντο ποιεῖν, εἰ μὴ διαίτῃ μετρίᾳ ἐχρῶντο *they would not be able (as they are) to do this if they did not lead an abstemious life,* X. C. 1, 2, 16; πολὺ ἂν θαυμαστότερον ἦν εἰ ἐτιμῶντο *it would be far more wonderful if they were honored,* Plat. Rep. 489 b; εἰ ἦσαν ἄνδρες ἀγαθοί, ὡς σὺ φής, οὐκ ἄν ποτε ταῦτα ἔπασχον *if they had been good men, as you say, would never have suffered these things* (referring to several cases), Plat. G. 516 e; καὶ ἴσως ἂν ἀπέθανον, εἰ μὴ ἡ ἀρχὴ κατελύθη *and perhaps I should have been put to death, if their government had not been overthrown,* Plat. Ap. 32 d; εἰ ἀπεκρίνω, ἱκανῶς ἂν ἤδη ἐμεμαθήκη *if you had answered, I should already have learned enough* (or *I should now be sufficiently instructed, which now I am not, cf.* 1265), Plat. Euthyph. 14 c; εἰ μὴ ὑμεῖς ἤλθετε, ἐπορευόμεθα ἂν ἐπὶ τὸν βασιλέα *if you had not come (aor.), we should now be on our way (impf.) to the King,* X. An. 2, 1, 4.

1408. In Homer the imperfect in this class of sentences is always past (see Il. 7, 273; 8, 130), and the present optative is used where the Attic would have the imperfect referring to *present* time; e.g. εἰ μέν τις τὸν ὄνειρον ἄλλος ἔνισπεν, ψεῦδός κεν φαῖμεν *if any other had told this dream (1407), we should call it a lie,* Il. 2, 80; see 24, 222.

1409. In Homer the optative with κέ is occasionally past in apodosis; e.g. καί νύ κεν ἔνθ' ἀπόλοιτο Αἰνείας, εἰ μὴ νόησε 'Αφροδίτη *and now Aeneas would there have perished, had not Aphrodite perceived him*, *Il.* 5, 311. Here ἀπώλετο with κεν or ἄν would be the regular form in Homer, as in other Greek. Homer has also a past potential optative; see *Il.* 5, 85.

1410. *a.* The imperfects ἔδει, χρῆν or ἐχρῆν, ἐξῆν, εἰκὸς ἦν, and other impersonal expressions denoting *obligation, propriety, possibility*, and the like, are often used without ἄν to form an apodosis implying that the duty is not or was not performed, or the possibility not realized. E.g.

ἔδει σε τοῦτον φιλεῖν *you ought to love him* (*but do not*), or *you ought to have loved him* (*but did not*), is substantially equivalent to *you would love him*, or *would have loved him* (ἐφίλεις ἄν τοῦτον), *if you did your duty* (τὰ δέοντα). So ἐξῆν σοι τοῦτο ποιῆσαι *you might have done this* (*but you did not do it*); εἰκὸς ἦν σε τοῦτο ποιῆσαι *you would properly* (εἰκότως) *have done this*. The actual apodosis is here always in the infinitive, and the reality of the action of the infinitive is generally denied.

b. When the present infinitive is used, the construction generally refers to the present or to continued or repeated action in the past; when the aorist is used, it refers to the past. E.g.

τούσδε μὴ ζῆν ἔδει *these ought not to be living* (*as they are*), S. *Ph.* 418; μένειν γὰρ ἐξῆν *for he might have stood his ground* (*but did not*), Dem. 3, 17; θανεῖν σε χρῆν πάρος τέκνων *you ought to have died before your children*, E. *Andr.* 1208; εἰ ἐβούλετο δίκαιος εἶναι, ἐξῆν αὐτῷ μισθῶσαι τὸν οἶκον *if he had wanted to be honest, he might have let the estate*, Lys. 32, 23; χρῆν σε τότε παρακαλεῖν τοὺς παριόντας μάρτυρας *you ought immediately to have summoned the passers-by as witnesses*, Lys. 7, 20.

1411. When the actual apodosis is in the verb of *obligation* etc., ἔδει ἄν can be used; e.g. εἰ τὰ δέοντα οὗτοι συνεβούλευσαν, οὐδὲν ἄν ὑμᾶς νῦν ἔδει βουλεύεσθαι *if these men had given you the advice you needed, there would now be no need of your deliberating*, Dem. 4, 1.

1412. *a.* Other imperfects, especially ἐβουλόμην, may be used without ἄν; e.g. ἐβουλόμην οὐκ ἐρίζειν ἐνθάδε *I could wish that the contest should not take place here*, Ar. *R.* 866; see Plat. *Rep.* 408 *c*, where οὐκ ἦν αἰσχροκερδής, though the apodosis of a simple supposition (**1400**), may be rendered *he could not have been avaricious*.

b. So ὤφελον or ὤφελλον *ought*, aorist and imperfect of ὀφέλλω *owe* (epic for ὀφείλω), in Homer; whence comes the use of ὤφελον in wishes (**1360**); e.g. ὤφελε Κῦρος ζῆν *would that Cyrus were alive*, X. *An.* 2, 1, 4.

c. So ἔμελλον with the infinitive; e.g. φθίσεσθαι ἔμελλον, εἰ μὴ ἔειπες *I should have perished if thou hadst not spoken*, *Od.* 13, 383. So Dem. 19, 159.

III. *Future Conditions, More Vivid Form*

SUBJUNCTIVE IN PROTASIS WITH FUTURE APODOSIS

1413. When a supposed future case is stated *distinctly* and *vividly* (as in English *if I shall go* or *if I go*), the protasis has the subjunctive with ἐάν (epic εἴ κε), and the apodosis has the future indicative or some other form expressing future time. E.g.

εἰ μέν κεν Μενέλαον ᾿Αλέξανδρος κ α τ α π έ φ ν ῃ, αὐτὸς ἔπειθ᾿ Ἑλένην ἐχέτω καὶ κτήματα πάντα *if Alexander shall slay Menelaus, then let him have Helen and all the goods himself, Il.* 3, 281; ἄν τις ἀ ν θ ι σ τ ῆ τ α ι, πειρασόμεθα χειροῦσθαι *if anyone oppose us, we shall try to overcome him,* X. *An.* 7, 3, 11; ἐὰν οὖν ἴ ῃ ς νῦν, πότε ἔσει οἴκοι; *if therefore you go now, when shall you be at home?* X. *C.* 5, 3, 27.

Note that the character of the apodosis distinguishes these future conditions from present general suppositions (**1403** *a*).

1414. The older English forms *if he shall go* and *if he go* both express the force of the Greek subjunctive and future indicative in protasis; but ordinary modern English uses *if he goes* even when the time is clearly future.

1415. The future indicative with εἰ is very often used in future conditions implying strong likelihood of fulfilment, especially in appeals to the feelings and in threats and warnings. E.g.

εἰ μὴ κ α θ έ ξ ε ι ς γλῶσσαν, ἔσται σοι κακά *if you do not restrain your tongue, you will have trouble,* E. *frag.* 5. This common use of the future must not be confounded with that of **1401**.

1416. In Homer εἰ (without ἄν or κε) is sometimes used with the subjunctive in future conditions, apparently in the same sense as εἴ κε or ἤν; e.g. εἰ δὲ νῆ᾿ ἐθέλῃ ὀλέσαι *but if he shall wish to destroy our ship, Od.* 12, 348. This is more common in general conditions in Homer (see **1406**). The same use of εἰ for ἐάν is found occasionally even in Attic poetry.

1417. For the Homeric subjunctive with κέ in the apodosis of a future condition, see **1305** *b*.

IV. *Future Conditions, Less Vivid Form*

OPTATIVE IN BOTH PROTASIS AND APODOSIS

1418. When a supposed future case is stated in a *less distinct* and *vivid* form (as in English *if I should go*, often *if I went*), the protasis has the optative with εἰ, and the apodosis has the optative with ἄν. E.g.

εἴης φορητὸς οὐκ ἄν, εἰ πράσσοις καλῶς *you would not be endurable if you should prosper*, Aesch. *Pr.* 979; οὐ πολλὴ ἂν ἀλογία εἴη, εἰ φοβοῖτο τὸν θάνατον ὁ τοιοῦτος; *would it not be a great absurdity if such a man should fear death?* Plat. *Ph.* 68 b; οἶκος δ' αὐτός, εἰ φθογγὴν λάβοι, σαφέστατ' ἂν λέξειεν *but the house itself, if it should find a voice, would speak most plainly*, Aesch. *Ag.* 37.

Note that the character of the apodosis distinguishes these future conditions from past general suppositions (1403 b).

1419. The optative with ἄν in apodosis is the potential optative (1328).

1420. The *future* optative cannot be used in protasis or apodosis, except in indirect discourse representing the future indicative after a past tense (see the second example under 1512 b).

1421. Εἰ κε is sometimes found with the optative in Homer, in place of the simple εἰ (1418); e.g. εἰ δέ κεν Ἄργος ἱκοίμεθ', . . . γαμβρός κέν μοι ἔοι *and if we should ever come to Argos, he would be my son-in-law*, *Il.* 9, 141.

1422. For the Homeric optative used like the past tenses of the indicative in unreal conditions, see 1408 and 1409.

Peculiar Forms of Conditional Sentences

ELLIPSIS AND SUBSTITUTION IN PROTASIS OR APODOSIS

1423. The protasis sometimes is not expressed in its regular form with εἰ or ἐάν, but is contained in a participle, or implied in an adverb or some other part of the sentence. When a participle represents the protasis, its *tense* is always that in which the verb itself would have stood in the indicative, subjunctive, or optative, — the present (as usual) including the imperfect. E.g.

πῶς δίκης οὔσης ὁ Ζεὺς οὐκ ἀπόλωλεν; *how is it that Zeus has not been destroyed, if Justice exists?* (εἰ δίκη ἐστίν), Ar. *Nub.* 904; σὺ δὲ κλύων εἴσει τάχα *but you will soon know, if you listen* (= ἐὰν κλύῃς), Ar. *Av.* 1390; τοιαῦτά τἂν γυναιξὶ συνναίων ἔχοις *such things would you surely have to endure if you dwelt among women* (i.e. εἰ συνναίοις), Aesch. *Sev.* 195; ἠπίστησεν ἄν τις ἀκούσας *anyone would have disbelieved* (*such a thing*) *if he had heard it* (i.e. εἰ ἤκουσεν), Thuc. 7, 28; μαμμᾶν δ' ἂν αἰτήσαντος (sc. σοῦ) ἧκόν σοι φέρων ἂν ἄρτον *and if you* (*ever*) *cried for food* (εἰ αἰτήσειας, 1403 b), *I used to come to you with bread* (1297), Ar. *Nub.* 1383.

διά γε ὑμᾶς αὐτοὺς πάλαι ἂν ἀπολώλειτε *if it had depended on yourselves* (cf. 1424 a, second example), *you would long ago have been ruined*, Dem. 18, 49; οὕτω γὰρ οὐκέτι τοῦ λοιποῦ πάσχοιμεν ἂν κακῶς *for in that case we should no longer suffer harm* (the protasis being in οὕτω), X. *An.* 1, 1, 10; οὐδ' ἂν δικαίως ἐς κακὸν πέσοιμί τι *nor should I justly* (i.e. *if I were treated justly*) *fall into any trouble*, S. *Ant.* 240.

1424. *a.* There is a (probably unconscious) suppression of the verb of the protasis in several phrases introduced by εἰ μή *except.* E.g.

τίς τοι ἄλλος ὁμοῖος, εἰ μὴ Πάτροκλος; *who else is like you, except Patroclus* (i.e. *unless it is Patroclus*)? *Il.* 17. 475; εἰ μὴ διὰ τὸν πρύτανιν, ἐνέπεσεν ἄν *had it not been for the Prytanis (except for the Prytanis), he would have been thrown in* (*to the Pit*), Plat. *G.* 516 e (1213 *b*).

b. The protasis or the apodosis, or both, may be suppressed with the Homeric ὡς εἰ or ὡς εἴ τε; e.g. τῶν νέες ὠκεῖαι ὡς εἰ πτερὸν ἠὲ νόημα *their ships are swift as a wing or thought (as they would be if they were,* etc.), *Od.* 7, 36. For the double ellipsis in ὥσπερ ἂν εἰ, see **1313**.

1425. In neither of the cases of **1424** is it probable that any definite verb was in the speaker's mind.

1426. The apodosis is sometimes entirely suppressed for rhetorical effect (*aposiopesis*) ; e.g. εἰ μὲν δώσουσι γέρας *if they shall give me a prize —very well, Il.* 1, 135, cf. 1, 580; εἰ μὲν γὰρ ἕνεκα χρημάτων με συκοφαντεῖ — *for if he is trying to play the informer against me to get my money —* (the supposition is too absurd), Lys. 24, 2.

1427. Εἰ δὲ μή without a verb often has the meaning *otherwise,* even where the clause would not be negative if completed, or where the verb if supplied would be a subjunctive; e.g. μὴ ποιήσῃς ταῦτα · εἰ δὲ μή, αἰτίαν ἕξεις *do not do this; otherwise (if you do not do what I say) you will be blamed,* X. *An.* 7, 1, 8.

1428. The apodosis may be expressed by an infinitive or participle in indirect discourse, each tense representing its own tenses of the indicative or optative (**1282, 1286**). If the finite verb in the apodosis would have taken ἄν, this particle is used with the infinitive or participle. E.g.

ἡγοῦμαι, εἰ τοῦτο ποιεῖτε, πάντα καλῶς ἔχειν *I believe that if you are doing this all is well;* ἡγοῦμαι, ἐὰν τοῦτο ποιῆτε, πάντα καλῶς ἕξειν *I believe that if you (shall) do this all will be well;* οἶδα ὑμᾶς, ἐὰν ταῦτα γένηται, εὖ πράξοντας *I know that you will prosper if this is (shall be) done.* For examples of the infinitive and participle with ἄν, see **1308.**

1429. The apodosis may be expressed in an infinitive not in indirect discourse (**1273**), especially one depending on a verb of *wishing, commanding, advising,* etc., from which the infinitive receives a future meaning. E.g.

βούλεται ἐλθεῖν ἐὰν τοῦτο γένηται *he wishes to go if this (shall) be done;* κελεύω ὑμᾶς ἐὰν δύνησθε ἀπελθεῖν *I command you to depart if you can.* For the principle of indirect discourse which appears in the *protasis* here after past tenses, see **1510, 1517** *a.*

1430. Sometimes the apodosis is merely implied in the context,

and in such cases εἰ or ἐάν is often to be translated *supposing that,
in case that, if perchance,* or *if haply.* E.g.

ἄκουσον καὶ ἐμοῦ, ἐάν σοι ταὐτὰ δοκῇ *hear me also, in case the same shall please
you* (i.e. *that then you may assent to it*), Plat. *Rep.* 358 b. So πρὸς τὴν
πόλιν, εἰ ἐπιβοηθοῖεν, ἐχώρουν *they marched toward the city, in case they
(the citizens) should rush out* (i.e. *to meet them if they should rush out*),
Thuc. 6, 100. On this principle we must explain αἴ κέν πως βούλεται *if
haply he may wish* (i.e. *in hope that he may wish*), *Il.* 1, 66; αἴ κ' ἐθέλησθα,
Od. 3, 92; and similar passages. For this construction, both in Homer
and elsewhere, see *Moods and Tenses,* §§ 486–491. See **1380.**

1431. The protasis and apodosis sometimes belong to different
forms.

a. Especially any tense of the indicative with εἰ in the protasis
may be followed by a potential optative with ἄν in the apodosis. E.g.

εἰ κατ' οὐρανοῦ εἰλήλουθας, οὐκ ἂν θεοῖσι μαχοίμην *if you have come down from
heaven, I cannot fight against the gods, Il.* 6, 128 ; εἰ νῦν γε δυστυχοῦμεν,
πῶς τἀναντί' ἂν πράττοντες οὐ σῳζοίμεθ' ἄν; *granted that today we have
bad luck, how could we help coming out right if we should do the opposite?*
Ar. *R.* 1449 (here πράττοντες = εἰ πράττοιμεν) ; εἰ οὗτοι ὀρθῶς ἀπέστησαν,
ὑμεῖς ἂν οὐ χρεὼν ἄρχοιτε *if these had a right to secede, you cannot possibly
hold your power rightfully,* Thuc. 3, 40.

b. Sometimes a subjunctive or a future indicative in the protasis has a potential optative in the apodosis. E.g.

ἢν ἐφῇς μοι, λέξαιμ' ἄν *if you (will) permit me, I would fain speak,* S. *El.*
554 (**1328**); οὐδὲ γὰρ ἂν πολλαὶ γέφυραι ὦσιν, ἔχοιμεν ἂν ὅποι φυγόντες
σωθῶμεν *for not even if there prove to be many bridges could we find a
place to fly to and be saved,* X. *An.* 2, 4, 19 (**1367**) ; ἀδικοίημεν ἂν εἰ μὴ
ἀποδώσω *I should be guilty of wrong if I fail to restore her,* E. *Hel.* 1010.

c. A potential optative (with ἄν) may express a present condition, and
a potential indicative (with ἄν) may express a present or past condition ;
e.g. καὶ ἐγώ, εἴπερ ἄλλῳ τῳ πειθοίμην ἄν, καὶ σοὶ πείθομαι *I also, if* (it is true,
as I think it is, that) *I would trust any man, certainly trust you,* Plat. *Prot.*
329 b ; εἰ τοῦτο ἰσχυρὸν ἦν ἂν τούτῳ τεκμήριον, κἀμοὶ γενέσθω τεκμήριον *if this
would have been a strong proof in his favor* (as it would have been), *so let
it be also a proof in mine,* Dem. 49, 58.

d. The optative in protasis sometimes depends on the present of a verb
expressing *obligation, propriety, possibility,* or *expediency* ; e.g. εἰ γὰρ
εἴησαν δύο τινὲς ἐναντίοι νόμοι, οὐκ ἀμφοτέροις ἔνι δήπου ψηφίσασθαι *for if there
should be two contradictory laws, you could not, of course, vote for both,*
Dem. 24, 35.

This use is more common in the corresponding relative condition (**1449**).

Δέ in Apodosis

1432. The apodosis is sometimes introduced by δέ, ἀλλά, or αὐτάρ *yet, still*. This is a relic of parataxis, or the coördination of sentences, and is common in Homer. In Attic prose δέ is sometimes used after a number of protases, and it is then resumptive, *I say*. E.g.

εἰ δέ κε μὴ δώωσιν, ἐγὼ δέ κεν αὐτὸς ἕλωμαι *but if they do not give her up, then I will take her myself*, *Il.* 1, 137. See Plat. *Ap.* 28 c.

Εἰ after Verbs of Wondering etc.

1433. Some verbs expressing *wonder, delight, contentment, disappointment*, and *indignation* may have the cause of the emotion stated by a protasis with εἰ (ἐάν) instead of by ὅτι *because* (**1463**). E.g.

θαυμάζω δ' ἔγωγε εἰ μηδεὶς ὑμῶν μήτ' ἐνθυμεῖται μήτ' ὀργίζεται *and I wonder that no one of you is either concerned or angry* (lit. *if no one of you is*, etc., *I wonder*), Dem. 4, 43 ; ἀγανακτῶ εἰ ἃ νοῶ μὴ οἷός τ' εἰμὶ εἰπεῖν *I am indignant that I am not able to say what I mean*, Plat. *Lach.* 194 a. See also **1512 b** for the principle of indirect discourse applied to these sentences.

1434. Such verbs are especially θαυμάζω, αἰσχύνομαι, ἀγαπάω, and ἀγανακτέω, with δεινόν ἐστιν.

Concessive Clauses

1435. Conditional clauses introduced by καὶ εἰ (κεἰ), καὶ ἐάν (κἄν), *even if*, and εἰ καί or ἐὰν καί *although*, denote *concession*.

1436. Concession is expressed also by the participle, with or without καίπερ. See **1566 f**. Also by a clause with μέν contrasted with a δέ clause; e.g. οἴεται μὲν εἶναι σοφός, ἔστι δ' οὔ *although he thinks he is wise, he really is not*, cf. Plat. *Ap.* 21 d.

VIII. Relative and Temporal Sentences

1437. The principles underlying the different types of conditional sentences (**1398**) apply also to relative and temporal sentences. Temporal clauses introduced by ἕως, πρίν, and other particles meaning *until* have special peculiarities, and are therefore treated separately (**1478–1489**). Relative clauses may be introduced by relative pronouns or relative adverbs.

1438. The antecedent of a relative is either *definite* or *indefinite*. It is definite when the relative refers to a definite person or thing, or to some definite time, place, or manner; it is indefinite when no such definite person, thing, time, place, or manner is referred to. Both definite and indefinite antecedents may be either expressed or understood. E.g.

DEFINITE: ταῦτα ἃ ἔχω ὁρᾷς *you see these things which I have*, or ἃ ἔχω ὁρᾷς *you see the things which I have*; ὅτε ἐβούλετο ἦλθεν (once) *when he wished, he came.*

INDEFINITE: πάντα ἃ ἂν βούλωνται ἕξουσιν *they will have everything which they may want*, or ἃ ἂν βούλωνται ἕξουσιν *they will have whatever they may want*; ὅταν ἔλθῃ, τοῦτο ποιήσω *when he shall come* (or *when he comes*), *I will do this*; ὅτε βούλοιτο, τοῦτο ἐποίει *whenever he wished, he (always) did this*; ὡς ἂν εἴπω, ποιῶμεν *let us do as I say*; ἃ ἔχει βούλομαι λαβεῖν *I want to take whatever he has.*

Definite Antecedent

1439. A relative *as such* has no effect on the mood of the following verb. A relative with a definite antecedent therefore may take the indicative (with οὐ for its negative) or any other construction which could occur in an independent sentence. E.g.

τίς ἔσθ' ὁ χῶρος δῆτ' ἐν ᾧ βεβήκαμεν; *what is the place wherein we now stand?* S. O. C. 52; ἕως ἐστὶ καιρός, ἀντιλάβεσθε τῶν πραγμάτων (now) *while there is opportunity, take a hand in the business*, Dem. 1, 20; τοῦτο οὐκ ἐποίησεν, ἐν ᾧ τὸν δῆμον ἐτίμησεν ἄν *this he failed to do, although he might have honored the people therein*, Dem. 21, 69. So ὃ μὴ γένοιτο *and may this not happen*, Dem. 27, 67.

Indefinite Antecedent

1440. *a.* A relative clause with an indefinite antecedent has a conditional force, and is called a conditional relative clause. Its negative is always μή.

b. Relative words, like εἰ *if*, take ἄν before the subjunctive. See **1299 *b*, 1311.** Ἅ *what* with ἄν may form ἅν. In Homer we generally find ὅτε κε etc. (like εἴ κε, **1413**), or ὅτε etc. alone (**1448**).

CONDITIONAL RELATIVE SENTENCES

1441. I. (*a*) Present or past condition *simply stated*, with the indicative, — *chiefly* in particular suppositions (**1400**). E.g.

ἃ μὴ οἶδα, οὐδὲ οἴομαι εἰδέναι *what I do not know, I do not even think I know* (like εἴ τινα μὴ οἶδα *if there are any things which I do not know*), Plat. *Ap.*

21 d ; οὓς μὴ ηὕρισκον, κενοτάφιον αὐτοῖς ἐποίησαν *for any whom they did not find* (= εἴ τινας μὴ ηὕρισκον) *they raised a cenotaph,* X. *An.* 6, 4, 9.

1442. (*b*) *a*. Present general condition, depending on a present form denoting repetition, with subjunctive (**1403** *a*). E.g.

συμμαχεῖν τούτοις ἐθέλουσιν ἅπαντες, οὓς ἂν ὁρῶσι παρεσκευασμένους *all wish to be allies of those whom they see prepared,* Dem. 4, 6 ; ἡνίκ' ἂν οἴκοι γένωνται, δρῶσιν οὐκ ἀνασχετά *when they get home, they do things unbearable,* Ar. *Pax* 1179.

b. Past general condition, depending on a past form denoting repetition, with optative (**1403** *b*). E.g.

οὓς μὲν ἴδοι εὐτάκτως ἰόντας, τίνες τε εἶεν ἠρώτα, καὶ ἐπεὶ πύθοιτο ἐπήνει *he (always) asked those whom he saw (at any time) marching in good order, who they were; and when he learned, he praised them,* X. *C.* 5, 3, 55 ; ἐπειδὴ δὲ ἀνοιχθείη, εἰσῇμεν παρὰ τὸν Σωκράτη *and (each morning) when the prison was opened, we went in to visit Socrates,* Plat. *Ph.* 59 d.

1443. The indicative sometimes takes the place of the subjunctive or optative here, as in other general suppositions (**1405**). This occurs especially with ὅστις, which itself expresses the same idea of indefiniteness that ὅς with the subjunctive or optative usually expresses; e.g. ὅστις μὴ τῶν ἀρίστων ἅπτεται βουλευμάτων, κάκιστος εἶναι δοκεῖ *whoever clings not to the best counsels is accounted most base,* S. *Ant.* 178. Here ὃς ἂν μὴ ἅπτηται would be the common expression.

1444. II. Present or past condition stated so as to imply that the condition *is not* or *was not fulfilled* (*supposition contrary to fact*), with the secondary tenses of the indicative (**1407**). E.g.

οὐκ ἂν ἐπεχειροῦμεν πράττειν ἃ ἠπιστάμεθα *we should not be undertaking to do* (*as we now are*) *things which we did not understand* (like εἴ τινα μὴ ἠπιστάμεθα *if there were any things which we did not understand,* the whole belonging to a supposition not realized), Plat. *Ch.* 171 e ; ὁπότερα τούτων ἐποίησεν, οὐδενὸς ἂν ἧττον 'Αθηναίων πλούσιοι ἦσαν *whichever of these things he had done, they would have been second to no Athenian in wealth,* Lys. 32, 23. So ὃν γῆρας ἔτετμεν *Od.* 1, 218.

1445. III. Future condition in the *more vivid* form, with ἄν and the subjunctive (**1413**). E.g.

ὅταν μὴ σθένω, πεπαύσομαι *when I* (*shall*) *have no more strength, I shall cease,* S. *Ant.* 91 ; ἀλόχους καὶ νήπια τέκνα ἄξομεν ἐν νήεσσιν, ἐπὴν πτολίεθρον ἕλωμεν *we will carry off their wives and young children in our ships, when we* (*shall*) *have taken the city, Il.* 4, 238. This use may be extended by analogy to clauses where there is little or no condition ; e.g. ἔσσεται ἦμαρ ὅτ' ἄν ποτ' ὀλώλῃ Ἴλιος *a day there shall be when Ilios is entirely destroyed, Il.* 6, 448.

1446. The future indicative cannot be substituted for the subjunctive here, as it can in common protasis. When the future indicative occurs in a relative protasis it usually denotes a simple supposition (**1439**), and the future expresses a present intention (**1401**). A rare case is X. C. 1, 5, 13 : ὅ τι γὰρ μὴ τοιοῦτον ἀποβήσεται παρ' ὑμῶν, εἰς ἐμὲ τὸ ἐλλεῖπον ἔσται *whatever you accomplish* (lit. *results from your actions*) *which is not of that quality, the loss will fall on me.* Here there is an emotional appeal (**1415**). Cf. also Luke 17, 22 : ἐλεύσονται ἡμέραι ὅτε ἐπιθυμήσετε μίαν τῶν ἡμερῶν τοῦ υἱοῦ τοῦ ἀνθρώπου ἰδεῖν καὶ οὐκ ὄψεσθε *days will come when ye shall desire to see one of the days of the Son of Man and ye shall not see it.*

1447. IV. Future condition in the *less vivid* form, with the optative (**1418**). E.g.

πεινῶν φάγοι ἂν ὁπότε βούλοιτο *if he were hungry, he would eat whenever* (i.e. *at such time in the future as*) *he might wish* (like εἴ ποτε βούλοιτο *if he should ever wish*), X. M. 2, 1, 18.

1448. Conditional relative sentences have most of the peculiarities and irregularities of common protasis. E.g., the protasis and apodosis may have different forms (**1431**); the relative without ἄν or κέ is sometimes found in poetry with the subjunctive (like εἰ for ἐάν or εἴ κε, **1406**, **1416**), especially in general conditions in Homer; the relative (like εἰ, **1421**) in Homer may take κέ or ἄν with the optative; the relative clause may depend on an infinitive, participle, or other construction (**1428**, **1429**); and the conjunction δέ may connect the relative clause to the antecedent clause (**1432**).

1449. The optative in a relative clause sometimes depends on the present of a verb expressing *obligation, propriety, possibility,* or *expediency*; e.g. ὃν πόλις στήσειε, τοῦδε χρὴ κλύειν *we should obey any one whom the state may appoint*, S. Ant. 666.

This is more common than the corresponding construction with εἰ (**1431** *d*).

1450. Homeric similes often have (besides the aorist indicative, **1295**) the subjunctive with ὡς ὅτε (occasionally ὡς ὅτ' ἄν), sometimes with ὡς or ὥς τε; e.g. ὡς ὅτε κινήσῃ Ζέφυρος βαθὺ λήιον *as (happens) when the west wind moves a deep grain-field*, Il. 2, 147; ὡς γυνὴ κλαίῃσι . . . ὣς Ὀδυσεὺς δάκρυον εἶβεν *as a wife weeps . . . so did Ulysses shed tears*, Od. 8, 523.

Assimilation in Conditional Relative Clauses

1451. When a conditional relative clause expressing either a future or a general supposition depends on a subjunctive or optative, it regularly takes the same mood by *assimilation*. E.g.

ἐάν τινες οἳ ἂν δύνωνται τοῦτο ποιῶσι, καλῶς ἕξει *if any who may be able shall do this, it will be well*; εἴ τινες οἳ δύναιντο τοῦτο ποιοῖεν, καλῶς ἂν ἔχοι *if*

any who should be (or *were*) *able should do this, it would be well*; εἴθε πάντες
οἳ δύναιντο τοῦτο ποιοῖεν *O that all who may be* (or *were*) *able would do
this* (here the optative ποιοῖεν (**1355**) makes οἳ δύναιντο preferable to οἳ
ἂν δύνωνται, which would express the same idea); ἐπειδὰν ὦν ἂν πρίηται
κύριος γένηται *when* (in any case) *he becomes master of what he has bought*,
Dem. 18, 47; ὡς ἀπόλοιτο καὶ ἄλλος, ὅ τις τοιαῦτά γε ῥέζοι *perish any other,
also, who should do the like! Od.* 1, 47; τεθναίην ὅτε μοι μηκέτι ταῦτα
μέλοι *may I die when I no longer care for these delights* (ὅταν μέλῃ would
express the same idea), Mimn. 1, 2.

1452. Likewise, when a conditional relative sentence depends
on a secondary tense of the indicative implying the non-fulfilment
of a condition, it takes by assimilation a similar form. E.g.

εἴ τινες οἳ ἐδύναντο τοῦτο ἐποίησαν, καλῶς ἂν εἶχεν *if any who had been able
had done this, it would have been well*; εἰ ἐν ἐκείνῃ τῇ φωνῇ τε καὶ τῷ τρόπῳ
ἔλεγον ἐν οἷς ἐτεθράμμην *if I were speaking to you in the accent and the
dialect in which I had been brought up* (all introduced by εἰ ξένος ἐτύγχανον
ὤν *supposing I happened to be a foreigner*), Plat. *Ap.* 17 d.

1453. All clauses which come under this principle of assimilation belong (as
conditional forms) equally under **1445, 1447, 1442, 1444**. This principle often
decides which form shall be used in future conditions (**1272** *b*).

Greek requires *sequence of mood*; Latin, *sequence of tense*. But see **1504.**

Relative Clauses Expressing Purpose

1454. The relative with the future indicative may express a
purpose. E.g.

πρεσβείαν πέμπειν ἥτις ταῦτ' ἐρεῖ καὶ παρέσται τοῖς πράγμασιν *to send an embassy to say this and to be present at the transactions*, Dem. 1, 2; οὐ γὰρ
ἔστι μοι χρήματα ὁπόθεν ἐκτείσω *for I have no money to pay the fine with*,
Plat. *Ap.* 37 c.

The antecedent here may be definite or indefinite; but the negative
particle is always μή, as in final clauses (**1373**).

1455. Homer generally has the subjunctive (with κέ joined to the relative) in this construction after primary tenses, and the optative (without
κέ) after secondary tenses. The optative is sometimes found even in Attic
prose. The earlier Greek here agrees with the Latin.

1456. In this construction the future indicative is very rarely changed
to the future optative after past tenses.

Relative Clauses Expressing Result

1457. The relative with any tense of the indicative, or with a
potential optative, may express a result. The negative is οὐ. E.g.

τίς οὕτω μαίνεται ὅστις οὐ βούλεταί σοι φίλος εἶναι; *who is so mad that he does not wish to be your friend?* X. *An.* 2, 5, 12; οὐδεὶς ἂν γένοιτο οὕτως ἀδαμάντινος, ὃς ἂν μείνειεν ἐν τῇ δικαιοσύνῃ *no one would ever become so like adamant that he would remain firm in his justice,* Plat. *Rep.* 360 b.

1458. With this construction compare the use of ὥστε with the finite moods (**1467, 1470**). It occurs chiefly after negative leading clauses or interrogatives implying a negative.

1459. The relative with a future (sometimes a present) indicative may express a result which is *aimed at.* The negative here is μή. E.g.

ηὔχετο μηδεμίαν οἱ συντυχίην γενέσθαι, ἥ μιν παύσει καταστρέψασθαι τὴν Εὐρώπην *he prayed that no such chance might befall him as to prevent him from subjugating Europe* (= ὥστε μιν παῦσαι), Hdt. 7, 54; βουληθεὶς τοιοῦτον μνημεῖον καταλιπεῖν ὃ μὴ τῆς ἀνθρωπίνης φύσεώς ἐστιν *when he wished to leave such a memorial as might be beyond human nature* (= ὥστε μὴ εἶναι), Isoc. 4, 89.

1460. Compare the construction of ὥστε with the infinitive (**1467**).

Causal Relative

1461. A relative clause may express a *cause.* The verb is in the indicative, as in causal sentences (**1463**), and the negative is generally οὐ. E.g.

θαυμαστὸν ποιεῖς, ὃς ἡμῖν οὐδὲν δίδως *you do a strange thing in giving us nothing* (like ὅτι σὺ οὐδὲν δίδως), X. *M.* 2, 7, 13; δόξας ἀμαθέα εἶναι, ὃς ... ἐκέλευε *believing him to be stupid because he commanded,* etc., Hdt. 1, 33.

1462. When the negative is μή, the sentence is conditional as well as causal; e.g. ταλαίπωρος εἶ, ᾧ μήτε θεοὶ πατρῷοί εἰσι μήθ' ἱερά *unfortunate you are, since you have neither ancestral gods nor temples* (implying also *if you really have none*), Plat. *Euthyd.* 302 b. This is equivalent to a clause introduced by εἴπερ, Lat. siquidem.

IX. Causal Sentences

1463. Causal sentences express a *cause,* and are introduced by ὅτι and ὡς *because*; ἐπεί, ἐπειδή, ὅτε, ὁπότε, *since*; εἴπερ *seeing that, since*; and by other particles of similar meaning. They have the indicative after both primary and secondary tenses. The negative particle is οὐ. E.g.

κήδετο γὰρ Δαναῶν, ὅτι ῥα θνήσκοντας ὁρᾶτο *for she pitied the Danai, because she saw them dying,* *Il.* 1, 56; ὅτε τοῦθ' οὕτως ἔχει, προσήκει προθύμως ἐθέλειν ἀκούειν *since this is so, it is becoming that you should be willing to hear eagerly,* Dem. 1, 1.

A potential optative or potential indicative may stand in a causal sentence: see Dem. 18, 49 and 79.

1464. On the principle of indirect discourse (**1517**), a causal sentence after a past tense may have the optative, to imply that the cause is assigned on the authority of some other person than the writer; e.g. τὸν Περικλέα ἐκάκιζον ὅτι στρατηγὸς ὢν οὐκ ἐπεξάγοι *they abused Pericles, because (as they said) although he was general he did not lead them out,* Thuc. 2, 21. This assigns the *Athenians'* reason for abusing Pericles, but does not show the historian's opinion.

1465. Besides the construction of **1461** and **1463**, cause may be expressed by a participle (**1566**) and by διὰ τό with the infinitive (**1549**).

X. Consecutive Clauses

1466. Ὥστε (sometimes ὡς) *so as, so that,* is used with the infinitive and with the indicative to express a result.

1467. With the infinitive (the negative being μή), the result is stated as one which the action of the leading verb *tends* to produce; with the indicative (the negative being οὐ), as one which that action actually *does* produce. E.g.

πάντας οὕτω διατιθεὶς ὥστε αὐτῷ μᾶλλον φίλους εἶναι *putting all in such a frame of mind that they were (tended to be) more friendly to him,* X. *An.* 1, 1, 5; πᾶν ποιοῦσιν ὥστε δίκην μὴ διδόναι *they do anything and everything (calculated) to result in not being punished,* i.e. *they aim at not being punished,* not implying that they actually escape, Plat. *G.* 479 c; οὕτως ἀγνωμόνως ἔχετε, ὥστε ἐλπίζετε αὐτὰ χρηστὰ γενήσεσθαι; *are you so senseless that you expect them to become good?* Dem. 2, 26. But with ὥστε ἐλπίζειν the meaning would be *so senseless as to expect,* i.e. *senseless enough to expect,* without implying necessarily that you do expect.

1468. These two constructions are essentially distinct in their nature, even when it is indifferent to the general sense which is used in a given case; e.g. οὕτως ἐστὶ δεινὸς ὥστε δίκην μὴ διδόναι *he is so skilful as not to be punished,* and οὕτως ἐστὶ δεινὸς ὥστε δίκην οὐ δίδωσιν *he is so skilful that he is not punished.* Idiomatic English usually requires the latter construction in translation (see the first example in **1467**).

The use of μή with the infinitive and of οὐ with the indicative shows that the distinction was really felt. When the infinitive with ὥστε has οὐ, it generally represents, in indirect discourse, an indicative with οὐ of the direct form (see Plat. *Ap.* 26 d and *Moods and Tenses,* §§ 594–598).

1469. The infinitive with ὥστε may express a purpose like a final clause: see ὥστε δίκην μὴ διδόναι (= ἵνα μὴ διδῶσι), quoted in **1467**. It may also be equivalent to an object clause with ὅπως (**1382**); e.g. μηχανὰς εὑρήσομεν ὥστ' ἐς τὸ πᾶν σε τῶνδ' ἀπαλλάξαι πόνων *we will find devices to free you wholly from these troubles* (= ὅπως σε ἀπαλλάξομεν), Aesch. *Eum.* 82.

1470. As ὥστε with the indicative has no effect on the form of the verb, it may be used in the same way with any verbal form which can stand in an independent sentence; e.g. ὥστ' οὐκ ἂν αὐτὸν γνωρίσαιμι *so that I should not know him*, E. *Or.* 379 ; ὥστε μὴ λίαν στένε *so do not lament overmuch*, S. *El.* 1172.

1471. Ὣς τε (written as two words) in Homer has the infinitive of result only twice ; elsewhere it means simply *as*, like ὥσπερ.

1472. Ὣς is sometimes used like ὥστε with the infinitive and the finite moods, but chiefly in Aeschylus, Sophocles, Herodotus, Xenophon, and late Greek.

1473. Verbs, substantives, and adjectives which commonly take the simple infinitive occasionally have the infinitive with ὥστε or ὡς ; e.g. ψηφισάμενοι ὥστε ἀμύνειν *having voted to defend them*, Thuc. 6, 88 ; πείθουσιν ὥστε ἐπιχειρῆσαι *they persuade them to make an attempt*, Thuc. 3, 102 ; φρονιμώτεροι ὥστε μαθεῖν *wiser in learning*, X. *C.* 4, 3, 11 ; ὀλίγοι ὡς ἐγκρατεῖς εἶναι *too few to have the power*, X. *C.* 4, 5, 15 ; ἀνάγκη ὥστε κινδυνεύειν *a necessity of incurring risk*, Isoc. 6, 51.

1474. In the same way (**1473**) ὥστε or ὡς with the infinitive may follow the comparative with ἤ ; e.g. ἐλάττω ἔχοντα δύναμιν ἢ ὥστε τοὺς φίλους ὠφελεῖν *having too little power to aid his friends*, X. *H.* 4, 8, 23. See **1535.**

1475. Ὣστε or ὡς is occasionally followed by a participle, generally where the participle is caused by assimilation with a preceding participial construction ; e.g. ὥστε σκέψασθαι δέον *so that we must consider*, Dem. 3, 1.

XI. Stipulative Clauses

1476. The infinitive with ὥστε may express a *condition* or *stipulation.* E.g.

ἐξὸν αὐτοῖς τῶν λοιπῶν ἄρχειν Ἑλλήνων, ὥστ' αὐτοὺς ὑπακούειν βασιλεῖ *although they might have ruled over the rest of the Greeks, provided (on the terms that) they themselves obeyed the King*, Dem. 6, 11.

1477. Ἐφ' ᾧ or ἐφ' ᾧτε *on condition that* is followed by the infinitive, and occasionally (in Herodotus and Thucydides) by the future indicative. E.g.

ἀφίεμέν σε, ἐπὶ τούτῳ μέντοι ἐφ' ᾧτε μηκέτι φιλοσοφεῖν *we release you, but on this condition, that you shall no longer pursue philosophy*, Plat. *Ap.* 29 c ; ἐπὶ τούτῳ ὑπεξίσταμαι, ἐφ' ᾧτε ὑπ' οὐδενὸς ὑμέων ἄρξομαι *I withdraw on this condition, that I shall be ruled by none of you*, Hdt. 3, 83. See **1217 b.**

XII. Temporal Particles Signifying *Until* and *Before*

ἕως, ἔστε, ἄχρι, μέχρι, ὄφρα

1478. When ἕως, ἔστε, ἄχρι, μέχρι, and the epic ὄφρα mean *while, so long as*, they are not distinguished in their use from other relatives. But when they mean *until*, they have many peculiarities. Homer has ἦος (sometimes written εἷος or εἵως) for ἕως (**33**).

1479. When ἕως, ἔστε, ἄχρι, μέχρι, and ὄφρα *until* refer to a definite past action they take the indicative, usually the aorist. E.g.

νῆχον πάλιν, ἦος ἐπῆλθον εἰς ποταμόν *I swam on again, until I came into a river, Od.* 7, 280; ταῦτα ἐποίουν, μέχρι σκότος ἐγένετο *this they did until darkness came on,* X. *An.* 4, 2, 4; οὐ πρότερον ἐπαύσαντο ἕως τὴν πόλιν εἰς στάσεις κατέστησαν *they did not stop until they had put the city into a turmoil of faction,* Lys. 25, 26.

This is the construction of the relative with a definite antecedent (**1439**).

1480. These particles, when they mean *until*, follow the construction of conditional relatives in both forms of future conditions, in unfulfilled conditions, and in present and past general suppositions. E.g.

ἐπίσχες, ἔστ' ἂν καὶ τὰ λοιπὰ προσμάθης *wait until you (shall) learn the rest besides* (**1445**), Aesch. *Pr.* 697; εἴποιμ' ἂν . . . ἕως παρατείναιμι τοῦτον *I should tell him . . . until I put him to torture* (**1447**), X. *C.* 1, 3, 11; ἡδέως ἂν τούτῳ ἔτι διελεγόμην, ἕως αὐτῷ . . . ἀπέδωκα *I should have been glad to continue conversing with him until I had given him back,* etc. (**1444**), Plat. *G.* 506; ἃ δ' ἂν ἀσύντακτα ᾖ, ἀνάγκη ταῦτα ἀεὶ πράγματα παρέχειν, ἕως ἂν χώραν λάβῃ *whatever is in disorder must necessarily make trouble until it is put in order* (**1442 a**), X. *C.* 4, 5, 37; περιεμένομεν ἑκάστοτε, ἕως ἀνοιχθείη τὸ δεσμωτήριον *we waited each day until the prison was opened* (**1442 b**), Plat. *Ph.* 59 d.

1481. The omission of ἄν after these particles, when the verb is in the subjunctive, is more common than it is after εἰ or ordinary relatives (**1416**), occurring sometimes in Attic prose; e.g. μέχρι πλοῦς γένηται *until the ship sails,* Thuc. 1, 137.

1482. Clauses introduced by ἕως etc. frequently imply a *purpose*; see the examples under **1480**. When such clauses depend upon a past tense, they admit the double construction of indirect discourse (**1517 c**), like final clauses (**1378**).

1483. Homer uses εἰς ὅ κε *until* like ἕως κε; and Herodotus uses ἐς ὅ and ἐς οὖ like ἕως.

Πρίν *before, until*

1484. Πρίν is followed by the infinitive, and also (like ἕως) by the finite moods. It is often correlated with πρότερον.

1485. *a.* In Homer πρίν generally has the infinitive without reference to its meaning or to the nature of the leading verb. But in other Greek it has the infinitive chiefly when it means simply *before* (and not *until*) and when the leading clause is affirmative.

b. The finite moods are used with πρίν when it means *until* (as well as *before*), and chiefly when the leading verb is negative or implies a negative. It has the subjunctive and optative only after negatives.

1486. *a.* Examples of πρίν with the infinitive:

ναῖε δὲ Πήδαιον πρὶν ἐλθεῖν υἷας Ἀχαιῶν *and he dwelt in Pedaeum before the coming of the sons of the Achaeans, Il.* 13, 172 (here πρὶν ἐλθεῖν = πρὸ τοῦ ἐλθεῖν); οὐ μ' ἀποτρέψεις πρὶν χαλκῷ μαχέσασθαι *you shall not turn me away before* (i.e. *until*) *we have fought together, Il.* 20, 257 (here the Attic would prefer πρὶν ἂν μαχεσώμεθα); ἀποπέμπουσιν αὐτὸν πρὶν ἀκοῦσαι *they send him away before* (i.e. *without*) *hearing him,* Thuc. 2, 12; Μεσσήνην εἵλομεν πρὶν Πέρσας λαβεῖν τὴν βασιλείαν *we took Messene before the Persians obtained their kingdom,* Isoc. 6, 26; πρὶν ὡς Ἄφοβον ἐλθεῖν μίαν ἡμέραν οὐκ ἐχήρευσεν *she was not a widow a single day before she went to Aphobus,* Dem. 30, 33 (here the infinitive is required, as πρίν does not mean *until*).

b. Examples of πρίν *until*, with the indicative (generally after negatives), and with the subjunctive and optative (*always* after negatives), the constructions being the same as those with ἕως (1479–1482):

οὐκ ἦν ἀλέξημ' οὐδέν, πρὶν γ' ἐγώ σφισιν ἔδειξα etc. *there was no relief, until I showed them,* etc. (1479), Aesch. *Pr.* 479; οὐ χρή με ἐνθένδε ἀπελθεῖν, πρὶν ἂν δῶ δίκην *I must not depart hence until I am punished* (1445), X. *An.* 5, 7, 5; οὐκ ἂν εἰδείης πρὶν πειρηθείης *you cannot know until you have tried it* (1447), Theognis 125; ἐχρῆν μὴ πρότερον συμβουλεύειν, πρὶν ἡμᾶς ἐδίδαξαν etc. *they ought not to have given advice until they had instructed us,* etc. (1444), Isoc. 4, 19; ὁρῶσι τοὺς πρεσβυτέρους οὐ πρόσθεν ἀπιόντας, πρὶν ἂν ἀφῶσιν οἱ ἄρχοντες *they see that the elders never go away until the authorities dismiss them* (1442 *a*), X. *C.* 1, 2, 8; ἀπηγόρευε μηδένα βάλλειν, πρὶν Κῦρος ἐμπλησθείη θηρῶν *he forbade any one to shoot until Cyrus had had his fill of hunting* (1482, 1517 *c*), X. *C.* 1, 4, 14.

1487. In Homer πρὶν γ' ὅτε (never the simple πρίν) is used with the indicative, and πρὶν γ' ὅτ' ἄν (sometimes πρίν, without ἄν) with the subjunctive.

1488. Πρίν, like ἕως etc. (1481), sometimes has the subjunctive without ἄν, even in Attic Greek; e.g. μὴ στέναζε πρὶν μάθῃς *weep not before you know* (or *until you have heard*), S. *Ph.* 917.

1489. Πρὶν ἤ (a developed form for πρίν) is used by Herodotus (rarely by Homer), and πρότερον ἤ *sooner than, before,* by Herodotus and Thucydides, in most of the constructions of πρίν. So πάρος *before* in Homer with the infinitive. Even ὕστερον ἤ *later than* once takes the infinitive by analogy. E.g.

πρὶν γὰρ ἢ ὀπίσω σφέας ἀναπλῶσαι, ἥλω ὁ Κροῖσος *for before they had sailed back, Croesus was overthrown,* Hdt. 1, 78; οὐδὲ ᾔδεσαν πρότερον ἤ περ ἐπύθοντο Τρηχινίων *they did not even know of it until they heard from the Trachinians,* Hdt. 7, 175; μὴ ἀπανίστασθαι ἀπὸ τῆς πόλιος πρότερον ἤ ἐξέλωσι *not to withdraw from the city until they capture it,* Hdt. 9, 86; πρότερον ἢ αἰσθέσθαι αὐτούς *before they perceived them,* Thuc. 6, 58; see Thuc. 1, 69, 2, 65; τέκνα ἐξείλοντο πάρος πετεηνὰ γενέσθαι *they took away the nestlings before they were fledged,* Od. 16, 218. So also ἔτεσιν ὕστερον ἑκατὸν ἢ αὐτοὺς οἰκῆσαι *a hundred years after their own settlement,* Thuc. 6, 4.

XIII. Indirect Discourse or Oratio Obliqua

General Principles

1490. A *direct quotation* or question gives the exact words of the original speaker or writer (i.e. of the *oratio recta*). In an *indirect* quotation or question (*oratio obliqua*) the original words conform to the construction of the sentence in which they are quoted.

E.g. the words ἐπιστολὴν γράφω *I am writing a letter* may be quoted either directly, λέγει τις "ἐπιστολὴν γράφω," or indirectly, λέγει τις ὅτι ἐπιστολὴν γράφει or φησί τις ἐπιστολὴν γράφειν *some one says that he is writing a letter.* So ἐρωτᾷ "τί γράφεις;" *he asks, "what are you writing?"* but indirectly ἐρωτᾷ τί γράφει *he asks what he is writing.*

1491. Indirect quotations may be expressed by ὅτι or ὡς *that,* with a finite verb, or by the infinitive (see 1509); or by the participle (1590).

1492. Ὅτι *that* often introduces a direct quotation; e.g. εἶπον ὅτι ἱκανοί ἐσμεν *they said, "we are able,"* X. *An.* 5, 4, 10; so ἔλεξε τάδε (ὧδε) *he spoke as follows,* since quotation marks were unknown.

1493. *a.* Homer sometimes has ὅ (neuter of ὅς) for ὅτι *that;* e.g. λεύσσετε γὰρ τό γε πάντες, ὅ μοι γέρας ἔρχεται ἄλλῃ *for you all see this, that my prize goes another way,* Il. 1, 120; so 5, 433.

b. Ὅπως is sometimes used, especially in poetry; e.g. τοῦτο μή μοι φράζ', ὅπως οὐκ εἶ κακός *tell me not that thou art not base,* S. *O. T.* 548.

c. Οὕνεκα and ὁθούνεκα *that* sometimes introduce indirect quotations in poetry.

1494. Indirect *questions* follow the same principles as indirect quotations with ὅτι or ὡς in regard to their moods and tenses.

For the words used to introduce indirect questions, see **1607** and **1608**.

1495. The term *indirect discourse* applies to all clauses (even single clauses in sentences of different construction) which indirectly express the words or thought of any person, even those of the speaker himself (see **1517**).

1496. Indirect quotations after ὅτι and ὡς and indirect questions follow these general rules:

a. After primary tenses, each verb retains both the *mood* and the *tense* of the direct discourse.

b. After past tenses, each indicative or subjunctive of the direct discourse may be either changed to the *same tense* of the optative or retained in its original *mood and tense*. But all secondary tenses of the indicative in conditions contrary to fact (**1407, 1444**) or in iterative constructions (**1297**), all aorist indicatives in dependent clauses (**1514**), and all optatives remain unchanged.

1497. The imperfect and pluperfect, having no tenses in the optative, generally remain unchanged in all kinds of sentences (but see **1503**). Observe that in Greek the *mood*, not the *tense*, is changed after a secondary tense (for exceptions, see **1504**); and that the subjunctive is never used *because of* the indirect discourse. When the subjunctive stands in indirect discourse it represents a subjunctive of the direct statement.

1498. When the quotation depends on a verb which takes the infinitive or participle, its leading verb is changed to the *corresponding tense* of the infinitive or participle (ἄν being retained when there is one), and its dependent verbs follow the preceding rule (**1496**).

1499. Ἄν is never omitted with the indicative or optative in indirect discourse, if it was used in the direct form; but when a particle or a relative word has ἄν with the subjunctive in the direct form, as in ἐάν, ὅταν, ὅς ἄν, etc. (**1299 b**), the ἄν is dropped when the subjunctive is changed to the optative after a past tense in indirect discourse.

1500. Ἄν is never *added* in indirect discourse when it was not used in the direct form.

1501. The negative particle of the direct discourse is regularly retained in the indirect form. But see **1511**.

Simple Sentences in Indirect Discourse

INDICATIVE AND OPTATIVE WITH ὅτι AND ὡς, AND IN INDIRECT QUESTIONS

1502. After primary tenses an indicative (without ἄν) retains both its mood and its tense in indirect discourse. After past tenses it is either changed to the same tense of the optative or retained in the original mood and tense. E.g.

λέγει ὅτι γράφει *he says that he is writing,* λέγει ὅτι ἔγραφεν *he says that he was writing,* λέγει ὅτι ἔγραψεν *he says that he wrote,* λέξει ὅτι γέγραφεν *he will say that he has written;* ἐρωτᾷ τί (or ὅ τι) βούλονται *he asks what they want,* ἀγνοῶ τί (or ὅ τι) ποιήσουσιν *I do not know what they will do.* εἶπεν ὅτι γράφοι or ὅτι γράφει *he said that he was writing* (he said γράφω); εἶπεν ὅτι γράψοι or ὅτι γράψει *he said that he should write* (he said γράψω *I shall write*); εἶπεν ὅτι γράψειεν or ὅτι ἔγραψεν *he said that he had written* (he said ἔγραψα *I wrote*); εἶπεν ὅτι γεγραφὼς εἴη or ὅτι γέγραφεν *he said that he had written* (he said γέγραφα *I have written*). OPTATIVE: ἐπειρώμην αὐτῷ δεικνύναι ὅτι οἴοιτο μὲν εἶναι σοφὸς, εἴη δ᾽ οὔ *I tried to show him that although he thought he was wise, he really was not* (i.e. οἴεται μὲν ... ἔστι δ᾽ οὔ), Plat. *Ap.* 21 c; ὑπειπὼν ὅτι αὐτὸς τἀκεῖ πράξοι, ᾤχετο *intimating that he would himself attend to the business there, he departed* (he said αὐτὸς τἀκεῖ πράξω), Thuc. 1, 90; ἔλεξαν ὅτι πέμψειε σφᾶς ὁ Ἰνδῶν βασιλεύς, κελεύων ἐρωτᾶν ἐξ ὅτου ὁ πόλεμος εἴη *they said that the king of India had sent them, commanding them to ask what the cause of the war was* (they said ἔπεμψεν ἡμᾶς, and the question was ἐκ τίνος ἐστὶν ὁ πόλεμος;), X. *C.* 2, 4, 7; ἤρετο εἴ τις ἐμοῦ εἴη σοφώτερος *he asked whether there was any one wiser than I* (i.e. ἔστι τις σοφώτερος;), Plat. *Ap.* 21 a. INDICATIVE: ἔλεγον ὅτι ἐλπίζουσι σὲ καὶ τὴν πόλιν ἕξειν μοι χάριν *they said that they hoped you and the state would be grateful to me* (they said ἐλπίζομεν, and the hope was σὺ καὶ ἡ πόλις ἕξετέ μοι χάριν), Isoc. 5, 23; ἧκε δ᾽ ἀγγέλλων ὡς Ἐλάτεια κατείληπται *some one had come with a report that Elatea had been taken* (here the perfect optative might have been used), Dem. 18, 169; ἀποκρινάμενοι ὅτι πέμψουσι πρέσβεις, εὐθὺς ἀπήλλαξαν *replying that they would send ambassadors, they immediately dismissed them,* Thuc. 1, 90; ἠπόρουν τί ποτε λέγει *I was uncertain what he meant* (τί ποτε λέγει;), Plat. *Ap.* 21 b; ἐβουλεύοντο τίν᾽ αὐτοῦ καταλείψουσιν *they were considering (the question) whom they should leave here,* Dem. 19, 122.

1503. Occasionally the present optative represents the imperfect indicative in this construction; e.g. ἀπεκρίναντο ὅτι οὐδεὶς μάρτυς παρείη *they replied that there had been no witness present* (οὐδεὶς παρῆν), Dem. 30, 20 (here the context makes it clear that παρείη does not stand for πάρεστι).

1504. *a.* In a number of cases, contrary to the rules given above, the Greek changes a present indicative to the imperfect, or a perfect to the pluperfect, in indirect discourse, instead of retaining it or changing it to the optative; e.g. ἐν ἀπορίᾳ ἦσαν, ἐννοούμενοι ὅτι ἐπὶ ταῖς βασιλέως θύραις ἦσαν, προυδεδώκεσαν δὲ αὐτοὺς οἱ βάρβαροι *they were in a quandary, reflecting that they were at the king's gates, and that the barbarians had betrayed them*, X. *An.* 3, 1, 2. Here the author gives his own point of view as he recalls these past events in his own experience. This is also the English usage. It occurs oftenest with verbs of *knowing* and *perceiving*.

b. In Homer this is the ordinary construction: γίγνωσκον ὅ δὴ κακὰ μήδετο δαίμων *I knew that the god plotted mischief, Od.* 3, 166.

SUBJUNCTIVE OR OPTATIVE REPRESENTING THE
INTERROGATIVE SUBJUNCTIVE

1505. An interrogative subjunctive (1367), after a primary tense, retains its mood and tense in an indirect question; after a past tense, it may be either changed to the same tense of the optative or retained in the subjunctive. E.g.

βουλεύομαι ὅπως σε ἀποδρῶ *I am trying to think how I shall escape you* (πῶς σε ἀποδρῶ;), X. *C.* 1, 4, 13; οὐκ οἶδ' εἰ Χρυσάντᾳ τούτῳ δῶ *I don't know whether to give (them) to Chrysantas here*, ibid. 8, 4, 16; οὐκ ἔχω τί εἴπω *I do not know what to say* (τί εἴπω;), Dem. 9, 54 (cf. non habeo quid dicam); ἐπήροντο εἰ παραδοῖεν τὴν πόλιν *they asked whether they should give up the city* (παραδῶμεν τὴν πόλιν; *shall we give up the city?*), Thuc. 1, 25; ἠπόρει ὅ τι χρήσαιτο τῷ πράγματι *he was at a loss how to deal with the matter* (τί χρήσωμαι;), X. *H.* 7, 4, 39; ἐβουλεύοντο εἴτε κατακαύσωσιν εἴτε τι ἄλλο χρήσωνται *they were debating whether they should burn them or dispose of them in some other way*, Thuc. 2, 4.

1506. In these questions εἰ (not ἐάν) is used for *whether*, with both subjunctive and optative (see the second example in 1505).

1507. An interrogative subjunctive may be changed to the optative when the leading verb is optative, contrary to the general usage of indirect discourse (1272 *b*); e.g. οὐκ ἂν ἔχοις ὅ τι χρήσαιο σαυτῷ *you would not know what to do with yourself* (τί χρήσωμαι ἐμαυτῷ;), Plat. *G.* 486 b.

INDICATIVE OR OPTATIVE WITH ἄν

1508. An indicative or optative with ἄν retains its mood and tense (with ἄν) unchanged in indirect discourse after ὅτι or ὡς and in indirect questions. E.g.

λέγει (or ἔλεξεν) ὅτι τοῦτο ἂν ἐγένετο *he says (or said) that this would have happened*; ἔλεξεν ὅτι οὗτος δικαίως ἂν ἀποθάνοι *he said that this man would justly die*; ἠρώτων εἰ δοῖεν ἂν τὰ πιστά *they asked whether they would give the pledges* (δοίητε ἄν;), X. *An.* 4, 8, 7.

Infinitive and Participle in Indirect Discourse

1509. Each tense of the infinitive or participle in indirect discourse represents the tense of the finite verb which would be used in the direct form, the present and perfect including the imperfect and pluperfect. Each tense with ἄν can represent the corresponding tenses of either indicative or optative with ἄν. E.g.

ἀρρωστεῖν προφασίζεται *he pretends that he is sick*; ἐξώμοσεν ἀρρωστεῖν τουτονί *he took an oath that this man was sick*, Dem. 19, 124; κατασχεῖν φησι τούτους *he says that he detained them*, ibid. 39; ἔφη χρήμαθ' ἐαυτῷ τοὺς Θηβαίους ἐπικεκηρυχέναι *he said that the Thebans had offered a reward for him*, ibid. 21; ἐπαγγέλλεται τὰ δίκαια ποιήσειν *he promises to do what is right*, ibid. 48.

ἤγγειλε τούτους ἐρχομένους *he announced that these were coming* (οὗτοι ἔρχονται); ἀγγέλλει τούτους ἐλθόντας *he announces that these came* (οὗτοι ἦλθον); αἰσθάνεται τοῦτο γενησόμενον *he perceives that this will be done*; ᾔσθετο τοῦτο γενησόμενον *he perceived that this would be done*; εἶδε τοῦτο γεγενημένον *he saw that this had been done* (τοῦτο γεγένηται).

See examples of ἄν with infinitive and participle in **1308**. For the present infinitive and participle as imperfect, see **1286** and **1290**.

1510. The infinitive or participle is said *to stand in indirect discourse*, and its tenses correspond to those of the finite moods, when it depends on a verb implying thought or the expression of thought, and when *also* the thought, *as originally conceived*, would have been expressed by some tense of the indicative (with or without ἄν) or optative (with ἄν), so that it can be transferred without change of tense to the infinitive (or participle). E.g. in βούλεται ἐλθεῖν *he wishes to go*, ἐλθεῖν represents no form of either aorist indicative or aorist optative, and is not in indirect discourse (**1523**). But in φησὶν ἐλθεῖν *he says that he went*, ἐλθεῖν represents ἦλθον of the direct discourse. It is important to observe this *grammatical* distinction, though it cannot in all cases be maintained *logically*. A verb of commanding is also a verb of saying, though it takes the object infinitive, not the infinitive in indirect discourse; e.g. οἱ δὲ σφάττειν ἐκέλευον · οὐ γὰρ ἂν δύνασθαι πορευθῆναι *they told him to (go ahead and) kill them; for (said they, implied in ἐκέλευον) they could not go on*, X. *An.* 4, 5, 16. See **1429, 1517**, and *Greek Moods and Tenses*, § 684.

1511. The regular negative of the infinitive and participle in indirect discourse is οὐ, but exceptions occur. Especially the infinitive after verbs of *hoping*, *promising*, and *swearing* (see **1287**) regularly has μή for its negative; e.g. ὤμνυε μηδὲν εἰρηκέναι *he swore that he had said nothing*, Dem. 21, 119.

Indirect Quotation of Complex Sentences

1512. *a.* When a complex sentence is indirectly quoted, its *leading* verb follows the rule for simple sentences (1502–1509).

b. The *dependent* verbs after primary tenses retain the same mood and tense. After past tenses, dependent primary tenses of the indicative and all dependent subjunctives may either be changed to the *same tense* of the optative or retain their original mood and tense. When a subjunctive becomes optative, ἄν is dropped, ἐάν, ὅταν, etc. becoming εἰ, ὅτε, etc. But dependent *secondary* tenses of the indicative remain unchanged. E.g.

(*a*) ἂν ὑμεῖς λέγητε, ποιήσειν (φησὶν) ὃ μήτ' αἰσχύνην μήτ' ἀδοξίαν αὐτῷ φέρει *if you say so, he declares he will do whatever does not bring either shame or discredit to him*, Dem. 19, 41. Here no change is made, except in ποιήσειν (1509).

(*b*) ἀπεκρίνατο ὅτι μανθάνοιεν ἃ οὐκ ἐπίσταιντο *he replied that they were learning what they did not understand* (he said μανθάνουσιν ἃ οὐκ ἐπίστανται, which might have been retained), Plat. *Euthyd.* 276 e; εἴ τινα φεύγοντα λήψοιτο, προηγόρευεν ὅτι ὡς πολεμίῳ χρήσοιτο *he announced that if he should catch any one running away he should treat him as an enemy* (he said εἴ τινα λήψομαι, χρήσομαι), X. *C.* 3, 1, 3 (**1415**); νομίζων, ὅσα τῆς πόλεως προλάβοι, πάντα ταῦτα βεβαίως ἕξειν *believing that he should hold securely all regions belonging to our city which he should seize first* (ὅσ' ἂν προλάβω, ἕξω), Dem. 18, 26; ἐδόκει μοι ταύτῃ πειρᾶσθαι σωθῆναι, ἐνθυμουμένῳ ὅτι, ἐὰν μὲν λάθω, σωθήσομαι *I resolved to try to gain safety in this way, reflecting that if I escaped detection I should be saved* (we might have had εἰ λάθοιμι, σωθησοίμην), Lys. 12, 15; ἔφασαν τοὺς ἄνδρας ἀποκτενεῖν οὓς ἔχουσι ζῶντας *they said that they should kill the men whom they had alive* (ἀποκτενοῦμεν οὓς ἔχομεν, which might have been changed to ἀποκτενεῖν οὓς ἔχοιεν), Thuc. 2, 5; πρόδηλον ἦν (τοῦτο) ἐσόμενον, εἰ μὴ κωλύσετε *it was plain that this would be so unless you should prevent* (ἔσται, εἰ μὴ κωλύσετε, which might have become εἰ μὴ κωλύσοιτε), Aeschin. 3, 90; ἤλπιζον τοὺς Σικελοὺς ταύτῃ οὓς μετεπέμψαντο ἀπαντήσεσθαι *they hoped the Sikels whom they had sent for would meet them here*, Thuc. 7, 80.

1513. One verb may be changed to the optative while another is retained; e.g. δηλώσας ὅτι ἕτοιμοί εἰσι μάχεσθαι, εἴ τις ἐξέρχοιτο *having shown that they were ready to fight if any one should come forth* (ἕτοιμοί ἐσμεν, ἐάν τις ἐξέρχηται), X. *C.* 4, 1, 1. This sometimes causes a variety of constructions in the same sentence.

1514. The *aorist* indicative is not changed to the aorist optative in dependent clauses, because in these the aorist optative generally represents the aorist subjunctive.

318   GREEK GRAMMAR

The present indicative is seldom changed to the present optative in dependent clauses, for a similar reason. For the imperfect and pluperfect, see 1497.

1515. A dependent optative of the direct form of course remains unchanged in all indirect discourse (1496 *b*).

1516. Occasionally a dependent present or perfect indicative is changed to the imperfect or pluperfect, as in the leading clause (1504).

1517. The principles of 1512 apply also to all dependent clauses after past tenses, which express indirectly the past thought of any person. This applies especially to the following constructions:

a. Clauses depending on an infinitive after verbs of *wishing, commanding, advising,* and others which imply *thought* but do not take the infinitive in indirect discourse (1510).

b. Clauses containing a protasis with the apodosis implied in the context (1430), or with the apodosis expressed in a verb like θαυμάζω (1433).

c. Temporal clauses expressing a past intention, purpose, or expectation, especially those introduced by ἕως or πρίν.

d. Ordinary relative sentences, regularly taking the indicative.

(*a*) ἐβούλοντο ἐλθεῖν, εἰ τοῦτο γένοιτο *they wished to go if this should happen.* (We might have ἐὰν τοῦτο γένηται, expressing the form *if this shall happen,* in which the wish would be conceived.) Here ἐλθεῖν is not in indirect discourse (1510). ἐκέλευσεν ὅ τι δύναιντο λαβόντας μεταδιώκειν *he commanded them to take what they could and pursue* (we might have ὅ τι ἂν δύνωνται, representing ὅ τι ἂν δύνησθε), X. C. 7, 3, 7 ; προεῖπον αὐτοῖς μὴ ναυμαχεῖν Κορινθίοις, ἢν μὴ ἐπὶ Κέρκυραν πλέωσι καὶ μέλλωσιν ἀποβαίνειν *they instructed them not to engage in a sea-fight with Corinthians, unless these should be sailing against Corcyra and should be on the point of landing* (we might have εἰ μὴ πλέοιεν καὶ μέλλοιεν), Thuc. 1, 45.

(*b*) φύλακας συμπέμπει, ὅπως φυλάττοιεν αὐτὸν καὶ εἰ τῶν ἀγρίων τι φανείη θηρίων *he sent* (1270) *guards along to protect him and (to be ready) in case any wild animals should appear* (the thought being ἐάν τι φανῇ), X. C. 1, 4, 7 ; τἆλλα, ἢν ἔτι ναυμαχεῖν οἱ Ἀθηναῖοι τολμήσωσι, παρεσκευάζοντο *they made all other preparations (to be ready) in case the Athenians should still venture a naval battle,* Thuc. 7, 59 ; ᾤκτιρον εἰ ἁλώσοιντο *they pitied them, if they were to be caught* (the thought being *we pity them if they are caught,* εἰ ἁλώσονται, which might be retained), X. An. 1, 4, 7 (1415) ; ἔχαιρον ἀγαπῶν εἴ τις ἐάσοι *I rejoiced, being content if anyone was going to let it pass* (the thought was ἀγαπῶ εἴ τις ἐάσει), Plat. *Rep.* 450 a ; ἐθαύμαζεν εἴ τις ἀργύριον πράττοιτο *he wondered that anyone demanded money,* X. M. 1, 2, 7 ; but in the same book (1, 1, 13) we find ἐθαύμαζε δ᾽ εἰ μὴ φανερὸν αὐτοῖς ἐστιν *he wondered that it was not plain to them.*

(c) σπονδὰς ἐποιήσαντο ἕως ἀπαγγελθείη τὰ λεχθέντα εἰς Λακεδαίμονα *they made a truce, (to continue) until what had been said should be reported at Sparta* (their thought was ἕως ἂν ἀπαγγελθῇ), X. H. 3, 2, 20; οὐ γὰρ δή σφεας ἀπίει ὁ θεὸς τῆς ἀποικίης, πρὶν δὴ ἀπίκωνται ἐς αὐτὴν Λιβύην *for the god did not mean to release them from the colony until they should actually come to Libya* (we might have ἀπίκοιντο), Hdt. 4, 157 (see 1482, 1488); μένοντες ἔστασαν ὁππότε πύργος Τρώων ὁρμήσειε *they stood waiting until (for the time when) a serried line should rush upon the Trojans,* Il. 4, 334.

(d) καὶ ᾔτεε σῆμα ἰδέσθαι, ὅττι ῥά οἱ γαμβροῖο πάρα Προίτοιο φέροιτο *he asked to see the token, which he was bringing* (as he said) *from his son-in-law Proetus,* Il. 6, 176; κατηγόρεον τῶν Αἰγινητέων τὰ πεποιήκοιεν προδόντες τὴν Ἑλλάδα *they accused the Aeginetans for what* (as they said) *they had done in betraying Greece,* Hdt. 6, 49.

For the same principle in causal sentences, see **1464**.

1518. On this principle, clauses introduced by ἵνα, ὅπως, ὡς, ὄφρα, and μή admit the double construction of indirect discourse, and allow the subjunctive or future indicative to stand unchanged after past tenses (see **1378**). The same principle extends to all conditional and all conditional relative and temporal sentences depending on clauses with ἵνα etc., as these too belong to the indirect discourse.

οὐχ ὅτι, οὐχ ὅπως, μὴ ὅτι, μὴ ὅπως, *not only not*

1519. These expressions, by the ellipsis of a verb of *saying*, often mean *I do not speak of,* or *not to speak of.* With οὐχ an indicative (e.g. λέγω) was originally understood, and with μή an imperative or subjunctive (e.g. λέγε or εἴπῃς). E.g.

οὐχ ὅπως τὰ σκεύη ἀπέδοσθε, ἀλλὰ καὶ αἱ θύραι ἀφῃρπάσθησαν *not only did you fail to sell the furniture, even the doors were carried off,* Lys. 19, 31; μὴ ὅτι θεός, ἀλλὰ καὶ ἄνθρωποι . . . οὐ φιλοῦσι τοὺς ἀπιστοῦντας *not only God (not to speak of God), but men also love not those who distrust them,* X. C. 7, 2, 17; πεπαύμεθ' ἡμεῖς, οὐχ ὅπως σε παύσομεν *we have been stopped ourselves; there is no talk of stopping you,* S. El. 796.

When these forms were thus used, the original ellipsis was probably never present to the mind.

THE INFINITIVE

1520. *a.* The infinitive is in origin a neuter substantive, with many attributes of a verb. Thus, like a verb, it has voices and tenses; it may have a subject or object; and it is qualified by adverbs, not by adjectives.

b. When the definite article came into use with other nouns (see **935 d**), it was used also with the infinitive, which thus became more distinctly a noun with four cases.

For the subject of the infinitive, see **883**. For the case of predicate substantives and adjectives when the subject is omitted, see **923** and **924**.

Infinitive without the Article

As Subject, Predicate, Object, or Appositive

1521. The infinitive may be the subject nominative of a finite verb (especially of an impersonal verb, **887**, or of ἐστί), or the subject accusative of another infinitive. It may be a predicate nominative (**896**), and it may stand in apposition to a substantive (**900**). E.g.

συνέβη αὐτῷ ἐλθεῖν *it happened that he went,* ἐξῆν μένειν *it was possible to stay,* ἡδὺ πολλοὺς ἐχθροὺς ἔχειν; *is it pleasant to have many enemies?* φησὶν ἐξεῖναι τούτοις μένειν *he says it is possible for them to stay* (μένειν being subject of ἐξεῖναι); τὸ γνῶναι ἐπιστήμην λαβεῖν ἐστιν *to learn is to acquire knowledge,* Plat. *Th.* 209 e; τὸ γὰρ θάνατον δεδιέναι οὐδὲν ἄλλο ἐστὶν ἢ δοκεῖν σοφὸν εἶναι μὴ ὄντα *for to fear death (the fear of death) is nothing else than pretending to be wise without being so,* Plat. *Ap.* 29 a; εἷς οἰωνὸς ἄριστος, ἀμύνεσθαι περὶ πάτρης *one omen is best, to fight for our country,* Il. 12, 243. See also **1116 a**.

For the subject infinitive with the article, see **1545**.

1522. The infinitive may be the object of a verb. It generally has the force of an object accusative, sometimes that of an accusative of kindred signification (**1049**), and sometimes that of an object genitive.

1523. The object infinitive not in indirect discourse (**1510**) follows verbs whose action naturally implies another action as its object, especially those expressing *wish, command, advice, cause, attempt, intention, prevention, ability, fitness, necessity,* or their opposites. Such verbs are in general the same in Greek as in English, and others will be learned by practice. The negative is μή. E.g.

βούλεται ἐλθεῖν *he wishes to go;* βούλεται τοὺς πολίτας πολεμικοὺς εἶναι *he wishes the citizens to be warlike;* παραινοῦμέν σοι μένειν *we advise you to remain;* προείλετο πολεμῆσαι *he preferred to make war;* κελεύει σε μὴ ἀπελθεῖν *he commands you not to depart;* ἀξιοῦσιν ἄρχειν *they claim the right to rule;* ἀξιοῦται ἀποθανεῖν *he is deemed worthy of death;* δέομαι ὑμῶν συγγνώμην μοι ἔχειν *I ask you to pardon me.* So ἀναβάλλεται τοῦτο ποιεῖν *he postpones doing this*; φοβεῖται ἀποθανεῖν *he is afraid to die* (cf. **1389** and X. *An.* 1, 3, 17); ἐπίσταται νεῖν *he knows how to swim* (**1594 b**).

1524. The tenses here used are chiefly the present and aorist, and these do not differ in their time, but solely in the character of their action (**1274**). In this construction the infinitive has no more reference to *time* than any other verbal noun would have, but the meaning of the verb generally gives it a reference to the future; e.g. in ἀξιοῦται ἀποθανεῖν (above) ἀποθανεῖν expresses time only in so far as θανάτου would express it.

1525. The infinitive may depend on a noun and a verb (generally ἐστί) which together are equivalent to a verb which takes an object infinitive (**1523**). E.g.

ἀνάγκη ἐστί πάντας ἀπελθεῖν *all must withdraw*; κίνδυνος ἦν αὐτῷ παθεῖν τι *he was in danger of suffering something*; ἐλπίδας ἔχει τοῦτο ποιῆσαι *he has hopes of doing this*; ὥρα ἀπιέναι *it is time to go away*, Plat. *Ap.* 42 a; τοῖς στρατιώταις ὁρμὴ ἐνέπεσε ἐκτειχίσαι τὸ χωρίον *an impulse to fortify the place fell upon the soldiers*, Thuc. 4, 4.

For the infinitive with τοῦ depending on a noun, see **1550**.

1526. *a.* The infinitive in indirect discourse (**1510**) is generally the object of a verb of *saying* or *thinking* or some equivalent expression. Here each tense of the infinitive corresponds in time to the same tense of some finite mood. See **1509**, with the examples.

b. Many verbs of this class (especially the passive of λέγω) allow both a personal and an impersonal construction. Thus we can say λέγεται ὁ Κῦρος ἐλθεῖν *Cyrus is said to have gone*, or λέγεται τὸν Κῦρον ἐλθεῖν *it is said that Cyrus went*. Δοκέω *seem* is generally used personally; e.g. δοκεῖ εἶναι σοφός *he seems to be wise (has the reputation of being wise)*.

1527. *a.* Of the three common verbs meaning *to say*,

(1) φημί regularly takes the infinitive in indirect discourse;

(2) εἶπον regularly takes ὅτι or ὡς with the indicative or optative;

(3) λέγω allows either construction, but in the *active* voice it generally takes ὅτι or ὡς, in the passive it takes the infinitive.

Most verbs meaning *to think* or *believe* regularly take the infinitive in indirect discourse; the commonest are οἶμαι (οἴομαι), ἡγοῦμαι, νομίζω, and δοκῶ (Ionic, poetic, and in Plato in this sense).

b. Exceptional cases of εἶπον with the infinitive are more common than those of φημί with ὅτι or ὡς, which are very rare except in late Greek.

Εἶπον and λέγω in the sense of *command* take the infinitive by the rule (1523).

For the two constructions allowed after verbs of *hoping, expecting, promising,* and *swearing,* see 1287.

1528. A relative or temporal clause depending on an infinitive in indirect discourse sometimes takes the infinitive by assimilation; e.g. ἐπειδὴ δὲ γενέσθαι ἐπὶ τῇ οἰκίᾳ, (ἔφη) ἀνεῳγμένην καταλαμβάνειν τὴν θύραν *and when they had come to the house, (he said) they found the door open,* Plat. *Symp.* 174 d. Herodotus allows this assimilation even after εἰ *if* and διότι *because.*

1529. In narration, the infinitive often seems to stand for the indicative, when it depends on some word like λέγεται *it is said,* expressed or implied in what precedes. E.g.

ἀπικομένους δὲ ἐς τὸ Ἄργος, διατίθεσθαι τὸν φόρτον *and they had arrived at Argos and were (it is said) setting out their cargo for sale,* Hdt. 1, 1; διατίθεσθαι is an imperfect infinitive (1286 a): see also Hdt. 1, 24 and X. *C.* 1, 3, 5.

INFINITIVE WITH ADJECTIVES

1530. The infinitive may depend on adjectives corresponding in meaning to verbs which take an object infinitive (1523), especially those expressing *ability, fitness, desert, willingness,* and their opposites. E.g.

δυνατὸς τοῦτο ποιεῖν *able to do this;* δεινὸς λέγειν *skilled in speaking;* ἄξιος τοῦτο λαβεῖν *worthy to receive this;* πρόθυμος λέγειν *eager to speak;* μαλακοὶ καρτερεῖν *too effeminate to endure,* Plat. *Rep.* 556 c; ἐπιστήμων λέγειν τε καὶ σιγᾶν *knowing how to speak as well as to be silent,* Plat. *Phdr.* 276 a (1594 b).

So μὴ τοιοῦτοι ἔσονται οἷοι πονηροῦ τινος ἔργου ἐφίεσθαι *that they may not be capable of aiming at any vicious act,* X. *C.* 1, 2, 3; οἷος ἀεί ποτε μεταβάλλεσθαι *one likely to be always changing,* X. *H.* 2, 3, 45.

1531. Δίκαιος *just* and some other adjectives may thus be used *personally* with the infinitive; e.g. δίκαιός ἐστι τοῦτο ποιεῖν *he has a right to do this* (equivalent to δίκαιόν ἐστιν αὐτὸν τοῦτο ποιεῖν). Cf. 1591.

LIMITING INFINITIVE WITH ADJECTIVES, ADVERBS, AND SUBSTANTIVES

1532. Any adjective or adverb may take an infinitive to limit its meaning to a particular action (*epexegetic infinitive*). E.g.

θέαμα αἰσχρὸν ὁρᾶν *a sight disgraceful to behold;* λόγοι ὑμῖν χρησιμώτατοι ἀκοῦσαι *words most useful for you to hear;* τὰ χαλεπώτατα εὑρεῖν *the things hardest to find;* πολιτεία ἥκιστα χαλεπὴ συζῆν *a government least hard to live under,* Plat. *Pol.* 302 b; οἰκία ἡδίστη ἐνδιαιτᾶσθαι *a house most pleasant to live in*, X. *M*. 3, 8, 8; κάλλιστα (adv.) ἰδεῖν *in a manner most delightful to behold*, X. *C*. 8, 3, 5.

1533. This infinitive is generally active rather than passive; e.g. πρᾶγμα χαλεπὸν ποιεῖν *a hard thing to do*, rather than χαλεπὸν ποιεῖσθαι *hard to be done*.

1534. Nouns and even verbs may take the infinitive as a limiting accusative (**1056**); e.g. θαῦμα ἰδέσθαι *a wonder to behold*, *Od*. 8, 366; ἀριστεύεσκε μάχεσθαι *he was the best in fighting* (like μάχην), *Il*. 6, 460; δοκεῖς διαφέρειν αὐτοὺς ἰδεῖν; *do you think they differ in appearance?* Plat. *Rep*. 495 e.

1535. Here belongs the infinitive after a comparative with ἤ *than*; e.g. νόσημα μεῖζον ἢ φέρειν *an affliction too heavy to bear*, S. *O.T.* 1293.

For ὥστε with this infinitive, see **1474**.

INFINITIVE OF PURPOSE

1536. a. The infinitive may express a *purpose* with a few verbs. E.g.

οἱ ἄρχοντες, οὓς εἵλεσθε ἄρχειν μου *the officers whom you chose to command me*, Plat. *Ap*. 28 e; τὴν πόλιν φυλάττειν αὐτοῖς παρέδωκαν *they delivered the city to them to guard*, X. *H*. 4, 4, 15; θεάσασθαι παρῆν τὰς γυναῖκας πιεῖν φερούσας *the women were to be seen bringing them (something) to drink*, X. *H*. 7, 2, 9.

b. The verbs which allow this construction in prose instead of the more common final clause (**1374**) are a few meaning *to appoint, give, take, send, bring*. Here, as with adjectives (**1533**), the infinitive is active rather than passive; e.g. κτανεῖν ἐμοί νιν ἔδοσαν *they gave her to me to kill (to be killed)*, E. *Tro*. 874; οὔτοι παῖδας παρήσω τοὺς ἐμοὺς καθυβρίσαι *verily I shall not give over my children to outrage*, E. *Med*. 1061.

Cf. the infinitive with τοῦ expressing purpose, **1551**.

c. With verbs of *naming* and *calling* a redundant εἶναι is often added; e.g. ὄνομα τοῦτο λέγεσθαι σοφὸς εἶναι *to be called this by name, "wise,"* Plat. *Ap*. 23 a. Cf. **1539**.

1537. In Homer, where ὥς τε only twice has the sense of *so as* (**1471**), the simple infinitive may express a *result*; e.g. τίς σφωε ξυνέηκε μάχεσθαι; *who brought them together to contend?* *Il*. 1, 8.

ABSOLUTE INFINITIVE

1538. The infinitive may stand *absolutely* in parenthetical phrases, generally with ὡς or ὅσον.

The most common of these expressions is ὡς ἔπος εἰπεῖν or ὡς εἰπεῖν *to put it in a word* or *if one may say so*, used to soften a statement. Others are ὡς συντόμως (or συνελόντι, 1172 b) εἰπεῖν to speak concisely; τὸ ξύμπαν εἰπεῖν in a word, in general; ὡς ἀπεικάσαι as far as we can judge; ὅσον γέ μ' εἰδέναι as far as I know; ὡς ἐμοὶ δοκεῖν or ἐμοὶ δοκεῖν as it seems to me; ὡς οὕτω γ' ἀκοῦσαι at first hearing (or without ὡς). So ὀλίγου δεῖν and μικροῦ δεῖν to want little, i.e. almost (see 1116 b).

Herodotus has ὡς λόγῳ εἰπεῖν and οὐ πολλῷ λόγῳ εἰπεῖν not to make a long story, in short; Plato, ὡς πρὸς ἡμᾶς εἰρῆσθαι between ourselves.

1539. In certain cases εἶναι seems to be superfluous; especially in ἑκὼν εἶναι willingly, which generally stands in a negative sentence. So in τὸ νῦν εἶναι at present; τὸ τήμερον εἶναι today; τὸ ἐπ' ἐκείνοις εἶναι and similar phrases as far as depends on them; τὴν πρώτην εἶναι at first, Hdt. 1, 153; κατὰ τοῦτο εἶναι so far as concerns this, Plat. Prot. 317 a; ὡς παλαιὰ εἶναι considering their age, Thuc. 1, 21; and some other phrases. Cf. 1536 c.

INFINITIVE IN COMMANDS, WISHES, LAWS

1540. The infinitive with a subject nominative is sometimes used like the second person of the imperative, especially in Homer. E.g.

μή ποτε καὶ σὺ γυναικί περ ἤπιος εἶναι be thou never indulgent to thy wife, Od. 11, 441; οἷς μὴ πελάζειν do not approach them (= μὴ πέλαζε), Aesch. Pr. 712.

1541. The infinitive with a subject accusative sometimes expresses a wish, like the optative (1355); and sometimes a command, like the third person of the imperative. E.g.

Ζεῦ πάτερ, ἢ Αἴαντα λαχεῖν ἢ Τυδέος υἱόν Father Zeus, may the lot fall either on Ajax or on the son of Tydeus (= Αἴας λάχοι, etc.), Il. 7, 179; θεοὶ πολῖται, μή με δουλείας τυχεῖν gods of our city, may slavery not be my lot, Aesch. Sev. 253; Τρῶας ἔπειθ' Ἑλένην ἀποδοῦναι after that let the Trojans surrender Helen (= ἀποδοῖεν), Il. 3, 285.

1542. This construction has been explained by supplying a verb like δός or δότε grant (see δὸς τείσασθαι grant that I may take vengeance, Il. 3, 351), or γένοιτο may it be.

1543. In laws, treaties, and proclamations, the infinitive often depends on ἔδοξε or δέδοκται be it enacted, or κεκέλευσται it is commanded; which may be expressed in a previous sentence or understood. E.g.

δικάζειν δὲ τὴν ἐν Ἀρείῳ πάγῳ φόνου and (be it enacted) that the Council of the Areopagus shall have jurisdiction in cases of murder, Dem. 23, 22; ἔτη δὲ εἶναι τὰς σπονδὰς πεντήκοντα and that the treaty shall continue fifty years, Thuc. 5, 18; ἀκούετε λεῴ· τοὺς ὁπλίτας ἀπιέναι πάλιν οἴκαδε hear ye people! let the heavy-armed go back home again, Ar. Av. 448.

Infinitive with the Article

1544. When the infinitive has the article, its character as a neuter substantive becomes more distinct, while it loses none of its attributes as a verb. The addition of the article extends its use to many new constructions, especially to those with prepositions; and the article is sometimes allowed even in many of the older constructions in which the infinitive regularly stands alone.

INFINITIVE WITH τό AS SUBJECT OR OBJECT

1545. The subject infinitive (1521) may take the article to make it more distinctly a substantive. E.g.

τὸ γνῶναι ἐπιστήμην λαβεῖν ἐστιν *to learn is to acquire knowledge*, Plat. *Th.* 209 e; τοῦτό ἐστι τὸ ἀδικεῖν *this is wrong-doing*, Plat. *G.* 483 c; τὸ γὰρ θάνατον δεδιέναι οὐδὲν ἄλλο ἐστὶν ἢ δοκεῖν σοφὸν εἶναι μὴ ὄντα *the fear of death is nothing else than pretending to be wise without being so*, Plat. *Ap.* 29 a. The predicate infinitives here omit the article (1521). See **954**.

1546. The object infinitive takes the article chiefly after verbs which do not regularly take the simple infinitive (see 1523), or when the relation of the infinitive to the verb is less close than it usually is. E.g.

τὸ τελευτῆσαι πάντων ἡ πεπρωμένη κατέκρινεν *fate has appointed the death of all things* (like θάνατον πάντων κατέκρινεν), Isoc. 1, 43; εἰ τὸ κωλῦσαι τὴν τῶν Ἑλλήνων κοινωνίαν ἐπεπράκειν ἐγὼ Φιλίππῳ *if I had sold to Philip the prevention of the unity of the Greeks* (i.e. *had prevented this as Philip's hireling*), Dem. 18, 23; τὸ ξυνοικεῖν τῆδ' ὁμοῦ τίς ἂν γυνὴ δύναιτο; *to live with her — what woman could do it?* S. *Tr.* 545.

1547. Sometimes in poetry the distinction between the object infinitive with and without τό is hardly perceptible; e.g. τλήσομαι τὸ κατθανεῖν *I shall dare death*, Aesch. *Ag.* 1290; τὸ δρᾶν οὐκ ἠθέλησαν *they refused to act*, S. *O. C.* 442; τὸ λαλαγῆσαι θέλων *willing to babble*, Pind. *O.* 2, 97.

INFINITIVE WITH τό DEPENDING ON NOUNS

1548. The infinitive with τό is sometimes used with the adjectives and substantives which regularly take the simple infinitive (1530). E.g.

τὸ βίᾳ πολιτῶν δρᾶν ἔφυν ἀμήχανος *I am helpless to act in defiance of the citizens*, S. *Ant.* 79; τὸ ἐς τὴν γῆν ἡμῶν ἐσβάλλειν ... ἱκανοί εἰσι *they have the power to invade our land*, Thuc. 6, 17.

INFINITIVE WITH τοῦ, τῷ, OR τό IN VARIOUS CONSTRUCTIONS

1549. The genitive, dative, or accusative of the infinitive with the article may depend on a preposition. E.g.

πρὸ τοῦ τοὺς ὅρκους ἀποδοῦναι *before taking the oaths*, Dem. 18, 26; πρὸς τῷ μηδὲν ἐκ τῆς πρεσβείας λαβεῖν *besides receiving no profit from the mission*, Dem. 19, 229; διὰ τὸ ξένος εἶναι οὐκ ἂν οἴει ἀδικηθῆναι; *do you think you would not be wronged on account of your being a stranger?* X. M. 2, 1, 15; ὑπὲρ τοῦ τὰ μέτρια μὴ γίγνεσθαι *that moderate counsels may not prevail* (= ἵνα μὴ γίγνηται), Aeschin. 3, 1.

1550. The genitive and dative of the infinitive, with the article, can stand in most of the constructions belonging to those cases; as in that of the attributive genitive, the genitive after a comparative or with verbs and adjectives, the dative of *cause, manner,* or *means,* and the dative with verbs and adjectives. E.g.

τοῦ πιεῖν ἐπιθυμία *a desire to drink*, Thuc. 7, 84; νέοις τὸ σιγᾶν κρεῖττόν ἐστι τοῦ λαλεῖν *for the young silence is better than too much talk*, Men. Mon. 387 (1147); ἐπέσχομεν τοῦ δακρύειν *we restrained our tears*, Plat. *Ph.* 117 e; ἀήθεις τοῦ κατακούειν τινός εἰσιν *they are unused to obeying any one*, Dem. 1, 23; τῷ φανερὸς εἶναι τοιοῦτος ὤν *by having it evident that he was such a man*, X. M. 1, 2, 3; τῷ κοσμίως ζῆν πιστεύειν *to trust in an orderly life*, Isoc. 15, 24; ἴσον τῷ προστένειν *equal to lamenting beforehand*, Aesch. *Ag.* 253.

1551. The infinitive with τοῦ may express a purpose, generally a negative purpose, where with ordinary genitives ἕνεκα is regularly used (see **1122, 1536**). E.g.

ἐτειχίσθη Ἀταλάντη, τοῦ μὴ λῃστὰς κακουργεῖν τὴν Εὔβοιαν *Atalante was fortified, that pirates might not ravage Euboea*, Thuc. 2, 32; Μίνως τὸ λῃστικὸν καθῄρει, τοῦ τὰς προσόδους μᾶλλον ἰέναι αὐτῷ *Minos put down piracy, that the revenues might come to him rather (than to them)*, Thuc. 1, 4; ἐξῆλθεν ὁ σπείρων τοῦ σπείρειν *the sower went forth to sow*, Matthew 13, 3.

1552. Verbs and expressions denoting *hindrance* or *freedom* from anything allow either the infinitive with τοῦ (**1550**) or the simple infinitive (**1523**). As the infinitive with such verbs can take the negative μή without affecting the sense (**1618**), we have a third and fourth form, still with the same meaning. See **1554**. E.g.

εἴργει σε τοῦτο ποιεῖν, εἴργει σε τοῦ τοῦτο ποιεῖν, εἴργει σε μὴ τοῦτο ποιεῖν, εἴργει σε τοῦ μὴ τοῦτο ποιεῖν, all meaning *he prevents you from doing this*; τὸν Φίλιππον παρελθεῖν οὐκ ἐδύναντο κωλῦσαι *they could not hinder Philip from passing through*, Dem. 5, 20; τοῦ δραπετεύειν ἀπείργουσι; *do they restrain them from running away?* X. M. 2, 1, 16; ὅπερ ἔσχε μὴ τὴν Πελοπόννησον πορθεῖν *which prevented* (*him*) *from ravaging Pelopon-nesus,* Thuc. 1, 73; δύο ἄνδρας ἕξει τοῦ μὴ καταδῦναι *it will keep two men from sinking,* X. *An.* 3, 5, 11.

1553. When the leading verb is negatived (or is interrogative implying a negative), the double negative μὴ οὐ is generally used with the infinitive rather than the simple μή (1619), so that we can say οὐκ εἴργει σε μὴ οὐ τοῦτο ποιεῖν *he does not prevent you from doing this;* τοῦ μὴ οὐ ποιεῖν is rarely (if ever) used.

1554. The infinitive with τὸ μή may be used after expressions denoting *hindrance,* and also after all which even imply *preven-tion, omission,* or *denial.* This infinitive with τό is less closely connected with the leading verb than are the forms before men-tioned (1552), and it may often be considered an accusative of *specification* (1056), and sometimes (as after verbs of *denial*) an object accusative. Sometimes it expresses merely a *result.* E.g.

τὸν ὅμιλον εἶργον τὸ μὴ τὰ ἐγγὺς τῆς πόλεως κακουργεῖν *they prevented the crowd from injuring the neighboring parts of the city,* Thuc. 3, 1; Κίμωνα παρὰ τρεῖς ἀφεῖσαν ψήφους τὸ μὴ θανάτῳ ζημιῶσαι *they allowed Cimon by three votes to escape the punishment of death* (*they let him off from the punishment of death*), Dem. 23, 205; φόβος ἀνθ' ὕπνου παραστατεῖ, τὸ μὴ βλέφαρα συμβαλεῖν *fear stands by me instead of sleep, preventing me from closing my eyelids,* Aesch. *Ag.* 15.

Thus we have a *fifth* form, εἴργει σε τὸ μὴ τοῦτο ποιεῖν, added to those given in 1552, as equivalents of the English *he prevents you from doing this.*

1555. Here, as above (1553), μὴ οὐ is generally used when the leading verb is negatived; e.g. οὐδὲν γὰρ αὐτῷ ταῦτ' ἐπαρκέσει τὸ μὴ οὐ πεσεῖν *for this will not at all suffice to prevent him from falling,* Aesch. *Pr.* 918.

1556. The infinitive with τοῦ μή and with τὸ μή may also be used in the ordinary negative sense; e.g. οὐδεμία πρόφασις τοῦ μὴ δρᾶν ταῦτα *no ground for not doing this,* Plat. *Tim.* 20 c.

1557. The infinitive with its subject, object, or other adjuncts (sometimes including dependent clauses) may be preceded by τό, the whole standing as a single noun in any ordinary construction. E.g.

τὸ δὲ μήτε πάλαι τοῦτο πεπονθέναι, πεφηνέναι τέ τινα ἡμῖν συμμαχίαν τούτων ἀντίρροπον, ἂν βουλώμεθα χρῆσθαι, τῆς παρ' ἐκείνων εὐνοίας εὐεργέτημ' ἂν ἔγωγε θείην *but the fact that we have not suffered this long ago, and that, more-over, an alliance has appeared in our favor to balance these dangers, if we wish to use it,* — *this I should ascribe as a benefaction to their good-will,* Dem. 1, 10. Here the whole sentence τὸ . . . χρῆσθαι is the object accusative of θείην ἄν. This construction corresponds more or less generally to the English gerund in *-ing.*

Infinitive in Exclamations

1558. *a.* The infinitive with τό may be used in exclamations, to express surprise or indignation. E.g.

τῆς μωρίας · τὸ Δία νομίζειν, ὄντα τηλικουτονί *what foolishness! believing in Zeus now you are so big!* Ar. *Nub.* 819. See **1124.**

b. The article here is sometimes omitted; e.g. τοιουτονί τρέφειν κύνα *to keep a dog like that!* Ar. *V.* 835.

1559. *a.* For the infinitive as well as the finite moods with ὥστε, ὡς, ἐφ' ᾧ and ἐφ' ᾧτε, see **1466–1477.**

b. For the infinitive and finite moods with πρίν, see **1484–1489.**

c. For the infinitive with ἄν, see **1308.**

THE PARTICIPLE

1560. The participle is a verbal adjective, in function partaking of the nature of verb and adjective. It has three uses. First, it may express an *attribute*, qualifying a noun like an ordinary adjective (**1562–1565**); secondly, it may define the *circumstances* under which an action takes place (**1566–1579**); thirdly, it may be joined to certain verbs to *supplement* their meaning, often having a force resembling that of the infinitive (**1580–1595**).

1561. These distinctions are not always exact, and the same participle may belong to more than one class. E.g. in ὁ μὴ δαρεὶς ἄνθρωπος *the unflogged man,* δαρείς is both attributive and conditional (**1566** *e*). Similarly, a circumstantial participle may denote more than one of the relations described in **1566.**

Attributive Participle

1562. The participle may qualify a substantive, like an attributive adjective. Here it may often be translated by a relative and a finite verb, especially when it has the article. E.g.

ὁ παρὼν καιρός *the present occasion,* Dem. 3, 3 ; θεοὶ αἰὲν ἐόντες *immortal gods (that live forever),* Il. 21, 518 ; πόλις κάλλει διαφέρουσα *a city excelling in beauty;* ἀνὴρ καλῶς πεπαιδευμένος *a man who has been well educated (or a well-educated man);* οἱ πρέσβεις οἱ ὑπὸ Φιλίππου πεμφθέντες *the ambassadors whom Philip had sent;* ἄνδρες οἱ τοῦτο ποιήσοντες *men who are to do this.*

1563. *a.* The participle with the article may be used substantively, like any adjective. It is then equivalent to *he who, they who, that which,* etc., with a finite verb. E.g.

οἱ κρατοῦντες *the conquerors*; οἱ πεπεισμένοι *those who have been convinced*; παρὰ τοῖς ἀρίστοις δοκοῦσιν εἶναι *among those who are accounted best*, X. M. 4, 2, 6; ὁ τὴν γνώμην ταύτην εἰπών *the man who gave this opinion*, Thuc. 8, 68; τοῖς Ἀρκάδων σφετέροις οὖσι ξυμμάχοις προεῖπον *they proclaimed to those Arcadians who were their allies*, Thuc. 5, 64; τοὺς ἀεὶ ἐγγυτάτω ἑαυτῶν ὄντας *those who for the time being* (or *whoever*) *are nearest them*, Plat. *Ap.* 25 c.

b. The article is sometimes omitted; e.g. πολεμούντων πόλις *a city of belligerents*, X. C. 7, 5, 73.

1564. *a.* Sometimes a participle becomes so completely a substantive that it takes an object genitive instead of an object accusative; e.g. ὁ ἐκείνου τεκών *his father* (for ὁ ἐκεῖνον τεκών), E. *El.* 335. Contrast **1048.**

b. A participle should often be rendered by an English substantive; e.g. τῇ Μυτιλήνῃ ἑαλωκυίᾳ *since the capture of Mitylene* (**1166**). So in Latin, ab urbe condita, *since the founding of Rome*.

1565. The neuter participle with the article is sometimes used as an abstract substantive, like the infinitive; e.g. τὸ δεδιός *fear*, τὸ θαρσοῦν *courage*, like τὸ δεδιέναι and τὸ θαρσεῖν, Thuc. 1, 36. Cf. τὸ καλόν for τὸ κάλλος *beauty*. In both cases the adjective is used substantively. *ΝΒ*

Circumstantial Participle

1566. The participle may define the *circumstances* of an action. It may express the following relations:

a. Time; the tenses denoting various points of time, which is relative to that of the verb of the sentence (**1289**). E.g.

ταῦτα ἔπραξε στρατηγῶν *he did this while he was general*; ταῦτα πράξει στρατηγῶν *he will do this while he is general*; τυραννεύσας δὲ ἔτη τρία Ἱππίας ἐχώρει ἐς Σίγειον *and after he had been tyrant three years Hippias withdrew to Sigeum*, Thuc. 6, 59.

b. Cause. E.g.

λέγω δὲ τοῦδ' ἕνεκα, βουλόμενος δόξαι σοι ὅπερ ἐμοί *and I speak for this* (*immediate*) *reason — I want you to come to the same opinion that I have*, Plat. *Ph.* 102 d.

c. Means, manner, and similar relations, including *manner of employment.* E.g.

προείλετο μᾶλλον τοῖς νόμοις ἐμμένων ἀποθανεῖν ἢ παρανομῶν ζῆν *he preferred to die abiding by the laws rather than to live transgressing them*, X. M. 4, 4, 4; τοῦτο ἐποίησε λαθών *he did this secretly*; ἀπεδήμει τριηραρχῶν *he was absent on duty as trierarch*; ληζόμενοι ζῶσιν *they live by plunder*, X. C. 3, 2, 25.

d. Purpose or *intention*; generally expressed by the future (sometimes by the present) participle. E.g.

ἦλθε λυσόμενος θύγατρα *he came to ransom his daughter, Il.* 1, 13; πέμπειν πρέσβεις ταῦτα ἐροῦντας καὶ Λύσανδρον αἰτήσοντας *to send ambassadors to say this and to ask for Lysander, X. H.* 2, 1, 6.

e. Condition; the tenses of the participle here represent the corresponding tenses of the indicative, subjunctive, or optative, in all classes of protasis. The negative is μή.

See **1423**, where examples will be found.

f. Opposition, limitation, or *concession;* where the participle is generally to be translated by *although* and a verb. The negative is οὐ. E.g.

ὀλίγα δυνάμενοι προορᾶν πολλὰ ἐπιχειροῦμεν πράττειν *although we are able to foresee few things, we try to carry out many things, X. C.* 3, 2, 15.

Ὤν is sometimes omitted in this construction; e.g. Ζεύς, καίπερ αὐθάδης φρενῶν *Zeus, albeit stubborn in mind,* Aesch. *Pr.* 907. See **1573**.

For other modes of expressing concession, see **1435, 1436.**

g. Any *attendant* circumstance, the participle being merely *descriptive.* This is one of the most common relations of the circumstantial participle. E.g.

ἔρχεται τὸν υἱὸν ἔχουσα *she came bringing her son, X. C.* 1, 3, 1; παραλαβόντες Βοιωτοὺς ἐστράτευσαν ἐπὶ Φάρσαλον *they took Boeotians with them and marched against Pharsalus,* Thuc. 1, 111.

h. That *in which* the action of the verb *consists.* E.g.

τόδ' εἶπε φωνῶν *thus he spake saying,* Aesch. *Ag.* 205; εὖ γ' ἐποίησας ἀναμνήσας με *you did well in reminding me,* Plat. *Ph.* 60 c.

For the time of the aorist participle here, see **1291.**

1567. These participles denoting time, cause, manner, condition, concession, and attendant circumstance are best translated by finite verbs. Certain participles of *time* and *manner* have almost the force of adverbs by idiomatic usage. Such are ἀρχόμενος *at first;* τελευτῶν *at last, finally;* διαλιπὼν χρόνον *after a while;* φέρων *hastily;* φερόμενος *with a rush;* κατατείνας *earnestly;* φθάσας *sooner (anticipating);* λαθών *secretly;* ἔχων *continually;* ἀνύσας *quickly;* κλαίων *to one's sorrow;* χαίρων *with impunity.* E.g.

ἅπερ ἀρχόμενος εἶπον *as I said at first,* Thuc. 4, 64; ἐσέπεσον φερόμενοι ἐς τοὺς Ἕλληνας *they fell upon the Greeks with a rush,* Hdt. 7, 210; τί κυπτάζεις ἔχων; *why do you keep poking about?* Ar. *Nub.* 509; κλαίων ἅψῃ τῶνδε *you will lay hands on them to your sorrow,* E. *Heraclid.* 270.

1568. Ἔχων, φέρων, ἄγων, λαβών, and χρώμενος may often be translated *with*. E.g.

μία ᾤχετο πρέσβεις ἄγουσα *one (ship) was gone with ambassadors*, Thuc. 7, 25. See X. *C.* 1, 3, 1 in **1566** *g.* βοῇ χρώμενοι *with a shout*, Thuc. 2, 84.

1569. *a.* Τί παθών *what has happened to him?* or *what ailed him?* and τί μαθών *what has he taken into his head?* are used in the general sense of *why? how comes he to? how is it that?* etc. E.g.

τί τοῦτο μαθὼν προσέγραψεν; *with what idea did he add this clause?* Dem. 20, 127; τί παθοῦσαι θνηταῖς εἴξασι γυναιξίν; *what makes them look like mortal women?* Ar. *Nub.* 340.

b. The corresponding relative forms ὅ τι παθών and ὅ τι μαθών hardly differ in meaning from the causal ὅτι; e.g. τί ἄξιός εἰμι παθεῖν ἢ ἀποτεῖσαι, ὅ τι μαθὼν ἐν τῷ βίῳ οὐχ ἡσυχίαν ἦγον; *what do I deserve to suffer or to pay because in the course of my life I have never kept quiet?* Plat. *Ap.* 36 b.

GENITIVE AND ACCUSATIVE ABSOLUTE

1570. When a circumstantial participle belongs to a noun or pronoun which is not grammatically connected with the main construction of the sentence, they stand together in the *genitive absolute*. E.g.

ἀνέβη οὐδενὸς κωλύοντος *he made the ascent with no one interfering*, X. *An.* 1, 2, 22; καὶ μεταπεμπομένου αὐτοῦ οὐκ ἐθέλω ἐλθεῖν *although he keeps sending for me, I do not want to go*, X. *An.* 1, 3, 10. See **1156**.

a. Sometimes a participle stands alone in the genitive absolute, when a subject can easily be supplied from the context, or when some general subject like ἀνθρώπων or πραγμάτων is understood; e.g. οἱ πολέμιοι, προσιόντων, τέως μὲν ἡσύχαζον *but the enemy, as they* (men before mentioned) *came on, kept quiet for a time*, X. *An.* 5, 4, 16; οὕτω δ' ἐχόντων, εἰκός (ἐστιν), κ.τ.λ. *and this being the case* (sc. πραγμάτων), *it is likely* etc., X. *An.* 3, 2, 10. So with verbs like ὕει (**886** *e*); e.g. ὕοντος πολλῷ *when it was raining heavily* (where originally Διός was understood), X. *H.* 1, 1, 16.

b. The genitive absolute is regularly used only when a *new* subject is introduced into the sentence and not when the participle can be joined with any noun or pronoun already belonging to the construction. Yet this principle is sometimes violated in order to make the participial clause more prominent; e.g.

ὡς δεινόν τι οἰομένους πείσεσθαι εἰ ἀποθανοῦνται, ὥσπερ ἀθανάτων ἐσομένων ἂν ὑμεῖς μὴ ἀποκτείνητε *because they think they will suffer something dreadful if they die, as though they were never going to die if you do not put them to death*, Plat. *Ap.* 35 b. So Thuc. 7, 48. Cf. **1595** *b.*

1571. The participles of *impersonal* verbs stand in the *accusative absolute*, in the neuter singular, when others would be in the genitive absolute. So passive participles and ὄν, when they are used impersonally. E.g.

τί δή, ὑμᾶς ἐξὸν ἀπολέσαι, οὐκ ἐπὶ τοῦτο ἤλθομεν; *why now, when we might have destroyed you, did we not proceed to do it?* X. *An.* 2, 5, 22.

οἱ δ' οὐ βοηθήσαντες δέον ὑγιεῖς ἀπῆλθον; *and did those who brought no aid when it was needed escape safe and sound?* Plat. *Alc.* 115 b. So εὖ δὲ παρασχόν *and when a good opportunity offers,* Thuc. 1, 120; οὐ προσῆκον *improperly (it being not becoming),* Thuc. 4, 95; τυχόν *by chance (it having happened)*; προσταχθέν μοι *when I had been commanded*; εἰρημένον *when it has been said*; ἀδύνατον ὂν ἐν νυκτὶ σημῆναι *it being impossible to signal by night,* Thuc. 7, 44.

1572. The participles of personal verbs sometimes stand with their subjects in the accusative absolute; but very seldom unless they are preceded by ὡς or ὥσπερ. E.g.

σιωπῇ ἐδείπνουν, ὥσπερ τοῦτο προστεταγμένον αὐτοῖς *they ate their dinner in silence, as if this had been the command given to them,* X. *Symp.* 1, 11.

1573. Ὤν as a circumstantial participle is seldom omitted, except with the adjectives ἑκών *willing* and ἄκων *unwilling,* and after ἄτε, οἷα, ὡς, or καίπερ; e.g. ἐμοῦ οὐχ ἑκόντος *against my will* (**1615**) S. *Aj.* 455; also ἀπόρρητον πόλει *when it is forbidden to the state,* S. *Ant.* 44. Cf. **1566** *f,* **1588**.

ADVERBS WITH CIRCUMSTANTIAL PARTICIPLE

1574. The adverbs ἅμα, μεταξύ, εὐθύς, αὐτίκα, ἄρτι, and ἐξαίφνης are often connected (in position and in sense) with the temporal participle, though grammatically they qualify the leading verb; e.g. ἅμα καταλαβόντες προσεκεάτο σφι *as soon as they overtook them, they began to attack them,* Hdt. 9, 57; Νεκὼς μεταξὺ ὀρύσσων ἐπαύσατο *Necho stopped in the midst of digging (the canal),* i.e. *before it was completed,* Hdt. 2, 158.

1575. The participle denoting *opposition* (**1566** *f*) is often strengthened by καί or καίπερ *even* (Homeric also καί . . . περ), and in negative sentences by οὐδέ or μηδέ; also by καὶ ταῦτα *and that too*; e.g. ἐποικτίρω νιν, καίπερ ὄντα δυσμενῆ *I pity him, even though he is an enemy,* S. *Aj.* 122; οὐκ ἂν προδοίην, οὐδέ περ πράσσων κακῶς *I would not be faithless, even though I am in a wretched state,* E. *Ph.* 1624.

While περ is common in Homer with a concessive participle, the participle with περ is not *always* concessive.

1576. Circumstantial participles, especially those denoting *cause* or *purpose,* are often preceded by ὡς. This particle shows that they express the idea or the assertion of the subject of the leading verb or that of some other person prominent in the sentence, *without implying* that it is also the idea of the speaker or writer. E.g.

τὸν Περικλέα ἐν αἰτίᾳ εἶχον ὡς πείσαντα σφᾶς πολεμεῖν *they found fault with Pericles because (as they thought) he had persuaded them to engage in war*, Thuc. 2, 59; ἀγανακτοῦσιν ὡς μεγάλων τινῶν ἀπεστερημένοι *they are indignant because (as they say) they have been deprived of some great blessings*, Plat. *Rep.* 329 a.

1577. The causal participle is often emphasized by ἅτε and οἷον or οἷα *as, inasmuch as*; but these particles have no such force as ὡς (**1576**); e.g. ἅτε παῖς ὢν ἥδετο *like the child that he was, he showed his delight*, X. *C.* 1, 3, 3. Here the cause is given on the authority of the writer.

1578. Ὥσπερ *as, as it were*, with the participle expresses a comparison between the action of the verb and that of the participle. E.g.

ὠρχοῦντο ὥσπερ ἄλλοις ἐπιδεικνύμενοι *they danced as if they were showing off to others* (i.e. *they danced, apparently showing off*), X. *An.* 5, 4, 34; τί τοῦτο λέγεις, ὥσπερ οὐκ ἐπὶ σοὶ ὂν ὅ τι ἂν βούλῃ λέγειν; *why do you say this, as if it were not in your power to say what you please?* X. *M.* 2, 6, 36. Although we find *as if* a convenient translation, there is really no condition, as appears from the negative οὐ (not μή). See **1615**.

1579. Ὥσπερ, like other words meaning *as*, may be followed by a protasis; e.g. ὥσπερ εἰ παρεστάτεις *as (it would be) if you had lived near*, Aesch. *Ag.* 1201. For ὥσπερ ἂν εἰ, see **1313**.

Supplementary Participle

1580. The supplementary participle completes the idea expressed by the verb, by showing to what its action relates. It may belong to either the subject or the object of the verb, and agree with it in case. E.g.

παύομέν σε λέγοντα *we stop you from speaking*, παυόμεθα λέγοντες *we cease speaking*.

1581. This participle has many points of resemblance to the infinitive in similar constructions. In the use of the participle (as in that of the infinitive) we must distinguish between indirect discourse (where each tense preserves its force) and other constructions.

Participle not in Indirect Discourse

1582. The supplementary participle is used with verbs signifying *to begin, to continue, to endure, to persevere, to cease, to repent,* *to be weary, to be pleased, displeased,* or *ashamed*; and with the object of verbs signifying *to permit* or *to cause to cease.* E.g.

ἦρχον χαλεπαίνων *I was the first to be angry, Il.* 2, 378; οὐκ ἀνέξομαι ζῶσα *I shall not endure my life,* E. *Hipp.* 354; ἑπτὰ ἡμέρας μαχόμενοι διετέλεσαν *they continued fighting seven days,* X. *An.* 4, 3, 2; τιμώμενοι χαίρουσιν *they delight in being honored,* E. *Hipp.* 8; ἐλεγχόμενοι ἤχθοντο *they were displeased at being put to the proof,* X. *M.* 1, 2, 47; τοῦτο οὐκ αἰσχύνομαι λέγων *I say this without shame* (see **1583**), X. *C.* 5, 1, 21; τὴν φιλοσοφίαν παῦσον ταῦτα λέγουσαν *make Philosophy stop talking in this style,* Plat. *G.* 482 a.

1583. Some of these verbs also take the infinitive, but generally with some difference of meaning; e.g. αἰσχύνεται τοῦτο λέγειν *he is ashamed to say this* (and does not say it), — see **1582**; ἀποκάμνει τοῦτο ποιεῖν *he ceases to do this, through weariness,* but ἀποκάμνει τοῦτο ποιῶν *he is weary of doing this.* So ἄρχεται λέγειν *he begins to speak,* but ἄρχεται λέγων *he begins by speaking* or *he is at the beginning of his speech*; παύω σε μάχεσθαι *I prevent you from fighting,* but παύω σε μαχόμενον *I stop you while fighting.*

1584. The participle may be used with verbs signifying *to perceive, to find,* or *to represent,* denoting an act or state in which the object is perceived, found, or represented. E.g.

ὁρῶ σε κρύπτοντα χεῖρα *I see you hiding your hand,* E. *Hec.* 342; ἤκουσά σου λέγοντος *I heard you speak*; ἐὰν ἀκούητέ μου ἀπολογουμένου *if you hear me making my defence,* Plat. *Ap.* 17 c; ηὗρε Κρονίδην ἄτερ ἥμενον ἄλλων *he found the son of Cronos sitting apart from the others, Il.* 1, 498; βασιλέας πεποίηκε τοὺς ἐν Ἅιδου τιμωρουμένους *he has represented kings in Hades as suffering punishment,* Plat. *G.* 525 d.

1585. This must not be confounded with indirect discourse, in which ὁρῶ σε κρύπτοντα would mean *I see that you are hiding,* ἀκούω σε λέγοντα *I hear that you say*; for *I hear you speaking* the genitive is used (**1103**): ἀκούω σου λέγοντος. See **1590**.

1586. The participles βουλόμενος *wishing,* ἡδόμενος *pleased,* προσδεχόμενος *expecting,* and some others, may agree in case with a dative which depends on εἰμί, γίγνομαι, or some similar verb. E.g.

τῷ πλήθει οὐ βουλομένῳ ἦν *it was not pleasing to the people (it was not to their liking),* Thuc. 2, 3; προσδεχομένῳ μοι τὰ τῆς ὀργῆς ὑμῶν ἐς ἐμὲ γεγένηται *I have been expecting the manifestations of your wrath against me* (i.e. *they have come as I expected*), Thuc. 2, 60. Cf. **1165**.

1587. With verbs signifying *to overlook* or *see,* in the sense of *to allow* or *let happen* (περιορῶ and ἐφορῶ, with περιεῖδον and ἐπεῖδον, sometimes εἶδον), the participle may be used in a sense which approaches that of the object infinitive, the present and aorist participles differing merely as the present and aorist infinitives would differ in similar constructions. E.g.

μὴ περιίδωμεν ὑβρισθεῖσαν τὴν Λακεδαιμονα καὶ καταφρονηθεῖσαν *let us not allow Lacedaemon to be insulted and despised*, Isoc. 6, 108; μή μ' ἰδεῖν θανόνθ' ὑπ' ἀστῶν *not to see me killed by citizens*, E. Or. 746; περιιδεῖν τὴν γῆν τμηθεῖσαν *to let the land be ravaged*, i.e. *to look on and see it ravaged*, Thuc. 2, 18; but in 2, 20 we have περιιδεῖν τὴν γῆν τμηθῆναι *to permit the land to be ravaged*, referring to the same thing from another point of view, τμηθῆναι being strictly future to περιιδεῖν, while τμηθεῖσαν is coincident with it. The infinitive is generally preferred in Hdt. and Thuc.

1588. The participle with λανθάνω *escape the notice of*, τυγχάνω *happen*, and φθάνω *anticipate*, contains the leading idea of the expression and is usually translated by a verb. The aorist participle here coincides in time with the verb (unless this expresses duration) and does not denote past time in itself. See **1291**. E.g.

φονέα τοῦ παιδὸς ἐλάνθανε βόσκων *he was unconsciously supporting the slayer of his son*, Hdt. 1, 44; ἔτυχον καθήμενος ἐνταῦθα *I happened to be sitting there*, Plat. Euthyd. 272 e; αὐτοὶ φθήσονται τοῦτο δράσαντες *they will do this themselves first* (= τοῦτο δράσουσι πρότεροι), Plat. Rep. 375 c; τοὺς δ' ἔλαθ' εἰσελθών *and he entered unnoticed by them* (= εἰσῆλθε λάθρᾳ), Il. 24, 477; ἔφθησαν πολλῷ τοὺς Πέρσας ἀπικόμενοι *they arrived long before the Persians*, Hdt. 4, 136; τοὺς ἀνθρώπους λήσομεν ἐπιπεσόντες *we shall rush in unnoticed by the men*, X. An. 7, 3, 43; ἄλλα τε πολλὰ λανθάνει καὶ σὺ τοὐμὸν ἐν οὐδενὶ ποιούμενος *there are many things that people don't see, and among them, that you hold my interest of no importance*, Libanius Epist. 98; here λανθάνεις (understood) is contrasted with a preceding εἰ ᾔδεσαν.

The perfect participle here has its ordinary force. With τυγχάνω the present participle ὤν is sometimes omitted (cf. **1573**).

1589. The participle with διατελέω *continue* (**1582**), οἴχομαι *be gone* (**1256**), θαμίζω *be wont* or *be frequent*, and some others, expresses the leading idea; e.g. οἴχεται φεύγων *he has taken flight*, Ar. Pl. 933; οὐ θαμίζεις καταβαίνων εἰς τὸν Πειραιᾶ *you don't come down to the Peiraeus very often*, Plat. Rep. 328 c. So with the Homeric βῆ and ἔβαν or βάν from βαίνω; e.g. βῆ φεύγων *he took flight*, Il. 2, 665; so 2, 167. The aorist participle, if used here, does not denote antecedent time (**1291**).

PARTICIPLE IN INDIRECT DISCOURSE

1590. With many verbs the participle stands in indirect discourse, each tense representing the corresponding tense of a finite mood.

Such verbs are chiefly those signifying *to see, to hear* or *learn, to perceive, to know, to be ignorant of, to remember, to forget, to show, to appear, to prove, to acknowledge,* and ἀγγέλλω *announce.* E.g.

ὁρῶ δέ μ' ἔργον δεινὸν ἐξειργασμένην but *I see that I have done a dreadful deed,* S. *Tr.* 706; ἤκουσε Κῦρον ἐν Κιλικίᾳ ὄντα *he heard that Cyrus was in Cilicia* (cf. 1585), X. *An.* 1, 4, 5; ὅταν κλύῃ ἥξοντ' Ὀρέστην *when she hears that Orestes will come,* S. *El.* 293; οἶδα οὐδὲν ἐπιστάμενος *I know that I understand nothing;* οὐκ ᾔδεσαν αὐτὸν τεθνηκότα *they did not know that he was dead,* X. *An.* 1, 10, 16; ἐπειδὰν γνῶσιν ἀπιστούμενοι *after they find out that they are distrusted,* X. *C.* 7, 2, 17; μέμνημαι ἐλθών *I remember that I went;* μέμνημαι αὐτὸν ἐλθόντα *I remember that he went;* δείξω τοῦτον ἐχθρὸν ὄντα *I shall show that this man is an enemy* (passive οὗτος δειχθήσεται or φανήσεται ἐχθρὸς ὤν); αὐτῷ Κῦρον ἐπιστρατεύοντα πρῶτος ἤγγειλα *I was the first to report to him that Cyrus was marching against him,* X. *An.* 2, 3, 19.

See **1509** and **1593**; also **1308** for examples of the participle with ἄν representing both indicative and optative with ἄν.

1591. Δῆλός εἰμι and φανερός εἰμι take the participle in indirect discourse, where we use an impersonal construction; e.g. δῆλος ἦν οἰόμενος *it was evident that he thought,* X. *An.* 2, 5, 27 (like δῆλον ἦν ὅτι οἴοιτο). Cf. **1531.**

1592. With σύνοιδα or συγγιγνώσκω and a dative of the reflexive, a participle may be in either the nominative or the dative; e.g. σύνοιδα ἐμαυτῷ ἠδικημένῳ or ἠδικημένος *I am conscious that I have been wronged;* ἐμαυτῷ ξυνῄδη οὐδὲν ἐπισταμένῳ *I felt sure that I understood nothing,* Plat. *Ap.* 22 c. But if the dative is not a reflexive, the participle is in the dative only; e.g. ξυνίσασι Μελήτῳ μὲν ψευδομένῳ, ἐμοὶ δὲ ἀληθεύοντι *they know as well as Meletus does that he is lying, but (know as well as I do) that I am telling the truth,* Plat. *Ap.* 34 b.

1593. Most of the verbs included in **1590** (especially ἀγγέλλω) may also take a clause with ὅτι or ὡς in indirect discourse.

1594. *a.* Some of these verbs have the infinitive of indirect discourse in nearly or quite the same sense as the participle. Others have the infinitive in a different sense: e.g. φαίνεται σοφὸς ὤν generally means *it is plain that he is wise,* and φαίνεται σοφὸς εἶναι *he seems to be wise;* but sometimes this distinction is not observed. Here, as in **1591,** the Greek prefers the personal to the impersonal construction. Cf. **1583.**

b. Others, again, may be used in a peculiar sense, in which they have the infinitive *not* in indirect discourse. E.g. οἶδα and ἐπίσταμαι regularly have this infinitive when they mean *know how;* e.g. οἶδα τοῦτο ποιῆσαι *I know how to do this* (but οἶδα τοῦτο ποιήσας *I know that I did this*). Μανθάνω, μέμνημαι, and ἐπιλανθάνομαι, in the sense of *learn, remember*, or *forget to do* anything, take the regular object infinitive. See also the uses of γιγνώσκω, δείκνυμι, δηλῶ, φαίνομαι, and εὑρίσκω in the Lexicon.

1595. *a.* Ὡς may be used with the participle of indirect discourse in the sense explained in 1576. E.g.

ὡς μηκέτ' ὄντα κεῖνον ἐν φάει νόει *think of him as no longer living*, S. *Ph.* 415. For the negative, see **1617.** Δῆλος ἦν Κῦρος ὡς σπεύδων *Cyrus was evidently hurrying*, X. *An.* 1, 5, 9. Thus an ordinary circumstantial participle may sometimes be rendered as in indirect discourse; e.g. τὴν πρόφασιν ἐποιεῖτο ὡς Πισίδας βουλόμενος ἐκβαλεῖν *he made the excuse that he wanted to drive out the Pisidians*, X. *An.* 1, 2, 1; νῦν δέ μοι δοκεῖ οὐδεπώποτε διανοηθῆναι ὡς φανερὰν καταστήσων τὴν οὐσίαν *but as it is, I do not believe that he ever once thought of converting the property into real estate*, Lys. 32, 23.

b. The genitive absolute with ὡς is sometimes found where we should expect the participle to agree with the object of the verb; e.g. ὡς πολέμου ὄντος παρ' ὑμῶν ἀπαγγελῶ; *shall I announce from you that there is war?* (lit. *assuming that there is war, shall I announce it from you?*), X. *An.* 2, 1, 21, — where we might have πόλεμον ὄντα with less emphasis and in closer connection with the verb. So ὡς ὧδ' ἐχόντων τῶνδ' ἐπίστασθαί σε χρή *you must understand that this is so* (lit. *believing this to be so, you must understand it*), S. *Aj.* 281. Cf. **1570** *b.*

VERBAL ADJECTIVES IN -τέος AND -τέον

1596. The verbal in -τέος has both a *personal* and an *impersonal* construction; the impersonal is more common. The negative is always οὐ.

1597. In the personal construction it is passive in sense, and expresses *necessity*, like the Latin participle in -dus, agreeing with the subject. E.g.

ὠφελητέᾱ (fem.) σοι ἡ πόλις ἐστίν *you must benefit the state*, X. *M.* 3, 6, 3; ἄλλας μεταπεμπτέας εἶναι (ἔφη) *he said that other (ships) must be sent for*, Thuc. 6, 25.

1598. The noun denoting the agent is here in the dative (**1174** *b*)· This construction is of course confined to transitive verbs.

1599. In the impersonal construction the verbal is in the neuter of the nominative singular (sometimes plural), with ἐστί expressed or understood. The expression is equivalent to δεῖ (*one*) *must*, with the infinitive. It is practically active in sense, and allows transitive verbals to have an object like their verbs.

The agent is generally expressed by the dative, sometimes by the accusative. E.g.

ταῦτα ἡμῖν (or ἡμᾶς) ποιητέον ἐστίν we must do this (equivalent to ταῦτα ἡμᾶς δεῖ ποιῆσαι); οἰστέον τάδε we must bear these things (sc. ἡμῖν), E. Or. 769; τί ἂν αὐτῷ ποιητέον εἴη; what would he be obliged to do? (= τί ἂν δέοι αὐτὸν ποιῆσαι;), X. M. 1. 7, 2 (1600); ἐψηφίσαντο πολεμητέα (neut. plur. 888 b) εἶναι they voted that they must go to war (= δεῖν πολεμεῖν), Thuc. 1, 88; ξύμμαχοι, οὓς οὐ παραδοτέα τοῖς Ἀθηναίοις ἐστίν allies, whom we must not abandon to the Athenians, Thuc. 1, 86.

1600. Though the verbal in -τέον allows both the dative and the accusative of the agent (1174), the equivalent δεῖ with the infinitive allows only the accusative (1162).

INTERROGATIVE SENTENCES

1601. All interrogative pronouns, pronominal adjectives, and adverbs can be used in both direct and indirect questions. The relative ὅστις (rarely ὅς) and the relative pronominal adjectives (408) may be used in indirect questions. E.g.

τί λέγει; what does he say? πότε ἦλθεν; when did he come? πόσα εἶδες; how many did you see? ἤροντο τί λέγοι (or ὅ τι λέγοι) they asked what he said; ἤροντο πότε (or ὁπότε) ἦλθεν they asked when he came (or had come) ; ὁρᾷς ἡμᾶς ὅσοι ἐσμέν; do you see how many of us there are? Plat. Rep. 327 c.

Prolepsis (anticipation of the subject of the dependent clause) is very common, as in the last example; οἶδά σε τίς εἶ "I know thee who thou art."

1602. The Greek, unlike the English, freely uses two or more interrogatives with the same verb. E.g.

ἡ τίσι τί ἀποδιδοῦσα τέχνη δικαιοσύνη ἂν καλοῖτο; Justice might be called the art which renders what to what? Plat. Rep. 332 d. See the five interrogatives (used for comic effect) in Dem. 4, 36: πρόοιδεν ἕκαστος τίς χορηγὸς, . . . πότε καὶ παρὰ τοῦ καὶ τί λαβόντα τί δεῖ ποιεῖν, meaning everybody knows who the choregus is to be, what he is to get, when and from whom he is to get it, and what he is to do with it.

1603. An interrogative word often belongs to a subordinate part of the sentence, and is not, as in English, attached to the main verb; e.g. τίνα ποτὲ ψυχὴν ἔχων ἀξιοῖ τοιαύτῃ γνώμῃ χρῆσθαι; what heart could he possibly have that he thought it right to adopt such a policy? Lys. 32, 12. The participle is causal. Cf. the first sentence in 1602. Πῶς με φῂς διαφθείρειν τοὺς νεωτέρους; how, say you, do I corrupt the young men? Plat. Ap. 26 b; ἐγὼ οὖν τὸν ἐκ ποίας πόλεως στρατηγὸν προσδοκῶ ταῦτα πράξειν; from what city do I expect the general to be who is to do this? X. An. 3, 1, 14.

1604. An interrogative sometimes stands as a predicate with a demonstrative; e.g. τί τοῦτο ἔλεξας; *what is this that you said?* (= ἔλεξας τοῦτο, τί ὄν;* lit. *you said this, being what?*); τίνας τούσδ' εἰσορῶ; *who are these that I see?* E. *Or.* 1347.

1605. The principal direct interrogative particles are ἆρα and ἦ. These imply nothing as to the answer expected; but ἆρα οὐ implies an *affirmative* and ἆρα μή a *negative* answer. Οὐ and μή are used alone with the same force as with ἆρα, μή suggesting the impossibility of the thing questioned. So μῶν (for μὴ οὖν) implies a negative answer; and οὐκοῦν *therefore* (with no negative force) implies an affirmative answer. E.g.

ἦ σχολὴ ἔσται; *will there be leisure?* ἆρ' εἰσί τινες ἄξιοι; *are there any deserving ones?* ἆρ' οὐ βούλεσθε ἐλθεῖν;* or οὐ βούλεσθε ἐλθεῖν; *do you not wish to go* (i.e. *you wish, do you not*)? ἆρα μὴ βούλεσθε ἐλθεῖν; *or μὴ (or μῶν) βούλεσθε ἐλθεῖν; *do you wish to go* (*you don't wish to go, do you*)? οὐκοῦν σοι δοκεῖ σύμφορον εἶναι; *does it seem to you to be of advantage?* X. *C.* 2, 4, 15. This distinction between οὐ and μή does not apply to questions with the interrogative subjunctive (**1367**), which allow only μή.

1606. Ἄλλο τι ἤ; *is it anything else than?* or (more frequently) ἄλλο τι; *is it not?* is used as a direct interrogative, expecting an affirmative answer. E.g.

ἄλλο τι ἢ ὁμολογοῦμεν; *do we not agree?* (*do we do anything else than agree?*), Plat. *G.* 470 b; ἄλλο τι οὖν δύο ταῦτα ἔλεγες; *did you note all these "two"?* *ibid.* 495 c.

1607. Indirect questions may be introduced by εἰ *whether*; and in Homer by ἦ or εἰ. E.g.

ἠρώτησα εἰ βούλοιτο ἐλθεῖν *I asked whether he wished to go*; ᾤχετο πευσόμενος ἤ που ἔτ' εἴης *he was gone to inquire whether you were still living*, *Od.* 13, 415; τὰ ἐκπώματα οὐκ οἶδα εἰ τούτῳ δῶ (**1505**) *I do not know whether I am* (or simply *whether*) *to give him the cups*, X. *C.* 8, 4, 16. Here εἰ is used even with the subjunctive: see **1506**.

1608. **Alternative** questions (both direct and indirect) may be introduced by πότερον (πότερα) . . . ἤ *whether . . . or. Indirect* alternative questions can also be introduced by εἰ . . . ἤ or εἴτε . . . εἴτε *whether . . . or.* Homer has ἦ (ἦε) . . . ἦ (ἦε) in direct, and ἦ (ἠέ) . . . ἦ (ἦε) in indirect, alternatives, — never πότερον. E.g.

πότερον ἐᾷς ἄρχειν ἢ ἄλλον καθίστης; *do you permit him to rule, or do you appoint another?* X. *C.* 3, 1, 12; ἐβουλεύετο εἰ πέμποιέν τινας ἢ πάντες ἴοιεν *he was deliberating whether they should send some or should all go*, X. *An.* 1, 10, 5.

NEGATIVES

1609. The Greek has two negative adverbs, οὐ and μή. What is said of each of these generally applies to its compounds, — οὐδείς, οὐδέ, οὔτε, etc., and μηδείς, μηδέ, μήτε, etc.

1610. Οὐ is used with the indicative and optative in all *independent* sentences, except *wishes*; also in *indirect discourse* after ὅτι and ὡς, in *causal* sentences, and in dependent clauses of *result*.

1611. In indirect *questions*, introduced by εἰ *whether*, μή can be used as well as οὐ; e.g. βουλόμενος ἐρέσθαι εἰ μαθών τίς τι μεμνημένος μὴ οἶδεν *wishing to ask whether one who has learnt a thing and remembers it does not know it*, Plat. *Th.* 163 d. In the second part of an indirect alternative question (**1608**) both οὐ and μή are allowed; e.g. σκοπῶμεν εἰ ἡμῖν πρέπει ἢ οὔ *let us look and see whether it suits us or not*, Plat. *Rep.* 451 d; εἰ δὲ ἀληθὲς ἢ μή, πειράσομαι μαθεῖν *but I will try to learn whether it is true or not*, *ibid.* 339 a.

1612. The adherescent (or privative) οὐ adheres closely to the following word, practically forming a compound with negative meaning; e.g. οὐκ εἴα ὑπείκειν *he would not let them yield*, Thuc. 1, 127; οὐκ ἔφη ἰέναι *he refused to go*, X. *An.* 1, 3, 8. Thus οὐ may occur even in protasis, **1394 b**.

1613. Μή is used with the subjunctive and imperative in all constructions, except with the Homeric subjunctive (**1364**), which has the force of a future indicative. Μή is used in all final and object clauses with ἵνα, ὅπως, etc. and the subjunctive, optative, and indicative; except after μή *lest*, which takes οὐ. It is used in all conditional and conditional relative clauses, and in the corresponding temporal sentences after ἕως, πρίν, etc., in relative sentences expressing a *purpose* (**1454**), and in all expressions of a wish with both indicative and optative (**1355, 1359**).

For causal relative clauses with μή (also conditional), see **1462**.

For εἰ οὐ occasionally used in protasis, see **1394 b**.

1614. Μή is used with the infinitive in all constructions, both with and without the article, except in *indirect discourse*. The infinitive in indirect discourse regularly has οὐ, to retain the negative of the direct discourse; but some exceptions occur (**1511**).

For ὥστε οὐ with the infinitive, see **1468**. For μή with the infinitive after verbs of *hoping, promising, swearing*, etc., see **1511**.

1615. When a participle expresses a *condition* (**1566 e**) it takes μή; so when it is equivalent to a conditional relative clause, e.g. οἱ μὴ βουλόμενοι *any who do not wish*; and when the participle denotes character, assigning the subject to a general class (the *generic μή*), e.g. ὁ μὴ λεύσσων *he who cannot see*, S. *Tr.* 829. Otherwise the participle takes οὐ. In indirect discourse it sometimes, like the infinitive, takes μή irregularly (1511).

1616. Adjectives follow the same principle as participles, taking μή only when they do not refer to definite persons or things (i.e. when they can be expressed by a relative clause with an indefinite antecedent).

E.g. οἱ μὴ ἀγαθοὶ πολῖται is *(any) citizens who are not good* (generic μή), but οἱ οὐκ ἀγαθοὶ πολῖται means *special citizens who are not good*; οὗτος ἐδόκει καὶ πρότερον πολλὰ ἤδη ἀληθεῦσαι τοιαῦτα, τὰ ὄντα ὡς ὄντα καὶ τὰ μὴ ὄντα ὡς οὐκ ὄντα *he had the reputation of having spoken the truth in many similar instances* (1049) *before this, (reporting) things that were so as being so, and things that were not so as being not so* (or *that facts were facts and non-facts were not*), X. *An.* 4, 4, 15.

1617. Participles or adjectives connected with a protasis, a command, or an infinitive which would be negatived by μή, generally take μή; e.g. κελεύει μεῖναι ἐπὶ τοῦ ποταμοῦ μὴ διαβάντας *he orders them to halt by the river without crossing*, X. *An.* 4, 3, 28.

1618. When verbs which contain a *negative* idea (as those of *hindering, forbidding, denying, concealing*, and *distrusting*) take the infinitive, μή can be added to the infinitive to strengthen the negation. Such a negative cannot be translated in English, and can be omitted in Greek. For examples see 1552–1554.

1619. An infinitive which would regularly be negatived by μή, either in the ordinary way (1614) or to strengthen a preceding negation (1618), generally takes the double negative μὴ οὐ if the verb on which it depends itself has a negative.

Thus δίκαιόν ἐστι μὴ τοῦτον ἀφεῖναι *it is just not to acquit him*, if we negative the leading verb, generally becomes οὐ δίκαιόν ἐστι μὴ οὐ τοῦτον ἀφεῖναι *it is not just not to acquit him.* So ὡς οὐχ ὅσιόν σοι ὂν μὴ οὐ βοηθεῖν δικαιοσύνῃ *since (as you said) it was a failure in piety for you not to vindicate justice*, Plat. *Rep.* 427 e. Here the subordinate negative must be translated (cf. **1556**), the context determining the sense. But with the verbs of **1618** μή or μὴ οὐ are not translated, i.e. εἶργέ σε μὴ τοῦτο ποιεῖν (**1553**) *he prevents you from doing this* becomes, with εἶργε negatived, οὐκ εἶργεί σε μὴ οὐ τοῦτο ποιεῖν *he does not prevent you from doing this*; οὐδὲν αὐτοὺς ἐπιλύεται ἡ ἡλικία τὸ μὴ οὐχὶ ἀγανακτεῖν τῇ παρούσῃ τύχῃ *their age does not at all prevent them from being upset by their impending fate*, Plat. *Crito* 43 c.

1620. *a.* Μὴ οὐ is used also when the leading verb is interrogative implying a negative; e.g. τί ἐμποδὼν μὴ οὐχὶ ὑβριζομένους ἀποθανεῖν; *what is there to prevent (us) from being put to death with insult?* X. *An.* 3, 1, 13.

b. It is sometimes used with participles, or even nouns, to express an *exception* to a negative (or implied negative) statement; e.g. πόλεις χαλεπαὶ λαβεῖν, μὴ οὐ πολιορκίᾳ *cities hard* (i.e. *not easy*) *to capture, except by siege,* Dem. 19, 123. For the synizesis of μὴ οὐ see **54** *a.*

1621. When a negative is followed by a *simple* negative (οὐ or μή) in the same clause, each retains its own force. If they belong to the same word or expression, they make an *affirmative*; but if they belong to different words, each is independent of the other. Here οὐ and μή may frequently be translated *fail to, refuse to.* E.g.

οὐδὲ τὸν Φορμίωνα οὐχ ὁρᾷ *nor does he fail to see Phormio* (i.e. *he sees Phormio well enough*), Dem. 36, 46; οὐ δι' ἀπειρίαν γε οὐ φήσεις ἔχειν ὅ τι εἴπῃς *it is surely not through inexperience that you will deny that you have anything to say,* Dem. 19, 120; εἰ μὴ Πρόξενον οὐχ ὑπεδέξαντο *if they had not refused to receive Proxenus* (*had not not-received him*), Dem. 19, 74. So μὴ οὖν . . . διὰ ταῦτα μὴ δότω δίκην *do not then on this account let him escape punishment* (*do not let him fail to be punished*) Dem. 19, 77; οὐδὲ χρήματα μὲν λαμβάνων διαλέγομαι, μὴ λαμβάνων δ' οὔ *and I do not converse* (*with a man*) *if I get money* (*for it*), *but refuse to converse if I don't,* Plat. *Ap.* 33 a. See **1612.**

1622. But when a negative is followed by a *compound* negative (or by several compound negatives) in the same clause, the negation is strengthened. E.g.

οὐδεὶς εἰς οὐδὲν οὐδενὸς ἂν ἡμῶν οὐδέποτε γένοιτο ἄξιος *no one of us* (*in that case*) *would ever come to be of any value for anything,* Plat. *Ph.* 19 b; ὥστε μηδεπώποτέ μοι μηδὲ πρὸς ἕνα μηδὲν ἔγκλημα γενέσθαι *so that there has never arisen against me any ground of complaint whatsoever on the part of a single solitary person* (**1223** *c*), Lys. 16, 10. But when οὐ (ἆρ' οὐ) introduces a question (**1605**), the negative following retains its own force; e.g. οὐ νῦν ἐκεῖνοι παιόμενοι, κεντούμενοι, ὑβριζόμενοι οὐδὲ ἀποθανεῖν οἱ τλήμονες δύνανται *is it not now true that those poor wretches, beaten, goaded, and insulted, are unable even to die?* X. *An.* 3, 1, 29.

For the double negative οὐ μή, see **1369** and **1370.** For οὐχ ὅτι, μὴ ὅτι, οὐχ ὅπως, μὴ ὅπως, see **1519.**

PART V

VERSIFICATION

RHYTHM AND METRE

1623. Greek verse, being developed in intimate connection with music, is regulated by the quantity of syllables, not by the accent of words, which in Greek was marked by differences in pitch, not stress (**127**). Sometimes word-accent seems to correspond with metre, e.g.

Ὅν   Τυνδαρὶς   παῖς   ἤδ'   ἀπόντα   κενοταφεῖ

$>$ $\_\cup\acute{\_}$ $>$ $\_$ $\cup\acute{\_}\cup$ $\cup\cup\cup\acute{\_}$ (E. *Hel.* 1546)

but in general we may disregard accent, and understand that Greek verse consists in the combination of syllables of differing quantities. This is *rhythm* (ῥυθμός *regular movement* or *order*). In some forms of verse the number of syllables is not fixed.

1624. It is common to regard a long syllable as having twice the length of a short, especially in pure anapaestic or dactylic verse; but it was observed in ancient times that this is not always the case. Not all long syllables are of the same length, and short syllables are not all equally short.

1625. Although in English poetry the rhythm depends on the regular succession of *accented* and *unaccented* syllables and, except in blank verse, is also marked by rime, in Greek poetry rhythm depends on *measures* (μέτρα), or the proper combinations of longs and shorts. There is no rime, in the modern sense. The elements composing measures are called *feet*. Thus, in the trochaic verse

Φήσομεν πρὸς τοὺς στρατηγούς

$\acute{\_}\cup\_>|\acute{\_}\cup\_>\|$

we have two measures, each composed of two trochaic feet. For the rhythm compare the English

Fár from mórtal cáres retreáting.

1626. In each foot one part is inevitably distinguished from the other by a stress of voice, called the *ictus* (*stroke*). The part of the foot on which the ictus falls is called the *thesis* (θέσις *setting*, *down-beat*), and the rest of the foot is called the *arsis* (ἄρσις *raising*, *up-beat*). The regular alternation of thesis and arsis in successive feet produces the rhythm of the verse.

a. The terms ἄρσις and θέσις, as they were used by nearly all the Greek writers on rhythm, referred to the *raising* and *putting down* of the foot in marching, dancing, or beating time, so that θέσις denoted the part of the foot on which the ictus fell, and ἄρσις the lighter part. Most of the Roman writers, however, inverted this use, and referred *arsis* to the raising of the voice and *thesis* to the lowering of the voice in reading. Much confusion has arisen from the Roman inversion of the terms. As to ictus, although it plays no part in the theories of rhythm and foot advanced by Greek metricians, it is difficult, if not impossible, for a modern reader to render a Greek verse without it. It has, of course, nothing to do with the written word-accent (1623).

1627. The change from metrical to accentual rhythm can best be seen in modern Greek poetry, in which, even when the forms of the ancient language are retained, the rhythm is generally accentual, and quantitative metre is no more regarded than it is in English poetry. These are the first two verses in a modern translation of the Odyssey:

Ψάλλε τὸν | ἄνδρα, Θε|ά, τὸν πο|λύτροπον, | ὅστις το|σούτους
Τόπους δι|ῆλθε, πορ|θήσας τῆς | Τροίας τὴν | ἔνδοξον | πόλιν.

The original verses are:

Ἄνδρα μοι | ἔννεπε, | Μοῦσα, πο|λύτροπον, | ὃς μάλα | πολλὰ
Πλάγχθη, ἐ|πεὶ Τροί|ης ἱε|ρὸν πτολί|εθρον ἔ|περσεν.

If the former verses set our teeth on edge, it is only through force of acquired habit; for these verses have much more of the nature of modern poetry than the Homeric originals, and their rhythm is precisely what we are accustomed to in English verse, where

Still stands the | forest pri|meval; but | under the | shade of its | branches
is dactylic, and

And the ol|ive of peace | spreads its branch|es abroad
is anapaestic.

FEET

1628. *a.* The unit of measure in Greek verse is the short syllable (⏑), which for convenience may be given the value of ♪ or an eighth note in music. This is called a *time* or *mora*. The long syllable (‿) has generally twice the length of a short one, and has the value of a quarter note or ♩ in music. See 1624.

b. But a long syllable sometimes has the length of three shorts, and is called a *triseme* (⌞), and sometimes that of four shorts, and is called a *tetraseme* (⌞⌟). The triseme has roughly the value of ♩. in music, and the tetraseme that of ♩ ; see 1634. Greek musical notation lacked the bar.

1629. Feet are distinguished according to the number of *times* which they contain. The most common feet are the following:

a. OF THREE TIMES

Trochee	— ◡	φαῖνε
Iambus	◡ —	ἔφην
Tribrach	◡ ◡ ◡	λέγετε

b. OF FOUR TIMES

Dactyl	— ◡ ◡	φαίνετε
Anapaest	◡ ◡ —	σέβομαι
Spondee	— —	εἰπών
Proceleusmatic	◡ ◡ ◡ ◡	ἔτι βρέφος

c. OF FIVE TIMES

Cretic	— ◡ —	φαινέτω
Paeon primus	— ◡ ◡ ◡	ἐκτρέπετε
Paeon quartus	◡ ◡ ◡ —	καταλέγω
Bacchīus	◡ — —	ἀφεγγής
Antibacchīus	— — ◡	φαίνητε

d. OF SIX TIMES

Ionic *a maiore*	— — ◡ ◡	ἐκλείπετε
Ionic *a minore*	◡ ◡ — —	προσιδέσθαι
Choriambus	— ◡ ◡ —	ἐκτρέπομαι
Antispast	◡ — — ◡	ταλαίπωρα
Molossus	— — —	βουλεύων

e. The pyrrhic, or ◡ ◡, is never counted as a foot.
For the dochmius, ◡ — — ◡ —, see **1683.** For the epitrite, see **1689.**

1630. The feet in $\frac{3}{8}$ time (*a*), in which the thesis is twice as long as the arsis, form the *double* class (γένος διπλάσιον), as opposed to those in $\frac{2}{4}$ time (*b*), in which the thesis and arsis are of equal length, and which form the *equal* class (γένος ἴσον). Where the ratio of thesis to arsis is as 3 to 2, as in the feet of five times, the foot belongs to the γένος ἡμιόλιον.

1631. The ictus falls naturally on a long syllable, but it sometimes falls on a short. The first syllable of the trochee and the dactyl, and the last syllable of the iambus and the anapaest, therefore, form the thesis, the remainder of the foot being the arsis; e.g. –́ ⏑, –́ ⏑ ⏑, ⏑ –́, ⏑ ⏑ –́.

1632. When a long syllable in the thesis is resolved into two short syllables (**1633**), the ictus properly belongs on the two taken together, but in reading it is usually placed on the first. Thus a tribrach used for a trochee (–́ ⏑) is ⏑́ ⏑ ⏑; one used for an iambus (⏑ –́) is ⏑ ⏑́ ⏑. Likewise a spondee used for a dactyl is –́ –; one used for an anapaest is – –́. So a dactyl used for an anapaest (– ⏑ ⏑ for – – for ⏑ ⏑ –) is – ⏑́ ⏑. The only use of the tribrach and the chief use of the spondee are (as above) to represent other feet which have their thesis naturally marked by a long syllable.

Resolution and Contraction — Irrational Time — Syllaba Anceps

1633. A long syllable, being ordinarily the metrical equivalent of two short ones (**1628**), is often resolved into these; as when a tribrach ⏑ ⏑ ⏑ stands for a trochee – ⏑ or an iambus ⏑ –. On the other hand, two short syllables are often contracted into one long syllable; as when a spondee – – stands for a dactyl – ⏑ ⏑ or an anapaest ⏑ ⏑ –. The mark for a long resolved into two shorts is ⏕; that for two shorts contracted into one long is ⏔.

1634. A syllable or syllables forming the arsis may be omitted. If this occurs in the middle of a verse it is called protraction (τονή); if at the beginning, the verse is said to be *acephalous* (*headless*); if at the end, the verse is *catalectic* (καταληκτικός *stopping short*). A trochee with arsis omitted may be indicated either by a triseme (⏗) or by a long mark and a dot (– .). This occurs frequently in syncopated verses. See **1641**, **1666** *b*.

1635. On the other hand, a long syllable may in certain cases take the place of a short syllable. Such a syllable is called *irrational*, and is marked > or ⏒. The foot in which it occurs is also called *irrational* (ποὺς ἄλογος). Thus, in ἀλλ' ἀπ' ἐχθρῶν ($\_ \cup \_ \smile$), the apparent spondee which takes the place of the second trochee is called an *irrational trochee*; in δοῦναι δίκην ($\smile \_ \cup \_$) that which takes the place of the first iambus is called an *irrational iambus*.

1636. A similar shortening occurs in the so-called *cyclic* dactyl (marked $\_\cup \cup$) and *cyclic* anapaest (marked $\cup \cup\_$), which have the time of only three short syllables instead of four. The cyclic dactyl may take the place of a trochee $\_ \cup$. The cyclic anapaest takes the place of an iambus $\cup \_$, and is found especially in the iambic trimeter of comedy (**1659**).

1637. The last syllable of every verse may be common, i.e. it may be made long or short to suit the metre, without regard to its usual quantity. It is called *syllaba anceps*. But the continuous *systems* described in **1656, 1668**, and **1679** allow this only at the end of the system.

RHYTHMICAL SERIES — VERSE — CATALEXIS — PAUSE

1638. A *rhythmical series* is a continuous succession of feet of the same measure. A *verse* may consist of one such series, or of several such united.

Thus the verse

πολλὰ τὰ δεινὰ, κοὐδὲν ἀν‖θρώπου δεινότερον πέλει

$\_ \cup \cup \_ \cup \_ \cup \_ \_\_ \_\cup\cup\_ \cup \_$

consists of a First Glyconic (**1688** *d*), $\_\cup \cup | \_ \cup | \_ \cup | \_$, followed by a Second Glyconic, $\_ \check{\circ} | \_\cup \cup | \_ \cup | \_ \wedge$. Each part forms a series, the former ending with the first syllable of ἀνθρώπου (see above); and either series might have formed a distinct verse.

1639. The verse must close in such a way as to be distinctly marked off from what follows.

a. It must end with the end of a word.

b. It allows the last syllable (*syllaba anceps*) to be either long or short (**1637**).

c. It allows *hiatus* (**38**) before a vowel in the next verse.

1640. A verse which has an unfinished foot at the close is called *catalectic* (**1634**). A complete verse is called *acatalectic*.

1641. *a.* If the omitted syllable or syllables in a catalectic verse are the arsis of the foot (as in trochaic and dactylic verses), their place is filled by a *pause*. A pause of one time, equivalent to a short syllable ($\cup$), is marked $\wedge$ (for Λ, the initial of λεῖμμα); a pause of two times (__) is marked $\overline{\wedge}$.

b. But in catalectic iambic and anapaestic verses the arsis of the last foot is lost, and the place may be filled by prolonging the preceding thesis (**1634**): thus we have $\cup \sqcup \_$ or $\cup \_ . \_$ as the catalectic form of $\cup \_ \cup \_$; and $\cup \cup \sqcup \_$ as that of $\cup \cup \_ \cup \cup \_$. See **1666** and **1667**.

1642. A verse measured by dipodies (**1647**) is called *brachycatalectic* if it wants a complete foot at the end, and *hypercatalectic* if it has a single syllable beyond its last complete dipody.

Caesura and Diaeresis

1643. *a.* Caesura (τομή i.e. *cutting*) *of the foot* occurs whenever a word ends before a foot is finished; e.g. in three cases in the following verse, i.e. in the third, fourth, and fifth feet:

πολλᾱ̀ς | δ' ἰφθί|μους ψῡ|χᾱ̀ς "Αϊ|δι προῑ̂|αψεν.

b. This becomes important only when it coincides with the *caesura of the verse* (as after ἰφθίμους). This caesura is a metrical device introduced to vary the rhythm and to facilitate the rendering of verse which was spoken or recited; it does not occur in sung verses (called *melic*, **1650**). In some verses, as in the iambic trimeter acatalectic (**1660**) and the heroic hexameter (**1671**), it follows definite principles, but with great freedom.

1644. When the end of a word coincides with the end of a foot, the double division is called *diaeresis* (διαίρεσις *division*); as after the first foot in the line just quoted. Diaeresis becomes important only when it coincides with a natural pause produced by the ending of a rhythmic series; as in the trochaic tetrameter (**1653**) and the so-called dactylic pentameter (**1672**).

1645. The following verse of Aristophanes (*Nub.* 519) shows the irrational long (**1635**) in the first, second, and sixth feet; and at the end catalexis and pause (**1640, 1641**), with *syllaba anceps* (**1637**):

τᾱ̓ληθῆ νὴ | τὸν Διόνῡ‐||σον τὸν ἐκθρέ‐|ψαντά με.
$\underline{\diagup} \overline{\cup} \_ \overline{\cup} \mid \underline{\diagup} \cup \cup \_ \parallel \underline{\diagup} \cup \_ \overline{\cup} \mid \underline{\diagup} \cup \underline{\cup}$

A rhythmical series (**1638**) ends with the penult of Διόνῡσον, consisting of two measures (dimeter) of eight syllables; the second measure is a choriamb (**1686**). The entire verse is "Aeolic," and is called a *Eupolidean* tetrameter.

VERSES

1646. Verses are called *Trochaic, Iambic, Dactylic*, etc., from their fundamental foot (1629).

1647. In most kinds of verse, a *monometer* consists of one foot, a *dimeter* of two feet, a *trimeter, tetrameter, pentameter,* or *hexameter* of three, four, five, or six feet. But in trochaic, iambic, and anapaestic verses, which are measured by *dipodies* (i.e. *pairs of feet*), a monometer consists of one *dipody* (or two feet), a dimeter of four feet, a trimeter of six feet, and a tetrameter of eight feet.

1648. When trochaic or iambic verses are measured by single feet, they are called *tripodies, tetrapodies, hexapodies*, etc. (as having three, four, six, etc. feet). Here irrational syllables (1635) seldom occur. See 1658.

1649. Rhythms are divided into *ascending* and *descending* rhythms. In ascending rhythms the thesis follows the arsis, as in the iambus and anapaest; in descending rhythms the arsis follows the thesis, as in the trochee and the dactyl.

1650. Verses may be spoken or recited; such was the iambic trimeter. They may be chanted or delivered in recitative, with or without instrumental accompaniment; in the former case they are called *melodramatic*. They may be sung (*melic* or *lyric* verse).

1651. The same kind of verse may be used *by the line* (κατὰ στίχον), that is, repeated continuously, as in the heroic hexameter (ἔπη) and the iambic trimeter of the drama. Secondly, similar verses may be combined into groups called *strophes*, of which the simplest is the distich or couplet (1672). Thirdly, in lyric poetry (μέλη), which was composed to be sung to music, verses may be combined into strophes of complex rhythmical and metrical structure, with *antistrophes* corresponding to them in form. A strophe and antistrophe may be followed by an epode (*after-song*) in a different metre, as in most of the odes of Pindar. The combination of these three elements is called a *triad*.

Trochaic Rhythms

1652. Trochaic verses generally occur in measures of two feet each, or dipodies (1647). The irrational trochee ⌣ > (1635) in the form of a spondee can stand in the *second* place of each trochaic dipody except the last, that is, in the *even* feet (second, fourth, etc.), so that the dipody has the form $\angle \cup \_ \overline{\cup}$. An apparent anapaest ($\breve{\cup} \cup >$ for $\angle >$) is sometimes used as the equivalent of the irrational trochee. The cyclic dactyl $\frown\cup \cup$ (1636) sometimes stands for the trochee in proper names in both parts of the dipody, except at the end of the verse.

The tribrach ($\breve{\cup} \cup \cup$) may stand for the trochee (1633) in every foot except the last. Other substitutions for the pure trochee are the triseme $\sqsubset$ (1628 b) and long syllable with pause $\angle \wedge$ (1641).

1653. The chief trochaic verse which is used *by the line* (1651) is the TETRAMETER CATALECTIC, consisting of four measures, of which the last is catalectic, and divided into two rhythmical series (1638) by a diaeresis (1644) after the second dipody. E.g.

(1) ὢ σοφώτα|τοι θεᾱταί, ‖ δεῦρο τὸν νοῦν | προσέχετε.[1]

    $\angle \cup \_ \cup | \angle \cup \_ > \| \angle \cup \_ > | \breve{\cup} \cup \cup \_ \wedge$

(2) κατὰ σελήνην | ὡς ἄγειν χρὴ ‖ τοῦ βίου τὰς | ἡμέρᾱς.[2]

    $\breve{\cup} \cup \cup \_ > | \angle \cup \_ > \| \angle \cup \_ > | \angle \cup \_ \wedge$

(3) ξύγγονόν τ' ἐ|μὴν Πυλάδην τε ‖ τὸν τάδε ξυν|δρῶντά μοι.[3]

    $\angle \cup \_ \cup | \frown\cup \cup \_ \cup \| \angle \cup \_ > | \angle \cup \_ \wedge$

Notice the tribrach in the first place of (2), and the cyclic dactyl in the third place of (3), due to a proper name.

This verse is familiar in English poetry, e.g.

> Tell me not in mournful numbers, life is but an empty dream.

1654. The *lame* tetrameter (τετράμετρον χωλόν or σκάζον), called Hipponactean from Hipponax (see 1665), is the preceding verse with the last syllable but one long. E.g.

    ἀμφιδέξι-|ος γάρ εἰμι | κοὐχ ἁμαρτά-|νω κόπτων.[4]

    $\angle \cup \_ \cup | \angle \cup \_ \cup | \angle \cup \_ \cup | \angle \_ \_$

1655. The following are some of the more important lyric trochaic verses:

a. Tripody acatalectic (the ithyphallic):

    μήποτ' ἐκτακείη.[5] $\angle \cup \angle \cup \angle \overline{\cup}$ (1648)

[1] Ar. *Nub.* 575.   [3] E. *Or.* 1535.   [5] Aesch. *Pr.* 535 (551).
[2] *ibid.* 626.   [4] Hippon. 83.

b. Tripody catalectic:

ὅς γε σᾶν λιπών.[1]   — ⏑ — ⏑ — ⋀

c. Tetrapody or dimeter acatalectic:

τοῦτο τοῦ μὲν ἦρος ἀεὶ   — ⏑ — ⏑ | — ⏑ — ⏡
βλαστάνει καὶ σῦκοφαντεῖ.[2]   — ⏑ — > | — ⏑ — ⏡

d. Tetrapody or dimeter catalectic:

δεινὰ πράγματ' εἴδομεν.[3]   — ⏑ — ⏑ | — ⏑ — ⋀
ἀσπίδας φυλλορροεῖ.[4]   — ⏑ — > | — ⏑ — ⋀

e. Hexapody or trimeter catalectic:

ἁρπαγαὶ δὲ διαδρομᾶν ὁμαίμονες.[5]
— ⏑ — ⏑ | ⏑ ⏑ ⏑ — ⏑ | — ⏑ — ⋀

1656. A series of dimeters acatalectic (**1655** *c*), rarely with an occasional monometer (— ⏑ — ⏑), and ending in a dimeter catalectic (**1655** *d*), is called a trochaic *system* or *hypermeter.* E.g.

ταῦτα μὲν πρὸς ἀνδρός ἐστι   — ⏑ — ⏑ | — ⏑ — ⏑
νοῦν ἔχοντος καὶ φρένας καὶ   — ⏑ — > | — ⏑ — >
πολλὰ περιπεπλευκότος.[6]   — ⏑ ⏑ ⏑ ⏑ | — ⏑ — ⋀

For iambic and anapaestic systems, formed on the same principle, see **1668** and **1679**. See also **1637**.

1657. The following contain examples of syncopated trochaic verses, in which ⌞ . may be written instead of ⌞ (**1634**):

νῦν καταστροφαὶ νέων   — ⏑ — ⏑ | — ⏑ — ⋀
θεσμίων, εἰ κρατήσει δίκᾱ τε καὶ βλάβᾱ
— ⏑ ⌞ | — ⏑ ⌞ | — ⏑ — ⏑ | — ⏑ — ⋀
τοῦδε μᾱτροκτόνου.[7]   — ⏑ ⌞ | — ⏑ — ⋀
δωμάτων γὰρ εἰλόμᾱν   — ⏑ — ⏑ | — ⏑ — ⋀
ἀνατροπᾱς, ὅταν "Αρης τιθασὸς ὢν φίλον ἔλῃ.[8]
⏑ ⏑ ⏑ ⌞ | ⏑ ⏑ ⏑ ⌞ | ⏑ ⏑ ⏑ ⌞ | ⏑ ⏑ ⏑ — ⋀

1658. In lyric trochaic and iambic verses, the irrational syllable is found chiefly in comedy, and is avoided in tragedy; in comedy, moreover, it is less common in lyric or sung trochaic verse than in that which was spoken.

Iambic Rhythms

1659. Iambic verses generally occur in measures of two feet each, or dipodies (**1647**). The irrational iambus > — (**1635**) in

[1] S. *Ph.* 1215.   [4] *ibid.* 1481.   [7] Aesch. *Eum.* 490 ff.
[2] Ar. *Av.* 1478, 1479.   [5] Aesch. *Sev.* 351 (338).   [8] *ibid.* 354 ff.
[3] *ibid.* 1472.   [6] Ar. *R.* 534 ff.

the form of a spondee can stand in the *first* place of each iambic dipody, that is, in the *odd* places (first, third, etc.), so that the dipody has the form ⏓ ⏑́ ⏑ – . An apparent dactyl (> ⏑́ ⏑ for > –́) is sometimes used as the equivalent of the irrational iambus; and the cyclic anapaest ⏑ ⏑–́ (**1636**) is used for the iambus in both parts of the dipody, except in the last foot, especially by the Attic comedians (**1660**). The tribrach (⏑ ⏑́ ⏑) may stand for the iambus in every foot except the last.

1660. The most common of all iambic verses is the TRIMETER ACATALECTIC, in which most of the dialogue of the Attic drama is composed. It never allows any substitution in the last foot. With this exception it may have the tribrach in any place. The irrational iambus > –́ in the form of a spondee can stand in the first place of every dipody. The *tragedians* allow the (apparent) dactyl > ⏑́ ⏑ only in the first and third places, and the cyclic anapaest only in the first place; but in proper names they allow the anapaest in every place except the last. The *comedians* allow the dactyl > ⏑́ ⏑ in all the *odd* places, and the cyclic anapaest in every place except the last (**1659**). The most common caesura is that after the arsis of the third foot.

1661. The following scheme shows the tragic and the comic iambic trimeter compared, — the forms peculiar to comedy being inclosed in [ ].

⏑ –́	⏑ –	⏑ –́	⏑ –	⏑ –́	⏑ –
> –		> –		> –	
⏑ ⏑ ⏑	⏑ ⏑ ⏑	⏑ ⏑ ⏑	⏑ ⏑ ⏑	⏑ ⏑ ⏑	
> ⏑ ⏑		> ⏑ ⏑		[> ⏑ ⏑]	
⏑ ⏑–	[⏑ ⏑–]	[⏑ ⏑–]	[⏑ ⏑–]	[⏑ ⏑–]	

From this it is seen that the greater number of equivalents of the pure iambus occur in the *first* half of the measure. The tribrach occurs in the *second* half both in tragedy and in comedy; the anapaest occurs in the *second* half in comedy, and then only in trimeters which are not sung. In general the tragedians avoid the feet of three syllables, even where they are allowed.

1662. *Porson's Rule.* When the *tragic* trimeter ends in a word forming a cretic (– ⏑ –), this is regularly preceded by a short syllable or by a monosyllable.[1] The following line (E. *I. T.* 580) violates this rule:

κἀμοί. τὸ δ' εὖ μάλιστά γ' οὕτω γίγνεται.

[1] R. Porson, *Suppl. ad Praef. ad Hecubam.*

1663. The following are examples of both the tragic and the comic form of the iambic trimeter:

TRAGIC χθονὸς μὲν εἰς | τηλουρὸν ἥκομεν πέδον,
Σκύθην ἐς οἶμον, ἄβατον εἰς | ἐρημίαν.
Ἥφαιστε, σοὶ | δὲ χρὴ μέλειν | ἐπιστολᾶς. Aesch. *Pr.* 1–3.

COMIC ὦ Ζεῦ βασιλεῦ · | τὸ χρῆμα τῶν | νυκτῶν ὅσον
ἀπέραντον · οὐδέποθ' ἡμέρα | γενήσεται;
ἀπόλοιο δῆτ', | ὦ πόλεμε, πολ|λῶν οὕνεκα. Ar. *Nub.* 2, 3, 6.

1664. The iambic trimeter is a much livelier verse in Greek than in English, where it appears as the Alexandrine, which is seldom used except at the end of a stanza:

> That líke a wounded snáke drags its slow léngth along.
> And hópe to mer|it Heáven by mak|ing Eárth a Hell.

1665. The *lame* trimeter (σκάζον), called the *Choliambus* and the Hipponactean (see **1654**), is the preceding verse with the last syllable but one long. It is said to have been invented by Hipponax (about 540 B.C.), and it is used in the mimes of Herodas (third century B.C.) and the fables of Babrius (second century A.D. ?). E.g.

ἀκούσαθ' Ἱππώνακτος · οὐ γὰρ ἀλλ' ἥκω.[1]
οὕτω τί σοι δοίησαν αἱ φίλαι Μοῦσαι.[2]
⏝ _́ ⏝ _ | ⏝ _́ ⏝ _ | ⏝ _́ _ _

1666. a. The TETRAMETER CATALECTIC, consisting of four measures, of which the last is catalectic, occurs often in Attic comedy. There is a regular diaeresis (**1644**) after the second dipody, where the first rhythmical series ends (**1638**).

εἴπερ τὸν ἄνδρ' | ὑπερβαλεῖ, ‖ καὶ μὴ γέλωτ' | ὀφλήσεις.[3]
> _́ ⏝ _ | ⏝ _́ ⏝ _ ‖ > _́ ⏝ _ | ⏝ _́   **1641 b)**

In English poetry we have

> A cáptain bold | of Hálifax, ‖ who lived in coun|try quárters.

b. A protracted or syncopated (**1634**) iambic tetrameter also occurs, sometimes called *versus Euripideus*:

νῦν καὶ τὸν ὡ|ραῖον θεὸν | παρακαλεῖ|τε δεῦρο.[4]
> _́ ⏝ _ |> _́ ⏝ _ | · ⏝́ ⏝ ⏝ _|⏝ _́ · _
or > _́ ⏝ _ |> _́ ⏝ _ | ⏝́ ⏝ ⏝ _ |⏝ _́ _

1667. The following are some of the more important lyric iambic verses:

a. Dipody or monometer:

τί δῆθ' ὁρᾷς;[5]   ⏝ _́ ⏝ _

[1] Hippon. 47.   [3] Ar. *Nub.* 1035.   [5] *ibid.* 1098.
[2] Herod. 3, 1.   [4] Ar. *R.* 397.

b. Tripody (acatalectic and catalectic):

τί τῶνδ' ἄνευ κακῶν; [1]   ∪ $\underline{\prime}$ ∪ $\underline{\prime}$ ∪ $\underline{\prime}$

ἐπ' ἄλλο πήδα. [2]   ∪ $\underline{\prime}$ ∪ $\underline{\prime}$. $\underline{\prime}$

c. Dimeter (acatalectic and catalectic):

ἰαλτὸς ἐκ | δόμων ἔβᾱν. [3]   ∪ $\underline{\prime}$ ∪ — | ∪ $\underline{\prime}$ ∪ —

ζηλῶ σε τῆς | εὐβουλίᾱς. [4]   > $\underline{\prime}$ ∪ — | > $\underline{\prime}$ ∪ —

καὶ τὸν λόγον | τὸν ἥττω. [5]   > $\underline{\prime}$ ∪ — | ∪ $\underline{\prime}$. —   (1641 *b*)

d. Hexapody or trimeter catalectic:

πρέπει παρηὶς φοινίοις ἀμυγμοῖς. [6]

∪ $\underline{\prime}$ ∪ — | > $\underline{\prime}$ ∪ — | ∪ $\underline{\prime}$ —

1668. Iambic *systems* are formed on the same principle as trochaic systems (**1656**), of acatalectic dimeters with an occasional monometer, ending with a catalectic dimeter. E.g.

ἡττήμεθ' · ὦ κῑνούμενοι,   > $\underline{\prime}$ ∪ — | > $\underline{\prime}$ ∪ —

πρὸς τῶν θεῶν δέξασθέ μου   > $\underline{\prime}$ ∪ — | > $\underline{\prime}$ ∪ —

θοἰμάτιον, ὡς   > $\underline{\prime}$ ∪ ∪ —

ἐξαυτομολῶ πρὸς ὑμᾶς.   > $\underline{\prime}$ ∪ ⌣ | ∪ $\underline{\prime}$. —

These verses end a long iambic system in Ar. *Nub.* 1090–1104; see also *Nub.* 1447–1451, and *Eq.* 911–940.

1669. For the irrational syllable in lyric verse, see **1658.**

Dactylic Rhythms

1670. The only regular substitute for the dactyl is the spondee, which arises by contraction of the two short syllables of the dactyl ($\underline{\prime}$ — from $\underline{\prime}$ ∪ ∪).

1671. The most common of all Greek verses is the HEROIC HEXAMETER, the Homeric verse. It has a spondee or trochee in the last place; and a spondee may occur in any of the first four places, *less commonly* in the fifth (the verse being then called *spondaic*). There is commonly a caesura in the third foot, either after the thesis or (rather more frequently) dividing the arsis. There is sometimes a caesura after the thesis of the fourth foot, and rarely one in the arsis. The caesura after the thesis is called *masculine*, that in the arsis *feminine* or *trochaic*. E.g.

[1] Aesch. *Ag.* 211.   [3] Aesch. *Ch.* 22.   [5] Ar. *Nub.* 1451.

[2] Ar. *Nub.* 703.   [4] Ar. *Ach.* 1008.   [6] Aesch. *Ch.* 24.

ἄνδρα μοι ἔννεπε, Μοῦσα, πολύτροπον, ὃς μάλα πολλὰ

‑ ◡ ◡|‑ ◡ ◡|‑ ◡, ◡|‑ ◡ ◡|‑ ◡ ◡|‑ ◡

πλάγχθη ἐπεὶ Τροίης ἱερὸν πτολίεθρον ἔπερσεν.[1]

‑ ◡ ◡|‑ ‑|‑, ◡ ◡|‑ ◡ ◡|‑ ◡ ◡|‑ ◡

A diaeresis after the fourth foot is called *bucolic*, since it was thought to be more common in bucolic poetry. E.g.

τίπτ' αὖτ', αἰγιόχοιο Διὸς τέκος, εἰλήλουθας;[2]

‑ ‑|‑ ◡ ◡|‑ ◡ ◡|‑ ◡ ◡,|‑ ‑|‑ ◡

εἰπέ μοι, ὦ Κορύδων, τίνος αἱ βόες; ἦρα Φιλώνδα;[3]

‑ ◡ ◡|‑ ◡ ◡|‑ ◡ ◡|‑ ◡ ◡,|‑ ◡ ◡|‑ ◡

1672. In the Homeric verse a long vowel or a diphthong in the arsis (not in the thesis) is often shortened at the end of a word when the next word begins with a vowel or a diphthong (35). This sometimes occurs in the middle of a word. E.g.

ὦ πόποι, | ἦ μάλα | δὴ μετε|βούλευ|σαν θεοὶ | ἄλλως.[4]

χρῡσέῳ ἀ|νὰ σκή|πτρῳ, καὶ | λίσσετο | πάντας 'Α|χαιούς (54).[5]

βέβληαι, οὐδ' ἄλιον βέλος ἔκφυγεν, ὡς ὄφελόν τοι.[6]

But   ἡμετέρῳ ἐνὶ οἴκῳ ἐν "Αργεϊ, τηλόθι πάτρης.[7]

1673. When a short vowel stands in Homer where a long one is required by the verse, it may be explained in various ways.

a. By supposing λ, μ, ν, ρ, or σ to be doubled at the beginning of certain words; e.g. πολλὰ λισσομένῳ (‑ ‑ ‑ ◡ ◡ ‑), *Il.* 22, 91 (we have ἐλλίσσετο written in *Il.* 6, 45). See 535, cf. 64.

b. By the original presence of ϝ making position (see 3, 102); e.g. τοῖον ϝοι πῦρ (‑ ‑ ‑ ‑), *Il.* 5, 7. So before δείδω *fear* and other derivatives of the stem δϝει, and before δήν (for δϝην).

c. By a pause in the verse prolonging the time; e.g.

φεύγωμεν · ἔτι γάρ κεν ἀλύξαιμεν κακὸν ἦμαρ.[8]

‑ ‑ ‑, ◡ ◡ ‑◡◡‑ ‑ ‑ ◡ ◡ ‑ ‑

For rules relating to quantity see 119–125.

1674. The ELEGIAC DISTICH consists of a heroic hexameter followed by the so-called *elegiac pentameter*. This latter verse consists really of two dactylic trimeters with protraction (1634) and catalexis in the last measure; e.g.

Παλλὰς 'Α|θηναί|η ‖ χεῖρας ὕ|περθεν ἔ|χει.[9]

‑ ◡ ◡ | ‑ ‑|◡⌐‖‑ ◡ ◡ | ‑ ◡ ◡|‑ Λ

[1] *Od.* 1, 1 and 2.   [4] *Od.* 5, 286.   [7] *Il.* 1, 30.
[2] *Il.* 1, 202.   [5] *Il.* 1, 15.   [8] *Od.* 10, 269.
[3] Theocr. 4, 1.   [6] *Il.* 11, 380.   [9] Solon 4, 4.

At the end of the pentameter verse the pause ($\bar{\wedge}$) takes the place of protraction ($\sqcup$) in the middle. The verse probably arose from the repetition of the first *penthemimer* (πενθ-ημι-μερές, *composed of five halves*) of the hexameter; i.e. if the part of the hexameter extending to the masculine caesura be repeated (μῆνιν ἄειδε θεᾶ) the result is the "pentameter." But *syllaba anceps* and hiatus are not allowed after the first trimeter, but only at the end of the verse (**1639**). The last two complete feet are always dactyls. A diaeresis (**1644**) divides the two parts of the verse. The pentameter used by itself is not common.

1675. The following is an elegiac distich :

τίς δὲ βί|ος, τί δὲ | τερπνὸν ἄ|νευ χρῡ|σέης ᾿Αφρο|δίτης; (**54**)
τεθναί|ην ὅτε | μοι ‖ μηκέτι | ταῦτα μέ|λοι.[1]

$$\text{–} \cup \cup | \text{–} \cup \cup | \text{–} \cup, \cup | \text{–} \_ | \text{–} \cup \cup | \text{–} \_$$
$$\text{–} \_ | \text{–} \cup \cup | \overset{\smile}{\text{–}} \| \text{–} \cup \cup | \text{–} \cup \cup | \text{–} \bar{\wedge}$$

1676. The following are some of the chief lyric dactylic verses :

a. Dimeter :

μυστοδό|κος δόμος.[2] $\text{–} \cup \cup | \text{–} \cup \cup$
μοῖρα δι|ώκει.[3] $\text{–} \cup \cup | \text{–} \_$

b. Trimeter (acatalectic and catalectic) :

παμπρέπτοις ἐν ἕδραισιν.[4] $\text{–} \_ | \text{–} \cup \cup | \text{–} \smile$
παρθένοι | ὀμβροφό|ροι.[5] $\text{–} \cup \cup | \text{–} \cup \cup | \text{–} \bar{\wedge}$

Opening with a short syllable :

ἐγείνατο μὲν μόρον αὐτῷ $\cup \text{–} \cup \cup | \text{–} \cup \cup | \text{–} \_$
πατροκτόνον Οἰδιπόδᾶν.[6] $\cup \text{–} \cup \cup | \text{–} \cup \cup | \text{–} \bar{\wedge}$

c. Tetrameter (acatalectic and catalectic) :

πέμπει ξὺν δορὶ καὶ χερὶ πράκτορι.[7] $\text{–} \_ | \text{–} \cup \cup | \text{–} \cup \cup | \text{–} \cup \cup$
οὐρανίοις τε θεοῖς δω|ρήματα.[8] $\text{–} \cup \cup | \text{–} \cup \cup | \text{–} \_ | \text{–} \cup \cup$
ἔλθετ᾿ ἐ|ποψόμε|ναι δύνα|μιν.[9] $\text{–} \cup \cup | \text{–} \cup \cup | \text{–} \cup \cup | \text{–} \bar{\wedge}$

Anapaestic Rhythms

1677. Anapaestic verses are generally measured by dipodies (**1647**). The spondee and the dactyl ($\_ \text{–}$ and $\_ \cup \cup$) may stand for the anapaest ($\cup \cup \text{–}$).

The long syllable of an anapaest is sometimes resolved into two short, making $\cup \cup \cup \cup$ or *proceleusmatic* (**1629** *b*).

[1] Mimn. 1, 1 and 2.
[2] Ar. *Nub.* 303.
[3] E. *Heraclid.* 612.
[4] Aesch. *Ag.* 117.
[5] Ar. *Nub.* 299.
[6] Aesch. *Sev.* 751, 752.
[7] Aesch. *Ag.* 111.
[8] Ar. *Nub.* 305.
[9] Ar. *R.* 879.

1678. The following are the most common anapaestic verses:

a. The monometer:

τρόπον αἰγυπιῶν.[1]   ∪ ∪ _́_ ∪ ∪ _

καὶ θέμις αἰνεῖν.[2]   _ _́_ ∪ _ _

ξύμφωνος ὁμοῦ.[3]   _ _́_ ∪ ∪ _

b. The dimeter acatalectic:

μέγαν ἐκ θυμοῦ | κλάζοντες Ἄρη.[4]   ∪ ∪ _́_ _ _ | _ _́_ ∪ ∪ _

ἄλγεσι παίδων | ὕπατοι λεχέων.[5]   _ _́_ ∪ _ _ | ∪ ∪ _́_ ∪ ∪ _

And the ó|live of peáce | sends its bránch|es abroád.

c. The dimeter catalectic, or *paroemiac*:

ἦραν στρατιῶ|τιν ἀρωγήν.[6]   _ _́_ ∪ ∪ _ | ∪ ∪ _́_ _   (**1641** *b*)

οὕτω πλουτή|σετε πάντες.[7]   _ _́_ | _ _ | ∪ ∪ _́_ | _

The Lórd | is advánc|ing. Prepáre | ye!

d. The TETRAMETER CATALECTIC, consisting of four measures, of which the last is protracted and catalectic, like the paroemiac. There is a regular diaeresis after the second measure. This verse is frequently used *by the line* (**1651**) in long passages of Aristophanes.

προσέχετε τὸν νοῦν | τοῖς ἀθανάτοις ‖ ἡμῖν, τοῖς αἰ|ἐν ἐοῦσι,

τοῖς αἰθερίοις, | τοῖσιν ἀγήρῳς, ‖ τοῖς ἄφθιτα μη|δομένοισιν.[8]

∪ ∪ _⌣_ _ _ | _ _⌣_ _⌣_ _ ‖ _ _́_ _ _ | ∪ ∪ _́_ _

1679. An ANAPAESTIC SYSTEM consists of a series of anapaestic dimeters acatalectic, with occasionally a monometer, ending always with the paroemiac (or dimeter catalectic). These systems are very frequently employed in both tragedy and comedy. E.g.

δέκατον μὲν ἔτος τόδ' ἐπεὶ Πριάμου   ∪ ∪ _́_ ∪ ∪ _ | ∪ ∪ _́_ ∪ ∪ _

μέγας ἀντίδικος,   ∪ ∪ _́_ ∪ ∪ _

Μενέλαος ἄναξ ἠδ' Ἀγαμέμνων,   ∪ ∪ _́_ ∪ ∪ _ | _ _́_ ∪ _ _

διθρόνου Διόθεν καὶ δισκήπτρου   ∪ ∪ _́_ ∪ ∪ _ | _ _́_ _ _

τῖμῆς ὀχυρὸν ζεῦγος Ἀτρειδᾶν,   _ _́_ ∪ ∪ _ | _ _́_ ∪ _ _

στόλον Ἀργείων χῑλιοναύτᾱν   ∪ ∪ _́_ _ _ | _ _́_ ∪ _ _

τῆσδ' ἀπὸ χώρᾱς   _ _́_ ∪ _ _

ἦραν, στρατιῶτιν ἀρωγήν.[9]   _ _́_ ∪ ∪ _ | ∪ ∪ _́_   _

[1] Aesch. *Ag.* 49.   [4] Aesch. *Ag.* 48.   [7] Ar. *Av.* 736.

[2] *ibid.* 98.   [5] *ibid.* 50.   [8] *ibid.* 688.

[3] Ar. *Av.* 221.   [6] *ibid.* 47.   [9] Aesch. *Ag.* 40–47.

1680. Anapaestic systems are especially common in march movements. The following rules are to be noted:

a. Except in lyric anapaests, a proceleusmatic is not common, nor a dactyl followed by an anapaest, because a succession of four short syllables was avoided.

b. In a paroemiac a dactyl occurs only in the first foot; the third usually has a pure anapaest.

c. There is no syllaba anceps or hiatus except at the end of a period. Thus the last syllable of ἀντίδικος (verse 2 above) is long by position, since it is chanted in close connection with the word Μενέλαος (verse 3). This is called συνάφεια *tying together.*

Rhythms with Feet of Five Times

1681. The basic foot is the *paeon*, of which the forms in use are the *first* (— ∪ ∪ ∪) and the *fourth paeon* (∪ ∪ ∪ —). These are often interchanged with the *cretic* (— ∪ —). Trochaic measures are sometimes mingled with them.

οὐκ ἀνα|σχήσομαι · | μηδὲ λέγε | μοι σὺ λόγον ·
ὡς μεμί|σηκά σε Κλέ|ωνος ἔτι | μᾶλλον, ὃν ἐ-
γὼ κατατε|μῶ ποθ' ἰπ|πεῦσι κατ|τύματα.[1]

— ∪ — | — ∪ — | — ∪ ∪ ∪| — ∪ ∪ ∪
— ∪ — | — ∪ ∪ ∪| — ∪ ∪ ∪| — ∪ ∪ ∪
— ∪ ∪ ∪| — ∪ — | — ∪ — | — ∪ ῡ

1682. *Bacchic* rhythms have the *bacchius* ∪ — — as the fundamental foot:

τίς ἀχώ, | τίς ὀδμὰ | προσέπτα | μ' ἀφεγγής;[2]
∪ — — | ∪ — — | ∪ — — | ∪ — —
στενάζω;| τί ῥέξω;
∪ — — | ∪ — —
γελῶμαι · | δυσοίστα
∪ —.. | ∪ — ◡
πολίταις | ἔπαθον.[3]
∪ — — | ∪∪ ◡

Dochmiacs

1683. *Dochmiac* verses, which are used in tragedy to express great excitement and in comedy for the sake of parody, are based upon a measure called the *dochmius*, compounded of an iambus

---

[1] Ar. *Ach.* 299–301. [2] Aesch. *Pr.* 115. [3] Aesch. *Eum.* 788.

and a cretic (or a bacchius and an iambus) ∪ — | — ∪ — (or
∪ — — | ∪ —). This may appear in nineteen different forms, by
resolving the long syllables and admitting irrational longs in place
of the two shorts. Its most common forms are ∪ — | — ∪ — and
∪ ∪ ∪ | — ∪ —. As examples may be given

δυσαλγεῖ τύχᾳ.[1]   ∪ —́ — ∪ —́
πτεροφόρον δέμας.[2]   ∪ ∪ ∪́ ∪ — ∪ —́
μῖσόθεον μὲν οὖν.[3]   > ∪́ ∪ — ∪ —́ (for > —́ — ∪ —́)
μεγάλα μεγάλα καί.[4]   ∪ ∪́ ∪ ∪ ∪ ∪ —́ (for ∪ —́ — ∪ —́)
μετοικεῖν σκότῳ θανὼν ὁ τλᾶμων.[5]   ∪ —́ — ∪ —́ | ∪ —́ — > —́
μεθεῖται στράτος, στρατόπεδον λιπών.[6]   ∪ —́ — ∪ —́ | ∪ ∪́ ∪ — ∪ —́

Cf. in English: Rebél, serfs, rebél, | Resént wrongs so díre.

Rhythms with Feet of Six Times

1684. a. The *ionic* rhythm, if ascending (**1649**), has the arsis
preceding the thesis, ∪ ∪ — —, and is called ionic *a minore*; if it
is descending, the arsis follows the thesis, — — ∪ ∪, and forms the
ionic *a maiore*:

> πεπέρᾱκεν | μὲν ὁ περσέ|πτολις ἤδη
> βασίλειος | στρατὸς εἰς ἀν|τίπορον γεί|τονα χώρᾱν,
> λινοδέσμῳ | σχεδίᾳ πορ|θμὸν ἀμείψ ᾱς
> Ἀθαμαν|τίδος Ἑλλᾱ̂ς.[7]

∪ ∪ —́ — | ∪ ∪ —́ — | ∪ ∪ —́ —
∪ ∪ —́ — | ∪ ∪ —́ — | ∪ ∪ —́ — | ∪ ∪ —́ —
∪ ∪ —́ — | ∪ ∪ —́ — | ∪ ∪ —́ —
∪ ∪ ⏑́ | ∪ ∪ —́ —

> ὤρχηντ' ἀπά|λοισ' ἀμφ' ἐρό|εντα βῶμον [8]

— — ∪ ∪ | — — ∪ ∪ | — ∪ — ∪

b. Trochaic measures are often interspersed with pure ionics, but the
double shorts make the character of the rhythm clear. This is called
anaclăsis (ἀνάκλασις *breaking up*). E.g.

> τίς ὁ κραιπνῷ | ποδὶ πηδή|μα τόδ' εὐπε|τῶς ἀνάσσων; [9]

∪ ∪ —́ — | ∪ ∪ —́ — | ∪ ∪ —́ ∪ | — ∪ —́ —

c. A dimeter composed of an ionic and a choriambic measure (**1686**)
is called a *prosodiac*. E.g.

> σᾶς ἀπτόμε|νος φαρέτρᾱς [10]

— — ∪ ∪ | — ∪ ∪ —

[1] Aesch. *Ag.* 1165.   [4] E. *Bacch.* 1198.   [7] Aesch. *Pers.* 65–70.   [9] *ibid.* 95.
[2] *ibid.* 1147.   [5] E. *Hipp.* 837.   [8] Sapph. 54.   [10] Ar. *Eq.* 1272.
[3] *ibid.* 1090.   [6] Aesch. *Sev.* 79.

d. A dimeter composed of a choriambic and an ionic measure is called an *enoplius*. It is sometimes catalectic. E.g.

ἦν δέ σε καρ|κίνος ἐλθὼν [1]
— ∪ ∪ — | ∪ ∪ — —
φροντίδ' ἐπι|σταμένην [2]
— ∪ ∪ — | ∪ ∪ —

1685. *a.* The *Anacreontic* verse is an ionic dimeter with anaclasis:

πολιοὶ μὲν ἡμὶν ἤδη
∪ ∪ —́ ∪ — ∪ —́ —
κρόταφοι κάρη τε λευκόν
∪ ∪ —́ ∪ — ∪ —́ —
χαρίεσσα δ' οὐκέτ' ἥβη
∪ ∪ —́ ∪ — ∪ —́ —
πάρα, γηράλεοι δ' ὀδόντες
∪ ∪ —́ ∪ — ∪ —́ —
γλυκεροῦ δ' οὐκέτι πολλός.[3]
∪ ∪ —́ — ∪ ∪ —́ ∪

b. With these verses may be compared the so-called *hemiambi*, or iambic dimeters catalectic, used in some of the *Anacreontea*:

Ἀνακρέων ἰδών με
∪ —́ ∪ — ∪ —́ ⏓
ὁ Τήιος μελῳδός
∪ —́ ∪ — ∪ —́ ⏓ [4]

1686. The *choriamb* (— ∪ ∪ —) is closely related to the iambic measure (∪ — ∪ —). Pure choriambs appear in the following trimeter and tetrameter:

παῖδα τὸν αὐτᾶς πόσιν αὐτᾷ θεμένᾱ.[5]
— ∪ ∪ — | — ∪ ∪ — | — ∪ ∪ —
δεινὰ μὲν οὖν, δεινὰ ταράσσει σοφὸς οἰωνοθέτᾱς.[6]
— ∪ ∪ — | — ∪ ∪ — | — ∪ ∪ — | — ∪ ∪ —

1687. Some variations on the pure choriambic series are seen in the following. Resolution, irrational syllables, and protraction may occur:

πῑ́νειν ἀεὶ καὶ μεθύειν πρὶν ἀγορὰν πεπληθέναι.[7]
⏒ — ∪ — | — ∪ ∪ — | . ∪ ∪ ∪ — | ∪ — ∪ — (**1688** ***k***)
ἀναπέτομαι δὴ πρὸς Ὄλυμπον πτερύγεσσι κούφαις.[8]
∪ ∪ ∪ ∪ — | — ∪ ∪ — | — ∪ ∪ — | ∪ ∟ —

[1] Ar. *Pax* 782.
[2] Ar. *Eccl.* 572.
[3] Anacr. *fr.* 43 B.
[4] Ps.-Anacr. 1 B.
[5] Aesch. *Sev.* 929.
[6] S. *O. T.* 484.
[7] Pherecr. 29.
[8] Anacr. 24.

1688. The choriamb is an important element in many verses commonly called "logaoedic." See also **1684** c. E.g.

a. *Adonic:* σύμμαχος ἔσσο.[1] $-\cup\cup\llcorner|\cup$ This is the closing verse of the Sapphic strophe (**1688** g).

b. *First Pherecratic:* ἐπταπύλοισι Θήβαις.[2] $-\cup\cup-\ \ \cup--$
　　Catalectic 　 ἃς τρέμομεν λέγειν.[3] 　 $-\cup\cup-\ \ \cup--$

c. *Second Pherecratic:* παιδὸς δύσφορον ἄτᾱν.[4] 　 $-\triangledown-\cup\ \ \cup--$
　　Catalectic 　 ἐκ μὲν δὴ πολέμων.[5] 　 $-\triangledown-\cup\ \ \cup-$

d. *First Glyconic:* ἵππι᾽ ἄναξ Πόσειδον, ᾧ.[6] 　 $-\cup\cup-\ \ \cup-\cup-$

e. *Second Glyconic:* Θήβᾳ τῶν προτέρων φάος.[7] 　 $-\triangledown-\cup\ \ \cup-\cup-$
　　　　　　δίπαις τοί σ᾽ ἐπιτύμβιος.[8] 　 $\cup--\cup\ \ \cup-\cup-$

f. *Third Glyconic:* φῶτα βάντα πανσαγίᾳ.[9] 　 $-\cup-\cup\ \ -\cup\cup-$
　　　　　　Ἔρως ἀνίκᾱτε μάχᾱν.[10] 　 $\cup-\cup-\ \ -\cup\cup-$

g. *Sapphic hendecasyllable,* making with the Adonic (a) the *Sapphic strophe:*

　　ποικιλόθρον᾽ ἀθάνατ᾽ ᾽Αφροδῑ́τᾱ,
　　$-\cup-\cup\ \ -\cup\cup-\ \ \cup\llcorner\triangledown$
　　παῖ Δίος, δολόπλοκε, λίσσομαί σε,
　　$-\cup-\cup\ \ -\cup\cup-\ \ \cup\llcorner\underset{\smile}{}$
　　μή μ᾽ ἄσαισι μηδ᾽ ὀνίαισι δάμνα,[11]
　　$-\cup-\cup\ \ -\cup\cup-\ \ \cup\llcorner\triangledown$
　　πότνια, θῦμον.
　　$-\cup\cup\ \ \llcorner\triangledown$

h. *Alcaic strophe:*

　　ἀσῠνέτημι τῶν ἀνέμων στάσιν.
　　$\cup-\cup-\ \ \cup-\cup\cup\ \ -\cup-$
　　τὸ μὲν γὰρ ἔνθεν κῦμα κυλίνδεται
　　$\cup-\cup-\ \ --\cup\cup\ \ -\cup-$
　　τὸ δ᾽ ἔνθεν · ἄμμες δ᾽ ὂν τὸ μέσσον νᾶι φορήμεθα σὺν μελαίνᾳ.[12]
　　$\cup-\cup-\ \ --\cup-\ \ --\cup\cup\ \ -\cup\cup-\ \ \cup\llcorner\triangledown$

i. *Lesser Asclepiadean:* 　 ἦλθες ἐκ περάτων γᾶς ἐλεφαντίναν
　　(three choriambs) 　 $-\cup|-\cup\cup-|-\cup\cup-|\cup-$
　　　　　　λάβᾱν τῶ ξίφεος χρῡσοδέτᾱν ἔχων.[13]
　　　　　　$\cup-|-\cup\cup-|-\cup\cup-|\cup-$

[1] Sapph. 1, 28.　　[5] S. *Ant.* 150.　　[8] Aesch. *Ch.* 334.　　[11] Sapph. 1, 1–4.
[2] Pind. *P.* 11, 11.　[6] Ar. *Eq.* 551.　　[9] S. *Ant.* 107.　　[12] Alcae. 6, 1–4.
[3] S. *O. C.* 129.　　[7] S. *Ant.* 101.　　[10] *ibid.* 781.　　[13] Alcae. 36,
[4] S. *Aj.* 643.

j. Greater Asclepiadean: μηδὲν ἄλλο φυτεύσῃς πρότερον δένδριον ἀμπέλω.[1]
   (four choriambs)   _ ∪ | _ ∪ ∪ _ | _ ∪ ∪ _ | _ ∪ ∪ _ | ∪ _

k. Eupolidean: ὦ θεώμενοι, κατερῶ πρὸς ὑμᾶς ἐλευθέρως.[2]
    _ ‾ _ ‾ _ ∪ ∪ _ ‾ _ _ ‾ _ ∪ ᵜ

l. Priapean: ἄριστον μὲν ὕδωρ, ὁ δὲ χρυσὸς αἰθόμενον πῦρ.[3]
    ∪ _ _ ∪ ∪ _ ∪ _ ∪ _ ∪ ∪ ∟ _

Dactylo-Epitritic Rhythms

1689. About half of the odes of Pindar are composed in a measure called *dactylo-epitritic*, which consists of dactyls, with their equivalent spondees and protracted forms (⎣⎦), and epitrites. The epitrite was said to be a foot of *seven times*, in these forms: ∪ _ _ _, _ ∪ _ _, _ _ ∪ _, _ _ _ ∪. The dactylic parts of the verse generally have the form _́ ∪ ∪ _́ ∪ ∪ _́ _ or (catalectic) _́ ∪ ∪ _́ ∪ ∪ _́ ∧. The epitrite also may be catalectic, _ ∪ _ ∧.

1690. The first strophe of Pindar's third Olympian ode is an example of this measure:

Τυνδαρίδαις τε φιλοξείνοις ἀδεῖν καλ‖‖λιπλοκάμῳ θ' Ἑλένᾳ
_́ ∪ ∪ _ ∪ ∪ _ _ _́ ∪ _ _ ‖ _́ ∪ ∪ _ ∪ ∪ _ ∧
κλεινὰν Ἀκράγαντα γεραίρων εὔχομαι,
_ _́ ∪ ∪ _ ∪ ∪ _ _ _́ ∪ _
Θήρωνος Ὀλυμπιονίκᾱν | ὕμνον ὀρθώσαις, ‖ ἀκαμαντοπόδων
_ _́ ∪ ∪ _ ∪ ∪ _ _ | _́ ∪ _ _ ‖ _́ ∪ ∪ _ ∪ ∪ _ ∧
ἵππων ἄωτον. Μοῖσα δ' οὕτω ποι παρέστᾱ μοι νεοσίγαλον εὑρόντι τρόπον
_ _́ ∪ _ _ | _ ∪ _ _ _ ∪ _ _ ‖ _́ ∪ ∪ _ ∪ ∪ _ _ _́ ∪ _
Δωρίῳ φωνὰν ἐναρμόξαι πεδίλῳ.
_́ ∪ _ _ _ ∪ _ _ _ ∪ _ _

[1] Alcae. 46.   [2] Ar. *Nub.* 518.   [3] Pind. *O.* 1, 1.

APPENDIX

CATALOGUE OF VERBS

This catalogue professes to contain all verbs in ordinary use in classic Greek which have any such peculiarities as to present difficulties to a student. No verb is introduced which does not occur in some form before Aristotle; and no forms are given which are not found in writers earlier than the Alexandrian period, except sometimes the present indicative of a verb which is classic in other tenses, and occasionally a form which is given for completeness and marked as *later*.

The forms printed in heavy type (except the lemmata and unless otherwise noted) are those which were in good Attic use, and may be employed by the student in writing Greek prose.

The verb stem, with any other important forms of the stem, is given in parentheses directly after the present indicative. The class of each verb is given by Arabic numeral in parentheses at the end, unless it is of the first class (608), or is a contract verb like τῑμάω (634).

A hyphen prefixed to a form (e.g. -ἐδρᾶν) indicates that it is found only in composition. This is omitted, however, if the simple form occurs even in later Greek; and it is often omitted when the occurrence of cognate forms, or any other reason, makes it probable that the simple form was in use. It would be extremely difficult to point out an example of every tense of even the best English verbs in a writer of established authority within a fixed period.

The imperfect or pluperfect is generally omitted when the present or perfect is given. Second perfects which are given among the principal parts of a verb (463) are not specially designated (see βλάπτω).

(ἀα-, ἀϝα-) *injure, infatuate*, stem with aor. ἄασα (ἄᾱσα), ἄσα; aor. p. ἀάσθην; pres. mid. ἀᾶται, aor. ἀασάμην *erred*. Vb. ἄᾱτος, in compos. ἀ-ἄᾱτος, ἄν-ᾱτος. Epic.

ἀγάλλω (ἀγαλ-) *ornament, honor*, ἀγαλῶ, ἤγηλα; ἀγάλλομαι *take pride in*, pres. and impf. (2)

ἄγαμαι (ἀγασ-, ἀγα-) *admire*, epic fut. ἀγάσ(σ)ομαι, ἠγάσθην, ἠγασάμην. Hom. also ἀγάομαι *admire*, Archil. ἀγαίομαι *envy*. Vb. ἀγαστός.

ἀγγέλλω (ἀγγελ-) *announce*, ἀγγελῶ [ἀγγελέω], ἤγγειλα, ἤγγελκα, ἤγγελμαι, ἠγγέλθην, fut. p. ἀγγελθήσομαι; aor. m. ἠγγειλάμην; 2 aor. pass. ἠγγέλην, Att. inscr. (2)

ἀγείρω (ἀγερ-) *collect*, ἤγειρα; epic plpf. p. ἀγηγέρατο; aor. p. ἠγέρθην, aor. m. (ἠγειράμην) ξυν-αγείρατο, 2 aor. m. ἀγερόμην with part. ἀγρόμενος. See ἠγερέθομαι. (2)

ἄγνῡμι (ϝαγ-), in comp. also ἀγνύω *break*, ἄξω, ἔαξα (537) rarely epic ἦξα, 2 pf. ἔᾱγα, Ion. ἔηγα, 2 aor. p. ἐάγην, epic ἐάγην or ἄγην. (3)

ἄγω *lead*, ἄξω, ἦξα (rare), ἦχα, ἦγμαι, ἤχθην, ἀχθήσομαι; 2 aor. ἤγαγον, ἠγαγόμην; fut. m. ἄξομαι (as pass.), Hom. aor. m. ἀξάμην, 2 aor. act. imv. ἄξετε, inf. ἀξέμεναι (654 h).

(ἀδε-) *be sated*, stem with aor. opt. ἀδήσειεν, pf. part. ἀδηκώς. Epic.

ᾄδω *sing*, ᾄσομαι (ᾄσω, rare), ᾖσα, ᾔσθην. Ion. and poet. ἀείδω, ἀείσω and ἀείσομαι, ἤεισα.

(ἀε-) *rest*, stem with aor. ἄεσα, ἄσα. Epic.

ἀέξω : Hom. for αὔξω.

ἄημι (ἀη-, ἀε-) *blow*, ἄητον, ἀεῖσι, inf. ἀῆναι, ἀήμεναι, part. ἀείς; impf. ἄην. Mid. ἄηται and ἄητο, part. ἀήμενος. Poetic, chiefly epic.

αἰδέομαι, poet. αἴδομαι *respect*, αἰδέσομαι, ᾔδεσμαι, ᾐδέσθην (as mid.), ᾐδεσάμην (chiefly poet., in prose *showed mercy*), Hom. imv. αἰδεῖο. 596, 597.

αἰνέω *praise*, αἰνέσω, ᾔνεσα, ᾔνεκα, ᾔνημαι, ᾐνέθην, 596, 599. Epic and lyric αἰνήσω, ᾔνησα. Usually in comp. Prose fut. usually -αινέσομαι.

αἴνυμαι *take*, impf. αἰνύμην. Epic. (3)

αἱρέω (αἱρε-, ἑλ-) *take*, mid. *choose*, αἱρήσω, ᾕρηκα, ᾕρημαι, Hdt. ἀραίρηκα, ἀραίρημαι, ᾑρέθην, αἱρεθήσομαι; fut. pf. ᾑρήσομαι (rare); 2 aor. εἷλον, ἕλω, etc.; εἱλόμην, ἕλωμαι, etc. (5)

αἴρω (ἀρ-) *take up*, ἀρῶ, ἦρα (689), ἦρκα, ἦρμαι, ἤρθην, ἀρθήσομαι; ἠράμην (689). Ion. and poet. ἀείρω (ἀερ-), ἤειρα, ἠέρθην. Hom. plpf. ἄωρτο (from ἤορτο) = ἤερτο; aor. m. ἀειράμην. Fut. ἀροῦμαι and 2 aor. ἠρόμην (with ἄρωμαι (ᾰ) etc.) belong to ἄρνυμαι (ἀρ-) *win*. (2)

αἰσθάνομαι (αἰσθ-, αἰσθε-) *perceive*, αἰσθήσομαι, ᾔσθημαι; ᾐσθόμην. Pres. αἴσθομαι (doubtful). (3)

αἰσχύνω (αἰσχυν-) *disgrace*, αἰσχυνῶ, ᾔσχῡνα, pf. p. part. epic ᾐσχυμμένος, ᾐσχύνθην *felt ashamed*, αἰσχυνθήσομαι; fut. m. αἰσχυνοῦμαι. (2)

ἀΐττω (ἀικ-, orig. ϝαι-ϝικ-) *rush*, ἀΐξω, ἤϊξα, ἠΐχθην, ἠϊξάμην. Also ᾄττω or ᾄσσω, ᾄξω, ᾖξα. Both rare in prose. (2)

ἀΐω *hear*, imp. ἄϊον, ᾖον, aor. -ήϊσα or -ῆσα. Vb. ἐπ-άϊστος. Ionic and poetic. ἀΐω *breathe out*, only impf. ἄϊον. Epic. See ἄημι.

ἀκαχίζω (ἀχ-, ἀκ-αχ-, 561, 617) *afflict*, redupl. pres., with ἀχέω and ἀχεύω *be grieved* (only in pres. part. ἀχέων, ἀχεύων) and ἄχομαι *be grieved*; fut. ἀκαχήσω, aor. ἀκάχησα; pf. p. ἀκάχημαι (ἀκηχέδαται), ἀκάχησθαι, ἀκαχήμενος or ἀκηχέμενος; 2 aor. ἤκαχον, ἀκαχόμην. See ἄχνυμαι and ἄχομαι. Epic. (2)

ἀκαχμένος (ἀκ-αχ-, 561, cf. ἄκ-ρον *edge*) *sharpened*, epic pf. part. with no present indicative in use.

ἀκέομαι (ἀκε-, ἀκεσ-) *heal,* aor. ἠκεσάμην. (2)

ἀκηδέω (ἀκηδε- for ἀκηδεσ-) *neglect,* aor. ἀκήδεσα epic (634). Epic and poetic. (2)

ἀκούω (ἀκου- for ἀκοϝ-) *hear,* ἀκούσομαι, ἤκουσα, pf. ἀκήκοα (for ἀκ-ηκοϝα, 721), plpf. ἠκηκόη or ἀκηκόη; ἠκούσθην, ἀκουσθήσομαι. 600.

ἀλαλάζω (ἀλαλαγ-) *raise the war-cry,* ἀλαλάξομαι, ἠλάλαξα. (2)

ἀλάομαι *wander,* pf. ἀλάλημαι (as pres.), w. inf. ἀλάλησθαι, part. ἀλαλήμενος, aor. ἀλήθην. Chiefly poetic.

ἀλδαίνω (ἀλδαν-) *nourish,* epic 2 aor. ἤλδανον. Pres. also ἀλδήσκω. Poetic. (2)

ἀλείφω (ἀλειφ-, ἀλιφ-) *anoint,* ἀλείψω, ἤλειψα, ἀλήλιφα (554), ἀλήλιμμαι, ἠλείφθην, ἀλειφθήσομαι (rare), 2 aor. p. ἠλίφην (rare). Mid. ἀλείψομαι, ἠλειψάμην.

ἀλέξω (ἀλεξ-, ἀλεξε-, ἀλεκ-, ἀλκ-) *ward off,* fut. ἀλέξομαι, epic ἀλεξήσω (590), Hdt. ἀλεξήσομαι; aor. ἠλέξησα (ἤλεξα, rare), ἠλεξάμην; epic 2 aor. ἄλαλκον.

ἀλέομαι *avoid,* epic; aor. ἠλεάμην. 37, 611. Cf. ἀλεύω.

ἀλεύω *avert,* ἀλεύσω, ἤλευσα. Mid. ἀλεύομαι *avoid,* aor. ἠλευάμην, with subj. ἐξ-αλεύσωμαι. Poetic. Cf. ἀλύσκω.

ἀλέω *grind,* ἤλεσα, ἀλήλεμαι (ἀλήλεσμαι). 596, 597.

ἄλθομαι (ἀλθ-, ἀλθε-) *be healed,* ἀλθήσομαι. Ionic and poetic.

ἁλίσκομαι (ἁλ-, ἁλο-) *be captured,* ἁλώσομαι, ἑάλωκα or ἥλωκα, 2 aor. ἑάλων or ἥλων, ἁλῶ (epic ἁλώω), ἁλοίην, ἁλῶναι, ἁλούς (694); all passive in meaning. 592, 604. No active ἁλίσκω, but see ἀν-ᾱλίσκω. (4)

ἀλιταίνομαι (ἀλιτ-, ἀλιταν-), with epic pres. act. ἀλιτραίνω *sin;* 2 aor. ἤλιτον, ἀλιτόμην, pf. part. ἀλιτήμενος *sinning.* Poetic, chiefly epic. (2, 3)

ἀλλάττω (ἀλλαγ-) *change,* ἀλλάξω, ἤλλαξα, ἤλλαχα, ἤλλαγμαι, ἠλλάχθην and ἠλλάγην, ἀλλαχθήσομαι and ἀλλαγήσομαι. Mid. fut. ἀλλάξομαι, aor. ἠλλαξάμην. (2)

ἄλλομαι (ἁλ-) *leap,* ἁλοῦμαι, ἡλάμην; 2 aor. ἡλόμην (rare). Epic 2 aor. ἆλσο, ἆλτο, ἄλμενος, athematic. 696 b. (2)

ἀλυκτάζω and ἀλυκτέω *be excited,* impf. ἀλύκταζον Hdt., pf. ἀλαλύκτημαι Hom. Ionic. (2)

ἀλύσκω (ἀλυκ-) *avoid,* ἀλύξω (epic ἀλύξομαι), ἤλυξα (rarely -άμην). Poetic. Ἀλύσκω is for ἀλυκ-σκω (648). Hom. also ἀλυσκάζω and ἀλυσκάνω. (4)

ἀλφάνω (ἀλφ-) *find, acquire,* epic 2 aor. ἦλφον. (3)

ἁμαρτάνω (ἁμαρτ-, ἁμαρτε-) *err,* ἁμαρτήσομαι, ἡμάρτηκα, ἡμάρτημαι, ἡμαρτήθην; 2 aor. ἥμαρτον, epic and Aeolic ἤμβροτον (108). (3)

ἀμβλίσκω (ἀμβλ-), ἀμβλόω in compos., *miscarry,* ἤμβλωσα, ἤμβλωκα, ἤμβλωμαι, ἠμβλώθην. (4)

ἀμείβω *change,* ἀμείψω, ἤμειψα. Mid. ἀμείβομαι *make return,* ἀμείψομαι, ἠμειψάμην; poetic ἠμειψάμην, ἠμείφθην *answered.* Mostly poetic.

ἀμείρω (ἀμερ-) and ἀμέρδω *deprive,* ἤμερσα, ἠμέρθην. Poetic. (2, 1)

ἀμπ-έχω and ἀμπ-ίσχω (ἀμφί and ἔχω, 105 d) wrap about, clothe, ἀμφέξω, 2 aor. ἤμπι-σχον; epic impf. ἄμπεχον. Mid. ἀμπέχομαι, ἀμπίσχομαι, ἀμπισχνέομαι; impf. ἠμπειχόμην; fut. ἀμφέξομαι; 2 aor. ἠμπι-σχόμην and ἠμπ-εσχόμην, 567. See ἔχω and ἴσχω.

ἀμπλακίσκω (ἀμπλακ-, ἀμπλακε-) err, miss, ἠμπλάκημαι; 2 aor. ἤμπλακον, part. ἀμπλακών or ἀπλακών. Poetic. (4)

ἄμπνυε, ἀμπνύνθην, ἄμπνῦτο, all epic: see ἀναπνέω.

ἀμύνω (ἀμυν-) ward off; fut. ἀμυνῶ, ἀμυνοῦμαι; aor. ἤμῡνα, ἠμῡνάμην. Also impf. ἠμύναθον, imv. ἀμῡνάθετε·(601). (2)

ἀμύττω (ἀμυχ-) scratch, epic ἀμύξω, ἤμυξα (Theocr.), ἠμυξάμην. Poetic and Ionic. (2)

ἀμφι-γνοέω doubt, ἠμφεγνόουν, ἠμφεγνόησα; aor. pass. part. ἀμφιγνοηθείς. 567.

ἀμφι-έννῡμι (see ἕννῡμι) clothe, fut. epic ἀμφιέσω, Att. ἀμφιῶ (678 c); ἠμφίεσα, ἠμφίεσμαι; ἀμφιέσομαι, ἀμφιεσάμην (poet.). 567. (3)

ἀμφισβητέω dispute, augmented ἠμφισ- and ἠμφεσ- (567); otherwise regular.

ἀναίνομαι (ἀναν-) refuse, impf. ἠναινόμην, poetic aor. ἠνηνάμην, ἀνήνασθαι. (2)

ἀναλίσκω (ἀλ-, ἀλο-, 592), and ἀναλόω expend, ἀνᾱλώσω, ἀνήλωσα (κατ-ηναλωσα late), ἀνήλωκα, ἀνήλωμαι (κατ-ηνᾱλωμαι late), ἀνηλώθην, ἀνᾱλωθήσομαι. See ἀλίσκομαι. (4)

ἀναπνέω take breath; see πνέω (πνευ-, πνυ-). Epic 2 aor. imv. ἄμπνυε, aor. p. ἀμπνύνθην, 2 aor. m. ἄμπνῦτο.

ἀνδάνω (ϝαδ- for σϝαδ-, ἀδ-, ἀδε-, 88) please, impf. Hom. ἄνδανον and ἑάνδανον, Hdt. ἤνδανον (ἑάνδανον?); fut. ἀδήσω Hdt.; pf. ἕᾱδα, epic; 2 aor. ἄδον, Ion. ἔαδον, epic εὔαδον for ἐϝϝαδον from ἐσϝαδον. Ionic and poetic. Cf. ἄσ-μενος pleased, as adj. (3)

ἀνέχω hold up, ἀνέχομαι endure, impf. ἠνειχόμην, fut. ἀνέξομαι and ἀνασχήσομαι, 2 aor. ἠνεσχόμην. See ἔχω, and 567.

ἀνήνοθε (ἀνεθ-, ἀνοθ-) defect. 2 pf. springs, sprung; in Il. 11, 266 as 2 plpf. (654 d). Epic.

ἀν-οίγνῡμι and ἀνοίγω (see οἴγνῡμι) open, impf. ἀνέῳγον (ἤνοιγον, rare), epic ἀνέῳγον with synizesis; ἀνοίξω, ἀνέῳξα (ἤνοιξα, rare), Hdt. MSS. ἄνοιξα; ἀνέῳχα, ἀνέῳγμαι, ἀνεῴχθην (subj. ἀνοιχθῶ etc.); fut. pf. ἀνεῴξομαι (pf. ἀνέῳγα late, very rare in Attic). (3)

ἀν-ορθόω set upright, augment ἀνωρ- and ἠνωρ-. 567.

ἀνύω, Attic also ἀνύτω accomplish; fut. ἀνύσω, Hom. -ανύω, ἀνύσομαι; aor. ἤνυσα, ἠνυσάμην; pf. ἤνυκα, ἤνυσμαι. 596. Poetic also ἄνω.

ἄνωγα, 2 pf. as pres., command, 1 pl. ἄνωγμεν, subj. ἀνώγω, opt. ἀνώγοιμι, imv. ἄνωγε (rare), also ἄνωχθι (with ἀνώχθω, ἄνωχθε), epic inf. ἀνωγέμεν; 2 plpf. ἠνώγεα, ἠνώγει (or ἀνώγει), epic also ἤνωγον (or ἄνωγον), see 654 d. Present forms ἀνώγει and ἀνώγετον (as if from ἀνώγω) occur in epic; also fut. ἀνώξω, aor. ἤνωξα. Poetic and Ionic.

ἀπ-αυράω *take away*, not found in present; impf. ἀπηύρων (as aor.); kindred forms are epic fut. ἀπουρήσω, and aor. part. ἀπούρας, ἀπουράμενος. Ἀπούρας is for ἀπο-ϝρᾱς, and ἀπηύρων for ἀπ-εϝρων (with η for ε). Poetic.

ἀπαφίσκω (ἀπ-αφ-, ἀπ-αφε-) *deceive*, -απάφησα (rare), 2 aor. -ήπαφον, m. opt. -απαφοίμην. Poetic. (4)

ἀπεχθάνομαι (ἐχθ-, ἐχθε-) *be hated*, ἀπεχθήσομαι, ἀπήχθημαι; 2 aor. ἀπηχθόμην. Late pres. ἀπέχθομαι. (3)

ἀπό(ϝ)ερσε *swept off*, subj. ἀποέρσῃ, opt. ἀποέρσειε (only in 3 pers.). Epic.

ἀποκτείνῡμι and -ύω, forms of ἀποκτείνω (sometimes written ἀποκτείννῡμι, -ύω, κτῑννῡμι, -ύω). See κτείνω.

ἀπόχρη *it suffices*, impersonal. See χρή.

ἅπτω (ἀφ-) *fasten, touch*, fut. ἅψω, ἅψομαι; aor. ἧψα, ἡψάμην; pf. ἧμμαι; aor. p. ἥφθην (see ἐάφθη). (2)

ἀράομαι *pray*, ἀράσομαι, ἠρᾱσάμην, ἤρᾱμαι. Ion. ἀρέομαι, ἀρήσομαι, ἠρησάμην. Epic act. inf. ἀρήμεναι.

ἀραρίσκω (ἀρ-) *fit*, ἧρσα, ἤρθην; 2 pf. ἄρᾱρα, Ion. ἄρηρα, plpf. ἀρήρεα and ἠρήρεα and ἠρήρει(ν); 2 aor. ἤραρον; 2 aor. m. part. ἄρμενος (as adj.) *fitting*. With form of Attic redupl. in pres. (646). Poetic. (4)

ἀράττω (ἀραγ-) *strike*, ἀράξω, ἤραξα, ἠράχθην. (2)

ἀρέσκω (ἀρε- for ἀρεσ-) *please*, ἀρέσω, ἤρεσα, ἠρέσθην; ἀρέσομαι, ἠρεσάμην. 596. (4)

ἀρημένος *oppressed*, perf. pass. part. Epic.

ἀρκέω (ἀρκε- for ἀρκεσ-) *assist, suffice*, ἀρκέσω, ἤρκεσα. 596.

ἁρμόττω, poet. ἁρμόζω (ἁρμοδ-) *fit*, ἁρμόσω, ἥρμοσα (συνάρμοξα Pind.), ἥρμοκα (Aristot.), ἥρμοσμαι, ἡρμόσθην, fut. p. ἁρμοσθήσομαι; aor. m. ἡρμοσάμην. (2)

ἄρνυμαι (ἀρ-) *win, secure*, fut. ἀροῦμαι, 2 aor. ἠρόμην (ἀρόμην). Chiefly poetic. See αἴρω. (3)

ἀρόω *plough*, ἤροσα, perf. mid. Ion. ἀρήρομαι, ἠρόθην. 596.

ἁρπάζω (ἁρπαγ-) *seize*, ἁρπάσω and ἁρπάσομαι, epic ἁρπάξω, ἥρπασα, epic ἥρπαξα, ἥρπακα, ἥρπασμαι (late ἥρπαγμαι), ἡρπάσθην, Hdt. ἡρπάχθην, ἁρπασθήσομαι. On the Attic forms, see 617, 624. (2)

ἀρύω and ἀρύτω *draw water*, aor. ἤρυσα, ἠρυσάμην, -ηρύθην, Ion. ἠρύσθην. 596.

ἄρχω *begin, rule*, ἄρξω, ἦρξα, (ἦρχα) ἦργμαι (mid.), ἤρχθην, ἀρχθήσομαι (Aristot.), ἄρξομαι (sometimes pass.), ἠρξάμην.

ἄσσω and ἄττω: see ἀίττω.

ἀτιτάλλω (ἀτιταλ-) *tend*; aor. ἀτίτηλα. Epic and lyric. (2)

αὐαίνω (αὐαν-) or αὑαίνω *dry*; fut. αὐανῶ; aor. ηὔηνα, ηὐάνθην or αὐάνθην, αὐανθήσομαι; fut. m. αὐανοῦμαι (as pass.). Augment ην- or αυ- (542). Chiefly poetic and Ionic. (2)

αὐξάνω or αὔξω (αὐξ-, αὐξε-) *increase,* αὐξήσω, αὐξήσομαι (sometimes pass.), ηὔξησα, ηὔξηκα, ηὔξημαι, ηὐξήθην, αὐξηθήσομαι. Also Ion. pres. ἀέξω, impf. ἄεξον. (3)

ἀφάσσω (see 623 and 625) *feel, handle,* aor. ἤφασα; used by Hdt. for ἀφάω or ἀφάω. (2)

ἀφ-ίημι *let go,* impf. ἀφίην or ἠφίην (567); fut. ἀφήσω, etc. See the inflection of ἵημι, 514.

ἀφύσσω (ἀφυγ-) *draw, pour,* ἀφύξω. Poetic, chiefly epic. See ἀφύω. (2)

ἀφύω *draw* (liquids), ἤφυσα, ἠφυσάμην. Poetic, chiefly epic.

ἄχθομαι (ἀχθ-, ἀχθε- for ἀχθεσ-, 596) *be displeased,* ἀχθέσομαι, ἠχθέσθην, ἀχθεσθήσομαι.

ἄχνυμαι (ἀχ-) *be troubled,* impf. ἀχνύμην. Poetic. (3) Also epic pres. ἄχομαι. See ἀκαχίζω.

ἄω (ἀ- for ἀ-, σα-, 87, cf. ἄ-δην, Lat. sa-tis) *satiate,* ἄσω, ἄσα; 2 aor. subj. ἔωμεν or ἑῶμεν from ἤομεν, pres. inf. ἄμεναι *to satiate one's self.* Mid. (ἄομαι) ἄαται (to be written ἄεται) as fut.; fut. ἄσομαι, aor. ἀσάμην. Epic.

βάζω (βακ-) *speak, utter,* βάξω, epic pf. βέβακται. Poetic. (2)

βαίνω (βα-, βαν-) *go,* βήσομαι, βέβηκα, βέβαμαι, ἐβάθην (rare); 2 aor. ἔβην (694); 2 pf., see 727; epic aor. mid. ἐβησάμην (rare) and ἐβησόμην, 654 *h.* In active sense, *cause to go,* βήσω, ἔβησα, poetic. See 643. The *simple* form is used in Attic prose only in the pres. and pf. active. 604. (2, 3)

βάλλω (βαλ-, βλη-, 169, 107, βαλλε-) *throw,* epic fut. βαλέω, βαλῶ, rarely βαλλήσω, βέβληκα, βέβλημαι, opt. δια-βεβλῇσθε (766), ἐβλήθην, βληθήσομαι; 2 aor. ἔβαλον, ἐβαλόμην; fut. m. βαλοῦμαι; fut. pf. βεβλήσομαι. Epic 2 aor. dual ξυμ-βλήτην; 2 aor. m. ἐβλήμην, with subj. βλήεται, opt. βλῇο or βλεῖο, inf. βλῆσθαι, part. βλήμενος; fut. ξυμβλήσεαι, pf. p. βέβληαι and βεβόλημαι. (2)

βάπτω (βαφ-) *dip,* βάψω, ἔβαψα, βέβαμμαι, ἐβάφην and (Aristoph.) ἐβάφθην; fut. m. βάψομαι. (2)

βάσκω (βα-) poetic form of βαίνω *go.* (4)

βαστάζω (see 618) *carry,* βαστάσω, ἐβάστασα. Later forms from stem βασταγ-. Poetic. (2)

βήττω (βηχ-) *cough,* βήξω, ἔβηξα. (2)

βιβάζω (βα-) *make go,* -βιβάσω and -βιβῶ (678), -εβίβασα. Cf. βαίνω. (2)

βίβημι (βα-) *go,* pres. part. βιβάς. Epic.

βιβρώσκω (βρω-) *eat,* pf. βέβρωκα, βέβρωμαι, ἐβρώθην Hdt.; 2 aor. ἔβρων; fut. pf. βεβρώσομαι Hom.; 2 pf. part. pl. βεβρῶτες. Hom. 2 pf. opt. βεβρώθοις from βρώθω (601). (4)

βιόω *live,* βιώσομαι, ἐβίωσα (rare), βεβίωκα, βεβίωμαι; 2 aor. ἐβίων (694). For ἐβιωσάμην see βιώσκομαι.

βιώσκομαι (βιο-), usually comp. ἀνα-βιώσκομαι *restore to life*, -εβιωσάμην *restored to life*, 2 aor. -εβίων intr. (4)

βλάπτω (βλαβ-) *injure*, βλάψω, ἔβλαψα, βέβλαφα, βέβλαμμαι, ἐβλάφθην; 2 aor. p. ἐβλάβην, 2 fut. βλαβήσομαι; fut. m. βλάψομαι; fut. pf. βεβλάψομαι Ion. 622 b. (2)

βλαστάνω (βλαστ-) *sprout*, βλαστήσω, βεβλάστηκα and ἐβλάστηκα (546); 2 aor. ἔβλαστον. (3)

βλέπω *look*, βλέψομαι, Hdt. ἀνα-βλέψω, ἔβλεψα.

βλίττω (μλιτ-, βλιτ-, 108) *take honey*, aor. ἔβλισα. (2)

βλώσκω (μολ-, μλω-, βλω-, 108) *go*, fut. μολοῦμαι, pf. μέμβλωκα, 2 aor. ἔμολον. Poetic. (4)

βοάω *shout*, βοήσομαι, ἐβόησα. Ion. (stem βο-) βώσομαι, ἔβωσα, ἐβωσάμην, (βέβωμαι) βεβωμένος, ἐβώσθην.

βόσκω (βο-, βοσκ-, βοσκε-) *feed*, βοσκήσω. (4)

βούλομαι (βουλ-, βουλε-) *will*, *wish* (augm. ἐβουλ- or ἠβουλ-); βουλήσομαι, βεβούλημαι, ἐβουλήθην; epic 2 pf. προ-βέβουλα *prefer*. Epic pres. also βόλομαι. 536.

(βραχ-) stem, only 2 aor. ἔβραχε and βράχε *resounded*. Epic.

βρίζω (see 618) *be drowsy*, aor. ἔβριξα. Poetic. (2)

βρίθω *be heavy*, βρίσω, ἔβρῑσα, βέβρῑθα. Rare in Attic prose.

(βροχ-) stem, *swallow*, aor. ἔβροξα (opt. -βρόξειε), 2 aor. p. ἀναβροχείς; 2 pf. ἀναβέβροχε *Il*. 17, 54 (Zenodotus). Epic. Cf. κατα-βροχθίζω *gulp down* (Ar.).

βρῡχάομαι (βρῡχ-, βρῡχα-, 591) *roar*, 2 pf. βέβρῡχα; -εβρῡχησάμην; βρῡχηθείς.

βῡνέω or βύω (βῠ- for βυσ-) *stop up*, βύσω, ἔβῡσα, βέβυσμαι. 639. Chiefly poetic. (3)

γαμέω (γαμ-, γαμε-) *marry* (said of a man), fut. γαμῶ, aor. ἔγημα, pf. γεγάμηκα; pf. p. γεγάμημαι (of a woman). Mid. *marry* (of a woman), fut. γαμοῦμαι, aor. ἐγημάμην. 590, 1245.

γάνυμαι *rejoice*, epic fut. γανύσσομαι. Chiefly poetic. (3)

γέγωνα (γων-, γωνε-), 2 pf. as pres. *shout*, subj. γεγώνω, imv. γέγωνε, epic inf. γεγωνέμεν, part. γεγωνώς; 2 plpf. ἐγεγώνει, with ἐγέγωνε and 1 sing. ἐγεγώνευν (654 d). Derived pres. γεγωνέω, w. fut. γεγωνήσω, aor. ἐγεγώνησα. Chiefly poetic. Present also γεγωνίσκω.

γείνομαι (γεν-) *be born*; aor. ἐγεινάμην *begat*. (2)

γελάω (γελα- for γελασ-) *laugh*, γελάσομαι, ἐγέλασα, ἐγελάσθην. 596, 597.

γέντο *seized*, epic 2 aor., *Il*. 18, 476. (See ἐγένετο, γίγνομαι).

γηθέω (γηθ-, γηθε-) *rejoice*, poetic γηθήσω, ἐγήθησα; pf. γέγηθα as pres. 590.

γηράσκω and less common γηράω (γηρα-) *grow old*, γηράσομαι, less often γηράσω, ἐγήρᾱσα, γεγήρᾱκα *am old*; 2 aor. (694) inf. γηρᾶναι, Hom. part. γηράς. (4)

γίγνομαι (γεν-, γενε-, γον-, γν-) *become* (605), γενήσομαι, γεγένημαι, ἐγενήθην
Dor. and Ion., γενηθήσομαι (rare); 2 aor. ἐγενόμην (epic γέντο for ἐγένετο);
2 pf. γέγονα *am*. For γεγάᾱσι, γεγώς, and other athematic forms, see
727. After 300 B.C. γίγνομαι in Attic became γίνομαι, as in New Ionic
and Doric. 586, 604.

γιγνώσκω (γνω-, γνο-) *know*, γνώσομαι, ἀν-έγνωσα, ἔγνωκα, ἔγνωσμαι, ἐγνώσθην;
2 aor. ἔγνων *perceived* (694). New Ionic, and Attic after 300 B.C.,
γῑνώσκω. (4)

γλύφω *carve*, ἐν-έγλυψα Hdt., ἐγλυψάμην Theocr., γέγλυμμαι and ἔγλυμμαι
(546).

γνάμπτω (γναμπ-) *bend*, γνάμψω, ἔγναμψα, ἐγνάμφθην. Poetic, chiefly epic.
See κάμπτω. (2)

γοάω (γο-, 591) *bewail*, 2 aor. γόον, only epic in active. Mid. γοάομαι,
poetic; epic fut. γοήσομαι.

γράφω *write*, γράψω, ἔγραψα, γέγραφα, γέγραμμαι, 2 aor. p. ἐγράφην (ἐγράφθην
late); 2 fut. p. γραφήσομαι; fut. pf. γεγράψομαι, aor. m. ἐγραψάμην.

γρύζω (γρυγ-) *grunt*, γρύξομαι (γρύξω late), ἔγρυξα. Chiefly Att. comedy. (2)

(δα-) *teach, learn*, no pres., (δαε-) δαήσομαι, δεδάηκα, δεδάημαι; 2 aor. mid.
inf. δεδαέσθαι (MSS. δεδάασθαι); 2 pf. pt. δεδαώς (726); 2 aor. ἔδαον
learned, redupl. δέδαον *taught*; 2 aor. p. ἐδάην *learned*. Cf. Hom. δήω
shall find, and διδάσκω. Poetic, chiefly epic.

δαιδάλλω (δαιδαλ-, δαιδαλο-) *deck out, ornament*, epic and lyric. Pindar has
pf. p. part. δεδαιδαλμένος, aor. part. δαιδαλθείς; also fut. inf. δαιδαλωσέμεν
(592). (2)

δαΐζω (δαϊγ-) *rend*, δαΐξω, ἐδάϊξα, δεδάϊγμαι, ἐδαΐχθην. Epic, lyric, and
tragic. (2)

δαίνῡμι (δαι-) *entertain*, δαίσω, ἔδαισα, (ἐδαίσθην) δαισθείς. Epic δαίνῡ, impf.
and pres. imv. Mid. δαίνυμαι *feast*, δαίσομαι, ἐδαισάμην; epic pres. opt.
δαινῦτο for δαινυ-το, δαινῡατο for δαινυ-ατο (654 c): see 766. (3)

δαίομαι (δασ-, δασι-, δαι-, 636) *divide*, epic fut. δάσομαι, aor. ἐδασάμην, pf. p.
δέδασμαι, epic δέδαιμαι. (2) See also δατέομαι.

δαίω (δαϝ-, δαϝι-, δαι-, 636) *kindle*, epic 2 pf. δέδηα, 2 plpf. 3 pers. δεδήει;
2 aor. (ἐδαόμην) subj. δάηται. Poetic. (2)

δάκνω (δηκ-, δακ-) *bite*, δήξομαι, δέδηγμαι, ἐδήχθην, δηχθήσομαι; 2 aor. ἔδακον.
(3)

δάμνημι (642), (δαμνάω?) (δαμ-, δμη-, δαμα-), also pres. δαμάζω (620), *tame*,
subdue, fut. δαμάσω, δαμάω, δαμῶ (with Hom. δαμάᾳ, δαμᾷ, δαμόωσι), aor.
ἐδάμασα, pf. p. δέδμημαι, aor. p. ἐδμήθην and ἐδαμάσθην; epic also 2 aor. p.
ἐδάμην (with δάμεν); fut. pf. δεδμήσομαι; fut. m. δαμάσομαι; aor. ἐδαμασάμην. In Attic prose only δαμάζω, ἐδαμάσθην, ἐδαμασάμην. 659, 678 b.
(3, 2)

CATALOGUE OF VERBS   371

δαρθάνω (δαρθ-, δαρθε-) *sleep*, 2 aor. ἔδαρθον, poet. ἔδραθον; p. **κατα-δεδαρθηκώς**. (Usually in comp. κατα-δαρθάνω, except 2 aor.) **(3)**

δατέομαι (δατ-, δατε-) *divide*, δάσ(σ)ομαι, **-εδασάμην** (in prose rare), epic ἐδασ(σ)άμην; Hes. δατέασθαι (should be written δατέεσθαι). See δαίομαι.

δέαμαι *appear*, only in impf. δέατο Od. 6, 242. Cf. δοάσσατο Il. 13, 458.

δέδια *fear*: see δέδοικα.

δέδοικα, pf. as pres. (δϝει-, δϝοι-, δϝι-, 34), epic δείδοικα, 552, *fear*. Epic fut. δείσομαι, aor. ἔδεισα; 2 pf. **δέδια**, epic δείδια; for full forms see 727. From stem δϝι- Homer forms impf. δίον, δίε *feared, fled*. Epic present δείδω *fear*. See also δίεμαι.

δείδεκτο *welcomed* Il. 9, 224, pf. δειδέχαται Od. 7, 72, plpf. δειδέχατο Il. 4, 4, probably belong with δέχομαι (652); some refer to δείκνῡμι or to a still different base δηκ-. Cf. δεικανόωντο *made welcome* Il. 15, 86.

δείκνῡμι (δεικ-) *show*: for synopsis and inflection see 503, 504, and 507. Ion. (δεκ-), δέξω, ἔδεξα, δέδεγμαι, ἐδέχθην, ἐδεξάμην. Epic pf. m. δείδεγμαι *greet* (for δέδεγμαι) probably comes from another stem δεκ- or δηκ- (see δέχομαι). 552, 553. **(3)**

δέμω (δεμ-, δμη-) *build*, ἔδειμα, δέδμημαι, ἐδειμάμην. Ionic and poetic.

δέρκομαι (δερκ-, δορκ-, δρακ-) *see*, ἐδέρχθην; 2 aor. ἔδρακον, (ἐδράκην) δρακείς; pf. δέδορκα (585, 587). Poetic.

δέρω (δερ-, δαρ-) *flay*, **δερῶ**, ἔδειρα, δέδαρμαι; 2 aor. ἐδάρην. Ionic and poetic also **δείρω** (δερ-). 585, 633.

δέχομαι *receive, await, accept*, δέξομαι, δέδεγμαι, ἐδέχθην, ἐδεξάμην; 2 aor. m. (chiefly epic) ἐδέγμην, δέκτο, imv. δέξο (788 a), inf. δέχθαι, part. δέγμενος (sometimes as pres.). So Hom. 3 pl. δέχαται (652).

δέω *bind*, δήσω, ἔδησα, δέδεκα (δέδηκα doubtful), δέδεμαι, ἐδέθην, δεθήσομαι; fut. pf. δεδήσομαι, aor. m. ἐδησάμην.

δέω (δεϝ-, δε-, δεε-) *want, need*, δεήσω, ἐδέησα, epic ἔδησα, δεδέηκα, δεδέημαι, ἐδεήθην. Mid. **δέομαι** *ask*, δεήσομαι. From epic stem δενε- come ἐδένησα Od. 9, 540 and δεύομαι, δευήσομαι. Impersonal **δεῖ**, debet, *there is need, (one) ought*, δεήσει, ἐδέησε.

δηριάω and **δηρίω**, act. rare (δηρι-, δηρια-, 591), *contend*, aor. ἐδήρῑσα (Theocr.), aor. p. δηρίνθην as middle (Hom.). Mid. δηριάομαι and δηρίομαι, as act., δηρίσομαι (Theocr.), ἐδηρῑσάμην (Hom.). Epic and lyric.

δήω, epic present with future meaning, *shall find*. See stem δα-.

διαιτάω *arbitrate*, with double augment in pf. and plpf. and in compounds (565 and 567); διαιτήσω, διῄτησα (ἀπ-εδιῄτησα), δεδιῄτηκα, δεδιῄτημαι, διῃτήθην (ἐξ-εδιῃτήθην, late); διαιτήσομαι, κατ-εδιῃτησάμην *effected a settlement*.

διᾱκονέω *wait on*, ἐδιᾱκόνουν; διᾱκονήσω, (aor. inf. διᾱκονῆσαι), δεδιᾱκόνημαι, ἐδιᾱκονήθην. Later and doubtful (poetic) earlier forms with augment διη- or δεδιη-. See 565.

διδάσκω (διδαχ-) for διδαχ-σκω (648) *teach*, **διδάξω, ἐδίδαξα**, epic ἐδιδάσκησα (stem διδασκε-), **δεδίδαχα, δεδίδαγμαι, ἐδιδάχθην**; **διδάξομαι**, ἐδιδαξάμην. See stem **δα-**. (**4**)

δίδημι (δη-, δε-) *bind*, chiefly poetic form for **δέω**; Xen. **διδέᾱσι**.

διδράσκω (δρᾱ-) only in comp., *run away*, **-δρᾱσομαι, -δέδρᾱκα**; 2 aor. **-έδρᾱν**, Ion. **-έδρην**, -δρῶ, -δραίην, -δρᾶναι, -δρᾶς (694). (**4**)

δίδωμι (δω-, δο-) *give*, **δώσω, ἔδωκα, δέδωκα**, etc.; see synopsis and inflection in **503, 504, 507**. Ep. δόμεναι or δόμεν (= δοῦναι), fut. διδώσω (= δώσω), 2 aor. iterative δόσκον (**606**).

δίεμαι (διε-) *be frightened, flee* (612), inf. δίεσθαι *to flee* or *to drive* (*chase*); δίωμαι and διοίμην (cf. δύνωμαι, **761**, and τιθοίμην, **773**) *chase*, part. διόμενος *chasing*. Impf. act. ἐν-δίεσαν *set on* (of dogs) *Il.* 18, 584.

δίζημαι (δι-διη-, cf. **ζητέω**) *seek*; διζήσομαι, ἐδιζησάμην. Ionic and poetic. (**δικ-**) stem, 2 aor. ἔδικον *threw, cast*. In Pindar and the tragedians.

διψάω (διψη-, διψα-) *thirst*, **διψήσω, ἐδίψησα**. See **486**.

διώκω *pursue*, **διώξομαι** (διώξω), **ἐδίωξα, δεδίωχα, ἐδιώχθην**. For ἐδιώκαθον see **601**.

δοκέω (δοκ-, δοκε-) *seem, think*, **δόξω, ἔδοξα, δέδογμαι, ἐδόχθην** (rare). Poetic δοκήσω, ἐδόκησα, δεδόκηκα, δεδόκημαι, ἐδοκήθην. Impersonal, **δοκεῖ** *it seems*, etc. **590**.

δουπέω (δουπ-, δουπε-) *sound heavily*, ἐδούπησα; epic δούπησα and ἐπι-γδούπησα, 2 pf. δέδουπα, δεδουπώς *fallen*. Chiefly poetic. **590**.

δράττομαι or **δράσσομαι** (δραγ-) *grasp*, aor. ἐδραξάμην, pf. δέδραγμαι. (**2**)

δράω *do*, **δράσω, ἔδρᾱσα, δέδρᾱκα, δέδρᾱμαι** (doubtful δέδρᾱσμαι), **ἐδράσθην**. **598**.

δύναμαι *be able*, augm. usually ἐδυν-, also ἠδυν- (536); 2 p. sing. pres. (poet.) δύνᾳ, Ion. δύνη, impf. ἐδύνω (ἐδύνασο late, **667**); **δυνήσομαι, δεδύνημαι, ἐδυνήθην** (ἐδυνάσθην, chiefly Ionic).

δύω *enter* or *cause to enter*, also *go down*, and **δύνω** (δῡ-, δυ-) *enter*; **δύσω, ἔδῡσα, δέδῡκα, δέδυμαι, ἐδύθην**, fut. p. δυθήσομαι; 2 aor. **ἔδῡν**, inflected p. 125, see **503** and **694**; fut. m. δύσομαι, aor. m. ἐδῡσάμην, epic ἐδῡσόμην (654 *h*).

ἐάφθη with ἐπί, *was hurled upon* (? *Il.* 13, 543; 14, 419), aor. pass. commonly referred to ἅπτω; also to ἕπομαι; possibly it should be referred to stem ϝαπ (ἰάπτω).

ἐάω *permit, let alone*, **ἐάσω, εἴᾱσα, εἴᾱκα, εἴᾱμαι, εἰάθην**; **ἐάσομαι** (as pass.). Ep. εἰάω, impf. ἔᾱ, aor. ἔᾱσα. For augment, see **537**.

ἐγγυάω *pledge, betroth*, augm. ἠγγυ- or ἐνεγυ- (ἐγγεγυ-), see **565, 567**.

ἐγείρω (ἐγερ-, ἐγορ-, ἐγρ-, **34**) *raise, rouse*, **ἐγερῶ, ἤγειρα, ἐγήγερμαι, ἠγέρθην**; 2 pf. **ἐγρήγορα** *am awake*, Hom. ἐγρηγόρθᾱσι, imv. ἐγρήγορθε, inf. ἐγρήγορθαι or -ορθαι; 2 aor. m. ἠγρόμην, epic ἐγρόμην. For ἐγρήγορα see **557**. (**2**)

CATALOGUE OF VERBS 373

ἔδω *eat*, poetic (chiefly epic) present: see ἐσθίω.

ἕζομαι (ἑδ- for σεδ-; cf. sed-eo) *sit*, fut. inf. ἐφ-έσσεσθαι trans. (Hom.); aor. εἰσάμην, epic ἐσσάμην and ἑεσσάμην. Active aor. εἶσα and ἔσσα (Hom.). 87, 88. Chiefly poetic. (2). See ἵζω and καθέζομαι.

ἐθέλω (ἐθελ-, ἐθελε-) and θέλω *wish*, impf. ἤθελον; ἐθελήσω or θελήσω, ἠθέλησα, ἠθέληκα. Ἐθέλω is the more common form except in the tragic trimeter. Impf. always ἤθελον; aor. (probably) always ἠθέλησα, but subj. etc. ἐθελήσω and θελήσω, inf. ἐθελῆσαι and θελῆσαι, etc.

ἐθίζω (see 620) *accustom*, ἐθιῶ (678 c), εἴθισα, εἴθικα, εἴθισμαι, εἰθίσθην. The base is σϝεθ- (see 537). (2)

ἔθων (σϝεθ-) Hom. pres. part.: see εἴωθα.

εἶδον (ἰδ-, ϝιδ-), vid-i, 2 aor. *saw*, no present (see 537): ἴδω, ἴδοιμι, ἴδε or ἰδέ, ἰδεῖν, ἰδών. Mid. (chiefly poet.) εἴδομαι (ϝειδ-) *seem*, epic εἰσάμην and ἐεισάμην; 2 aor. εἰδόμην (in prose rare and only in comp.) *saw* = εἶδον. Οἶδα, 2 pf. as pres. (ϝοιδ-) *know*, plpf. ᾔδη *knew*, fut. εἴσομαι; see 529. (5)

εἰκάζω (see 620) *make like*, ᾔκαζον, εἰκάσω, ᾔκασα, ᾔκασμαι (εἴκασμαι), εἰκάσθην, εἰκασθήσομαι. (2)

εἴκω, not used in pres. (εἰκ-, οἰκ-, ἰκ-), *resemble, appear*, impf. εἶκον, fut. εἴξω (rare), 2 pf. ἔοικα, Ion. οἶκα (with ἔοιγμεν, εἴκτον (728), εἴξασι, εἰκέναι, εἰκώς, chiefly poetic); 2 plpf. ἐῴκη, with ἔϊκτην. Impersonal ἔοικε *it seems*, etc. For ἔοικα, see 537, 549.

εἴκω *yield*, εἴξω, εἶξα. For εἴκαθον see 601.

εἰλέω (εἰλ-, εἰλ-) *press, roll up* (590), aor. ἔλσα, pf. p. ἔελμαι, 2 aor. p. ἐάλην or ἄλην w. inf. ἀλήμεναι. Pres. pass. εἴλομαι. Epic. Hdt. has (in comp.) -είλησα, -είλημαι, -ειλήθην (Thuc.). Pind. has plpf. ἐόλει. The Attic has εἰλέομαι, and εἴλλω or εἴλλω. See ἴλλω.

εἰμί *be* and εἶμι *go*. See 509-513.

εἶπον (ἐπ- for ϝεπ-) *said*, epic ἔειπον, 2 aor., no present; εἴπω, εἴποιμι, εἰπέ, εἰπεῖν, εἰπών; Ion. and late Att. 1 aor. εἶπα, poet. ἔειπα (opt. εἴπαιμι, imv. εἶπον, inf. εἶπαι, part. εἴπας), Hdt. ἀπ-ειπάμην. Other tenses are supplied by a stem ἐρ-, ῥε- (for ϝερ-, ϝρη-, Lat. ver-bum): Hom. pres. (rare) εἴρω, fut. ἐρέω, ἐρῶ; pf. εἴρηκα, εἴρημαι (552); aor. p. ἐρρήθην, rarely ἐρρέθην, Ion. εἰρέθην; fut. pass. ῥηθήσομαι; fut. pf. εἰρήσομαι. See ἐνέπω. (5)

εἴργνῡμι and (rarely) εἰργνύω, also εἴργω (εἰργ-), *shut in*; εἴρξω, εἶρξα, εἴργμαι, εἴρχθην. Also ἔργω, ἔρξω, ἔρξα, Hom. pf. (ἔργμαι) 3 pl. ἔρχαται, plpf. ἔρχατο (652), ἔρχθην. Often with smooth breathing, εἴργω, εἴρξω, etc., Soph. ἔρξεται. Epic also ἐέργω. (3, 1)

εἴρομαι (εἰρ-, εἰρε-) Ion. *ask*, fut. εἰρήσομαι. Hom. ἐρέϝω (rare), subj. ἐρείομεν (for ἐρεγομεν); ἐρέϝομαι, imv. ἔρειο or ἐρεῖο. See ἔρομαι.

εἴρω (ϝερ-) *say*, epic in present. See εἶπον.

εἴρω (ἐρ- for σερ-, Lat. sero) *join*, aor. -εῖρα, Ion. -έρσα, pf. -εῖρκα, εἴρμαι, epic ἔερμαι. Rare except in composition. (2)

ἴσκω (ϝικ-, redupl. ϝεϝικ-) *liken, compare* (561, 648); poetic, chiefly epic: pres. also ἴσκω. Προσ-ήϊξαι *art like* (Eur.) and epic ἤϊκτο or ἔϊκτο, sometimes referred to εἴκω. See εἴκω. (4)

εἴωθα, Ionic ἔωθα (ἐθ- for σϝεθ-, 537, 719), pf. *am accustomed*, plpf. εἰώθη. Hom. has pres. act. part. ἔθων.

ἐκκλησιάζω *hold an assembly*; augm. ἠκκλη- and ἐξεκλη- (565).

ἐλαύνω, for ἐλα-νυ-ω (641), poetic ἐλάω (ἐλα-) *drive, march*, fut. (ἐλάσω) ἐλῶ (678 b), epic ἐλάσσω, ἐλόω; ἤλασα, ἐλήλακα, ἐλήλαμαι, Ion. and late ἐλήλασμαι, Hom. plpf. ἐληλέδατο (558), ἠλάθην, ἠλασάμην. (3)

ἐλέγχω *test, confute*, ἐλέγξω, ἤλεγξα, ἐλήλεγμαι (497 b), ἠλέγχθην, ἐλεγχθήσομαι.

ἐλίττω (rarely εἰλίττω, Hdt. εἰλίσσω, stem ἑλικ- for ϝελικ-) *roll*, ἑλίξω, εἵλιξα (537), εἵλιγμαι, εἰλίχθην, ἐξ-ελιχθήσομαι. Epic aor. m. ἐλιξάμην, plpf. m. ἐέλικτο (MSS. ἐλέλικτο), aor. p. ἐελίχθησαν (MSS. ἐλελίχθησαν). Written also ἑλίττω etc. (2)

ἕλκω (ἑλκ- for σελκ-, ἑλκυ-) *pull*, ἕλξω (Ion. and late Att. ἑλκύσω), εἵλκυσα, εἵλκυκα, εἵλκυσμαι, εἱλκύσθην. Pres. ἑλκύω late. 537.

ἐλπίζω (ἐλπιδ-) *hope*, aor. ἤλπισα; aor. p. part. ἐλπισθέν. (2)

ἔλπω (ἐλπ- for ϝελπ-) *cause to hope*, pf. ἔολπα (for ϝε-ϝολπα) *hope*; plpf. ἐώλπεα (585). Mid. ἔλπομαι *hope*, like Attic ἐλπίζω. Epic.

ἐμέω *vomit*, fut. ἐμοῦμαι, ἐμῶ (rare); aor. ἤμεσα. 596.

ἐναίρω (ἐναρ-) *kill*, 2 aor. ἤναρον. Hom. aor. m. ἐνήρατο. Poetic. (2)

ἐνέπω (ἐν and stem σεπ-, σπ-, σπε-) or ἐννέπω *say, tell*, epic fut. ἐνι-σπήσω and ἐνίψω; 2 aor. ἔνι-σπον, w. imv. ἔνισπε, epic ἐνίσπες, 2 pl. ἔσπετε for ἐν-σπετε, inf. ἐνισπεῖν, epic -έμεν. Poetic. See εἶπον.

ἐνίπτω (ἐνιπ-) *chide*, epic also ἐνίσσω, 2 aor. ἐνένιπον and ἠνίπαπον (559). (2)

ἕννῡμι (ἑ- for ϝεσ-, cf. ves-tio) *clothe*, pres. act. only in comp.; epic fut. ἕσσω, aor. ἕσσα, ἐσ(σ)άμην or ἑεσσάμην (for ἑϝεσσάμην); pf. ἕσμαι or εἷμαι, εἱμένος in trag. In comp. -έσω, -εσα, -εσάμην. Chiefly epic: ἀμφι-έννῡμι is the common form in prose. (3)

ἐνοχλέω *bother*, w. double augment (567); ἠνώχλουν, ἐνοχλήσω, ἠνώχλησα, ἠνώχλημαι.

ἔοικα *seem*, perfect: see εἴκω.

ἑορτάζω (see 616), Ion. ὀρτάζω *keep festival*; impf. ἑώρταζον (for ἠορταζον, 33). (2)

ἐπ-αυρέω and ἐπ-αυρίσκω (αὐρ-, αὐρε-) *enjoy*, both rare, 2 aor. Dor. and epic ἐπαῦρον; epic fut. m. ἐπαυρήσομαι, aor. ἐπηυράμην, 2 aor. ἐπηυρόμην. Chiefly poetic. 590. (4)

ἐπ-ενήνοθε, defect. 2 pf. *sit on, lie on*; also as 2 plpf. (654 d). Epic. See ἀνήνοθε.

ἐπίσταμαι *understand*, 2 p. sing. (poet.) ἐπίστᾳ, Ion. ἐπίστεαι, impf. ἠπιστά-μην, 2 p. sing. ἠπίστασο or ἠπίστω (667); fut. ἐπιστήσομαι, aor. ἠπιστήθην. Not to be confounded with forms of ἐφίστημι.

ἕπω (σεπ-, σπ-) *be after, be busy with,* impf. εἶπον (poet. ἕπον); fut. -έψω, 2 aor. -έσπον (for ἐ-σεπ-ον), aor. p. περι-έφθην (Hdt.): active chiefly Ionic or poetic, and in compos. Mid. ἕπομαι *follow,* fut. ἕψομαι; 2 aor. ἑσπόμην (σπῶμαι, σποίμην, σποῦ, σπέσθαι, σπόμενος). Hom. imv. σπεῖο for σποῦ. 87, 537.

ἐράω *love,* ἠράσθην *fell in love,* ἐρασθήσομαι, epic ἠρασ(σ)άμην. Poetic pres. ἔραμαι, impf. ἠράμην.

ἐργάζομαι (ϝεργ-) *work, do;* ἐργάσομαι, εἴργασμαι, ἠργάσθην, ἠργασάμην, ἐργασθήσομαι. 537, 616. (2)

ἔργω and εἴργω: see εἴργνῡμι (εἴργω).

ἔρδω and ἔρδω *work, do* (ϝεργ-ι̯ω, ϝρεγ-ι̯ω, 618, 537); fut. ἔρξω, aor. ἔρξα, Ion. 2 pf. ἔοργα, 2 plpf. ἐώργεα (for ἐϝεϝοργεα), Ion. ἐόργεα. Ionic and poetic. See ῥέζω.

ἐρείδω *prop,* ἐρείσω (later), ἤρεισα, Ion. -ήρεικα, epic ἐρήρεισμαι with ἐρηρέδαται and -ατο, 654 c, 558, ἠρείσθην; ἐρείσομαι (Aristot.), ἠρεισάμην.

ἐρείκω (ἐρεικ-, ἐρικ-) *tear, burst,* ἤρειξα, ἐρήριγμαι, 2 aor. ἤρικον. Ionic and poetic.

ἐρείπω (ἐρειπ-, ἐριπ-) *throw down,* ἐρείψω, epic ἤρειψα, 2 pf. ἐρήριπα *have fallen,* pf. p. ἐρήριμμαι (plpf. ἐρέριπτο, Hom.), 2 aor. ἤριπον, ἠρίπην, aor. m. ἀν-ηρειψάμην (Hom.), aor. p. ἠρείφθην.

ἐρέσσω (ἐρετ-) *row,* epic aor. δι-ήρεσ(σ)α. 625. (2)

ἐρέω *ask,* epic. See εἴρομαι and cf. ἔρομαι.

ἐριδαίνω *contend,* aor. m. inf. ἐρῑδήσασθαι. Epic. (3)

ἐρίζω (ἐριδ-) *contend,* ἤρισ(σ)α, ἐρήρισμαι. Poetic. (2)

ἔρομαι (rare), Ion. εἴρομαι, epic ἐρέω or ἐρέομαι (ϝερ-, ϝερε-) for the Attic ἐρωτάω *ask,* fut. ἐρήσομαι, Ion. εἰρήσομαι, 2 aor. ἠρόμην. See εἴρομαι.

ἕρπω (σερπ-) *creep,* impf. εἷρπον; fut. ἕρψω. Also ἑρπύζω, aor. εἵρπυσα. Poetic. 537.

ἔρρω (ἐρρ-, ἐρρε-) *go to destruction,* ἐρρήσω, ἤρρησα, εἰσ-ήρρηκα.

ἐρυγγάνω (ἐρυγ-) *eruct,* 2 aor. ἤρυγον. (3). Ion. ἐρεύγομαι, ἐρεύξομαι.

ἐρύκω *hold back,* epic fut. ἐρύξω, ἤρυξα (Xen.), epic 2 aor. ἠρύκακον.

ἔρῡμαι (ϝερῡ-) and εἴρυμαι (ἐϝρῡ-) *protect;* 3 pl. εἰρύαται and εἴρᾱται, inf. ἔρυσθαι or εἴρυσθαι; impf. ἔρῡτο and εἴρῡτο, εἴρυατο; fut. ἐρύσ(σ)ομαι and εἰρύσ(σ)ομαι, aor. ἐρυσ(σ)άμην and εἰρυσ(σ)άμην. See ῥύομαι.

ἐρύω (ϝερυ-, ϝρῡ-) *draw,* fut. ἐρύω, aor. εἴρυσ(σ)α and ἔρυσ(σ)α, pf. p. εἴρῡμαι and εἴρυσμαι. Mid. ἐρύομαι *draw to one's self;* ἐρύσσομαι, ἐρυσ(σ)άμην and εἰρυσ(σ)άμην, εἴρῡμαι and εἴρυσμαι, εἰρύμην, ἐρύσθην and εἰρύσθην. Epic and Ion., with poetic and New Ion. pres. εἰρύω. 537, 596.

ἔρχομαι (ἐρχ-, ἐλθ-, ἐλευθ-, ἐλυθ-) *go, come,* fut. ἐλεύσομαι (Ion. and poet.), 2 pf. ἐλήλυθα, epic ἐλήλουθα and εἰλήλουθα, 2 aor. ἦλθον (poet. ἤλυθον). In Attic *prose,* εἶμι is used for ἐλεύσομαι (1257). 166 b. (5)

ἐσθίω, also poetic ἔσθω and ἔδω (ἐδ-, φαγ-, edo) *eat*, fut. ἔδομαι, pf. ἐδήδοκα, ἐδήδεσμαι, epic ἐδήδομαι(?), ἠδέσθην ; 2 aor. ἔφαγον ; epic pres. inf. ἔδμεναι ; 2 pf. part. ἐδηδώς. 681. (5)

ἑστιάω *entertain*, augment εἱστι- (537).

εὕδω (εὐδ-, εὐδε-) *sleep*, impf. εὗδον (ἐ-κάθ-ευδον) or ηὗδον (καθ-ηὗδον, 541), εὐδήσω, Ion. -εὐδησα. Commonly in καθ-εύδω. 590.

εὐεργετέω *do good*, εὐεργετήσω, ηὐεργέτησα, etc., regular : sometimes (wrongly) augmented εὐηργ-. See 567.

εὑρίσκω (εὑρ-, εὑρε-, 604) *find*, εὑρήσω, ηὕρηκα, ηὕρημαι, ηὑρέθην, εὑρεθήσομαι ; 2 aor. ηὗρον, ηὑρόμην. 596, 597. Often found with augment εὑ- (541). (4)

εὐφραίνω (εὐφραν-) *cheer*, fut.' εὐφρανῶ ; aor. ηὔφρᾱνα ; aor. p. ηὐφράνθην, fut. p. εὐφρανθήσομαι ; fut. m. εὐφρανοῦμαι. 541. (2)

εὔχομαι *pray, boast*, εὔξομαι, ηὐξάμην, ηὗγμαι. 541.

ἐχθαίρω (ἐχθαρ-) *hate*, fut. ἐχθαροῦμαι, aor. ἤχθηρα. Epic and poetic. (2)

ἔχω (σεχ-, σχ-, σχε-) *have*, impf. εἶχον (537) ; ἕξω or σχήσω, ἔσχηκα, ἔσχημαι, ἐσχέθην (chiefly Ion.) ; 2 aor. ἔσχον, σχῶ, σχοίην and -σχοιμι, σχές, σχεῖν, σχών ; poet. ἔσχεθον etc. (601). Hom. pf. part. συν-οχωκώς for ὀκ-οχ-ως (585, 554), plpf. ἐπ-ώχατο *were shut Il.* 12, 340. Mid. ἔχομαι *cling to, be next to*, ἕξομαι and σχήσομαι, ἐσχόμην. See ἀμπέχω, ἴσχω, and ὑπισχνέομαι. 1250 f.

ἕψω (ἑψ-, ἐψε-) *cook, boil*, fut. ἑψήσομαι, ἑψήσω (in comedy), aor. ἥψησα, Ion. ἥψημαι, ἡψήθην. 590.

ζάω *live⁻* (ζα-, ζη-), with ζῇς, ζῇ, etc. (486), impf. ἔζων ; ζήσω, ζήσομαι. Later are ἔζησα, ἔζηκα, for which Att. uses ἐβίων, βεβίωκα. Ion. ζώω in the drama.

ζεύγνῡμι (ζευγ-, ζυγ-, cf. iug-um) *yoke*, ζεύξω, ἔζευξα, ἔζευγμαι, ἐζεύχθην (rare) ; 2 aor. p. ἐζύγην. (3)

ζέω (ζε- for ζεσ-) *boil* (poet. ζείω), ζέσω, ἔζεσα, -ἐζεσμαι Ion. 596.

ζώννῡμι (ζω- for ζωσ-) *gird*, ἔζωσα, ἔζωμαι (inscr.) and ἔζωσμαι. (3)

ἡβάσκω (ἡβα-) *come to manhood*, with ἡβάω *be at manhood* : -ηβήσω, ἥβησα, -ἥβηκα. For epic ἡβώωντα etc. see 659 b.

ἠγερέθομαι *be collected*, poetic passive, see ἀγείρω (ἀγερ-) and 601. Only in 3 pl. ἠγερέθονται, the subj. and infin., and ἠγερέθοντο.

ἥδομαι *be pleased* ; aor. p. ἥσθην, fut. p. ἡσθήσομαι, aor. m. ἥσατο *Od.* 9, 353. The act. ἥδω with impf. ἧδον, aor. ἧσα, occurs very rarely.

ἠερέθομαι *be raised*, poetic passive, see ἀείρω (ἀερ-) and 601. Only in 3 pl. ἠερέθονται (impf. ἠερέθοντο is late).

ἧμαι *sit* : see 521.

ἠμί say, chiefly in impf. ἦν δ᾽ ἐγώ said I and ἦ δ᾽ ὅς said he (1023 b). Epic ἦ he said. Ἠμί I say is colloquial.

ἠμύω bow, sink, aor. ἤμῡσα, Hom. pf. ὑπ-εμν-ήμῡκε (with an inexplicable ν inserted, for ὑπ-εμ-ημῡκε, 554). Poetic, chiefly epic.

θάλλω (θαλ-) bloom, 2 pf. τέθηλα as present. 589. Poetic. (2)

θαπ- or ταφ-, stem : see θηπ-.

θάπτω (ταφ- for θαφ-) bury, θάψω, ἔθαψα, τέθαμμαι, Ion. ἐθάφθην, rare ; 2 aor. p. ἐτάφην ; 2 fut. ταφήσομαι ; fut. pf. τεθάψομαι. 105 e. (2)

θαυμάζω (see 620) wonder, θαυμάσομαι, ἐθαύμασα, τεθαύμακα, ἐθαυμάσθην, θαυμασθήσομαι. (2)

θείνω (θεν-) smite, θενῶ, ἔθεινα Hom., 2 aor. ἔθενον. Poetic, Att. comedy. (2)

θέλω wish : see ἐθέλω.

θέρομαι warm one's self, epic fut. θέρσομαι (682), 2 aor. p. (ἐθέρην) subj. θερέω. Chiefly epic.

θέω (θευ-, θεϝ-, θυ-) run, fut. θεύσομαι. 611.

(θη-), inf. θῆσθαι milk, ἐθησάμην. Epic.

(θηπ-, θαπ-, or ταφ-) astonish, stem with epic 2 pf. τέθηπα am astonished, epic plpf. ἐτεθήπεα ; 2 aor. ἔταφον, also intransitive. 34, 105 e.

θιγγάνω (θιγ-) touch, θίξομαι, 2 aor. ἔθιγον. 638. Chiefly poetic. (3)

θλάω bruise, ἔθλασα, τέθλασμαι (Theocr.), ἐθλάσθην (Hippocr.). Ionic and poetic. See φλάω.

θλίβω (θλῑβ-, θλῐβ-) squeeze, ἔθλῑψα, τέθλῑφα, τέθλιμμαι, ἐθλίφθην ; ἐθλίβην ; fut. m. θλίψομαι, Hom.

θνῄσκω, pres. also written θνήσκω, Doric and Aeolic θνάσκω (θαν-, θνη-) die, θανοῦμαι, τέθνηκα ; fut. pf. τεθνήξω (736), later τεθνήξομαι ; 2 aor. ἔθανον ; 2 pf. see 727 and 802. In Attic prose always ἀπο-θανοῦμαι and ἀπ-έθανον, but τέθνηκα. 594, 647. (4)

θράττω (θρᾱχ-, τρᾱχ-) disturb, aor. ἔθρᾱξα, ἐθρᾱχθην (Soph.) ; 2 pf. τέτρηχα be disturbed, Hom. See ταράττω. (2)

θραύω bruise, θραύσω, ἔθραυσα, τέθραυμαι and τέθραυσμαι, ἐθραύσθην (600).

θρύπτω (τρυφ- for θρυφ-) crush, ἔθρυψα Hippocr., τέθρυμμαι, ἐθρύφθην, epic 2 aor. p. ἐτρύφην, θρύψομαι. 105 e. (2)

θρώσκω and θρώσκω (θορ-, θρω-) leap, fut. θοροῦμαι, 2 aor. ἔθορον. Chiefly poetic. Cf. Hdt. θορνύομαι. (4)

θύω (θῡ-, θυ-) sacrifice, impf. ἔθυον ; θύσω, ἔθῡσα, τέθυκα, τέθυμαι, ἐτύθην ; θύσομαι, ἐθῡσάμην. 105 a and c.

θύω or θύνω rage, rush. Poetic : classic only in present and imperfect. Hes. θῡνέω.

ἰάλλω (ἰαλ-) send, fut. -ιαλῶ, ep. aor. ἴηλα. Poetic (in Ar. comp. with ἐπί). (2)

ἰάχω and ἰαχέω (ϝιϝαχ-) *shout*, pf. (ἴαχα) ἀμφ-ιαχυῖα. Poetic, chiefly epic. In tragedy commonly written ἰακχ-.

(ἰδ-, ϝιδ-), in εἶδον for ἔϝιδον.

ἱδρόω *sweat*, ἱδρώσω, ἵδρωσα: for irregular contraction ἱδρῶσι etc. see 488.

ἱδρύω *place*, ἱδρύσω, ἵδρῡσα, ἵδρῡκα, ἵδρῡμαι, ἱδρύθην, epic ἱδρύνθην (740), ἱδρύσομαι, ἱδρῦσάμην.

ἵεμαι (ϝῖε-, Lat. in-vī-tus) *strive*, in Att. chiefly in comp. παρ-ίεμαι *entreat*; ep. aor. ἐεισάμην and εἰσάμην. Distinguish from mid. of ἵημι (ση-, σε-) *send*.

ἵζω (σεδ-, redupl. σι-σδ-, 561) *seat* or *sit*, mid. ἵζομαι *sit*; used chiefly in καθ-ίζω, which see. See also ἕζομαι and ἧμαι. (2) By-form ἱζάνω.

ἵημι (ση-, σε-, redupl. σι-ση-, 561) *send*: for inflection see 514.

ἱκνέομαι (ἱκ-), poet. ἵκω, *come*, ἵξομαι, ἷγμαι; 2 aor. ἱκόμην. In prose usually ἀφ-ικνέομαι. From ἵκω, epic impf. ἷκον, aor. ἷξον, 654 *h*. Also ἱκάνω, epic and tragic. (3)

ἱλάσκομαι (ἱλα-) *propitiate*, ἱλάσομαι, ἱλάσθην, ἱλασάμην. (4) Epic pres. ἱλάομαι, aor. ἱλασσάμην.

ἵλημι (ἱλη-, ἱλα- for σι-σλη-, σι-σλα-) *be propitious*, pres. only imv. ἵληθι or ἵλαθι; pf. subj. and opt. ἱλήκω, ἱλήκοιμι (Hom.). Mid. ἵλαμαι *propitiate*, epic. Poetic, chiefly epic.

ἵλλω and ἵλλομαι *roll*, aor. ἵλα. See εἰλέω. (2)

ἱμάσσω (ἱμαντ-, see 625) *lash*, aor. ἵμασα or ἵμασσα epic. (2)

ἱμείρω (ἱμερ-) *long for*, ἱμειράμην (epic), ἱμέρθην (Ion.). Poetic and Ionic. (2)

ἵπταμαι *fly*, late present: see πέτομαι.

ἴσᾱμι, Doric for οἶδα *know*, with ἴσᾱς or ἴσαις, ἴσᾱτι, ἴσαμεν, ἴσατε, ἴσαντι, part. ἴσᾱς.

ἴσκω: see ἔϊσκω.

ἵστημι (στη-, στα-, redupl. σι-στη-, σι-στα-) *set, place*, for synopsis and inflection see 503, 504, 507: στήσω *shall set*, ἔστησα *set, brought to a stop*, ἔστην *came to a stand*, ἕστηκα *am standing*, εἰστήκη *was standing*, 2 pf. ἔστατον (506), pf. mid. ἕσταμαι (rare), fut. pf. ἑστήξω *shall stand*, aor. pass. ἐστάθην *was placed*.

ἰσχναίνω (ἰσχναν-) *make lean, make dry*, fut. ἰσχνανῶ, aor. ἴσχνᾱνα (688), ἴσχνηνα Ion., aor. p. ἰσχνάνθην; fut. m. ἰσχνανοῦμαι. (2)

ἴσχω (for σι-σχ-ω, 561) *have, hold*. See ἔχω.

(καδ-, καδε-) in Hom. redupl. 2 aor. κεκαδών *depriving*, fut. κεκαδήσω. For κεκάδοντο see χάζω.

καθαίρω (καθαρ-) *purify*, καθαρῶ, ἐκάθηρα (and ἐκάθᾱρα), κεκάθαρμαι, ἐκαθάρθην; καθαροῦμαι, ἐκαθηράμην. (2)

καθ-έζομαι (σεδ-, ἑδ-) *sit down*, impf. ἐκαθεζόμην, fut. καθεδοῦμαι. See ἕζομαι.

καθεύδω (εὐδ-, εὐδε-) *sleep*, impf. **ἐκάθευδον** and **καθηῦδον**, epic καθεῦδον, see 567; fut. **καθευδήσω.** See **εὕδω.**

καθίζω *set, sit*, fut. **καθιῶ** (678 *c*), καθιζήσομαι; aor. ἐκάθισα or καθῖσα, Hom. καθεῖσα, Hdt. κατεῖσα, ἐκαθισάμην. See ἵζω. For inflection of **κάθημαι** see 522. (**2**)

καίνυμαι, perhaps for καδ-νυμαι (καδ-), *excel*, impf. ἐκαίνυτο, pf. κέκασμαι, Dor. κεκαδμένος. Poetic. (**3**)

καίνω (καν-, κον-) *kill*, fut. κανῶ, 2 aor. ἔκανον, 2 pf. κέκονα, κατα-κεκονότες (Xen.). Chiefly poetic. (**2**)

καίω (καιϝω for καϝ-ιω, καυ-, και-, 635), in Attic prose generally **κάω** (not contracted), *burn*; **καύσω**; **ἔκαυσα**, epic aor. ἔκηα, part. κήᾱς, Att. κέᾱς Eur., Ar.; **κέκαυκα, κέκαυμαι, ἐκαύθην, καυθήσομαι,** 2 aor. ἐκάην (poetic); fut. mid. καύσομαι (rare), ἀν-εκαυσάμην, Hdt. (**2**)

καλέω (καλε-, κλη-) *call*, **καλῶ** (678 *a*), **ἐκάλεσα, κέκληκα, κέκλημαι** (opt. κεκλῇο, κεκλήμεθα), **ἐκλήθην, κληθήσομαι**; fut. m. **καλοῦμαι**, aor. **ἐκαλεσάμην**; fut. pf. **κεκλήσομαι.** Aeol. pres. κάλημι, epic inf. καλήμεναι, fut. καλέω (Hom.), καλέσω (Aristotle), aor. ἐκάλεσσα. Epic pres. κι-κλή-σκω, iterative καλέεσκον. 596, 597, 766.

καλύπτω (καλυβ-) *cover*, **καλύψω, ἐκάλυψα, κεκάλυμμαι, ἐκαλύφθην, καλυφθήσομαι**; aor. m. ἐκαλυψάμην. In prose chiefly in compounds. (**2**)

κάμνω (καμ-, κμη-) *labor, be sick*, **καμοῦμαι, κέκμηκα**, epic 2 pf. part. κεκμηώς; 2 aor. ἔκαμον, epic ἐκαμόμην. (**3**)

κάμπτω (καμπ-) *bend*, **κάμψω, ἔκαμψα, κέκαμμαι** (81), **ἐκάμφθην.** (**2**)

κατηγορέω *accuse*, regular except in augment, κατηγόρουν etc. (565).

(**καφε-**) *pant*, in Hom. pf. part. κεκαφηώς.

κεδάννῡμι epic for σκεδάννῡμι *scatter*, ἐκέδασσα, ἐκεδάσθην. (**3**)

κεῖμαι *lie*, **κείσομαι**; inflected in 525.

κείρω (κερ-, καρ-) *shear*, fut. **κερῶ**, aor. ἔκερσα, poet. ἔκερσα, **κέκαρμαι**, ἐκέρθην (Pind.); 2 aor. p. ἐκάρην; fut. m. κεροῦμαι, aor. m. ἐκειράμην with poet. part. κερσάμενος. 689 *b*. (**2**)

κέκαδον in Hom. part. κεκαδών *depriving*. See (**καδ-**) and **χάζω.**

κελαδέω *shout, roar*, fut. κελαδήσω, κελαδήσομαι, aor. ἐκελάδησα; Hom. pres. part. κελάδων. Epic and lyric.

κελεύω *command*, **κελεύσω, ἐκέλευσα, κεκέλευκα, κεκέλευσμαι, ἐκελεύσθην** (600). Mid. (chiefly in compounds) κελεύσομαι, ἐκελευσάμην.

κέλλω (κελ-) *run ashore*, **κέλσω, ἔκελσα.** 682, 689. Poetic: the Att. prose form is **ὀκέλλω.** (**2**)

κέλομαι (κελ-, κελε-) *command*, κελήσομαι, ἐκελησάμην; 2 aor. m. ἐκεκλόμην (559, 692). Poetic, chiefly epic; Att. prose **κελεύω.**

κεντέω (κεντ-, κεντε-) *goad*, κεντήσω, ἐκέντησα, κεκέντημαι Ion., ἐκεντήθην later, συγκεντηθήσομαι Hdt. Hom. aor. inf. κένσαι, from stem κεντ-. 590. Chiefly Ionic and poetic.

κεράννῡμι and κεραννύω (κερα-, κρᾱ-) *mix*, ἐκέρασα, κέκρᾱμαι, ἐκρᾱ́θην and ἐκεράσθην; fut. p. κρᾱθήσομαι; aor. m. ἐκερασάμην. Ion. ἔκρησα, poet. ἐκέρασσα, κέκρημαι, ἐκρήθην. Other pres. forms are κεράω, κεραίω, κίρνημι, κιρνάω. (3)

κερδαίνω (κερδ-, κερδε-, κερδαν-) *gain*, fut. κερδανῶ, aor. ἐκέρδᾱνα (688), Ion. ἐκέρδηνα, fut. κερδήσομαι and aor. ἐκέρδησα (Hdt.); pf. προσ-κεκερδήκᾱσι (Dem.). 643. (3, 2)

κεύθω (κευθ-, κυθ-) *hide*, κεύσω, ἔκευσα; 2 pf. κέκευθα (as pres.); epic 2 aor. κύθον, redupl. aor. subj. κεκύθω. Epic and tragic.

κήδω (κηδ-, κηδε-, καδ-) *cause distress*, κηδήσω, -εκήδησα; 2 p. κέκηδα; active only epic. Mid. κήδομαι *sorrow*, ἐκηδεσάμην, epic fut. pf. κεκαδήσομαι.

κηρῡ́ττω (κηρῡκ-) *proclaim*, κηρῡ́ξω, ἐκήρῡξα, κεκήρῡχα, κεκήρῡγμαι, ἐκηρῡ́χθην, κηρῡχθήσομαι; κηρῡ́ξομαι, ἐκηρῡξάμην. (2)

κιγχάνω, epic κιχάνω (κιχ-, κιχε-) *find*, κιχήσομαι, epic ἐκιχησάμην; 2 aor. ἔκιχον. Epic forms as if from pres. κίχημι, 2 aor. pass. with intrans. meaning ἐκίχην: (ἐ)κίχεις, κίχημεν, κιχήτην, κιχήω (κιχείω MSS.), κιχείη, κιχῆναι and κιχήμεναι, κιχείς, κιχήμενος. Poetic. 638 (b). (3)

κίδνημι (κιδ-να-) *spread*, Ion. and poetic for σκεδάννῡμι. See σκίδνημι. (3)

κίνυμαι *move* (intrans.), pres. and impf.; as mid. of κῑνέω. Epic. (3)

κίρνημι and κιρνάω: epic forms (in pres. and impf.) for κεράννῡμι.

κίχρημι (χρη-, χρα-) *lend*, χρήσω Hdt., ἔχρησα, κέχρημαι; ἐχρησάμην *borrowed*.

κλάζω (κλαγγ-, κλαγ-) *clang*, κλάγξω, ἔκλαγξα; 2 pf. κέκλαγγα, epic pf. part. formed like pres. κεκλήγοντες; 2 aor. ἔκλαγον; fut. pf. κεκλάγξομαι. Chiefly poetic. (2)

κλαίω (κλαιϝω for κλαϝ-ῖω, κλαυ-, κλαι-, κλαιε-, 634, 635), in Attic prose and Ar. generally κλᾱ́ω (not contracted) *weep*, κλαύσομαι (rarely κλαυσοῦμαι, sometimes κλαιήσω or κλᾱήσω), ἔκλαυσα and ἐκλαυσάμην, κέκλαυμαι; fut. pf. (impers.) κεκλαύσεται. (2)

κλάω *break*, ἔκλασα, κέκλασμαι, ἐκλάσθην; generally in composition. 2 aor. part. ἀποκλᾱς Ion.

κλέπτω (κλεπ-, κλοπ-) *steal*, κλέψω (rarely κλέψομαι), ἔκλεψα, κέκλοφα (585, 723), κέκλεμμαι, (ἐκλέφθην) κλεφθείς; 2 aor. p. ἐκλάπην. (2)

κλῄζω *sound the praises of*, κλήσω, ἔκλησα. Dor. aor. ἐκλέϊξα from κλεΐζω. Poetic. (2)

κλῄω, later Attic κλείω *shut*, κλῄσω, ἔκλῃσα, κέκλῃκα, κέκλῃμαι, ἐκλῄσθην; κλῃσθήσομαι, κεκλήσομαι, ἐκλῃσάμην (also κλείσω, ἔκλεισα, etc.). Ion. κληΐω, ἐκλήϊσα, κεκλήϊμαι, ἐκληΐσθην.

κλῑ́νω (κλιν-) *bend, incline*, κλῐνῶ, ἔκλῑνα, κέκλιμαι, ἐκλίθην, epic ἐκλίνθην, 740; κλιθήσομαι; 2 aor. p. ἐκλίνην, 2 fut. κλινήσομαι; fut. m. κλινοῦμαι, aor. ἐκλῑνάμην. 602. (2)

κλύω *hear*, impf. ἔκλυον (really 2 aor., as from a present κλεϝ-ω); 2 aor. imv. κλῦθι, κλῦτε, epic κέκλυθι, κέκλυτε. Part. κλύμενος *renowned*. Poetic.

κναίω *scrape, scratch* (in compos.), -κναίσω, -έκναισα, -κέκναικα, -κέκναισμαι, -εκναίσθην, -κναισθήσομαι. Also Att. κνῶ (as from κνα-ω, κνη-, κνα-), with αε, αη contracted to η, and αει, αη to ῃ (486).

κομίζω (κομιδ-) *care for, carry,* κομιῶ, ἐκόμισα, κεκόμικα, κεκόμισμαι, ἐκομίσθην; κομισθήσομαι; fut. m. κομιοῦμαι (678 c), aor. ἐκομισάμην. (2)

κόπτω (κοπ-) *cut,* κόψω, ἔκοψα, κέκοφα (724), part. κεκοπώς Hom., κέκομμαι; 2 aor. p. ἐκόπην, 2 fut. p. κοπήσομαι; fut. pf. κεκόψομαι; aor. m. ἐκοψάμην. (2)

κορέννῡμι (κορεσ-, κορε-) *satiate,* fut. κορέσω (Hdt.), κορέω (Hom.), aor. ἐκόρεσα (poet.), κεκόρεσμαι, Ion. κεκόρημαι, ἐκορέσθην; epic 2 pf. part. κεκορηώς, aor. m. ἐκορεσάμην. 596. (3)

κορύσσω (κορυθ-) *arm,* Hom. aor. part. κορυσσάμενος, pf. pt. κεκορυθμένος. Poetic, chiefly epic. (2)

κοτέω *be angry,* aor. ἐκότεσα, ἐκοτεσάμην, 2 pf. part. κεκοτηώς *angry,* epic.

κράζω (κρᾱγ-, κραγ-) *cry out,* fut. pf. κεκράξομαι (rare); 2 pf. κέκρᾱγα (imv. κέκραχθι and κεκρᾱγετε, Ar.), 2 plpf. ἐκεκρᾱγετε (Dem.); 2 aor. ἔκραγον. (2)

κραίνω (κραν-) *accomplish,* κρανῶ, ἔκρᾱνα, Ion. ἔκρηνα, ἐκράνθην, κρανθήσομαι; pf. p. 3 sing. κέκρανται (cf. πέφανται), fut. m. inf. κρανέεσθαι, Hom. Ionic and poetic. Epic pres. also κραιαίνω (possibly for κρᾱαίνω), aor. ἐκρήηνα, pf. and plpf. κεκράανται and κεκράαντο; aor. p. 3 pl. ἐκρᾱανθεν (Theocr.). (2)

κρέμαμαι (κρεμα-) *hang* (intrans.), κρεμήσομαι. See κρεμάννῡμι and κρίμνημι.

κρεμάννῡμι (κρεμα-) *hang* (trans.), κρεμῶ (κρεμάσω in comedy), ἐκρέμασα, ἐκρεμάσθην. For the mid. (intrans.) see κρέμαμαι. (3)

κρίζω (κρικ-, κριγ-) *creak, squeak,* epic 2 aor. κρίκε or κρίγε, 2 p. part. κεκρῑγότες *squeaking* (Ar.). (2)

κρίμνημι (κριμ-νη-, κριμ-να-) *hang* (trans.), rare in act. Mid. κρίμναμαι = κρέμαμαι. Poetic (often wrongly written κρήμνημι); used only in pres. and impf. (3)

κρίνω (κριν-) *judge,* fut. κρινῶ, ἔκρῑνα, κέκρικα, κέκριμαι, ἐκρίθην (epic ἐκρίνθην), κριθήσομαι; fut. m. κρινοῦμαι (rarely pass.). 602. (2)

κρούω *beat,* κρούσω, ἔκρουσα, -κέκρουκα, -κέκρουμαι and -κέκρουσμαι, -εκρούσθην.

κρύπτω (κρυφ-) *conceal,* κρύψω, ἔκρυψα, κέκρυμμαι, ἐκρύφθην; 2 aor. p. ἐκρύφην (rare), 2 fut. κρυβήσομαι (rare). (2)

κτάομαι *acquire,* κτήσομαι, ἐκτησάμην, κέκτημαι (rarely ἔκτημαι) *possess* (subj. κεκτῶμαι, opt. κεκτήμην or κεκτῴμην, 766), ἐκτήθην (as pass.); κεκτήσομαι (rarely ἐκτήσομαι) *shall possess.*

κτείνῡμι and **κτεινύω**, in compos., only pres. and impf. See κτείνω. (3)

κτείνω (κτεν-, κτον-, κτα-ν-) *kill,* fut. κτενῶ, Ion. κτενέω, epic also κτανέω, aor. ἔκτεινα, 2 pf. ἀπ-έκτονα, epic aor. p. ἐκτάθην; 2 aor. ἔκτανον (for poetic ἔκταν and ἐκτάμην see 694); epic fut. m. κτανέομαι. In Attic prose ἀποκτείνω is generally used; pass. supplied from ἀποθνῄσκω. 585, 1242. (2)

382 GREEK GRAMMAR

κτίζω (see 620) *found*, κτίσω, ἔκτισα, ἔκτισμαι, ἐκτίσθην; aor. m. ἐκτισάμην (rare); epic 2 aor. m. part. κτίμενος as pass. *founded*. (2)

κτυπέω (κτυπ-, κτυπε-) *sound, cause to sound*, ἐκτύπησα, Hom. 2 aor. ἔκτυπον. Chiefly poetic. 590.

κυλίνδω and κυλινδέω, later κυλίω, *roll*, ἐκύλῑσα, -κεκύλῑσμαι, ἐκυλίσθην, -κυλῑσθήσομαι.

κυνέω (κυ-) *kiss*, ἔκυσα. Poetic. προσ-κυνέω *do homage to*, fut. προσκυνήσω, aor. προσεκύνησα (poet. προσέκυσα), are common in prose and poetry. (3)

κύπτω (κυφ-) *stoop*, κύψω and κύψομαι, aor. ἔκυψα, 2 p. κέκῡφα. (2)

κύρω (κυρ-, κυρε-) *meet, happen*, κύρσω, ἔκυρσα (682, 689). Chiefly poetic. (2) κυρέω is regular.

λαγχάνω (λαχ-, ληχ-) *obtain by lot*, fut. m. λήξομαι, Ion. λάξομαι, 2 pf. εἴληχα, Ion. and poet. λέλογχα, pf. m. εἴληγμαι, aor. p. ἐλήχθην; 2 aor. ἔλαχον, epic ἔλλαχον (redupl. λέλαχον). 559, 638. (3)

λαμβάνω (λαβ-, ληβ-) *take*, λήψομαι, εἴληφα, εἴλημμαι (poet. λέλημμαι), ἐλήφθην, ληφθήσομαι; 2 aor. ἔλαβον, ἐλαβόμην (epic inf. λελαβέσθαι, 559). Ion. λάμψομαι (better λάψομαι), λελάβηκα, λέλαμμαι, ἐλάμφθην; Dor. fut. λαψοῦμαι, aor. p. ἐλάφθην. 604, 638. (3)

λάμπω *shine*, λάμψω, ἔλαμψα, pf. λέλαμπα (poetic).

λανθάνω (λαθ-, ληθ-) *lie hid, escape the notice of*, λήσω, 2 pf. λέληθα, 2 aor. ἔλαθον. Mid. *forget*, ἐπιλήσομαι, -λέλησμαι, fut. pf. λελήσομαι, 2 aor. ἐλαθόμην. Epic 2 aor. λέλαθον, λελαθόμην (559), Dor. 2 pf. λέλᾱθα, Hom. pf. m. λέλασμαι. Poetic pres. λήθω, aor. ἔλησα. 638. (3)

λάπτω (λαβ- or λαφ-) *lap, lick*, λάψω, ἔλαψα, pf. λέλαφα (724); fut. m. -λάψομαι, ἐλαψάμην. (2)

λάσκω for λακ-σκω (λακ-, λακε-) *speak*, λακήσομαι, ἐλάκησα, 2 pf. λέλᾱκα, epic λέληκα with fem. part. λελᾱκυῖα; 2 aor. ἔλακον, epic λελακόμην. Poetic. 648. (4)

λάω, λῶ *wish*, λῇς, λῇ, etc.; inf. λῆν. 486. Doric.

λέγω *say*, λέξω, ἔλεξα, λέλεγμαι (δι-είλεγμαι), ἐλέχθην; fut. λεχθήσομαι, λέξομαι, λελέξομαι, all passive. For pf. act. εἴρηκα is used (see εἴρω, εἶπον).

λέγω *gather, arrange, count* (Attic only in comp.), λέξω, ἔλεξα, εἴλοχα, εἴλεγμαι or λέλεγμαι, ἐλέχθην (rare); aor. m. ἐλεξάμην, 2 aor. p. ἐλέγην, fut. λεγήσομαι. Epic 2 aor. m. (ἐλέγμην) λέκτο *counted*. See stem λεχ-.

λείπω (λειπ-, λοιπ-, λιπ-, 585) *leave*, λείψω, λέλειμμαι, ἐλείφθην; 2 pf. λέλοιπα; 2 aor. ἔλιπον, ἐλιπόμην. See synopsis in 477, and inflection of 2 aor., 2 pf., and 2 plpf. in 481.

λελίημαι, see λιλαίομαι.

λεύω *stone*, generally κατα-λεύω *stone to death*, -λεύσω, -έλευσα, -ελεύσθην (600), -λευσθήσομαι.

(λεχ-), cf. λέχ-ος; 2 aor. m. (ἐλέγμην) ἔλεκτο *laid himself to rest*, with imv.

λέξο (also λέξεο), inf. κατα-λέχθαι, part. κατα-λέγμενος (696 b). Also ἔλεξα *laid to rest*, with mid. λέξομαι *will go to rest* and ἐλεξάμην *went to rest*. Only epic.

λήθω, poetic: see λανθάνω.

ληΐζω (ληϊδ-) *plunder*, act. rare, only impf. ἐλήϊζον. Mid. ληΐζομαι (as act.), Ion. fut. ληΐσομαι, aor. ἐληϊσάμην. Eurip. has ἐλησάμην, and pf. p. λέλησμαι. (2)

λιλαίομαι (λασ-, λα-) *desire eagerly*, only pres., impf., and pf. λελίημαι, part. λελιημένος *eager*. Hom. Cf. λάω. (2)

λίσσομαι or (rare) λίτομαι (λιτ-) *supplicate*, epic ἐλλισάμην, 2 aor. ἐλιτόμην. (2)

λοέω (λοϝε-) epic for λούω; λοέσσομαι, ἐλόεσσα, ἐλοεσσάμην.

λούω *wash, bathe*, regular. In Attic writers and Hdt. the pres. and impf. generally have contracted forms (λου- becoming λο-) where a short thematic vowel would appear; e.g. λούω, λούεις, λούει, but λοῦμεν, λοῦτε, λοῦσι; ἔλου, λοῦται, λοῦσθαι; aor. ἔλουσα, pf. λέλουμαι. 488.

λύω (λῡ-, λυ-) *loose*, see synopsis and full inflection in 475 and 480. Hom. also λύω (ῠ). Epic 2 aor. m. ἐλύμην (as pass.), λύτο and λῦτο, λύντο; pf. opt. λελῦτο and λελῦντο (766). 604.

μαίνω (μαν-, μην-) *madden*, aor. ἔμηνα, pf. μέμηνα *am mad*, 2 aor. p. ἐμάνην. Mid. μαίνομαι *be mad*; μανοῦμαι (Hdt.); poetic are ἐμηνάμην and μεμάνημαι. (2)

μαίομαι (μασ-, μασι-, μαι-, 636) *desire, seek*. Ep. μάσσομαι, ἐμασ(σ)άμην. Also Aeolic pres. μάομαι (contracted μῶται, μῶνται, μῶσο, μῶσθαι, μώμενος) and epic and poetic μαιμάω belong here. (2)

μανθάνω (μαθ-, μαθε-) *learn*, μαθήσομαι, μεμάθηκα; 2 aor. ἔμαθον. Hom. ἔμμαθον. 638. (3)

μάρναμαι (μαρ-να-) *fight* (subj. μάρνωμαι, impf. μάρναο); only in pres. and impf. Poetic. (3)

μάρπτω (μαρπ-) *seize*, μάρψω, ἔμαρψα, epic 2 pf. μέμαρπα, 2 aor. μέμαρπον (559). Poetic. (2)

μάττω (μαγ-) *knead*, μάξω, ἔμαξα, μέμαχα, μέμαγμαι; 2 aor. p. ἐμάγην. (2)

μάχομαι (μαχ-, μαχε-) *fight*, fut. μαχοῦμαι, aor. ἐμαχεσάμην, pf. μεμάχημαι. Ion. forms are Hom. pres. μαχέομαι, part. μαχεούμενος and μαχειόμενος, fut. μαχέσσομαι (μαχήσομαι) and μαχέομαι, Hdt. μαχήσομαι, aor. ἐμαχεσ(σ)άμην.

μέδομαι (μεδ-, μεδε-) *think of, plan*, μεδήσομαι (rare). Epic.

μεθ-ίημι *let loose*; see ἵημι (514). Hdt. pf. part. μεμετιμένος.

μεθύσκω (μεθυ-) *make drunk*, ἐμέθυσα. Pass. μεθύσκομαι *be made drunk*, aor. p. ἐμεθύσθην *became drunk*. See μεθύω. (4)

μεθύω *be drunk*, only pres. and impf.

μείγνῡμι (μειγ-, μιγ-) *mix*, also μειγνύω and μίσγω, fut. μείξω, ἔμειξα, μέμειγμαι, ἐμείχθην, 2 aor. p. ἐμίγην; μειχθήσομαι (rare); epic 2 fut. pass. μιγήσομαι, 2 aor. m. ἔμικτο (or ἔμεικτο); poetic fut. pf. μεμείξομαι. Formerly written μῑγνῡμι; the spelling with ει is attested by the inscriptions. (3)

μείρομαι (μερ- for σμερ-, μορ-, μαρ-) *obtain a share*, epic, 2 pf. 3 sing. ἔμμορε; impers. εἵμαρται (552) *it is fated*, εἱμαρμένη (as subst.) *Fate*. (2)

μέλλω (μελλ-, μελλε-) *am going to*, augm. ἐμ- or ἠμ- (536); μελλήσω, ἐμέλλησα.

μέλω (μελ-, μελε-) *concern, care for*, μελήσω, epic μελήσομαι, 2 pf. μέμηλα; μεμέλημαι, epic μέμβλεται, μέμβλετο, for μεμλεται, μεμλετο (108); (ἐμελήθην) μεληθείς. Poetic. μέλει *it concerns*, impers.; μελήσει, ἐμέλησε, μεμέληκε, — used in Attic prose, with ἐπιμέλομαι and ἐπιμελέομαι, ἐπιμελήσομαι, ἐπιμεμέλημαι, ἐπεμελήθην.

μέμονα (μεν-, μον-, μα- for μη-) *desire*, 2 pf. with present meaning; dual μέματον, pl. μέμαμεν, μέματε, μεμάᾱσι, impf. μεμάτω, part. μεμαώς and μεμαώς, μεμαυῖα, inf. μεμονέναι (Hdt.). See 728. Epic and poetic.

μένω (μεν-, μενε-) *remain*, fut. μενῶ (Ion. μενέω), ἔμεινα, μεμένηκα. 633.

μερμηρίζω (see 620) *ponder*, ἀπεμερμήρισα (Ar.), but μερμήριξα epic. (2)

μήδομαι *devise*, μήσομαι, ἐμησάμην. Poetic.

μηκάομαι (μηκ-, μακ-, 591) *bleat*, Hom. 2 aor. part. μακών; 2 pf. part. μεμηκώς, μεμακυῖα; 2 plpf. ἐμέμηκον (654 d). Chiefly epic. 728.

μητιάω (μητι-, 591) *plan*. Mid. μητιάομαι, μητίομαι (Pind.), μητίσομαι, ἐμητῑσάμην. Epic and lyric.

μιαίνω (μιαν-) *stain*, μιανῶ, ἐμίᾱνα, μεμίασμαι, ἐμιάνθην, μιανθήσομαι. (2)

μίγνῡμι *mix*, see μείγνῡμι.

μιμνήσκω and (older) μιμνήσκω (μνα-, 647) *remind*; mid. *remember*; μνήσω, ἔμνησα, μέμνημαι *remember*, ἐμνήσθην (as mid.) *mentioned*; μνησθήσομαι, μνήσομαι, μεμνήσομαι *shall keep in mind*; ἐμνησάμην (poet.). μέμνημαι (memini) has subj. μεμνῶμαι (754), opt. μεμνήμην (766), imv. μέμνησο, Hdt. μέμνεο, inf. μεμνῆσθαι, part. μεμνημένος. (4). From epic μνάομαι come ἐμνώοντο, μνωόμενος. 659.

μίμνω (μεν-, μν-) for μι-μν-ω (604, 605) *remain*, poetic form of μένω.

μίσγω (μιγ-) for μι-μ-σγω (604, 648) *mix*, pres. and impf. See μείγνῡμι. (4)

μύζω *suck*, Ion. μυζέω, aor. -εμύζησα (Hom.).

μύζω (μυγ-) *grumble, mutter*, aor. ἔμυξα. (2)

μῡκάομαι (μῡκ-, μυκ-, μῡκα-, 591) *bellow*, epic 2 pf. μέμῡκα; 2 aor. μύκον, ἐμυκησάμην. Chiefly poetic.

μύττω (μυκ-) *wipe*, ἀπο-μυξάμενος, plpf. ἀπ-εμέμυκτο. In comedy. (2)

μύω *shut* (*the lips* or *eyes*), aor. ἔμυσα, pf. μέμῡκα.

(να-, νη-) in νῶ *spin*, pres. νῆς, νῇ (486), inf. νῆν, part. νῶν; fut. νήσω, ἔνησα, ἐνήθην.

ναίω (ναϝ-, ναϝι-, ναι-, 636) *swim, be full*, impf. ναῖον *Od.* 9, 222. (2)

ναίω (νασ-, να-, 636) *dwell*, ἔνασσα *caused to dwell*, ἐνασσάμην *came to dwell*, ἐνάσθην *was settled, dwelt.* Poetic. (2)

νάττω (ναδ-, ναγ-) *stuff*, ἔναξα (epic and Ion.), νένασμαι (Ar.) or νέναγμαι (Hippocr.). 624. (2)

(νάω) νῶ *spin*, see stem να-.

νεικέω and νεικείω (νεικεσ-, νεικε-, 597) *chide*, νεικέσω, ἐνείκεσ(σ)α. Ionic, chiefly epic. (2)

νείφει *it is snowing*; -ένειψε. Formerly written νῖφει.

νέμω (νεμ-, νεμε-) *distribute*, νεμῶ, ἔνειμα, νενέμηκα, νενέμημαι, ἐνεμήθην; νεμοῦμαι, ἐνειμάμην. 590.

νέομαι (νεσ-) *go, come*, also in future sense. Chiefly poetic. See νίσομαι.

νέω (νευ-, νεϝ-, νυ-, orig. σνευ-) *swim*, νευσοῦμαι (679), ἔνευσα, νένευκα. 611.

νέω *heap up*, ἔνησα, νένημαι (? νένησμαι). For the pres. Att. generally uses χόω. Epic and Ion. νηέω, νήησα, ἐνηησάμην.

νήθω *spin*, νήσω, ἔνησα, ἐνήθην; epic aor. m. νήσαντο. See (να-).

νίζω (νιβ-, νιγ-), later νίπτω, Hom. νίπτομαι, *wash*, νίψω, ἔνιψα, νένιμμαι, -ενίφθην (Hippocr.); νίψομαι, ἐνιψάμην. 619. (2)

νίσομαι (νεσ-, redupl. νι-ν(ε)σ-ι̯ομαι) *go*, fut. νίσομαι. Cf. 604. (2) See νέομαι.

νοέω *think, perceive*, νοήσω, etc., regular in Attic. Mid. usually in comp., as fut. διανοηθήσομαι. Ion. ἔνωσα, νένωκα, νένωμαι, ἐνωσάμην.

νομίζω (see 620) *believe*, fut. νομιῶ (678 c), aor. ἐνόμισα, pf. νενόμικα, νενόμισμαι, aor. p. ἐνομίσθην, fut. p. νομισθήσομαι, fut. m. νομιοῦμαι (Hippocr.). (2)

νῶ *spin*, see (να-).

ξέω (ξεσ-, ξε-) *scrape*, aor. ἔξεσα and ξέσσα, chiefly epic, ἔξεσμαι. 597, 598.

ξηραίνω (ξηραν-) *dry*, ξηρανῶ, ἐξήρᾱνα, ἐξήρασμαι and late ἐξήραμμαι, ἐξηράνθην. Ion. aor. ἐξήρηνα. 732. (2)

ξύω *polish*, ἔξῡσα, ἔξῡσμαι, ἐξύσθην. 598.

ὁδοιπορέω *travel*, regular; but pf. ὁδοιπεπόρηκα for ὠδοιπόρηκα (565).

ὁδοποιέω *make a way*, regular; but pf. part. ὠδοπεποιημένος for ὠδοποιημένος occurs (566).

(ὀδυ-) *be angry*, only Hom. ὠδυ(σ)σάμην, ὀδώδυσμαι.

ὄζω (ὀδ-, ὀζε-) *smell*, ὀζήσω, ὤζησα, Ion. ὀζέσω, ὤζεσα, Hom. plpf. ὀδώδει as impf. 590. Aeol. has ὄσδω. (2)

οἴγω *open*, poetic οἴξω and ᾦξα, aor. p. part. οἰχθείς. οἴγνῡμι, simple form late in active, impf. p. ᾠϊγνύμην Hom. (ᾠειγνύμην?), aor. ᾦξα (ᾦειξα?). In prose in composition: see ἀν-οίγνῡμι.

οἶδα (ϝοιδ-), 2 pf. as pres. *know*, see εἶδον. 529.

οἰδέω *swell*, ᾤδησα, ᾤδηκα. Also οἰδάνω.

οἰκτίρω (οἰκτιρ-), later written οἰκτείρω, pity (630), aor. ᾤκτῑρα. (2)

οἰνοχοέω pour wine, οἰνοχοήσω, οἰνοχοῆσαι (epic and lyric). Impf. epic 3 pers. οἰνοχόει, ᾠνοχόει, ἐῳνοχόει. 566.

οἴομαι (οἰ-, οἰε-) think (582 g), in prose generally οἶμαι and ᾤμην in 1 pers. sing.; οἰήσομαι, ᾠήθην. Epic act. οἴω (only 1 sing.), often ὀΐω; ὀΐομαι, ὀΐσάμην, ὠΐσθην. οἶμαι is probably a perfect.

οἴσω shall bear, see φέρω.

οἴχομαι (οἰχ-, οἰχε-, οἰχο-) be gone, οἰχήσομαι, οἴχωκα or ᾤχωκα (592); Ion. οἴχημαι or ᾤχημαι, doubtful.

ὀκέλλω (ὀκελ-) run ashore, aor. ὤκειλα. Prose form of κέλλω. (2)

ὀλισθάνω (ὀλισθ-, ὀλισθε-), also -ολισθαίνω slip, Ion. -ωλίσθησα, ὠλίσθηκα; 2 aor. ὤλισθον (poetic). (3)

ὄλλῡμι (ὀλ-, ὀλε-, ὀλο-, 640), for ὀλ-νῡ-μι, also -ολλύω destroy, lose, ὀλῶ, ὤλεσα, -ολώλεκα; 2 pf. ὄλωλα am ruined, 2 plpf. -ωλώλη (558). Mid. ὄλλυμαι be lost, -ολοῦμαι, 2 aor. -ωλόμην, epic part. οὐλόμενος ruinous. Epic also fut. ὀλέσ(σ)ω. In prose ἀπ-όλλῡμι, also δι- and ἐξ-. (3)

ὀλοφύρομαι (ὀλοφυρ-) bewail, fut. ὀλοφυροῦμαι, ὠλοφῡράμην, part. ὀλοφυρθείς made to lament (Thuc.). (2)

ὄμνῡμι and ὀμνύω (ὀμ-, ὀμο-, 592) swear, ὀμοῦμαι, ὤμοσα, ὀμώμοκα ὀμώμοσμαι (with ὀμώμοται), ὠμόθην and ὠμόσθην; ὀμοσθήσομαι, aor. m. ὠμοσάμην. (3)

ὀμόργνῡμι (ὀμοργ-) wipe, ὀμόρξομαι, ὤμορξα, ὠμορξάμην; ἀπ-ομορχθείς. Chiefly poetic. (3)

ὀνίνημι (ὀνη-, ὀνα-, probably for ὀν-ονη-μι, 605) benefit, ὀνήσω, ὤνησα, ὠνήθην; ὀνήσομαι; 2 aor. m. ὠνήμην, ὀναίμην, ὄνασθαι (ὠνάμην late), Hom. imv. ὄνησο, pt. ὀνήμενος. 707. ⦙

ὄνομαι insult, inflected like δίδομαι, with opt. ὄνοιτο (Hom.), fut. ὀνόσσομαι, aor. ὠνο(σ)σάμην (ὤνατο Il. 17, 25), aor. p. κατ-ονοσθῇς (Hdt.). Ionic and poetic.

ὀξύνω (ὀξυν-) sharpen, -οξυνῶ, ὤξῡνα, -ώξυμμαι, -ωξύνθην, -οξυνθήσομαι Hippocr. 732. In Attic prose only in compos. (usually παρ-). (2)

ὀπυίω (ὀπυ-, 636) take to wife, fut. ὀπύσω (Ar.). (2)

ὁράω (ὁρα- for ϝορα-, ὀπ-) see, imperf. ἑώρων (537, Ion. ὥρων), ὄψομαι, ἑόρᾱκα or ἑώρᾱκα (plpf. ἑωρᾱκη), ὦμμαι or ἑόρᾱμαι, ὤφθην, ὀφθήσομαι; 2 pf. ὄπωπα (Ion. and poet.). For 2 aor. εἶδον etc., see εἶδον. Hom. pres. mid. 2 sing. ὅρηαι, 659 d. Aeol. pres. ὄρημι (ὄρημμι), New Ion. ὁρέω. (5)

ὀργαίνω (ὀργαν-) be angry, aor. ὤργᾱνα enraged. Only in tragedy. (2)

ὀρέγω reach, ὀρέξω, ὤρεξα, Ion. pf. ὤρεγμαι, Hom. 3 plur. ὀρωρέχαται, plpf. ὀρωρέχατο, aor. pass. as mid. ὠρέχθην; ὀρέξομαι, ὠρεξάμην. Epic ὀρέγνῡμι, pres. part. ὀρεγνύς.

ὄρνῡμι (ὀρ-) raise, rouse, ὄρσω, ὦρσα, 2 pf. ὄρωρα am roused, epic 2 aor. ὤρορον; mid. rise, rush, fut. ὀροῦμαι, pf. ὀρώρεμαι, 2 aor. ὠρόμην with ὦρτο, imv. ὄρσο, ὄρσεο, ὄρσευ, inf. ὄρθαι, part. ὄρμενος. Poetic. (3)

ὀρύττω (ὀρυγ-) *dig*, ὀρύξω, ὤρυξα, -ορώρυχα (rare), ὀρώρυγμαι (ὤρυγμαι rare and doubtful), ὠρύχθην; fut. p. κατ-ορυχθήσομαι, 2 fut. κατορυχήσομαι; ὠρυξάμην *caused to dig* Hdt. (2)

ὀσφραίνομαι (ὀσφραν-, ὀσφρε-, 643) *smell*, ὀσφρήσομαι, ὠσφράνθην (rare), 2 aor. m. ὠσφρόμην, Hdt. ὤσφραντο. (2, 3)

οὐρέω *mingo*, impf. ἐούρουν, fut. οὐρήσομαι, aor. ἐούρησα, pf. ἐούρηκα. New Ionic has οὐρ- for Attic ἐουρ-.

οὐτάζω (616) *wound*, οὐτάσω, οὔτασα, οὔτασμαι. Chiefly epic. (2)

οὐτάω *wound*, οὔτησα, οὐτήθην; athematic 2 aor. 3 sing. οὖτα (cf. 696), inf. οὐτάμεναι and οὐτάμεν; 2 aor. m. οὐτάμενος as passive. Epic.

ὀφείλω (ὀφελ-, ὀφειλε-, 631) *owe*, ὀφειλήσω, ὠφείλησα, ὠφείληκα, aor. p. part. ὀφειληθείς; 2 aor. ὤφελον, used in wishes (1360), *O that*. Hom. has the Aeol. form ὀφέλλω. (2)

ὀφέλλω (ὀφελ-) *increase*, aor. opt. ὀφέλλειε Hom. Poetic, especially epic. (2)

ὀφλισκάνω (ὀφλ-, ὀφλε-, ὀφλισκ-) *owe, be guilty, incur a penalty*, ὀφλήσω, ὤφλησα (?), ὤφληκα, ὤφλημαι; 2 aor. ὤφλον (ὄφλειν and ὄφλων, for ὀφλεῖν and ὀφλών, are said by grammarians to be Attic forms of inf. and part., as from a later present ὄφλω). (3, 4)

ὄψομαι, see ὁράω.

παίζω (παιδ-, παιγ-) *sport*, παιξοῦμαι, ἔπαισα, πέπαικα, πέπαισμαι. Att. fut. probably παίσομαι. 618, 679. (2)

παίω (παι-, παιε-) *strike*, παίσω and παιήσω (Ar.), ἔπαισα, πέπαικα, ἐπαίσθην (598).

παλαίω *wrestle*, ἐπάλαισα, ἐπαλαίσθην (598); fut. παλαίσω in epic.

πάλλω (παλ-) *brandish*, ἔπηλα, πέπαλμαι; Hom. redupl. 2 aor. ἀμ-πεπαλών, as if from πέπαλον; 2 aor. m. ἔπαλτο and πάλτο. (2)

παρανομέω *transgress the law*, augm. παρενόμουν and παρηνόμουν, παρανενόμηκα (565).

παροινέω *insult* (*as a drunken man*), impf. ἐπαρῴνουν; ἐπαρῴνησα, πεπαρῴνηκα, παρῳνήθην (Dem.) and ἐπαρῳνήθην (567).

πάσομαι fut. *shall acquire* (no pres.), pf. πέπᾱμαι *possess*, ἐπᾱσάμην. Poetic = κτάομαι. Not to be confounded with πάσομαι, ἐπασάμην, etc. (with ᾰ) of πατέομαι *eat*.

πάσχω (πενθ-, πονθ-, παθ- for πνθ-), for παθ-σκω (648) *suffer*, πείσομαι (for πενθ-σομαι, 70), 2 pf. πέπονθα (Hom. πέποσθε or πέπασθε for πεπόνθατε, and πεπαθυῖα); 2 aor. ἔπαθον. 585. (4)

πατάσσω *strike*, pres. and impf. epic. Att. uses τύπτω or παίω in pres. system, but has πατάξω, ἐπάταξα; Hom. ἐκ-πεπάταγμαι; ἐπατάχθην late. Perf. and aor. pass. in Att. from πλήττω (πέπληγμαι, ἐπλήγην). (2)

πατέομαι (πατ-, πατε-) *eat*, fut. πάσονται (?), ἐπᾰ(σ)σάμην (Hom.); epic plpf. πεπάσμην. 590. Epic and New Ionic. Not to be confounded with πάσομαι.

πάττω (623, 625) *sprinkle*, πάσω, ἔπασα, ἐπάσθην; usually in comp. and chiefly in comedy. Hom. has only pres. and impf. (2)

παύω *stop, cause to cease*, παύσω, ἔπαυσα, πέπαυκα, πέπαυμαι, ἐπαύθην (ἐπαύσθην and ἐπαύθην Hdt.), παυθήσομαι, πεπαύσομαι. Mid. παύομαι *cease* (intrans.), παύσομαι, ἐπαυσάμην.

πείθω (πειθ-, ποιθ-, πιθ-) *persuade*, πείσω, ἔπεισα, πέπεικα, πέπεισμαι *am convinced, believe*, ἐπείσθην (66), πεισθήσομαι; fut. m. πείσομαι; 2 pf. πέποιθα *trust*, with imv. πέπεισθι (perhaps for πέπισθι) Aesch. *Eum.* 599, Hom. plpf. ἐπέπιθμεν for ἐπεποίθεμεν, 728; poet. 2 aor. ἔπιθον and ἐπιθόμην, epic redupl. πέπιθον (559). From πιθε-, epic πιθήσω *shall obey*, πεπιθήσω *shall persuade*, πιθήσας *trusting* (590).

πείκω, epic pres. = πεκτέω *comb*.

πεινάω (πεινη-, πεινα-) *hunger*, regular, except in η for α in contract forms, inf. πεινῆν, epic πεινήμεναι, etc. See 486.

πείρω (περ-, παρ-) *pierce*, epic in pres.; ἔπειρα, πέπαρμαι, ἀν-επάρην Hdt. 587. Ionic and poetic. (2)

πεκτέω (πεκ-, πεκτε-, 590) *comb, shear*, Dor. fut. πεξῶ, aor. ἔπεξα (Theocr.), epic ἐπεξάμην; aor. p. ἐπέχθην. See epic πείκω. Poetic. Att. uses κτενίζω or ξαίνω *comb*, κείρω *shear*.

πελάζω (cf. πέλας *near*; see 620) *bring near, approach*, fut. πελάσω, Att. πελῶ (678 b), ἐπέλασα, πέπλημαι (epic), ἐπελάσθην (epic), ἐπλάθην (trag.); epic ἐπέλασσα, with mid. ἐπελασάμην; 2 aor. m. ἐπλήμην *approached*. Also poetic presents πελάω, πελάθω, πλάθω, πίλναμαι. (2)

πέλω and πέλομαι (πελ-, πλ-) *be*, impf. ἔπελον, ἐπελόμην; 2 aor. ἔπλε, ἔπλεο (ἔπλευ), ἔπλετο; so ἐπι-πλόμενος and περι-πλόμενος. Poetic.

πέμπω (πεμπ-, πομπ-) *send*, πέμψω, ἔπεμψα, πέπομφα (585, 724), πέπεμμαι (81, 499 a), ἐπέμφθην, πεμφθήσομαι; πέμψομαι, ἐπεμψάμην. (2)

πεπαίνω (πεπαν-) *make soft, ripen*, ἐπέπᾱνα (688), ἐπεπάνθην, πεπανθήσομαι. (2)

πεπορεῖν or πεπαρεῖν *show*, 2 aor. inf. in Pind. *P.* 2, 57, see (πορ-).

πέπρωται *it is fated*: see (πορ-).

πέρδομαι (περδ-, πορδ-, παρδ-), Lat. pedo, 2 fut. παρδήσομαι, 2 pf. πέπορδα, 2 aor. ἔπαρδον. See 585, 587.

πέρθω (περθ-, πραθ-) *destroy, sack*, πέρσω (πέρσομαι Hom.), ἔπερσα, epic 2 aor. ἔπραθον (587), m. ἐπραθόμην (as pass.) with inf. πέρθαι for περθ-σθαι. Poetic. Prose πορθέω.

πέρνημι (περ-να-) *sell*, fut. περάω, ἐπέρασ(σ)α; mid. πέρναμαι, pf. part. πεπερημένος. Chiefly epic. Prose πωλέω and ἀποδίδομαι; cf. πιπράσκω. 642. (3)

πετάννῡμι (πετα-, πτα-) *expand*, πετῶ, ἐπέτασα, πέπταμαι. Fut. ἐκ-πετάσω Eur., pf. mid. πεπέτασμαι late, aor. p. πετάσθην Hom. See πίτνημι. (3)

πέτομαι (πετ-, πετε-, πτ-) *fly*, πτήσομαι (poet. πετήσομαι); 2 aor. m. ἐπτόμην. To πέταμαι (poet.) belong 2 aor. ἔπτην and ἐπτάμην (694). The forms πεπότημαι and ἐποτήθην (Dor. -άμαι, -άθην) belong to ποτάομαι. Late is ἵπταμαι.

πέττω (πεκ-, πεπ-) cook, πέψω, ἔπεψα, πέπεμμαι (79, 499 a), ἐπέφθην. See 626. (2)

πεύθομαι (πευθ-, πυθ-) : see πυνθάνομαι.

πέφνον slew, see (φεν-).

πήγνῡμι (πηγ-, παγ-) fasten, πήξω, ἔπηξα, ἐπήχθην (rare and poet.) ; 2 aor. p. ἐπάγην, 2 fut. p. παγήσομαι ; 2 pf. πέπηγα be fixed, be frozen ; epic 2 aor. m. κατ-έπηκτο ; πηγνῦτο (Plat.) pres. opt. for πηγνυ-ῖ-το (766) ; πήξομαι, ἐπηξάμην, Ion. (3)

πῑαίνω (πῑαν-) fatten, πῑανῶ, ἐπῑανα, πεπίασμαι. Chiefly poetic and Ionic. (2)

πίλναμαι (πιλ-να-) approach, only in pres. and impf. 642. Epic. See πελάζω. (3)

πίμπλημι (πλη-, πλα-, with μ assimilated) fill, πλήσω, ἔπλησα, πέπληκα, πέπλησμαι, ἐπλήσθην, πλησθήσομαι ; aor. m. ἐπλησάμην (trans.) ; 2 aor. m. ἐπλήμην (707), chiefly epic, with ἐν-έπλητο, opt. ἐμ-πλήμην, ἐμ-πλῆτο, impf. ἔμ-πλησο, part. ἐμ-πλήμενος, in Aristoph. 613. Cf. πλήθω, in prose only πλήθουσα, also poet. πληθύω and πληθύνομαι, and πληρόω.

πίμπρημι (πρη-, πρα-, with μ assimilated) burn, πρήσω, ἔπρησα, πέπρημαι and πέπρησμαι (Hdt.), ἐπρήσθην ; Ion. fut. πρήσομαι, fut. pf. πεπρήσομαι. 613. Cf. πρήθω blow.

πινύσκω (πινυ-) make wise, Hom. aor. ἐπίνυσσα. Poetic. See πνέω. (4)

πίνω (πι-, πο-, πω-) drink, fut. πίομαι (πιοῦμαι rare) ; πέπωκα, πέπομαι, ἐπόθην, ποθήσομαι ; 2 aor. ἔπιον. Aeol. πώνω. 681. (3)

πιπίσκω (πῑ-) give to drink, πῑσω, ἔπῑσα. New Ionic and poetic (πῑσᾱς Aristotle). See πίνω. (4)

πιπράσκω (πρᾱ-) sell, epic περάσω, ἐπέρασα, πέπρᾱκα, πέπρᾱμαι, Hom. πεπε-ρημένος, ἐπράθην (Ion. -ημαι, -ήθην) ; fut. pf. πεπρᾱσομαι. The Attic uses forms of ἀποδίδομαι and πωλέω for pres., fut., and aor. (4)

πίπτω (πετ-, πτ-, πτω-, 605) fall, fut. πεσοῦμαι, Ion. πεσέομαι ; pf. πέπτωκα, 2 pf. part. πεπτώς, epic πεπτηώς or -εώς ; 2 aor. ἔπεσον, Dor. Aeol. ἔπετον. πίτνημι (πιτ-να-) spread, pres. and impf. act. and mid. ; also πιτνάω. 642. Epic and lyric. See πετάννῡμι. (3)

πίτνω, poetic for πίπτω. (3)

πλάζω (πλαγγ-) cause to wander, ἔπλαγξα. Pass. and mid. πλάζομαι wan-der, πλάγξομαι will wander, ἐπλάγχθην wandered. Ionic and poetic. (2)

πλάττω (see 625) form, mould, ἔπλασα, πέπλασμαι, ἐπλάσθην ; ἐπλασάμην. Ion. fut. ἀνα-πλάσω. (2)

πλέκω (πλεκ-, πλοκ-, πλακ-) plait, knit, πλέξω, ἔπλεξα, πέπλεγμαι, ἐπλέχθην, πλεχθήσομαι ; 2 aor. p. ἐπλάκην ; aor. m. ἐπλεξάμην. Ion. πλέξω, -πέπλοχα (probably also Att.) and -πέπλεχα.

πλέω (πλευ-, πλεϝ-, πλυ-) *sail*, πλεύσομαι or πλευσοῦμαι, ἔπλευσα, πέπλευκα, πέπλευσμαι, ἐπλεύσθην (later). 600, 611. Ion. and poet. πλώω, πλώσομαι, ἔπλωσα, πέπλωκα, epic 2 aor. ἔπλων. Epic pres. also πλείω, Att. πλῴζω.

πλήττω (πληγ-, πλαγ-, 34) *strike*, πλήξω, ἔπληξα, πέπληγμαι, ἐπλήχθην (rare) ; 2 pf. πέπληγα ; 2 aor. p. ἐπλήγην, in comp. -επλάγην (745) ; 2 fut. p. πληγήσομαι and -πλαγήσομαι ; fut. pf. πεπλήξομαι ; epic 2 aor. πέπληγον (or ἐπέπλ-), πεπληγόμην ; Ion. aor. m. ἐπληξάμην. Att. uses comp. forms in pres., impf., fut., and aor., or substitutes τύπτω and παίω. Cf. πατάσσω. (2)

πλύνω (πλυν-) *wash*, πλυνῶ, ἔπλῡνα, πέπλυμαι, ἐπλύθην ; fut. m. (as pass.) ἐκ-πλυνοῦμαι. 602. (2)

πλώω, Ionic and poetic : see πλέω.

πνέω (πνευ-, πνεϝ-, πνυ-) *breathe, blow*, -πνεύσομαι and πνευσοῦμαι, ἔπνευσα, πέπνευκα, epic πέπνῡμαι *be wise*, part. πεπνῡμένος *wise*, plpf. πέπνῡσο ; late ἐπνεύσθην, Hom. ἀμ-πνύνθην. For epic ἄμ-πνυε etc., see ἀνα-πνέω and ἄμπνυε. See πινύσκω.

πνίγω (πνῑγ-, πνιγ-) *choke*, πνίξω, Dor. πνιξοῦμαι, ἔπνιξα, πέπνῑγμαι, ἐπνίγην, πνιγήσομαι. 584.

ποθέω *desire*, ποθήσω or ποθέσομαι, ἐπόθησα or ἐπόθεσα. 596, 597.

πονέω *labor*, πονήσω etc., regular, but Ionic πονέσω and ἐπόνεσα (Hippocr. MSS.). 596, 597. Older pres. πονέομαι (1244), Dor. and Aeol. πονάω.

(πορ-, πρω-) *give, allot*, 2 aor. ἔπορον (poet.), pf. p. πέπρωμαι, chiefly impers., πέπρωται *it is fated* (with ἡ πεπρωμένη *Fate*) ; redupl. 2 aor. inf. πεπορεῖν (πεπαρεῖν) in Pind. *to show*. Poetic except in perf. part.

πράττω (πρᾱγ-) *do*, πρᾱ́ξω, ἔπρᾱξα, πέπρᾱχα (trans. *have effected*, a later form, 725), πέπρᾱγμαι, ἐπρᾱ́χθην, πρᾱχθήσομαι, fut. pf. πεπρᾱ́ξομαι ; intrans. pf. πέπρᾱγα *am faring* (*well* or *ill*, 1250 c), also *have done* ; mid. fut. πρᾱ́ξομαι, aor. ἐπρᾱξάμην. Ionic πρήσσω (πρηγ-), πρήξω, ἔπρηξα, πέπρηχα, πέπρηγμαι, ἐπρήχθην ; πέπρηγα ; πρήξομαι, ἐπρηξάμην. (2)

(πρια-) *buy*, only 2 aor. ἐπριάμην, inflected throughout in 504 ; see synopsis in 503.

πρίω *saw*, ἔπρῑσα, πέπρῑσμαι, ἐπρίσθην. 598.

προΐσσομαι (προϊκ-) *beg*, once in Archil. (cf. προῖκα *gratis*) ; fut. only in κατα-προΐξομαι (Ar.) ; Ion. κατα-προΐξομαι. (2)

πτάρνυμαι (πταρ-) *sneeze* ; 2 aor. ἔπταρον ; also 1 aor. ἔπταρα, 2 aor. pass. ἐπτάρην (Aristotle). (3)

πτήσσω (πτηκ-, πτακ-) *cower*, ἔπτηξα, ἔπτηχα ; 2 aor. part. καταπτακών (Ar.). From stem πτα- epic 2 aor. καταπτήτην, dual ; 2 pf. part. πεπτηώς. Poetic also πτώσσω (cf. πτωχ-ός *beggar*, πτώξ *hare*). (2)

πτίττω *pound* (πτισ-), ἔπτισα (Hdt.), -έπτισμαι (Ar.), late -επτίσθην. (2)

πτύσσω (πτυχ-) *fold*, πτύξω, ἔπτυξα, ἔπτυγμαι, ἐπτύχθην ; πτύξομαι, ἐπτυξάμην ; 2 aor. pass. -επτύγην (Hippocr.). Usually comp. in prose. (2)

πτύω *spit*, πτύσω, πτύσομαι, ἐπτύσθην, Hippocr.; aor. ἔπτυσα.

πυνθάνομαι (πευθ-, πυθ-) *hear, inquire*, fut. πεύσομαι, Dor. πευσοῦμαι, pf. πέπυσμαι; 2 aor. ἐπυθόμην (with Hom. redupl. opt. πεπύθοιτο). (3). Poetic also πεύθομαι.

ῥαίνω (ῥα-, ῥαν-) *sprinkle*, ῥανῶ, ἔρρανα, ἐρράνθην. From a stem ῥαδ- epic aor. ἔρασσα, pf. p. ἔρρασμαι, ἔρρανται Aeschyl., epic ἐρράδαται, plpf. ἐρράδατο, 654 c. See 643. Ionic and poetic. (2, 3)

ῥαίω *strike*, ῥαίσω, ἔρραισα, ἐρραίσθην; fut. m. (as pass.) ῥαίσομαι. Poetic, chiefly epic.

ῥάπτω (ῥαφ-) *stitch*, ῥάψω, ἔρραψα, ἔρραμμαι;˙ 2 aor. p. ἐρράφην; aor. m. ἐρραψάμην. (2)

ῥάττω (ῥαγ-), late for ἀράττω *throw down*, ῥάξω, ἔρραξα, ἐρράχθην. See ἀράττω. (2)

ῥέζω (ϝρεγ-, 617) *do*, ῥέξω, ἔρεξα; Ion. aor. p. ῥεχθείη, ῥεχθείς. See ἔρδω. (2)

ῥέω (ῥευ-, ῥεϝ-, ῥυ-, ῥυε-) *flow*, ῥεύσομαι, ἔρρευσα (rare in Attic), ἐρρύηκα; 2 aor. p. ἐρρύην, ῥυήσομαι. 611.

(ῥη-) stem of εἴρηκα, εἴρημαι, ἐρρήθην, ῥηθήσομαι, εἰρήσομαι. See εἶπον and εἴρω.

ῥήγνῡμι (ϝρηγ-, ῥωγ-, ῥαγ-) *break*; ῥήξω, ἔρρηξα, ἔρρηγμαι and ἐρρήχθην Ion.; 2 aor. p. ἐρράγην; ῥαγήσομαι; 2 pf. ἔρρωγα *am broken* (719, 1250 c). (3)

ῥῑγέω (ῥῑγε-, ῥῑγ-) *shudder*, epic fut. ῥῑγήσω, aor. ἐρρίγησα, pf. ἔρρῑγα (as pres.). Poetic, chiefly epic. 590.

ῥῑγόω *shiver*, ῥῑγώσω, ἐρρίγωσα; pres. ind. and subj. ῥῑγῷ for ῥῑγοῖ, opt. ῥῑγῴην, inf. ῥῑγῶν and ῥῑγοῦν: see 488.

ῥίπτω (ῥῑπ-, ῥιπ-) *throw*, ῥίψω, ἔρρῑψα, ἔρρῑφα, ἔρρῑμμαι, ἐρρίφθην, ῥῑφθήσομαι; 2 aor. p. ἐρρίφην. Pres. also ῥῑπτέω (590). (2)

ῥύομαι, epic also ῥῦομαι (ϝρῡ-) *defend*, ῥύσομαι, ἐρρῡσάμην. Athematic forms: 3 pers. ἔρρῡτο (ἔρῦτο, 696 a), pl. ῥύατο, inf. ῥῦσθαι. Chiefly poetic. See ἔρῡμαι.

ῥυπάω *be dirty*, epic ῥυπόω *soil*; Ion. pf. part. ῥερυπωμένος. 547.

ῥώννῡμι (ῥω-, ῥωσ-, 86 c) *strengthen*, ἔρρωσα, ἔρρωμαι, imv. ἔρρωσο *farewell*, part. ἐρρωμένος as adj. *strong*, ἐρρώσθην. (3)

σαίνω (σαν-) *fawn on*, aor. ἔσηνα, Dor. ἔσᾱνα. Poetic. (2)

σαίρω (σηρ-, σαρ-) *sweep*, aor. (ἔσηρα) part. σήρᾱς; 2 pf. σέσηρα *grin*, esp. in part. σεσηρώς, Dor. σεσᾱρώς. (2)

σαλπίζω (σαλπιγγ-) *sound a trumpet*, aor. ἐσάλπιγξα. (2)

σαόω *save*, pres. rare and poet., σαώσω, ἐσάωσα, ἐσαώθην; 3 sing. impf. σάω (for ἐσάω), imv. σάω, as if from Aeol. σάωμι (or read σάου for σαο-ε). Epic subj. σόῃς, σόῃ (MSS.) should perhaps be σαῷς, σαῷ, or σάως, σάῳ (cf. 659). See σῴζω. Epic.

σάττω (σαγ-) *pack, load*, aor. ἔσαξα, pf. p. σέσαγμαι. (2)

σβέννῡμι (σβε- for σβεσ-, 86 c) *extinguish*, σβέσω, ἔσβεσα, ἔσβηκα *have gone out* (of fire), ἐσβέσθην; 2 aor. ἔσβην (706) *went out*, with inf. σβῆναι, part. ἀποσβείς Hippocr.; fut. m. σβήσομαι. (3)

σέβω *revere*, aor. p. ἐσέφθην, with part. σεφθείς *awe-struck*.

σείω *shake*, σείσω, ἔσεισα, σέσεικα, σέσεισμαι, ἐσείσθην (598).

σεύω (σευ-, συ-) *urge*, mid. *rush*, aor. ἔσσευα, ἐσσευάμην; ἔσσυμαι *be in haste*, ἐσσύθην or ἐσύθην; 2 aor. m. ἐσ(σ)ύμην (with ἔσυτο, σύτο, σύμενος). The Attic poets have σοῦται (σεῦται MSS.), σοῦνται, σοῦσθε (ind. and imv.), σοῦ, σούσθω (all probably from σοέομαι or σόομαι). 696 a. Poetic; Xen. has ἀπ-εσσύᾰ (ἀπ-έσσουα). The forms σοῦ and σοῦσθε in comedy may be imitative, *shoo!*

σημαίνω (σημαν-) *show*, σημανῶ, ἐσήμηνα, σεσήμασμαι, ἐσημάνθην, σημανθή-σομαι; mid. σημανοῦμαι, ἐσημηνάμην; aor. act. ἐσήμᾱνα in Xen. MSS., but not good Att. (2)

σήπω (σηπ-, σαπ-) *rot*, σήψω, 2 pf. σέσηπα *am rotten*; σέσημμαι (Aristot.), 2 aor. p. ἐσάπην, fut. σαπήσομαι.

σίνομαι (σιν-) *injure*, aor. ἐσῑνάμην Ion. 630. (2)

σκάπτω (σκαφ-) *dig*, σκάψω, ἔσκαψα, ἔσκαφα, ἔσκαμμαι, ἐσκάφην. (2)

σκεδάννῡμι (σκεδα- for σκεδασ-) *scatter*, fut. σκεδῶ, ἐσκέδασα, ἐσκέδασμαι with part. ἐσκεδασμένος, ἐσκεδάσθην; ἐσκεδασάμην; fut. σκεδάσω poetic. Epic also κεδάννῡμι, Ion. σκίδνημι and κίδνημι. (3)

σκέλλω (σκελ-, σκλη-) *dry up*, Hom. aor. ἔσκηλα, Ion. pf. ἔσκληκα; 2 aor. (ἔσκλην) ἀπο-σκλῆναι (694) Aristophanes. (2)

σκέπτομαι (σκεπ-) *view*, σκέψομαι, ἐσκεψάμην, ἔσκεμμαι, fut. pf. ἐσκέψομαι; ἐσκέφθην Ion. For pres. and impf. the better Attic writers use σκοπῶ, σκοποῦμαι, etc. (see σκοπέω). (2)

σκήπτω (σκηπ-) *prop*, σκήψω, ἔσκηψα, ἔσκημμαι, ἐσκήφθην; σκήψομαι, ἐσκηψά-μην. In prose usually comp. ἐπισκήπτω *lay an injunction upon*. (2)

σκίδνημι (σκιδνη-, σκιδ-να-), mid. σκίδναμαι, *scatter*, also κίδνημι: chiefly poetic for σκεδάννῡμι. (3)

σκοπέω *view*, in better Attic writers only pres. and impf. act. and mid. For the other tenses σκέψομαι, ἐσκεψάμην, and ἔσκεμμαι of σκέπτομαι are used. See σκέπτομαι.

σκώπτω (σκωπ-) *jeer*, σκώψομαι, ἔσκωψα, ἐσκώφθην. (2)

σμάω *smear*, only in contr. σμῶ (σμα-, σμη-) *smear*, with η for ᾱ in contracted forms (486), σμῇς, σμῇ, etc.; aor. ἔσμησα, mid. ἐσμησάμην Hdt. Ion. σμέω and σμήχω, aor. p. διασμηχθείς (Aristoph.).

σπάω (σπα- for σπασ-) *draw*, σπάσω, ἔσπασα, ἔσπακα, ἔσπασμαι, ἐσπάσθην, σπασθήσομαι; σπάσομαι, ἐσπασάμην. 596, 597.

σπείρω (σπερ-, σπαρ-) *sow*, σπερῶ, ἔσπειρα, ἔσπαρμαι; 2 aor. p. ἐσπάρην. (2)

σπένδω *pour libation*, σπείσω (for σπενδ-σω, 70), ἔσπεισα, ἔσπεισμαι (see 499 c); mid. σπένδομαι *make a treaty*, σπείσομαι, ἐσπεισάμην.

στάζω (σταγ-) *drop*, ἔσταξα, ἔσταγμαι, ἐστάχθην. Late fut. στάσω, Theocr. σταξεῦμαι. (**2**)

στείβω (στειβ-) *tread*, ἔστειψα, ἐστίβημαι (from a stem στιβε-, 590, or possibly a pres. στιβέω). Poetic.

στείχω (στειχ-, στιχ-) *go*, ἔστειξα, 2 aor. ἔστιχον. Poetic and Ionic.

στέλλω (στελ-, σταλ-) *send*, στελῶ, ἔστειλα, ἔσταλκα, ἔσταλμαι; 2 aor. p. ἐστάλην; σταλήσομαι; aor. m. ἐστειλάμην. 587. In prose comp. with ἀπό and ἐπί. (**2**)

στενάζω (στεναγ-) *groan*, στενάξω, ἐστέναξα. Epic or poetic are στένω, στενάχω, στεναχίζω, στοναχέω. (**2**)

στέργω (στεργ-, στοργ-) *love*, στέρξω, ἔστερξα; 2 pf. ἔστοργα (585).

στερέω *deprive*, στερήσω, ἐστέρησα, ἐστέρηκα, ἐστέρημαι, ἐστερήθην, στερηθήσομαι; 2 aor. p. ἐστέρην (poetic), part. στερείς, 2 fut. (pass. or mid.) στερήσομαι. Epic aor. ἐστέρεσα. In prose usually comp. ἀπο-στερέω. Also pres. στερίσκω. Pres. στέρομαι *be in want*.

(στεῦμαι) *pledge one's self*; only in 3 pres. στεῦται, στεῦνται, impf. στεῦτο. Poetic, chiefly epic.

στίζω (στιγ-) *tattoo*, στίξω, ἔστιγμαι; ἔστιξα Hdt. (**2**)

στόρνῡμι (στορ-, στορε-) *spread out*, στορῶ, ἐστόρεσα, ἐστορέσθην (Ion.). Late fut. στορέσω, Theocr. στορεσῶ. (**3**)

στρέφω (στρεφ-, στροφ-, στραφ-) *turn*, στρέψω, ἔστρεψα, ἔστραμμαι, ἐστρέφθην (rare in prose), usually 2 aor. p. ἐστράφην. 2 pf. ἀν-έστροφε trans. (comedy); Ion. aor. p. ἐστράφθην; fut. στραφήσομαι; mid. στρέψομαι, ἐστρεψάμην. 585, 587.

στρώννῡμι (στρω-), στρώσω, ἔστρωσα, ἔστρωμαι, ἐστρώθην. Cf. στόρνῡμι. (**3**)

στυγέω (στυγ-, στυγε-, 590) *dread, hate*, fut. στυγήσομαι (as pass.), aor. ἐστύγησα (epic ἔστυξα *made terrible*, Ion. pf. ἐστύγηκα), aor. p. ἐστυγήθην; epic 2 aor. ἔστυγον. Ionic and poetic.

στυφελίζω (στυφελιγ-) *dash*, aor. ἐστυφέλιξα. Ionic, chiefly epic. (**2**)

σύρω (συρ-) *draw*, aor. ἔσῡρα, ἐσῡράμην, σέσυρκα. In prose comp. with ἀπό, διά, ἐπί. (**2**)

σφάλλω (σφαλ-) *trip, deceive*, σφαλῶ, ἔσφηλα, ἔσφαλμαι; 2 aor. p. ἐσφάλην, fut. p. σφαλήσομαι; fut. m. σφαλοῦμαι (rare). (**2**)

σφάττω (σφαγ-) *cut the throat of*, σφάξω, ἔσφαξα, ἔσφαγμαι, ἐσφάχθην (rare); 2 aor. p. ἐσφάγην, fut. σφαγήσομαι; aor. m. ἐσφαξάμην. 624. (**2**) Trag. pres. σφάζω, 617.

σχάζω (620) *cut open, let go*, σχάσω, ἔσχασα, ἐσχασάμην; Ion. ἐσχάσθην. From pres. σχάω impf. ἔσχων (Aristoph.). (**2**)

σώζω, later σώζω, epic usually σώω (σω-, σωι-), *save*, epic pres. subj. σόῃς (σάῳς, σόῳς), σόῃ (σάῳ, σόῳ), σόωσι; σώσω, ἔσωσα (Att. inscr. ἔσωσα), σέσωκα, σέσωμαι or σέσωσμαι, ἐσώθην, σωθήσομαι; σώσομαι, ἐσωσάμην. See σαόω. (**2**)

ταγ- *seize*, in Hom. 2 aor. pt. *τεταγών.* Cf. Lat. tango.

τανύω (τεν-, τα- for τῃ + -νυ-ω) *stretch*, τανύσω, ἐτάνυ(σ)σα, τετάνυσμαι, ἐτανύσθην; aor. m. ἐτανυσσάμην. Pres. pass. athematic τάνυται. Epic form of **τείνω.** (3)

ταράττω (ταραχ-) *disturb*, **ταράξω, ἐτάραξα, τετάραγμαι, ἐταράχθην**; fut. m. **ταράξομαι**; epic 2 pf. (τέτρηχα) τετρηχώς *disturbed*; plpf. τετρήχει. (2)

τάττω (ταγ-) *arrange*, **τάξω, ἔταξα, τέταχα, τέταγμαι, ἐτάχθην, ταχθήσομαι**; τάξομαι, ἐταξάμην; 2 aor. p. ἐτάγην; fut. pf. **τετάξομαι.** 624. (2)

(**ταφ-** for θαφ-, 105) in 2 aor. ἔταφον *was amazed*; see (**θηπ-**).

τείνω (τεν-, τα- for τῃ) *stretch*, **τενῶ, ἔτεινα, τέτακα, τέταμαι, ἐτάθην, ταθήσομαι**; τενοῦμαι, ἐτεινάμην. 27, 585, 587. See **τανύω** and **τιταίνω.** (2)

τεκμαίρομαι (τεκμαρ-) *judge, infer*, fut. **τεκμαροῦμαι**, aor. **ἐτεκμηράμην.** Act. **τεκμαίρω**, rare and poetic, aor. ἐτέκμηρα. (2)

τελέω (τελεσ-, τελε-) *finish*, (τελέσω) **τελῶ, ἐτέλεσα, τετέλεκα, τετέλεσμαι, ἐτελέσθην**; fut. m. (τελέομαι) τελοῦμαι, aor. m. ἐτελεσάμην. 596, 597, 600. Epic also τελείω.

τέλλω (τελ-, ταλ- for τλ-) *cause to rise, rise*, aor. ἔτειλα; plpf. p. ἐτέταλτο. In compos. **ἐν-τέταλμαι, ἐν-ετειλάμην.** See 27, 585, 587. (2)

(**τεμ-, τμ-**) *find*, in Hom. redupl. 2 aor. τέτμον or ἔτετμον (559).

τέμνω (τεμ-, ταμ-, τμη-), Ion. and Dor. **τάμνω**, Hom. once τέμω, *cut*, fut. **τεμῶ, τέτμηκα, τέτμημαι, ἐτμήθην**, τμηθήσομαι; 2 aor. ἔτεμον, ἐτεμόμην, poet. and Ion. ἔταμον, ἐταμόμην; fut. m. τεμοῦμαι; fut. pf. **τετμήσομαι.** See **τμήγω.** (3)

τέρπω (τερπ-, ταρπ-, τραπ-) *amuse*, **τέρψω, ἔτερψα, ἐτέρφθην**, epic ἐτάρφθην, 2 aor. p. ἐτάρπην (with subj. τραπήομεν), 2 aor. m. (τ)εταρπόμην (559); fut. m. τέρψομαι (poet.), aor. ἐτερψάμην epic. See 585, 587.

τέρσομαι *become dry*, 2 aor. p. ἐτέρσην intrans. Chiefly epic. Fut. act. τέρσω in Theocr.

τεταγών *having seized*: see stem (**ταγ-**).

τετίημαι Hom. perf. *am troubled*, in dual τετίησθον and part. τετιημένος; also τετιηώς *troubled*.

τέτμον or **ἔτετμον** (Hom.) *found*, redupl. 2 aor. (559). See (**τεμ-**).

τετραίνω (τετραν-, also τερ-, τρη-) *bore*, late pres. τιτραίνω and τιτράω; Ion. fut. τετρανέω, aor. **ἐτέτρāνα** and **ἔτρησα**, ἐτετρηνάμην (688); pf. p. **τέτρημαι.** 643. (2, 3)

τεύχω (τευχ-, τυχ-, τυκ-) *prepare, make*, **τεύξω, ἔτευξα**, epic τετευχώς as pass., τέτυγμαι, τετεύχαται, ἐτετεύχατο, ἐτύχθην Hom., ἐτεύχθην Hippocr., fut. pf. **τετεύξομαι** Hom.; fut. m. τεύξομαι, epic aor. ἐτευξάμην, 2 aor. τετυκεῖν, τετυκόμην. Poetic.

τῆ (τα- in τανύω, τείνω) imperative *take*. Hence pl. τῆτε (Sophron). More probably instrumental case of demonstrative stem το- *here!*

τήκω (τηκ-, τακ-) melt, Dor. τάκω, τήξω, ἔτηξα, ἐτήχθην (rare); 2 aor. p. ἐτάκην; 2 pf. τέτηκα am melted.

τίθημι (θη-, θε-) put; see synopsis and inflection in 503, 504, 507.

τίκτω (τεκ-, τοκ-) for τι-τκ-ω (106, 605) beget, bring forth, τέξομαι, poet. also τέξω, rarely τεκοῦμαι, ἐτέχθην (rare); pf. τέτοκα; 2 aor. ἔτεκον, ἐτεκόμην.

τίλλω (τιλ-) pluck, τιλῶ, ἔτῖλα, τέτιλμαι, ἐτίλθην. Chiefly poetic. (2)

τίνω (τει-, τι-) pay, τείσω, ἔτεισα, τέτεικα, τέτεισμαι, ἐτείσθην. Mid. τίνομαι take payment, τείσομαι, ἐτεισάμην. The futures, aorists, and perfects are written τίσω, ἔτισα, etc. in MSS.; the spelling ει is attested by inscriptions. Hom. τίνω (for τι-νϝ-ω), τίω. Parallel mid. pres. τείνυμαι take vengeance (MSS. τίνυμαι). See τίω. (3)

τιταίνω (redupl. τι-ταν-) stretch, aor. ἐτίτηνα, τιτήνᾱς. Epic for τείνω. (2)

τιτρώσκω (τρω-) wound, τρώσω, ἔτρωσα, τέτρωμαι, ἐτρώθην, τρωθήσομαι; fut. m. τρώσομαι as passive, Hom. Rarely epic τρώω. (4)

τίω honor, Hom. τίω (? τείω) or τίω, fut. τίσω, aor. ἔτῑσα (προ-τίσᾱς, S. Ant. 22), pf. p. τέτῑμαι. After Homer chiefly in pres. and impf. Attic τείσω, ἔτεισα, etc. belong to τίνω. See τίνω.

(τλα-, τλη-, ταλα-) endure, τλήσομαι, τέτληκα, 2 aor. ἔτλην (see 694). Epic forms of 2 pf. τέτλαμεν, τετλαίην, τέτλαθι, τετλάμεναι and τετλάμεν, τετληώς (728). From (ταλα-) Hom. aor. ἐτάλασσα. Poetic. Prose uses τολμάω.

τμήγω (τμηγ-, τμαγ-) cut, poet. for τέμνω; τμήξω (rare), ἔτμηξα, 2 aor. ἔτμαγον, ἐτμάγην, 3 pl. τμάγεν (cf. 741).

τορέω (τορ-, τορε-) pierce, pres. only in epic ἀντι-τορεῦντα; epic fut. τορήσω, τετορήσω (Ar.), epic aor. ἐτόρησα, 2 aor. ἔτορον. 590.

τρέπω (τρεπ-, τροπ-, τραπ-) [turn, τρέψω, ἔτρεψα, τέτροφα (τέτραφα rare), τέτραμμαι, ἐτρέφθην; fut. m. τρέψομαι, aor. m. ἐτρεψάμην; ἐτράπην, ἐτραπόμην fled. Ion. Dor. pres. τράπω; epic and poetic 2 aor. ἔτραπον; Hom. and Hdt. aor. pass. ἐτράφθην. This verb has all the six aorists (746). 585, 587.

τρέφω (τρεφ- for θρεφ-, 105 e, τροφ-, τραφ-) nourish, θρέψω, ἔθρεψα, τέτροφα, τέθραμμαι with inf. τεθράφθαι, ἐθρέφθην with inf. θρεφθῆναι (rare); 2 aor. p. ἐτράφην; fut. m. θρέψομαι, aor. m. ἐθρεψάμην. Dor. pres. τράφω, epic 2 aor. ἔτραφον intrans. 585, 587.

τρέχω (τρεχ- for θρεχ-, 105 e, τρεχε-, δραμ-) run, fut. δραμοῦμαι (-θρέξομαι only in comedy), ἔθρεξα (rare), δεδράμηκα, δεδράμημαι; 2 pf. δέδρομα (poet.) in comp. with ἀνά, ἀμφί, ἐπί, 2 aor. ἔδραμον. (5)

τρέω (τρεσ-, τρε-) tremble, aor. ἔτρεσα. Chiefly poetic.

τρίβω (τρῖβ-, τρῐβ-) rub, τρίψω, ἔτρῑψα, τέτριφα, τέτρῑμμαι (497, 499), ἐτρίφθην; more often 2 aor. p. ἐτρίβην, 2 fut. p. τριβήσομαι; fut. pf. τετρίψομαι; fut. m. τρίψομαι, aor. m. ἐτρῑψάμην.

τρίζω (τρῑγ-, τρῐγ-) squeak, 2 pf. τέτρῑγα as present (with epic part. τετρῑγῶτες, τετρῑγυῖα). Ionic and poetic. (2)

τρῡχόω *exhaust*, fut. τρῡχώσω, aor. ἐτρῡχωσα, pf. part. τετρῡχωμένος, aor. p. ἐτρῡχώθην Ion. Parallel are τρῡχω, epic τρῡξω, and τρύω, τρύσω (Aesch.), pf. τέτρῡμαι.

τρώγω (τρωγ-, τραγ-, 585) *gnaw*, τρώξομαι, ἔτρωξα (Hippocr.), τέτρωγμαι; 2 aor. ἔτραγον.

τυγχάνω (τευχ-, τυχ-, τυχε-) *hit, happen*, τεύξομαι, pf. τετύχηκα; 2 aor. ἔτυχον. Epic aor. ἐτύχησε, Ion. 2 pf. τέτευχα (cf. τεύχω). (**3**)

τύπτω (τυπ-, τυπτε-) *strike*, τυπτήσω, ἐτύπτησα (Aristot.), 2 aor. p. ἐτύπην, fut. p. τυπτήσομαι or τυπήσομαι. Ionic and lyric aor. ἔτυψα, pf. p. τέτυμμαι, 2 aor. ἔτυπον; ἀπο-τύψωνται (Hdt.). This verb, once the grammarian's model, was scarcely used in Att. prose except in the pres. and fut. systems (Aristoph. MSS. have fut. m. as pass. τυπτήσομαι). The other tenses are supplied in ἔπαισα or ἐπάταξα, πέπληγα, πέπληγμαι, ἐπλήγην. (**2**)

τύφω (τῡφ- or τῠφ-, for θυφ-, 105 *e*) *raise smoke, smoke*, τέθῡμμαι, 2 aor. p. ἐτύφην, 2 fut. p. τυφήσομαι (Menander).

ὑπισχνέομαι (ἰσχ- + νε-, cf. ἴσχω), Ion. and poet. ὑπίσχομαι (strengthened from ὑπέχομαι) *promise*, ὑποσχήσομαι, ὑπέσχημαι; 2 aor. m. ὑπεσχόμην. See ἴσχω and ἔχω. (**3**)

ὑφαίνω (ὑφαν-) *weave*, ὑφανῶ, ὕφηνα, ὕφασμαι (603), ὑφάνθην; aor. m. ὑφηνάμην. (**2**)

ὕω *rain*, ὕσω, ὗσα, ὗσμαι, ὕσθην. Hdt. ὕσομαι as pass.

φαείνω (φαεν-) *appear, shine*, aor. p. ἐφαάνθην (αα- for αε-, cf. 659) *appeared*. Epic. See φαίνω. (**2**)

φαίνω (φαν-) *show*, fut. φανῶ, aor. ἔφηνα, πέφαγκα, πέφασμαι (603), ἐφάνθην (rare in prose); 2 aor. p. ἐφάνην, 2 fut. φανήσομαι; 2 pf. πέφηνα *have appeared*; fut. m. φανοῦμαι, aor. m. ἐφηνάμην (rare and poet.) *showed*, but ἀπ-εφηνάμην *declared*; epic iter. 2 aor. φάνεσκε *appeared*. For full synopsis see 478; for inflection of certain tenses see 492. From stem φα- (cf. βαίνω, 643) Hom. impf. φάε *appeared*, fut. pf. πεφήσεται *will appear*. For ἐφαάνθην see φαείνω. (**2**)

φάσκω (φα-) *say, allege*, only pres. and impf. See φημί. (**4**)

φείδομαι (φειδ-, φιδ-) *spare*, φείσομαι, ἐφεισάμην, Hom. redupl. 2 aor. m. πεφιδόμην (559), fut. πεφιδήσομαι.

(φεν-, φν-, φα-) *kill*, stems whence Hom. πέφαμαι, πεφήσομαι; 2 aor. redupl. πέφνον or ἔπεφνον with part. κατα-πέφνων (or -νών). Related to φόνος *murder*, θείνω *smite*.

φέρω (φερ-, οἰ-, ἐνεκ-, ἐνεγκ- for ἐν-ενεκ-) *bear, carry*, fut. οἴσω, aor. ἤνεγκα, pf. ἐνήνοχα, ἐνήνεγμαι (3 s. ἐνήνεγκται inscr.), aor. p. ἠνέχθην; fut. p. ἐνεχθήσομαι and οἰσθήσομαι; 2 aor. ἤνεγκον; fut. m. οἴσομαι (sometimes as pass.); aor. m. ἠνεγκάμην, 2 aor. m. imv. ἐνεγκοῦ (Soph.). 686. Ion.

ἤνεικα and -άμην, Dor. Aeol. ἤνικα, Ion. ἤνεικον, ἐνήνειγμαι, ἠνείχθην; Hdt.
aor. inf. ἀν-οῖσαι (or ἀν-ῷσαι); Hom. aor. (also Ar.) imv. οἶσε for οἶσον
(654 h), pres. imv. φέρτε for φέρετε. (5)

φεύγω (φευγ-, φυγ-) *flee,* **φεύξομαι** and **φευξοῦμαι** (678), pf. **πέφευγα** (585), 2
aor. **ἔφυγον**; Hom. pf. part. πεφυγμένος and πεφυζότες, as from φύζω.
Parallel form **φυγγάνω** New Ion. and Att. poetry.

φημί (φη-, φα-) *say,* **φήσω, ἔφησα**; pf. p. imv. πεφάσθω (πεφασμένος belongs
to φαίνω). Mid. Dor. fut. φάσομαι. For the full inflection see 517–520.

φθάνω (φθη-, φθα-) *anticipate,* **φθήσομαι, ἔφθασα**; 2 aor. act. **ἔφθην** (like
ἔστην, 504), epic 2 aor. m. φθάμενος. Fut. φθάσω doubtful. Hom. pres.
φθἄνω from φθανϝω. (3)

φθείρω (φθερ-, φθορ-, φθαρ-) *corrupt,* fut. **φθερῶ**, aor. **ἔφθειρα**, pf. **ἔφθαρκα**,
ἔφθαρμαι; 2 aor. p. **ἐφθάρην**, 2 fut. p. **φθαρήσομαι**; 2 pf. **διέφθορα**; fut. m.
φθεροῦμαι. Ion. fut. -φθερέω Hdt., -φθέρσω Hom. 585. (2)

φθίνω (φθι-) *waste, decay,* φθίσω, ἔφθισα, ἔφθιμαι; epic aor. p. ἐφθίθην, fut. m.
φθίσομαι; 2 aor. m. ἐφθίμην *perished,* subj. φθίωμαι, opt. φθῑμην for φθι-ῑ́-
μην (766), imv. 3 sing. φθίσθω, inf. φθίσθαι, part. φθίμενος. All these
forms in Hom. or Att. poetry. Hom. also pres. φθίω, assumed from
φθίης and ἔφθιεν, which have been doubted; fut. φθῑσω, ἔφθῑσα (φθείσω,
ἔφθεισα?). Parallel is φθινύθω. Present generally intransitive; future
and aorist active transitive. (3)

φιλέω (φιλε-) *love,* **φιλήσω**, etc., regular. 482. Epic aor. m. (φιλ-) ἐφῑλάμην,
inf. pres. φιλήμεναι (659 f). 590. Aeolic φίλημι.

φλάω *bruise,* fut. **φλάσω** (Dor. φλασσῶ), aor. ἔφλασ(σ)α, ἔφλασμαι, ἐφλάσθην.
See **θλάω.**

φράγνῡμι (φραγ-) *fence,* mid. **φράγνυμαι**; only in pres. and impf. Also
φάργνῡμι. See **φράττω.** (3)

φράζω (φραδ-) *tell,* mid. *consider, devise,* **φράσω, ἔφρασα, πέφρακα, πέφρασμαι**
(epic part. πεφραδμένος), **ἐφράσθην** (as mid.); φράσ(σ)ομαι epic, ἐφρα(σ)-
σάμην chiefly epic. Epic 2 aor. πέφραδον or ἐπέφραδον. (2)

φράττω (φραγ-) *fence,* **ἔφραξα** (Att. inscr. ἔφαρξα), **πέφραγμαι** (πέφαργμαι),
ἐφράχθην; ἐφραξάμην. See **φράγνῡμι.** (2)

φρίττω (φρῑκ-) *shudder,* **ἔφρῑξα, πέφρῑκα**, pf. part. πεφρῑκόντας Pind. (cf. epic
κεκλήγοντες from κλάζω). (2)

φρύγω (φρῡγ-, φρυγ-) *roast,* **φρύξω, ἔφρυξα, πέφρῡγμαι**, ἐφρύγην (Hippocr.).

φυλάττω (φυλακ-) *guard,* **φυλάξω, ἐφύλαξα, πεφύλαχα, πεφύλαγμαι, ἐφυλάχθην**;
φυλάξομαι (as pass. in Soph.), ἐφυλαξάμην. (2)

φύρω (φυρ-) *mix,* ἔφυρσα (Hom.), **πέφυρμαι**, ἐφύρθην; fut. pf. πεφύρσομαι Pind.
φῡράω *mix* is regular, φῡράσω etc. (2)

φύω (φυ-, φῡ-), with ῠ in Homer and rarely in Attic, *produce,* **φύσω, ἔφῡσα,
πέφῡκα** *be (by nature),* with 2 pf. forms, epic πεφύᾱσι, ἐμ-πεφύῃ, πεφυώς;
plpf. ἐπέφῡκον (654 d); 2 aor. **ἔφῡν** *came into being, was* (694); 2 aor. p.
ἐφύην (subj. φυῶ); fut. m. φύσομαι.

χάζω (χαδ-) *force back*, χάζομαι *yield* (pres. only in ἀνα-χάζω), fut. χάσ(σ)ομαι, aor. -έχασσα (Pind.), aor. m. ἐχασάμην (Xen.); from stem καδ- (different from stem of κήδω) 2 aor. m. κεκαδόμην, fut. pf. κεκαδήσω *will deprive* (736), 2 aor. κέκαδον *deprived*. Poetic, chiefly epic; except ἀναχάζοντες and διαχάσασθαι in Xenophon. See (καδ-). (2)

χαίρω (χαρ-, χαιρε-, χαρε-) *rejoice*, χαιρήσω, κεχάρηκα, κεχάρημαι and κέχαρμαι, 2 aor. p. ἐχάρην, epic aor. m. χήρατο, 2 aor. m. κεχαρόμην; 2 pf. part. κεχαρηώς; fut. pf. κεχαρήσω, κεχαρήσομαι (736). (2)

χαλάω *loosen* (χαλάσω Ion.), ἐχάλασα (-αξα Pind.), ἐχαλάσθην. 596, 597.

χαλεπαίνω (χαλεπαν-) *be offended*, χαλεπανῶ, ἐχαλέπηνα, ἐχαλεπάνθην. (2)

χανδάνω (χενδ-, χονδ-, χαδ- for χνδ-) *hold*, 2 aor. ἔχαδον; fut. χείσομαι (70), 2 pf. κέχανδα (should be κέχονδα? 585). Poetic (chiefly epic) and Ionic. (3)

χάσκω, later χαίνω (χην-, χαν-, χν-σκω) *gape*, fut. χανοῦμαι, pf. κέχηνα as pres. (589), 2 aor. ἔχανον. Ionic and poetic. (4)

χέζω (χεδ-) Lat. caco, fut. χεσοῦμαι (rarely χέσομαι), ἔχεσα, 2 pf. κέχοδα (585), 2 aor. ἔχεσον (rare); aor. m. only in χέσαιτο, Ar. *Eq.* 1057; pf. p. part. κεχεσμένος. (2)

χέω (χευ-, χεϝ-, χυ-), epic χείω (660 c), *pour*, fut. χέω, epic χεύω, aor. ἔχεα, epic ἔχευα, κέχυκα, κέχυμαι, ἐχύθην, χυθήσομαι; aor m. ἐχεάμην, epic ἐχευάμην, 2 aor. m. ἐχύμην as pass. (696 a). 611.

(χλαδ-), in 2 pf. part. κεχλᾱδώς *swelling* (Pind.), with acc. pl. κεχλάδοντας and inf. κεχλάδειν.

χόω (χοϝ-) *heap up*, χώσω, ἔχωσα, κέχωκα, κέχωσμαι (600), ἐχώσθην, χωσθήσομαι.

χραισμέω (χραισμε-, χραισμ-) *help*, late in present; Hom. χραισμήσω, ἐχραίσμησα; 2 aor. ἔχραισμον. 590.

χράομαι (always χρῶμαι) *use*, χρήσομαι, ἐχρησάμην, κέχρημαι, ἐχρήσθην; fut. pf. κεχρήσομαι Theocr. For χρῆται, χρῆσθαι (Hdt. χρᾶται, χρέωνται, imv. χρέω, χρᾶσθαι, part. χρεώμενος), etc., see 486, 487.

χράω (always χρῶ) *give oracles* (Attic χρῇς, χρῇ, etc., 486); χρήσω, ἔχρησα, κέχρηκα, κέχρησμαι Hdt., ἐχρήσθην. Mid. *consult an oracle*, χρήσομαι, ἐχρησάμην. For χρῇς and χρῇ = χρῄζεις and χρῄζει, see χρήζω.

χρή (impers.), orig. a noun meaning *need* (cf. χρεία) with ἐστί understood, *there is need*, (one) *ought*, *must*, subj. χρῇ, opt. χρείη, inf. χρῆναι (poet. χρῆν); impf. χρῆν (= χρὴ ἦν) or ἐχρῆν; ἀπόχρη *it suffices*, inf. ἀποχρῆν, impf. ἀπέχρη, Ion. ἀποχρᾷ, ἀποχρᾶν, ἀπέχρα; ἀποχρήσει, ἀπέχρησε. 528.

χρήζω (620), Ion. χρηΐζω, *want, ask*, χρήσω, Ion. χρηΐσω, ἔχρησα, Ion. ἐχρήϊσα; χρῆς and χρῇ (as if from χράω) occasionally have the meaning of χρῄζεις, χρῄζει. (2)

χρίω (χρῑ- for χρῑσ-) *anoint, sting*, χρῑσω, ἔχρῑσα, κέχρῑμαι (or κέχρῑσμαι?), ἐχρῑσθην; χρῑσομαι Hom., ἐχρῑσάμην.

χρῴζω, poet. also χροΐζω (620), *color, stain*, κέχρωσμαι (κέχρῳσμαι?), ἐχρώσθην (ἐχρῴσθην?). (2)

ψάω (always ψῶ) *rub*, with η for ᾱ in contracted forms (486), ψῇ, ψῆν, ἔψη, etc.; generally in composition; ἀποψήσω, ἔψησα; pf. κατέψηγμαι from parallel form ψήχω.

ψεύδω *deceive*, ψεύσω, ἔψευσα, ἔψευσμαι, ἐψεύσθην, ψευσθήσομαι; ψεύσομαι, ἐψευσάμην. 66, 69.

ψήχω (ψυχ-, ψῡχ-) *cool*, ψύξω, ἔψῡξα, ἔψῡγμαι, ἐψύχθην, ψῡχθήσομαι (Ion.); 2 aor. p. -εψύχην or (generally later) ἐψύγην.

ὠθέω (ὠθ- for ϝωθ-, ὠθε-) *push*, impf. gen. ἐώθουν (537); ὤσω, poet. ὠθήσω, ἔωσα, Ion. ὦσα, ἔωσμαι, Ion. ὦσμαι, ἐώσθην: ὠσθήσομαι; fut. m. ὤσομαι, aor. m. ἐωσάμην, Ion. ὠσάμην. 590.

ὠνέομαι (ϝωνε-) *buy*, impf. ἐωνούμην (537) or ὠνούμην (in comp.); ὠνήσομαι, ἐώνημαι (mid. and pass.), ἐωνήθην. Classic writers use ἐπριάμην (503–504) for later (Ionic) ἐωνησάμην.

INDEXES

N.B. In these Indexes the numerals refer to the SECTIONS of the Grammar, except occasionally when the pages are specifically mentioned. Forms not found in the Greek Index should be sought in the list of Irregular Substantives (pp. 62–64) or in the Catalogue of Verbs (pp. 363–399).

GREEK INDEX

βασιλεία 187 c, 820
βασίλεια 187 c, 825
βασιλεύς, transfer of quantity in
33; gen. not contracted 48; declined 265, 268; compared 363;
used without article 955
βασιλεύω, denom. 465, 851; w. gen.
1109; w. dat. (Hom.) 1164;
aor. of 1262
βασιλικός 814 a, 843
βεβαιοτέρως 422
βείω in Hom. 670 b
βέλτερος, βέλτατος, and βελτίων,
βέλτιστος 357
βέομαι in Hom. 681
βιβάζω, future of 678 b
βίβλος, fem. 201 c
βίη Διομήδεος 1084
βίηφι 292
βιόω, athem. 2 aor. 694
βλ-, how reduplicated 546 b
βλάπτω 622, 723; aor. pass. 744
βλέπω w. acc. 1053 b
βλίττω (μελιτ-), 108, 625
βλώσκω 108
βοή 188
βοηθέω w. dat. 1163
βορέας, βορρᾶς declined 194
Βουλή, in documents 28
βούλομαι, augment of 536; stem
βουλε-, 590 c, 594; βούλει in indic.
(never βούλῃ) 582 g; βουλοίμην ἄν
and ἐβουλόμην ἄν 1326, 1338; see
ἐβουλόμην; βούλει or βούλεσθε w.
interrog. subj. 1367; βουλομένῳ
τινί ἐστιν etc. 1586, cf. 1171
βοῦς, declined 265; formation of
37, 266; not contracted 48;
Hom. forms of 271; compounds
of 858
βρέτας, declension of 234
βροτός (μορ-) 108 a
βσ, written ψ 19

βυνέω (βυ-νε-) 639
βύρσα 71

Γ, voiced stop 18, 23, 617; palatal
17; nasal (w. sound of ng) before
κ, γ, χ, or ξ 21, 68, 603; see
Palatals
γαμῶ and γαμοῦμαι 1245
γάρ 963, 1202
γαρύεν (Pind.) 657 b
γαστήρ, declension of 274 b
γγμ changed to γμ 81, 499 b
γέ, elided 57 c; enclitic 159, 963,
1202
γέγονα as pres. 1265
γελασείω, desiderative verb 855
γελάω 596, 597, 598, 855
γεννάδας, adj. of one ending 341
γένος 90, 43; declined 232
γέντο grasped 696 b: see also
γίγνομαι
γεραιός compared 348
γέρας 41; declined 232
γεύω w. acc. and gen. 1107; γεύομαι
w. gen. 1103
γέφυρα declined 183
γῆ omitted after article 929 b
γηράσκω 644, 649; athem. 2 aor. 694
γι gave ζ 19, 96, 617, 624; or δ 96
γίγας declined p. 51
γίγνομαι 561, 604; athem. pf. 802;
copul. vb. 896; w. gen. 1125;
w. poss. dat. 1173, 1586
γιγνώσκω redupl. in pres. 546, 561,
605, 644; athem. 2 aor. 694; inflect. of ἔγνων 695; w. part. 1590
γλ-, how reduplicated 546
γλυκύς declined 315
γν-, how reduplicated 546
γνάθος, fem. 201 c
γνώμη declined 183
γνωρίζω, augment of 546 b
γνώω (Hom.) 670 b

γξ, pronunciation 21

Γοργώ 815 e

γραῦς, declined 265; formation of 266; Hom. forms of 271

γράφω 499 a, 716; and γράφομαι 1245; ἐγράφην 1247; γράφομαι w. cogn. accus. 1049, 1074, 1127

γρηῦς, γρηΰς, Hom. for γραῦς 271

γσ written ξ 19

γυμνής 339

γυμνός w. gen. 1140

γχ before μ 499 b

Δ, voiced stop 18, 19; see Dentals; inserted in ἀνδρός (ἀνήρ) 109; before -αται and -ατο (in Hom.) 654 c

δα-, intens. prefix 862

δαήρ, voc. δᾶερ 142 d

δαίμοσι 76; δαίμων 214 b, 229

δαίνυμι, pres. opt. mid. 766

δαίομαι (δασ-) divide 636

δαίω (δαϝ-) burn 636

δάμαρ, nom. of 215 a

δαμνάω (δαμ-) and δάμνημι 642

δανείζω and δανείζομαι 1245

δᾷς, accent of gen. du. and pl. 148

δέ, position 963, 1202 b; elided 57; in ὁ μέν . . . ὁ δέ 979–983; in apodosis 1432

-δε, local ending 292, 413, 415; enclit. 159 d

δεδιέναι 727, 798

δέδοικα 712

δεῖ, impers.: see δέω want

δείδια and δείδοικα, redupl. of (Hom.) 552 b; δέδια 727

δείκνυμι 501, 640, 760, 775, 786; synopsis 503, 507; inflection of μι forms 504. Synt. w. partic. 1590; partic. δεικνύς declined 329

δεῖνα, indef. pron., declined 398; always w. art. 945

δεινόν ἐστιν εἰ 1434

δελφίς (δελφιν-) 215 b, 281 b

δεξιά 929 b, 956, 1205

δέομαι 485 a; w. gen. or w. gen. and acc. 1114

δέρη (δερϝη) 188

δέρκομαι 587; Ἄρη δεδορκέναι 1053 b

δεσμός (-σ-) 815 b, 819; heterog. 288

δεσπότης, voc. of 192

δεύτατος 362

δέχαται (Hom.) 553, 652

δέχομαι, 2 aor. mid. of 696 b; w. acc. and dat. (Hom.) 1169

δέω bind, contraction of 485 b; vowel grades in 596 b, 734

δέω want, contraction of 485 a; in Hdt. 660. Impers. δεῖ 887, 1162; w. gen. and dat. (rarely acc.) 1115, 1161; πολλοῦ δεῖ, ὀλίγου δεῖ 1116; ὀλίγου for ὀλίγου δεῖν almost 1116 b; δέον (acc. abs.) 1571; ἑνός etc. w. δέοντες 441 c; ἔδει in apod. without ἄν 1410. See δέομαι

δή in crasis 49; with indef. rel. 410; position 963

δηλοῖ without subject 886 c

δῆλός εἰμι w. partic. 1591

δηλόω, contracted 43–45; inflect. of partic. 337; other contr. forms 482; stem of 593, 634; synopsis of 484; infin. 45 e

Δημήτηρ, declined 277, 278; accent of voc. 142 d

Δημοσθένης, acc. of 237; voc. of 142 c

-δην, adverbs in 420

δήποτε added to indef. rel. 410

-δης, patronym. in 833

δι gave ζ 19, 96, 616

διά w. gen. and acc. 1207, 1208, 1213; διὰ φιλίας 1189

διαιτάω, augm. 542 b

ἐγείρω 630, 632; pf. and plpf. mid. 499 d; aor. mid. 692; Att. redupl. 557

ἔγχελυς, decl. of 264

ἐγώ declined 364; Hom. and Hdt. 369; generally omitted 984; emphatic 985; enclitic forms 998 b

ἐγῷδα in crasis 51

ἔδδεισε 535

ἔδει etc. without ἄν in apod. 1410

ἔδομαι 681

ἔδυν (of δύω) 502, 694; synopsis 503, 694; inflected 504; Hom. opt. 776

ἐδωδή 815 e

-εε in dual of nouns in ις, υς 255

ἐέ for ἕ, Hom. pron. 369

ἔεδνα for ἑ-ϝεδνα 36

ἐείκοσι 431

ἐθέλω or θέλω 537, 590 c

ἔθεν for οὗ 369

ἐθίζω, augment 537; pf. and plpf. mid. 499 c

ει, diphthong 7; genuine and spurious ει 8, 32, 45 e, 75, 100, 793; pronunc. of 28, 29; augment of 540, 541 b; as augm. or redupl. (for εε) 537, 552; normal grade in vowel mutation 585, 610

εἰ if, proclitic 155; 1392, 1432; whether 1506, 1607, 1608; εἰ γάρ, εἴθε 1355, 1359; εἰ causal 1433; in wishes, O if 1355; in Hdt. 1528

εἶ name of epsilon 4

-ει for -εσαι, -εαι in 2d pers. sing. 582 g, 654 b

-ειᾱ, nouns in, denoting action 820

-ειᾰ, nouns in 187 c, 825

-ειας, -ειε, -ειαν in aor. opt. act. 575, 764

εἶδον 102, 537; w. partic. 1584, 1587

εἰδώς declined 329

εἰκάθω, εἰκάθοιμι 601

εἰκών, decl. of 251; gender 280 b

εἵμαρται, augm. of 552

εἰ μή except 1213 b, 1424

εἰμί 86, 612; inflection of 509, 664; dialect forms of 510; as copula 878, 879; w. pred. nom. 896; w. poss. or part. gen. 1094; w. dat. 1173, 1586; ἔστιν οἵ, ἔστιν οὗ, ἔστιν ᾗ or ὅπως 1029; w. opt. without ἄν 1332; ἐκὼν εἶναι, τὸ νῦν εἶναι, κατὰ τοῦτο εἶναι 1539; accent (enclitic) 159 c, 161; accent of ὤν, ὄντος 149

εἶμι, inflection of 511; dial. forms of 513; pres. as fut. 1257

εἶναι, redundant 1077, 1536 c, 1539

εἴνατος for ἔνατος 435

εἵνεκα 165 g

εἴνυμι 86: see ἕννυμι

εἶο for οὗ 369

-εῖον, nouns of place in 829

εἶος, Hom. for ἕως 1478

-εῖος, patronymic suffix 835

εἶπα, first aorist 686, 699

εἶπον, accent 151; w. ὅτι or ὡς 1527; ὡς (ἔπος) εἰπεῖν 1538; εἰπών, formation of 330; Aeol. εἴπην 657 b

εἴργω etc. w. gen. 1117; w. infin. or infin. w. τοῦ and μή (5 forms) 1552, 1554, 1619

εἴρηκα, augment of 552

εἰς proclitic 155; w. accus. 1207, 1214; for ἐν w. dat. 1204; w. numerals 946; ἐς χεῖρας ἐλθεῖν 1189

εἷς, μία, ἕν declined 432, 433; compounds of 434

-εις, -εσσα, -εν, adj. in 847; decl. 323, 324; compar. 351

-εις in acc. pl. of 3d decl. (for -εας) 240; late in nouns in ευς 255

εἴσω, adv. w. gen. 1152, 1227

εἴτε ... εἴτε accent 163; synt. 1608
εἶχον, augment of 90, 537
-είω, Hom. pres. in, for -έω 660 c, cf. 670 b
εἴωθα, 2 pf. 552, 719
εἴως, Hom. for ἕως 1478
ἐκ: see ἐξ
ἕκαστος, ἑκάτερος, 363; w. article 974
ἐκεῖ 423
ἐκεῖθεν 413, 425, 1205
ἐκεῖνος 388, 391, 923, 943, 972, 1004, 1005; ἐκεινοσί 392
ἐκεῖσε 413, 423
ἐκεχειρία 105 d
ἐκκλησιάζω 565
ἔκπλεως, neut. pl. ἔκπλεω 301
ἐκποδών 412
ἐκτός, adv. w. gen. 1152, 1227
ἑκών declined 327; compar. 353; as adv. 922; ὤν omitted 1573; ἑκὼν εἶναι 1539
ἐλάσσων, ἐλάττων 63, 357, 1150
ἐλαύνω, form of pres. 641; fut. 678 b (see ἐλόω); Att. redupl. 554; Hom. ἐληλάδαται 654 c; sense 1232
ἐλαφη-βόλος 858, 871
ἐλάχεια (Hom.), ἐλάχιστος 357
ἐλέγχω, pf. and plpf. 81; inflected 497, 499 b, 554
ἐλεύσομαι 34, 511 c
ἐλθέ, accent 151
ἔλιπον inflected p. 111]
ἔλλαβον, ἔλλαχον (Hom.) for ἔλαβον, ἔλαχον 535
Ἑλληνιστί 420
ἐλόω, Hom. fut. of ἐλαύνω 659 b, 678 b
ἐλπίζω 616, 620; w. fut. infin. or pres. and aor. 1287
ἐλπίς declined p. 51; accus. sing. 218 c; voc. 223

ἐμαυτοῦ declined 377; syntax of 960, 993
ἐμέθεν, ἐμεῖο, ἐμέο, ἐμεῦ 369
ἐμεωυτοῦ (Hdt.) 379
ἐμίν (Dor. for ἐμοί) 374
ἔμμεν or ἔμμεναι, ἔμεν or ἔμεναι, ἔμμι (Hom.) 510
ἐμός 380, 998
ἐμπίπλημι and ἐμπίπρημι 613
ἔμπροσθεν w. gen. 1152, 1227
ἐν proclitic 155; w. dat. 1215, 1179; as adv. 1201; w. dat. for εἰς w. acc. 1204 b; in expr. of time 1195; phon. change before liquid or nasal 73; before ζ or σ 77
ἔν: see εἷς
-εν for -ησαν, aor. pass. 654 i, 741, 747
-εν, verbs in 100; infin. in 657 b
ἐναντίος w. gen. 1146; w. dat. 1175
ἐνδεής w. gen. 1140
ἕνεκα w. accented pron. 161 d; w. gen. 1155, 1227
ἔνεστι, impers. 887
ἔνθα, ἔνθεν 414, 423, 424
ἐνθάδε 414, 423
ἐνθαῦτα, ἐνθεῦτεν (Ion.) 425
ἔνθεν 292 b; ἔνθεν καὶ ἔνθεν 424, 1205
ἔνι for ἔνεστι 1203
ἔνιοι and ἐνίοτε 1028
ἐννέα not contracted 48
ἕννυμι 86, 105 f, 553, 640
ἔνοχος w. gen. 1140
ἐνταῦθα 423
ἐντεῦθεν 424
ἐντός w. gen. 1153, 1227
ἐξ or ἐκ 25, 67, 80, 84, 116, 362, 564; ἐκ long before liquid or nasal 123; proclitic 155; accented 156; w. gen. 1207, 1216; for ἐν w. dat. 1204; w. agent of pass. vb. 1208

εὖ, compared 421; augm. of verbs compounded with 568; w. ποιέω, πάσχω, ἀκούω, etc. 1072, 1242; w. ἔχω and gen. 1092

εὖ, pron. for οὗ 369

εὐδαίμων declined 307; accent 142 b

εὐελπις 311; accus. 218 c

εὐεργετέω, augm. 568

εὐθύ w. gen. 1152, 1227

εὐθύς w. partic. 1574

εὐκλεής, contr. of 309

εὔνοια 814

εὔνοος, εὔνους, compared 349

εὑρίσκω 604, 644; w. partic. 1584, 1590

εὖρος, acc. of specif. 1056

εὐρύς wide, Hom. acc. of 317

-εύς, nouns in 265–269, 825, 840; Hom. forms of 267; original forms of 267; contracted forms of 269

εὐφυής, contr. of 309

εὔχαρις, decl. of 311

-εύω, denom. vbs. in 634, 851

εὐώδης 308

ἔφηνα for ἔφαν-σα 32, 92, 687

ἐφοράω w. partic. 1587

ἐφ' ᾧ or ἐφ' ᾧτε 402; w. infin. and fut. ind. 1476, 1477

ἐχθρός compared 354

ἐχρῆν or χρῆν in apod. without ἄν 1410

ἔχω 105, 692; augment 537; w. partic. for perf. 1264; ἔχομαι 1245; w. gen. 1099; ἔχω w. adv. and part. gen. 1092; ἔχων continually 1567; with 1568; ἕξω and σχήσω 1250 f

-εω and -εων, Ion. gen. of 1st decl. 131, 165 h, 196 e

-έω, denom. verbs in 634, 851; inflection of contract forms 482, 485, 660 d

-έω for -άω in vbs. (Hdt.) 659 e

-έω in fut. of liquid stems 677

ἐᾠκη, plpf. 551

ἕως dawn 105 f; acc. of 206, 244

ἕως, conj. 1478; while 1439; until 1478–1483; expr. purpose 1482; in indir. disc. 1517 c

-εως, Att. 2d decl. in 131, 203, 299

ἑωυτοῦ for ἑαυτοῦ (Hdt.) 379

Ϝ, equivalent to w 3: see Digamma

Z, double cons. 19; voiced 23; origin of 19; probable pronunciation of 29; makes position 120; except for α, ι, υ 125 d; ε for redupl. before 545

ζα-, intens. prefix 862

ζάω, contr. form of 486

-ζε, adv. in 86 d, 292

Ζεύς 291, 886 e

-ζω, verbs in 616–620; fut. of vbs. in -άζω and -ιζω 678 b, c

H, open long vowel 5, 6; orig. aspirate 13, 28; in Ion. for Dor. ᾱ 164; ᾰ and ε length. to η 31, 532, 536, 538, 539, 593; after σ 188; in contr. 42, 45, 486; as thematic vowel in subj. 467; fem. nouns and adj. in 817, 841

ἤ whether (Hom.), or, interrog. 1607, 1608; than 1149, 1474, 1535; om. 1150; in synizesis 54

ἥ rel. pron. 399; ᾗ 412, 423, 425

ἤ, interrogative 1605, 1608

ῃ, improper diphthong 7

-ῃ for -εσαι or -ησαι in 2d pers. sing. 45 c, 582 g, 654 b: see -ει

ἡγεμών decl. 229

ἡγέομαι w. gen. 1109; w. dat. (Hom.) 1164; w. infin. 1527

ἥδε accent 159, 160, 390

ἥδομαι 460, 465; w. cogn. acc. 1049

ἡδομένῳ σοί ἐστιν etc. 1586

ᾗ δ' ὅς: see ἠμί

ἡδύς 89; compared 354; ἡδίων declined 355

ἠέ, ἦε, interrog. (Hom.) 1608

ᾔδης etc. (οἶδα) 530 b, 538

-ῄεις, adj. in, contracted in Hom. 325

ἥκιστα (superl.) 357, 421

ἥκω as perf. 1256

ἡλίκος 408

ἤλωθον 34, 718

ἧμαι 664; inflection of 521; dial. forms of 524

ἡμάς or ἧμας 372

-ημενος in athem. partic. (Hom.) 674

ἡμέτερος 380, 1003; w. αὐτῶν 1003

ἠμί 612, 1023

ἡμι-, insepar. particle 88, 861

ἡμῖν, ἧμιν 372

ἥμισυς 318

ἦμος 425

ἤν for ἐάν (εἰ ἄν) 1393

ἤνεγκα 686, 699

ἡνίκα, rel. adv. 423

ἠνίπαπον 559

ἦος (Hom.) 1478

ἧπαρ declined p. 51; form of nom. 216

ἤπειρος, fem. 201 b

Ἡρακλέης 45 f, 48, 241

ἥρως declined 246

-ης, adj. in 841, 867; inflection of 307, cf. 232, 237

-ῆς (for -ῆες), in nom. pl. of nouns in -εύς (older Attic) 268

-ῃσι or -ης, in dat. pl. 1st decl. (Ion.) 196 f

ἥσσων, ἥττων 94, 165; comp. 357, 360, 421

ἥσυχος comp. 348

ἥττωμαι w. gen. 1120

ην, diphthong 7; augm. of ευ 540

ἠχώ decl. 248

ἠώς (Ion.) 105; decl. 244

Θ, voiceless aspirate 18, 23; dental 17; in πλήθω etc. 601, 815 c; see Dentals

-θα, local ending 414

-θα, pers. ending (see -σθα) 582

θάλασσα, θάλαττα decl. 141, 186

θαμίζω w. partic. 1589

θάπτω (ταφ-) 620; aspirates in 105 e

θάρσος 107

θάσσων, θάττων 94, 354; aspirate in 105 e

θάτερον etc. 53

θαῦμα w. infin. 1534

θαυμάζω w. gen. 1103, 1121; θαυμάζω εἰ 1433; θαυμάζω ὅτι 1433

θεά 196

θείω (Hom.) 670 b

θέλεις or θέλετε 537, 590 c; w. interrog. subjunctive 1367

-θεν, local ending 113, 292, 413, 415

θεός, in synizesis 54; vocative 202, 886 a

θέρομαι, fut. of 682

θέω (θεϝ) 54, 485, 611

Θήβαζε 86 d, 292

θῆλυς 318

θήρ declined 229; nom. 214

θής declined p. 51

-θη-τι' for -θη-θι in 1 aor. pass. imperat. 105 b, 672, 784–789

-θι, local ending 159, 292 b, 413, 415

θνήσκω (θαν-, θνη-) 647, 714 d; fut. pf. act. τεθνήξω 736, 1268; perf. as pres. 1265; athem. 2 perf. 500, 790; part. τεθνεώς, Hom. τεθνηώς 802

θοἰμάτιον (by crasis) 51

θράσος 107

θρίξ, τριχός, aspirates in 105 e; declension of 227
-θρον, nouns in 822
θρύπτω (τρυφ-) 105 e
θυγάτηρ declined 274; poetic forms 275
θύραζε 292
θύρᾱσι 412

I, close vowel 5, 6; rarely contr. w. foll. vowel 46; contr. w. preceding vowel 41; α after 32, 185, 187; length. to ῑ 31, 32; interchanged w. ει and οι 34; mood suffix in opt. 573, 574, 763; in redupl. of pres. stem 547, 561, 604, 612; before ς 125 d; noun stems in 250, 257; phon. changes caused by 93–101; semivowel ι 26, 37, 212; subscript 7, 10, 12
-ι, local ending 412, 413
-ι class of verbs 615–636
-ί, deictic suffix 392
ἵα for μία (Hom.) 435
-ια, fem. partic. in 332; nouns in 819, 826, 827
-ιάζω, imitative verbs in 854
ἰάομαι 593
-ιάω, desideratives in 855
-ιδ, stems in 223
ἰδεῖν, accent of 791
-ίδεος, suffix 839
-ίδης (fem. -ίς) and -ιάδης (fem. -ιάς), patronym. in 833, 836
-ίδιον, diminutive in 830
ἴδιος w. poss. gen. 1143
ἴδμεν 82
ἴδρις declined (one ending) 340
ἱδρόω, contraction of 488
ἱδρύνθην (ἱδρύω), Hom. aor. pass. 740
ιε- or ιη- as mood suffix in opt. 573, 574, 769, 771

ἱερός w. poss. gen. 1143
-ίζω, denom. vbs. in 620, 851, 854
ἵημι, inflection of 514, 612; dial. forms of 516; augment 537; aor. in -κα 685; opt. πρόοιτο etc. 514 c, 668, 773; εἶναι 798
ἴθι come! w. subj. and imperat. 1344
ἱκνέομαι 639
-ικος, adjectives in 843
ἵλεως, adj. declined 204, 299
Ἰλιόθι πρό 292 b, 415
-ιμος, suffix 844
ἵν (ϝίν) Doric for οἷ 374
-ιν in acc. sing. 218 c
-ιν, verbs in 100
ἵνα, final conj. 1371, 1372, 1374, 1376, 1377
-ινος, adj. of material in 845; adj. of time in -ινός 846
-ιον, suffix 829, 830
-ιος, adj. in 842; patronymic 835
ἵππος 63; fem., cavalry, w. sing. numerals 442
ἱππότᾰ, nom. (Hom.) 196 b
-ιρ, verbs in 100
-ις, feminines in 840 b
Ἰσθμοῖ 412
-ισι, dat. case ending 180
-ισκᵒ/ε-, pres. stems in 644
-ίσκος, -ίσκη, dimin. in 830
ἴσμεν for ἴδμεν 82, 530
ἴσος w. dat. 1176; comp. 348; γένος ἴσον 1630
ἵστημι, synopsis 503, 507; inflect. of μι forms 504, 506, 785; redupl. of pres. 501, 561, 612; fut. perf. act. 736; partic. ἱστάς declined 329
-ιτις, suffix 829
ἰχθύς declined 260; acc. pl. of 262; gender 281 b
Ἰώ, acc. Ἰοῦν (Hdt.) 250

quantity of ν 584 : see 75, 95, 101, 151 b, 223

λῴων, λῷστος 357

M, nasal 21 ; and sonant 27 ; stops before 79, 122 ; becomes ν 24 ; ν becomes μ 732 ; σ before μ 82 ; μβλ and μβρ for μλ and μρ 108

μά in oaths w. acc. 1065–1067

-μα, neut. nouns in 821

μαίομαι (μασ-) 636

μακρός, decl. of 294 ; comp. 357 ; μακρῷ w. comp. 1184

μάλα 420 ; comp. (μᾶλλον, μάλιστα) 351, 421

-μᾱν, Dor. ending for -μην 654

μανθάνω 450, 638 ; w. gen. of source 1125 ; w. infin. 1594 b ; τί μαθών 1569

Μαραθῶνι, dat. of place 1193

μαρτύρομαι 630

μάχομαι, fut. -εσομαι, -οῦμαι 590 c, 596, 678 ; w. dat. 1189

Μέγαράδε 292

μέγας, decl. 342 ; comp. 357, 358

μέζων for μείζων 96, 165, 357, 358

-μεθον in first person dual 582 b

μεθύσθην 657 b

μείζων 358

μείρομαι, redupl. of pf. 552

μείων, μεῖστος 357, 360

μέλας 32, 75 ; declined 319 ; fem. of 320 ; nom. 215 b ; comp. 346

μέλει pf. (Hom.) 722 ; w. dat. and gen. 1106, 1161

μέλι 24, 108, 214 d

μέλισσα, μέλιττα 63 c, 95

μέλλω, augment of 536 ; w. infin., as periphr. fut. 1254

μέμβλωκα 108

μέμνημαι 547, 654 a ; pf. subj. and opt. 754, 766 ; as pres. 1265 ; w.

gen. 1103, 1105 ; w. part. 1590 ; w. infin. 1594 b

μέμφομαι w. dat. 1160 ; w. acc. 1163

μέν 963, 1202 ; in ὁ μέν . . . ὁ δέ 979

-μεναι, -μεν, in infin. (Hom.) 657, 673

Μενέλᾱος and Μενέλεως 33, 205 ; accent 131

μένος Ἀτρείδαο 1084

μεντᾶν (by crasis) 51

μέρος in fractions 443, 1090 ; w. gen. 1091, 1098

-μες, -μεσθα for -μεν, -μεθα 578, 582 d, 654

μεσημβρία 108

μέσος, μέσσος 95 b ; compar. 348, 361 ; w. art. 976

μεστός w. gen. 1140

μετά w. gen., dat., and acc. 1207, 1219 ; as adv. 1201 ; μέτα (Hom.) for μέτεστι 1203

μεταμέλει w. gen. and dat. 1106, 1161

μεταξύ w. gen. 1155, 1227 ; w. part. 1574

μεταποιέομαι w. gen. 1097, 1099

μέτεστι w. gen. and dat. 1097 b, 1161

μετέχω w. gen. 1097 b, 1098

μετέωρος 33

μέτοχος w. gen. 1140

-μέτρης, compounds in, 190

μεῦ 369 ; enclitic 159

μέχρι, as prep. w. gen. 1227 ; as conj. 1478 ; w. subj. without ἄν 1481

μή, adv. not 1609–1622 ; w. ἵνα, ὅπως, etc. in final clauses 1371, 1373 ; with vbs. of fearing, w. subj. and opt. 1389 ; w. indic. 1391 ; in protasis 1394 ; in rel. cond. sent. 1440 ; in wishes 1355, 1359, 1613 ; w. imperat. and

subj. in prohibitions 1343, 1345;
w. subj. expressing fear 1347,
1348; for ὅπως μή 1386; w. subj.
(also μὴ οὐ) in cautious assertions
1349; w. indic. 1350; w. dubi-
tative subj. 1367; w. infin. 1614;
in clauses of result 1459; in
causal sentences 1462; w. infin.
after negative verb 1554, 1618;
generic 1616; μὴ ὅτι, μὴ ὅπως 1519.
See οὐ μή and μὴ οὐ

-μη, fem. nouns in 819

μηδαμοῦ etc. 427

μηδέ, μήτε 1608; μηδὲ εἷς 434; w.
concess. part. 1575

μηδείς 396, 411, 434, 1609; μηδένες
etc. 434

μηδέτερος 411

μηκάομαι 591

μηκέτι 115

μὴ οὐ 1553, 1618, 1619; one syllable in poetry 54; μὴ . . . οὐ in
final cl. 1373; w. subj. or indic.
in cautious negations 1349, 1350

μήτε 1609; accent 163

μήτηρ 169; declined 274

μῆτις (poet.) 411; accent 163, 396

μήτρως 246

-μι, conj. of verbs in 500–532, 662–
674; in 1st pers. sing. 578, 582,
637, 763; dependent moods 755–
761, 771–777; Aeol. vbs. in, for
-αω, -εω, -οω 659 f, 660 d

μία 88, 429, 432, 433

μικρός 88; compared 357; μικροῦ
(δεῖν) 1116 b

μιμνῄσκω 647; augment of pf. 547;
w. gen. 1107. See μέμνημαι

μίν and νίν 371, 374

Μίνως, acc. 206; gen. 247

μίσγω 648

μισέω w. acc. 1163

μμμ changed to μμ 81

μνάα, μνᾶ, declined 193

μοῖρα 88, 99, 187, 443

μολ- in pf. of βλώσκω 108, 644

μοναχῇ 445 b

μόνος 165, 445 c

μορ- in βροτός 108

-μος, nouns in 819; adj. in 844

μοῦνος (μόνος) 165

Μοῦσα declined 183; Aeol. Μοῖσα
165 g

μυῖα 187 c

μυριάς 430

μύριοι and μυρίοι 442

μυρίος, μυρία 442 b

μῦς, μυός, declined 260

μῶν (μὴ οὖν), interrog. 1605

-μων, adj. in 841 d

N, nasal 21; sonant 27; can end
word 24; movable 59, 110, 489;
before labial, dental, and palatal
72; before liquid and nasal 73,
78 b; before σ 75; ντ, νδ, νθ,
dropped before σ 70; in ἐν and
σύν 77; after voiced stop 122;
dropped in some vbs. in -νω 92,
499 d, 602; changed to σ before
μαι 74, 499 d, 603, 732; dropped
before σ in dat. pl. 85; added in
aor. pass. 740; adj. in 319; in 3d
class of verbs 637–643

να- added to verb stem 642

ναί yes 1066; ναίχι, accent 159 d,
163

-ναι, infin. in 579, 795, 797, 798.
See -μεναι

ναίω (ναϝ-) 636

νᾱός, νηός, and νεώς 203

ναῦς declined 265; Dor. and Ion.
decl. of 270; ναῦφι 292; formation of 37, 266; compounds of
(ναυμαχία, ναυσίπορος, νεώσοικος,
etc.) 858

ὅποι *whither* 412, 413; of place where 1205

ὁποῖος, ὁπόσος 408

ὁπότε, rel. 423, 1437; causal 1463; ὁπόταν w. subj. 1440 b, 1299 b

ὁπότερος 363, 408, 410 c

ὅπου 412, 423

ὁππότε etc. 426, 409

ὀπυίω (ὀπυ-), ὀπύσω 636

ὅπως, rel. adv. 412; as indir. interrog. w. subj. or opt. 1505; as final particle 1371, 1374, 1377; sometimes w. ἄν or κὲ 1376; w. past t. of indic. 1381; rarely w. fut. ind. 1375; in obj. cl. w. fut. ind. 1382; sometimes w. ἄν 1387; in obj. cl. in Hom. 1388; ὅπως μή after vbs. of fearing, 1390; ὅπως and ὅπως μή w. fut. in commands and prohib. 1351; ὅπως for ὡς in indir. quot. 1493. Μὴ ὅπως and οὐχ ὅπως 1519

-ορ, verbs in 99

ὁράω 650; augm. and redupl. of 537; Hom. forms 659; w. ὅπως 1382; w. μή 1389; w. suppl. part. 1584; w. part. in indir. disc. 1590, 1585

ὀρέγομαι w. gen. 1099

ὄρνις declined p. 51; acc. sing. of 218 c, 219. See 291

ὄρνυμι, fut. 682; aor. 689 b

ὁρόω etc. 659 b

ὅς, rel. pron. 399, 408; fem. dual rare 400; Hom. forms of 401; as demonstr. 1023

ὅς *his*, poss. pron. (poet.) 89, 380, 382, 1000

-ος, -ον, nouns in 197, 817; adj. in 293, 841, 857; neuters in -ος (stems in εσ-) 232, cf. 243, 821

ὅσον w. absol. infin. 1538

ὅσος, ὁπόσος 408, 1035, 1038

ὅσπερ 402

ὅσσος Hom. 409

ὀστέον, ὀστοῦν, declined 208

ὅστις declined 403–405; Hom. form 406; as indir. interrog. 407, 408, 1012, 1601; sing. w. pl. antec. 1021; ὅστισοῦν 410

ὀσφραίνομαι, formation 643; w. gen. 1103

ὅτε, rel. 420, 423; causal 1463; elided 57; ὅταν w. subj. 1440 b

ὅτευ or ὅττευ, ὅττεῳ, ὅτεων, ὀτέοισι 406

ὅτι *that* 404; in indir. quot. 1491, 1502, 1593; in direct quot. 1492; causal (*because*) 1463; not elided 57

ὅ τι (neut. of ὅστις) 403, 404

ὅ τι μαθών, ὅ τι παθών 1569

ὅτις, ὅτινα, ὅτινος, ὅττεο, ὅττι 406

ου, diphthong 7; genuine and spurious ου 8, 32, 45 e, 75, 793; pronunc. of 28, 29; length. from ο 32; for ο in Ion. 165; not augmented 542 d; stems in 265

οὐ, οὐκ, οὐχ 25, 103, 115; proclitic 155; accented 115, 156; uses of 1439, 1457, 1461, 1468, 1609–1622; οὐκ ἔσθ' ὅπως etc. w. opt. (without ἄν) 1332; οὐχ ὅπως and οὐχ ὅτι 1519. See οὐ μή and μὴ οὐ

οὖ, name of omicron 4

οὔ, οἷ, ἕ, etc. 159, 161, 364; syntax of 986, 987

οὖ, rel. adverb 412, 423

-ου in gen. sing. 191, 199; for -εσο in 2d pers. mid. 582 g, 702

οὐδαμοῦ etc. 427

οὐδας 234

οὐδέ 1609; οὐδ' εἷς and οὐδείς 434; οὐδ' ὥς 156 c; οὐδὲ πολλοῦ δεῖ 1116; w. concess. participle 1575

οὐδείς 396, 411, 434, 1609; οὐδένες

πόθι and ποθί 159, 425
ποῖ 412, 423
ποί, indef. 412, 423; enclitic 159
ποιέω w. two accus. 1071, 1073; w.
  partic. 1566 h, 1584; εὖ and
  κακῶς ποιῶ 1072; derivatives 808,
  815; ποιοῦμαι value 1133
ποιμήν declined 229
ποῖος, ποιός 408
πολεμέω, πολεμίζω w. dat. 1188;
  disting. from πολεμόω 853
πόλις declined 253; voc. 224;
  πόλεως 131, 254; πόλινδε 415;
  Ion. forms 257
πολίτης declined 189
πολλός, Ion. = πολύς 63, 343
πολύς declined 342; Ion. forms
  343; compared 357; οἱ πολλοί
  and τὸ πολύ 966, 1090; πολύ and
  πολλά as adv. 412; as pred. 922;
  πολλῷ w. comp. 1184; πολλοῦ δεῖ
  and οὐδὲ πολλοῦ δεῖ 1116; ἐπὶ πολύ
  1217
πομπὴν πέμπειν 1049
πόρρω or πρόσω 422; w. gen. 1153
Ποσειδάων, Ποσειδῶν, accus. 220;
  voc. 142 d, 223 b
πόσος, ποσός 408, 1014
ποταμός after proper noun 969
ποτάομαι 34
πότε 423
ποτέ, indef. 423, 427; enclitic 159
πότερον or πότερα, interrog. 363,
  1608
πότερος, πότερος 408
ποῦ 412, 423; w. part. gen. 1088,
  1092
πού, indef. 420; enclitic 159
πούς, nom. sing. 215; compounds
  of 345; ὡς ποδῶν εἶχον 1092
ππ Aeol. 409, 426
πράγματα, omitted after article
  951

πρᾷος, declined 342; two stems of
  344; πρηΰς 344
πράττω (πραγ-), 2 perf. 97, 120,
  499 b, 624, 724; w. ὅπως and obj.
  cl. 1382
πρέπει, impers. 887
πρέσβα 318
πρεσβευτής, πρεσβύτης, πρέσβυς 291
πρεσβεύω, denom. verb 851; πρεσβεύειν εἰρήνην 1053
πρηΰς (epic) 344
πρίν w. infin. and indic. 1484; w.
  infin. 1485, 1486; w. indic.,
  subj., and opt. 1486 b; w. subj.
  without ἄν 1488; πρὶν ἤ 1489
πρίωμαι and πριαίμην, accent of 761,
  774
πρό in crasis 49, 51; w. gen. 1207,
  1222; not elided 57; compared
  362; contracted w. augment 563,
  or w. foll. ε or ο 860 b; φροῦδος
  and φρουρός 105
προβέβουλα Hom. 722
προῖκα gratis, as adv. 1059
πρόκειμαι w. gen. 1132
πρόοιτο, etc. 514 c, 668, 773. See
  ἵημι
πρός w. gen. 1208, dat., and acc.
  1207, 1223, 1179; as adv., besides 1201
προσδεχομένῳ μοί ἐστιν 1586
προσήκει 887; w. gen. and dat.
  1097 b, 1161; προσῆκον, acc. abs.
  1571
πρόσθεν 113, 414; w. gen. 1152
πρόσω w. gen. 1153; ἰέναι τοῦ πρόσω
  1138
προσῳδία 127
πρότερος 362; πρότερον ἤ (like πρὶν ἤ)
  1489
πρὸ τοῦ or προτοῦ 983
προύργου and προύχω 51, 860
πρώτιστος 362

opt. act. 655 *d*, 656; in indic. of vbs. in μι 669 *d*

-σθαι (-θαι) 579; elided 58

-σθᾱν, Dor. ending for -σθην 654

-σθε (-θε) 83, 499 *b*

-σθον and -σθην in 2d and 3d pers. dual 578; -σθον for -σθην in 3d pers. 582 *c*

-σι in 2d pers. sing. (in ἐσσί) 582; in 3d pers. 578

-σι (for -ντι, -νσι) 91, 101; in 3d pers. pl. 582 *e*

-σι in dat. pl. 180, 225, 285 *b*; -ισι 180, 196

-σι as locative ending 412, 413

-σιᾱ, fem. nouns in 819

-σις, fem. nouns in 819

σῖτος and σῖτα 288

σκάζον verse 1654, 1665

σκεδάννυμι, fut. of (-άσω, -ῶ) 678 *b*

σκέλλω, ἀπο-σκλῆναι 694, 706

-σκον, -σκομην, Ion. iterative endings 606; w. ἄν 1298

σκοπέω w. ὅπως and fut. ind. 1371, 1382

σκότος, declension of 286

Σκύθης, Σκύθις 326

-σκω, verbs in 644

σμάω, contraction of 486

σμικρός 88

-σο in 2d pers. sing. 578, 582 *g*, 786, 788: see -σαι

-σ°/ε-, tense suffix in future and fut. pf. 572, 675, 734

σόος: see σῶς

σορός, fem. 201 *c*

σός, poss. pron. 380, 998

σοφός declined 294; comp. 346

σπένδω, fut. σπείσω 70; pf. and plpf. mid. 499 *c*

σπεύδω and σπουδή 34

σποδός, fem. 201 *c*

σσ = ττ 63, 85, 94, 623–626, 827;

σσ > σ 69, 85, 235; retained 86, 91

στ abbreviated 3

-στᾱ for στῆθι 787 *c*

σταθμός 82, 815 *d*

στᾶς 32

στέλλω 34, 587, 628; pf. and plpf. mid. inflected 497, 499 *d*, 545

στήῃς 670 *b*

στίχος: κατὰ στίχον 1651

στοχάζομαι w. gen. 1099

στρατηγέω w. gen. 1109

στρέφω 587, 739

σύ 101; declined 364; Hom. and Hdt. 369; omitted 885

συγγενής w. gen. 1144; w. dat. 1176

συγγιγνώσκω w. partic. (nom. or dat.) 1592; w. gen. 1121

συμβαίνει, impers. 887

σύν or ξύν, w. dat. 1207, 1224; in compos. 1179; becomes συσ- or συ- in compos. 77

συνελόντι (or ὡς συνελόντι) εἰπεῖν 1172 *b*

-σύνη, nouns in 826

συνίημι w. acc. 1105; w. gen. 1103

σύνοιδα w. partic. (nom. or dat.) 1592

συντρίβω w. gen. 1098

σφάζω, σφάττω 97, 617, 624

σφέ 367, 370; enclit. 159

σφέα 369; σφέας, σφέων 369; enclit. 159

σφέτερος 380, 1000, 1003

σφί or σφίν 367

σφίγξ 21

σφίσι 364; not enclitic 161 *e*

σφός for σφέτερος 381

σφώ, σφῶϊ, etc., σφωέ, σφωΐν 364, 369

σφωΐτερος 381

σφῶν αὐτῶν etc. 377

σχεδόν 420

σχές and σχοίην (of ἔχω) 574 c, 694, 705, 787; σχήσω 1250 f

σῴζω 620

Σωκράτης, decl. of 232; acc. 237, 286; voc. 142, 224

σῶμα 24; declined 223; nom. formed 214; dat. pl. 226

σῶs (Hom. σόοs) 302

σώτειρα 100

σωτήρ, voc. σῶτερ 142 d, 223 b; decl. 229

σωφροσύνη 815

σώφρων compared 349

T, voiceless stop 18, 23; dental 17: see Dentals; dropped 24, 214 c; assimilated 63, 69; ντ dropped before σ 70

-τᾰ (Hom.) for -της in nom. of first decl. 196 b

τᾱ́ and ταῖν (dual of ὁ), rare 386

-ται in 3d pers. sing. 578; elided 58

τάλας, adj., decl. of 319; nom. of 215 b

τἄλλα (τὰ ἄλλα) 50 b, 1059

τᾶν (τοι ἄν) 51

-τᾶν, Doric ending for -την 654

τἀνδρί 51

τἄρα 51

ταράττω 94, 623; pf. mid. 499 b

-τατος, superl. in 346

τάττω 498, 624; w. part. gen. 1096

ταὐτά, ταὐτό, ταὐτόν, ταὐτοῦ 51, 114, 376

ταυτᾶν 391

ταύτῃ, adv. 423

ταφ- for θαφ- (θάπτω) 105 e

τάχα 420; w. ἄν (τάχ' ἄν) 1315

ταχύς compared 94, 105 e, 354; τὴν ταχίστην 1059

τάων (= τῶν) 386

τέ (enclitic), Doric for σέ 374

τέ and, enclitic 159; elided 57; w.

relatives 402, 1024; w. οἷος 1024; position 963, 1202

τεθάφθαι 105 e

τεθνεώς 338, 802

τεθνήξω, fut. pf. act. of θνήσκω 736

τεθράφθαι 105 e

τείν (Ion. = σοί) 369

τείνω 100, 587, 602, 630, 731, 738

-τειρα, fem. nouns in 818

τειχομαχία 858

τεκών as subst. 1564

τελευτῶν finally 1567

τελέω, stem in σ 85, 91, 596; fut. in -ῶ, -οῦμαι 678; pf. and plpf. mid. inflected 497, 499 e; cf. 598, 599, 634, 660 c

τέλος finally, adv. acc. 1059

τέμνω 637, 714 c; 2 aor. 107, 169, 691

τέο, τεῦ, τέος, τεῦς, τεοῦ (= σοῦ) 374

τέο, τεῦ (= τοῦ for τίνος or τινός), τέῳ, τέων, τέοισι 394 b

-τέον, verbal adj. in 581, 804; impers., w. subj. in dat. or acc. 1599

-τέος, verbal adj. in 581, 804; passive 1174 b, 1597

τεός, Doric and Aeolic (= σός) 381

τέρας 216; declined 234

τέρην, decl. of 319; fem. of 320

-τερος, comparative in 346

τέρπω, 2 aor. redupl. 559; 2 aor. pass. 655 c

τέσσαρες, τέτταρες, Ion. τέσσερες 165 e, 437, etc.; declined 432

τέταχθε 83, cf. 499 b

τέτορες (Dor.) 437

τετραίνω 643; aor. 688

τέτρασι (dat.) 437

Τέως, accus. of 206

τῇ, τῇδε 423, 1191

τήκω 34, 720, 745

τηλίκος, τηλικοῦτος 393, 408, 945

τήμερον 412

τῆμος 425

-την in 3d pers. dual 578; for -τον in 2d pers. 582 c. See -σθον and -σθην

τηνίκα, τηνικάδε, τηνικαῦτα 423

-τήρ, masc. nouns in 273, 818

-τήριον, nouns of place in 829; adj. in 844

-της, masc. nouns in 189, 196 b, 818, 825, 840; fem. (denom.) in 826

τῆσι and τῆις (= ταῖς) 386

τῇ ὑστεραίᾳ 929 b

τθ for θθ 63

τι becomes σσ (ττ) or σ 95, 827

τί, adv. acc. 1059

-τι, adverbs in 420

-τι 101; ending of 3d pers. sing. 106, 578, 582, 654, 669 d

τίθημι 101, 105, 466; synopsis 503, 507; inflection 504, 665, 785; redupl. in pres. 561, 614; imperf. 665; aor. in -κα and -κάμην 685, 701; opt. mid. in -οίμην and accent 668, 773; θεῖναι 579; partic. τιθείς declined 329; w. 2 acc. 1073

-τικος, adj. in 843 b

τίκτω 106, 604

τιμάω, denom. verb 634, 851; stem of 593; inflect. of contr. forms 39, 43–45, 482; synopsis of 484; infin. 45 e, 793; partic. τιμάων, τιμῶν declined 336; w. gen. of value 1133; τιμᾶν τινί τινος and τιμᾶσθαί τινος 1133

τιμή declined 183

τιμήεις, τιμῆς, contraction of 325

τιμωρέω and τιμωρέομαι 1245; w. acc. and dat. 1163; w. gen. 1121; w. 2 acc. (poetic) 1069

τίν, Doric (= σοί) 374

τί παθών 1569

τίς, interrog. 408; declined 394; accent 134, 149, 398; Ion. forms 395; subst. or adj. 1011; in direct and ind. questions 1012, 1078, 1601

τις, indef. 408; declined 394; indef. article 387, 1015; accent 159, 394 b; Ion. forms 395; position 963; subst. or adj. 1015; like πᾶς τις 1017; sort of 1016

-τις, fem. nouns in 818, 819, 825, 840 b

τό (τοῦ, τῷ) and infin. 1545, 1549

τόθεν, τόθι 425

τοί, enclitic 50, 51, 159, 963

τοί, ταί 386, 401, 938

τοί, Ion. and Dor. (= σοι) 369, 374

τοῖος, τοιόσδε, τοιοῦτος 393, 408, 945, 974

τοιοῦτος, τοσοῦτος 393; w. article 945; position 974, 975; τοιοῦτον 114, 393 b

τοῖσδεσσι or τοῖσδεσι (= τοῖσδε) 390

τόλμα 186

-τον, in 2d and 3d pers. dual 578; for -την in 3d pers. (Hom.) 582 c. See -την

τὸν καὶ τόν 983

-τος, verb. adj. in 581, 804

τόσος, τοσόσδε, τοσοῦτος 393, 408; τοσούτῳ w. compar. 1184; τοσοῦτον 114, 393 b

τότε 423; w. art. 950

τοῦ for τίνος, του for τινός 394, 395 b

τοὐναντίον (by crasis) 51

τοὔνομα 51

τοῦ πρόσω 1138

τουτέων (Hdt.), fem. 391

τουτογί, τουτοδί 392

τοῦτο μέν . . . τοῦτο δέ 1010, 1059

-τρᾱ, fem. nouns in 822, 829

τρεῖς, τρία, declined 432

ENGLISH INDEX

See note on page 402